INTERNATIONAL BORROWING

Negotiating and Structuring International Debt Transactions

Second Edition

Daniel D. Bradlow, Editor

International Negotiation and Development
Sourcebooks on Policy and Practice
Don Wallace, Jr. and Willis W. Jourdin Jr., General Editors

INTERNATIONAL LAW INSTITUTE

K
4450
.I576
1986

This book is published and distributed in the United States and Canada by the International Law Institute. Orders or requests for information may be sent to:

Publications Department
International Law Institute
1330 Connecticut Avenue, N.W.
Washington, D.C. 20036

Outside the United States, this book is published and distributed by Martinus Nijhoff Publishers. Orders should be sent to:

United Kingdom and Ireland:

Kluwer Academic Publishers
MTP Press Ltd.
Falcon House
Queen Square
Lancaster LA1 1RN
UNITED KINGDOM

All other countries:

Kluwer Academic Publishers Group
  Distribution Center
P.O. Box 322
3300 AH Dordrecht
THE NETHERLANDS

Copyright © 1986 by the International Law Institute

All rights reserved. No part of this book may be reproduced in any form or by any electronic or mechanical means including information storage and retrieval systems without permission in writing from the publisher, except by a reviewer who may quote brief passages in a review.

Library of Congress Catalog Number: 86-082157

ISBN: 0-935328-40-8 (International Law Institute)

  90-247-3402-9 (Martinus Nijhoff Publishers)

Printed and bound in the United States of America

Acknowledgments:

"Issues in External Debt Management," from *Finance & Development,* September 1983, pp. 23-25.

"Institutional Structure for External Debt Management," from Hassanali Mehran, ed., *External Debt Management* (Washington, DC: International Monetary Fund, 1985), pp. 88-98.

"LDC Capital Flight," from *World Financial Markets,* March 1986, pp. 13-15. Reprinted by permission of Morgan Guaranty Trust Company.

"Aid in the Context of Total Resource Flows," from *Twenty-Five Years of Development Co-operation: A Review,* Report of the Development Assistance Committee (Paris: OECD, 1985), pp. 157-170. Reprinted by permission of the OECD.

"The World Bank and the International Finance Corporation," from *The World Bank and the International Finance Corporation* (Washington, DC: The World Bank, 1983). Reprinted by permission.

"The World Bank: Lending for Structural Adjustment," from Richard E. Feinberg and Valeriana Kallab, eds., *Adjustment Crisis in the Third World,* U.S.-Third World Policy Perspective No. 1 (New Brunswick, NJ: Transaction Books in cooperation with the Overseas Development Council, 1984). Copyright Overseas Development Council. Reprinted with permission of the editors.

"Range of World Bank Lending Instruments," from *World Bank Annual Report* 1985 (Washington, DC: The World Bank, 1985), Table 3-1, pp. 50-51. Reprinted by permission.

"Sample IBRD Loan Agreement and Guarantee Agreement." Reprinted by permission of The World Bank.

"General Conditions Applicable to Development Credit Agreements." Reprinted by permission of the International Development Association.

"The African Development Bank, The Inter-American Development Bank and The Asian Development Bank," from UNCTAD Secretariat, *Multilateral Development Finance Institutions of Developing Countries and the Promotion of Economic Cooperation and Integration,* United Nations Document No. TD/B/C.7/64 (New York: United Nations, 1984).

"Cofinancing: An Overview," from **Cofinancing** (Washington, DC: The World Bank, 1983). Reprinted by permission.

"Note on Documentation for IBRD's New Co-Financing Program." Reprinted by permission of The World Bank.

"Classification of Bilateral Economic Cooperation," from *OECF Loans and Loan Procedures* (Japan: Overseas Economic Cooperation Fund., n.d.).

"Recent Aid Trends and Prospects in Historical Perspective," from *Twenty-Five Years of Development Co-operation: A Review,* Report of the Development Assistance Committee (Paris: OECD, 1985), pp. 91-134 with omissions. Reprinted by permission of the OECD.

"Comecon Connection," from *South Magazine,* February 1985, pp. 63-69. Reprinted by permission of the publisher.

"Co-operation with Non-Governmental Organizations," from *Twenty-Five Years of Development Cooperation: A Review,* Report of the Development Assistance Committee (Paris: OECD, 1985), pp. 151-156. Reprinted by permission of the OECD.

"What Is Export Finance?" from A. Dunn and M. Knight, *Export Finance* (London: Euromoney Publications, 1982), pp. 7-14. Reprinted by permission.

"The Role of Export Credits in Economic Development," from *Resources for Development,* Development Committee Report No. 4 (Washington, DC: The World Bank, 1985), pp. 35-54. Reprinted by permission.

"International Capital Markets," abridged from *International Banking* edited by Emmanuel N. Roussakis. Copyright © 1982 Praeger Publishers. Reprinted by permission of Praeger Publishers. Table reprinted by permission of Export Credits Guarantee Department, London.

"Arranging and Marketing Syndicated Eurocurrency Loans," from *Bankers Magazine,* November/December 1978, Vol. 161, No. 6, Copyright © 1978, Warren, Gorham & Lamont, Inc., 210 South Street, Boston, MA 02111. Reprinted with permission. All Rights Reserved.

"Guide for Private Corporations from Developing Countries to Doing a Eurobond or Foreign Bond Issue." Reprinted by permission of the International Finance Corporation, Washington, DC.

"Direct and Portfolio Investments: Their Role in Economic Development," from *Resources for Development,* Development Committee Report No. 4 (Washington, DC: The World Bank, 1985), pp. 12-29, 32-34. Reprinted by permission.

"The Project Cycle." Copyright © 1982 by the International Bank for Reconstruction and Development. Reprinted by permission.

"An Introduction to International Project Financing," from Robert Hellawell and Don Wallace, Jr., eds., *Negotiating Foreign Investments: A Manual for the Third World* (Washington, DC: International Law Institute, 1982). Reprinted with permission.

"Leasing," from Charles J. Gmür, ed., *Trade Financing* (London: Euromoney Publications, 1981), pp. 105-116 with omissions. Reprinted by permission.

"Documentary Collection and Letters of Credit," from Charles J. Gmür, ed., *Trade Financing* (London: Euromoney Publications, 1981), pp. 43-61. Reprinted by permission.

"How to Negotiate Countertrade Deals," from *International Financial Law Review,* March 1984, pp. 20-26. Reprinted by permission of Euromoney Publications.

"Country Risk and International Bank Lending," from *University of Illinois Law Review,* 1982, pp. 71-88. © 1982 Ingo Walter, Ralph Reisner, Michael Gruson. Reprinted by permission.

"**The Mechanics of Eurodollar Transactions,**" from Emilio J. Cardenas, Antonio Mendes, and Ralph Reisner, eds., *International Financial Transactions: Selected Issues* (Washington, DC: Inter-American Development Bank, 1983), pp. 84–100. Reprinted by permission.

"**Checklist of Items for Negotiation with Commercial Banks.**" Reprinted with permission of Merrill Lynch.

"**Legal Aspects of International Lending,**" from Emilio J. Cardenas, Antonio Mendes, and Ralph Reisner, eds., *International Financial Transactions: Selected Issues* (Washington, DC: Inter-American Development Bank, 1983), pp. 103–111. Reprinted with permission.

"**Annotated Sample Loan Agreement.**" Copyright © 1986 by Cleary, Gottlieb, Steen & Hamilton. Reprinted by permission.

"**Negotiations with Transnational Banks: A Sovereign Borrower's Perspectives,**" from United Nations Centre on Transnational Corporations, *Issues in Negotiating International Loan Agreements with Transnational Banks,* United Nations Document No. ST/CTC/48 (New York: United Nations, 1983).

"**Enhancing the Effectiveness of Surveillance,**" from *Finance & Development,* December 1985, pp. 2–6.

"**Procedures in Establishing Adjustment Programs,**" excerpted from *Finance & Development,* June 1982, pp. 10–15.

"**Do Fund-Supported Adjustment Programs Retard Growth?**" from *Finance & Development,* March 1986, pp. 30–32.

"**Towards a Real Economy Approach,**" from *The Quest for Economic Stabilization,* edited by Tony Killick. © Overseas Development Institute 1983, and reprinted by permission of St. Martin's Press, Inc. and Gower Publishing.

"**Coordination of Paris and London Club Reschedulings,**" from *New York University Journal of International Law & Politics* 17 (1985): 553–571. Reprinted by permission.

"**Legal Issues in the Restructuring of Commercial Bank Loans to Sovereign Borrowers,**" from Michael Gruson and Ralph Reisner, eds., *Sovereign Lending: Managing Legal Risk* (London: Euromoney Publications, 1984). Reprinted by permission.

"**Terms and Conditions of Bank Debt Restructurings and Bank Financing Packages, 1978 - June 1985,**" from K. Burke Dillon et al., *Recent Developments in External Debt Rescheduling,* IMF Occasional Paper #40 (Washington, DC: International Monetary Fund, 1985), Table 17, pp. 48–62.

"**The International Financial System and the Management of the International Debt Crisis,**" from David Suratgar, ed., *Default and Rescheduling: Corporate and Sovereign Borrowers in Difficulty* (London: Euromoney Publications, 1984), pp. 151–160. Reprinted by permission.

PREFACE

This volume is the first published in "International Negotiation and Development: Sourcebooks on Policy and Practice," a new series of reference works and documentary collections on important issues in international trade, finance, and economic development. The series is being published in conjunction with the Negotiation and Development Training Program of the International Law Institute.

The Institute was founded in 1955 at Georgetown University (as the Institute for International and Foreign Trade Law) to promote a better understanding of the legal problems of international trade. Today the Institute is devoted to training, research, and practical responses to problems in social and economic development and to complex international policy issues and negotiation problems involving governments and multinational corporations. In this endeavor it hosts conferences and colloquia, presents training seminars, conducts research, advises, and publishes. Regular seminars are given in foreign investment and financing, procurement and contracting, arbitration, intellectual property and transfer of technology (including telecommunications, informatics, biotechnology, and computer policy), trade, petroleum and mining, management, public enterprises, national budgeting, lawmaking and constitutional administration of justice. In 1983 the Institute became an independent non-profit entity but continues to work in cooperation with Georgetown University in many of its programs.

In the past decade, the Institute's Negotiation and Development Training Program has trained over 2,000 officials and professionals, in both the public and private sectors, from 115 countries. Participants in the ILI program are trained to manage their organizations effectively, to carry out policies and effect change, and to negotiate on an equal footing with foreign investors and financiers, multilateral organizations, contractors, experts, consultants, exporters, suppliers and licensors, taking into account the latest developments in law, finance, economics, technology and public administration.

The books in this series will incorporate materials used in the Institute's seminars. Each volume will include articles, case studies, and essential documents on the substance and practice of negotiation, policy execution, and management in its respective field. The strong emphasis in ILI seminars is on the practical application of theory and on how the real (as opposed to the ideal) world works. That same emphasis on practical success in the real world will be embodied in the sourcebooks in this series.

Don Wallace, Jr.
Director

Willis W. Jourdin Jr.
Deputy Director

International Law Institute
Washington, D.C.
August 1986

Contents

Introduction ... 1

Section I: THE MANAGEMENT OF EXTERNAL DEBT
Chapter 1: Debt Management

1A. Issues in External Debt Management ... 5
Nicholas Hope and Thomas Klein

1B. Institutional Structure for External Debt Management ... 8
Guillermo de la Dehesa

1C. LDC Capital Flight ... 13

Section II: SOURCES OF FUNDS
Chapter 2: Introduction

Aid in the Context of Total Resource Flows ... 19
OECD

Chapter 3: The World Bank

3A. The World Bank and the International Finance Corporation ... 31
The World Bank

3B. The World Bank: Lending for Structural Adjustment ... 37
Stanley Please

3C. Range of World Bank Lending Instruments ... 45
The World Bank

3D. Sample IBRD Loan Agreement and Guarantee Agreement ... 47

3E. General Conditions Applicable to Development Credit Agreements ... 83
International Development Association

Chapter 4: Other Multinational Financial Institutions

4A. The African Development Bank, The Inter-American Development Bank and The Asian Development Bank ... 91
UNCTAD

4B. Selected Multilateral Financial Institutions ... 99

Chapter 5: Cofinancing

5A. Cofinancing: An Overview ... 105
The World Bank

5B. Note on Documentation for IBRD's New Co-Financing Program ... 111
The World Bank

Chapter 6: National Aid

6A. Classification of Bilateral Economic Cooperation ... 117

6B. Recent Aid Trends and Prospects in Historical Perspective ... 118
   OECD

6C. Comecon Connection ... 142

6D. Co-operation with Non-Government Organizations ... 149
   OECD

Chapter 7: Export Credits

7A. What is Export Finance? ... 155
   A. Dunn and M. Knight

7B. The Role of Export Credits in Economic Development ... 163
   The World Bank

7C. Export Credit Agencies ... 173

Chapter 8: Commercial Sources

8A. International Capital Markets ... 179
   David K. Eiteman

8B. Arranging and Marketing Syndicated Eurocurrency Loans ... 185
   Henry S. Terrell and Michael G. Martinson

8C. Guide for Private Corporations from Developing Countries to Doing a Eurobond or Foreign Bond Issue ... 190
   International Finance Corporation

8D. Direct and Portfolio Investments: Their Role in Economic Development ... 200
   The World Bank

Section III: SELECTED FINANCING TECHNIQUES

Chapter 9: Project Financing

9A. The Project Cycle ... 211
   Warren C. Baum

9B. An Introduction to International Project Financing ... 220
   John M. Niehuss

Chapter 10: Lease Financing

Leasing ... 237
   Charles J. Gmur

Chapter 11: Documentary Credits

Documentary Collection and Letters of Credit   245
Paul O'Hanlon

Chapter 12: Countertrade

How to Negotiate Countertrade Deals   267
Stanley J. Marcuss and Jay D. Grushkin

Section IV: NEGOTIATING AND STRUCTURING LOAN AGREEMENTS

Chapter 13: Financial Issues

13A. Country Risk and International Bank Lending   277
Ingo Walter

13B. The Mechanics of Eurodollar Transactions   286
Thomas Moffett

13C. Checklist of Items for Negotiation with Commercial Banks   295
Merrill Lynch

Chapter 14: Legal Issues

14A. Legal Aspects of International Lending: Basic Concepts of a Loan Agreement   299
Michael Gruson

14B. Annotated Sample Loan Agreement   304

Chapter 15: Negotiations

Negotiations with Transnational Banks: A Sovereign Borrower's Perspective   389
Jose Angel Gurria-Trevino

Section V: INTERNATIONAL MONETARY FUND

Chapter 16: International Monetary Fund

16A. The International Monetary Fund: An Overview of its Structure and Functions   399
Daniel D. Bradlow

16B. Enhancing the Effectiveness of Surveillance   414
G.G. Johnson

16C. Procedures in Establishing Adjustment Programs   418
Andrew Crockett

16D. Do Fund-Supported Adjustment Programs Retard Growth?   420
Mohsin Khan and Malcolm Knight

16E. Towards a Real Economy Approach   424
    Tony Killick, Graham Bird, Jennifer Sharpley and Mary Sutton

Section VI: LOAN RENEGOTIATION

Chapter 17: Loan Renegotiation

17A. Coordination of Paris and London Club Reschedulings   451
    Karen Hudes

17B. Legal Issues in the Restructuring of Commercial   459
    Bank Loans to Sovereign Borrowers
    Mark A. Walker and Lee C. Buchheit

17C. Terms and Conditions of Bank Debt Restructurings   475
    and Bank Financial Packages, 1978 - June 1985

Chapter 18: Proposed Solutions to Sovereign Debt Problems

The International Financial System and the Management   493
of the International Debt Crisis
    David Suratgar

Introduction

This book is a reference work and training manual for officials in developing countries who are responsible for their nation's international financial transactions. It should also prove useful to academics, students, and practitioners in international finance.

The book is meant to inform readers about the technical aspects of international finance, particularly the financing of specific projects. The complex issues of public policy raised by general-purpose financing are outside the scope of this book. Nevertheless, the relationship between macroeconomic issues and project financing is such that the book would not be complete without some discussion of the International Monetary Fund, structural adjustment loans, and debt management. However, the chapters on these topics are intended only to be introductory.

The material in this collection falls into three categories. First, there are articles that describe particular financing sources and techniques. Second, resource materials are included to direct readers to further information. Finally, there are sample documents. The articles will illuminate the advantages and disadvantages of each type of financing source and technique, and the reference materials and documents will help government officials to plan the most effective use of available financing.

In selecting material for the book, there has been no attempt to advocate a particular perspective on international borrowing in general or to promote any financing source or technique in particular. The intention has been to provide officials with the technical information necessary to make their own informed decisions on these issues and to help them make the most effective use of their country's development financing opportunities.

The book is organized to follow the steps that a government official would take when structuring a financing package for a development project. It begins with a discussion of external debt management, because the debt-management policies of a developing country determine the parameters within which an official must operate. The articles in section 1 address some of the important considerations in developing efficient debt-management programs and policies.

Section 2 describes sources of funds for developing countries. The seven chapters in section 2 contain a great deal of factual information about each source, and a number of reference materials are included. Chapters 2-5 discuss multilateral financial institutions, in particular the World Bank. Chapter 6, on national aid, describes the aid programs of the OECD countries, Comecon countries, developing countries, and non-OECD industrialized countries, as well as nongovernmental sources of aid. Chapter 7 explains the mechanics of export financing and compares the positive and negative contributions that export financing can make to economic development. The chapter includes a list of many official export financing agencies. Chapter 8, which discusses commercial sources of funds, contains articles describing international capital markets and the process of raising debt through syndicated loans and bonds. It also includes a discussion of the role of foreign investment in economic development.

The third section of the book is devoted to the financing techniques most often used by developing countries. Chapter 9 is a discussion of project planning and project financing, followed in chapter 10 by a description of the under-utilized technique of lease financing. Chapter 11, which is a discussion of letters of credit and other forms of documentary credits, is a counterpart to chapter 12, an overview of countertrade. The focus of all of the chapters in section 3 is on describing the mechanics, benefits, detriments, and utility of these financing techniques.

Once an official has chosen a financing source and technique, attention shifts to the negotiation and structuring of the transaction. Section 4 is concerned with negotiating and structuring a loan transaction. The section begins with a chapter on the financial issues in loan agreements. The articles in chapter 13 discuss such issues as credit analysis, interest rates, interest periods, grace periods, and repayments. A checklist of key financial issues is included to assist readers in preparing for a loan negotiation. Chapter 14 analyzes the legal considerations relevant to loan transactions. An annotated loan agreement enables the reader to understand the key clauses in such an agreement. Section 4 concludes with chapter 15, a review of some factors that developing countries should consider when negotiating a loan agreement.

Inevitably, the process of negotiating a loan presents unexpected twists and turns. Sections 5 and 6 are concerned with some of the problems that can arise and with the institutions involved in sovereign debt renegotiations. Chapter 16 examines the International Monetary Fund (IMF) and its role in international finance, explaining the structure and functions of the IMF and providing the reader with insight into the present controversies surrounding IMF policies. This chapter, however, is only an introduction to this complex subject.

Chapter 17 focuses on the sovereign debt renegotiations that have characterized the first half of the 1980s. Again, this section is intended only as an introduction to the subject, but it gives the reader a good overview of the technicalities of debt renegotiations. A discussion of the renegotiation of official and private debt is included as well as articles on the financial and legal issues raised in debt renegotiations.

The final chapter in the book proposes a possible solution to the debt situation in the developing world. It is included not because the editor endorses its proposals but to stimulate readers into further thought about the dimensions of the debt crisis.

The characteristics and conditions of international financial transactions are subject to sudden change. This book can only elucidate the general outlines of international finance, and the editors caution that the information on the specific features of each financing source or technique should be treated as merely illustrative and subject to change. Consequently, readers should be aware that material in this book may not apply exactly to their financing programs.

A book such as this is never the product of only one person's work. It was originally developed in conjunction with the International Law Institute's training programs, "Financing Sources and Techniques" and "International Loan Negotiation and Renegotiations." Many people should share the credit for creation of this book. I especially wish to thank the International Law Institute, its director, Prof. Don Wallace Jr., and its executive director, Frank Loftus, for providing me with the opportunity and the support for this project; Willis W. Jourdin Jr., deputy director at the Institute, who gave me valued guidance and encouragement in developing courses on international borrowing out of which this book developed; Veronica Johns, who provided valued research assistance; Peter Whitten, who oversaw editing and production; and Vernita Greenfield, without whose secretarial skills this book would not have been completed. Furthermore, I particularly with to thank David Suratgar for all the advice and assistance he has given me; and Paul Reichler and my colleagues at Reichler & Appelbaum for encouraging me to persevere with this book and for allowing me the time to complete a project that they perceived to be as important as I did.

Washington, D.C.　　　　　　　　　　　　　　Daniel D. Bradlow
August 1986

Section I:
The Management of External Debt
Chapter 1: Debt Management

1A. Issues in External Debt Management

Nicholas Hope and
Thomas Klein***

Since 1973, more than 30 developing countries have had to reschedule their debts, some of them two or three times. Although the amounts involved are not very substantial measured against the total outstanding debt, they have increased considerably: debt relief agreements covered an annual average of US$2 billion of debts between 1974 and 1981; but some $10 billion was renegotiated in 1982. By mid-1983, debt in excess of $35 billion was under negotiation,, including short-term credits that would normally be "rolled-over" for countries not in economic difficulty.

As the accompanying article on rescheduling explains, debt problems may arise from many reasons—for instance in recent years depressed export markets and high interest rates have been important factors. But poor debt management policies also had contributed to the debt difficulties of developing countries during the past decade. What pitfalls for debt management—as distinct from overall economic management—must be avoided, if developing countries are to reduce costly debt servicing problem in the future?

The problems of managing external debt in the postwar period became apparent during the late 1950s and early 1960s when first Turkey, then Argentina, Brazil, Chile, Ghana, and Indonesia encountered severe debt servicing difficulties. In each country, large shares of capital formation by the public sector were financed through suppliers' creditors of five to seven years maturity. While this investment, for the most part, had a positive effect on economic growth, it did not lead to an acceleration of exports, nor did the returns from the projects always conform to the timing of sevice payments. For these countries, debt service obligations rose rapidly; foreign exchange earnings did not. Adding to their problems was the lack of timely information on the external debt. Borrowing was monitored poorly, if at all; in some countries (Turkey in the late 1950s; Ghana and Indonesia in the 1960s) there was a virtual absence of statistics on debt and debt servicing obligations. The common characteristics of all these countries were: excessive foreign borrowing relative to profitability and to export earnings, inappropriate borrowing terms, and inadequate information about the volume and composition of external debt. All these difficulties could have been alleviated by more effective debt management.

Developing countries borrow to promote their growth—generally by augmenting the resources available for investment. At the same time, borrowing imposes constraints on their future policies. Specifically, projected export earnings, possibly augmented by further borrowings and other foreign finance, must be sufficient to accommodate the required debt service obligations; and projected government revenue must be enough to provide the local currency equivalent of the government's debt service obligations. The latter requirement will be met more easily when the projects financed are successful; but even where returns are more than adequate to cover costs, the government's ability to raise revenues may constrain severely its ability to manage debt.

To manage debt effectively, authorities must project accurately the time profile of their debt service obligations, and forecast export earnings, domestic revenues, and future access to various sources of finance. They must also monitor the potential for prepaying or refinancing their debt: (1) to take advantage of new borrowings on better terms; (2) to adapt loan maturities to the revenues generated by the projects financed, or (3) to cope with shortfalls in earnings from exports or unanticipated expenditures on imports.

A major problem for a government is to view foreign borrowing in the broader framework of its overall economic policy decisions. Where policies are chosen so that key economic variables especially interest and exchange rates convey true economic costs to decisionmakers and where governments underpin their public investment programs with effective resource budgeting and measures to raise domestic savings, debt problems will rarely arise. But, as the past few years have shown, countries can find that they have "overborrowed" in deteriorating economic circumstances, making them vulnerable to painful deflationary pressures and slow growth. Beyond good macroeconomic policy, however, the effective management of external debt comprises three specific interrelated processes: knowing the debt;

---
* Chief, External Debt Division of the World Bank.
** Economist, External Debt Division of the World Bank.

deciding how much to borrow; and selecting the appropriate available financing.

KNOWING THE DEBT

Information on external debt and associated debt service payments is essential for the day-to-day management of foreign exchange transactions as well as for managing debt and planning foreign borrowing strategies. At the most detailed level, the information enables central authorities to ensure that individual creditors are paid promptly; at more aggregated levels, it is important for assessing current foreign exchange needs, and for projecting future debt service obligations and the consequences of further foreign borrowing.

In most countries, debt statistics are the responsibility of a debt recording agency affiliated with the ministry of finance or the central bank. The collection of these statistics has accounting, statistical, and analytical implications. Details of each loan contract and schedules of future service payments msut be recorded, figures on loan utilizations collected, and the payment of debt service obligations ordered promptly. The statistical and analytical aspect involves assembling summary figures on foreign borrowing, tabulating debt outstanding, and projecting debt service due. From these statistics, inputs are prepared for the government budget and for balance of payments projections. With the help of a macroeconomic model, the statistics department of a debt office can simulate the impact of alternative future borrowing patterns on the budget and on the balance of payments.

Developing countries typically encounter problems with the accounting of public sector debt. New loans are not always reported to the debt agency: in some countries, government agencies have considerable autonomy to borrow abroad, and this makes it difficult to have an overall picture of the country's external debt commitments. Another problem concerns loan disbursement. Autonomous public corporations are sometimes uncooperative in supplying figures on these to the central debt office responsible for monitoring debt transactions. Occasionally debt service payments are not made because of disorderly work procedures and ineffective management. Because of these administrative failures, a country that is able to service its debts may incur penalty charges and impair its creditworthiness. Even well-organized debt offices have experienced accounting difficulties when faced with a rapid growth in the volume of external debt transactions. In response to this, countries that have taken on large numbers of relatively small loans have benefited from computerizing their accounting operations.

The statistical and analytical function is an essential complement to the accounting exercise. A number of countries with well-developed accounting systems have been unable to generate useful statistics from the basic accounting records because their bookkeeping staff has not been complemented by economists or financial analysts. This work, too, has become more complex in recent years. Most financial credits from commercial banks now carry variable interest rates, so budget and balance of payments projections should allow for the effects of alternative interest charges. Similarly, the volatility of exchange rates necessitates several sets of projections to test the sensitivity of debt service payments. Even with a small volume of debt, this sensitivity assessment is difficult without the help of economic analysis and computer based models. In an increasing number of countries, the private sector borrows substantial sums abroad, in some countries, private borrowing comprises three quarters of the medium and long term debt. Debt offices are usually informed regarding private sector debt guaranteed by government, but data collection systems for private nonguaranteed debt are frequently inadequate.

A characteristic of recent debt problems is the important role of short-term debt; payments crises have erupted when countries failed in their attempts to refinance short maturities. Monitoring short-term debt is difficulty, however, and this is as true for the lender as for the borrower. Some short-term liabilities can be measured easily-for example, payments arrears on trade credits that arise when officials block transfers requiring approval under exchange controls. More difficult to monitor is the growth of new short-term financing arrangements, such as the Turkish convertible lira deposit system of the mid-1970s and lending to Mexico in 1981-82.

HOW MUCH TO BORROW

The amount of debt to contract is a basic policy decision, and the correct decision will depend on the skill and judgment of those responsible for making it. Formal models and related technical analyses cannot substitute for good policymaking, but they can aid it by providing information on the future implications of alternative borrowing strategies—especially their impact on a country's capacity to invest wisely in the light of its balance of payments prospects.

The amount that any country ought to borrow is governed by two factors: how much foreign capital the economy can absorb efficiently, and how much debt it can service without risking external payments problems. Each factor will depend on the effectiveness of overall economic management. But, considered narrowly, after the debt servicing capacity of the economy is projected, the volume of external borrowing will depend on the terms on which it is made available. The policy decision is complicated by different terms and currencies for borrowings and by uncertainty about the evolving debt servicing capacity of the economy (including the capacity to borrow further to service the debt). The interaction between debt servicing capacity, the type of finance available, and the borrowing decision increases in complexity as the number of loans increases. Computer-assisted models are important aids to the policy-maker in coping with this complexity.

Most governments, in assessing the feasibility of a borrowing strategy, pay particular attention to the risk of overtaxing their debt servicing capacity and causing balance of payments problems. But they also examine the costs, in terms of foregone growth of underborrowing. In foreign borrowing both over-optimism and excessive pessimism can be costly.

FINANCING TECHNIQUES

The best combination must be chosen from the available sources of external finance—whether loans, grants, or direct investment to suit the needs of individual projects and of the economy as a whole. The preceding discussion makes clear that a major concern in the selection is to avoid problems in making service payments on foreign capital. (These payments include profits and dividends remitted by direct investment enterprises, and obligations resulting from barter, prepayments for exports, or other similar arrangements.)

Authorities will have other objectives in choosing among sources of finance. For many, a major concern is to make the maximum use of—or obtain the most "leverage" from—those external capital flows that are scarce. Grants and foreign loans on concessional terms are clearly the cheapest form of financing, but these are generally inadequate to meet a country's needs. Maximum leverage can be obtained from them by combining them with other types of financing; for countries with limited ability for borrowing from financial markets, the leverage obtained from these funds can be very important.

Loans from international banks provide a flexible source of foreign exchange contrasting with much official capital and export related financng that is specific to particular projects or goods. Bank loans provide governments with the foreign exchange needed for participation in joint ventures, for the down payments on capital goods often required to secure preferential export credit finance, and for meeting unanticipated shortfalls of foreign exchange earnings, when the ability to "roll over" debts or meet debt service payments through new borrowing may be very important.

Commercial bank loans in recent years have carried high interest rates compared with official loans and guaranteed export credits, and many countries (such as China and Indonesia) have endeavored to minimize their use in project financing. Clearly, authorities should ensure that credits from the financial markets are part of a package that provides the best possible external financing mix for the economy as well as for an individual project. At the project level the best mix could mean one with: (1) the highest possible grant element; (2) the minimum amount of market finance; (3) the maximum amount of capital that can be rolled over easily; or (4) the minimum debt service due in the first five to ten years of the project.

As well as eveluating alternative financing packages for each major project, the authorities must ensure that the aggregate financing package meets national financial priorties. This involves an assessment of such aspects as the sources of finance the amounts of each type that could be borrowed and the prospects for future supply; the currency composition of foreign borrowing that would minimize exposure to exchange rate fluctuations; the exposure to interest rate fluctuations over the life of the loan; and the impact of new borrowing on the structure of debt service obligations and the overall future access to external finance. Analysis of this kind is not easy, but all developing countries must perform it effectively if they are to continue to benefit from foreign borrowing while avoiding balance of payments, problems.

A CONTINUING PRIORITY

Many countries are encountering the need to consolidate and restructure their external borrowing in an orderly fashion, and many more, less publicly, have experienced reduced growth as debt has become an increasing constraint on their development budgets. The resolution of these difficulties lies, to a large extent, in a restoration of economic health to the global economy, and a resumption of strong growth in international trade. But careful debt management—the most effective use of scarce borrowed resources—will remain an important function of national authorities.

1B. Institutional Structure for External Debt Management
Guillermo de la Dehesa

There seems to be an international consensus that a country's external debt is its liabilities in foreign currencies to nonresidents with an original or extended maturity of over one year. Most statistics on debt, national as well as international, cover only medium-term and long-term liabilities because of the difficulties involved in obtaining accurate data on short-term debt.

This definition of external debt is, in principle, appropriate for a discussion of liability management, but it would be completely misleading to use it to analyze a country's liquidity or solvency. When asset management and country risk are at issue, gross external liabilities are not relevant; by that measure, the United States is by far the most externally indebted country in the word, for instance, yet hardly constitutes a solvency or liquidity risk. For this risk, the net external position of a country is relevant, and this should include not only short-term, medium-term, and long-term liabilities in foreign currency, but also external assets. The maturities of assets and liabilities are also important — as an extreme example, a country that builds up foreign liabilities to increase its foreign investment and its short-term reserves may have an equilibrium net position, but incur risk from the different maturity and country structure of its assets and liabilities.

Complete knowledge of a country's external position should therefore include the short-term position of its banking institutions, both on the liability and on the asset side. This comprises short-term accounts, trade credits and documents, deposit acounts, foreign and domestic currency reserves (both public and private), and, finally, foreign investments — direct, portfolio, and others. Once the global external position is known, the scope of any solvency or liquidity problems of a given country can be identified. Nevertheless, only the standard and more limited definition of foreign debt is used in this discussion of external debt management. This definition does not include countries' liabilities with the International Monetary Fund, nor any "off-shore" activity of banks conducted among nonresidents.

Apart from the issue of whether to include short-term debt, assets, and information on maturities, the definition of external debt also raises the question of how to define public and private debt. In principle, all private foreign debt guaranteed by the government or other public institutions should be considered as public, since it will be submitted to the same regulations and procedures as debt that is unambiguously public. The latter should include not only government debt, but also liabilities of the central bank, government agencies, and the states, and — where a country is a federation — the debt of provincial and local governments, and so on. As regards public enterprises, in some countries firms are only considered public if the government (or a government institution or agency) holds the majority of the shares. A more realistic view, however, is to include in the definition of public those enterprises in which the public sector controls the management team — be it as a majority shareholder or as a large minority shareholder.

For this study, therefore, the definition of public foreign debt includes the liabilities of the central government, state, provincial, and local governments, government agencies, public companies (as defined above), and private debt guaranteed by the public sector.

MANAGEMENT OF FOREIGN DEBT

The theory of debt management is very simple. Developing countries resort to foreign financing to foster internal growth and to increase the resources available for investment. But before receiving foreign funds, plans must be made on how to repay them, and the limits such debt will impose on future economic policy must be considered. Investment projects financed with foreign debt should yield enough foreign currency to cover the servicing of the debt. In theory, therefore, debt management involves knowing the level of the debt, keeping it within the desired limits, and obtaining the best available terms for it.

In reality, debt management is very different. First of all, public foreign debt has been used mainly to create (or maintain) fiscal deficits, caused not by greater public investment but by higher public current consumption or, in some cases, grandiose and unprofitable investments.

Second, the volume of foreign debt incurred by a given country has been independent of the size of its current account deficit plus net foreign direct investment. The reason is that all three elements are determined by different forces. The current account is determined in the goods and services market and varies according to domestic and foreign demand as well as the competitiveness of exports and imports of goods and services. Net foreign direct investment depends mainly on the development of the real sector of the economy. The volume of debt in every period is mostly determined in the money market and is a function of differential net borrowing costs as well as expectations regarding exchange and interest rates. As a result, in most years the volume of foreign debt has been either greater than the current account deficit plus net foreign direct investment — and has led to a build-up of reserves — or else it has been smaller — and reserves have fallen. In fact, the latter case is very rare, since governments have preferred, rather than lose reserves, either to force the public sector or to encourage the private sector to obtain additional foreign financing. But these higher reserves from an unnecessarily large foreign debt have proved unprofitable. The cost of borrowing has been much greater than the return on the reserves because markets have generally exhibited a normal upward-sloping yield curve, with higher yields on debt of longer maturities, and reserves have tended to be invested in short-term securities with lower returns. The result has been a serious debt-servicing problem, the "debt crisis," attributable in most countries largely to the absence of debt management.

Debt management should take place at two levels: the macroeconomic and the administrative level. Macroeconomic management is the most important since the management of the economy as a whole is the main factor in determining the volume of foreign debt. When debt servicing can no longer be covered by more borrowing, there are only two alternatives. One is to create a bigger surplus in the trade and service accounts by reducing expenditures relative to output. The other alternative is normally to create a fiscal surplus — since in developing countries most foreign debt is owed by the public sector while most foreign assets are held by the private sector (partly because private foreign investment has been a way of generating external income and evading exchange controls and taxes by not repatriating the principal). The debt-service problem is, therefore, more a fiscal issue than one related to the balance of payments. Turning fiscal deficits into fiscal surpluses could be called macroeconomic debt management today.

The main purpose of this paper, however, is administrative management — the control, by administrative measures, of the volume, currency, instruments, and terms of foreign currency borrowing, both for the public as well as the private sector.

INSTITUTIONAL MANAGEMENT OF FOREIGN DEBT

The institutional management of foreign debt is organized in a very similar way in most countries, with minor differences due mainly to peculiarities in the historical formation of administrative institutions. A grouping of the institutional structure in selected countries permits some broad conclusions.

First, there are a few countries without exchange controls; any institution or citizen is free to sell foreign debt instruments, and pay interest and principal. In these countries, only a statistical ex-post control exists through the information that banks provide periodically to the central bank or the monetary authority. Germany, Kuwait, Saudi Arabia, Singapore, the United Kingdom, and the United States are in this category.

In a second group of countries, all foreign borrowing is free, but the central bank or monetary authority must be notified ex ante, to allow direct statistical control of the volume of the foreign debt. The Netherlands, among others, falls into this group.

In a third group, the largest, some prior authorization is required, whether for private or for public debt, or both. Some countries also treat nonbank and bank borrowing differently.

In most countries, controls imposed on foreign debt only affect nonbanks. Bank borrowing is generally not subject to restrictions, although in some cases it is bound by regulations aimed at matching maturities. In Israel, for instance, nonbank residents cannot borrow abroad directly (except for import credits of over 30 months) but only through resident banks at a surcharge interest rate of 1 per cent. There is a general tendency to channel nonbank borrowing through resident banks, since the latter are subject to safety regulations imposed by the central bank, have a better knowledge of foreign markets, and are usually able to obtain better terms. These conditionas apply to Austria, Cameroon, France, Greece, India, Malaysia, South Africa, and Japan.

Although both public and private foreign debt need prior approval in most countries, they are usually subject to different institutional treatment, public debt being controlled more than private.

Public debt is usually approved in advance by the ministry of finance, as in Austria, Belgium, Brazil, Cameroon, Canada, France, Indonesia, Italy, Korea, Mexico, Nigeria, Senegal, South Africa, Sweden, and Turkey. In other countries the ministry of finance has delegated the approval to the central bank (this has happened in Argentina, Costa Rica, Denmark, Finland, Greece, Iceland, India, Ireland, Malaysia, New Zealand, Philippines, Thailand, Yugoslavia, and Zaire). Finally, there are some countries, mainly Spanish speaking, where public foreign borrowing is approved by a joint committee of the ministry of finance and the central bank; such is the case in Bolivia (Comite de Politica Cambiaria), Colombia (Junta Monetaria), Dominican Republic (Junta Monetaria), Ecuador (Junta Monetaria), Guatemala (Junta Monetaria), Peru (Comite de Financiacion Exterior), Portugal (Consejo Coorinador de Financiacion Exterior), and Spain (CIFEX). In some cases public debt, and in most, central government debt, is subject to an annual ceiling established in the budget law. Overall public debt ceilings are established in Brazil, Peru and Yugoslavia; central government ceilings are established by parliament in Belgium, the Dominican Republic, Norway and Spain.

In some countries, private debt is not subject to prior approval and only ex-post registration with the central bank or the ministry of finance is needed. Argentina, Canada, Chile, Denmark, Mexico, and Uruguay fit into this group. It is striking that some of the heavily indebted countries have such a liberal stance on private borrowing. Private debt in most countries has to be approved by the central bank. Only in a few countries is a distinction made between commercial and pure financial debt, the former being approved by the ministry of commerce. Brazil, Japan, Mexico and Spain, among others, share this peculiarity, the reason being that the regulation of import financing can be a way of imposing a nontariff protection, and is therefore a trade policy instrument.

In Bolivia, only large private borrowing (of more than $b 100,000) is subject to the approval of the Ministry of Finance, while smaller borrowings must be approved by the Central bank. Something similar occurs in Colombia. On the other hand, in Sweden no borrowing is authorized under Skr 10 million and, in Costa Rica, the minimum is set at C 50,000.

Certain terms are imposed on private borrowing in some countries to stretch maturities as much as possible. In Brazil no financial borrowing is allowed with maturities shorter than eight years, while in Sweden the minimum maturity is two years, and in Colombia, three years. Ecuador taxes all borrowing of maturities less than two years. Other countries, such as Chile and Brazil, have imposed different deposit requirements on different maturities.

France exempts borrowing of firms for work undertaken abroad, for import and export financing, and all borrowing under F 50 million. Austria grants automatic approval to borrowing for productive investment, import and export finance, and loans from nonresident relatives. In Denmark, private borrowing is exempted from prior authorization provided its maturity is over five years. In Italy some financial loans from countries in the European Economic Community are exempted.

In most countries, commitments and disbursements as well as the payment of interest and the repayment of principal come under the control of the central bank. While ministries of finance provide the main criteria and regulations for borrowing abroad, the real management and control of the debt is usually delegated to the central bank. This function is, most frequently, delegated further by the central bank to authorized banks, which are then responsible for checking that outflows of capital and interest derived from the original borrowing coincide with the approved maturities, rates, spreads, dates, and so on. In other cases every inflow and outflow of capital subsequent to the authorized borrowing requires central bank approval.

Central banks also have, in most countries, a statistical unit for foreign debt. This is also an important factor in foreign debt management. It is almost impossible to manage something whose dimensions are not known with a certain degree of accuracy. Such statistics are obtained through the authorized banks if exchange control regulations are delegated to the banks, or else directly from the central bank. Authorized banks send the central bank a monthly or quarterly computer tape or written lists of all transactions that have entailed the purchase or sale of foreign currency, with the identification of the transaction among the different items of the balance of payments. Central banks can thus keep a record of all transactions between residents and nonresidents.

INSTITUTIONAL PRIORITIES

The evidence on the institutional structures of different countries forms the basis for a few comments on the efficient institutional management of foreign debt.

The first institutional priority for foreign debt management is the statistical unit. This unit depends very much on the strength and the organization of exchange control regulations. The difficulties of some Latin American and African countries in ascertaining the level and characteristics of their foreign debt are well known. In some of these countries, the absence of exchange controls also means a lack of statistical control. To get rid of exchange controls can be good economic policy but without statistics on capital flows it is impossible to make adequate economic policy decisions. One wonders how these countries could produce statistics for the current and capital account of the balance of payments without knowing inflows and outflows of capital. They only had data on trade and and part of the service balance, and on those foreign investment inflows that needed prior approval;

the rest of the balance of payments was calculated from foreign currency reserve movements.

Mexico, for example, had to ask all resident borrowers to register their foreign liabilities at the Central Bank and at the Secretariat of Commerce in order to calculate its foreign debt on a given date. Some borrowers did not register their debt, although they knew that if they did not do so they could not service it through official channels and the official or controlled market. Later Nigeria introduced a more sophisticated registration system to obtain information on its foreign debt. Resident borrowers had to register their borrowings with the Ministry of Finance in Lagos and foreign lenders had to register loans with a given nonresident bank in London. The simplest way to have a good statistical record (as mentioned earlier) is to oblige residents to make all their foreign transactions through authorized banks. This did not happen in many developing countries before the debt crisis.

The second most important institutional priority is to have a control unit for debt service and for foreign debt commitments and disbursements. The key factor in debt management is to be able to service the annual burden. The main priority is, therefore, to establish, through balance of payments forecasting, the sustainable level of the foreign debt-servicing burden, and then to incur the foreign borrowing appropriate to that level. The only way to avoid the accumulation of debt service above sustainable levels is to control commitments and disbursements. Since there is usually a lag between the approval of a loan and its commitment, and another between commitment and disbursement, controlling approval is not as important as controlling commitments, and either controlling or knowing disbursements and putting a limit on the annual debt-service burden. The interest burden is always difficult to forecast since most foreign debt today is committed at floating rates.

The unit must have a global picture of the evolution and movements of external debt and its service, to be able to make efficient debt management decisions. If, at any time such a unit is aware of a dangerous short-run accumulation of debt servicing, it must be able to make prompt decisions to offset it — by delaying public sector commitments, slowing down private sector approvals, or regulating short-term borrowing in an effort to extend average maturities. Central banks, for the reasons indicated earlier, are the most suitable institutions to fulfill the tasks of the debt control unit, and to run the statistical unit as well, since both units are so interrelated that they should not be located in different institutions.

A third institutional priority is an advisory unit. Up to now the discussion has focused on the defensive or passive management of debt, which involves avoiding unsustainable debt servicing and foreign financial crises. But active

Chart 3.
Spain: Flows of Information for Foreign Debt Management

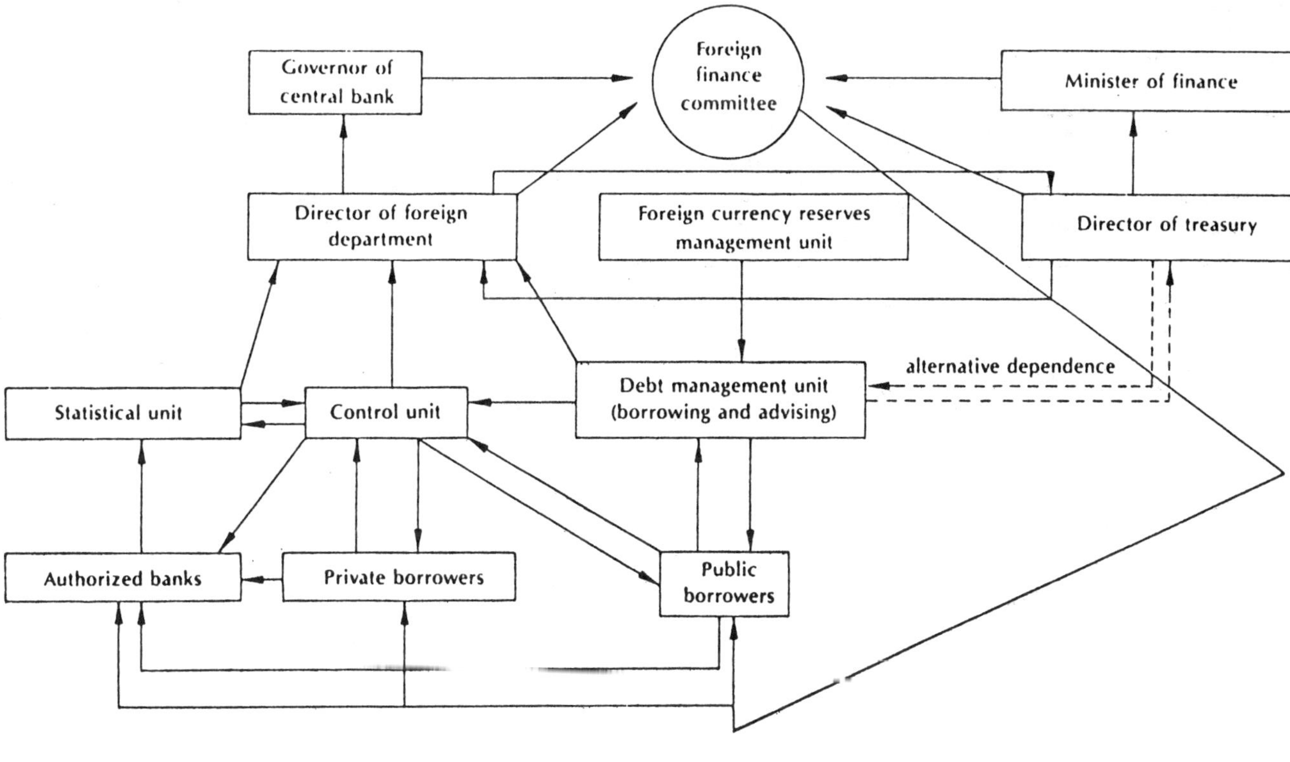

management is also very important. Active management consists of the daily analysis of the foreign markets, and the study of future options. This advisory unit should be able to advise both the government and the public sector on the best available borrowing opportunities in the markets, and to inform the control unit and the approval committee, if one exists, so that both have adequate terms of reference for authorizing new borrowings.

A priority, but one of lesser importance, is a foreign finance committee to provide general criteria for the approval and management of foreign debt in the light of the macroeconomic performance of the economy and the situation of the markets. This committee should include high-ranking economic policy decision makers, so that it has close connections with the decisions affecting monetary and fiscal policy. It should meet as often as possible to be able to adapt its criteria to the changing conditions of both foreign capital markets and macroeconomic performance.

Finally, one institutional problem that affects many countries is whether the ministry of finance or the central bank should be in charge of negotiating the central government and public sector borrowing, or whether it should be done only for the central government, leaving other government agencies and public sector companies to negotiate and manage their own foreign borrowing. To have a single public borrowing unit avoids problems of image in the markets that may arise when agencies or public firms approach the markets under conditions that adversely affect implicit rating of the country (although this problem can be avoided if there is loan-by-loan control of public sector borrowings). On the other hand, it is convenient for public agencies and companies to enter markets in their own name and try to obtain a solid and solvent image.

In my opinion, there should be a public borrowing unit that concentrates only on central government and government-guaranteed debt. This unit should coincide with the advisory unit since it is almost impossible to have a deep knowledge of the markets without being permanently active in them.

CONCLUSIONS

In the last few years there has been increasing government intervention in foreign debt management due to serious problems of solvency and liquidity in many developing and developed countries. In some cases, the institutional structure has become too complicated and cumbersome for flexible debt management. If all public borrowing needs to be approved by a council of ministers and to be signed by the prime minister, as happens in some countries, debt management cannot be flexible enough to adapt to the ever-changing conditions of the markets. Countries that have had more control (even from the statistical point of view) over their foreign debts have not incurred the abnormal debt levels of countries that had no control.

Foreign debt control should, therefore, be as minimal and as flexible as possible. Both objectives can be achieved at very little cost for the government, provided debt managers have a fair knowledge of foreign capital markets and debt management techniques.

A debt management unit consisting of three small components, preferably in the central bank, covering the statistical, the control, and the borrowing and advisory aspects of debt management is more than enough for efficient foreign debt management in any indebted country (see Chart 3). There are two reasons this unit should be located in the central bank: it needs to be under a single direction; and that of the central bank provides the additional necessary expertise of its foreign currency reserve management team that is in permanent contact with the markets. The entire management of foreign debt could thus be under the head of the foreign department of the central bank, who would act as secretary to the foreign finance committee. The minister of finance, the governor of the central bank, and the director of the treasury (plus the minister of economy or commerce, if neccesary), should be the other members of such a committee. Nevertheless, the committee should restrict itself to study general annual criteria, regulations, and difficult cases. The other possible alternative would be to put the debt management unit under the director of the treasury.

1C. LDC Capital Flight

Capital flight is a serious problem for a number of LDCs, depriving them of resources for economic development and symbolizing the poor policies and performance contributing to external debt troubles. As clearly stated in the Baker initiative, dealing with capital flight is a prerequisite for mobilizing additional foreign credit for troubled LDCs. While particular instances of capital flight have achieved some notoriety, comprehensive quantitative estimates are hard to come by. This note presents an attempt at such quantification for 18 developing countries that are prominent international borrowers.

Capital flight can be defined as the reported and unreported acquisition of foreign assets by the non-bank private sector and some elements of the public sector. This is an expansive definition, in that it includes foreign-currency working balances of local enterprises engaged in international trade and trade credit extended directly by local exporters to foreign importers.

Since, in practice, capital flight cannot be well measured directly, Table 10 estimates it indirectly as the counterpart of recorded net direct investment inflows *plus* increases in gross external debt, *less* recorded outflows through current account deficits, and *less* the build-up of foreign assets by the banking system and the official monetary authorities. The resulting estimates are necessarily rough and are subject to several sources of both downward and upward bias. These biases are intrinsic to the indirect estimation method, arising principally from errors and omissions in recorded transactions and valuation changes in assets and liabilities induced by exchange rate changes. The overall direction and magnitude of bias cannot be established conclusively. However, with few exceptions, the estimates seem likely to understate actual capital flight—by as much as half in one or two cases. Further, the estimates are presented on a net basis—gross capital flight could be substantially higher.

SOURCES OF UNDERSTATEMENT

Misreporting. Underinvoicing enables exporters to acquire foreign exchange in excess of that declared and normally required to be sold to the central bank or its agents. The difference may be invested abroad, by the exporters themselves or after sale to others through unofficial markets offering an advantageous rate of exchange. Much the same applies to the proceeds from goods smuggled abroad. Some prime examples are: Argentina in 1983-84, when underreporting of exports is thought to have been a main channel for capital flight; Malaysia in 1976-84, when reported exports fell roughly $10 billion short of their FOB value recorded by trading partners; and Nigeria in 1979, when reported oil exports were about $4 billion less than volume and price data implied. In the area of service export receipts, underreporting also is prevalent in relation to tourism and the interest and dividends earned on assets held abroad.

Overinvoicing enables importers to purchase more foreign exchange at official rates—sometimes preferential—than they owe to foreign exporters. Again, the difference may be invested abroad, directly or by others through the unofficial markets. For example, during several years in the 1970s and 1980s Nigeria's reported imports substantially exceeded those recorded by its trading partners.

Valuation effects. When the dollar appreciates, as it did between end-1979 and end-1984, the dollar equivalent of debts denominated in other currencies decreases. Net borrowing from abroad is then understated when measured by changes in year-end debt outstandings—the more so with the growing practice of borrowing in currencies other than the dollar. The currency composition of external debt varies from country to country: almost 90% of Mexico's public-sector debt is dollar denominated, but less than half of Indonesia's. Unfortunately, the lack of full information concerning currency composition prevents reliable estimation of appropriate valuation adjustments.

On the asset side—quantitatively less important—it is when the dollar depreciates, as during 1985, that valuation effects cause capital flight measures based on year-end outstandings to be understated.

SOURCES OF OVERSTATEMENT

Misreporting. Imports also are sometimes underreported—obviously so in connection with smuggled goods, to evade duties or controls, but also when governments seek to prevent public disclosure, for example, of military purchases. Such underreporting results in understatement of the current

14 International Borrowing

Table 10

Estimated net capital flight
cumulative flows during 1976-85
billions of dollars, minus sign indicates outflows

	Net direct investment inflows	Change in gross external debt	Current account balance*	Change in selected gross foreign assets**	Capital flight*** Total	1976-82	1983-85
Argentina	4	42	—15	—4	—26	—27	1
Bolivia	0	3	—2	—0	—1	—1	0
Brazil	20	80	—77	—13	—10	—3	—7
Chile	2	16	—16	—3	1	0	1
Colombia	2	10	—11	—2	0	0	0
Ecuador	1	7	—5	—1	—2	—1	—1
Mexico	11	75	—29	—3	—53	—36	—17
Peru	0	8	—6	—2	—0	1	—1
Uruguay	1	4	—3	—1	—1	—1	—0
Venezuela	—0	26	10	—5	—30	—25	—6
Subtotal	40	270	—154	—33	—123	—93	—30
India	0	22	—8	—5	—10	—6	—4
Indonesia	2	27	—15	—9	—5	—6	1
Korea	0	40	—22	—6	—12	—6	—6
Malaysia	9	19	—12	—4	—12	—8	—4
Nigeria	2	18	—15	4	—10	—7	—3
Philippines	1	23	—16	1	—9	—7	—2
South Africa	—2	16	2	2	—17	—13	—4
Thailand	2	17	—17	—1	—0	1	—1
Subtotal	14	181	—102	—18	—75	—52	—23
Total for 18 countries	54	451	—256	—51	—198	—145	—53

*Minus sign indicates deficit.

**Official reserve assets and other foreign assets of official monetary authorities plus foreign assets of commercial banks and certain other banking institutions. Minus sign indicates increase in foreign assets.

***Apparent change in other foreign assets (minus sign indicates increase) through residual capital flows measured as the counterpart of the sum of net direct investment inflows, change in gross external debt, current account balance, and change in selected gross foreign assets. Direct investment and current account data are taken from the reported balance of payments. Debt and asset changes are derived from estimated year-end outstandings in dollar terms.

Note: Due to rounding columns and rows may not add.

account deficit and, following the indirect estimation approach, overstatement of apparent net capital flight.

Valuation effects. When the dollar depreciates, as between end-1975 and end-1979 and again during 1985, the dollar equivalent of debt denominated in other currencies increases. Capital inflows measured by changes in the value of external debt outstandings from one year-end to the next are correspondingly overstated.

On the asset side, it is when the dollar appreciates, as during the early 1980s, that valuation effects cause capital flight measures based on year-end outstandings to be overstated.

WHERE IS THE MONEY?

Only a fraction of the specific assets accumulated through capital flight can be identified. The BIS and the IMF report bank deposits held by nonbank entities in foreign banks by residence of depositor. Last September, for the 18 LDCs listed in Table 11, such deposits amounted to nearly $63 billion, an increase of about $15 billion in less than three years. Only a small fraction is believed to be collateral for loans. Approximately half of all identified deposits were held in banks in the United States; only about 10% of those in U.S. banks were demand deposits. Undoubtedly there are additional holdings in U.S. and foreign banks by residents of these countries, but their use of addresses or intermediaries in countries other than their own prevents identification. Virtually no data are published on other foriegn assets acquired through capital flight, such as currency, securities, businesses, and real estate.

COMMENT

During the past decade the 18 LDCs listed in Table 9 experienced net capital flight of nearly $200 billion, while simultaneously accumulating $450 billion additional foreign debt.

Table 11
Identifiable nonbank residents' deposits in foreign banks, September 1985
billions of dollars

	Total in all foreign banks*	Banks in U.S.**	Other foreign banks
Argentina	8.2	4.1	4.1
Bolivia	0.4	n.a.	n.a.
Brazil	8.5	1.7	6.8
Chile	2.2	1.6	0.6
Colombia	1.6	1.8	0.8
Ecuador	1.3	0.7	0.6
Mexico	15.3	11.1	4.2
Peru	1.5	1.0	0.5
Uruguay	2.0	1.2	0.8
Venezuela	12.6	7.1	5.5
Subtotal	54.6	30.3	24.3
India	1.7	0.1	1.6
Indonesia	0.7	0.2	0.5
Korea	0.4	0.1	0.3
Malaysia	1.0	0.0	1.0
Nigeria	1.4	n.a.	n.a.
Philippines	1.1	0.7	0.4
South Africa	1.3	0.0	1.3
Thailand	0.4	0.2	0.2
Subtotal	8.0	1.3	6.7
Total for 18 countries	62.6	31.6	31.0

*Source: IMF, *International Financial Statistics*.
**Source: U.S. Treasury *Bulletin*. Banks in the U.S. include the U.S. agencies, branches, and subsidiaries of foreign banks.

Table 12
Impact of capital flight on debt
billions of dollars, unless otherwise noted

	Gross external debt, end-1985 Actual	Without capital flight**	Gross debt as percent of exports of goods and services* Actual	Without capital flight**
Argentina	50	1	493	16
Brazil	106	92	358	322
Mexico	97	12	327	61
Venezuela	31	—12	190	—55
Malaysia	20	4	103	18
Nigeria	19	7	161	62
Philippines	27	15	327	195
South Africa	24	1	131	15

*Debt-to-export ratios are based on the average of debt at beginning and end of 1985.
**Assumes that in the absence of capital flight, debt accumulation and related interest payments would have been reduced, and other flows (direct investment, changes in foreign assets of official monetary authorities and banks, and current account transactions other than interest payments) would not have differed from actual.

This was no coincidence. The policies and track records that engendered capital flight also generated demands for foreign credit that, for much of the time, was readily available. Had the earnings on foreign assets acquired through capital flight been repatriated, rather than reinvested abroad, the servicing of existing debts would have been facilitated. Moreover, foreign debt accumulation would have been much smaller in the absence of capital flight. On the admittedly oversimplified assumption that capital flight served only to inflate debt buildup and related interest charges, several of the eight countries in Table 12 might have been practically debt-free today—were it not for capital flight.

Section II: Sources of Funds
Chapter 2: Introduction

Aid in the Context of Total Resource Flows
OECD

1. CONTINUITY AND CHANGE IN THE ROLE OF AID

In the 1950s and early 1960s aid, provided by a small number of major industrial countries, was the pre-eminent mechanism through which capital flowed to the developing countries. In the mid-1980s aid, provided now by a much greater range and number of donors, remains the largest single inflow in the capital account of developing countries as a group, as it has been throughout the past three or four decades.

The persistence and strength of aid efforts implied by this record reflect the firm establishment of the concept of co-responsibility for development. Earlier chapters in this volume have described how the institutional and political underpinnings of this commitment were put in place.

It is also clear, however, that over the course of the decades much has changed—the sources and distribution of aid, the role and magnitudes of other sources of finance for developing countries' imports of capital, and the sources of the savings which have released real resources to flow from the richer countries to the developing ones. This chapter attempts to place this history of continuity and change in the role of aid on the larger international economic and financial co-operation canvas.

2. CAPITAL FLOWS TO DEVELOPING COUNTRIES AND INTERNATIONAL ECONOMIC BALANCES

The First Two Post-War Decades

In contrast to the current situation, the 1950s and 1960s presented a relatively clear-cut and readily explainable pattern of international capital flows. Initially, the United States was the sole source of capital for both developed and developing countries. The United States current account surplus provided the real goods and services needed for post-war reconstruction and development elsewhere. By the end of the 1950s, however, the rapid recovery in Europe had restored Europe's traditional position as a net exporter of capital. For the following decade and a half, until 1974, the major industrial countries, including Japan to an increasing extent, collectively generated surplus savings for transfer to the rest of the world. Some of this surplus was absorbed by the traditional importers of capital among the developed countries—Canada, Australia, New Zealand, Denmark, etc. Some was absorbed by Eastern Europe. But the bulk of it was taken up by developing countries in what was generally regarded as a logical and healthy process in which savings flowed from capital-rich to capital-poor countries. Table VI-I, taken from the 1985 World Development Report, illustrates the broad picture which held through the 1960s and into the early 1970s—a current account (savings) surplus in industrial countries of around 0.7-1.0 per cent of their combined GNPs and a current account (savings) deficit in developing countries, taken together, in the region of 2.0-2.5 per cent of their combined GNPs.

These averages conceal wide variations in the situations of individual countries. Nevertheless, it is fair to say that it was during this reasonably stable period of a decade and a half that many of the assumptions, expectations and issues which came to play an important role in international discussions on development and finance were established. It might be noted, with this in mind, that the magnitude of the capital transfers from developed to developing countries during this period was significant but not spectacular, falling a long way short of the peak international cpaital flows of the nineteenth and early twentieth centuries. No doubt this perception helped to engender the claim that capital flows to developing countries could be, and should be, lifted to higher levels to the advantage of both developed and developing countries.

The Oil Shocks and Their Impact

The first oil shock, at the end of 1973, radically disturbed the pattern that had become established during the 1960s. While the savings surplus of the major industrial countries contracted sharply, the savings (current account) deficit of the developing countries, excluding the high-income oil exporters, increased sharply. These movements had as their counterpart the enormous increase in the savings of the very small number of capital surplus oil producers located in the Gulf. Although the subsequent adjustment on all sides was, especially in retrospect, relatively rapid, the five years 1974-78 taken

Table VI-1. CURRENT ACCOUNT BALANCE AS A PERCENTAGE OF GNP IN SELECTED GROUPS OF DEVELOPING COUNTRIES AND YEARS, 1960-84

Data source and country group	1960[a]	1965[a]	1970	1971	1972	1973	1974	1975	1976	1977	1978	1979	1980	1981	1982	1983	1984
BASED ON NATIONAL ACCOUNTS																	
Low-income countries	-1.6	-1.8	-1.1	-1.6	-1.0	-0.9	-1.7	-2.1	-0.9	-0.7	-1.2	-1.4	-2.2	-1.4	-0.9	-1.0	-1.3
Asia	-1.4	-1.6	-0.9	-1.0	-0.5	-0.6	-1.1	-1.2	-0.1	0.4	-0.1	-0.6	1.4	-0.5	-0.2	0.2	-0.6
Africa	-3.3	-4.1	-3.4	-7.3	5.6	-4.4	-7.8	-10.2	-7.3	-7.6	-8.3	-7.7	-9.8	-10.5	-12.0	-10.0	-9.4
Middle-income oil importers	-2.9	-2.0	-3.2	-3.6	-1.2	-0.8	-4.8	-5.3	-2.9	-2.3	-2.2	-3.2	-4.1	-5.2	-4.7	-4.4	-2.7
Exporters[b]	-2.7	-2.0	-3.2	-3.5	-0.9	-0.9	-5.7	-5.5	-2.8	-1.6	-1.7	-3.1	-3.6	-4.2	-4.0	-3.1	-1.3
Other	-3.5	-2.0	-3.0	-4.0	-2.2	-0.2	-1.8	-4.5	-3.4	-4.5	-3.9	-3.7	-5.9	-8.3	-7.3	-8.6	-7.4
Middle-income oil exporters	-1.6	-2.4	-3.0	-3.0	-2.4	-1.1	3.3	-3.4	-2.4	-3.6	-5.1	-0.2	0.8	-3.8	-4.4	-2.1	-0.7
All developing countries	-2.2	-2.0	-2.3	-2.7	-1.4	-0.9	-1.9	-3.9	-2.2	-2.2	-2.6	-2.0	-2.3	-3.9	-3.7	-2.8	-1.8
Oil-importing developing countries	-2.3	-1.9	-2.2	-2.7	-1.1	-0.8	-3.5	-4.0	-2.2	-1.7	-1.8	-2.6	-3.4	-3.9	-3.4	-3.1	-2.1
High-income oil exporters	9.7	20.9	15.7	26.2	22.5	21.2	51.5	40.2	35.0	26.3	15.5	21.2	31.4	32.2	20.1	-4.7	..
Industrial countries	1.0	0.9	0.8	1.0	0.9	0.7	-0.2	0.6	0.1	0.1	0.7	0.0	-0.5	0.0	0.0	0.3	-0.4
BASED ON BALANCE OF PAYMENTS[c]																	
All developing countries	..	..	-2.6	-3.0	-1.7	-1.3	-2.3	-4.2	-2.8	-2.6	-3.3	-2.9	-3.3	-4.9	-4.8	-2.8	-1.8
Oil-importing developing countries	..	..	-2.5	-3.0	-1.5	-1.1	-3.9	-4.3	-2.6	-2.1	-2.5	-3.4	-4.6	-5.1	-4.2	-3.1	-2.1

a) Data for 1960 and 1965 do not include net private transfers.
b) Major exporters of manufactures.
c) Excluding official transfers.

Source: World Development Report, 1985 (based on World Bank data).

as a whole saw a fall in the industrial countries' net savings surplus of at least half a percentage point of GNP and an increase in the developing countries' net savings deficit of at least one percentage point of GNP. The current account surpluses of the Gulf countries over the period were sufficient in magnitude, however, (at their peak more than 2 per cent of OECD countries' combined GNP) to produce, on balance, a "world savings surplus" which, with prevailing policy settings in the major countries, actually lowered world real interest rates.

As can be seen from Table VI-1, the second oil shock produced an additional shift along the same lines in world savings balances. New features appeared, however, and therefore new consequences. The further fall in industrial countries' net savings was bound up with growing public sector deficits, a trend under way for some time previously, but now emerging unmistakably as an important economic phenomenon. In addition, resurgent inflation and a falling dollar produced a new stringency in monetary policies in the major countries. These factors combined to produce a "world savings shortage" and high real interest rates. And although the recession in the industrial countries was shallower than its predecessor it proved more persistent. Commodity prices, including oil prices, were not able to attain (or retain in the case of oil) previous peaks, and indeed have remained remarkably weak even in the face of world economic recovery. The oil-price situation eliminated even the Gulf countries as a source of surplus savings and oil exporters in general became significant claimants on the shrunken pool of available world savings.

The consequential adjustment process involved an inevitable reduction in developing-country absorption of foreign savings. The developing countries' use of external resources fell from the 1981 peak of 5.0 per cent of developing countries' GNP—the highest ever registered in the post-war period—to 3.0 per cent by 1983. This adjustment was effected under conditions of world-wide recession, and itself contributed not insignificantly to that recession. (In contrast, the previous adjustment had been eased by an expanding world economy.)

Recent Developments and Longer-Term Trends

In 1984 a new chapter in the international adjustment process was written. The strong United States recovery which spread economic expansion around the world, including to a large part of the developing world, also produced an unprecedented United States current account deficit. The dynamic export expansion which this entailed for the rest of the world produced a further fall in the developing countries' deficit of one per cent of their GNP (see Table VI-1) to around two per cent, the lowest recorded since 1972-73 (which had reflected a major commodity-price boom).

The extent to which the current pattern of international balances and capital flows departs from the "logical" and historical norm is only partly revealed in Table VI-1. What is clear there is the marked reduction in the savings surplus generated collectively by the industrial countries, dominated at this point by the large deficit of the United States which more than offsets the surpluses of Japan and Europe. But there is also what appears to be a longer-term trend towards a lower industrial-country savings surplus, discernible especially if one sees the history in terms of three periods—1960-73, 1974-78 and 1979-84. This trend is probably exaggerated by Table VI-1, especially for the final period, by the dramatic growth in the world current-account discrepancy, which makes it impossible to reach definitive conclusions about the magnitudes, or even the direction, of international capital flows. Thus, if the current account deficit of the developing countries is accepted as more or less reflecting the actual situation, then there must be at the present time—with no oil surpluses —a positive current balance for the industrial countries.

But behind these aggregate figures lie other factors which are essential to an adequate appreciation of how much the situation has changed. It is already clear in Table VI-1 that there are major differences among the developing countries—that low-income Asia (dominated by India and China) has a traditionally low and recently declining reliance on external resources while low-income Africa, from relatively restrained imports of capital in the 1960s, has in the 1980s a relatively large reliance on external resources. Similarly, among the middle-income oil importers, the major exporters of manufactures clearly have the capacity to adjust reasonably rapidly their call on external resources, while the more commodity-dependent have had a more persistent and growing use of capital imports.

Recent IMF analysis provides a further dimension to these indications. (See *World Economic Outlook,* April 1985, Supplementary Note No. 9 and Appendix Tables 32 and 33.) Expressed in terms of the ratio of current account balances to exports of goods and services, it is apparent that almost all of the reduction in developing-country current deficits and hence external resource use is accounted for by the countries which can be defined as "market borrowers" (i.e., more than two-thirds of external financing is from commercial sources). These countries are now very close to current-account balance. Official borrowers (with more than two-thirds of external financing from official sources), on the other hand, have adjusted much less; their deficits are still some 45 per cent of their export receipts, compared with a peak of 50 per cent in 1981-82.

A third group of countries which draws on both commercial and official financing in roughly equal proportions would appear to have adjusted little more, if at all, than the official borrowers.

In other words, all the recent large adjustment of the developing countries as a group has been effected by the market borrowers and little or none by the countries that rely for one-third or more of their financing on official sources. And among the market borrowers the bulk of the adjustment has been made by those countries, notably in Latin America, which have experienced debt problems. The adjustment by these countries, as is well known, has been of truly massive proportions, since they faced rapidly mounting interest obligations requiring the generation of very significant trade surpluses if they were to be serviced. Market borrowers who have avoided debt-servicing problems also adjusted, usually at an earlier stage. But they have remained in a position where moderate continuing use of external resources is open to them: hence the phenomenon of a stark division between those market borrowers who are able to finance current-account deficits of some significance and those who, for the foreseeable future, can make only very limited use of external resources relative to past experience.

The Post-War History in Review

It may be useful at this point to recapitulate the historical evolution of resource flows to developing countries suggested by the analysis set out above. First, the "normal" pattern of capital flows established in the 1960s did not evolve according to textbook principles or any programme established in the international fora. Rather than an orderly, expansionary process of resource flow from more advanced to less advanced countries, the savings balance of the developed countries deteriorated after the first oil shock in a seemingly secular trend which has yet to be reversed and which appears increasingly to be associated with structural imbalances in their economies, specifically in public sector finances. While the oil surpluses lasted, the aggregate flow of resources to developing countries was nevertheless able to increase markedly. With the adoption of a strong anti-inflationary policy stance in the major economies, high real interest rates, the emergence of recession conditions and then the disappearance of the oil surplus, the economics of debt-financing changed radically. Those developing countries which had made heavy use of bank finance at floating interest rates, without at the same time building economies with robust debt-servicing and adjustment capacities, suddenly lost their creditworthiness. A significant proportion of the flow of world savings to developing countries thus stopped abruptly; and countries which had retained their creditworthiness curtailed their demand for external capital as a logical reaction to the changed economics of foreign borrowing. The aggregate use of external resources by developing countries fell, as a consequence, to an historically low level. (See Table VI-2.) Subsequently, a new factor has entered the scene in the form of a large external financing requirement on the part of the United States, arising essentially from domestic developments. In the mid-1980s, therefore, the United States, rather than the developing countries, is the world's major importer of capital. This is one of the new situations in the world economy which involve increasingly complex interlinkages between policies and developments in both developed and developing countries.

The history then is one of sharp discontinuities and disparities among the developing countries. Indeed, it is much less possible now to think in terms of a single developing-country aggregate. For the behaviour of the resource-flow aggregates have, for the past decade and more, been dominated by a few major "market borrowers" and especially by the current major "debt problem" countries, which have accounted for the large shifts in both expansionary and contractionary directions. If the "market borrowers" are removed from the picture, the resource flow history for the remaining developing countries, leaving aside for the moment the special cases of India and China, looks much more like the steady secular expansion that has been the vision underlying international discussions and debates on resource flows to developing countries. This much is apparent from Table VI-1, in the lines for low-income Africa and "other" middle-income oil importers. For both these groups, the importance of external resource flows in their economies has grown apace over the past twenty-five years, assuming very considerable proportions in the 1980s. As discussed elsewhere in this Report, the increased use of external resources by these groups of countries in the 1980s has necessarily reflected a counteroffensive against deteriorating economic conditions and performance rather than a new offensive for development. But the needs have been critical and the resource flow to these countries has expanded in response.

The present situation and future prospects can now be summarised briefly, in terms of the developing-country groups identified in this analysis.

First, and most paradoxically, the "market borrowers," accounting for more than 65 per cent of developing-country GNP (see *Development Co-operation–1983 Review,* Chapter III, Table III-4, for breakdowns based on 1980-81 data), have practically ceased, collectively at least, to be net importers of capital from the rest of the world. A not unlikely prognosis is that net resource flows to them will be negligible for the rest of the decade, marking a major departure from previous experience and expectations. A change in this prognosis depends on both convincing repair of the economies of the debt-problem countries and a favourable evolution of the world economy, in particular a reduction in real interest rates, which is dependent upon policies in the major industrial countries.

Second, the "official borrowers" have reached an historically high level of reliance on external resource flows, which may now diminish slightly as they succeed in making some further essential external adjustment. But the IMF prognosis suggests that these countries' external resource use will remain

Table VI-2. TOTAL RESOURCE FLOWS TO DEVELOPING COUNTRIES BY MAJOR TYPES OF FLOW, 1950-84

$ billion at 1983 prices and exchange rates

	1950-55	1960-61	1970	1971	1972	1973	1974	1975	1976	1977	1978	1979	1980	1981	1982	1983	1984
I. Official Development Assistance	(8.35)	19.54	22.18	23.37	22.13	23.93	28.62	31.59	29.50	27.98	32.06	32.93	36.05	36.23	33.69	33.80	35.75
1. Flows from bilateral sources	8.35	18.60	19.38	20.22	19.12	20.24	23.77	25.88	23.92	21.59	25.25	26.53	28.75	28.52	26.21	26.23	27.35
a) DAC countries	8.35	15.87	14.82	15.32	14.40	13.34	14.15	14.56	13.70	13.34	14.87	16.74	16.99	17.71	18.35	18.53	20.10
b) OPEC countries		—	1.02	1.07	1.44	3.82	7.13	8.44	7.46	5.66	7.82	7.13	8.19	7.46	4.56	4.33	3.79
c) CMEA countries		1.80	2.60	2.53	2.24	2.19	1.69	2.23	2.07	2.01	1.87	2.20	2.48	2.88	2.86	2.94	2.95
d) Non-DAC/OECD		0.02	0.01	0.02	0.02	0.02	0.01	0.02	0.05	0.11	0.16	0.14	0.81	0.21	0.18	0.07	0.10
e) LDC donors		0.91	0.93	1.28	1.02	0.87	0.79	0.63	0.64	0.47	0.53	0.32	0.28	0.26	0.26	0.26	0.41
2. Flows from multilateral agencies		0.94	2.80	3.15	3.01	3.69	4.85	5.71	5.58	6.39	6.81	6.40	7.30	7.71	7.48	7.57	8.40
II. Grants by private voluntary agencies			2.25	2.21	2.27	2.58	2.10	1.99	1.94	1.97	1.87	2.00	2.17	1.97	2.30	2.34	2.50
III. Non-concessional flows	7.54	15.29	28.66	28.72	28.98	37.41	34.06	51.01	54.59	58.53	64.79	53.45	55.66	68.56	60.10	82.12	54.00
1. Official or officially supported		6.57	10.36	11.94	8.17	9.15	13.14	15.66	19.21	20.79	21.29	18.84	22.91	21.55	21.90	19.82	20.00
a) Private export credits (DAC)		2.03	5.47	6.58	3.14	2.18	4.13	6.57	9.72	11.70	11.00	9.07	10.43	10.99	7.06	5.50	5.00
b) Official export credits (DAC)		2.80	1.54	1.75	1.61	2.13	1.38	1.78	2.00	1.91	2.52	1.77	2.31	1.95	2.65	2.10	2.50
c) Multilateral		0.80	1.86	2.23	2.20	2.47	3.11	3.76	3.66	3.56	3.50	4.26	4.55	5.57	6.58	7.22	7.50
d) Other off. & private flows (DAC)	0.94	0.65	0.68	0.98	1.92	1.43	1.12	1.15	0.83	1.54	1.17	2.10	1.91	2.62	3.00	3.00	
e) Other donors			0.84	0.70	0.24	0.45	3.09	2.42	2.67	2.79	2.73	2.57	3.52	1.13	2.99	2.00	2.00
2. Private		8.72	18.30	16.78	20.81	28.25	20.92	35.35	35.38	37.74	43.50	34.61	32.75	47.01	38.21	62.30	34.00
a) Direct investment		6.54	9.66	8.04	9.22	8.89	3.25	16.89	11.98	12.99	13.14	13.75	9.89	16.77	11.81	7.80	9.50
b) Bank sector[a]		2.18	7.85	8.01	10.46	18.27	17.19	17.84	21.63	20.51	25.93	20.16	21.57	29.19	25.89	54.00[a]	24.00[a]
c) Bond lending			0.79	0.73	1.13	1.09	0.48	0.62	1.76	4.23	4.43	0.70	1.29	1.05	0.51	0.50	0.50
Memo: Official development finance[a]	8.35	20.34	24.04	25.60	24.33	26.40	31.73	35.35	33.16	31.54	35.56	37.19	40.60	41.80	40.27	40.92	43.25
Total resource flows (I + II + III)	(15.89)	34.83	53.09	54.30	53.38	63.92	64.78	84.59	86.03	88.48	98.72	88.38	93.88	106.76	96.09	118.26	92.25
For information:																	
ODA to developing countries and multilateral agencies, total		20.80	22.86	23.30	24.93	24.29	30.31	32.81	31.75	31.54	34.53	33.88	37.60	36.37	36.88	36.39	37.40
DAC countries	8.8	18.02	18.19	18.33	20.05	17.14	19.96	20.59	20.12	20.82	22.66	23.38	25.57	24.85	27.61	27.54	29.30
OPEC countries		—	1.05	1.09	1.54	4.02	7.87	9.28	8.80	8.03	9.23	7.84	9.06	8.14	5.80	5.43	4.60
CMEA countries		1.85	2.62	2.55	2.26	2.20	1.71	2.25	2.08	2.03	1.88	2.22	2.50	2.84	2.92	3.04	3.00
Non-DAC/OECD		0.02	0.03	0.02	0.02	0.03	0.03	0.04	0.10	0.17	0.21	0.20	0.19	0.27	0.27	0.12	0.20
LDC donors		0.91	0.97	1.31	1.06	0.90	0.74	0.65	0.65	0.49	0.55	0.24	0.28	0.27	0.28	0.26	0.30
Total bank lending										41.68	45.20	36.56	45.96	50.59	40.83	35.00	18.00
of which:																	
Short-term										21.17	19.27	16.40	24.39	21.40	14.94	−19.00	−6.00
IMF purchases, net			0.89	0.12	0.65	0.68	2.99	4.82	4.30	−0.57	−0.96	0.53	2.45	6.01	6.38	12.48	5.50

a) Bank Sector includes, for 1983 and 1984, significant amounts of rescheduled short-term debt. The real evolution of bank lending is best reflected in the line showing "Total bank lending" at the bottom of the table above. The evolution of total resource flows needs to be adjusted accordingly.
b) Bilateral and multilateral ODA plus multilateral non-concessional flows.

23

near its high current level in relation to their export revenue and GNP through to the end of the decade. And for the next year or two the "official borrowers," accounting for only 7 per cent of developing country GNP, will be the recipients of the largest absolute volume of real resource flows among the developing countries, as they have been since 1983. (See *World Economic Outlook,* April 1985, Appendix Table 51.)

Third, the remaining group of developing countries, those who draw fairly evenly on both official and commercial finance and including in this group both India and China (although they have very different financing patterns), are likely to remain in the near future at their current levels of external resource use. This group accounts for some 26 per cent of developing-country GNP (of which China 12 per cent and India 7 per cent). It could, potentially, become a much larger user of capital imports but this depends very much on China and India and how their economic objectives, policies and performance evolve in the years immediately ahead.

A basic implication which emerges from this prognosis is that by far the greatest proportion of the substantially reduced resource flows to developing countries is currently (i.e., from 1984) directed towards countries that are reliant on official finance or use significant amounts of official finance. With this pattern predicted to continue for the next few years, a major change in the pattern of developing-country financing is now under way, with official finance clearly becoming more predominant. Against this background, the next section of this chapter examines the historical evolution of the "financing mix" of developing countries.

3. THE CHANGING MIX OF FINANCIAL FLOWS

The previous section examined the history of resource flows in terms of "real resource flows," that is the transfer of real goods and services through current-account surpluses and deficits, reflecting domestic savings surpluses and deficits. This section moves to the analysis of the financing of this resource transfer, that is, to the composition of the capital account of the developing countries.

The mix of financing flows to developing countries as it has evolved over time is illustrated in the two associated tables, Table VI-2 (showing volumes, estimated at 1983 prices and exchange rates) and Table VI-3 (showing percentage shares).

A useful point of departure for the analysis of this history is to consider the progress of "privatisation" of development finance—a trend which attracted much attention in the 1970s. That such a process should occur is not at all surprising given the point of departure, determined by historical circumstances, of a predominant role for official finance. This was not simply a matter of political inclination. In the 1950s, present-day international capital markets had hardly begun to develop. As a practical matter therefore (and given that the multilateral institutions were still in their infancy), significant development financing meant official bilateral financing.

The Initial Dominance of Official Bilateral Financing

That is what the numbers in Tables VI-2 and VI-3 show—a dynamic increase during the 1950s in official bilateral flows. It was this major new thrust in the 1950s that provided the raison d'etre for the Development Assistance Group, which first met in 1960, and in 1961 was transformed into the Development Assistance Committee. At that stage official development financing (including a still very small component of multilateral financing), accounted for nearly 60 per cent of total flows to developing countries. Of the non-concessional flows, the two major components were export credits (more than half of which were direct official export credits, in contrast to the later pattern where officially guaranteed private export credits predominated), with a share in total flows of some 14 per cent, and private direct foreign investment, with a share of about 19 per cent. Bank loans had established, at this stage, only a very minor presence.

From the mid-1960s, as private international capital markets began to grow (the birth of the Eurodollar market being particularly significant) and as a number of the more advanced developing countries became creditworthy, a natural process of transformation of the pattern of financial flows set in. The component almost solely responsible for this change over the course of the 1960s was bank lending, which increased its share of total financial flows by nearly 9 percentage points in the course of the decade, while the share of foreign direct investment remained practically steady and bond lending established a very modest presence.

Yet this was not the whole story of the 1960s. For the fall in the share of official development assistance over this decade reflected also the very small increase in the volume of aid. Aid from DAC countries as a group increased only marginally during the decade, increases being largely offset by the termination or reduction of aid to some major recipients. The diverse developments in national aid programmes that, taken together, produced such a result are described in some detail in Chapter III (see Section 2 in particular). While bilateral aid actually fell in volume during the 1960s, it was in this period that a significant role for multilateral aid was established, following the foundation of IDA in 1960 (see Chapter IV). A further indication that the 1960s was a period when the idea of a permanent aid effort was becoming firmly entrenched is the appearance of a small but durable presence on the part of private voluntary agencies, amounting by 1970 to about 4 per cent of total financial flows.

The near-stagnation of aid volumes in the 1960s did not, in the prevailing world economic environment of growth and

Table VI-3. TOTAL RESOURCE FLOWS TO DEVELOPING COUNTRIES BY MAJOR TYPES OF FLOW, 1950-84

Percentage shares of long-term total flows

	1950-55	1960-61	1970	1971	1972	1973	1974	1975	1976	1977	1978	1979	1980	1981	1982	1983[a]	1984[a]
I. Official Development Assistance	(52.5)	55.9	41.8	43.0	41.4	37.4	44.2	37.3	34.3	31.6	32.5	37.2	38.4	33.9	35.1	35.9	41.9
1. Flows from bilateral sources	52.5	53.6	36.5	37.2	35.8	31.7	36.7	30.5	27.8	24.4	25.6	30.0	30.6	26.7	27.3	27.8	32.0
a) DAC countries	52.5	47.7	27.9	28.2	27.0	20.9	21.9	17.2	15.9	15.1	15.1	18.9	18.1	16.6	19.1	19.7	23.6
b) OPEC countries	—	—	1.9	1.9	2.7	6.0	11.0	10.0	8.7	2.3	1.9	2.5	2.6	2.7	3.0	4.6	4.4
c) CMEA countries	...	5.2	4.9	4.7	4.2	3.4	2.6	2.6	2.4	2.3	1.9	2.5	2.6	2.7	3.0	3.1	3.5
d) Non-DAC/OECD	...	0.1	x	x	x	x	x	x	x	0.1	0.2	0.2	0.9	0.2	0.2	0.1	0.1
e) LDC donors	...	2.6	1.8	2.4	1.9	1.4	1.2	0.7	0.8	0.5	0.5	0.4	0.3	0.2	0.3	0.3	0.5
2. Flows from multilateral agencies	...	2.3	5.3	5.8	5.6	5.8	7.5	6.8	6.5	7.2	6.9	7.2	7.8	7.2	7.8	8.0	9.9
II. Grants by private voluntary agencies	...	...	4.2	4.1	4.3	4.0	3.2	2.4	2.2	2.2	1.9	2.3	2.3	1.8	2.4	2.5	2.9
III. Non-concessional flows	47.5	44.1	54.0	52.9	54.3	58.5	52.6	60.3	63.5	66.2	65.6	60.5	59.3	64.2	62.5	61.6	55.2
1. Official or officially supported	...	18.9	19.5	22.0	15.3	14.3	20.3	18.5	22.3	23.5	21.5	21.3	24.4	20.2	22.8	21.0	23.5
a) Private export credits (DAC)	...	5.9	10.3	12.1	5.9	3.4	6.4	7.8	11.3	13.2	11.1	10.3	11.1	10.3	7.3	5.8	5.9
b) Official export credits (DAC)	...	8.1	2.9	3.2	3.0	3.3	2.1	2.3	2.2	2.6	2.6	2.0	2.5	1.8	2.8	2.2	2.9
c) Multilateral	...	2.3	3.5	4.1	4.1	3.9	4.8	4.4	4.3	4.0	3.5	4.8	4.8	5.2	6.8	7.7	8.8
d) Other off. & private flows (DAC)	...	...	1.2	1.3	1.8	3.0	2.2	1.3	1.3	0.9	1.5	1.3	2.2	1.8	2.7	3.2	3.5
e) Other donors	...	2.7	1.6	1.3	0.5	0.7	4.8	2.9	3.1	3.2	2.8	2.9	3.7	1.1	3.1	2.1	2.3
2. Private	...	25.1	34.5	30.9	39.0	44.2	32.2	41.8	41.1	42.7	44.1	39.2	34.9	44.0	39.8	40.6	31.7
a) Direct investment	...	18.8	18.2	14.8	17.3	13.9	5.0	20.0	13.9	14.7	13.3	15.6	10.5	15.7	12.3	8.3	11.2
b) Bank sector	...	6.3	14.8	14.8	19.6	28.6	26.5	21.1	25.1	23.2	26.3	22.8	23.0	27.3	26.9	31.8	20.0
c) Bond lending	...	...	1.5	1.3	2.1	1.7	0.7	0.7	2.0	4.8	4.5	0.8	1.4	1.0	0.5	0.5	0.6
Memo: Official development finance[b]	52.5	58.2	45.3	47.1	45.6	41.3	49.0	41.8	38.5	35.6	36.0	42.1	43.2	39.2	41.9	43.4	50.7
Total resource flows (I + II + III)	100.0	100.0	100.0	100.0	100.0	100.0	100.0	100.0	100.0	100.0	100.0	100.0	100.0	100.0	100.0	100.0	100.0
For information ODA to developing countries and multilateral agencies, total	100.0	100.0	100.0	100.0	100.0	100.0	100.0	100.0	100.0	100.0	100.0	100.0	100.0	100.0	100.0	100.0	100.0
DAC countries	...	86.6	79.6	78.7	80.4	70.5	65.9	62.7	63.4	66.0	65.6	69.0	68.0	68.3	75.0	75.7	78.4
OPEC countries	—	—	4.6	4.7	6.2	16.6	26.0	28.3	27.7	25.5	26.7	23.1	24.1	22.4	15.7	14.9	12.3
CMEA countries	...	8.9	11.5	11.0	9.1	9.1	5.6	6.9	6.6	6.4	5.5	6.5	6.6	7.8	7.9	8.4	8.0
Non-DAC/OECD	...	0.1	0.1	x	x	0.1	0.1	0.1	0.5	0.5	0.6	0.6	0.7	0.7	0.3	0.5
LDC donors	...	4.4	4.2	5.6	4.3	3.7	2.4	2.0	2.0	1.6	1.6	0.3	0.7	0.7	0.7	0.7	0.8

a) 1983 and 1984 percentages have been calculated using a baseline figure for ordinary long-term bank sector lending business, i.e., $30 billion instead of the $34 billion shown in Table VI-2 and $17 billion instead of $24 billion after excluding from long-term flows estimated amounts rescheduled from short-term in those years (see footnote to previous table).
b) Bilateral and multilateral ODA plus multilateral non-concessional flows.

25

trade and financial expansion, prevent the developing countries from enjoying a period of unprecedented development progress. Nor did it detract very much from a general consciousness that official finance remained the most important debt-creating flow by far. Thus, in the late 1960s and early 1970s, the DAC gave a considerable amount of attention to the implications of mounting stocks of official financial obligations, culminating in the publication in 1974 of an analytical study entitled "Debt Problems of Developing Countries." (This was a period when the cumulative volume of private bank debt remained insignificant and when the debt problems which had arisen in the 1960s were all connected with official debt.) But, as noted in the previous section, there was also by the end of the 1960s an appreciation that capital flows from developed to developing countries, including official aid volume, fell short of what history and economic principles would suggest might be both feasible and effective. This provided the background for the international debate on the level of resource flows and the introduction of the concept of targets for total resource flows and for aid.

The Rise of Bank Lending

The first half of the 1970s did indeed witness a spectacular increase in financial flows, both official and private, to developing countries. This was not, however, the consequence of a considered and agreed adjustment of objectives and policies, but rather a response to events which virtually no one had foreseen.

The most popular version of this change associates it with the recycling of the oil surplus by private banks after 1973. In fact, it is absolutely clear from Tables VI-2 and VI-3 that the most decisive and dramatic increase in bank lending to developing countries was associated with the major commodity price boom of 1972-73—before the oil shock, which struck in late 1973. From a 1971 figure of US$8 billion (at 1983 prices and exchange rates), bank lending expanded to more than US$18 billion in 1973, and as a share of total flows from 15 per cent in 1971 to 29 per cent in 1973. Bank lending thereafter levelled off for the next two years, despite the enormous increase in oil bills, because a good proportion of the borrowing had served to increase official reserves. Developing-country borrowers were thus in a very liquid position at the time of the first oil crisis. (It should be noted that as financial flows reached new heights in 1973, developing-country current-account deficits reached new lows, as is apparent in Table VI-1. This is a striking example of how real resource flows can differ from financial flows. Over the longer haul, of course, real resource flows and financial resource flows must broadly match up.)

A second phase of increase in bank lending occurred between 1976 and 1978, carrying the volume from the figure of roughly US$18 billion established by the first wave to a new peak of US$26 billion in 1978 (all figures at 1983 prices and exchange rates). Again this increase took place in the context of a commodity price boom, less dramatic than in 1972-73 but significant nonetheless. Again it coincided with a significant fall in developing-country current-account deficits to relatively low levels, thus flowing for the most part into a major build-up in developing countries' foreign exchange reserves. Again this process preceded the 1978-79 oil shock, which thus found oil-importing countries in a highly liquid position. Again long-term bank-lending receded in the immediately following two years.

The other major private flow, foreign direct investment, fluctuated considerably over this period, but around a fairly stable trend, holding more or less constant its percentage share in total financial flows. Thus the rise in the share of private flows in total flows reflected fully the rise in bank lending.

The Privatisation of Financial Flows — Processes and Problems

Against this background, the most plausible explanation for the "privatisation" of financial flows to developing countries would seem to be not the advent of the recycling of oil surpluses, but rather the continuation of the "natural" process identified earlier; that is, a process arising from the parallel evolution of international financial markets and creditworthy developing-country borrowers. The major increases in lending to developing countries by the international banks were effected against a record of strong economic growth, improving current-account balances and rising export volumes and prices. The rapid accumulation of financial obligations was indeed remarked and began to be tracked systematically by interested international organisations, including the OECD and the World Bank. But interest burdens remained relatively small and inflation consistently reduced the real burden of the accumulating debt stocks. For the international bankers, developing-country lending had a track record of being both profitable and low-risk.

This interpretation of the expansion of private bank lending reveals a deeper economic and historical logic to what is perhaps now too readily seen as a mistaken turn in development financing, in degree if not fundamentally. But, as the perspective provided by the subsequent debt crises indicates, there was a darker side to the evolution of bank lending. Part of this story is visible in Table VI-2, where it is very apparent that total bank funding of developing countries in the second half of the 1970s was in fact much greater than the figures mentioned so far. The estimates for short-term bank lending start only in 1977, so that it is not possible to say exactly how much this level of short-term lending exceeded previously established norms. But there is reason to believe, from the facts that came to light in the emergency rescheduling operations of 1982 and 1983, that short-term lending (including inter-bank market operations) escaped proper surveillance and control, either by the authorities in both lending and borrowing countries or by bank managements. Neither can the more organised forms of lending escape criticism. The mechanism of syndicated floating-interest-rate loans transferred the interest-rate risks of banks to the borrowing countries to an unrealistic degree, so that the bankers created for themselves a high degree of vulnerability to credit risks. The syndication technique itself appears to have reduced the incentive to base lending decisions on objective risk assessment, since the fees and margins of lenders and participants in developing-country loans depended on volume rather than attention either to prudent exposure limits or to the economic policies of borrowing countries.

These weaknesses in the conduct of bank lending proved to be profound in the context of the third wave of increased bank lending in 1981-82. In sharp contrast to the two previous episodes (1972-73 and 1976-78), the world economy was in a recession rather than a recovery, real interest rates were high and rising, commodity prices were depressed. The real burden of debt stocks was therefore increasing rapidly and developing-country borrowers were moving towards greater current-account and internal imbalances, with falling rather than rising external reserves. This was the background against which the private bank debt crises emerged in the autumn of 1982, engulfing those major developing-country borrowers whose economic policies had not been compatible with the development of a robust debt-servicing capacity.

New Developments in the Mid-1980s

In the wake of the debt crisis total bank lending, short- and long-term taken together, has fallen rapidly. Initially, the stabilization of the debt-problem required bank support to continue at a comparatively high level. But in 1984 the rapid development of the United States recovery and accompanying import demand both boosted the trade surpluses of the debt-problem countries, thus reducing significantly their financing requirements, and dramatically diverted major US bank lending from external to internal borrowers. As outlined in Section I of this chapter, the net new financing requirements of the "market borrowers" among developing countries are forecast to remain comparatively small as the debt-problem countries repair their balance sheets and concentrate on rapidly building up their export orientation and their creditworthiness. This does not imply, however, that developing countries have suddenly ceased to make use of private bank funding. Many "market borrowers" avoided debt problems. In fact, some 20 developing countries continue to have ready access to private capital markets. And it is not impossible that India and China may emerge in the next few years as larger users of private financing. But in the meantime the reduction in the bank financing requirements of what were previously the major borrowers seems almost certain to be the dominant factor. As far as the history of financial flows to developing countries is concerned, the next few years may thus appear as an epilogue to the story which began with the lending boom of the early 1970s. By the time an important new upward trend in private financing for developing countries becomes established, it may well have taken nearly two decades for the 1970s lending cycle to have played out.

Non-Banking Flows in the 1970s and 1980s

Bank lending to developing countries, with its interconnections with major events and economic policy trends and its successes and failures, has tended to dominate the analysis of developing country finances over the past decade, obscuring important new departures in aid and other financing flows.

i) Direct Investment

Direct investment fluctuated so strongly during the period that it is difficult to see any clear picture. It seems fair to say however, that, until 1983 and 1984, no definite trend either up or down in absolute volumes was discernible. The percentage share in total flows was reduced from its 1960s level, but this much was established by the early 1970s, and reflected the increase in bank lending volume rather than any tailing off in direct investment. The clear reductions in the past two years are mainly a reflection of the sharp curtailment of investment flows to Latin American countries whose domestic retrenchment in the face of debt problems adversely affected the prospects against which foreign investment decisions are taken. In Asia, the other main recipient region, investment flows appear to be continuing more or less as previously. It may be expected that flows to Latin American countries will recover as confidence in their economic future returns.

ii) Export Credits

A boom in officially guaranteed export credits, which began in 1975, carried through for another seven years, until 1982, when recession in the developing world cut back the demand for project financing in general. This surge in export credits reflected the buoyant investment activity in developing countries during a period when investment growth in OECD countries was faltering and manufacturers (and their governments) were anxious to find new outlets to preserve output and employment. The pace of private export credit lending, much of it during this period at subsidised interest rates, carried its share in total flows to around 11 per cent. With direct government export credits adding another 2.0-2.5 per cent share, total export credit lending played a role approximately of the same magnitude as in the 1960s. Clearly both borrowers and lenders found this form of financing useful and attractive. But it was not without problems or controversy, contributing in some cases to deteriorating debt structures and engendering conflicts among lending governments of the OECD over the trade-distorting features of interest-rate competition and the use of aid in association with export credits. As described in Chapter X, this latter practice also engendered a major debate about those aspects of associated financing which distorted aid and development. Despite the fall in 1983 and 1984 in export credit volumes, these debates and the attempt to find solutions to both the intergovernmental conflicts and the inherent policy problems continue.

iii) Multilateral Developing Lending

Non-concessional lending by the multilateral development banks (MDBs) grew steadily through the 1970s as the World Bank consolidated its standing in the international bond markets and strengthened its capacity to conduct well founded lending programmes, while the regional development banks also established recognised standing in the markets. By 1980 the share of MDB lending in total flows had risen to nearly 5 per cent, about one percentage point above its 1970 share. In the 1980s, this share began to ascend much more rapidly, even before the turn-around in private bank lending. This new thrust reflected in part the expansion of world bond markets. On the lending side, the kind of long-term development financing delivered by the MDBs patently was more in line with financial fundamentals and development priorities than either medium-term bank loans or much export-credit financing. By 1984, MDB non-concessional lending had reached over 8 per cent of total financial flows and a consensus was gathering that its role should grow further in the years ahead.

iv) Concessional Aid

Overshadowed by the dramatic evolution of private bank lending (and still little recognised) was the dynamic growth of official development aid in the 1970s, following the near-stagnation of aid volume in the 1960s.

A major new impulse in aid volume came in 1973-1975, when in the context of the oil price increases the major oil-surplus developing countries mounted an aid effort (including both bilateral and multilateral contributions), which climbed from US$1.5 billion in 1972 to US$7.9 billion in 1974, and to a peak of US$9.3 billion in 1975, reaching that year 2.71 per cent of the OPEC countries' GNP. (All amounts expressed in 1983 dollars.) This effort was maintained, with some fluctuations, until the significant oil price declines beginning in 1982 brought a sudden reduction. OPEC aid is currently less than half the volume established between 1975 and 1981. At its peak in 1974-75 OPEC aid constituted 10 per cent of total resource flows. Its share is now around 3.5 per cent. During the mid-1970s, DAC aid moved into a pronounced upward trend, and this has been maintained (but at a less steady pace) up to the present.

The decade and a half of concessional aid flows since 1970 can perhaps be best viewed as composed of two periods. In the first, from 1970 to 1978, the rise of OPEC aid was the headline news and the increase in multilateral aid flows the significant second-page feature. All of the still relatively modest increase in DAC aid in this period went towards funding this much expanded multilateral aid effort (nearly US$7 billion in 1978 compared with about US$3 billion in 1970). Bilateral DAC aid disbursements in this period remained static although a sharp rise in aid commitments at mid-decade foreshadowed a coming rise in net disbursements. The second period, from 1978 to 1984, has seen a shift in this pattern. In this period, DAC countries' aid increases went into bilateral aid, while the expansion of multilateral aid continued but at a noticeably slower pace. The marked increase in DAC aid was offset, however, by the even more marked decline in OPEC aid, so that global ODA declined in the early 1980s.

Prospects Ahead for Total Financial Flows

The prospects ahead for total financial flows are closely interrelated with the prospects for real resource flows, as outlined in the first half of this chapter. There are two dominant factors. First is the need for the major debt-problem countries to repair their financial positions and revise their economic structures and policies. This involves relying much more on domestic savings than foreign savings in comparison with the 1970s, when the relatively small number of big debtor countries accounted for a large proportion of total capital imports by developing countries. Second is the large demand for external savings of the United States economy. In combination, these two factors have dramatically reshaped the pattern of international capital flows.

For countries relying on concessional aid and other official financing, current flows will be maintained and may expand somewhat, but there seems little scope for further significant increases. Although aid flows are forecst to continue to rise in real terms, this is likely to be at a lower rate than the rather buoyant expansion of the past decade. At the same time a considerable number of official borrowers are in economic and financial trouble, with debt problems that seem likely to continue in many cases. A less constrained supply of multilateral concessional finance and more co-ordinated approaches to the financial problems of these countries seem essential.

The situation, then, is hardly a comfortable one; the strains are not just financial and economic but also social and political. Recognition of the real risks to stability that are involved has prompted new efforts, notably at the recent annual Fund/Bank meetings in Seoul, to ensure that enough finance is forthcoming to provide the basis for adjustment with growth. It is imperative to the success of these efforts that progress is made on all fronts at once—policy reform to establish real creditworthiness on the part of debtor countries and to improve the efficiency and flexibility of their economies, policy co-operation among the major OECD countries to maintain world economic activity while reducing interest rates and the present major imbalances, and, finally, consultation between official and private creditors to provide soundly-based increases in financial flows without compromising the integrity of the lending institutions.

Section II: Sources of Funds
Chapter 3: The World Bank

3A. The World Bank and the International Finance Corporation
The World Bank

The World Bank, which consists of the International Bank for Reconstruction and Development (IBRD) and the International Development Association (IDA), has one central purpose: to promote economic and social progress in developing nations by helping raise productivity so that their people may live a better and fuller life. This is also the aim of the International Finance Corporation (IFC), which works closely with private investors from around the world and invests in commercial enterprises in developing countries.

The IBRD, IDA, and IFC have three interrelated functions: to lend funds, to provide advice, and to serve as a catalyst to stimulate investments by others. The three institutions are closely associated; both IDA and IFC are affiliates of the IBRD. The IBRD and IDA share the same staff. While IFC has its own operating and legal staff, it shares certain administrative and other services with the Bank. The same person is President of all three institutions. Unlike the Bank, IFC lends without government guarantees, and can take equity positions in commercial companies.

Over the years, the IBRD, IDA, and IFC have served to reinforce one another's work in a variety of ways. Whether working separately or together through joint projects, their common objective has been to help poor nations move to that stage of economic strength at which development becomes self-sustaining, and eventually to a level that permits these same nations to contribute to the development process in countries that are less developed.

Of the three institutions, the IBRD, established in 1945, is the oldest and largest. It was conceived nearly forty years ago—at the United Nations Monetary and Financial Conference held in Bretton Woods, New Hampshire, United States of America, in July 1944.

Representatives of forty-four nations assembled there decided to establish two complementary financial institutions. The first—the International Monetary Fund (IMF)—was to promote international currency stability by helping finance temporary balance-of-payments deficits and by providing for the progressive elimination of exchange restrictions and the observance of accepted rules of international financial conduct. The second institution—the International Bank for Reconstruction and Development—was to help finance the reconstruction and development of its member countries.

The Articles of Agreement of the IBRD were formally accepted by a majority of the participants by December 27, 1945. Six months later, on June 25, 1946, the IBRD opened for business and proceeded to call up capital from its member governments. All the nations which participated in the Bretton Woods Conference, except the Soviet Union, eventually joined the Bank, although Cuba, Czechoslovakia, and Poland subsequently ceased to be members.

The IBRD is owned by the governments of the more than 140 countries that have subscribed to its capital. Under the Articles of Agreement, only countries that are members of the IMF can be considered for membership in the IBRD. Subscriptions by member countries to the capital stock of the IBRD are related to each member's quota in the IMF, which is designed to reflect the country's relative economic strength.

FINANCIAL STRENGTH

The IBRD makes loans only to creditworthy borrowers. Assistance is provided only to those projects that promise high real rates of economic return to the country. As a matter of policy, the Bank does not reschedule repayments, and it has suffered no losses on the loans it has made. It earns a net income which amounted to about $600 million in both fiscal years 1981 and 1982. A substantial part of the income is used to strengthen its reserves. The remainder is transferred to IDA.

The IBRD obtains most of its funds through medium-term and long-term borrowing in the capital markets of Eruope, Japan, the United States of America, and the Middle East. Its solid standing in these markets is based upon the combination of conservative lending policies, strong financial backing by its members, and prudent financial management.

Apart from borrowing, significant amounts also come from the IBRD's paid-in capital, from its retained earnings, and from the flow of repayments on its loans. These loans generally are repayable over fifteen to twenty years, with a grace period of three to five years. The interest rate they carry is related to the interest the IBRD has to pay on the money it borrows. In early 1983, the average rate on new IBRD loans was a little under 11 percent. Each loan must be made to, or be guaranteed by, the government concerned.

The International Development Association was established in 1960 to provide assistance to the poorer developing countries on terms that would bear less heavily on their balance of payments than IBRD loans. IDA's assistance is concentrated on the very poor countries—mainly those with an annual per capita gross national product (GNP) of $795 or less (in 1981 dollars). By this criterion, more than fifty countries are eligible. In practice, over 80 percent of IDA lending goes to countries with an annual per capita GNP of less than $410.

Membership in IDA is open to all members of the IBRD, and most of them have joined. The funds lent by IDA come mostly in the form of contributions from its richer member countries, although some developing countries contribute to IDA as well. A small part of IDA's resources come in the form of the transfers from the net earnings of the IBRD. IDA credits are made only to governments. They have to be repaid over fifty years and there is a grace period of ten years. They carry no interest, but there is an annual commitment charge of 0.5 percent on the undisbursed amount and a service charge of 0.75 percent on the disbursed amount of each credit. Although IDA is legally and financially distinct from the IBRD, it shares the same staff, and the projects it assists have to meet the same criteria as do projects supported by the IBRD.

The International Finance Corporation was established in 1956. Its function is to assist the economic development of less developed countries by promoting growth in the private sector of their economies and helping to mobilize domestic and foreign capital for this purpose. More than 120 countries are members of IFC. Legally and financially, IFC and the Bank are separate entities. IFC has its own operating and legal staff, but draws upon the Bank for administrative and other service.

GROWTH IN WORLD BANK ASSISTANCE

Between June 1946 and mid-1982, the World Bank—the IBRD and IDA—lent a total of over $105 billion for about 3,300 projects in more than 100 countries. Assistance has increased more than four-fold in the last ten years. The Bank has sought to meet the needs of the poorest people in the world as it has explored opportunities for high-priority, economically sound investments in developing countries that have a total population of more than 3 billion. These investments have covered a wide range of activities. They have helped to develop agriculture, improve education, increase the output of energy, expand industry, create better urban facilities, promote family planning, extend telecommunications networks, modernize transportation systems, improve water supply and sewerage facilities, and establish medical care.

More development assistance is provided by the Bank than any other single agency, multilateral or bilateral, in the world. The Bank is now assisting investments in over 1,600 projects costing, in the aggregate, nearly $200 billion. Finance from the Bank typically covers only a little more than a third of the cost of these projects. The largest share is generally raised by the developing country from its own resources.

The Bank's financing is intended primarily to help meet foreign-exchange costs. Every project supported by the Bank is designed in close collaboration with national governments and local agencies, and often in cooperation with other multilateral assistance organizations. Indeed, 40 percent of all Bank-assisted projects also receive financial support from others—bilateral and multilateral agencies, and, in recent years, commercial banks as well. Many of these institutions would not have participated in the development process on the present scale were it not for the Bank's leadership and expertise. Thus, the Bank has an important catalytic role, and its involvement in development assistance is greater than that indicated by the annual amount of its lending commitments of around $13 billion in the early 1980s.

LENDING CRITERIA

The success of the Bank's operations depends upon the trust it has established with borrowers, and this trust is based on the experience and technical skills the Bank has demonstrated over the years in working with its member developing countries.

Under its Articles of Agreement, the Bank cannot allow itself to be influenced in its decisions by the political character of a member country; only economic considerations are relevant. Thus, the Bank does not lend in support of military or political objectives. It seeks to ensure that the developing country gets full value for the money it borrows. Bank assistance, therefore, is "untied," in that it may be used to purchase goods and services from any member country—plus Switzerland, which, although not a member, is an important source of borrowig for the IBRD.

Most of the countries that are members of the IBRD are members also of IDA and IFC. The lsit includes almost all developing and developed countries. The People's Republic of China, with a population of more than 1 billion, is a member. So is Vanuatu, with a population of slightly more than 100,000. Yugoslavia, Romania, and Hungry are members. But other East European countries are not. The United Arab Emirates, with a per capita gross national product of more than $30,000, is a member; so is Bhutan, which has a per capita GNP of only $180.

THE GRADUATION PROCESS

In making loans to developing countries, the Bank does not compete with other sources of finance. It is enjoined to assist only those projects for which the capital required is not available from other sources on reasonable terms. Through its work, the Bank seeks to strengthen the economies of borrowing nations so that they can graduate from reliance on Bank resources and meet their financial needs, on terms they can afford, direct from conventional sources of capital.

Graduation from the IBRD and IDA has occurred for many years. Of the thirty-four very poor countries that borrowed money from IDA in the earliest years, twenty-seven have attained sufficient economic strength for them to need IDA money no longer. Of the twenty-seven, two—Colombia and the Republic of Korea—have not only moved from reliance on IDA credits, but have attained sufficient economic strength to be able to contribute to IDA. Similarly, about twenty countries that formerly borrowed money from the IBRD no longer need to do so. An outstanding example is Japan. For a period of fourteen years, it borrowed from the IBRD. Now, the IBRD borrows large sums in Japan.

This graduation process is an important index of the progress made by borrowing countries since the IBRD and IDA were established. A substantial number of countries have moved from being IDA borrowers to becoming IBRD borrowers. Similarly, many others which once were IBRD borrowers are now significant sources of funds for both the IBRD and IDA. Some countries which no longer rely on the IBRD's money continue to seek its technical assistance. Several others mobilize their financial requirements more and more from commercial sources and from IFC.

IFC'S COMPLEMENTARY ROLE

IFC complements the work of the Bank in a number of ways. It is active in areas of business where it is impractical for the Bank to operate. It can offer kinds of financial assistance that are unavailable from the Bank—equity, convertible debentures, underwritings, and standby commitments. Unlike the Bank, it makes loans without a government guarantee; in fact, it may not accept a government guarantee. The Bank and IFC have jointly financed a number of projects. Often enterprises assisted by IFC have been made possible by, or have depended on, infrastructure projects supported by the Bank. The IBRD has been the major source of IFC's borrowing. IFC benefits from the Bank's economic work.

While IFC is an integral part of the development efforts led by the World Bank, its special role is to help mobilize resources on commercial terms for business ventures and financial institutions where a market-oriented approach is not only applicable but economically preferable. IFC's immediate concern is to assist in raising funds needed by investors, often in conjunction with governments, to undertake promising projects that have been held back by inadequate financing. In addition to its own loan and equity financing, IFC helps investors mobilize resources from others through syndications and by encouraging parallel financing. IFC provides several kinds of technical assistance—for specific projects, for the development of capital markets, and for other purposes.

In recent years, there has been a rapid expansion in IFC's activities, made possible by a capital increase in 1978. The number of IFC investments has been growing by more than 10 percent a year on the average. Moreover, special attention is being paid to the smaller and poorer developing countries, where about one-half of IFC's investments are now being made.

Both IFC and the Bank play an important role in promoting the flow of private foreign investment to developing countries. With the increase in their activities, and in the cofinancing of projects, the role has expanded. New ways are being explored to stimulate the expansion. In order to promote the flow of direct foreign investment, for instance, the Bank is examining the need for a multilateral investment insurance agency (MIIA). A number of regional and national schemes for investment insurance already exist. In most cases, they work effectively. But they cover only a small portion of the total direct foreign investment flowing to developing countries. An MIIA could conceivably complement those schemes and thus help stimulate the flow.

OWNERSHIP AND DIRECTION

The IBRD, IDA, and IFC are owned and directed by their member countries. Although each of the three institutions has its distinctive features, the IBRD's ownership structure is broadly illustrative of the pattern.

In the IBRD, each country subscribes to shares in an amount based roughly on its relative economic strength. Each has 250 votes plus one vote for each share of stock it holds, thus increasing the relative voting powers of the poorer countries. For example, Malawi has subscribed $16.4 million, or 0.04 percent of the total, while its voting power is 0.09 percent. The United States of America, the Bank's largest shareholder, which provides 22.4 percent of the subscribed capital, has 20.6 percent of the voting power.

Direction in the IBRD is exercised through a Board of Governors, consisting of one governor for each member country, and twenty-one full-time Executive Directors. The governors meet once a year to review operations and basic policies. Most functions of the governors are delegated to the Executive Directors, who normally meet at least once a week at the Bank's headquarters in Washington. Five of the Executive Directors are appointed by the largest stockholders (the United States of America, the United Kingdom, France, the Federal Republic of Germany, and Japan), while sixteen are elected by the governors representing the other members. Each Executive Director has an Alternate.

All votes of an elected Executive Director are cast as a unit.

In practice, most decisions are made through consensus, rather than by formal vote. Although the Executive Directors have to approve all loans, only the management of the institution can propose that a loan be made. The Executive Directors are responsible for all matters of policy. They meet under the chairmanship of the President. They select him, and he is responsible for the conduct of the Bank's business and for its organization and staff under the direction of the Executive Directors.

The International Development Association

The International Development Association (IDA) is an affiliate of the IBRD. IDA's resources, provided primarily by the richer countries, are used to help finance development projects and programs in the poorest nations.

IDA does what the IBRD does, and it shares the same staff. IDA makes money available to help support high-priority projects that foster economic development in developing countries. However, the IBRD and IDA do not lend on the same terms. The terms for IDA "credits" (so-called to distinguish them from IBRD "loans") are fifty-year maturities, ten-year grace periods before repayments of principal begin, and no interest (but an annual commitment charge of 0.5 percent on the undisbursed portion, and a service charge of 0.75 percent on the disbursed portion, of each credit). The charges are intended to cover administrative costs.

The difference in terms of lending reflects the important difference in countries assisted by the IBRD and IDA. IDA credits are designed to assist mainly those very poor developing countries that cannot afford to borrow on IBRD terms. Some IDA borrowers also obtain some IBRD loans. Most IDA borrowers are in Africa south of the Sahara and in South Asia.

IDA lends only to governments. But governments commonly relend IDA funds to enterprises, both private and public, within the country. Such relending is generally on terms that reflect the cost of capital in the country.

Thus, the benefits of the concessionary terms IDA offers go to the country as a whole, and not to any particular enterprise or entity within it. The enterprises benefiting from IDA funds, under such conditions, remain subject to the financial discipline necessary for efficient operation.

The demand for IDA assistance has always exceeded the supply of available resources. IDA always, therefore, has had to ration its money carefully. In doing so, it takes four main criteria into consideration:
- The poverty level in member countries.
- The creditworthiness of the prospective borrower.
- The economic performance of the prospective borrower.
- The availability of projects suitable for IDA financing.

Per capita income levels in member countries affect the eligibility for credits. The income level beyond which IDA credits are severely rationed—currently $795 per capita in 1981 dollars—has been modified from time to time, chiefly to take account of rising price levels.

This $795 level is not regarded as a ceiling that cannot, under any circumstances, be pierced. But it has been thought of as establishing a strong presumption against lending to member countries in which the average annual income per inhabitant is higher.

On the other hand, an income level below $795 does not, of itself, create a presumption in favor of IDA lending. A number of countries in the $410-$795 range, and even a few in the "under $410" category, are considered capable of servicing some IBRD loans and IDA credits.

IDA has three main sources of funds. They are:
- Members' subscriptions.
- Contributions provided mainly by the richer countries, but, in recent years, by an increasing number of developing countries, as well.
- Transfers from the IBRD's income and repayments on IDA credits.

The initial subscription of each member of IDA was roughly proportional to its subscription to the capital stock of the IBRD. IDA's charter provides for two categories of membership: Part I, which includes the richer countries, and

Part II, which is composed of developing countries. Each Part I member pays its full subscription in convertible funds, all of which can be used by IDA in its lending activities. Each Part II member pays only 10 percent of its subscription in convertible funds. The other 90 percent is paid in the member's own currency and cannot be used for lending without the consent of the member. At present, there are twenty-two IDA members in the Part I category. The remaining members are in the Part II category.

Since its inception, there have been six replenishments of IDA resources. The first replenishment in 1964 involved contributions of $750 million from eighteen members, all in the Part I category, for commitments in the three-year period from July 1, 1964, to June 30, 1966. Over the years, the replenishments expanded to the point where, by 1980, thirty-three countries agreed to provide approximately $12 billion under the sixth replenishment covering the three years from July 1, 1980, to June 30, 1983.

Some of the newer donors under the more recent replenishment agreements have been oil-exporting countries like Saudi Arabia, the United Arab Emirates, and Venezuela. Others include such developing countries as the Republic of Korea and Yugoslavia.

A report entitled "IDA in Retrospect," published for the Bank in September 1982, comprehensively reviews the work IDA has done over the past two decades. The report notes that IDA has committed $27 billion to more than 1,300 projects in seventy-eight countries since 1960. Details are given of specific projects and programs assisted by IDA—failures as well as successes. The broad analysis reaches several conclusions:

- Twenty-seven nations, once eligible for IDA credits on the basis of their weak economies, have developed to the stage at which they can finance further growth on conventional borrowing terms.
- Dramatic increases in agricultural production in South Asia, where IDA has been particularly active, have sharply reduced the need for massive food imports in the region and, in India's case, have resulted in virtual self-sufficiency.
- IDA lending has been effective in promoting development.
- IDA has gained a vast amount of understanding by "doing," including learning from past mistakes.
- IDA has been remarkably successful in attracting financial support.
- IDA has a key role to play in meeting the needs for concessional aid to the poorest countries.

THE WORLD BANK

	International Bank for Reconstruction and Development (IBRD)	International Development Association (IDA)	International Finance Corporation (IFC)
Objectives of the institution	To promote economic progress in developing countries by providing financial and technical assistance, mostly for specific projects in both public and private sectors.		To promote economic progress in developing countries by helping to mobilize domestic and foreign capital to stimulate the growth of the private sector.
Year established	1945	1960	1956
Number of member countries (April 1983)	144	131	124
Types of countries assisted	Developing countries other than the very poorest. Some countries borrow a "blend" of IBRD loans and IDA credits.	The poorest: 80% of IDA credits go to countries with annual per capita incomes below $410. Many of these countries are too poor to be able to borrow part or any of their requirements on IBRD terms.	All developing countries, from the poorest to the more advanced.
Types of activities assisted	Agriculture and rural development, energy, education, transportation, telecommunications, industry, mining, development finance companies, urban development, water supply, sewerage, population, health, and nutrition. Some nonproject lending, including structural adjustment.		Agribusiness, development finance companies, energy, fertilizer, manufacturing, mining, money and capital markets institutions, tourism and services, utilities.
Lending commitments (fiscal 1982)	$10,330 million	$2,686 million	$580 million
Equity investments (fiscal 1982)	IBRD and IDA do not make equity investments.		$32 million
Number of operations (fiscal 1982)	150	97	65
Terms of lending:			
Average maturity period	Generally 15 to 20 years	50 years	7 to 12 years
Grace period	Generally 3 to 5 years	10 years	An average of 3 years
Interest rate (as of April 1, 1983)	10.97%	0.0%	In line with market rates
Other charges	Front-end fee of 0.25% on loan. Commitment charge of 0.75% on undisbursed amount of loan.	Annual commitment charge of 0.5% on undisbursed and service charge of 0.75% on disbursed amounts of the credit.	Commitment fee of 1% per year on undisbursed amount of loan.
Recipients of financing	Governments, government agencies, and private enterprises which can get a government guarantee for the IBRD loan.	Governments. But they may relend the funds to state or private organizations.	Private enterprises; government organizations that assist the private sector.
Government guarantee	Essential	Essential	Neither sought nor accepted.
Main method of raising funds	Borrowings in world's capital markets.	Grants from governments.	Borrowings and IFC's own capital, subscribed by member governments.
Main sources of funds	Financial markets in U.S., Germany, Japan, and Switzerland.	Governments of U.S., Japan, Germany, U.K., France, other OECD countries, and certain OPEC countries.	Borrowings from IBRD.

3B. The World Bank: Lending for Structural Adjustment
Stanley Please

At the start of the 1980s, the developing world faced the prospect of a marked deterioration in its external economic circumstances, including recession in developed countries, related declines in primary-product prices as well as in market access for other exports, high oil prices, and a rising burden of debt aggravated by high real interest rates. These unpropitious external circumstances were intensified further by a widespread failure of developing countries to take effective steps to assure their ability to meet the debt-service obligations on the large flows of funds obtained from commercial banks during the second half of the 1970s. It was clear that unless both these external and internal factors were recognized and addressed, the consequent deterioration in the balances of payments of developing countries would develop into financial crises that only the most draconian of demand-restricting measures would be able to handle. Such measures would inevitably fall heavily on investment programs and on other efforts essential in the developing world for stimulating growth, providing basic needs, and alleviating poverty.

It was with these concerns in mind that the World Bank[1] introduced its program of structural adjustment lending (SAL) in 1980. Despite some improvement in the global economic situation since then—revival in industrial countries, lower oil prices, and some increases in primary-product prices—these concerns remain as valid now as they were in 1980. Moreover, what was merely feared in 1980 has become reality in many countries as governments have found expenditure-cutting programs to be the only option available for dealing with an immediate external financial crisis.

Successful adjustment to the external shock of a deteriorated world economic environment requires programs that combine national financial discipline with measures that speed the reduction of the import dependency of countries in deficit and increase their export-earning effectiveness compared with countries in surplus. Programs supported by the International Monetary Fund have been directed at these twin objectives. It has been pointed out, for instance, that while "demand management measures and financial stability may have been *proximate* instruments and objectives of Fund policies, the full attainment of supply potential has always been the *ultimate* aim"; most policy measures—whether interest rates, measures to achieve greater financial viability of public enterprises, taxes and subsidies, or exchange rates—have impact both on aggregate demand and on the pattern of supply.[2]

But the process of speeding and deepening structural adjustment so that balance-of-payments viability can be achieved *at a higher level of real income and with greater attention to the needs of developmental policy* requires programs reaching beyond the measures included in IMF programs. Among these additional sectoral and sub-sectoral concerns that are important to the structural adjustment and development are:

- the relative roles of the public and private sectors in economic activity;
- the way markets are premitted to develop or are organized by governments;
- the process and criteria by which the level and structure of agricultural prices are determined;
- the industrial policy framework within which industry operates and expands, as determined by tariffs, import licensing systems, and investment promotion schemes;
- the appropriate structure of energy pricing and taxation that will both induce an efficient supply of energy to reflect projected comparative costs of imported and domestic sources and at the same time bring about whatever level of energy conservation is considered desirable; and
- a well-formulated public expenditure program.

IMF conditionality has not attempted to address these complex structural and sectoral issues to any great extent—and probably quite rightly so, given the other important responsibilities of the Fund and the specialties of its staff. In relation to these areas to policy, Fund conditionality has been limited to the most glaring cases of economically inappropriate prices, such as those of food, domestic oil, or exports. The World Bank, on the other hand, has always been deeply concerned with these issues. Its economic work has always given considerable emphasis to sectoral and sub-sectoral pricing issues—involving not only prices of the factors of production and selling prices, but also tariffs, subsidies, and industrial incentives. Institutional development also has been an important and growing part of the Bank's economic work.

However, despite the importance that the Bank attributes in its economic work to appropriate policies for achieving development and structural adjustment objectives, its Articles of Agreement legally preclude its engagement in anything other than project lending except in special circumstances. The Bank has interpreted this obligation fairly rigorously. Since the late 1960s, there has been an agreed ceiling of 10 per cent of World Bank commitments for non-project lending. Yet these operations have until recently represented no more than 6 per cent of annual commitments. In fact, prior to 1980, non-project operations were undertaken only in response to a few cases of immediate and urgent need stemming from natural disasters or "man-made" ones (Such as postwar reconstruction in Nigeria or Uganda); from serious declines in the terms of trade due to export price declines (such as Zambia's past experience with copper or Colombia's with coffee); from import price increases (most obviously in the price of oil in 1973-74, and again in 1979); or from other acute needs such as India's need for help in financing imports of intermediate goods and spare parts for more fully utilizing its existing industrial capacity rather than for financing new projects.

Until 1980, these non-project operations all emphasized the need for quick disbursement of World Bank funds and focused on policy issues only incidentally, if at all. Even sectoral and sub-sectoral lending that has gone beyond narrowly conceived project lending has been limited and has rarely made policy issues central in the design of operations. For instance, sectoral lending has been virtually restricted to a few highway authorities with which agreement has been reached on a program of projects to be prepared, appraised, and supervised by the national agency.

The Bank has thus always been confronted with the problem of how to make an effective link between its commitment and disbursement of project funds and its concern with broader issues of policy and institutional development. In this respect, the contrast with the IMF could not be starker. In making its more conditioned distribution of funds, the IMF commits and makes available its resources purely and simply against the willingness of a government to formulate and agree on a program of policy changes and subsequently to implement the agreed program. The Fund, therefore, is an operational institution that is mainly concerned with providing financial support for packages of policy reform. The Bank, however, is an operational institution that is close to being exclusively concerned with providing financial support for individual *projects*, notwithstanding its recognition of the fact that its mandate as an international development institution can only be implemented if policy packages that address issues of structural adjustment and development are being formulated and implemented by governments.

It was in the context of an increased need both for deeper, more sustained adjustment programs and for additional external financial support for such programs that the Bank launched its structural adjustment lending program in 1980. The SAL program represented the Bank's first attempt to introduce on a systematic basis a form of lending that focused expressly on policy and institutional reform. It was also an effort to provide more structure and discipline both within the Bank and in the Bank's relationship with its member countries regarding policy and institutional reform than had been possible previously.

Structural adjustment lending has been limited both in the number of countries participating—sixteen to date—and in the volume of World Bank funds allocated to SAL operations, which has risen from approximately $700 million in 1981 to about $1,250 million in 1983 (fiscal years). Despite this limited scale and extent, SAL operations already have had the obvious effect of forcing the Bank's operational management to take policy reform more seriously. It is, of course, another question whether SAL programs have had an impact on the willingness, or ability, of governments to adopt more far-reaching and sustained policy reforms than would have been adopted in the absence of SAL operations. An even more important question is whether SAL programs have encouraged governments undertaking policy reforms to provide for *sustaining* these reforms by simultaneously improving the political as well as technical institutional setting in which policy is formulated and implemented.

However difficult and tentative such a comprehensive evaluation of the SAL program would at this stage necessarily be (and it is not attempted here), it is a central issue for those interested in and responsible for determining the future role of the World Bank. The Bank's mandate is to engage in the financing of projects in support of the achievement of the long-term development objectives of its developing-country members. The SAL program has moved the institution into non-project lending on a systematic basis and has placed policy issues rather than project issues at center-stage. The context of its introduction is the financial crisis that most developing countries have been experiencing since 1980. But should the SAL program simply disappear when the immediate intensity of the crisis eases? Or does experience with the program to date suggest that the Bank should rethink its role and the design of its operations more generally? Is there a possibility that SAL lending will be seen in retrospect not so much as a diversion to meet an immediate crisis but as a watershed in the role of the Band and in the way it executes this role?

STRUCTURAL ADJUSTMENT LENDING

In each case structural adjustment lending consists of some three or four discrete lending operations over approximately five or six years. Its purpose is to provide quick-disbursing, balance-of-payments support to a country that is prepared both to formulate a structural adjustment program and to reach agreement with the Bank on such a program.[3] SAL programs have three components:

- a statement of structural objectives to be achieved in five to ten years;
- a statement of the measures that will be taken over approximately five years to achieve the objectives; and
- a monitorable set of actions to be taken by a government either before the Bank's Board approves the SAL operation or during the approximately year-long disbursement period.

The disbursement of funds under each SAL operation is typically tranched, or phased, to ensure both that the adjustment program in general is on track and that specific measures included in the monitorable program of action actually are implemented.

Quick disbursement of Bank funds to provide immediate support to a country's balance of payments has not been the primary focus of Bank attention under SAL, although it has been a necessary part of the concept. In any case, the aggregate amounts involved have been relatively small. Moreover, SAL funds are not additional; they do not increase the total agreed level of World Bank lending, which is determined by IDA replenishment decisions and by a slowly rising ceiling on IBRD lending related to the IBRD's capital base. In practice, SAL funds are disbursed more quickly than those committed under regular Bank operations and are not tied to particular commodities or particular country procurement, unlike many other sources of finance. For some countries, the financial "bridging" that is in effect provided by the SAL program (while policy measures take effect) may not be unimportant—even though the program's central purpose is to give greater urgency and robustness to the Bank's concerns and involvement in policy issues relating to structural adjustment.

Three features of SAL operations help achieve this central objective. First, the program's comprehensiveness of coverage applies to both economy-wide and sectoral issues of policy and of institutional reform. In terms of macro-economic policy, for instance, SAL operations typically cover agreements on the size and composition of the public investment program and sometimes on important components of recurrent expenditures. As regards sectoral coverage, the loans cover the directly productive sectors of agriculture and industry as well as the energy sector.

Second, SAL operations have a single-minded concern with policy reform. Bank project operations have never been weak on conditionality; on the contrary, it could be argued that they have attached too many conditions—conditions ranging from detailed technical, administrative, and financial issues relating to a project, through sub-sectoral policy and institutional concerns, to larger questions of sectoral and macro-economic policy. The problem with such a broad spectrum of conditionality is that it becomes diffused and weakened, with an understandable (and appropriate) priority given to the narrower project conditions and, to a lesser extent, sub-sectoral conditions. The broader agreements on sectoral and macro-economic issues tend always, because of their indirectness, to lose their strength and therefore their credibility. SAL conditionality, in contrast, is concerned entirely with macro-economic and sectoral policies. This focus has given the preparation, formulation, negotiation, monitoring, and disciplining of programs of policy reform far greater importance than these processes receive in project lending. The commitment of funds for a limited period of twelve months or so, with an intermediate tranching provision after, say, half the commitment has been disbursed, has made the monitoring of policy implementation a continuous process.

The third notable feature of SAL operations is that they involve agreement on a monitorable program of action. This program embodies precise and detailed actions of both policy and institutional changes that a government obligates itself to undertake. Some of these precise action programs emerge from studies that are, in their terms of reference and schedules of work, an integral part of the monitorable program. Actions based on these recommendations provide the basis for subsequent SAL policy agreements.

One of the Bank's major concerns at the macro-economic level has been with the public sector's use of resources—and particularly with the public investment program. SAL agreements have covered: specific changes in the institutional arrangements by which public investment programs are determined and monitored; changes in the sectoral and sub-sectoral balance of the investment program; agreement on project seleciton criteria; determination of a core program of highest priority projects that will be protected from budgetary cutbacks if financial resources are more limited than envisaged; and annual presentation of rolling, two- or three-year public investment programs.

This emphasis that SAL operations give to institutional reform is a feature of SAL operations that extends beyond public investment programs. For instance, in the case of agricultural pricing, which involves agreement on precise changes in output or input prices or in tax and subsidy ar rangements. considerable emphasis also has been given to agreement on institutional measures to improve the criteria used to determine the level and structure of agricultural prices, as well as the timeliness of announcements of price policy in relation to the cultivation cycle, etc. Moreover, SAL agreements have reflected the importance of improved marketing efficiency if pricing policy is to have the full intended impact on production. Thus SAL agreements have included measures both to limit the public sector's role in agricultural marketing (where this has exceeded the capacity of the public sector to provide marketing services efficiently) and to improve the efficiency of public-sector marketing agencies and their policies.

CONSTRAINTS ON THE PROGRAM

The introduction of the SAL program has resulted in the Bank's reaching its 10-per cent ceiling on non-project lending in the past two years. An important issue, therefore, is whether this ceiling is constraining the development of SAL operations and their effectiveness. The Bank's Board, while reaffirming the ceiling in 1982, indicated its willingness to review this decision if the ceiling is considered to constraining. Three separate questions shape this issue: Does the ceiling limit the number of countries with which the Bank could develop a SAL program? Does it limit the effectiveness of SAL operations? Does it encourage the development of alternative operational options that do not count as non-project operations and, therefore, fall outside the 10-per cent ceiling?

It is unlikely that the number of participating countries has been kept down by the 10-per cent ceiling. Only a few governments are interested in structural adjustment lending; many governments have been unable to formulate and implement structural adjustment programs of a scope and depth acceptable to the Bank, and among those who are prepared to move along these lines, some are unwilling to do so at the behest of the Bank. The first situation is clearly more worrisome than the second. It raises the question of whether these unwilling governments are pursuing structural adjustment poilicies that can achieve both their developmental objectives and their goal of medium- and long-term viability of their balances of payments—and therefore whether their programs justify existing levels of external assistance, including project lending by the Bank. Although project lending has a very important continuing role to play in the lending program of the Bank, it would clearly be undesirable if it came to be seen by some countries as the "easy option" for those unable to address critical policy issues.

In the future, the number of countries receiving SAL support will be determined not only by how many new countries request it, but also by how many "drop out" of the program. To some extent this will occur "automatically," as a consequence of the decision that a SAL program for any one country should be limited to a maximum of four or five operations over five to six years. (Only Turkey has reached this limit so far). Countries will also be phased out of the SAL program if they are unable to maintain in full the agreed program of structural adjustment measures (as has happened in the cases of Bolivia, Guyana, and Senegal). Finally, certain countries whose immediate balance-of-payments situation has improved might be pased out of SAL operations despite the fact that the structural adjustment measures required to avoid future balance-of-payments problems need to be sustained. If countries are phased out for this reason, it will be because a decision has been taken that structural adjustment lending is only justified in "special circumstances" and that improvement in the immediate balance-of-payments situation disqualifies a country from such assistance. The alternative view is that SAL should be used more actively to anticipate and avoid future balance-of-payments crises—and their "remedies," which inevitably mean severe reductions in developmental expenditures.

It is difficult, therefore, to estimate how binding a constraint the 10-per cent ceiling will be on the number of countries receiving SAL support. In a substantive sense it must be hoped that it will prove to be the main binding constraint, as this would imply that more countries are able to formulate ant sustain structural adjustment programs and are seeking Bank support for them. Consequently, any reconsideration of the ceiling on non-project lending should start from a recognition that, at a time when domestic policy reforms to achieve structural adjustment are still desperately required, it would be foolish to constrain the Bank from providing support to any government willing to implement such a program. The danger of this happening is not very great in the cases of small countries for which SAL operations can be handled within the 10-per cent ceiling. It is clearly much more of a constraint in relation to the larger and medium-size countries (such as Brazil, Mexico, and Nigeria), at least until some other larger recipients of SAL support (for example, the Republic of Korea, the Philippines, or Thailand) "graduate" from the program.

The number of countries that can be supported by the SAL program under the 10-per cent ceiling obviously depends on the size of the individual country programs that are then in operation. Although the dollar amount of each is flexible and certainly does not correspond to a country's need as reflected in its foreign exchange gap, there is a minimum amount below which the "seriousness" and "credibility" of the Bank's involvement in the monitoring and disciplining of major policy issues becomes suspect. It is difficult to define this lower limit in any precise way, but it has been considered to be best expressed as a percentage—about 30 per cent—of the Bank's lending program to a country. So far, this percentage, in combination with the number of countries seeking SAL support, also has been consistent with the 10-per cent ceiling.

Would a higher level of SAL support to a country have resulted in a broader, more extensive, or more rapidly implemented program of structural adjustment measures? Within the bounds of realistic levels of SAL support, probably no significant increase in the strength of the program would have occurred. There is no continuous supply curve of measures reflecting an increased willingness to improve the structural adjustment program for each $1-million, or $10-million, increase in SAL support. If the matter is thought of in there terms at all, the curve should be seen as very stepped: from zero willingness to discuss and agree to a program with the Bank unless a minimum loan commitment is made, to a step representing a much greater willingness by a government to improve its program provided that the level of support by the Bank is much higher than 30 per cent. This level of Bank support, however, would be inconsistent both with the Bank's total lending program to the developing world—fixed by the availability of IDA funding and the slowly rising ceiling on lending determined by the IBRD's capital structure—and with its other non-SAL responsibilities

It needs to be reemphasized in this connection that the funding of the SAL program has to be within existing IDA and IBRD levels of lending—that there is no "additionality" for SAL lending operations. Funds for a structural adjustment loan in any country have to be taken either from resources that would otherwise have been allocated to other operations in the country or from a reallocation of funds from other country programs—or, most likely, a little from both. As regards the second of these "sources" of funding, a government's willingness to formulate and agree on a SAL program is evidence of "good performance" and is therefore likely to result in an increase in the country's allocation of IDA and/or IBRD funds. However, the leeway both for country reallocations and for reducing longer-term development project lending to make room for SAL lending is clearly limited. It is this limited scope for SAL additionality *even to each country* that represents the major barrier to a more positive attitude toward SAL operations by many governments. Although the speed of disbursements from IDA and Bank funds is likely to be increased—and this is of course a very attractive feature of SAL—the increase is a once-only gain.

In summary, the absence of additionality for SAL represents the major constraint on SAL lending. But this constraint relates primarily to whether or not a country is willing to agree with the Bank on a SAL program in the first place. Once such a relationship is established, the 30-per cent guideline probably does not have any adverse impact on the strength of the program of measures agreed. To the extent that it has relevance in any one country, the 30-per cent guideline can and has been implemented flexibly.

A third factor to consider in examining the impact of the 10-per cent ceiling that applies to non-project lending is the definition of what is included within the ceiling. Since 1980, only a few non-SAL operations—such as Bangladesh's import credit (virtually a SAL operation in recent years) and the one-time reconstruction operations in Uganda and Zimbabwe—have in fact been counted as part of the ceiling. Of much greater significance is the list of operations that have been excluded from the definition of non-project lending: agricultural rehabilitation projects (Uganda, Sudan, Tanzania); export development projects (Jamaica, Mexico, Costa Rica); public-sector management projects (Peru, Turkey); and technical assistance projects (Mauritius, Mauritania, Bhutan, Tunisia). There clearly is a spectrum of operational lending concepts between "pure" project lending and the "pure" non-project lending of the SAL program. The line drawn for defining the 10-per cent ceiling on non-project lending is somewhat arbitrary, but the line itself has gained considerable significance in the design of Bank operations in support of structural adjustment programs. For the Bank has been able to use sectoral and sub-sectoral operations having an overwhelming focus on policy and institutional reforms in support of adjustment programs even in countries in which it does not formally have a SAL program. These operations have not been subject to the 10-per cent ceiling. Yet while these operations have been useful in supplementing SAL programs in countries in which such programs exist, they never have had—nor were they conceived as having—the same degrees of comprehensiveness in support of adjustment programs as actual SAL operations. On the contrary, in countries in which for political and/or technical reasons a full SAL program was not initially possible, these sectoral and sub-sectoral operations have been thought of as first steps toward the development of a SAL-supported program. Thus, although the development of these operations has eased the constraint of the 10-per cent ceiling, the ceiling still has relevance.

A question frequently asked, of course, is whether these operations *should* be excluded from the 10-per cent ceiling; some of the questioners suggest that these operations are designed to avoid the constraint of the ceiling. The feature that most concerns these critics is that the sectoral and sub-sectoral operations in question support policy reform *directly*, rather than *indirectly*, through project lending. This is of course the very feature considered most relevant and attractive by those who desire an active role for the Bank in support of adjustment programs.

QUALITATIVE EVALUATION

It is both too early and conceptually enormously difficult to undertake a full-scale evaluation of SAL operations. Clearly the easiest approach would be to list the component parts of the monitorable action programs supported under each SAL operation and then to determine the extent to which they were implemented. Indeed, this exercise is more easily undertaken for Bank SAL operations than it is for IMF operations. While IMF operations comprise a series of macroeconomic targets (such as those relating to the balance-of-payments deficit or to public-sector borrowing) that are determined by both policy actions and non-policy variables (such as the weather or export prices), SAL operations relate purely to policy actions taken by the government. Thus a SAL program might, for instance, include agreement to increase agricultural producer prices, to permit more freedom of entry into agricultural output and input marketing, and to take other actions to stimulate agricultural output. What is then monitored is not the target of increased agricultural output but the implementation of the agreed actions. If in fact, contrary to expectations, agricultural output should fall, this will either be due to non-policy factors or to an incorrect diagnosis of why agricultural output was not increasing as rapidly as expected. The government should not be held responsible for either of these situations.

If SAL operations were evaluated in this manner they would undoubtedly show a good track record. The Bank has been very strict in ensuring that governments adhere closely to certain agreed actions. This has not been for purely legalistic reasons. On the contrary, where actions have been taken that were not agreed upon but that were clearly effective substitutes, this has been fully acceptable. In addition, strict compliance with a SAL agreement has not always been interpreted as 100-per cent implementation, particularly where the defaults have involved relatively minor actions, or where it is known that the procedures for taking certain actions are well advanced but are taking somewhat longer to be completed than anticipated.

While the record of compliance under SAL agreements has in general been good, both governments and the Bank have tended to underestimate the time it takes to implement action to reform policies and institutions. In part this delay is simply due to the time it takes to mobilize political support for the agreed actions, often as much a problem in one-party dictatorial systems as in any other country. In large part, however, the delay results from the complex nature of the actions to be taken to reform policies and institutional arrangements once there is movement beyond the generalities of "providing incentive prices," "permitting more managerial autonomy to parastatal managers," and other broad recommendations that typically emanate from the general analysis of a problem.

Any substantive evaluation of SAL operations must, however, proceed beyond the simple test of whether structural adjustment measures have been implemented as agreed, including the timeliness of their implementation. To what extent have SAL operations induced governments to adopt reform measures they would not otherwise have implemented or would have implemented less rapidly? This line of examination would ultimately seek to determine whether SAL operations can be credited with some of the success a country might have had in achieving such structural adjustment objectives as the maintenance or revival of international creditworthiness, the stimulation of export earnings and foreign-exchange savings in economically efficient ways, and action on developmental priorities through the adoption of better targeted and more efficient public expenditure programs. Ambitious evaluation exercises of this hypothetical "with/without" type are notoriously difficult and speculative even at the project level; they are even more problematic at the level of broad policy and institutional reform. No such evaluation is attempted here.

Probably the most relevant question that can be asked at this stage is one that is more internal to the World Bank—although any answer to it is also fraught with some of the problems of comparing actual and hypothetical events. Has the Bank done all it possibly could within its mandate and within the limits of its financial and staff resources to encourage and support countries facing the severe and unexpected deterioration in the global economy in the early 1980s? Specifically, has the SAL program made such encouragement and support by the Bank more effective than would otherwise have been possible? Clearly governments are sovereign within their borders and are responsible for their own policies, whether these are well- or ill-suited to the development and structural adjustment needs of their countries. The relevant test for the Bank is whether it has used its resources in ways that maximized its positive impact on programs to meet these development and structural adjustment needs. If is has done so and the country in question nevertheless "collapses" in some sense (as some middle-income, semi-industrialized developing countries have in terms of their foreign debt crises, and some Sub-Saharan African countries have due to continuing production crises), the Bank can still maintain that it designed its operations as effectively as possible to try to avert such collapses.

Evaluated in this way, structural adjustment lending can claim to have been extremely effective. The Bank has been able to mobilize far greater attention to the reform of critical policy and institutional issues than was previously possible. The mere adoption of a form of lending expressly in support of reform programs has provided a clear signal to governments of the extent to which the Bank is willing to modify its own operational practices in major ways in the light of the crisis that they face—provided that governments show a comparable willingness to face up to the urgency of the need. In addition, as already noted, the SAL process has itself provided ways to make policies and institutional issues central in the Bank's operational relationship with a government. Thus the program forces both the Bank and the government to seek acceptable solutions to these issues at whatever level of decision making is appropriate. In fact, one of the program's major achievements is that in many cases it has helped to establish forums within governments for the handling of important policy issues that otherwise were likely to remain unresolved because they fell between the responsibilities of different ministries and agencies.

It is likewise very difficult to believe that any operational concept with a less direct focus on and support for programs of structural adjustment could have given this same degree of assistance. The frequently mentioned alternative to SAL—that the Bank's project lending program to a country, or part of this program, be based on agreement on a structural adjustment program—can in no way match the sharpness of focus and support provided under SAL operations.

PUBLIC EXPENDITURES

A major criticism of IMF-supported programs has always been that in concentrating on the total level of government expenditures, they countenance undesirable reductions in economic and social expenditures. One of the objectives of SAL was, in effect, to provide an external "lobby" for expenditures designed to achieve developmental objectives. To some significant extent, this has been achieved. In particular, some programs have been agreed upon to reduce or eliminate, in a phased manner, expenditures that no longer serve priority economic or social objectives. Most important in this connection is the phasing out of subsidy programs. Whatever their original objectives—and often, these were well conceived, as in ther case of encouraging fertilizer use during the early years of its introduction as part of a new agricultural package—many of these subsidies have become "counter-developmental" in terms of both efficiency and poverty-alleviation objectives. Furthermore, under SAL operations, considerable attention has been given to public investment programs, to their sectoral allocations, choices of projects, and other aspects. In particular, the Bank has attempted to ensure that the cutting back of public investment is done in an efficient manner. Instead of cutbacks across the whole range of projects (with the consequence that all projects take longer to complete), a more selective exercise is undertaken, with some projects being excluded from funding completely while others proceed on a priority basis.

The Bank has probably been insufficiently active, however, in stressing that if a structural adjustment program is to be supported under SAL, aggregate social and economic expenditures should not be the residual recipient of government resources in order that IMF targets can be met. There has been a tendency for the Bank to accept this aggregate as a "given" arising out of the IMF-supported program and simply to address the question of how the expenditure can be more efficiently allocated. Of course, in a situation of falling domestic real incomes and balance-of-payments problems, government real expenditures are bound to fall. It is unlikely that economic and social expenditures will escape these reductions. Yet a too passive attitude by the Bank in accepting whatever emerges from IMF agreements could subvert the objective of structural adjustment lending, which is to ensure that development momentum is maintained while macro-economic balance is achieved. In a very few instances, SAL programs have included agreements to maintain or increase real expenditures on priority social and economic services, but these have been exceptions.

The Bank also has not gone very far in assisting governments to design expenditure programs that help achieve developmental objectives within a tight budgetary situation. Expenditures on education, health, or housing can be more effectively targeted toward poverty groups and can be designed in ways that reduce unit costs very considerably. The Bank and other external donors have been working with developing-country governments for many years to develop low-cost, replicable program to provide basic infrastructure or services, such as housing, sewage, water supply, and health and education delivery systems. Most of these activities have been at the level of *projects*. The present and prospective economic situation facing developing countries now makes it even more urgent to help intensify the implementation of efficient but low-cost and replicable socio-economic *programs*. Structural adjustment lending provides an operational channel through which these policy issues can be handled more effectively than typically has been the case under project operations. By strengthening emphasis on this area, SAL would be contributing not only to the adjustment process, but to the longer-term needs of development.

Discussion of these issues provides a fuller context for attempting to answer, at least in part, the questions raised at the beginning of this chapter: Is structural adjustment lending to be regarded as a diversion to help deal with a global crisis or as a watershed in the Bank's mandate and operational design? If an appropriate framework of policies is as important as investment for achieving growth and poverty alleviation objectives, should not the Bank put policy issues at the center of its operations as a matter of long-term strategy? If so, is this consistent with a mandate that makes the Bank overwhelmingly a *project* lender in the absence of exceptional circumstances?

The SAL program has for the first time disciplined Bank staff and management to treat policy issues as central to its operations and not simply as add-ons to project operations. The view expressed in this chapter is that the attempt to make *policy* conditionality the "tail" of *project* lending — especially with too wide a span of conditionality — almost inevitably means inadequate discipline toward policy issues. The absence of priority attention for policy considerations does not arise from lack of concern about or commitment toward policy reform on the part of staff and management. If this view is accepted, and if it is also accepted that the Bank, acting alongside the IMF, has a comparative advantage over other financial agencies in pursuing policy issues with governments, then SAL should be regarded as a watershed in the evolution of the Bank. The SAL program has provided an experience upon which governments and the Bank's management should build when looking to the institution's future role in the international effort to eradicate poverty.

NOTES

1. The term World Bank includes the International Bank for Reconstruction and Development (IBRD) and the International Development Association (IDA). IBRD lends to governments or against a government guarantee on non-concessional terms (17-20 years at 10.08 per cent, May 1984). IDA lends on concessional terms (50 yeras at 0.75 per cent service charge).

2. Manual Guitian, "Fund Conditionality and the Intenrational Adjustment Process: The Early Period, 1950-70," *Finance and Development,* Vol. 17, No. 4 (December 1980), pp. 23-27.

3. For earlier descriptions of structural adjustment lending and the considerations that led to its introduction, see especially Pierre M. Landell-Mills, "Structural Adjustment Lending: Early Experience," *Finance and Development,* Vol. 18, No. 4 (December 1981), pp. 17-21, and Ernest Stern, "World Bank Financing of Structural Adjustment," in John Williamson, ed., *IMF Conditionality* (Washington, D.C.: Institute for International Economics, 1983), pp. 87-107.

# 3C. Range of World Bank Lending Instruments
The World Bank

Instrument	Objective	Focus and content	Use of loan proceeds	Disbursement period[a]	Commitments, 1985[b]
Specific investment loan	To create new productive assets and economic and social infrastructures, to restore them to full capacity, or to ensure their maintenance.	Focuses on technical, financial, economic, and institutional viability of a specific investment and its maintenance, and on those aspects of the sector policy framework that bear directly upon the productivity of the investment (for example, input and output prices, operational efficiency of enterprises). Assists in the design of investments and in preparing management and training programs. Investment proposals are appraised by Bank staff. Requires agreement on viability and specifics of investments.	Preidentified equipment, materials, and services, and civil works for specific investments.	Four to nine years.	7,140.3
Sector Operations					
Sector-investment and maintenance loan	To bring sector investments in line with economic priorities and ensure they are efficiently operated and maintained.	Focuses on sector expenditures, especially balance between new investments and rehabilitation and maintenance, and on institutional capacity to plan, implement, and monitor investments. Requires agreement on well-designed sector program to meet priority development needs, as well as on specific measures to strengthen management and policies, and a sector institution capable of carrying out the program using agreed appraisal criteria for individual parts of program.	Broad categories of equipment, materials, services, and civil works related to the whole, or a time slice, of the sector program.	Three to seven years.	4,001.8
Financial intermediary loan	To provide funds for enterprises and small and medium-size farmers through an intermediary within a competitive environment.	Focuses on categories of clients, types of investments, service levels, and cost of capital. Requires agreement on criteria to select subborrowers and appraise their needs, on on-lending rates and on specific actions for institution building.	Credit for investment and working capital needs of subborrowers selected in accordance with agreed criteria.	Three to seven years.	1,598.6
Sector-adjustment loan	To support comprehensive policy changes and institutional reforms in a specific sector.	Focuses on major sectoral issues and investment programs, especially incentive framework (tariffs, prices, taxes), and institutional capability. Usually either in countries lacking administrative and political capability to formulate and implement comprehensive economywide structural-adjustment programs, or not requiring such comprehensive programs, or as follow-up to stabilization programs to deepen reforms in a sector. Requires agreement on specific monitorable action program in these areas on specific schedule and on investment programs for the sector.	Mainly imports required for sector, with actual users either preidentified or to be selected following agreed criteria.	One to four years.	1,058.1
Structural-adjustment loan	To support, through a series of loans, specific policy changes and institutional reforms to achieve efficient use of resources and contribute to a sustainable balance of payments in the medium and long term, while maintaining growth.	Focuses on major macroeconomic issues, as well as on major sectoral issues covering several sectors, especially trade policy (for example, tariff reform, import liberalization, export incentives), resource mobilization (for example, role of parastatals, budget policy, interest rates, debt management), efficient use of resources (for example, public-investment program criteria, pricing, incentive system), and institutional reforms, economywide and in specific sectors. Requires agreement on effective stabilization program with monitorable policy modifications in these areas on specific schedule.	General imports subject to negative list of prohibited imports.	One to three years.	238.8[c]

46 International Borrowing

Technical-assistance loan	To strengthen local institutions concerned with (i) designing and adopting policies, strategies, and institutional approaches promoting further development in a sector or in the economy as a whole, or (ii) preparing, implementing, or operating specific investments, or to carry out specific tasks related to the preparation, implementation, or operation of investments.	Focuses on capacity (e.g., organization, management, staffing, methods, physical or financial resources) or institutions directly concerned with sector or economywide policies and strategies or with investments, and on specific gaps (studies and personnel) preventing efficient investments. Requires agreement on specific time-bound action programs to strengthen institution through technical assistance and training, on appointment of local counterparts, or on the carrying out of studies with agreed terms of reference.	Specialized consultants and services, studies, and training.	Two to six years.	206.1
Emergency reconstruction loan	To support rebuilding activities and rapid restoration of physical structures and productive activities after disasters.	Focuses mainly on restoring predisaster situations with emphasis on strengthening institutions to handle reconstruction effort and prepare them for future.	Broad positive list related to reconstruction needs.	Two to five years.	148.6

a. This is the normal range of expected disbursements. There may be a small number of exceptional cases where the disbursement period is shorter or longer than shown.

b. Fiscal year; US $ millions.

c. Includes program-loan amounts.

3D. Sample IBRD Loan Agreement and Guarantee Agreement

LOAN AGREEMENT

AGREEMENT, dated May 21, 1980, between INTERNATIONAL BANK FOR RECONSTRUCTION AND DEVELOPMENT (hereinafter called the Bank) and the NATIONAL ELECTRICITY BOARD OF THE STATES OF MALAYA (hereinafter called the Borrower).

ARTICLE I

General Conditions; Definitions

Section 1.01. The parties to this Agreement accept all the provisions of the General Conditions Applicable to Loan and Guarantee Agreements of the Bank, dated March 15, 1974, with the same force and effect as if they were fully set forth herein (said General Conditions Applicable to Loan and Guarantee Agreements of the Bank being hereinafter called the General Conditions).

Section 1.02. Wherever used in this Agreement, unless the context otherwise requires, the several terms defined in the General Conditions have the respective meanings therein set forth and the following additional terms have the following meanings.

(a) "Malaysian Dollars" and "M$" mean dollars in the currency of the Guarantor;

(b) "1963 Loan Agreement" means the Loan Agreement, No. 350 MA, dated August 7, 1963, as amended, between the Bank and the Central Electricity Board of the Federation of Malaya;

(c) "1966 Loan Agreement" means the Loan Agreement, No. 458 MA, dated July 26, 1966, as amended, between the Bank and the Borrower;

(d) "1969 Loan Agreement" means the Loan Agreement, No. 579 MA, dated January 9, 1969, as amended, between the Bank and the Borrower;

(e) "1970 Loan Agreement" means the Loan Agreement, No. 700 MA, dated July 16, 1970, as amended, between the Bank and the Borrower;

(f) "1974 Loan Agreement" means the Loan Agreement, No. 1031 MA, dated July 25, 1974, as amended, between the Bank and the Borrower;

(g) "1975 Loan Agreement" means the Loan Agreement, No. 1178 MA, dated December 17, 1975, as amended, between the Bank and the Borrower; and

(h) "1977 Loan Agreement" means the Loan Agreement, No. 1443 MA, dated August 3, 1977, between the Bank and the Borrower.

ARTICLE II

The Loan

Section 2.01. The bank agrees to lend to the Borrower, on the terms and conditions set forth or referred to in the Loan Agreement, an amount in various currencies equivalent to fifty million dollars ($50,000,000).

Section 2.02. The amount of the Loan may be withdrawn from the Loan Account in accordance with the provisions of Schedule 1 to this Agreement, as such Schedule may be amended from time to time by agreement between the Borrower and the Bank, for expenditures made (or, if the Bank shall so agree, to be made) in respect of the reasonable cost of goods and services required for the Project described in Schedule 2 to this Agreement and to be financed out of the proceeds of the Loan.

Section 2.03. Except as the Bank shall otherwise agree, procurement of the goods and services to be financed out of the proceeds of the Loan, shall be governed by the provisions of Schedule 4 to this Agreement.

Section 2.04. The Closing date shall be August 31, 1985 or such later date as the Bank shall establish. The Bank shall promptly notify the Borrower and the Guarantor of such later date.

Section 2.05. The Borrower shall pay to the Bank a commitment charge at the rate of three-fourths of one per cent (¾ of

1%) per annum on the principal amount of the Loan not withdrawn from time to time.

Section 2.06. The Borrower shall pay interest at the rate of eight and one-fourth per cent (8.25%) per annum on the principal amount of the Loan withdrawn and outstanding from time to time.

Section 2.07. Interest and other charges shall be payable semiannually on June 15 and December 15 in each year.

Section 2.08. The Borrower shall repay the principal amount of the Loan in accordance with the amortization schedule set forth in Schedule 3 to this Agreement.

ARTICLE III

Execution of the Project

Section 3.01. The Borrower shall carry out the Project with due diligence and efficiency and in conformity with appropriate administrative, financial, engineering and public utility practices, and shall provide, promptly as needed, the funds, facilities, services and other resources required for the purpose.

Section 3.02. In order to assist the Borrower in preparing detailed Project designs, procurement and the supervision of the construction of the Project, the Borrower shall continue to employ engineering consultants whose qualifications, experience and terms and conditions of employment shall be satisfactory to the Bank and the Guarantor.

Section 3.03. The Borrower shall maintain its panel of experts to review Project designs and assist the Borrower in resolving any special problems which may arise during the carrying out of the Project.

Section 3.04. (a) The Borrower undertakes to insure, or make adequate provision for the insurance of, the imported goods to be financed out of the proceeds of the Loan against hazards incident to the acquisition, transportation and delivery thereof to the place of use or installation, and for such insurance any indemnity shall be payable in a currency freely usable by the Borrower to replace or repair such goods.

(b) Except as the Bank shall otherwise agree, the Borrower shall cause all goods and services financed out of the proceeds of the Loan to be used exclusively for the Project.

Section 3.05. (a) The Borrower shall furnish to the Bank, promptly upon their preparation, the plans, specifications, reports, contract documents and construction and procurement schedules for the Project, and any material modifications thereof or additions thereto, in such detail as the Bank shall reasonably request.

(b) The Borrower: (i) shall maintain records and procedures adequate to record and monitor the progress of the Project (including its cost and the benefits to be derived from it), to identify the goods and services financed out of the proceeds of the Loan, and to disclose their use in the Project; (ii) shall enable the Bank's accredited representatives to visit the facilities and construction sites included in the Project and to examine the goods financed out of the proceeds of the Loan and any relevant records and documents; and (iii) shall furnish to the Bank at regular intervals all such information as the Bank shall reasonably request concerning the Project, its cost and, where appropriate, the benefits to be derived from it, the expenditure of the proceeds of the Loan and the goods and services financed out of such proceeds.

(c) Promptly after completion of the Project, but in any event not later than six months after the Closing Date or such later date as may be agreed for this purpose between the Borrower and the Bank, the Borrower shall prepare and furnish to the Bank a report, of such scope and in such detail as the Bank shall reasonably request, on the execution and initial operation of the Project, its cost and the benefits derived and to be derived from it, the performance by the Borrower and the Bank of their respective obligations under the Loan Agreement and the accomplishment of the purposes of the Loan.

(d) The Borrower shall enable the Bank's representatives to examine, except for reasons of national security, all plants, installations, sites, works, buildings, property and equipment of the Borrower and any relevant records and documents.

Section 3.06. The Borrower shall take or cause to be taken all such action as shall be necessary to acquire as and when needed all such land and rights in respect of land as shall be required for carrying out the Project and shall furnish to the Bank, upon request, evidence satisfactory to the Bank that such land and rights in respect of land are available for purposes related to the Project.

Section 3.07. The Borrower shall, whenever it is neccesary, make arrangements satisfactory to the Guarantor and the Bank to relocate any residents in the areas which will be flooded by the reservoirs of the dams constructed under Parts A and B of the Project, who are required to move as a result of the carrying out of such Parts of the Project.

Section 3.08. The Borrower shall take all reasonable measures to ensure that the execution and operation of the Project are carried out with due regard to ecological and environmental factors and in particular, except as the Bank may otherwise agree, the recommendations of the Pre-investment Report dated October 1976 of the Shawinigan Engineering Co., Ltd.

ARTICLE IV

Management and Operations of the Borrower

Section 4.01. The Borrower shall at all times conduct its business and operations and maintain its financial position, in accordance with sound public utility practices under the supervision of experienced and competent management.

Section 4.02. The Borrower shall take out and maintain with responsible insurers, or make other provision satisfactory to the Bank for, insurance against such risks and in such amounts as shall be consistent with appropriate practice.

Section 4.03. The Borrower shall operate and maintain its plants, equipment and property, and from time to time make all necessary renewals and repairs thereof, all in accordance with sound engineering standards; shall, except as the Bank shall otherwise agree, take all practical steps which may be reasonably necessary to maintain and renew all rights, powers, privileges and franchises which are necessary or useful in the conduct of its business and shall at all times operate and maintain its plants, equipment and properties in accordance with sound public utility practice.

Section 4.04. Without limiting the generality of Section 4.03, the Borrower shall under arrangements satisfactory to the Bank cause the dam, waterways, and reservoir banks constructed under Parts A and B of the Project to be periodically inspected in accordance with sound engineering practice in order to determine whether there are any deficiencies or potential deficiencies in the condition of such structures, or in the quality and adequacy of maintenance or methods of operation of such structures which may endanger the safety of such structures.

ARTICLE V

Financial Covenants

Section 5.01. The Borrower shall maintain records adequate to reflect in accordance with consistently maintained appropriate accounting practices its operations and financial condition.

Section 5.02. The Borrower shall: (i) have its accounts and financial statements (balance sheets, statements of income and expenses and related statements) for each fiscal year audited, in accordance with appropriate auditing principles consistently applied, by independent auditors acceptable to the Bank; (ii) furnish to the Bank as soon as available, but in any case not later than six months after the end of each such year, (A) certified copies of its financial statements for such year as so audited and (B) the report of such audit by said auditors, of such scope and in such detail as the Bank shall have reasonably requested; and (iii) furnish to the Bank such other information concerning the accounts and financial statements of the Borrower and the audit thereof as the Bank shall from time to time reasonably request.

Section 5.03. (a) The Borrower represents that at the date of this Agreement no lien exists on any of its assets as security for any debt.

(b) The Borrower undertakes that, except as the Bank shall otherwise agree, if any lien shall be created on any assets of the Borrower as security for any debt, such lien will *ipso facto* equally and ratably secure the payment of the principal of, and interest and other charges on, the Loan, and in the creation of any such lien express provision will be made to that effect, at no cost to the Bank; provided, however, that the foregoing provisions of this paragraph shall not apply to: (i) any lien created on property, at the time of purchase thereof, solely as security for the payment of the purchase price of such property; or (ii) any lien arising in the ordinary course of banking transactions and securing a debt maturing not more than one year after the date on which it is originally incurred.

Section 5.04. The Borrower shall:

(a) exchange views with the Bank on any proposed changes in its tariff structure; and

(b) review with the Guarantor, at least three months before the end of each fiscal year, with effect from the fiscal year ending August 31, 1981, measures necessary for the Borrower to comply with the requirements of Section 5.05 of this Agreement.

Section 5.05. Except as the Bank may otherwise agree, the Borrower shall take all such measures as shall be required to produce, during each of its fiscal years beginning on September 1, 1979, funds from internal sources equivalent to not less than 15% for fiscal year 1980, 25% for fiscal years 1981 to 1984 and 30% for fiscal year 1985 and thereafter, of the Borrower's average capital expenditures for electricity operations (excluding rural electrification) for three years comprising the year in question, the next preceding year and (on the basis of estimates acceptable to the Bank) the next following year.

For the purposes of this Section:

(a) The term "funds from internal sources" means the difference between:

(i) the sum of gross revenues from all sources related to electricity operations, cash consumer contributions in aid of construction, net non-operating income, and any other cash inflows (including subsidies for losses in operation of rural and diesel stations) but excluding external funds for financing capital expenditures (such as contributions from the Guarantor for financing rural electrification projects); and

(ii) The sum of all expenses of operation, including maintenance and administration (excluding depreciation and other non-cash operating charges), interest charged to operations, repayment of loans, cash dividends, investment in industries and increases in working capital.

(b) The term "capital expenditures" means all expenditures incurred on account of fixed or capital assets, including interest during construction but excluding investment in rural electrification programs.

Section 5.06. (a) Except as the Bank shall otherwise agree, the Borrower shall not incur any debt, if such debt would raise the Borrower's total debt to more than sixty per cent (60%) of the sum of its equity plus its total debt.

(b) For the purposes of this Section:

(i) the term "total debt" includes all debt contracted by the Borrower that matures more than twelve months after the date on which it is incurred, but excludes current maturities on such debt; and

(ii) the term "equity" means the total paid-in capital and surplus of the Borrower, with the exception of the surplus derived from the revaluation of its fixed assets.

Section 5.07. (a) It is hereby agreed that, with effect from the fiscal year commencing September 1, 1980, Section 5.08 of the 1977 Loan Agreement shall be deleted and that, except as the Bank may otherwise agree, the Borrower shall thenceforth ensure that its current liabilities do not exceed thirty-three per cent (33%) of its cash operating expenses during the preceding fiscal year.

(b) For the purposes of this Section:

(i) the term "current liabilities" shall include accounts payable to suppliers of goods and services (except those related to capital expenditures), accrued interest on loans, declared dividends, provisions for taxation, bank overdrafts and short-term loans maturing on demand or within twelve months after the date they are incurred; and

(ii) the term "cash operating expenses" shall include purchase of fuel and electricity, personnel costs, maintenance and administrative expenses, interests, taxes and dividends.

Section 5.08. Except as the Bank shall otherwise agree, the Borrower shall not invest in industry other than for the generation, transmission, distribution and sale of electricity more than an aggregate amount equivalent to one per cent (1%) of the gross value of its fixed assets as such assets shall have been revalued each year in accordance with methods of valuation and revaluation acceptable to the Bank and the Borrower. For the purposes of this Section the index to be used in such revaluation shall be the current fixed capital formation deflator used each year in the Borrower's national accounts, using fiscal year 1970 as the base year.

ARTICLE VI

Amendment of 1963 Loan Agreement, 1966 Loan Agreement, 1969 Loan Agreement, 1970 Loan Agreement, 1974 Loan Agreement, 1975 Loan Agreement and 1977 Loan Agreement

Section 6.01. For the purposes of the 1963 Loan Agreement Section 5.11 thereof and a letter supplemental thereto dated August 7, 1963 between the same parties are amended by the deletion of the provisions thereof and the substitution therefor of the provisions of Section 5.05 of this Agreement.

Section 6.02. For the purposes of the 1966 Loan Agreement Section 5.11 thereof and a letter supplemental thereto dated July 26, 1966 between the same parties are amended by the deletion of the provisions thereof and the substitution therefor of the provisions of Section 5.05 of this Agreement.

Section 6.03. For the purposes of the 1969 Loan Agreement Section 5.11 thereof is amended by the deletion of the provisions thereof and the substitution therefor of the provisions of Section 5.05 of this Agreement.

Section 6.04. For the purposes of the 1970 Loan Agreement Section 5.03 thereof is amended by the deletion of the provisions thereof and the substitution therefor of the provisions of Section 5.05 of this Agreement.

Section 6.05. For the purposes of the 1974 Loan Agreement Section 5.05 thereof is amended by the deletion of the provisions thereof and the substitution therefor of the provisions of Section 5.05 of this Agreement.

Section 6.06. For the purposes of the 1975 Loan Agreement Section 5.05 thereof is amended by the deletion of the provisions thereof and the substitution therefor of the provisions of Section 5.05 of this Agreement.

Section 6.07. For the purposes of the 1977 Loan Agreement Section 5.05 thereof is amended by the deletion of the provisions thereof and the substitution therefor of the provisions of Section 5.05 of this Agreement.

ARTICLE VII

Remedies of the Bank

Section 7.01. For the purposes of Section 6.02 of the General Conditions, the following additional events are specified pursuant to paragraph (k) thereof:

(a) Any loan edit to the Borrower shall have become due and payable prior to its agreed maturity pursuant to the terms thereof, or any security constituted thereunder shall have become enforceable.

(b) Any provision of the Electricity Act, 1949, as amended, shall have been amended, suspended, abrogated or terminated so as to affect adversely the ability of the Borrower to carry out its obligations under this Agreement.

(c) (i) Subject to subparagraph (ii) of this paragraph:

    (A) the right of the Borrower to withdraw the proceeds of any loan made to the Borrower for the financing of the Project shall have been suspended, cancelled or terminated in whole or in part, pursuant to the terms of the agreement providing therefor, or

    (B) any such loan shall have become due and payable prior to the agreed maturity thereof.

(ii) Subparagraph (i) of this paragraph shall not apply if the Borrower establishes to the satisfaction of the Bank that:

    (A) such suspension, cancellation, termination or prematuring is not caused by the failure of the Borrower to perform any of its obligations under such agreement, and

    (B) adequate funds for the Project are available to the Borrower from other sources on terms and conditions consistent with the obligations of the Borrower under this Agreement.

Section 7.02. For the purposes of Section 7.01 of the General Conditions, the following events are specified pursuant to paragraph (h) thereof:

(a) any event specified in paragraph (a), (b), or (c) of Section 7.01 of this Agreement shall occur.

ARTICLE VIII

Termination

Section 8.01. The date August 21, 1980, is hereby specified for the purpose of Section 12.04 of the General Conditions.

ARTICLE IX

Addresses

Section 9.01. The following addresses are specified for the purposes of Section 11.01 of the General Conditions:

For the Bank:

  International Bank for
    Reconstruction and Development
  1818 H Street, N.W.
  Washington, D.C. 20433
  United States of America

  Cable Address: Telex:
    INTBAFRAD   440098 (ITT)
    Washington, D.C. 248423 (RCA) or
                            64145 (WUI)

For the Borrower:

  National Electricity Board
    of the States of Malaya
  P.O. Box 1003
  Kuala Lumpur,
  Malaysia

  Cable Address: Telex:

    TRANG   MA 30426
    Kuala Lumpur

IN WITNESS WHEREOF, the parties hereto, acting through their representatives thereunto duly authorized, have caused this Agreement to be signed in their respective names in the District of Columbia, United States of America, as of the day and year first above written.

INTERNATIONAL BANK FOR
RECONSTRUCTION AND DEVELOPMENT

by /s/ S. Shahid Husain

Regional Vice President East Asia and Pacific

NATIONAL ELECTRICITY BOARD
OF THE STATES OF MALAYA

by /s/ Zain Azraai

Authorized Representative

SCHEDULE 1

Withdrawal of the Proceeds of the Loan

1. The table below sets forth the Categories of items to be financed out of the proceeds of the Loan, the allocation of the amounts of the Loan to each Category and the percentage of expenditures for items so to be financed in each Category.

Category	Amount of the Loan Allocated (Expressed in Dollar Equivalent)	% of Expenditures to be Financed
(1) Supply and installation of ancilliary mechanical and electrical equipment	23,900,000	
(a) directly imported		100% of foreign expenditures
(b) imported but procured locally		70%
(c) manufactured locally		100% of local expenditures (ex-factory)
(2) Supply and installation of transmission and substation equipment and materials	15,800,000	
(a) directly imported		100% of foreign expenditures
(b) imported but procured locally		70%
(c) manufactured locally		100% of local expenditures (ex-factory)
(3) Consultants' Services in Parts C and D of the Project	1,700,000	100% of foreign expenditures
(4) Unallocated	8,600,000	
TOTAL	50,000,000	

2. For the purposes of this Schedule:

(a) the term "foreign expenditures" means expenditures in the currency of any country other than the Guarantor and for goods or services supplied from the territory of any country other than the Guarantor; and

(b) the term "local expenditures" means expenditures in the currency of the Guarantor and for goods and services supplied from the territory of the Guarantor.

3. The disbursement percentages have been calculated in compliance with the policy of the Bank that no proceeds of the Loan shall be disbursed on account of payments for taxes levied by, or in the territory of, the Guarantor on goods or services, or on the importation, manufacture, procurement or supply thereof; to that end, if the amount of any such taxes levied on or in respect of any item to be financed out of the proceeds of the Loan decreases or increases, the Bank may, by notice to the Borrower, increase or decrease the disbursement percentage then applicable to such item as required to be consistent with the aforementioned policy of the Bank.

4. Notwithstanding the provisions of paragraph 1 above, no withdrawals shall be made in respect of payments made for expenditures prior to the date of this Agreement.

5. Notwithstanding the allocation of an amount of the Loan or the disbursement percentages set forth in the table in paragraph 1 above, if the Bank has reasonably estimated that the amount of the Loan then allocated to any Category will be insufficient to finance the agreed percentage of all expenditures in that Category, the Bank may, by notice to the Borrower: (i) reallocate to such Category, to the extent required to meet the estimated shortfall, proceeds of the Loan which are then allocated to another Category and which in the opinion of the Bank are not needed to meet other expenditures; and (ii) if such reallocation cannot fully meet the estimated shortfall, reduce the disbursement percentage then applicable to such expenditures in order that further withdrawals under such Category may continue until all expenditures thereunder shall have been made.

6. If the Bank shall have reasonably determined that the procurement of any item in any Category is inconsistent with the procedures set forth or referred to in this Agreement, no expenditures for such item shall be financed out of the proceeds of the Loan and the Bank may, without in any way restricting or limiting any other right, power or remedy of the Bank under the Loan Agreement, by notice to the Borrower, cancel such amount of the Loan as, in the Bank's reasonable opinion, represents the amount of such expenditures which would otherwise have been eligible for financing out of the proceeds of the Loan.

SCHEDULE 2

Description of the Project

The Project consists of:

Part A:

The construction and placing into operation of a concrete gravity dam about 244 meters long and 32 meters high at Bersia, on the Perak River, with a conventional above-ground powerhouse including three generating units (3 x 24 MW) and associated ancilliary electrical and mechanical equipment.

Part B:

The construction and placing into operation of a composite earthfill and concrete gravity dam about 610 meters long and 41 meters high at Kenering, on the Perak River, with a conventional above-ground powerhouse including three generating units (3 x 40 MW) and associated electrical and mechanical equipment.

Part C:

The construction, installation and placing into operation of the following associated transmission and sub-station facilities:

(i) about 136 kilometers of 275 kV transmission line between Temengor and Tanah Merah;

(ii) about 38 kilometers of 132 kV transmission line between Tanah Merah and Kota Bahru;

(iii) a sub-station with two 180 MVA 275/132 kV transformers, two 30 MVA 132/33 kV transformers and two 7.5 MVA 33/11 kV transformers at Tanah Merah; and

(iv) a sub-station with two 45 MVA 132/33 kV transformers and two 30 MVA 132/11 kv transformers at Kota Bahru.

Part D:

Preparation of a study for optimizing development and use of domestic energy resources.

The Project is expected to be completed by August 31, 1984.

SCHEDULE 3

Amortization Schedule

Date Payment Due	Payment of Principal (expressed in dollars)*
On each June 15 and December 15	
beginning December 15, 1984 through December 15, 1996	1,925,000
On June 15, 1997	1,875,000

*To the extent that any portion of the Loan is repayable in a currency other than dollars (see General Conditions, Section 4.02), the figures in this column represent dollar equivalents determined as for purposes of withdrawal.

Premiums on Prepayment

The following percentages are specified as the premiums payable on repayment in advance of maturity of any portion of the principal amount of the Loan pursuant to Section 3.05 (b) of the General Conditions:

Time of Prepayment	Premium
Not more than three years before maturity	1.45%
More than three years but not more than six years before maturity	2.90%
More than six years but not more than eleven years before maturity	5.35%
More than eleven years but not more than fifteen years before maturity	7.30%
More than fifteen years before maturity	8.25%

SCHEDULE 4

Procurement

A. International Competitive Bidding

1. All goods and services shall be procured under contracts awarded in accordance with procedures consistent with those set forth in the "Guidelines for Procurement under World Bank Loans and IDA Credits" published by the Bank in March 1977 (hereinafter called the Guidelines), on the basis of international competitive bidding as described in Part A of the Guidelines.

2. In addition to the requirements of paragraph 1.2 of the

Guidelines, the Borrower shall prepare and forward to the Bank as soon as possible, and in any event not later than 60 days prior to the date of availability to the public of the first tender or prequalification documents relating thereto, as the case may be, a general procurement notice, in such form and detail and containing such information as the Bank shall reasonably request; the Bank will arrange for the publication of such notice in order to provide timely notification to prospective bidders of the opportunity to bid for the goods and services in question. The Borrower shall provide the necessary information to update such notice annually so long as any goods or services remain to be procured on the basis of international competitive bidding.

3. For the purpose of evaluation and comparison of bids for the supply of goods to be procured on the basis of international competitive bidding: (i) bidders shall be required to state in their bid the c.i.f. (port of entry) price for imported goods, or the ex-factory price for domestically manufactured goods; (ii) customs duties and other import taxes on imported goods, and sales and similar taxes on domestically supplied goods, shall be excluded; and (iii) the cost to the Borrower of inland freight and other expenditures incidental to the delivery of goods to the place of their use or installation shall be included.

B. Preference for Domestic Manufacturers

In the procurement of goods in accordance with the procedures described in Part A of this Schedule, goods manufactured in Malaysia may be granted a margin of preference in accordance with, and subject to, the following provisions:

1. All bidding documents for the procurement of goods shall clearly indicate any preference which will be granted, the information required to establish the eligibility of a bid for such preference and the following methods and stages that will be followed in the evaluation and comparison of bids.

2. After evaluation, responsive bids will be classified in one of the following three groups:

(1) Group A: bids offering goods manufactured in Malaysia if the bidder shall have established to the satisfaction of the Borrower and the Bank that the manufacturing cost of such goods includes a value added in Malaysia equal to at least 20% of the ex-factory bid price of such goods.

(2) Group B: all other bids offering goods manufactured in Malaysia.

(3) Group C: bids offering any other goods.

3. All evaluated bids in each group shall be first compared among themselves, excluding any customs duties and other import taxes on goods to be imported and any sales or similar taxes on goods to be supplied domestically, to determine the lowest evaluated bid of each group. Such lowest evaluated bids shall then be compared with each other, and if, as a result of this comparison, a bid from Group A or Group B is the lowest, it shall be selected for the award.

4. If, as a result of the comparison under paragraph 3 above, the lowest bid is a bid from Group C, all Group C bids shall be further compared with the lowest evaluated bid from Group A after adding to the c.i.f. bid price of the imported goods offered in each Group C bid, for the purpose of this further comparison only, an amount equal to: (i) the amount of customs duties and other import taxes which a non-exempt importer would have to pay for the importation of the goods offered in such Group C bid; or (ii) 15% of the c.i.f. bid price of such goods if said customs duties and taxes exceed 15% of such price. If the Group A bid in such further comparison is the lowest, it shall be selected for the award; if not, the bid from Group C which as a result of the comparison under paragraph 3 is the lowest evaluated bid shall be selected.

C. Review of Procurement Decisions by the Bank 1.

(1) Review of invitations to bid and of proposed awards and final contracts:

With respect to all contracts for goods and services estimated to cost the equivalent of $200,000 or more:

(a) Before bids are invited, the Borrower shall furnish to the Bank, for its comments, the text of the invitations to bid and the specifications and other bidding documents, together with a description of the advertising procedures to be followed for the bidding, and shall make such modifications in the said documents or procedures as the Bank shall reasonably request. Any further modification to the bidding documents shall require the Bank's concurrence before it is issued to the prospective bidders.

(b) After bids have been received and evaluated, the Borrower shall, before a final decision on the award is made, inform the Bank of the name of the bidder to which it intends to award the contract and shall furnish to the Bank, in sufficient time for its review, a detailed report, by the consultants referred to in Section 3.02 of this Agreement, on the evaluation and comparison of the bids received, together with the recommendations for award or the said consultants and such other information as the Bank shall reasonably request. The Bank shall, if it determines that the intended award would be inconsistent with the Guidelines of this Schedule, promptly inform the Borrower and state the reasons for such determination.

(c) The terms and conditions of the contract shall not,

without the Bank's concurrence, materially differ from those on which bids were asked or prequalification invited.

(d) Two conformed copies of the contract shall be furnished to the Bank promptly after its execution and prior to the submission to the Bank of the first application for withdrawal of funds from the Loan Account in respect of such contract.

(2) With respect to each contract not governed by the preceding paragraph, the Borrower shall furnish to the Bank, promptly after its execution and prior to the submission to the Bank of the first application for withdrawal of funds from the Loan Account in respect of such contract, two conformed copies of such contract, together with the analysis of the respective bids, recommendations for award and such other information as the Bank shall reasonably request. The Bank shall, if it determines that the award of the contract was not consistent with the Guidelines of this Schedule, promptly inform the Borrower and state the reasons for such determination.

3. Before agreeing to any material modification or waiver of the terms and conditions of a contract, the Borrower shall inform the Bank of the proposed modification or waiver and the reasons therefor. The Bank, if it determines that the proposal would be inconsistent with the provisions of this Agreement, shall promptly inform the Borrower and state the reasons for its determination.

Guarantee Agreement

GUARANTEE AGREEMENT

AGREEMENT dated May 21, 1980, between MALAYSIA (hereinafter called the Guarantor) and INTERNATIONAL BANK FOR RECONSTRUCTION AND DEVELOPMENT (hereinafter called the Bank).

WHEREAS by the Loan Agreement of even date herewith between the Bank and the National Electricity Board of the States of Malaya (hereinafter called the Borrower) the Bank has agreed to make to the Borrower a loan in various currencies equivalent to fifty million dollars ($50,000,000) on the terms and conditions set forth in the Loan Agreement, but only on condition that the Guarantor agree to guarantee the obligations of the Borrower in respect of such loan as hereinafter provided; and

WHEREAS the Guarantor, in consideration of the Bank's entering into the Loan Agreement with the Borrower, has agreed to so guarantee such obligations of the Borrower;

NOW THEREFORE the parties hereby agree as follows:

ARTICLE I

General Conditions; Definitions

Section 1.01. The parties to this Agreement accept all the provisions of the General Conditions Applicable to Loan and Guarantee Agreements of the Bank dated March 15, 1974, with the same force and effect as if they were fully set forth herein (said General Conditions Applicable to Loan and Guarantee Agreements being hereinafter called the General Conditions).

Section 1.02. Wherever used in this Agreement, unless the context otherwise requires, the several terms defined in the General Conditions have the respective meanings therein set forth.

ARTICLE II

Guarantee; Provision of Funds

Section 2.01. Without limitation or restriction upon any of its other obligations under the Guarantee Agreement, the Guarantor hereby unconditionally guarantees, as primary obligor and not as surety merely, the due and punctual payment of the principal of, and interest and other charges on, the Loan, and the premium, if any, on the prepayment of the Loan and the punctual performance of all the other obligations of the Borrower, all as set forth in the Loan Agreement.

Section 2.02. Without limitation or restriction upon the provisions of Section 2.01 of this Agreement, the Guarantor specifically undertakes: (a) whenever there is reasonable cause to believe that the funds available to the Borrower will be inadequate to meet the estimated expenditures required for the carrying out of the Project, to make arrangements, consistent with the provisions of the Loan Agreement, promptly to provide the Borrower or cause the Borrower to be provided with such funds as are needed to meet such expenditures; and (b) to provide the Borrower, or cause the Borrower to be provided, with adequate funds to finance the Borrower's development programs as approved by the Guarantor, including an equity contribution of Malaysian $150,000,000 to be provided during the Borrower's Fiscal Year 1979-80.

ARTICLE III

Other Covenants

Section 3.01. (a) It is the policy of the Bank, in making loans to, or with the guarantee of its members not to seek, in normal circumstances, specific security from the member concerned but to ensure that no other external debt shall have priority over its loans in the allocation, realization or distribution of foreign exchange held under the control or for the benefit of such member. To that end, if any lien shall be created on any public assets (as hereinafter defined), as security for any external debt, which will or might result in a priority for the benefit of the creditor of such external debt in the allocation, realization or distribution of foreign exchange, such lien shall, unless the Bank shall otherwise agree, *ipso facto*, and at no cost to the Bank, equally and ratably secure the principal of, and interest and other charges on, the Loan, and the Guarantor, in creating or permitting the creation of such lien, shall make excess provision to that effect; provided, however, that, if for any constitutional or other legal reason such provision cannot be made with respect to any lien created on assets of any of its political or administrative subdivisions, the Guarantor shall promptly and at no cost to the Bank secure the principal of, and interest and other charges on, the Loan by an equivalent lien on other public assets satisfactory to the Bank.

(b) The foregoing undertaking shall not apply to: (i) any lien created on property, at the time of purchase thereof, solely as security for payment of the purchase price of such property; and (ii) any lien arising in the ordinary course of banking transactions and securing a debt maturing not more than one year after its date.

(c) As used in this Section, the term "public assets" means assets of the Guarantor, of any political or administrative subdivision thereof and of any entity owned or controlled by, or operating for the account or benefit of, the Guarantor or any such subdivision.

Section 3.02. The Guarantor covenants: (i) that it will not take, or cause or permit any of its political subdivisions or any of its agencies or any agency of any such political subdivisions to take, any action which would prevent or interfere with the performance by the Borrower of its obligations contained in the Loan Agreement and will take or cause to be taken all reasonable action necessary or appropriate to enable the Borrower to perform such obligations; and (ii) that it will use its best efforts to ensure that the time taken by its agencies in processing each application made to such agencies by the Borrower for the approval of a bid evaluation and the award of a contract for goods or services does not exceed three months.

Section 3.03. The Guarantor shall furnish to the Bank for its comments and review, not later than July 31, 1982, a study, prepared by consultants whose terms of reference and qualifications shall be satisfactory to the Guarantor and the Bank, on optimizing development and use of domestic energy resources.

ARTICLE IV

Representative of the Guarantor; Addresses

Section 4.01. The Minister of Finance or Deputy Minister of Finance of the Guarantor or such other person or persons as such Minister of Finance shall authorize in writing are designated as representatives of the Guarantor for the purposes of Section 11.03 of the General Conditions.

Section 4.02. The following addresses are specified for the purposes of Section 11.01 of the General Conditions:

For the Guarantor:

The Treasury
Kuala Lumpur 01-01
Malaysia

Cable Address: Telex:
TREASURY MA 30242
Kuala Lumpur

For the Bank:

International Bank for
 Reconstruction and Development
1818 H. Street, N.W.
Washington, D.C. 20433
United States of America

Cable Address: Telex:

INTBAFRAD 440098 (ITT)
Washington, D.C. 248423 (RCA) or
  64145 (WUI)

IN WITNESS WHEREOF, the parties hereto, acting through their representatives thereunto duly authorized, have caused this Agreement to be signed in their respective names in the District of Columbia, United States of America, as of the day and year first above written.

MALAYSIA

By /s/ Zain Ayraai
                              Authorized Representative

INTERNATIONAL BANK FOR
 RECONSTRUCTION AND DEVELOPMENT

By /s/ S. Shahid Husain
                              Regional Vice President
                              East Asia and Pacific

INTERNATIONAL BANK FOR
RECONSTRUCTION AND DEVELOPMENT

General Conditions Applicable to Loan and Guarantee Agreements

DATED JANUARY 1, 1985

INTERNATIONAL BANK FOR RECONSTRUCTION AND DEVELOPMENT

GENERAL CONDITIONS APPLICABLE TO LOAN AND GUARANTEE AGREEMENTS

TABLE OF CONTENTS

Article Number	Title
Article I	Application to Loan and Guarantee Agreements ....
Section 1.01	Application of General Conditions ....
Section 1.02	Inconsistency with Loan and Guarantee Agreements ....
Article II	Definitions; Headings ....
Section 2.01	Definitions ....
Section 2.02	References ....
Section 2.03	Headings ....
Article III	Loan Account; Interest and Other Charges; Repayment; Place of Payment ....
Section 3.01	Loan Account ....
Section 3.02	Commitment Charges ....
Section 3.03	Interest ....
Section 3.04	Repayment ....
Section 3.05	Place of Payment ....
Article IV	Currency Provisions ....
Section 4.01	Currencies in which Withdrawals are to be Made ....
Section 4.02	Central Disbursement Account; Loan's Share........................
Section 4.03	Principal Amount of the Loan ....
Section 4.04	Currency in which Principal is Payable; Maturities ....
Section 4.05	Central Disbursement Account; Repayments ....
Section 4.06	Currency in which Premium is Payable..
Section 4.07	Currency in which Interest and Other Charges are Payable ....
Section 4.08	Purchase of Currencies ....
Section 4.09	Valuation of Currencies ....
Section 4.10	Manner of Payment ....
Article V	Withdrawal of Proceeds of Loan ....
Section 5.01	Withdrawal from the Loan Account .....

59

Article Number	Title
Section 5.02	Special Commitment by the Bank ....
Section 5.03	Applications for Withdrawal or for Special Commitment ....
Section 5.04	Reallocation............................
Section 5.05	Evidence of Authority to Sign Applications for Withdrawal ....
Section 5.06	Supporting Evidence ....
Section 5.07	Sufficiency of Applications and Documents ....
Section 5.08	Treatment of Taxes.....................
Section 5.09	Payment by the Bank ....
Article VI	**Cancellation and Suspension** ....
Section 6.01	Cancellation by the Borrower ....
Section 6.02	Suspension by the Bank ....
Section 6.03	Cancellation by the Bank ....
Section 6.04	Amounts Subject to Special Commitment Not Affected by Cancellation or Suspension by the Bank ....
Section 6.05	Application of Cancellation to Maturities of the Loan ....
Section 6.06	Effectiveness of Provisions after Suspension or Cancellation ....
Section 6.07	Cancellation of Guarantee ....
Article VII	**Acceleration of Maturity** ....
Section 7.01	Events of Acceleration ....
Article VIII	**Taxes** ....
Section 8.01	Taxes ....
Article IX	**Cooperation and Information; Financial and Economic Data; Negative Pledge; Project Implementation** ....
Section 9.01	Cooperation and Information ....
Section 9.02	Financial and Economic Data ....
Section 9.03	Negative Pledge.......................
Section 9.04	Insurance..............................
Section 9.05	Use of Goods and Services.............
Section 9.06	Plans and Schedules...................
Section 9.07	Records and Reports...................
Section 9.08	Maintenance...........................
Section 9.09	Land Acquisition......................
Article X	**Enforceability of Loan Agreement and Guarantee Agreement; Failure to Exercise Rights; Arbitration** ......
Section 10.01	Enforceability ....

Article Number	Title	
Section 10.02	Obligations of the Guarantor	....
Section 10.03	Failure to Exercise Rights	....
Section 10.04	Arbitration	....
Article XI	**Miscellaneous Provisions**	....
Section 11.01	Notices and Requests	....
Section 11.02	Evidence of Authority	....
Section 11.03	Action on Behalf of the Borrower or Guarantor	....
Section 11.04	Execution in Counterparts	....
Article XII	**Effective Date; Termination**	....
Section 12.01	Conditions Precedent to Effectiveness of Loan Agreement and Guarantee Agreement	....
Section 12.02	Legal Opinions or Certificates	......
Section 12.03	Effective Date	....
Section 12.04	Termination of Loan Agreement and Guarantee Agreement for Failure to Become Effective	....
Section 12.05	Termination of Loan Agreement and Guarantee Agreement on Full Payment	....

General Conditions Applicable to Loan and Guarantee Agreements

Dated January 1, 1985

ARTICLE I

Application to Loan and Guarantee Agreements

Section 1.01. **Application of General Conditions.** These General Conditions set forth certain terms and conditions generally applicable to loans made by the Bank. They apply to any loan agreement providing for any such loan and to any guarantee agreement with a member of the Bank providing for the guarantee of any such loan to the extent and subject to any modifications set forth in such agreements. In the case of a loan agreement between the Bank and a member of the Bank, references in these General Conditions to the "Guarantor" and the "Guarantee Agreement" shall be disregarded.

Section 1.02. **Inconsistency with Loan and Guarantee Agreements.** If any provision of a loan agreement or guarantee agreement is inconsistent with a provision of these General Conditions, the provision of the loan agreement or guarantee agreement, as the case may be, shall govern.

ARTICLE II

Definitions; Headings

Section 2.01. **Definitions.** The following terms have the following meanings wherever used in these General Conditions:

1. "Bank" means the International Bank for Reconstruction and Development.

2. "Association" means the International Development Association.

3. "Loan Agreement" means the particular loan agreement to which these General Conditions apply, as such agreement may be amended from time to time. Loan Agreement includes these General Conditions as applied thereto, and all schedules and agreements supplemental to the Loan Agreement.

4. "Loan" means the loan provided for in the Loan Agreement.

5. "Guarantee Agreement" means the agreement between a member of the Bank and the Bank providing for the guarantee of the Loan, as such agreement may be amended from time to time. Guarantee Agreement includes these General Conditions as applied thereto, and all schedules and agreements supplemental to the Guarantee Agreement.

6. "Borrower" means the party to the Loan Agreement to which the Loan is made.

7. "Guarantor" means the member of the Bank which is a party to the Guarantee Agreement.

8. "Currency" includes the currency of a country, the Special Drawing Right of the International Monetary Fund, and any unit of account which represents a debt service obligation of the Bank to the extent of such obligation. "Currency of a country" means the coin or currency which is legal tender for the payment of public and private debts in that country.

9. "Dollars" and the sign "$" mean dollars in the currency of the United States of America.

10. "Loan Account" means the account opened by the Bank on its books in the name of the Borrower to which the amount of the Loan is credited.

11. "Project" means the project or program for which the Loan is granted, as described in the Loan Agreement and as the description thereof may be amended from time to time by agreement between the Bank and the Borrower.

12. "Central Disbursement Account" means the account maintained by the Bank on its books to record the amounts in each currency outstanding and not yet repayable under the Loan and under such other loans as the Bank shall determine from time to time.

13. "Common denominator" means a single currency or other unit of account selected by the Bank for the purpose of determining the aggregate value of the Central Disbursement Account and the Loan's share therein.

14. "External debt" means any debt which is or may become payable other than in the currency of the country which is the Borrower or the Guarantor.

15. "Effective Date" means the date on which the Loan Agreement and the Guarantee Agreement shall enter into effect as provided in Section 12.03.

16. "Lien" includes mortgages, pledges, charges, privileges and priorities of any kind.

17. "Assets" includes property, revenue and claims of any kind.

18. "Taxes" includes imposts, levies, fees and duties of any nature, whether in effect at the date of the Loan Agreement or Guarantee Agreement or thereafter imposed.

19. "Incurring of debt" includes the assumption and guarantee of debt and any renewal, extension, or modification of the terms of the debt or of the assumption or guarantee thereof.

20. "Closing Date" means the date specified in the Loan Agreement after which the Bank may, by notice to the Borrower, terminate the right of the Borrower to withdraw from the Loan Account.

Section 2.02. **References.** References in these General Conditions to Articles or Sections are to Articles or Sections of these General Conditions.

Section 2.03. **Headings.** The headings of the Articles and Sections and the Table of Contents are inserted for convenience of reference only and are not a part of these General Conditions.

ARTICLE III

Loan Account; Interest and Other Charges; Repayment; Place of Payment

Section 3.01. **Loan Account.** The amount of the Loan shall be credited to the Loan Account and may be withdrawn therefrom by the Borrower as provided in the Loan Agreement and in these General Conditions.

Section 3.02. **Commitment Charges.** The Borrower shall pay a commitment charge on the unwithdrawn amount of the Loan at the rate specified in the Loan Agreement. Such commitment charge shall accrue from a date sixty days after the date of the Loan Agreement to the respective dates on which amounts shall be withdrawn by the Borrower from the Loan Account or shall be cancelled. The Borrower shall pay an additional commitment charge at the rate of one-half of one per cent (1/2 of 1%) per annum on the principal amount outstanding from time to time of any special commitment entered into by the Bank pursuant to Section 5.02.

Section 3.03. **Interest.** The Borrower shall pay interest at the rate specified in the Loan Agreement on the amounts of the Loan withdrawn from the Loan Account and outstanding from time to time. Interest shall accrue from the respective dates on which such amounts shall have been withdrawn.

Section 3.04. **Repayment.** (a) The Borrower shall repay the principal amount of the Loan withdrawn from the Loan Account in accordance with the amortization schedule to the Loan Agreement. The portion of the Loan to be repaid on each maturity date shall be determined by multiplying the principal amount of the maturity specified for that date in said amortization schedule by the ratio of:

(i) the principal amount of the Loan not yet due, determined for that date in accordance with Section 4.03 (b), to

(ii) the outstanding aggregate equivalent of the amounts withdrawn from the Loan Account and not yet due, expressed in terms of the common denominator as of the respective dates of withdrawal.

(b) Upon payment of all accrued interest and of the premium specified in said amortization schedule and after giving not less than forty-five days' notice to the Bank, the Borrower shall have the right to repay, as of a date acceptable to the Bank, in advance of maturity: (i) all of the principal amount of the Loan then outstanding, or (ii) all of the principal amount of any one or more maturities, provided that after such prepayment no portion of the Loan maturing after the prepaid portion shall remain outstanding.

(c) It is the policy of the Bank to encourage the repayment prior to maturity of portions of its loans which the Bank has not sold or agreed to sell. Accordingly, the Bank will sympathetically consider any request of the Borrower that the Bank waive the payment of any premium payable under paragraph (b) of this Section on prepayment of any such portions of the Loan.

Section 3.05. **Place of Payment.** The principal (including premium, if any) of, and interest and other charges on, the Loan shall be paid at such places as the Bank shall reasonably request.

ARTICLE IV

Currency Provisions

Section 4.01. **Currencies in which Withdrawals are to be Made.** Except as the Bank and the Borrower shall otherwise agree, withdrawals from the Loan Account shall be made in the respective currencies in which the expenditures to be financed out of the proceeds of the Loan have been paid or are payable; provided, however, that withdrawals in respect of expenditures in the currency of the member of the Bank which is the Borrower or the Guarantor shall be made in such currency or currencies as the Bank shall from time to time reasonably select.

Section 4.02. **Central Disbursement Account; Loan's Share.**

(a) The Central Disbursement Account shall record the amounts in various currencies withdrawn under the Loan and under such other loans as the Bank shall determine from time to time. All amounts so withdrawn shall be recorded in the Central Disbursement Account in the currency or currencies withdrawn, except that if the Bank has purchased the currency withdrawn with another currency in order to provide for such withdrawal, then the amount of such other currency paid by the Bank shall be recorded in the Central Disbursement Account instead of the currency withdrawn. Each such amount shall be deleted from the Central Disbursement Account on the date it becomes due or such earlier date as may be accepted by the Bank for prepayment.

(b) The aggregate value of the Central Disbursement Account shall be the sum of the amounts of each currency outstanding in the Central Disbursement Account, valued in terms of the common denominator. The aggregate value of the Central Disbursement Account shall be readjusted before any withdrawals or deletions have been recorded on each date by revaluing, as of that date, such net amounts in terms of the common denominator.

(c) For the purposes of determining the Loan's share in the Central Disbursement Account, a sub-account shall be maintained by the Bank to record in terms of the common denominator amounts withdrawn from the Loan Account. Each such amount shall be deleted from such sub-account on the date it becomes due or such earlier date as may be accepted by the Bank for prepayment. Amounts withdrawn from the Loan Account shall be recorded initially in terms of the common denominator as of the date of withdrawal. Thereafter, the value of the amounts recorded in such sub-account shall be readjusted at the time and by the same proportion that the aggregate value of the Central Disbursement Account is readjusted pursuant to Section 4.02 (b).

(d) The Loan's share in the Central Disbursement Account for any date shall be the ratio of: (i) the aggregate readjusted value of the amounts in such sub-account as of that date, to (ii) the aggregate readjusted value of the Central Disbursement Account as of that date.

Section 4.03. **Principal Amount of the Loan.** (a) The principal amount of the Loan withdrawn from the Loan Account and outstanding shall for any date consist of the sum of the principal amount of the Loan not yet due and the principal amount of the Loan remaining due and payable after its scheduled maturity date.

(b) For any date, the principal amount of the Loan not yet due (including any principal amount due on that date and not yet deleted from the Central Disbursement Account pursuant to the provisions of Section 4.05 (a)) shall be the aggregate equivalent in terms of the common denominator of the amounts in various currencies found by multiplying each of the several currency amounts outstanding in the Central Disbursement Account as of that date by the Loan's share in the Central Disbursement Account, determined in accordance with Section 4.02 (d).

(c) For any date, the principal amount of the Loan remaining due and payable after its scheduled maturity date shall be the aggregate equivalent in terms of the common denominator of any currency amounts deleted from the Central Disbursement Account pursuant to the provisions of Section 4.05 (a) and not yet repaid.

Section 4.04. **Currency in which Principal is Payable; Maturities.** (a) The principal of the Loan shall be repayable from time to time in such currency or currencies as the Bank shall specify. The aggregate of all loan amounts repayable in each such currency and still outstanding in the Central Disbursement Account shall not exceed the amount of such currency outstanding in the Central Disbursement Account.

(b) The amount of any currency so specified for repayment of any portion of the Loan shall be the equivalent thereof in terms of such currency as of the date on which such portion of the Loan becomes due and payable.

Section 4.05. **Central Disbursement Account; Repayments.** (a) On each maturity date set forth in the Loan Agreement, the equivalent of the portion of the Loan to be repaid as of such date expressed in terms of the currency specified by the Bank for repayment pursuant to Section 4.04 shall be deleted from the Central Disbursement Account.

(b) If, on or before any date acceptable to the Bank, all or any portion of the Loan is prepaid in accordance with paragraph (b) of Section 3.04 and in the currency specified by the Bank pursuant to Section 4.04, the amount so prepaid shall be deleted from the Central Disbursement Account on such date.

(c) In the event of a notice given pursuant to Section 7.01, the principal amount of currency specified in such notice shall be deleted from the Central Disbursement Account on the date or the respective dates of its repayment.

Section 4.06. **Currency in which Premium is Payable.** Any premium payable under Section 3.04 on prepayment of any portion of the Loan shall be payable in the currency in which the principal of such portion of the Loan is repayable.

Section 4.07. **Currency in which Interest and Other Charges are Payable.** Interest and other charges on the Loan shall be payable in such currency or currencies as the Bank shall from time to time specify.

Section 4.08. **Purchase of Currencies.** The Bank shall, at the request of the Borrower and on such terms and conditions as the Bank shall determine, use its best efforts to purchase any currency needed by the Borrower for payment of principal, interest and other charges required under the Loan Agreement upon payment by the Borrower of sufficient funds therefor in a currency or currencies to be specified by the Bank from time to time. In purchasing the currencies required, the Bank shall be acting as agent of the Borrower and the Borrower shall be deemed to have made any payment required under the Loan Agreement only when and to the extent that the Bank has received such payment in the currency or currencies required.

Section 4.09. **Valuation of Currencies.** Whenever it shall be necessary for the purposes of the Loan Agreement or the Guarantee Agreement, or any other agreement to which these General Conditions apply, to determine the value of one currency in terms of another, such value shall be as reasonably determined by the

Bank. The Bank may value an amount of currency outstanding in the Central Disbursement Account in such manner as may be required to reflect the debt service obligation of the Bank in respect of such amount. Notwithstanding the provisions of Sections 4.04 (a) and 4.05, the Bank may specify, for repayment of the principal amount of the Loan, any currency needed by the Bank to discharge such debt service obligation and, in such a case, an equivalent amount of the currency outstanding in the Central Disbursement Account shall be deleted from such Account instead of the currency so specified.

Section 4.10. **Manner of Payment.** (a) Any payment required under the Loan Agreement or the Guarantee Agreement to be made to the Bank in the currency of a country shall be made in such manner, and in currency acquired in such manner, as shall be permitted under the laws of such country for the purpose of making such payment and effecting the deposit of such currency to the account of the Bank with a depository of the Bank in such country.

(b) The principal (including premium, if any) of, and interest and other charges on, the Loan shall be paid without restrictions of any kind imposed by, or in the territory of, the member of the Bank which is the Borrower or the Guarantor.

ARTICLE V

Withdrawal of Proceeds of Loan

Section 5.01. **Withdrawal from the Loan Account.** The Borrower shall be entitled to withdraw from the Loan Account amounts expended or, if the Bank shall so agree, amounts to be expended for the Project in accordance with the provisions of the Loan Agreement and of these General Conditions. Except as the Bank and the Borrower shall otherwise agree, no withdrawals shall be made on account of expenditures in the territories of any country which is not a member of the Bank (other than Switzerland) or for goods produced in, or services supplied from, such territories.

Section 5.02. **Special Commitment by the Bank.** Upon the Borrower's request and upon such terms and conditions as shall be agreed upon between the Bank and the Borrower, the Bank may enter into special commitments in writing to pay amounts to the Borrower or others in respect of expenditures to be financed out of the proceeds of the Loan notwithstanding any subsequent suspension or cancellation by the Bank or the Borrower.

Section 5.03. **Applications for Withdrawal or for Special Commitment.** When the Borrower shall desire to withdraw any amount from the Loan Account or to request the Bank to enter into a special commitment pursuant to Section 5.02, the Borrower shall deliver to the Bank a written application in such form, and containing such statements and agreements, as the Bank shall reasonably request. Applications for withdrawal, including the documentation required pursuant to this Article, shall be made promptly in relation to expenditures for the Project.

Section 5.04. **Reallocation.** Notwithstanding the allocation of an amount of the Loan or the percentages for withdrawal set forth or referred to in the Loan Agreement, if the Bank has reasonably estimated that the amount of the Loan then allocated to any withdrawal category set forth in the Loan Agreement or added thereto by amendment will be insufficient to finance the agreed percentage of all expenditures in that category, the Bank may, by notice to the Borrower:

(a) reallocate to such category, to the extent required to meet the estimated shortfall, proceeds of the Loan which are then allocated to another category and which in the opinion of the Bank are not needed to meet other expenditures; and

(b) if such reallocation cannot fully meet the estimated shortfall, reduce the percentage for withdrawal then applicable to such expenditures in order that further withdrawals under such category may continue until all expenditures thereunder shall have been made.

Section 5.05. **Evidence of Authority to Sign Applications for Withdrawal.** The Borrower shall furnish to the Bank evidence of the authority of the person or persons authorized to sign applications for withdrawal and the authenticated specimen signature of any such person.

Section 5.06. **Supporting Evidence.** The Borrower shall furnish to the Bank such documents and other evidence in support of the application as the Bank shall reasonably request, whether before or after the Bank shall have permitted any withdrawal requested in the application.

Section 5.07. **Sufficiency of Applications and Documents.** Each application and the accompanying documents and other evidence must be sufficient in form and substance to satisfy the Bank that the Borrower is entitled to withdraw from the Loan Account the amount applied for and that the amount to be withdrawn from the Loan Account is to be used only for the purposes specified in the Loan Agreement.

Section 5.08. **Treatment of Taxes.** It is the policy of the Bank that no proceeds of the Loan shall be withdrawn on account of payments for any taxes levied by, or in the territory of, the Borrower or the Guarantor on goods or services, or on the importation, manufacture, procurement or supply thereof. To that end, if the amount of any taxes levied on or in respect of any item to be financed out of the proceeds of the Loan decreases or increases, the Bank may, by notice to the Borrower, increase or decrease the percentage for withdrawal set forth or referred to in respect of such item in the Loan Agreement as required to be consistent with such policy of the Bank.

Section 5.09. **Payment by the Bank.** The Bank shall pay the amounts withdrawn by the Borrower from the Loan Account only to or on the order of the Borrower.

ARTICLE VI

Cancellation and Suspension

Section 6.01. **Cancellation by the Borrower.** The Borrower may, by notice to the Bank, cancel any amount of the Loan which the Borrower shall not have withdrawn, except that the Borrower may not so cancel any amount of the Loan in respect of which the Bank shall have entered into a special commitment pursuant to Section 5.02.

Section 6.02. **Suspension by the Bank.** If any of the following events of suspension shall have occurred and be continuing, the Bank may, by notice to the Borrower and the Guarantor, suspend in whole or in part the right of the Borrower to make withdrawals from the Loan Account:

(a) The Borrower shall have failed to make payment (notwithstanding the fact that such payment may have been made by the Guarantor or a third party) of principal or interest or any other amount due to the Bank or the Association: (i) under the Loan Agreement, or (ii) under any other loan or guarantee agreement between the Bank and the Borrower, or (iii) in consequence of any guarantee or other financial obligation of any kind extended by the Bank to any third party with the agreement of the Borrower, or (iv) under any development credit agreement between the Borrower and the Association.

(b) The Guarantor shall have failed to make payment of principal or interest or any other amount due to the Bank or the Association: (i) under the Guarantee Agreement, or (ii) under any other loan or guarantee agreement between the Guarantor and the Bank, or (iii) in consequence of any guarantee or other financial obligation of any kind extended by the Bank to any third party with the agreement of the Guarantor, or (iv) under any development credit agreement between the Guarantor and the Association.

(c) The Borrower or the Guarantor shall have failed to perform any other obligation under the Loan Agreement or the Guarantee Agreement.

(d) The Bank or the Association shall have suspended in whole or in part the right of the Borrower or the Guarantor to make withdrawals under any loan agreement with the Bank or any development credit agreement with the Association because of a failure by the Borrower or the Guarantor to perform any of its obligations under such agreement or any guarantee agreement with the Bank.

(e) As a result of events which have occurred after the

date of the Loan Agreement, an extraordinary situation shall have arisen which shall make it improbable that the Project can be carried out or that the Borrower or the Guarantor will be able to perform its obligations under the Loan Agreement or the Guarantee Agreement.

(f) The member of the Bank which is the Borrower or the Guarantor: (i) shall have been suspended from membership in or ceased to be a member of the Bank, or (ii) shall have ceased to be a member of the International Monetary Fund.

(g) After the date of the Loan Agreement and prior to the Effective Date, any event shall have occurred which would have entitled the Bank to suspend the Borrower's right to make withdrawals from the Loan Account if the Loan Agreement had been effective on the date such event occurred.

(h) Any material adverse change in the condition of the Borrower (other than a member of the Bank), as represented by the Borrower, shall have occurred prior to the Effective Date.

(i) A representation made by the Borrower or the Guarantor in or pursuant to the Loan Agreement or the Guarantee Agreement, or any statement furnished in connection therewith, and intended to be relied upon by the Bank in making the Loan, shall have been incorrect in any material respect.

(j) Any event specified in paragraph (f) or (g) of Section 7.01 shall have occurred.

(k) Any other event specified in the Loan Agreement for the purposes of this Section shall have occurred.

The right of the Borrower to make withdrawals from the Loan Account shall continue to be suspended in whole or in part, as the case may be, until the event or events which gave rise to suspension shall have ceased to exist, unless the Bank shall have notified the Borrower that the right to make withdrawals has been restored in whole or in part, as the case may be.

Section 6.03. **Cancellation by the Bank.** If (a) the right of the Borrower to make withdrawals from the Loan Account shall have been suspended with respect to any amount of the Loan for a continuous period of thirty days, or (b) at any time, the Bank determines, after consultation with the Borrower, that an amount of the Loan will not be required to finance the Project's costs to be financed out of the proceeds of the Loan, or (c) at any time, the Bank determines that the procurement of any item is inconsistent with the procedures set forth or referred to in the Loan Agreement and establishes the amount of expenditures in respect of such item which would otherwise have been eligible for financing out of the proceeds of the Loan, or (d) after the Closing Date, an amount of the Loan shall remain unwithdrawn from the Loan Account, or (e) the Bank shall have received notice from the Guarantor pursuant to Section 6.07 with respect to an amount of the Loan, the Bank may, by notice to the Borrower and the Guarantor, terminate the right of the Borrower to make withdrawals with respect to such amount. Upon the giving of such notice, such amount of the Loan shall be cancelled.

Section 6.04. **Amounts Subject to Special Commitment Not Affected by Cancellation or Suspension by the Bank.** No cancellation or suspension by the Bank shall apply to amounts subject to any special commitment entered into by the Bank pursuant to Section 5.02 except as expressly provided in such commitment.

Section 6.05. **Application of Cancellation to Maturities of the Loan.** Except as the Bank and the Borrower shall otherwise agree, any cancellation shall be applied **pro rata** to the several maturities of the principal amount of the Loan which shall mature after the date of such cancellation and shall not have been theretofore sold or agreed to be sold by the Bank.

Section 6.06. **Effectiveness of Provisions after Suspension or Cancellation.** Notwithstanding any cancellation or suspension, all the provisions of the Loan Agreement and the Guarantee Agreement shall continue in full force and effect except as specifically provided in this Article.

Section 6.07. **Cancellation of Guarantee.** If the Borrower shall have failed to make payment of principal or interest or any other payment required under the Loan Agreement (otherwise than as a result of any act or omission to act of the Guarantor) and such payment shall have been made by the Guarantor, the Guarantor may, after consultation with the Bank, by notice to the Bank and the Borrower, terminate its obligations under the Guarantee Agreement with respect to any amount of the Loan unwithdrawn from the Loan Account on the date of receipt of such notice by the Bank and not subject to any special commitment entered into by the Bank pursuant to Section 5.02. Upon receipt of such notice by the Bank, such obligations in respect of such amount shall terminate.

ARTICLE VII

Acceleration of Maturity

Section 7.01. **Events of Acceleration.** If any of the following events shall occur and shall continue for the period specified below, if any, then at any subsequent time during the continuance thereof, the Bank, at its option, may, by notice to the Borrower and the Guarantor, declare the principal of the Loan then outstanding to be due and payable immediately together with the interest and other charges thereon and upon any such declaration such principal, together with the interest and other charges thereon, shall become due and payable immediately:

(a) A default shall occur in the payment of principal or interest or any other payment required under the Loan Agreement and such default shall continue for a period of thirty days.

(b) A default shall occur in the payment of principal or interest or any other payment required under the Guarantee Agreement and such default shall continue for a period of thirty days.

(c) A default shall occur in the payment by the Borrower of principal or interest or any other amount due to the Bank or the Association: (i) under any other loan or guarantee agreement between the Bank and the Borrower, or (ii) in consequence of any guarantee or other financial obligation of any kind extended by the Bank to any third party with the agreement of the Borrower, or (iii) under any development credit agreement between the Borrower and the Association, and such default shall continue for a period of thirty days.

(d) A default shall occur in the payment by the Guarantor of principal or interest or any other amount due to the Bank or the Association: (i) under any loan or guarantee agreement between the Guarantor and the Bank, or (ii) in consequence of any guarantee or other financial obligation of any kind extended by the Bank to any third party with the agreement of the Guarantor, or (iii) under any development credit agreement between the Guarantor and the Association, under circumstances which would make it unlikely that the Guarantor would meet its obligations under the Guarantee Agreement; and such default shall continue for a period of thirty days.

(e) A default shall occur in the performance of any other obligation on the part of the Borrower or the Guarantor under the Loan Agreement or the Guarantee Agreement, and such default shall continue for a period of sixty days after notice thereof shall have been given by the Bank to the Borrower and the Guarantor.

(f) The Borrower (other than a member of the Bank) shall have become unable to pay its debts as they mature or any action or proceeding shall have been taken by the Borrower or by others whereby any of the assets of the Borrower shall or may be distributed among its creditors.

(g) The Guarantor or any other authority having jurisdiction shall have taken any action for the dissolution or disestablishment of the Borrower (other than a member of the Bank) or for the suspension of its operations.

(h) Any other event specified in the Loan Agreement for the purposes of this Section shall have occurred and shall continue for the period, if any, specified in the Loan Agreement.

ARTICLE VIII

Taxes

Section 8.01. **Taxes.** (a) The principal of, and interest and other charges on, the Loan shall be paid without deduction for, and free from, any taxes levied by, or in the territory of, the member of the Bank which is the Borrower or the Guarantor.

(b) The Loan Agreement and the Guarantee Agreement, and any other agreement to which these General Conditions apply, shall be free from any taxes levied by, or in the territory of, the member of the Bank which is the Borrower or the Guarantor on or in connection with the execution, delivery or registration thereof.

ARTICLE IX

Cooperation and Information; Financial and Economic Data; Negative Pledge; Project Implementation

Section 9.01. **Cooperation and Information.** (a) The Bank, the Borrower and the Guarantor shall cooperate fully to assure that the purposes of the Loan will be accomplished. To that end, the Bank, the Borrower and the Guarantor shall:

(i) from time to time, at the request of any one of them, exchange views with regard to the progress of the Project, the purposes of the Loan, and the performance of their respective obligations under the Loan Agreement and the Guarantee Agreement, and furnish to the other party all such information related thereto as it shall reasonably request; and

(ii) promptly inform each other of any condition which interferes with, or threatens to interfere with, the matters referred to in paragraph (i) above.

(b) The Guarantor shall ensure that no action which would prevent or interfere with the execution of the Project or with the performance of the Borrower's obligations under the Loan Agreement is taken or permitted to be taken by the Guarantor or any of its political or administrative subdivisions or any of the entities owned or controlled by, or operating for the account or benefit of, the Guarantor or such subdivisions.

(c) The member of the Bank which is the Borrower or the Guarantor shall afford all reasonable opportunity for representatives of the Bank to visit any part of its territory for purposes related to the Loan.

Section 9.02. **Financial and Economic Data.** The member of the Bank which is the Borrower or the Guarantor shall furnish to the Bank all such information as the Bank shall reasonably request with respect to financial and economic conditions in its territory, including its balance of payments and its external debt as well as that of its political or administrative subdivisions and of any entity owned or controlled by, or operating for the account or benefit of, such member or any such subdivision, and of any institution performing the functions of a central bank or exchange stabilization fund, or similar functions, for such member.

Section 9.03. **Negative Pledge.**

(a) It is the policy of the Bank, in making loans to, or with the guarantee of, its members not to seek, in normal circumstances, special security from the member concerned but to ensure that no other external debt shall have priority over its loans in the allocation, realization or distribution of foreign exchange held under the control or for the benefit of such member.

> (i) To that end, if any lien shall be created on any public assets (as hereinafter defined), as security for any external debt, which will or might result in a priority for the benefit of the creditor of such external debt in the allocation, realization or distribution of foreign exchange, such lien shall, unless the Bank shall otherwise agree, **ipso facto** and at no cost to the Bank, equally and ratably secure the principal of, and interest and other charges on, the Loan, and the member of the Bank which is the Borrower or the Guarantor, in creating or permitting the creation of such lien, shall make express provision to that effect; provided, however, that if for any constitutional or other legal reason such provision cannot be made with respect to any lien created on assets of any of its political or administrative subdivisions, such member shall promptly and at no cost to the Bank secure the principal of, and interest and other charges on, the Loan by an equivalent lien on other public assets satisfactory to the Bank.

> (ii) As used in this paragraph, the term "public assets" means assets of such member, of any political or administrative subdivision thereof and of any entity owned or controlled by, or operating for the account or benefit of, such member or any such subdivision, including gold and foreign exchange assets held by any institution performing the functions of a central bank or exchange stab-

lization fund, or similar functions, for such member.

(b) The Borrower which is not a member of the Bank undertakes that, except as the Bank shall otherwise agree:

(i) if such Borrower shall create any lien on any of its assets as security for any debt, such lien will equally and ratably secure the payment of the principal of, and interest and other charges on, the Loan and in the creation of any such lien express provision will be made to that effect, at no cost to the Bank; and

(ii) if any statutory lien shall be created on any assets of such Borrower as security for any debt, such Borrower shall grant at no cost to the Bank, an equivalent lien satisfactory to the Bank to secure the payment of the principal of, and interest and other charges on, the Loan.

(c) The foregoing provisions of this Section shall not apply to: (i) any lien created on property, at the time of purchase thereof, solely as security for the payment of the purchase price of such property or as security for the payment of debt incurred for the purpose of financing the purchase of such property; or (ii) any lien arising in the ordinary course of banking transactions and securing a debt maturing not more than one year after the date on which it is originally incurred.

Section 9.04. **Insurance.** The Borrower shall insure or cause to be insured, or make adequate provision for the insurance of, the imported goods to be financed out of the proceeds of the Loan against hazards incident to the acquisition, transportation and delivery thereof to the place of use or installation. Any indemnity for such insurance shall be payable in a freely usable currency to replace or repair such goods.

Section 9.05. **Use of Goods and Services.** Except as the Bank shall otherwise agree, the Borrower shall cause all goods and services financed out of the proceeds of the Loan to be used exclusively for the purposes of the Project.

Section 9.06. **Plans and Schedules.** The Borrower shall furnish, or cause to be furnished, to the Bank promptly upon their preparation, any plans, specifications, reports, contract documents and construction and procurement schedules for the Project, and any material modifications thereof or additions thereto, in such detail as the Bank shall reasonably request.

Section 9.07. **Records and Reports.** (a) The Borrower shall: (i) maintain records and procedures adequate to record and monitor the progress of the Project (including its cost and the benefits to be derived from it), to identify the goods and services financed out of the proceeds of the Loan, and to disclose their use in the Project; (ii) enable the Bank's representatives to visit any facilities and construction sites included in the Project and to examine the goods financed out of the proceeds of the Loan and any plants, installations, sites, works, buildings, property, equipment, records and documents relevant to the performance of the obligations of the Borrower under the Loan Agreement; and (iii) furnish to the Bank at regular intervals all such information as the Bank shall reasonably request concerning the Project, its cost and, where appropriate, the benefits to be derived from it, the expenditure of the proceeds of the Loan and the goods and services financed out of such proceeds.

(b) Upon the award of any contract for goods or services to be financed out of the proceeds of the Loan, the Bank may publish a description thereof, the name and nationality of the party to which the contract was awarded and the contract price.

(c) Promptly after completion of the Project, but in any event not later than six months after the Closing Date or such later date as may be agreed for this purpose between the Bank and the Borrower, the Borrower shall prepare and furnish to the Bank a report, of such scope and in such detail as the Bank shall reasonably request, on the execution and initial operation of the Project, its cost and the benefits derived and to be derived from it, the performance by the Borrower and the Bank of their respective obligations under the Loan Agreement and the accomplishment of the purposes of the Loan.

Section 9.08. **Maintenance.** The Borrower shall at all times operate and maintain, or cause to be operated and maintained, any facilities relevant to the Project, and promptly as needed, make or cause to be made all necessary repairs and renewals thereof.

Section 9.09. **Land Acquisition.** The Borrower shall take, or cause to be taken, all such action as shall be necessary to acquire as and when needed all such land and rights in respect of land as shall be required for carrying out the Project and shall furnish to the Bank, promptly upon its request, evidence satisfactory to the Bank that such land and rights in respect of land are available for purposes related to the Project.

ARTICLE X

Enforceability of Loan Agreement and Guarantee Agreement; Failure to Exercise Rights; Arbitration

Section 10.01. **Enforceability.** The rights and obligations of the Bank, the Borrower and the Guarantor under the Loan Agreement and the Guarantee Agreement shall be valid and enforceable in accordance with their terms notwithstanding the law of any State or political subdivision thereof to the contrary. Neither the Bank nor the Borrower nor the Guarantor shall be entitled in any proceeding under this Article to assert any claim that any provision of these General Conditions or of the Loan Agreement or the Guarantee Agreement is invalid or unenforceable because of any provision of the Articles of Agreement of the Bank.

Section 10.02. **Obligations of the Guarantor.** Except as provided in Section 6.07, the obligations of the Guarantor under the Guarantee Agreement shall not be discharged except by performance and then only to the extent of such performance. Such obligations shall not require any prior notice to, demand upon or action against the Borrower or any prior notice to or demand upon the Guarantor with regard to any default by the Borrower. Such obligations shall not be impaired by any of the following: (a) any extension of time, forebearance or concession given to the Borrower; (b) any assertion of, or failure to assert, or delay in asserting, any right, power or remedy against the Borrower or in respect of any security for the Loan; (c) any modification or amplification of the provisions of the Loan Agreement contemplated by the terms thereof; or (d) any failure of the Borrower to comply with any requirement of any law of the Guarantor.

Section 10.03. **Failure to Exercise Rights.** No delay in exercising, or omission to exercise, any right, power or remedy accruing to any party under the Loan Agreement or Guarantee Agreement upon any default shall impair any such right, power or remedy or be construed to be a waiver thereof or an acquiescence in such default. No action of such party in respect of any default, or any acquiescence by it in any default, shall affect or impair any right, power or remedy of such party in respect of any other or subsequent default.

Section 10.04. **Arbitration.** (a) Any controversy between the parties to the Loan Agreement or the parties to the Guarantee Agreement, and any claim by any such party against any other such party arising under the Loan Agreement or the Guarantee Agreement which has not been settled by agreement of the parties shall be submitted to arbitration by an Arbitral Tribunal as hereinafter provided.

(b) The parties to such arbitration shall be the Bank on the one side and the Borrower and the Guarantor on the other side.

(c) The Arbitral Tribunal shall consist of three arbitrators appointed as follows: one arbitrator shall be appointed by the Bank; a second arbitrator shall be appointed by the Borrower and the Guarantor or, if they shall not agree, by the Guarantor; and the third arbitrator (hereinafter sometimes called the Umpire) shall be appointed by agreement of the parties or, if they shall not agree, by the President of the International Court of Justice or, failing appointment by said President, by the Secretary-General of the United Nations. If either side shall fail to appoint an arbitrator, such arbitrator shall be appointed by the Umpire. In case any arbitrator appointed in accordance with this Section shall resign, die or become unable to act, a successor arbitrator shall be appointed in the same manner as herein prescribed for the appointment of the original arbitrator and such successor shall have all the powers and duties of such original arbitrator.

(d) An arbitration proceeding may be instituted under this Section upon notice by the party instituting such proceeding to the other party. Such notice shall contain a statement setting forth the nature of the controversy or claim to be submitted to arbitration and the nature of the relief sought and the name of the arbitrator appointed by the party instituting such proceeding. Within thirty days after such notice, the other party shall notify to the party instituting the proceeding the name of the arbitrator appointed by such other party.

(e) If within sixty days after the notice instituting the arbitration proceeding, the parties shall not have agreed upon an Umpire, any party may request the appointment of an Umpire as provided in paragraph (c) of this Section.

(f) The Arbitral Tribunal shall convene at such time and place as shall be fixed by the Umpire. Thereafter, the Arbitral Tribunal shall determine where and when it shall sit.

(g) The Arbitral Tribunal shall decide all questions relating to its competence and shall, subject to the provisions of this Section and except as the parties shall otherwise agree, determine its procedure. All decisions of the Arbitral Tribunal shall be by majority vote.

(h) The Arbitral Tribunal shall afford to all parties a fair hearing and shall render its award in writing. Such award may be rendered by default. An award signed by a majority of the Arbitral Tribunal shall constitute the award of such Tribunal. A signed counterpart of the award shall be transmitted to each party. Any such award rendered in accordance with the provisions of this Section shall be final and binding upon the parties to the Loan Agreement and the Guarantee Agreement. Each party shall abide by and comply with any such award rendered by the Arbitral Tribunal in accordance with the provisions of this Section.

(i) The parties shall fix the amount of the remuneration of the arbitrators and such other persons as shall be required for the conduct of the arbitration proceedings. If the parties shall not agree on such amount before the Arbitral Tribunal shall convene, the Arbitral Tribunal shall fix such amount as shall be reasonable under the circumstances. The Bank, the Borrower and the Guarantor shall each defray its own expenses in the arbitration proceedings. The costs of the Arbitral Tribunal shall be divided between and borne equally by the Bank on the one side and the Borrower and the Guarantor on the other. Any question concerning the division of the costs of the Arbitral Tribunal or the procedure for payment of such costs shall be determined by the Arbitral Tribunal.

(j) The provisions for arbitration set forth in this Section shall be in lieu of any other procedure for the settlement of controversies between the parties to the Loan Agreement and Guarantee Agreement or of any claim by any such party against any other such party arising thereunder.

(k) If, within thirty days after counterparts of the award shall have been delivered to the parties, the award shall not be complied with, any party may: (i) enter judgment upon, or institute a proceeding to enforce, the award in any court of competent jurisdiction against any other party; (ii) enforce such judgment by execution; or (iii) pursue any other appropriate remedy against such other party for the enforcement of the award and the provisions of the Loan Agreement or the Guarantee Agreement. Notwithstanding the foregoing, this Section shall not authorize any entry of judgment or enforcement of the award against any party that is a member of the Bank except as such procedure may be available otherwise than by reason of the provisions of this Section.

(1) Service of any notice or process in connection with any proceeding under this Section or in connection with any proceeding to enforce any award rendered pursuant to this Section may be made in the manner provided in Section 11.01. The parties to the Loan Agreement and the Guarantee Agreement waive any and all other requirements for the service of any such notice or process.

ARTICLE XI

Miscellaneous Provisions

Section 11.01. **Notices and Requests.** Any notice or request required or permitted to be given or made under the Loan Agreement or Guarantee Agreement and any other agreement between any of the parties contemplated by the Loan Agreement or the Guarantee Agreement shall be in writing. Except as otherwise provided in Section 12.03, such notice or request shall be deemed to have been duly given or made when it shall be delivered by hand or by mail, telegram, cable, telex or radiogram to the party to which it is required or permitted to be given or made at such party's address specified in the Loan Agreement or Guarantee Agreement or at such other address as such party shall have designated by notice to the party giving such notice or making such request.

Section 11.02. **Evidence of Authority.** The Borrower and the Guarantor shall furnish to the Bank sufficient evidence of the authority of the person or persons who will, on behalf of the Borrower or the Guarantor, take any action or execute any documents required or permitted to be taken or executed by the Borrower under the Loan Agreement or by the Guarantor under the Guarantee Agreement, and the authenticated specimen signature of each such person.

Section 11.03. **Action on Behalf of the Borrower or Guarantor.** Any action required or permitted to be taken, and any documents required or permitted to be executed, pursuant to the Loan Agreement or the Guarantee Agreement, on behalf of the Borrower or the Guarantor, may be taken or executed by the representative of the Borrower or the Guarantor designated in the Loan Agreement or the Guarantee Agreement for the purposes of this

Section or any person thereunto authorized in writing by such representative. Any modification or amplification of the provisions of the Loan Agreement or the Guarantee Agreement may be agreed to on behalf of the Borrower or the Guarantor by written instrument executed on behalf of the Borrower or the Guarantor by the representative so designated or any person thereunto authorized in writing by such representative; provided that, in the opinion of such representative, such modification or amplification is reasonable in the circumstances and will not substantially increase the obligations of the Borrower under the Loan Agreement or of the Guarantor under the Guarantee Agreement. The Bank may accept the execution by such representative or other person of any such instrument as conclusive evidence that in the opinion of such representative any modification or amplification of the provisions of the Loan Agreement or the Guarantee Agreement effected by such instrument is reasonable in the circumstances and will not substantially increase the obligations of the Borrower or of the Guarantor thereunder.

Section 11.04. **Execution in Counterparts.** The Loan Agreement and the Guarantee Agreement may each be executed in several counterparts, each of which shall be an original.

ARTICLE XII

Effective Date; Termination

Section 12.01. **Conditions Precedent to Effectiveness of Loan Agreement and Guarantee Agreement.** The Loan Agreement and the Guarantee Agreement shall not become effective until evidence satisfactory to the Bank shall have been furnished to the Bank:

(a) that the execution and delivery of the Loan Agreement and the Guarantee Agreement on behalf of the Borrower and the Guarantor have been duly authorized or ratified by all necessary governmental and corporate action;

(b) if the Bank shall so request, that the condition of the Borrower (other than a member of the Bank), as represented or warranted to the Bank at the date of the Loan Agreement, has undergone no material adverse change after such date; and

(c) that all other events specified in the Loan Agreement as conditions to effectiveness have occurred.

Section 12.02. **Legal Opinions or Certificates.** As part of the evidence to be furnished pursuant to Section 12.01, there shall be furnished to the Bank an opinion or opinions satisfactory to the Bank of counsel acceptable to the Bank or, if the Bank shall so request, a certificate satisfactory to the Bank of a competent official of the member of the Bank which is the Borrower or the Guarantor showing:

(a) on behalf of the Borrower, that the Loan Agreement has been duly authorized or ratified by, and executed and delivered on behalf of, the Borrower and is legally binding upon the Borrower in accordance with its terms;

(b) on behalf of the Guarantor, that the Guarantee Agreement has been duly authorized or ratified by, and executed and delivered on behalf of, the Guarantor and is legally binding upon the Guarantor in accordance with its terms; and

(c) such other matters as shall be specified in the Loan Agreement or as shall be reasonably requested by the Bank in connection therewith.

Section 12.03. **Effective Date.** (a) Except as the Bank and the Borrower shall otherwise agree, the Loan Agreement and the Guarantee Agreement shall enter into effect on the date upon which the Bank dispatches to the Borrower and to the Guarantor notice of its acceptance of the evidence required by Section 12.01.

(b) If, before the Effective Date, any event shall have occurred which would have entitled the Bank to suspend the right of the Borrower to make withdrawals from the Loan Account if the Loan Agreement had been effective, the Bank may postpone the dispatch of the notice referred to in paragraph (a) of this Section until such event or events shall have ceased to exist.

Section 12.04. **Termination of Loan Agreement and Guarantee Agreement for Failure to Become Effective.** If the Loan Agreement shall not have entered into effect by the date specified in the Loan Agreement for the purposes of this Section, the Loan Agreement and the Guarantee Agreement and all obligations of the parties thereunder shall terminate, unless the Bank, after consideration of the reasons for the delay, shall establish a later date for the purposes of this Section. The Bank shall promptly notify the Borrower and the Guarantor of such later date.

Section 12.05. **Termination of Loan Agreement and Guarantee Agreement on Full Payment.** If and when the entire principal amount of the Loan withdrawn from the Loan Account and the premium, if any, on the prepayment of the Loan and all interest and other charges which shall have accrued on the Loan shall have been paid, the Loan Agreement and the Guarantee Agreement and all obligations of the parties thereunder shall forthwith terminate.

3E. General Conditions Applicable to Development Credit Agreements
International Development Association

DATED JANUARY 1, 1985

Article Number Title

Article I Application to Development Credit Agreements
Section 1.01 Application of General Conditions
Section 1.02 Inconsistency with Development Credit Agreements

Article II Definitions; Headings
Section 2.01 Definitions
Section 2.02 References
Section 2.03 Headings

Article III Credit Account; Service Charges; Repayment; Place of Payment
Section 3.01 Credit Account
Section 3.02 Service Charges
Section 3.03 Computation of Service Charges
Section 3.04 Repayment
Section 3.05 Place of Payment

Article IV Currency Provisions
Section 4.01 Currencies in which Withdrawals are to be Made
Section 4.02 Currencies in which Principal and Service Charges are Payable
Section 4.03 Amount of Repayment
Section 4.04 Purchase of Currency of Withdrawal with Other Currency
Section 4.05 Valuation of Currencies
Section 4.06 Manner of Payment

Article V Withdrawal of Proceeds of Credit
Section 5.01 Withdrawal from the Credit Account
Section 5.02 Special Commitments by the Association
Section 5.03 Applications for Withdrawal or for Special Commitment
Section 5.04 Reallocation
Section 5.05 Evidence of Authority to Sign Applications for Withdrawal
Section 5.06 Supporting Evidence
Section 5.07 Sufficiency of Applications and Documents
Section 5.08 Treatment of Taxes
Section 5.09 Payment by the Association

Article VI Cancellation and Suspension
Section 6.01 Cancellation by the Borrower
Section 6.02 Suspension by the Association
Section 6.03 Cancellation by the Association
Section 6.04 Amounts Subject to Special Commitment Not Affected by Cancellation or Suspension by the Association
Section 6.05 Application of Cancellation to Maturities of the Credit
Section 6.06 Effectiveness of Provisions after Suspension or Cancellation

Article VII Acceleration of Maturity
Section 7.01 Events of Acceleration

Article VIII Taxes
Section 8.01 Taxes

Article IX Cooperation and Information; Financial & Economic Data; Project Implementation
Section 9.01 Cooperation and Information
Section 9.02 Financial and Economic Data
Section 9.03 Insurance
Section 9.04 Use of Goods and Services
Section 9.05 Plans and Schedules
Section 9.06 Records and Reports
Section 9.07 Maintenance
Section 9.08 Land Acquisition

Article X Enforceability of Development Credit Agreement; Failure to Exercise Rights; Arbitration
Section 10.01 Enforceability
Section 10.02 Failure to Exercise Rights
Section 10.03 Arbitration

Article XI Miscellaneous Provisions
Section 11.01 Notices and Requests
Section 11.02 Evidence of Authority
Section 11.03 Action on Behalf of the Borrower
Section 11.04 Execution in Counterparts

Article XII Effective Date, Termination
Section 12.01 Conditions Precedent to Effectiveness of Development Credit Agreement

Section 12.02   Legal Opinions or Certificates
Section 12.03   Effective Date
Section 12.04   Termination of Development Credit Agreement for Failure to Become Effective

Article I

APPLICATION TO DEVELOPMENT CREDIT AGREEMENTS

Section 1.01. *Application of General Conditions.* These General Conditions set forth certain terms and conditions generally applicable to development credits granted by the Association to its members. They apply to any development credit agreement providing for any such development credit to the extent and subject to any modifications set forth in such agreement.

Section 1.02. *Inconsistency with Development Credit Agreements.* If any provision of a development credit agreement is inconsistent with a provision of these General Conditions, the provision of the agreement shall govern.

Article II

DEFINITIONS; HEADINGS

Section 2.01. *Definitions.* The following terms have the following meanings wherever used in these General Conditions:

1. "Association" means the International Development Association.
2. "Bank" means the International Bank for Reconstruction and Development.
3. "Development Credit Agreement" means the particular development credit agreement to which these General Conditions apply, as such agreement may be amended from time to time. Development Credit Agreement includes these General Conditions as applied thereto, and all schedules and agreements supplemental to the Development Credit Agreement.
4. "Credit" means the development credit provided for in the Development Credit Agreement.
5. "Borrower" means the member of the Association to which the Credit is granted.
6. "Currency of a country" means the coin or currency which is legal tender for the payment of public and private debts in that country.
7. "Dollars" and the sign "$" means dollars in the currency of the United States of America.
8. "Credit Account" means the account opened by the Association on its books in the name of the Borrower to which the amount of the Credit is credited.
9. "Project" means the project or program for which the Credit is granted, as described in the Development Credit Agreement and as the description thereof may be amended from time to time by agreement between the Borrower and the Association.
10. "External debt" means any debt which is or may become payable other than in the currency of the country which is the Borrower.
11. "Effective Date" means the date on which the Development Credit Agreement shall enter into effect as provided in Section 12.03.
12. "Taxes" includes imposts, levies, fees and duties of any nature, whether in effect at the date of the Development Credit Agreement or thereafter imposed.
13. "Closing Date" means the date specified in the Development Credit Agreement after which the Association may, by notice to the Borrower, terminate the right of the Borrower to withdraw from the Credit Account.
14. "Special Drawing Rights" and the symbol "SDR" mean special drawing rights as valued by the International Monetary Fund in accordance with its Articles of Agreement.

Article III

CREDIT ACCOUNT; SERVICE CHARGES; REPAYMENT; PLACE OF PAYMENT

Section 3.02 *Service Charges.* The Borrower shall pay a service charge on the amount of the Credit withdrawn and outstanding from time to time at the rate specified in the Development Credit Agreement. The Borrower shall pay an additional service charge at the rate of one-half of one per cent (½ of 1%) per annum on the principal amount outstanding from time to time of any special commitment entered into by the Association pursuant to Section 5.02.

Section 3.03. *Computation of Service Charges.* Service charges shall be computed on the basis of a 360-day year of twelve 30-day months.

Section 3.04 *Repayment.* (a) The Borrower shall repay the principal amount of the Credit withdrawn from the Credit Account in installments as provided in the Development Credit Agreement.

(b) The Borrower shall have the right to repay in advance of maturity all or any part of the principal amount of one or more maturities of the Credit specified by the Borrower.

Article IV

CURRENCY PROVISIONS

Section 4.02. *Currencies in which Principal and Service Charges are Payable.* (a) The Borrower shall pay the principal amount of, and service charges on, the Credit in the currency specified in the Development Credit Agreement for the purposes of this Section or in such other eligible currency or currencies as may from time to time be designated or selected pursuant to paragraph (c) or (e) of this Section.

(b) For the purposes of this Section, the term "eligible currency" means the currency of any member of the Association which the Association from time to time determines to be freely convertible or freely exchangeable by the Association for currencies of other members of the Association for the purposes of its operations.

(c) If at any time the Borrower shall desire that, commencing on a given future payment date, such principal and service charges shall be payable in an eligible currency other than that so specified or than one previously designated pursuant to this paragraph (c) or selected pursuant to paragraph (e) below, the Borrower shall deliver to the Association, not less than three nor more than five months prior to such payment date, a notice in writing to that effect and designating such other eligible currency. Upon receipt of such notice and commencing on such payment date, the currency so designated shall be the currency in which such principal and service charges shall be payable.

(d) If at any time the Association shall determine that a currency payable pursuant to the provisions of this Section is not an eligible currency, the Association shall so notify the Borrower in writing and furnish the Borrower with a list of eligible currencies.

(e) Within thirty days from the date of such notice from the Association, the Borrower shall notify the Association in writing of its selection from such list of a currency in which payment shall be made, failing which the Association shall select a currency for such purpose from such list. Upon such selection in either manner, such principal and service charges shall, commencing on the payment date next succeeding such thirty-day period, be payable in the currency so selected.

Section 4.03. *Amount of Repayment*. The principal amount of the Credit repayable shall be the equivalent (determined as of the date, or the respective dates, of repayment) of the value of the currency or currencies withdrawn from the Credit Account expressed in terms of Special Drawing Rights as of the respective dates of withdrawal.

Section 4.04. *Purchase of Currency of Withdrawal with Other Currency*. If withdrawal shall be made in any currency which the Association shall have purchased with another currency for the purpose of such withdrawal, the portion of the Credit so withdrawn shall be deemed to have been withdrawn from the Credit Account in such other currency for the purposes of Section 4.03.

Section 4.05. *Valuation of Currencies*. Whenever it shall be necessary for the purposes of the Development Credit Agreement, or any other agreement to which these General Conditions apply, to determine the value of one currency in terms of another, such value shall be as reasonably determined by the Association.

Section 4.06. *Manner of Payment*. (a) Any payment required under the Development Credit Agreement to be made to the Association in the currency of a country shall be made in such manner, and in currency acquired in such manner, as shall be permitted under the laws of such country for the purpose of making such payment and effecting the deposit of such currency to the account of the Association with a depository of the Association in such country.

(b) The principal of, and service charges on, the Credit shall be paid without restrictions of any kind imposed by, or in the territory of, the Borrower.

Article VI

CANCELLATION AND SUSPENSION

Section 6.02. *Suspension by the Association*. If any of the following events of suspension shall have occurred and be continuing, the Association may, by notice to the Borrower, suspend in whole or in part the right of the Borrower to make withdrawals from the Credit Account:

(a) The Borrower shall have failed to make payment (notwithstanding the fact that such payment may have been made by a third party) of principal, interest, service charges or any other amount due to the Association or the Bank: (i) under the Development Credit Agreement, or (ii) under any other development credit agreement between the Borrower and the Association, or (iii) under any loan or guarantee agreement between the Borrower and the Bank, or (iv) in consequence of any guarantee or other financial obligation of any kind extended by the Bank to any third party with the agreement of the Borrower.

(b) The Borrower shall have failed to perform any other obligation under the Development Credit Agreement.

(c) (i) The Association or the Bank shall have suspended in whole or in part the right of the Borrower to make withdrawals under any development credit agreement with the Association or any loan agreement with the Bank because of a failure by the Borrower to perform any of its obligations under such agreement; or (ii) the Bank shall have suspended in whole or in part the right of any borrower to make withdrawals under a loan agreement with the Bank guaranteed by the Borrower because of a failure by such borrower to perform any of its obligations under such agreement.

(d) As a result of events which have occurred after the date of the Development Credit Agreement, an extraordinary situation shall have arisen which shall make it improbable that the Project can be carried out or that the Borrower will be able to perform its obligations under the Development Credit Agreement.

(e) The Borrower: (i) shall have been suspended from membership in or ceased to be a member of the Association; or (ii) shall have ceased to be a member of the International Monetary Fund.

(f) After the date of the Development Credit Agreement and prior to the Effective Date, any event shall have occurred which would have entitled the Association to suspend the Borrower's right to make withdrawals from the Credit Account if the Development Credit Agreement had been effective on the date such event occurred.

(g) A representation made by the Borrower, in or pursuant to the Development Credit Agreement, or any statement furnished in connection therewith, and intended to be relied upon by the Association in making the Credit, shall have been incorrect in any material respect.

(h) Any other event specified in the Development Credit Agreement for the purposes of this Section shall have occurred.

The right of the Borrower to make withdrawals from the Credit Account shall continue to be suspended in whole or in part, as the case may be, until the event or events which gave rise to suspension shall have ceased to exist, unless the Association shall have notified the Borrower that the right to make withdrawals has been restored in whole or in part, as the case may be.

Article VII

ACCELERATION OF MATURITY

Section 7.01. *Events of Acceleration.* If any of the following events shall occur and shall continue for the period specified below, if any, then at any subsequent time during the continuance thereof, the Association, at its option, may, by notice to the Borrower, declare the principal of the Credit then outstanding to be due and payable immediately together with the service charges thereon and upon any such declaration such principal, together with such charges, shall become due and payable immediately:

(a) A default shall occur in the payment of principal or any other payment required under the Development Credit Agreement and such default shall continue for a period of thirty days.

(b) A default shall occur in the payment by the Borrower of principal or interest or any other amount due to the Association or the Bank: (i) under any other development credit agreement between the Borrower and the Association, or (ii) under any loan or guarantee agreement between the Borrower and the Bank, or (iii) in consequence of any guarantee or other financial obligation of any kind extended by the Bank to any third party with the agreement of the Borrower; and such default shall continue for a period of thirty days.

(c) A default shall occur in the performance of any other obligation on the part of the Borrower under the Development Credit Agreement, and such default shall continue for a period of sixty days after notice thereof shall have been given by the Association to the Borrower.

(d) Any other event specified in the Development Credit Agreement for the purposes of this Section shall have occurred and shall continue for the period, if any, specified in the Development Credit Agreement.

Article X

ENFORCEABILITY OF DEVELOPMENT CREDIT AGREEMENT; FAILURE TO EXERCISE RIGHTS; ARBITRATION

Section 10.03. *Arbitration.* (a) Any controversy between the parties to the Developed Credit Agreement and any claim by either such party against the other arising under the Development Credit Agreement which has not been settled by agreement of the parties shall be submitted to arbitration by an Arbitral Tribunal as hereinafter provided.

(b) The parties to such arbitration shall be the Association and the Borrower.

(c) The Arbitral Tribunal shall consist of three arbitrators appointed as follows: one arbitrator shall be appointed by the Association; a second arbitrator shall be appointed by the Borrower; and the third arbitrator (hereinafter sometimes called the Umpire) shall be appointed by agreement of the parties or, if they shall not agree, by the President of the International Court of Justice or, failing appointment by said President, by the Secretary-General of the United Nations. If either of the parties shall fail to appoint an arbitrator, such arbitrator shall be appointed by the Umpire. In case any arbitrator appointed in accordance with this Section shall resign, die or become unable to act, a successor arbitrator shall be appointed in the same manner as herein prescribed for the appointment of the original arbitrator and such successor shall have all the powers and duties of such original arbitrator.

(d) An arbitration proceeding may be instituted under this

Section upon notice by the party instituting such proceeding to the other party. Such notice shall contain a statement setting forth the nature of the controversy or claim to be submitted to arbitration, the nature of the relief sought, and the name of the arbitrator appointed by the party instituting such proceeding. Within thirty days after such notice, the other party shall notify to the party instituting the proceeding the name of the arbitrator appointed by such other party.

(e) If within sixty days after the notice instituting the arbitration proceeding, the parties shall not have agreed upon an Umpire, either party may request the appointment of an Umpire as provided in paragraph (c) of this Section.

(f) The Arbitral Tribunal shall convene at such time and place as shall be fixed by the Umpire. Thereafter, the Arbitral Tribunal shall determine where and when it shall sit.

(g) The Arbitral Tribunal shall decide all questions relating to its competence and shall, subject to the provisions of this Section and except as the parties shall otherwise agree, determine its procedure. All decisions of the Arbitral Tribunal shall be by majority vote.

(h) The Arbitral Tribunal shall afford to the parties a fair hearing and shall render its award in writing. Such award may be rendered by default. An award signed by a majority of the Arbitral Tribunal shall constitute the award of such Tribunal. A signed counterpart of the award shall be transmitted to each party. Any such award rendered in accordance with the provisions of this Section shall be final and binding upon the parties to the Development Credit Agreement. Each party shall abide by and comply with any such award rendered by the Arbitral Tribunal in accordance with the provisions of this Section.

(i) The parties shall fix the amount of the remuneration of the arbitrators and such other persons as shall be required for the conduct of the arbitration proceedings. If the parties shall not agree on such amount before the Arbitral Tribunal shall convene, the Arbitral Tribunal shall fix such amount as shall be reasonable under the circumstances. Each party shall defray its own expenses in the arbitration proceedings. The costs of the Arbitral Tribunal shall be divided between and borne equally by the parties. Any question concerning the division of the costs of the Arbitral Tribunal or the procedure for payment of such costs shall be determined by the Arbitral Tribunal.

(j) The provisions for arbitration set forth in this Section shall be in lieu of any other procedure for the settlement of controversies between the parties to the Development Credit Agreement or of any claims by either party against the other party arising thereunder.

(k) The Association shall not be entitled to enter judgment against the Borrower upon the award, to enforce the award against the Borrower by execution or to pursue any other remedy against the Borrower for the enforcement of the award, except as such procedure may be available against the Borrower otherwise than by reason of the provisions of this Section. If, within thirty days after counterparts of the award shall have been delivered to the parties, the award shall not be complied with by the Association, the Borrower may take such action for the enforcement of the award against the Association.

(l) Service of any notice or process in connection with any proceeding under this Section or in connection with any proceeding to enforce any award rendered pursuant to this Section may be made in the manner provided in Section 11.01. The parties to the Development Credit Agreement waive any and all other requirements for the serivce of any such notice or process.

Article XII

EFFECTIVE DATE; TERMINATION

Section 12.01. *Conditions Precedent to Effectiveness of Development Credit Agreement.* The Development Credit Agreement shall not become effective until evidence satisfactory to the Association shall have been furnished to the Association that:

(a) the execution and delivery of the Development Credit Agreement on behalf of the Borrower have been duly authorized or ratified by all necessary governmental action; and

(b) all other events specified in the Development Credit Agreement as conditions to its effectiveness have occurred.

Section II: Sources of Funds
Chapter 4:
Other Multinational Financial Institutions

4A. The African Development Bank, The Inter-American Development Bank and The Asian Development Bank
UNCTAD

B. REVIEW OF EXPERIENCES OF SELECTED REGIONAL MDFIs

1. African Development Bank

(a) Organization and functions

35. The African Development Bank (AfDB) was established in 1963 and began operating in 1966. Its headquarters are in Abidjan, Ivory Coast. By 1973, 38 African countries had subscribed to the Bank's capital. In 1981, all the 50 member States of the Organization of African Unity were members of the Bank. Each member country has 625 votes, plus one vote for each share of the capital subscribed. The ultimate authority of the Bank rests with the Board of Governors which meets annually and is made up of a Governor and an alternate for each member country. The Board of Governors elects a Board of Directors which consists of 18 members. These, in turn, elect the President of the Bank and, on the latter's recommendation, one or more Vice-Presidents.

36. As stated in the Agreement setting it up, AfBD's main purpose is to contribute to the economic development and social progress of its member States.[4] In pursuit of this objective, the Bank uses the resources available to it to finance investment projects and programmes and to promote the study and preparation of projects. It also contributes to the mobilization of resources for the financing of such projects and provides such technical assistance as may be needed for the preparation, financing and execution of projects and programmes.

37. In this respect, two initiatives of the Bank are noteworthy. Soon after its establishment, the Bank concluded an agreement with UNDP* for the creation and funding of a Pre-Investment Unit within the Bank for the identification, preparation and appraisal of projects. UNDP funding of the Unit ceased in 1977, but the Bank has continued to act as the executing agency for UNDP-sponsored project studies in Africa. In addition, the Bank has throughout the period under review acted as an intermediary for channelling bilateral assistance to Africa within the framework of the technical and financial assistance agreements concluded with various aid agencies and individual countries. These agreements provide the Bank with additional resources to finance, *inter ali*, technical assistance, studies and training programmes for the benefit of member countries. In view of the strong demand for such assistance, the Bank has in addition drawn on its own resources to provide soft loans for financing pre-investment studies. The Bank also co-operates with FAO*, UNESCO and WHO in providing technical assistance to member countries for identifying and preparing projects in their respective fields.

38. The Bank's limited capital base, in part a function of the ineligibility for membership of non-regional countries, did not allow the Bank to borrow extensively on private capital markets and for a number of years acted as a constraint on its lending activities. In recognition of the need for additional sources of funds, AfDB requested developed countries to join in establishing the African Development Fund (AfDF), a concessional loan fund not dissimilar from the International Development Association (IDA). The Draft Articles of Agreement for the Fund were initialled by 15 developed countries in Abidjan in November 1972 and the Fund became operative in 1973. The purpose of the Fund is to assist the Bank in contributing to the economic and social development of its member countries and to promote co-operation and increase international trade, particularly among member countries.[5] The Fund was designed to provide finance on concessional terms for priority projects. Voting rights in the Fund are evenly divided between regional members and non-regional members.

39. The Bank's other major initiative conducive to the mobilization of additional external resources was the agreement reached with the Nigerian Government which led to the creation of the Nigeria Trust Fund (NTF) in 1976. The central purpose of the Fund is to enable Nigeria to contribute effectively towards the economic development of those

---

*Editor's Note: UNDP - United Nations Development Program

*Editor's Note: FAO - Food and Agricultural Organization of the United Nations
UNESCO - United Nations Economic, Social and Cultural Organizaiton
WHO - World Health Organization

member countries which are less developed and which have been adversely affected by natural disasters or by exogenous economic events. The resources of the Fund are earmarked primarily for the long-term financing of agricultural development, health, transport and water supply projects, but may also be allocated to meet the cost of engineering studies related to the approved projects.

(b) Resources and their utilization

40. AfDB's authorized capital was fixed at UA 250 million, divided into 25,000 shares of UA 10,000 each.[6] Of the capital subscribed by each member country, one half was to be payable in six instalments over a period of four and a half years; the other half was subject to call as and when the Bank's obligations required it. The subscriptions of the founding members of the AfDB were determined on the basis of such criteria as population, national income, foreign trade, tax receipts and currency reserves, while those of new members, as well as their form of payment; were to be subject to conditions established by the Board of Governors.

45. In the latter half of the 1970s, AfDB's lending activities were characterized by a marked effort to derive the greatest possible impact on African development from its limited resources. This is reflected in the rapid expansion of co-financing arrangements with other institutions such as IBRD*, various Arab funds and BADEA*. During the period 1977-1981 a total of 96 projects were jointly financed for a total cost of $5.3 billion, of which the Bank's share was $752.3 million. The relatively low proportion of total project costs financed by the Bank is, in fact, a reflection of the important catalytic role it has played in facilitating the participation of other financial institutions in Bank-supported projects.

(c) Institutional co-operation at the regional, subregional and interregional levels.

55. Since its inception, AfDB has maintained links with a growing number of institutions and has participated with several of them in a wide range of initiatives. These institutions include the World Bank Group and the United Nations agencies, ECA* and OAU.*

56. In Africa itself, the Bank has established contacts and joint activities with the regional and subregional bodies which promote economic co-operation and integration between groups of African countries.

57. In the financial sector, the Bank has been particularly active in promoting co-operation. Among its earliest initiatives was the organization of the first meeting of development banks in Africa in 1970. This led to the establishment in 1975, of the Association of African Development Finance Institutions (AADFI) for which the Bank provides logistical support.

58. In 1976 AfDB took the initiative to promote co-operation on a permanent basis with the East African Development Bank (EADB), the West African Development Bank (WADB), and the Central African States Development Bank (CASDB). A joint meeting of experts prepared the ground for co-operation in the fields of joint financing, harmonization of working methods, and the identification and preparation of projects.

59. In 1979 the Bank co-operated with ECA, OAU, UNIDO* and UNDP to create the African Industrial Development Fund, which is designed to ensure the availability of resources for pre-investment feasibility studies for multinational, regional and subregional projects in high priority sectors of industry. The ratification process for the actual launching of the Fund is nearing completion. At the interregional level, the Bank maintains, by way of regular consultations and co-operation agreements, close relations with the other two regional development banks, AsDB and IDB, as well as several Arab finance institutions.

60. The bank has also built up a portfolio of equity participations in development banks, including EADB and the Development Bank of the Great Lakes States, in AfDF, in the SIFIDA* Investment Company, in the International Financial Company for Investment and Development in Africa, and in Shelter Africa, for a total of UA 22.5 million in 1981.

61. Finally, the Bank has important links with a number of development banks in member countries, which it has provided with loans and lines of credit amounting to UA 171.5 million in the years 1973-1981.

(d) AfDB and multinational projects: Statutory provisions and policies

62. It has been observed earlier that AfDB was established through the efforts of OAU and ECA, and is therefore a product of the African concept of economic co-operation. The Bank's role in African economic integration is clearly stated in its founding statute. Article 2 of the Agreement requires the Bank "to use the resources at its disposal for the

---

*Editors Note: BADEA - Arab Bank for Economic Development in Africa.
IBRD - International Bank for Reconstruction and Development ("The World Bank").

*Editor's Note: ECA - Economic Commision for Africa
OAU - Organization for African Unity
UNIDO - United Nations Industrial Development Organization
SIFIDA - Societe Internationale Financiere pour les Investissements et le Developpement en Afrique

financing of investment projects and programmes relating to the economic and social development of its members, giving special priority to: (i) projects or programmes which by their very nature or scope concern several members; (ii) projects or programmes designed to make the economies of its members increasingly complementary and to bring about an orderly expansion of their foreign trade".

63. The Bank's role in economic co-operation has been emphasized in the Revised Statement of Policy and Procedure for Loans and Investments, which enjoins the Bank in its financing activities to ensure that "a special preference is accorded to all projects which benefit two or more member countries and thus stimulate intra-African co-operation. Such projects may include transportation links, telecommunications links, irrigation and flood control, joint production and/or distribution of electric power and vocational training projects".

64. Both the Bank's statute and its policy guidelines therefore suggest that the Bank gives priority to projects which are clearly multinational, though it would also give assistance to national projects which it considered to be "integrational" by virtue of the fact that they are conducive to making the economies of member countries complementary. Thus the Bank enjoys a high degree of flexibility with regard to the projects to which it might give preferential treatment.

65. With the establishment of AfDF, new resources became available to meet on a preferential basis the requirements of balanced development within the context of African economic integration schemes. In fact, under its constituent Agreement, AfDF is required to provide finance to member countries "whose economic situation and prospects require such financing to be on concessional terms."[13] Besides, priority is to be given to projects forming part of a national, regional or subregional programme, including the provision of financing for national development banks or "other suitable institutions", the latter reference being to subregional financial institutions.[14] Again, provision is made for financing regional or subregional institutions[15] as well as for arrangements for co-operation with such institutions.[16]

66. Though its resources and, therefore, also its potential impact on the process of economic co-operation and integration in Africa are limited, the NTF, too, is required to pursue this objective. In administering the Fund, the Bank is, in fact, required to pay particular attention to projects which are likely to strengthen intra-African economic co-operation and promote regional integration.

2. Inter-American Development Bank

(a) Organization and fucntions

78. The first proposal to create an inter-American financial institution seems to have been made at the first Inter-American Conference held at the end of the nineteenth century. The proposal was revived in 1940 when a charter was drawn up for such an institution. In 1957, the Economic Conference of the Organization of American States (OAS) authorized the Inter-American Economic and Social Council to study ways of financing Latin American development, including the establishment of a regional development lending institution. A special committee was convened in Washington in 1959 to negotiate the instrument for an inter-American financial institution and a draft "Agreement Establishing the Inter-American Development Bank" (IDB) was prepared. It was ratified and entered into force at the end of 1959. The Bank started operations early in 1961 with headquarters in Washington D.C..

79. The supreme authority of the Bank rests with the Board of Governors which meets annually and consists of one Governor and one alternate appointed by each member country. The Board elects the President while the Executive Vice-President is elected by the Board of Executive Directors. Each Director's vote is in relation to the capital subscribed by the countries he represents.

80. IDB was conceived and set up as a strictly regional organization with membership restricted to the member countries of OAS. The heavy demand for loans experienced by the Bank in its formative years pointed to the desirability of opening the Bank's membership to non-regional members. The entry of such countries stemmed from the Bank's 11th Annual Meeting held in 1970. At that Meeting, it was decided to begin action to bring additional capital-contributing countries into membership of the Bank as a means of broadening its financial structure. In 1973 the conditions relating to the admission of non-regional countries were established, and by 1976 the requisite amendments to the Agreement Establishing the Bank had been ratified by a sufficient number of countries.

83. Nine non-regional countries[17] became members of IDB in 1976, a further six[18] joined in 1977 and Portugal acceded to membership in 1980. In the meantime other regional countries became members, taking the total membership of the Bank to 43 countries in 1981, of which 16 were non-regional countries.

84. In accordance with its purpose as defined in the Agreement,[19] namely, to accelerate the process of economic development of the member countries individually and collectively, IDB provides financing for the public and private sectors of those countries. It also provides technical assistance for the preparation, financing and implementation of development plans and programmes and for specific projects.

(b) Resources and their utilization

85. The Bank began its operations with an authorized capital stock of $1,000 million. From $11,409 million in 1972, the Bank's combined resources, shown in table 5, expanded more than three times over to $35,311 million in 1981.[20] This substantial growth in the Bank's resources over the period under review highlights one of the key aspects of the Bank's operations, i.e., its role as a mobilizer of external capital for Latin American development. Only a minor share of the Bank's capital resources now consist of paid-in subscriptions. By far the largest proportion is in the form of callable capital, which serves as a guarantee for the funds borrowed by the Bank for relending to its members.

90. In addition to expanding its membership, replenishing its own resources and borrowing, the IDB has expanded its lending operations by administering special funds entrusted to it by various governments. In 1961 the Bank accepted the administration of Social Progress Trust Fund to which the United States contributed $525 million. The Fund was specifically designed to provide resources for Latin America's social development and to help the lowest income sectors of the region. Subsequently, the Bank accepted other funds from a number of countries, including Agrentina, Canada, Federal Republic of Germany, the Holy See, Sweden and the United Kingdom. More recently, in 1975, the Bank accepted the administration of a $500 million fund, primarily for developing the region's productive and exporting capacity. As at the end of 1981, the Bank had accepted the administration of a total of 15 funds, most of whose resources have been completely committeed in loans.

96. The Bank's lending, substantial as it is, represents only a minor proportion of the total Latin American investment effort. The Bank's cumulative lending up to 1972 financed projects with a total cost of $16,374 million, making for a share of 33 per cent. By 1981 this share had fallen to about 25 per cent, pointing to a greater involvement by the borrowing countries and other outside sources. In 1981, the Bank's loans were helping to finance projects valued at nearly $80 billion.

97. Apart from this, the Bank has employed a number of other mechanisms designed to channel additional private and public resources towards Latin America's development. In its early years, it sold participations in individual loans to private banks and other institutions. Subsequently, in 1975, it introduced the complementary financing concept into its lending operations in an effort to secure additional private financing. Under the programme, resources from private commercial banks and other financial institutions are channelled to projects in Latin America through loans complementary to those made by the Bank.

98. Such loans are made on prevailing commercial terms and participations for the full amount of the loans are sold to interested financial institutions. Loans extended directly by the Bank are made customarily for between 15 and 30 years at rates which may vary from 1 to 4 per cent on concessionary resources, to the 9.25 per cent rate in effect on conventional loans in 1981.

99. Financial institutions participating in complementary loans benefit from the fact that the Bank has thoroughly analysed the project, supervised its implementation and administered the loan until its full repayment.

100. In addition, the Bank has collaborated in the parallel financing of projects with such international agencies as EEC*, the OPEC Fund, IFAD*, the Venezuelan Investment Fund and the Saudi Arabian Fund.

101. In 1978 the Bank initiated a programme to finance small projects. The objective was to make credit available to individuals and groups of individuals who, owing to their financial conditions and lack of credit experience, failed to qualify for conventional sources of public and commercial credit. By 1981, the cumulative number of such small-scale financings had reached 60 for a total of $25.7 million.

102. Apart from its lending, the Bank extends grant and contingent recovery technical co-operation to its regional developing member countries. This assistance is increasingly related to the objectives of the Bank's lending programme. In 1981, for instance, nearly half of the Bank's regular technical co-operation commitments were specifically related to the identification, preparation or execution of loan projects.

(c) Institutional co-operation at the regional, subregional and interregional levels

107. Given the historical and politico-economic context of the origins of the IDB, it is not surprising that the Bank has developed strong links with the regional and subregional organizations engaged in the promotion of economic integration. These include, on the one hand, the technical

*Editor's Note: EEC - European Economic Community
IFAS - International Fund for Agricultural Development

secretariats of individual groups, such as OAS, LAFTA*, the Board of the Cartagena Agreement, SIECA* and CARICOM, and, on the other, subregional financing organizations such as CABEI,* ADC* and CDB*, with each of whom the Bank has signed general co-operation agreements. In the latter group, CABEI and CDB have the closest involvement with the Bank, which provided them with technical assistance for their establishment and subsequently granted them several lines of credit.

108. Also at the regional level, in 1975 the Bank enlisted various international and bilateral organizations in setting up the International Group for Agricultural Development in Latin America (GIDA-AL). The basic aims of GIDA-AL are to co-ordinate action by the participating agencies to consider agricultural problems common to the region and its subregional areas, and to channel the flow of external financial and technical co-operation resources for food production and urban development in Latin America.

109. Another long-standing co-operative endeavour, this time carried out with LAFTA, was the launching of Latin American Bankers' Acceptances on the New York capital market in 1976 as a new mechanism for financing the growing volume of regional trade.

110. A year later the Bank joined with IBRD, IMF* and CDB in a programme designed to increase the flow of additional financial resources and technical co-operation to accelerate the orderly growth of the Caribbean region. Finally, in 1980 the Bank signed an agreement on co-operation with the River Plate Development Fund.

111. At the interregional level, the IDB has maintained regular contacts with AsDB*, AfDB, IBRD and the OPEC Fund, with particular emphasis being placed on methods of mobilizing additional financial resources.

112. In 1978 the Bank financed an agreement with IFAD to co-operate in the identification, preparation and approval of projects and in the administration of loans and grants made by the Fund for agricultural development in member countries.

113. The Bank has also worked closely with United Nations agencies, particularly UNDP, and also with IBRD, with whom it has financed a number of substantial loans to Bank member countries. Similar co-financing operations have been carried out with EEC and the OPEC Fund. With the latter, the Bank initiated a new form of co-operation in 1981. This consists of OPEC channelling loans which it might make in support of a country's balance of payments to provide counterpart resources for Bank-financed projects. In the same year, the Bank entered into an agreement with EEC whereby the Community will provide up to 2 million ECUs to finance rural micro-enterprises in Latin America in co-operation with the Bank.

(d) IDB and multinational projects Statutory provisions and policies

114. The establishment of IDB coincided with the period of intense activity in the early 1960s which witnessed the formation of a number of integration groupings and institutions. In the same year as IDB was set up, the Central American Common Market (CACM) and the Latin American Free Trade Area (LAFTA) came into being. This coincidence of the birth of integrationalist movements and the establishment of IDB was emphasized during the first meeting of the Bank's Board of Governors and the Bank's first President described it as "the Integration Bank".

115. According to the Agreement Establishing IDB, the purpose of the Bank is "to contribute to the acceleration of the process of economic development of the member countries individually and collectively". However, among the functions set forth in the Agreement is that of co-operation "with the member governments to orient their development policies towards a better utilization of their resources, in a manner consistent with the objectives of making their economies more complementary and of fostering the orderly growth of their foreign trade". This clearly shows that the fundamental purpose of promoting development is to be pursued collectively and that the Bank must find policies, rules and procedures that make its activities consistent with the regional integration process in which it is involved.

116. Within this context, the Bank has supported the integration process of Latin America inasmuch as it constitutes one of the basic premises for its existence. This is reflected in several initiatives the Bank has taken over the years, as follows:

(i) The Bank set up an Office of the Integration Adviser in 1965, now called the Office of the Deputy Manager for Integration of the Economic and Social Development Department. In this Office, the Bank's policies for evaluating integration projects are formulated and its technical co-operation and loan programmes monitored. The Bank has formulated criteria defining the nature of an intergration project and, to sharpen those definitions, it applies formulae for quantifying specific factors;

---

*Editor's Note: LAFTA - Latin American Free Trade Association
SIECA - Permanent Secretorial of the General Treaty for the Economic Integration of Central America
CARICOM - Caribbean Community
CABEI - Central American Bank for Economic Integration
ADC - Andean Development Corporation
CDB - Caribbean Development Bank

*Editor's Note: IMF - International Monetary Fund
AsDB - Asian Development Bank

(ii) Another institutional effort of great significance was the establishment, also in 1965, of the Institute for Latin American Integration (INTAL). Among its more important objectives are its research in the economic, social and legal fields in the context of integration; the training of personnel of public or private enterprises concerned with the integration process; collaboration with units of the Bank in integration matters; and the compilation of documentation relating to the integration process and the dissemination of such information;

(iii) In 1966, the Bank set up the Pre-Investment Fund for Latin American Integration with resources from the Special Progress Trust Fund and member countries. This Fund finances studies and the preparation of projects which may help to accelerate the process of Latin American integration, through the mobilization of additional external financing;

(iv) On the premise that one of the major objectives of the integration programme is the increase in trade between member countries and the reduction of external dependence, the Bank has created a programme for financing intra-regional exports of goods. The initial limitation to capital goods has recently been relaxed to include also non-traditional exports of manufactured and semi-manufactured goods;

(v) Since 1972 the Bank has been keeping an updated Inventory of Multinational Projects for Physical Integration. The Inventory is used by countries as a guide for improving co-ordination of work on such projects;

(vi) Another way in which the Bank has supported the integration process is through its technical assistance activities either through its own staff or through consultants;

(vii) Finally, the Bank grants financial assistance to integration and subregional financial institutions and, of course, loans to member countries for integration projects.

3. Asian Development Bank

(a) Organization and functions

125. The Asian Development Bank (AsDB) was established in December 1965 and began its operations a year later after its Articles of Agreement had been ratified by its 31 original members. At the end of 1981, the Bank's membership consisted of 27 regional developing countries, 3 regional developed countries and 14 non-regional developed countries, for a total of 44 countries.[23] The Bank's headquarters are in Manila, Philippines.

126. The Bank's Board of Governors, which is composed of one Governor and one alternate for each member country, elects the Bank's President and a Board of Directors composed of 12 members. Eight Directors represent regional members and, of these, two represent the developed regional member countries. The non-regional members are represented by four Directors. Though the regional developing member countries have six Directors, or half of the Board, they control only 42.3 per cent of the votes, while the three developed regional members have a combined share of 20.7 per cent. The voting power of each member country consists of the sum of its basic vote, which results from the equal distribution to each member of 20 per cent of the aggregate sum of the total votes, and its proportional votes, which are equal to the number of shares it holds.

127. AsDB represents one of the more tangible expressions of regional co-operation in a region which houses more than one third of the world's population. The populations of its member countries range from hundreds of millions to less than 100,000. Furthermore, the member countries are in varying stages of economic development, and many are in the least developed category. Given the enormity of the financing requirements of these countries on the one hand, and the relatively limited scale of the Bank's resources on the other, the Bank regards itself as a catalyst, supplying the impetus for the influx of new investment funds into the region.

128. The availability of finance is not the only major constraint on the development process in Asia. The acute shortage of expertise to formulate, implement and administer development projects is another. For this reason, the Bank often incorporates specific and on-the-job training facilities in its project loans.

129. In its earlier years, the Bank followed a cautious approach to its lending activities, in fulfilment of the principles enumerated in its Charter which ends with the statement that "The Bank shall be guided by sound banking principles in its operations".[24] There was a strong measure of agreement among the Governors at the initial meeting that the Bank needed to adopt "strict economic criteria in its lending operations".[25] Indeed, John White has criticized the Bank for apparently believing "not merely that political and social development problems are no concern of the Bank, but that they did not exist".[26]

130. In the nine years covered by this report, the Bank has responded to this type of criticism by taking into greater consideration the social impact of its lending policies and by giving more importance to the needs of the poorest among its developing member countries. This is reflected in, among other things, the growing share of resources devoted to education, health, urban development and agriculture, and also in the rising proportion of concessional loans in the Bank's total lending. In this regard, a milestone was reached in 1974 with the birth of the Asian Development Fund (AsDF). In accor-

dance with its Articles, the Bank may establish special funds and allocate to them a proportion of its ordinary resources which is not greater than 10 per cent of the paid-up capital. Up to that point, the Bank had created the Multi-Purpose Special Fund and the Technical Assistance Special Fund, but these had limited resources. In contrast, AsDF was set up with contributions from developed members countries of the Bank and was designed to provide a mechanism for the systematic mobilization of resources for the Bank's concessional lending programme. Contributions to the Fund are untied for procurement in all developing member countries and in all contributor countries.

(b) Resources and their utilization

131. At the end of 1981 the authorized capital of the AsDB was $8,404 million, representing an almost threefold increase since the end of 1972. Of the subscribed capital of $8,297 million in 1981, developing countries of the region accounted for 37.5 per cent, the non-regional developed countries 37.2 per cent and the three developed countries of the region 25.3 per cent. The "callable" share capital, $6,681 million in 1981, is subject to call by the Bank only as and when required to meet the Bank's obligations incurred on borrowings or on guarantees. The "paid-in" share capital is payable in instalments, partly in convertible currencies and partly in the currency of the subscribing member. In accordance with article 6, paragraph 3, of the Articles, the Bank accepts non-negotiable, non-interest-bearing demand obligations in satisfaction of the portion payable in the currency of the member, when such currency is not required by the Bank for the conduct of its operations.

138. The Bank's efforts in helping the poor—nearly three quarters of the world's poor are found in the Asian and pacific regions—are embodied in a lending strategy which aims at:

(i) improving productivity and social infrastructure in rural areas;

(ii) providing better educational, health and housing facilities for the poor; and

(iii) moderating population growth.

139. Apart from the preference given to these sectors, which has been described above, this lending strategy is also reflected in two other facts:

(i) The proportion of concessional loans in total Bank and Fund lending has risen from 21 per cent in 1972 to 32 per cent in 1981;

(ii) In the latter year, almost 92 per cent of Fund loans went to developing member countries which had a *per capita* GNP of less than $300 in 1980, up from 88 per cent the previous year.

140. In addition to its own lending operations, the AsDB has made several efforts at mobilizing additional resources and at maximizing the impact of its financial assistance to member countries. Every dollar lent by the Bank is matched with an average additional investment of about $1.5 by the borrowing countries and by outside co-financiers. Cofinancing has, in fact, become an important element in the Bank's operations. At the end of 1981, 112 of the Bank's loan projects involved cofinancing of over $2.5 billion.

141. Simultaneously, the Bank has been devoting an increasing volume of resources to technical assistance, which enables developing member countries to make more effective use of development funds and also to generate new projects for Bank financing. No less than 38 per cent of the Bank's loans have resulted from earlier technical assistance. An outlay of $48.6 million in non-refundable technical assistance up to 1981 resulted in Bank lending of $3.6 billion for these projects.

143. As for the Bank's lending terms, these are largely determined by the cost of the Bank's borrowed funds. This explains why, until the creation of the AsDF, the Bank's concessional lending programme was relatively small. As at the end of 1981, the rate charged on loans financed from ordinary capital resources was 10.1 per cent. In addition, the Bank levies a commitment charge of 0.45 per cent on the undisbursed portion of loans. The repayment period is usually between 15 and 20 years.

144. In the case of the AsDF, loans do not carry interest but are subject to a service charge of 1 per cent. The repayment period may be as long as 40 years, including a 10-year grace period.

(c) Institutional co-operation at the regional, subregional and interregional levels

145. One of the Bank's functions under its Articles is to co-operate with the United Nations, in particular the Economic and Social Commission for Asia and the Pacific (ESCAP), which took the initiative in setting up the Bank, and with other institutions interested in development financing in the region.

146. In compliance with this provision, the Bank has maintained close relations with IBRD, with whom it has also financed a large project in Bangladesh, and also collaborates in the area of aid co-ordination. The Bank has further co-operated with IBRD in developing a series of pioneer agricultural projects under the aegis of the Committee for Co-ordination of Investigation of the Lower Mekong Basin. The Bank also maintains close links with FAO and with UNDP, for whom it acts as Executing Agency. With UNDP

the Bank co-operates in identifying projects for joint investment. Also at the interregional level, the Bank holds annual consultations with AfDB and IDB, as well as AFESD*, the Islamic Development Bank, the OPEC Fund and IFAD, among others.

147. At the regional level, the Bank promoted the agreement establishing the Association of Development Finance Institutions of Asia and the Pacific (ADFIAP), one of whose main objectives is the promotion of regional co-operation among development finance institutions.

(d) AsDB and multinational projects Statutory provisions and policies

148. As in the case of AfDB, the founding of AsDB may be traced to an initiative which originated within the appropriate United Nations regional commission. In this case, the Economic Commission for Asia and the Far East (ECAFE, now ESCAP) initiative resulted in the formation of a group of experts on regional economic co-operation who eventually proposed the establishment of a regional development bank. Accordingly, a commitment to the promotion of integration projects is implicit in the Agreement establishing the AsDB which states that the Bank's purpose is to "foster economic growth and co-operation in the region of Asia and the Far East and to contribute to the acceleration of the process of economic development of the developing member countries in the region collectively and individually".[27] "Region" is defined as including the member countries of ECAFE. Furthermore, the Bank is called on to utilize "the resources at its disposal for financing development of the developing member countries in the region, giving priority to those subregional as well as regional projects and programmes which will contribute most effectively to the harmonious economic growth of the region as a whole, and having special regard to the needs of the smaller or less developed member countries in the region". Finally, the Articles also state that the Bank will assist member countries "in the co-ordination of their development policies and plans with a view to achieveing better utilization of their resources, making their economices more complementary, and promoting the orderly expansion of their foreign trade, in particular intraregional trade".[28]

*Editor's Note: AFESD - Arab Fund for Economic and Social Development

NOTES

4. Agreement Establishing the African Development Bank, article 1.

5. Agreement Establishing the African Development Fund, article 2.

6. The Bank Unit of Account (UA) is valued at 0.88867088 gramme of fine gold in the Agreement. Since 1978 the Bank's Unit of Account has been deemed to be equivalent in value to SDR 1.

13. Agreement Establishing the African Development Fund, article 1, para. 1.

14. Ibid. article 1, para. 2.

15. Ibid. article 16, para. 3

16. Ibid. article 18.

17. Belgium, Denmark, Federal Republic of Germany, Israel, Japan, Spain Switzerland, United Kingdom and Yugoslavia.

18. Australia, Finland, France, Italy, Netherlands and Sweden.

19. Agreement Establishing the Inter-American Development Bank (United Nations, *Treaty Series*, vol. 389, p. 70).

20. These amounts are expressed in terms of current United States dollars and do not correspond with the figures published by the Bank in its financial statements, where the standard unit of measurement is the 1959 United States dollars (see foot-note a to table 5).

23. The regional developing countries and areas are the following: Afghanistan, Bangladesh, Burma, Cambodia, China, Republic of, Cook Islands, Fiji, Hong Kong, India, Indonesia, Kiribati, Korea, Republic of, Lao People's Democratic Republic, Malaysia, Maldives, Nepal, Pakistan, Paupa New Guinea, Philippines, Singapore, Solomon Islands, Sri Lanka, Thailand, Tonga, Vanuatu, Viet Nam, Republic of, and Western Samoa. (The terminology corresponds to that used in English by the Bank.) The three regional developed countries are: Australia, Japan and New Zealand. The 14 non-regional developed countries are: Austria, Belgium, Canada, Denmark, Finland, France, Germany, Federal Republic of, Italy, Netherlands, Norway, Sweden, Switzerland, United Kingdom of Great Britain and Northern Ireland, United States of America.

24. Articles of Agreement of the Asian Development Bank, article 14, para. XIV.

25. Asian Development Bank, *Inaugural Meeting Documents*, Manila, 1966, pp. 216-217.

26. J. White, *Regional Development Banks, A Study of Institutional Style* (London: Overseas Development Institute, 1970), p. 74.

27. Articles of Agreement of the Asian Development Bank, article 1.

28. Ibid., article 2.

4B. Selected Multilateral Financial Institutions

For further information on these institutions and for a more comprehensive list of such institutions see *Financial Resources for Industrial Projects in Developing Countries,* UNIDO (3rd éd. 1983) U.N. No. PI/64 Rev. 1.

REGIONAL DEV. BANKS & FUNDS

African Development Bank
P.O. Box 1387
Anoma Street
Abidjan 01
Ivory Coast

Arab African Int'l Bank (AAIB)
P.O. Box 1143
44 Abdel Khalek Sarwat Street
Cairo

Arab Fund for EC & Social Dev.
P.O. Box 21923 — Safat 5th Fl.
Souk el Safat Bldg.
Kuwait

Arab Petroleum Investments Corp.
P.O. Box 448
Dhahran Airport
King Abdul Aziz St.
al-Khobar

Asian Development Bank
P.O. Box 789
2330 Roxas Blvd.
Metro Manilla
Phillipines

Banco Centroamericano de Integracion Economia
Apartado Postal No. 772
Tegucigalpa
D.C. Honduras

Banque Arabe pour le Developpement Economique
  en Afrique
P.O. Box 2640
Baladia Rd.
Khartoum
Sudan

Banque Oest Africaine de Developement
P.O. Box 1172
68 Avenue de la Liberation
Lomé
Togo

Caribbean Development Bank
P.O. Box 408
Wildey
St. Michael
Barbados
West Indies

Caribbean Investment Corp.
P.O. Box 731
27 Brazil St.
Castries
Saint Lucia

Corporacion Andina de Fomenta
  (Andean Development Corp.)
P.O. Box 69011 or 69012
Torre Central
100 Piso
Altamira
Caracas
Venezuela

East African Development Bank
P.O. Box 7128
4 Nile Avenue
Kampala
Uganda

European Arab Bank S.A.
Avenue Des Arts 19H — Bte. 2
B-1040 Brussels
Belgium

European Arab Holding S.A.
76 Avenue de la Liberté
Luxembourg — Ville Grand Duche de Luxembourg

Gulf International Bank
P.O. Box 1017
Government Rd.
Tarek Bldg.
Manoma Bahrain

Inter-American Development Bank
808 17th Street N.W.
Washington, D.C. 20577
U.S.A.

International Investment Bank
17 Presnensky Val
123557 Moscow D-557
U.S.S.R.

Kuwait Fund for Arab Economic Development
P.O. Box 2921
Kuwait

Nordic Investment Bank
P.O. Box 249
Unioninkatu 30
Helsinki
Finland

Private Investment Company of Asia (PICA) S.A.
P.O. Box 3442
Maxwell Road
Singapore 9054

Société Internationale Financiére pour les
    Investissements et le Développement en Afrique
    (SIFIDA Investment Company)
B.P. 396
8c Avenue de Champel
CH-1211
Geneva Switzerland

The Inter-Arab Investment Guarantee Corporation
18 Al-Istiqlal Street
Kuwait
23568 Safat — Kuwait

INTERNATIONAL BANKING & AID-GIVING INSTITUTIONS

European Investment Bank
P.O. Box 2005
2 Place de Metz
Luxembourg

The OPEC Fund for International Development
P.O. Box 995
A-1011 Vienna I
Austria

United Nations Capital Development Fund
c/o UNDP
One United Nations Plaza
New York
N.Y. 10017
U.S.A.

United Nations Industrial Development Fund
Vienna International Center
A-1400 Vienna
Austria

The World Bank
1818 H Street, N.W.
Washington, D.C. 20433
U.S.A.

International Development Association
1818 H Street, N.W.
Washington, D.C. 20433
U.S.A.

International Finance Corporation
1818 H Street, N.W.
Washington, D.C. 20433
U.S.A.

REGIONAL ASSOCIATIONS OF DEVELOPMENT FINANCE INSTITUTIONS

Association of African Development Finance Institutions
P.O. Box 1387
c/o African Development Bank
Abidjan
Ivory Coast

The Association of Development Financing Institutions
  in Asia and the Pacific
Private Development Corporation of the Philippines
PDCP Building
Ayata Avenue
Makati, Metro Manilla, Philippines

International Association of Islamic Banks
P.O. Box 4992
Jeddah
Saudi Arabia

Latin American Association of Development Financing
  Institutions
P.O. Box 3988
Lima 27
Peru

DEVELOPMENT BANKING PROGRAMS OF INTERNATIONAL ORGANIZATIONS

Food and Agricultural Organization of the United Nations
Via delle Terme di Caracella
I-00100
Rome
Italy

Organization for Economic Cooperation and Development
94 rue Chardon Lagache
F-75016 Paris
France

United Nations Industrial Development Organization
Vienna International Centre
P.O. Box 300
A-1400 Vienna
Austria

INVESTMENT COOPERATION PROGRAMME

—run by United Nations Industrial Development
 Organization (UNIDO).
—promotes investment, assists in mobilizing financial
 resources, cooperates with World Bank.

Section II: Sources of Funds
Chapter 5: Cofinancing

5A. Cofinancing: An Overview
The World Bank

About one-third of the development projects assisted by the World Bank[1] now receive financial support from a cofinancer. Cofinancing is not a new activity for the Bank. However, in today's uncertain economic environment, it is even more important than in the past that different lenders should work closely together. Cofinancing is one of the most effective ways for the different sources of finance to collaborate. As a result, the World Bank is giving special emphasis to expanding its cofinancing activities and to putting in place arrangements that can be of benefit to all the entities involved: the borrower, the World Bank, and the cofinancer. What cofinancing means and the advantages it offers are the subject of this pamphlet.

Cofinancing and Its Benefits

The World Bank can provide only a small part of the external resources needed to stimulate the economic growth of its member developing countries. It, therefore, encourages and assists borrowers to augment the resources it provides with other external sources of investment finance, appropriate to each nation's borrowing situation, in support of high priority projects. This collaborative support is commonly known as cofinancing. The additional funds come from three principal sources:

- agencies or departments of governments administering bilateral development programs, and multilateral agencies such as regional development banks and funds;
- export credit agencies, which either lend directly or provide guarantees or insurance to commercial banks extending export credits; and
- commercial banks.

Lenders have found that cofinancing offers several advantages. For example, for official agencies cofinancing is an efficient way of combining professional development expertise; export credit agencies can be satisfied that their resources will be applied to well-conceived and appraised projects; and commercial lenders can be assured that loan proceeds will be used for the intended purposes. More generally, the risks attached to lending in developing countries can be reduced through cofinancing. The underlying quality of the project, as well as close supervision of project implementation, reduces the risk that the project may not earn a return. The financing of well-conceived projects helps improve the recipient countries' overall capacity to repay their external borrowings. The arrangements for association with the World Bank reduce the risk that the borrower may not repay even if the project goes well.

Borrowers also find cofinancing advantageous. In particular, it gives them greater assurance that high-priority investments can be financed on the best terms available. In addition, cofinancing can improve their access to each source of funding—official, export credit, and commercial.

World Bank Cofinancing Record

Between fiscal years 1974 and 1983, the total cost of projects supported by the World Bank amounted to $275 billion. Other lenders were associated in cofinancing projects with about half of these total costs. The Bank provided nearly the same amount of financing for those projects as the cofinancers.

Although, as noted earlier, cofinancing is not a new activity for the World Bank, the number of projects financed with other lenders has increased over time. Since fiscal 1981, an average of about 90 projects each year has involved the association of World Bank finance with that of other lenders, while in the mid-1970s there were only about 60 such projects a year. Over the same time span, the sources of cofinancing have become more diversified; the involvement of export credit agencies and commercial banks has grown faster than that of official agencies. Nevertheless, association with other official lenders remains the most prominent form of cooperation through cofinancing.

The second distribution of cofinanced projects reflects the fact that official agencies provide most of their aid to the poorer countries, in which the development of the agricultural and infrastructure sectors is particularly important. Export credit and commercial bank financing, on the other hand, is concentrated in those sectors in which the requirements for imported capital goods are large.

Arrangements with Cofinancers

Arrangements with cofinancers have to be tailored to the terms, conditions, and objectives of each source of cofinancing. Key features common to the arrangements with most cofinancers include provision for the sharing of information about the cofinanced project and the economic prospects of the borrowing country; understandings on the responsibility for preparation, appraisal, and implementation of the project; and understandings on how to proceed should difficulties arise with the project and the loan repayment. With the concurrence of the borrower, arrangements in each of these areas have to be responsive to the different concerns of the different lenders.

Cofinancing arrangements also depend on restrictions affecting the use of funds. For its part in cofinancing arrangements, the World Bank must ensure that the procurement of any goods and services financed by its loan is carried out efficiently and economically. All member countries of the World Bank, plus Switzerland, are afforded an equal opportunity to supply goods and services needed for implementing the World Bank-financed share of projects assisted. In most cases, International Competitive Bidding is used to achieve this objective. Since other lenders frequently have different procedures, the goods and services have to be divided into a number of "packages" and different packages financed from different sources. This method (used in about nine out of ten cases) is traditionally referred to as "parallel financing." With respect to the packages not financed by the World Bank, it satisfies itself that the goods and services involved are acceptable in both quality and price and that the financing is on terms consistent with the overall financial soundness of the project. Parallel financing ensures that the identity of each lender and its relationship with the borrower are fully recognized.

Although "joint financing" is another method of structuring procurement arrangements, it has been seldom used in recent years. In this case, funds from two or more sources in some agreed proportion can be used for the procurement of a common set of goods and services. This method is feasible when the procurement procedures of other lenders are compatible with the procurement guidelines of the Bank.

Organizing Cofinancing

Cofinancing is feasible only when all three parties to the transaction—the borrower, the cofinancers, and the World Bank—see advantages in the arrangements. The actual steps in arranging cofinancing and the roles of the parties vary from case to case.

What happens initially is that the World Bank consults with the borrower and identifies and selects projects to support that can best assist the borrowing country's economic development. Since the extent to which the Bank itself can support those projects is limited, it often assists the borrower in identifying other sources of financing that might be able to contribute to the total cost of the projects. Cofinancing, therefore, is a means of financing a borrower's development priorities and does not determine them.

For poorer countries, additional support is generally sought from official agencies on concessionary terms. For countries that can borrow on market-related terms and for projects that require significant amounts of capital goods and equipment from external sources, borrowers may be encouraged to obtain export credits. In such projects, potential suppliers of goods and services may take the initiative and ask that the borrower and the credit insurers or guarantors in their home countries organize the export finance. As for commercial sources, they may be encouraged to join in cofinancing because of the links in many cases between banks and major manufacturers of capital goods and equipment, or the perception that opportunities exist for widening their relationships with the borrowers through involvement with the project.

The World Bank's own role in this process varies according to the needs of the borrower or the complexity of the project. Borrowers who have less ready access to international capital markets or who have more limited contacts with official agencies need to be helped more. Technically complex projects, for which the procurement and financial "packaging" needs to be done systematically and for which difficult choices may be made among alternative packages may also require greater World Bank assistance. Ultimately, however, the decision on what cofinancing arrangements are beneficial and which sources to tap rests with the borrower.

THREE MAIN SOURCES

The different relationships that have evolved between the World Bank and the principal sources of cofinancing are examined separately in the next three secitons of this pamphlet.

Official Lenders

Historically, the World Bank's main associates in funding projects in developing countries have been agencies such as the Inter-American Development Bank, the Asian Development Bank, the African Development Bank, the United States Agency for International Development, the Federal Republic of Germany's Kreditanstalt fur Wiederaufbau, and Japan's Overseas Economic Cooperation Fund. Between fiscal years 1974 and 1983, official agencies lent $16.2 billion in association with the World Bank for 682 Bank-assisted projects. During that period, the annual volume of cofinancing grew from $790 million to more than $1.75 billion.

The two distinctive characteristics of official lenders such as these are that they were established to give priority to development objectives, and that they provide financing on concessionary terms, or, as in the case of the multilateral institutions, on market-related as well as concessionary terms. Many poorer developing countries cannot borrow on commercial or market-related terms. They, therefore, turn to the official agencies—including the concessionary window of the World Bank (the International Development Association)—for help in putting together a financial package on appropriate terms.

Because of their common developmental orientation, the official bilateral agencies have had a long and close association with the World Bank, as is reflected in the cofinancing record. By far the largest number of cofinancing operations has involved these agencies.

Ties among the multilateral development agencies have been equally close. Because most of these institutions lend on market-related as well as concessionary terms, their cofinancing association can cover countries at all stages of development.

Bilateral official agencies work within budget ceilings fixed by their governments, and multilateral agencies work within the constraint of the size of their capital bases provided by their government shareholders. As a result, financing from a combination of official lenders may not increase the total flow of finance to the developing countries. Nevertheless, such association is highly desirable for a number of reasons:

- Many investments are too large to be carried out by any one agency.
- The channeling of flows to the poorest countries most in need of concessionary finance is encouraged.
- Agreement on the financing of investments with the highest priority is facilitated.
- Association provides a practical opportunity for official lenders to consult and exchange views on all aspects of development.

Official colenders have found it important to work closely with borrowers in the early stages of project preparation and appraisal in order to establish early on whether there is a joint interest in combining forces, as well as to decide at an early point how functions are to be shared in carrying forward the financing. The practice of working together continues while the project is being implemented and enables both parties to identify what corrective action should be taken if adjustments are needed in the project. Early cooperation between official lenders is particularly important because:

- Potential financers are able to make their decisions to lend on the basis of their own broader sectoral and country priorities, rather than in response to a last-minute "gap" in a financing plan.
- The borrower and potential colenders are given an opportunity to discuss the borrower's overall investment priorities; as a result, lending decisions by individual agencies are not taken in isolation, but are made against the broader background of a borrower's investment priorities.
- The design of the project, in particular the possible source of the goods and services required, can be closely meshed with prospective financing arrangements.

Export Credit Institutions

Most industrialized countries have established national agencies such as the United States Export-Import Bank, the Export-Import Bank of Japan, the United Kingdom's Export Credit Guarantee Department (ECGD), or France's Compagnie Francaise d'Assurance pour le Commerce Exterieur (COFACE) to encourage the financing of the nation's exports. Sometimes, the agencies provide the needed finance directly themselves; in other cases, they provide insurance or guarantees under which commercial lenders provide finance for exports.

Between fiscal years 1974 and 1983, export credit financing associated with World Bank-assisted projects grew from $590 million to $2.92 billion a year, totaling $11.77 billion for the decade. The record shows that the number of projects financed together by the World Bank and export credit agencies is still limited. However, from the borrower's point of view, this kind of financing is well suited for projects since it provides the longer maturities appropriate for such investments. Further, this type of financing is more readily available than official assistance and, in many cases, export credit guarantees are necessary to encourage commercial bank lending.

An effective association between the World Bank and an export credit agency requires the two to exchange information at an early stage of the project cycle. This is because an export credit agency needs to know whether a national supplier is likely to be involved in providing goods and services for the project. Early information on the type of equipment that may be required enables the agency in turn to express to the World Bank and the borrower its interest in cofinancing. It thus facilitates the preparation of the financing plan.

In arranging a financing plan involving export credit, the borrower and the World Bank must package the items of equipment so that as many packages as possible are eligible for export credit financing. The items being financed by the Bank itself under its own procurement procedures must be arranged in relation to these other packages so as to ensure that the borrower gets the most advantageous overall financing. The size of the World Bank's financial participation also reflects the role that the borrower and the other lenders wish the Bank to play in implementing the project and its associated policy objectives.

The World Bank's continuing presence in implementing the entire project, together with the assurance that the project itself has met high standards of appraisal, has encouraged some export credit agencies to lend in association with the Bank more readily than might otherwise be the case. From the borrower's point of view, therefore, association between the World Bank and export credit agencies enhances the prospects of additional finance. An equally important point for the borrower is that cofinancing can help ensure that export credit offers are used productively and for suitable equipment.

Private Sources

Cofinancing with private sources refers to cofinancing with commercial banks, most of which are privately owned. An important stage in the evolution of cofinancing with these institutions began in 1975, when 16 banks, led by the Bank of America, provided a $55 million Eurocurrency loan alongside a $95 million World Bank loan, a $63 million Inter-American Development Bank loan, and $490 million in export credits to support the expansion of a large Brazilian steel company.

The major portion of loans outstanding from commercial banks to developing countries are held by approximately 50 lenders. Between 600 and 800 banks are internationally active on a smaller scale. About 200 of these banks have participated in loans that involve cofinancing arrangements with the World Bank. Banks from Japan and the United States have been particularly active.

A commercial bank loan that becomes part of a financial package for an investment together with a World Bank loan (and sometimes with export credit financing) is arranged on normal commercial terms. Therefore, most of the poorer developing countries are not able to look to this source of financing. Nevertheless, until the recent uncertainties in capital movements, commercial lending was the fastest growing source of funding for many developing countries. The cofinancing record also shows growing association between the World Bank and commercial lenders since 1975.

There are two main reasons why commercial lenders can find association with the World Bank attractive. First, the World Bank has a long-established expertise in ensuring that loans are employed for productive purposes and in supervising the end use of loan proceeds. Secondly, the Bank is an important source of information on the development policies and prospects of developing countries, and association with the World Bank can influence the perception of country economic risk. In addition, a commercial lender may be attracted to a particular cofinancing opportunity for more specific reasons:

- A domestic client may be involved in the investment as a supplier of goods and services.
- A lender may wish to establish or foster a client relationship with a particular borrower.
- Involvement may supplement a commercial bank's broader international strategy.

In the past, there have been some cases in which the relationship between the Bank and the commercial lender has been quite informal. In such cases, commercial loans have formed part of a financing plan involving the World Bank, but there has been no further connection between the two parties involved. In other cases, where such links were deemed desirable by the lenders and the borrower, a Memorandum of Agreement was arranged providing for an exchange of information on the progress of the project, and an "optional" cross-default clause has linked the World Bank loan with the commercial loan to signal that the World Bank would use its "good offices" in the event of loan difficulties.

The frequency of association between the World Bank and commercial lenders that has grown in this way has been less than the importance of this source of finance for developing countries would suggest, and less than has seemed desirable given the potential benefits of closer association for borrowers, the World Bank, and commercial lenders. The World Bank, therefore, has recently initiated a trial program of new instruments for cofinancing with commercial banks that offers closer association with commercial lenders and correspondingly greater benefits for borrowers. These and other changes in the manner of association with the other sources of cofinancing are described in the next section.

NEW THRUSTS IN COFINANCING

In recent years, developing countries have experienced new stresses stemming in part from a much more difficult external economic environment that has adversely affected the growth of export earnings and, more generally, their overall prospects for economic progress. The availability of capital has been uncertain, and commercial and export credit flows have become more costly. Many developing countries have had to undertake major adjustment programs that have reduced their short-run economic growth. The World Bank has embarked, therefore, on new measures to help developing countries undertake the necessary adjustments and to restore the basis for more rapid development. They imply that the Bank has to play a more active role, first, as a source of pragmatic policy advice on development strategy, for which it is uniquely qualified; and, second, as a catalyst in mobilizing the large-scale financial support which can only be provided by all sources of finance acting in closer concert. In order to play this more active role in mobilizing the financial resources needed to accompany the efforts of developing countries, the World Bank has taken several steps to expand its cofinancing activities.

Frame Agreements

One recent initiative has been the revival of "frame agreements" with some official cofinancers.[2] Because official cofinancers must work closely from an early stage in designing a loan, the process can be long and complicated. Frame agreements are intended to accelerate the process by recording the understandings reached between the World Bank and other agencies as to how the association should be carried out. Earlier frame agreements covered mainly procedural matters, but recently, in understandings reached with Italy and Belgium, they have included a volume target for cofinancing. Similar arrangements are currently under discussion with other official lenders. An effort is also under way to establish more frequent and systematic consultations with a broad range of official agencies.

New Instruments with Banks

Another potentially important development has been the introduction of new instruments designed to facilitate a greater number of cofinancing arrangements with private commercial banks. In early 1983, the World Bank's Executive Directors approved a trial program linking the finance provided by commercial lenders more closely with the Bank. The main feature of this program is that the World Bank, in addition to making its own loan for an investment, may participate in the parallel commercial loan. This participation may take the form of direct financial participation in the the later maturities of a loan made by commercial banks, the use of the World Bank guarantee, or a contingent participation by the World Bank in the commercial loan.

The new program offers greater comfort to lenders, particularly in their preception of country risk, because of the participation of the World Bank with a major stake in the commercial loan. This affords important protection to commercial lenders because of the special relationship between the World Bank and its borrowers. At the same time, the program has two important objectives from the point of view of the borrower: to increase the developing country's access to, and familiarity with, the commercial markets; and to extend maturities of commercial loans to lengths more appropriate for development investments. The benefits of closer association to lenders are contingent on these benefits being available to the borrower.

Other Steps

The World Bank is also taking steps to expand cofinancing with export credit agencies. In December 1982, it convened a meeting attended by 26 representatives of export credit agencies to explore the possibilities and discuss the issues involved. These discussions covered the means of improving the exchange of information between the World Bank and the agencies and ways of improving the combining of packages of goods and services with financial offers from export credit agencies and with the World Bank's own finance. Another subject of particular concern to the export credit agencies has been the financial risk they incur if a borrower runs into severe balance-of-payments difficulties. Whether combined financing can be arranged in forms that would mitigate this risk in order to improve prospects of ensuring a larger flow of finance to borrowers from this source is now under examination. Specific proposals in each of these areas will be reviewed at a follow-up meeting with export credit agencies scheduled for November 1983.

In addition, the World Bank has enlarged its role as a source of information on sound investment opportunities by sending detailed listings of projects suitable for cofinancing to official lenders, export credit agencies, and commercial banks. Projects are listed at the earliest opportunity and more detailed cofinancing briefs are available at a later stage of the project cycle.

To support this new activity, the World Bank has established a central cofinancing advisory unit that will enable the World Bank to be more responsive to the challenges posed by the cofinancing process. In addition, a staff member in each of the World Bank's six regional groupings and one sectoral grouping (Energy and Industry) has been appointed to coordinate cofinancing activities in these areas with the cofinancing unit.

COFINANCING'S FUTURE

The present international economic environment calls for much closer association between the different sources of financing for developing countries. The momentum of development will not be restored unless the developing countries' own efforts are accompanied by a sufficient inflow of new capital for productive investments. Efficient use of these inflows will itself help restore the confidence of lenders. The World Bank is ready to play its part in promoting a closer association between different lenders.

Cofinancing offers an important practical means for such cooperation. This pamphlet has summarized a number of steps that the World Bank is taking to improve its cofinancing procedures. The Bank recognizes that these measures will take time to yield results, and that it must continue to explore changes through which a closer association between lenders can be realized. The end results can benefit all parties concerned—the borrower, lenders, and the World Bank itself.

THREE NEW COFINANCING INSTRUMENTS

1. Direct Financial Participation Option

The World Bank participates in the later maturities of a commercial loan to provide comfort to colenders and to achieve a lengthening of maturities beyond a point to which the commercial banks would normally commit themselves. A sizable share of World Bank participation would be around 10 percent, but a larger share—up to a maximum of 25 percent—might be necessary to achieve the objective of lengthening maturities. The World Bank retains the right to reduce its share as the loan matures or if initial syndication is more successful than anticipated.

2. Guarantee Option

The World Bank guarantees the later maturities of a loan made by commercial banks and thus provides an incentive for the colenders to fund the later maturities with short-term funds for a significantly longer period than would otherwise be the case. Alternatively, the World Bank could, under certain conditions, offer its colenders a suitable "put" option on the later maturities of the loan, which would represent a World Bank commitment to purchase the designated maturities at the request of the colenders. A "guarantee fee," payable to the World Bank, would encourage a "take-out" by the commercial lenders as the guarantee portion progressively comes within the normal range of market maturities.

3. Contingent Obligation after Level Payment Option

The World Bank takes a contingent participation in the final maturity of a commercial loan designed with a fixed level of installments that combine floating-interest and variable-principal repayments. If the interest rate should rise above its initial rate, the amortization of the loans is not completed on the original schedule, and the World Bank accepts an obligation to finance the final repayment if the commercial banks are not willing to finance the balance of principal outstanding, if any, at final maturity.

In this trial program, the World Bank also has the authority to undertake "sale of participation" operations under which the commercial loan would be arranged by the World Bank but would be sold to participating commercial banks.

The world Bank has recently discussed these new instruments with commercial bankers in the United States, Hong Kong, Japan, France, the Middle East, and Britain and has disseminated information on them at meetings with others.

NOTES

1. "The World Bank" in this pamphlet refers to the Internationaal Bank for Reconstruction and Development (IBRD) and the International Development Association (IDA). The World Bank's purpose is to help raise the standard of living in its developing member countries by financing high priority development projects, by providing technical assistance, and by conducting an economic policy dialogue with borrower governments. The IBRD, founded in 1945, has 144 countries as members. It raises its funds mainly in the world's capital markets. Its affiliate, IDA, is funded by government contributions; IDA's purpose is to lend for development projects in the poorest countries at concessional terms.

2. The World Bank has entered into frame agreements with the Government of Italy (June 30, 1982), the Nordic Investment Bank (July 1, 1982), and the Government of Belgium (September 15, 1982).

5B. Note on Documentation for IBRD's New Co-Financing Program*
The World Bank

This Note contains a general summary of the documentation which has been used in the first three transactions (one in Thailand and two in Hungary) under IBRD's new co-financing program. Although the substance of the documentation described in this Note is expected to be reflected in future similar transactions, the precise language may vary depending upon the particular circumstances of each transaction.

Each of the three transactions involved IBRD taking a direct financial participation in the later maturities of commercially syndicated loans for projects approved by IBRD for financing under parallel IBRD loans. Consistent with market practice, the co-financing loan documentation was initially prepared by the lead manager, revised so as to incorporate special features associated with IBRD's participation, and subsequently negotiated with the borrower.

In each case, the documentation is basically in the form of a commercially syndicated loan agreement. Accordingly, although the text of each loan agreement differs (reflecting the preferences of the lead managing bank and its lawyers), the documentation incorporates usual provisions on such matters as definitions; the loan; conditions precedent to drawdown; interest and default interest; fees, charges and expenses; repayment, prepayment and application of payments; taxes; yield protection/increased costs; representations and warranties; financial information; negative pledge and other covenants; events of default and remedies; the agent bank and the managers; governing law, jurisdiction and waiver of sovereign immunity; and miscellaneous matters.

Additional provisions designed to reflect IBRD's participation in the loan are as follows:

Purpose of Loan and Application of Proceeds The purpose of each loan is clearly specified and, depending upon the drawdown period and the requirements of the project being financed, special provisions are added to ensure that the proceeds of the loan will be disbursed and used for that purpose and to enable IBRD to monitor such use.

---
* Issued by the International Bank for Reconstruction and Development, Washington, D.C. (September 1983)

Rescheduling of the Co-Financing Loan Given the particular characteristics of the co-financing loan and IBRD's participation in it, the parties agree not to reschedule the debt obligations under the loan without IBRD's consent (see attached sample debt rescheduling clause).

Government Guarantee of Commercial Bank Portion Whether a government guarantee of the commercial bank portion should be provided is a matter to be decided by the guarantor and the commercial banks on normal market considerations. If such a guarantee is provided, its terms may be included in the co-financing loan agreement, consistent with usual commercial practice.

Government Guarantee of IBRD Portion If a member State of IBRD is not the borrower, the Articles of Agreement of IBRD require that the IBRD portion must be fully guaranteed by the member State in whose territories the project is located. The terms of this guarantee are included in a separate guarantee agreement between the guarantor and IBRD. The guarantee agreement is made available to the commercial banks for their information.

Sharing of Debt Service Payments The co-financing loan agreement generally provides for pro rata sharing of loan service payments received or recovered by IBRD and the commercial banks from the borrower in discharge of the borrower's obligations under the loan agreement.

Voting Arrangements Decision making is by a majority which should not be less than two-thirds of the loan outstanding (after initial drawdown) or of commitments (before initial drawdown).

Cross Default Clause The co-financing loan may be declared in default if IBRD accelerates its parallel loan(s) for the project, or if there is a material debt service failure to IBRD by the borrower or the guarantor, if any. In addition, customary cross default clauses referring to general indebtedness of the borrower (other than indebtedness of the borrower to IBRD) are included (see attached sample cross default clause). However, since the general indebtedness cross default clauses are usually much broader than would be permitted by long-standing IBRD policy, IBRD reserves the right to instruct that any acceleration of the co-financing loan based upon such broad clauses not apply to its portion of the co-financing loan.

Option to Sell Part of IBRD Participation In order to provide IBRD with additional lending resources at the earliest opportunity, provisions enable IBRD to assign (without benefit of the IBRD guarantee, if any), or to sub-participate, its portion of the co-financing loan down to a specified minimum, by first offering such assignment or sub-participation to the commercial bank participants in the loan. An assignment or sub-participation below the specified minimum requires the consent of all lenders, so as to ensure IBRD's continued involvement in the loan at a significant level (see attached sample sell down clause).

Role of IBRD and Information Sharing Provisions are included defining the role and liability of IBRD and specifying the type of information concerning the project and the borrower which IBRD will exchange with the agent bank (see attached sample IBRD clause).

SAMPLE DEBT RESCHEDULING CLAUSE

Each of the parties hereto hereby expressly acknowledges that:

(a) The terms and conditions of the Loan are substantially more beneficial to the Borrower than would have been the case had IBRD not been a party hereto; and

(b) IBRD follows a policy of not taking part in debt rescheduling agreements and, without imposing any obligation or liability on any of the parties hereto, express or implied, each of the parties hereto intends that policy to apply to the payment by the Borrower of the amounts due to the Lenders hereunder.

Accordingly, notwithstanding any other provision of this agreement, each of the parties hereto hereby agrees that none of the payment obligations of the Borrower set forth in this Agreement shall be varied or waived without the consent of IBRD, which consent may be given on such terms and conditions (including amending the sharing provisions of section _____ of this Agreement) as IBRD in its absolute discretion may consider appropriate. IBRD shall incur no liability, express or implied, with respect to the withholding or granting of such consent, nor shall any of the parties hereto take any action to compel IBRD to agree to a variation or waiver of any of the obligations of the Borrower hereunder towards IBRD.

SAMPLE CROSS DEFAULT CLAUSE

I. Inclusion of the usual language of the lead manager as regards defaults under other loan and guarantee agreements, but expressly excluding defaults and IBRD loan and guarantee agreements.

II. Inclusion of the following language relating to IBRD loan and guarantee agreements:

(a) The Borrower [or the Guarantor] shall have failed to pay any amount due, whether in respect of principal, interest, fees, charges, or otherwise and whether by scheduled maturity, by required prepayment, by acceleration, by demand or otherwise under the IBRD Loan Agreement or under any other agreement involving a borrowing from IBRD to which the Borrower [or the Guarantor] is a party; provided, however, that: (1) the failure to pay such amount shall have continued for a period of not less than forty-five consecutive days and shall be continuing; and (2) the aggregate of the amounts due and payable under such agreements shall exceed the equivalent of _____ United States dollars (US$_____);*/or

(b) The IBRD shall have declared the principal of the IBRD Loan then outstanding to be due and payable before its stated maturity.

SAMPLE SELL-DOWN CLAUSE

IBRD may, with the prior written consent of each of the other Lenders, sell, transfer or assign to any person [without benefit of the IBRD Guarantee, if any,] any of its rights and benefits hereunder — and/or grant to any person sub-participations in its share of the Loan provided that the consent of other Lenders shall not be required if:

(a) IBRD has first (i) offered to sell, transfer, or assign such rights and benefits to the other Lenders (and/or grant such sub-participations to the other Lenders) in proportion to their respective shares of the Loan, (ii) granted to the other Lenders that accept such offer an option to acquire, in proportion to their respective shares in the Loan, any of such rights and benefits (and/or such sub-participations) as were offered to the other Lenders that

* The amount to be specified shall be about 1/24th of the aggregate amount payable by the borrower (and the Guarantor) to IBRD on existing loans (including the IBRD Loan for the project being co-financed) during the calendar year of the first scheduled repayment of the IBRD Loan for the project being co-financed.

do not accept such offer and (iii) given the other Lenders at least five business days from the date such offer was made to accept such offer and exercise such option; and

(b) such sale, transfer, assignment or sub-participation by IBRD does not cause IBRD's share of the Loan to fall below _____ per cent.

SAMPLE IBRD CLAUSE

(a) The parties hereto acknowledge that IBRD is acting hereunder solely in the capacity of one of the Lenders and in no other capacity. IBRD shall incur no liability hereunder nor have any other duties or responsibilities, except to the extent expressly specified in this Agreement. Without limitation upon the foregoing, IBRD makes no representations, express or implied, with respect to, nor shall IBRD be responsible to any of the other parties hereto for:

(i) the execution, effectiveness, genuineness, validity, enforceability or sufficiency of this Agreement or of the IBRD Loan Agreement [or the IBRD Guarantee] or of any documents connected herewith or therewith or for the collectibility of any part or all of the Loan;

(ii) any representations, warranties, recitals or statements contained herein or made in any written or oral statement or in any financial or other statements, instruments or any other documents connected herewith or with the IBRD Loan Agreement [or the Guarantee] (including, without limitation, the Information Memorandum and any information referred to in subclasses (c) and (d) below), furnished or made by the Borrower, [the Guarantor,] the Agent or any Manager to any of the Banks or by IBRD to the Agents, any Manager or any of the Banks;

(iii) ascertaining or enquiring as to the performance or observance of any of the terms, conditions, provisions, covenants or agreements contained herein or in the IBRD Loan Agreement [or the IBRD Guarantee] or as to the use of the proceeds of the Loan or as to the progress of the Project;

(iv) any failure or delay in performance, or any breach, of any of the obligations of any of the other parties hereto; or

(v) any covenants given solely for the benefit of IBRD.

(b) It is understood and agreed by the Agent and each Lender and Manager that:

(i) it has made an independent credit investigation and appraisal of the Borrower and the Project on the basis of such documents and information as it has deemed appropriate and that it has entered into this Agreement on the basis of such independent appraisal; and

(ii) it shall continue to make its own credit appraisals of the Borrower and of the Project and all decisions which it might take in connection with this Agreement (whether relating to matters under consideration or decided upon by the Majority Lenders or otherwise) shall be based solely on its own independent judgment.

(c) IBRD in its capacity as the lender under the IBRD Loan Agreement shall:

(i) make available to the Agent such information received from the Borrower concerning the service of the IBRD Loan Agreement and the implementation of the Project as the Agent shall have specifically requested unless such information is, in IBRD's sole judgment, of a confidential nature; and

(ii) to the extent IBRD shall in its sole judgment consider practicable under the circumstances, afford the Agent a reasonable opportunity to exchange views prior to taking any action which may lead to [the exercise of its rights under the IBRD Guarantee,] the suspension, cancellation, or acceleration of sums owed to IBRD under the IBRD Loan Agreement or a substantial amendment of the Project; provided that nothing in this sub-clause shall in any way limit or impair the independent right of decision or action Agreement or give rise to any liability or obligation on IBRD in respect of such decision or action.

(d) IBRD and the Agent shall at any time on the request of the other:

(i) exchange views on any substantial and adverse change in the financial condition of the Borrower or in the progress or cost of the Project; and

(ii) consult with each other and with the Borrower concerning any condition which interferes or threatens to interfere with the accomplishment of the purposes of the Loan, the maintenance of the service thereof, the performance by the Borrower of its obligations under this Agreement and any remedial measures which may be necessary or appropriate under the circumstances.

(e) No information concerning the Borrower, [the Guarantor,] the IBRD Loan Agreement or the Project made available by IBRD to the Agent, any Manager or any Bank shall be disclosed to any other person except with IBRD's prior consent and IBRD shall incur no liability or obligation with respect to any such information, except for its gross negligence or wilful misconduct.

Section II: Sources of Funds
Chapter 6: National Aid

6A. Classification of Bilateral Economic Cooperation

A country's activities in the field of economic cooperation with the developing countries are usually measured in terms of monetary flow. This flow is divided into three categories.

The first is Official Development Assistance (ODA), which is assistance satisfying the following three criteria:

(1) It must be made available to developing countries or multilateral institutions by governments or governmental agencies;
(2) It must be principally intended to further the economic development and welfare of developing countries;
(3) It must be concessional in character and contain a grant element of at least 25 percent.

The second category is Other Official Flow (OOF), which comprises the following types of financial flow:

(1) Official bilateral transactions which are not sufficiently concessional (i.e., having a grant element of less than 25 percent) or which, even though they have a concessional element of 25 percent of more, are primarily export-facilitating in purpose;
(2) The net acquisition on market terms by governments and central monetary institutions of securities issued by multilateral development banks.

The third is Private Flow (PF), which includes all financial flows not coming under either ODA or OOF. Funds provided by the private sector in the form of export credits, overseas investment, etc., are included in this category.

The development cooperation usually referred to as "Aid" comes in the first category, ODA. The grant element (GE) is determined by the financial terms of a transaction: rate, maturity (interval to final repayment) and grace period (interval to first repayment of capital). As regards ODA, it is a measure of the concessionality (i.e., softness) of a loan. The extent of the benefit depends on the difference between the ODA interest rate and the market rate and the length of time the funds are available to the borrower. To calculate this benefit, the present value at the market rate of interest of each repayment is ascertained. The excess of the loan's face value over the sum of these present values, expressed as a percentage of the face value, is the "grant element" of the loan. Conventionally the market rate is take as 10 per cent.

Thus, the grant element is nil for a loan carrying an interest rate of 10 per cent; it is 100 per cent for a grant; and it lies between these two limits for a soft loan. Generally speaking, a loan will not convey a grant element of over 25 per cent if its maturity is less than 10 years, unless its interest rate is well below 5 per cent. If the face value of a loan is multiplied by its grant element, the result is referred to as the grant equivalent of that loan.

6B. Recent Aid Trends and Prospects in Historical Perspective
OECD

This chapter sets out the record of the international aid effort since 1950 in quantitative terms. It seeks to set in historical perspective the major trends in geographic and sectoral allocation and in financial terms. It concludes with a general interpretation of factors determining comparative aid levels. The emphasis is on aid from DAC countries but data are also provided for non-DAC donors. The aid and resource flow concepts used by the DAC and some of the problems of statistical measurement and comparability are set out in the annex which follows Chapter VI.

1. AID IN 1984

In 1984, Official Development Assistance (ODA) from DAC countries combined reached $28.7 billion, $1.1 billion or 4 per cent above the total for 1983. In "real terms", i.e., measured in constant prices and exchange rates, DAC ODA rose by 6 per cent, considerably above the average annual rate of increase of 4 per cent reached during the past five years. As a result of faster GNP growth, the ODA/GNP ratio remained at its 1983 level of 0.36 per cent. While the 1984 increase was above average, there has been—as will be documented below—a regular and sustained expansion of ODA from DAC countries virtually since aid figures began to be collected.

Total net ODA flows in 1984 to developing countries from all sources (DAC and non-DAC bilateral aid and net disbursements by the multilateral aid agencies) were at nearly $36 billion, an increase in real terms of 5 per cent over 1983. This was due to increases in bilateral DAC aid and to expanded disbursements by multilateral agencies, more than offsetting a further decline in OPEC aid.

The strong increase in DAC aid in 1984 was the combined result of the sustained aid expansion of the countries with upward medium-term aid plans and exceptional emergency efforts for drought-stricken countries in Africa, largely in the form of food aid. The comparative performance of individual countries in a particular year continued to be affected by the erratic timing of contributions to multilateral institutions, especially IDA.

Among DAC Members the Netherlands ranked highest in 1984 in terms of the share of its GNP devoted to aid, with an ODA/GNP ratio of 1.02 per cent. Other donors exceeding an ODA/GNP ratio of 0.7 per cent were Norway, Denmark, Sweden and France (if aid to French overseas departments and territories is included). Particularly large percentage aid increases were recorded by Italy, Japan, Finland, the Netherlands, Denmark, Austria and Canada.

More detail on 1984 volume developments and future aid volume prospects of individual Members is given below.

Net disbursements from OPEC countries fell to $4.5 billion in 1984 compared with $5.4 billion in 1983. Aid from Saudi Arabia, the fourth largest source of economic assistance to developing countries after the United States, Japan and France, declined from $3.7 billion in 1983 to $3.3 billion in 1984, but in relation to GNP remained about 3.3 per cent. Kuwait maintained its aid in 1984 at the 1983 level at $1 billion, and Kuwaiti aid remained above 3.8 per cent of GNP.

CMEA countries' net disbursements are estimated to have declined from their peak level in 1983 of $3.2 billion to $3.0 billion in 1984, of which $2.5 billion was provided by the USSR and $0.5 billion by the East European countries (mainly by the German Democratic Republic, Czechoslovakia and Bulgaria).

2. AID VOLUME TRENDS IN HISTORICAL PERSPECTIVE

Taking the period since the Second World War as a whole, it is possible to distinguish three major periods in aggregate DAC aid flows:

— A rapid building up of economic assistance during the 1950s and early 1960s, resulting from the accumulation of new and broadened development assistance efforts and strategically motivated economic aid;

— Relative stability in aggregate levels of aid from DAC countries as a group from the mid-1960s to the early 1970s, in which the downward drift of United States aid was compensated for by offsetting increases in aid from the "new donors";

— Rapid increases in DAC aid from the mid-1970s in response to new pressing developing country needs resulting from the oil price shocks, a variety of external factors including serious havest failures, the effect of world economic recession and the Africal development crises.

The Early Build-up of Economic Assistance

The immediate post-war period, extending to the early 1960s, was characterised by major increases in economic assistance to developing countries. The earliest data collected by the OEEC on a reasonably comparable basis date back to 1950-55. During this period the United States alone accounted for about half of the total economic assistance, France for about 30 per cent and the United Kingdom for over 10 per cent. These three countries together made up 90 per cent of the early assistance effort.

...Assistance from the United States during the 1950s consisted mainly of non-project assistance to a group of countries stretching from Greece to South Korea along the periphery of what was then known as the Sino-Soviet bloc. Past, or still existing, colonial relationships tended to shape the aid programmers of what were the other major donors during that period. France's aid, heavily concentrated on the former colonies in francophone Africa, included a very substantial technical assistance component in the form of teachers and administrative personnel, and support for infrastructure development and maintenance. Aid from the United Kingdom, directed towards the newly independent Commonwealth countries, consisted—in addition to technical co-operation—of substantial amounts of budget support and project aid for the public sector. This period also saw the expansion of the Netherlands' programme (in the form mainly of budget support), directed to the overseas parts of the Kingdom.

The period of the early 1960s was characterised by continued major increases in economic assistance by the three leading donors and a substantial geographic broadening of participation in assistance efforts by other industrialised countries. The United States played a unique role in launching international development assistance. During this period it was the first country without colonial relations to have a global aid programme of importance, and its initiatives were essential to the establishment and orientation of a number of multilateral and bilateral programmes. In 1960 the United States provided 58 per cent of total economic assistance to the developing countries extended by the donors subsequently grouped in the DAC. American economic aid to developing countries reached a peak during the Kennedy presidency (1961-63), although falling short of the levels reached during th Marshall Plan era. Aid to India and Pakistan expanded; development co-operation with Latin America, which had been very modest until then, was launched on a substantial scale with the "Alliance for Progress"; and aid to Africa increased. Strategically motivated assistance continued to play a significant role in United States aid but its share in the total tended to decrease in the mid-1960s as aid to Taiwan declined and that to Indochina and Korea tended to stabilize. During this period the United States was also a major donor of food aid, partly prompted by large domestic surpluses, especially in response to food crises in the South Asian subcontinent

French economic assistance climbed to a peak of close to 1.5 per cent of France's GNP in the late 1950s and early 1960s. This reflected a major effort in Algeria aimed at the establishment of economic conditions for the continued attachment of that country to France; at the turn of the decade French aid to Algeria alone accounted for 0.7 per cent of France's GNP. Although declining, aid to Algeria remained at a high level for a number of years after that country's independence as provided for by the independence agreement. It was to fall off sharply in the mid-1960s and Algeria's share in French aid was to decline from about half to about 10 per cent before the end of the decade. The remainder of France's assistance continued to be concentrated on its former colonies and on the overseas departments and territories of France. A widening of the geographic scope of French aid began with the launching of lending to other independent countries in 1960.

Aid from the United Kingdom continued to increase as lending to independent Commonwealth and other countries, first extended in 1958, expanded alongside the technical assistance programmes and capital grant aid which had characterised it until then.

The two major new aid donors after postwar reconstruction and rehabilitation were Germany and Japan. These countries joined the multilateral aid effort and established their own bilateral aid programmes in the 1950s. The rapid increase of Germany and Japan's foreign aid in the 1950s was partly due to special factors (reparation and indemnification payments, refinancing of export credits). Financing and management were still characterised by improvisation. The beginning of a comprehensive German development aid programme occurred in the early 1960s. That of Japan can be dated to the same period, reparations programmes to South-East Asian countries being accompanied by an expanding government-to-government loan programme.

The programmes of Australia and Canada, which had initially been limited to technical assistance under the Colombo Plan, also began to expand—Australia's mainly in the then dependent Papua New Guinea, and Canada's in capital

Table III-1. LONG-TERM TRENDS IN AID BY MAJOR DONORS

	Volume of ODA ($ million at 1983 prices & exch. rates)					Share in World ODA					ODA as per cent of GNP				
	1950-55	60-61	70-71	75-76	83-84	1950-55	60-61	70-71	75-76	83-84	1950-55	60-61	70-71	75-76	83-84
United States	3 961	8 689	7 045	7 037	8 236	50.2	46.3	30.8	21.7	22.2	0.32	0.56	0.31	0.26	0.24
EEC members combined[a]	3 730	6 476	7 129	8 275	11 834	47.2	34.5	31.2	25.6	31.9	0.52	0.64	0.42	0.45	0.52
EEC members (excl. DOM/TOM)	..	4 084	6 399	7 267	10 512	..	24.9	28.9	23.1	29.4	..	0.40	0.38	0.40	0.49
of which:															
France (incl. DOM/TOM)	2 325	2 827	2 450	2 659	3 939	29.4	15.0	10.7	8.2	10.6	1.24	1.35	0.66	0.62	0.75
(excl. DOM/TOM)	..	(435)[b]	1 720	1 651	2 617	..	(2.7)[b]	7.8	5.3	7.3	..	(0.21)[b]	0.46	0.38	0.51
Germany	193	1 213	1 684	2 149	3 108	2.4	6.5	7.4	6.6	8.4	0.11	0.38	0.33	0.38	0.47
United Kingdom	888	1 605	1 523	1 583	1 578	11.2	8.6	6.7	4.9	4.3	0.42	0.56	0.42	0.39	0.34
Netherlands	105	220	587	884	1 288	1.3	1.2	2.6	2.7	3.5	0.27	0.38	0.60	0.79	0.96
Italy	183	270	409	326	1 009	2.3	1.4	1.8	1.0	2.7	0.23	0.19	0.17	0.12	0.28
Belgium	36	312	295	400	474	0.5	1.7	1.3	1.2	1.3	0.11	0.82	0.48	0.55	0.58
Denmark	—	29	172	258	438	—	0.2	0.7	0.8	1.2	—	0.11	0.40	0.57	0.79
Japan	67	558	1 568	1 794	4 027	0.8	3.0	6.9	5.5	10.9	0.22	0.22	0.23	0.22	0.34
Canada	91	212	885	1 346	1 544	1.1	1.1	3.9	4.2	4.2	0.10	0.16	0.41	0.50	0.48
Sweden	12	24	277	662	748	0.2	0.1	1.2	2.0	2.0	0.04	0.06	0.41	0.82	0.82
Australia	..	257	619	665	750	..	1.4	2.7	2.1	2.0	..	0.40	0.59	0.53	0.47
Norway	6	28	114	294	576	0.1	0.1	0.5	0.9	1.6	0.04	0.13	0.33	0.68	1.06
Switzerland	8	37	119	177	315	0.1	0.2	0.5	0.5	0.9	0.02	0.06	0.13	0.19	0.31
Austria	—	6	34	92	177	—	x	0.1	0.3	0.5	—	0.02	0.07	0.17	0.26
Finland	—	3	28	65	166	—	x	0.1	0.2	0.4	—	0.02	0.09	0.17	0.34
New Zealand	—	13	37	89	60	—	0.1	0.2	0.3	0.2	—	0.12	0.23	0.47	0.26
Total DAC	7 875	16 304	17 845	20 480	28 433	99.7	86.9	78.1	63.3	76.8	0.35	0.52	0.34	0.35	0.36
Spain	..	—	15	53	109	..	—	0.1	0.2	0.3	..	—	0.02	0.04	0.07
Ireland	..	—	4	11	36	..	—	x	x	0.1	..	—	..	0.09	0.22
Luxembourg	..	—	5	5	8	..	—	x	x	x	..	—	..	0.12	0.19
Portugal[c]	22	152	176	—	—	0.3	0.8	0.8	—	—	0.30	1.70	1.05	—	—
Total OECD	7 897	16 456	18 045	20 549	28 586	100.0	87.7	79.0	63.5	77.1	0.34	0.52	0.33	0.34	0.36
OPEC countries															
Saudi Arabia	—	—	486	4 085	3 526	—	—	2.1	12.6	9.5	—	—	5.31	6.86	3.29
Kuwait	—	—	323	1 236	1 023	—	—	1.4	3.8	2.8	—	—	4.79	6.13	3.83
U.A.E.	—	—	63	1 518	411	—	—	0.3	4.7	1.1	—	—	5.36	10.32	0.81
Other	—	—	184	2 141	67	—	—	0.8	6.6	0.2	—	—	..	0.85	(0.07)
Total OPEC	—	—	1 053	8 980	5 027	—	—	4.6	27.8	13.6	—	—	0.78	2.61	0.95
CMEA countries															
USSR	..	(1 605)	2 023	1 776	2 650	..	..	8.9	5.5	7.1	..	..	0.15	0.16	0.26
GDR	..	..	110	98	(169)	..	..	0.5	0.3	0.5	..	..	0.12	0.11	0.16
Eastern Europe, other	..	(250)	457	291	(316)	..	..	2.0	0.9	0.9	..	..	0.15	0.09	0.10
Total CMEA	..	1 855	2 590	2 165	3 135	..	9.9	11.3	6.7	8.5	..	..	0.15	0.14	0.21
LDC donors[d]	..	454	1 149	649	301	..	2.4	5.0	2.0	0.8					
Total World	7 897	18 765	22 837	32 343	37 049	100.0	100.0	100.0	100.0	100.0	(0.30)	(0.41)	0.33	0.40	0.37

a) Excluding Ireland and Luxembourg.
b) In 1960-61 DOM/TOM are defined to include Algeria receiving $1 295 million at 1983 prices and exchange rates.
c) Portugal was a member of DAC up to 1974 and is now on the list of developing countries.
d) China, India, Israel, Yugoslavia.

assistance, first to the South Asian subcontinent and subsequently to Africa and the Caribbean.

The 1960s: Divergent Trends Leading to Global Aid Stagnation

The 1960s were characterised by quite heterogeneous and contradictory trends in development assistance.

The years around 1960 were a period of extraordinary activity in the new field of international co-operation: establishment of the consortia for India and Pakistan (1958, 1960), the European Development Fund and the Inter-American Development Bank (1959), IDA and the DAC—initially named the Development Assistance Group (1960). Canada (1960), Kuwait (1961), Japan (1961), the United Kingdom (1961), Denmark, Sweden and Norway (1962) created development aid authorities, and France and Germany established ministries for co-operation. In 1961 the United Nations proclaimed the 1960s as the "Development Decade". The conversion of the OEEC, the organisation co-ordinating the Marshall Plan aid, into the OECD, the Organisation for Economic Co-operation and *Development*, and the creation of the Development Assistance Group (DAG) in 1960 are symbols of this evolution. The founding members of the DAG (the name was changed to the Development Assistance Committee in 1961) were the established donors (United States, France, United Kingdom, Netherlands, Belgium and Portugal) and the new donors (Germany, Japan, Italy and Canada).

It may appear as a paradox that, in spite of the flourishing of new aid initiatives, the first "Development Decade" witnessed a levelling off and, during two years, actual declines in the aggregate level of aid from the DAC countries as a group. However, the stagnation (in inflation adjusted terms) in total DAC aid during the 1960s (the first decade of the DAC's existence) was the result of major declines in United States and French aid from exceptionally high levels, determined by special factor, along with stability of United Kingdom aid on the one hand and, on the other hand, substantial increases in economic assistance from virtually all other DAC countries.

During the latter part of the 1960s The United States Congress and public opinion became increasingly hostile to foreign assistance. The intense controversy over all aspects of the war in Vietnam, in which economic aid prominently figured, led to a lasting incrimination of the aid idea in Congress and with the liberal groups which had traditionally been supporters of generous development assistance. In addition, the United States faced growing problems of balance-of-payments and budget deficits and inflation. Reduced support for aid also was an aspect of a certain withdrawal by the United States during its preoccupation with Vietnam from its role of global political and economic leadership. Finally, the American Government's room for manoeuvre with respect to development assistance is limited—compared to other parliamentary democracies—by the constitutional separation of powers and the independence of members of Congress. The Congress took an ever more important role in determining bilateral and multilateral development assistance, often substantially reducing the President's aid budget proposals.

United States economic assistance by the early 1970s nevertheless was still roughly one-thrid of total aid to developing countries. The United States worked towards an enlarged aid effort by other donor countries and remained a major supporter of multilateral programmes. During this period United States bilateral assistance consisted of three programmes of roughly equal size, which were in a process of transition: bilateral development assistance, which was increasingly moving away from large-scale non-project lending towards poverty-oriented project assistance (a tendency which was strongly accentuated in 1973 by the enactment of legislation oriented towards basic human needs); security-related aid in the form of commodity import support given, until 1976, primarily to Vietnam; and food aid, frequently for balance-of-payments support.

As already noted, French aid declined substantially in the first half of the 1960s both in real terms and as a proportion of GNP due to the sharp falling-off in aid to Algeria following that country's independence (by mid-decade aid to Algeria amounted to less than one-thrid of what it had been at the beginning of the 1960s). A moderate up-turn in real terms began in the second half of the decade because of a rapid expansion in disbursements to the DOM/TOM and a more modest increase in aid to independent countries. By the end of the decade France's aid programme, the second largest in the DAC, had acquired the features which were to characterise it in the 1970s: a marked concentration on Africa at a fairly stable volume, a substantial allocation to its DOM/TOM, and a heavy emhasis on technical co-operation.

The 1960s saw aid from the United Kingdom decline at a moderate rate in real terms and rather more rapidly as a proportion of GNP. As a result, the United Kingdom was overtaken during the decade first by Germany and then by Japan as a source of ODA. Throughout this period no significant changes took place in the geographic distribution of British aid, which remained heavily concentrated on Commonwealth countries, while the share of multilateral contributions in total ODA began to increase.

For many other DAC countries the 1960s were a period of substantial expansion in their aid programmes. Two previously smaller donors, Germany and Japan, had by the early 1970s become major contributors to the international assistance effort. In the case of Germany, which had become the third largest donor (in dollar terms) among DAC countries during these years, growth reflected in part increased participation in multilateral efforts as well as a general expansion of bilateral aid as the programme assum-

122 International Borrowing

ed a more global character. The expansion of Japan's aid, on the other hand, was largely the result of a continued increase in lending, primarily to Asian countries.

The most striking development of this period was the rapid expansion of aid from the Nordic countries and the Netherlands, which was sustained during the 1970s (see following section).

Aid from Canada continued to increase at a sustained pace. Aid from Australia also expanded but tended to level off towards the end of the decade, remaining at a relatively high level as a proportion of GNP. Belgium's aid, which had reached a peak at the time of Zaire's independence, tended to decline slightly in real terms, remaining nonetheless substantially above the DAC average. The much more modest aid programme of Switzerland recorded steady progress throughout the decade.

Responsiveness to New Needs of Developing Countries

From the early 1970s developing countries were facing major economic and financial problems resulting from oil price rises and subsequent world economic recession. The Sahel countries suffered from a series of drought years of catastrophic proportion. In addition, there was a growing awareness that progress in reducing mass poverty and in fulfilling basic human needs had been inadequate and that a major new attack on these problems was required. An intense international debate on aid requirements had led to the adoption by the United Nations in 1970 of the 0.7 per cent target. (See "Origin and Evolution of the International Aid and Resource Flow Targets" below.) The United Nations also identified a group of "least developed countries" as priority cases for international co-operation.

DAC Members responded to the new needs of the developing countries with substantial increases in aid. Between 1970-71 and 1983-84 total DAC ODA grew in real terms at an average annual rate of 3.5 percent, raising the level of aid (in 1983 prices and exchange rates) from nearly $18 to over $28 billion. Because of relatively fast GNP growth over the same period, there was only a limited increase in the aggregate DAC ODA/GNP ratio.

Table III-2 sets out average annual growth rates for individual DAC Members in 1970/71-1983/84 and in the latest five-year period.

The group of Nordic countries achieved very fast rates of growth during the 1970s (9.5 per cent per annum as a group during the reference period) and three—Denmark, Norway, and Sweden—first reached, and then substantially surpassed, the 0.7 per cent target.

These three countries had set themselves ambitious budgetary targets in the late 1960s (Denmark in 1967, Norway and Sweden in 1968) which were in some cases revised upwards subsequently. Sweden achieved the 0.7 per cent target in 1974, Norway in 1976 and Denmark in 1978. As their aid budgets were growing faster than their aid administrative capacities, the Nordic countries became major contributors to the multilateral programmes, mainly those of

Table III-2. RECENT GROWTH RATES IN AID VOLUME BY DAC DONORS

Percentages

	Annual average growth rates		Contribution to DAC aid growth	
	1978/79-1983/84	1970/71-1983/84	1978/79-1983/84	1970/71-1983/84
Australia	0.2	1.5	0.2	1.2
Austria	4.8	13.5	0.7	1.3
Belgium	1.2	3.7	0.5	1.7
Canada	0.8	4.4	1.2	6.2
Denmark	3.7	7.5	1.4	2.5
Finland	16.5	14.6	1.7	1.3
France incl. DOM/TOM	6.9	3.7	21.7	14.1
France excl. DOM/TOM	9.3	4.1	20.0	5.1
Germany	3.9	4.8	10.5	13.5
Italy	21.8	7.2	12.3	5.7
Japan	10.5	7.5	30.8	23.2
Netherlands	2.6	6.2	3.0	6.6
New Zealand	-1.4	3.9	x	0.2
Norway	5.2	13.3	2.5	4.3
Sweden	-0.3	8.0	-0.2	4.5
Switzerland	10.4	7.8	2.4	1.9
United Kingdom	-6.1	0.3	-11.3	0.5
United States	3.1	1.2	22.6	11.3
DAC Total	4.1	3.6	100.0	100.0

the United Nations. They concentrated most of their bilateral aid on the poorest countries.

The Netherlands also became one of the DAC "frontrunner" countries. Historical links with Indonesia and the overseas parts of the Kingdom played a part in launching the effort, but there was strong support also for the multilateral programmes and aid for the poorest countries.

Other countries with very fast aid expansion during the 1970s and early 1980s include Japan and Italy. The expansion of Japan's ODA (which grew by $2 billion over this period) was the result of political decisions to increase aid by means of two successive medium-term plans. The first, which aimed at doubling ODA in dollars between 1977 and 1980, was exceeded by a substantial margin; the second (1981-85), aiming at doubling in dollars the amounts disbursed during the previous five years, brought Japan to second position in absolute volume among all aid donors.

In Italy, strong parliamentary and public concern with hunger and malnutrition in the developing countries was instrumental in leading to the adoption at the turn of the decade of successive three-year plans for increasing aid. As a result, aid appropriations grew by some 80 per cent in real terms from 1981 to 1985 and a comprehensive development programme came into being in a short period of time. Total aid appropriations in 1985 were nearly $2 billion.

Substantial increases also took place in the aid programmes of France and Germany. French aid, which had tended to remain relatively stable for much of the 1970s, began to expand rapidly at the end of the decade and in the early 1980s as bilateral lending and multilateral contributions increased substantially. The decision taken in 1981 to raise ODA to independent countries to 0.7 per cent of GNP in 1988 (while continuing to assist the DOM/TOM) gave further impetus to the growth of French aid, and in particular to ODA to independent countries—which is the fourth largest among DAC countries in dollar terms and substantially exceeds the DAC average. Total French aid (including the DOM/TOM) increased somewhat more slowly in real terms but has exceeded 0.7 per cent of GNP in every year since 1981.

German aid, which had shown no clear upward trend in relation to GNP during the period 1970-77, began to expand rapidly in 1978 following a substantial increase in the planned growth rates of the medium-term assistance plan. Although growth rates were significantly reduced in subsequent plans, ODA in real terms expanded by an annual average of 8 per cent during the 1977-83 period and the ODA/GNP ratio rose from 0.33 to 0.48 per cent. In 1984, however, the Government's current policy of public expenditure restraint began to affect ODA disbursements, which declined to 0.45 per cent of GNP. Although aid has been accorded priority in the Federal Budget, the envisaged annual growth rate for aid in the present aid budget plan of about 3.5 per cent may be sufficient only to maintain the future volume of aid in real terms.

The United States remained the largest DAC donor country and its share in total DAC ODA, which had fallen from about one-third in 1970-71 to one-fifth in 1975-76, has remained roughly constant since then as aid grew modestly in real terms and tended to decline as a proportion of GNP. United States aid grew substantially in 1984-85 inter alia in response to the African food crisis. During the 1970s the geographic distribution of United States aid underwent marked changes. The end of the war in Vietnam and of United States aid programmes there in 1975 was soon followed by a marked upsurge in aid to Israel and Egypt in connection with United States efforts to promote an Arab-Israeli peace settlement. Aid to these two countries rapidly exceeded the peak amounts received by Vietnam and continued at these high levels. The Reagan administration sharply increased aid to the Caribbean and Central American regions as part of an increasing concentration of aid to countries of strategic and political interest to the United States. A concomitant of this trend was a stronger preference for bilateral over multilateral aid channels.

The United Kingdom's ODA in 1983-84 was in real terms only slightly higher than it had been in 1970. This reflected a gradual decline in real terms which set in early in the 1980s as part of a general policy of budgetary restraint and which had the effect of erasing the modest gains of the 1970s.

Aid from the other DAC countries grew in real terms during the 1970s and early 1980s, but growth was on the whole slower and more irregular than in the case of the more rapidly expanding programmes cited earlier. Australia, Belgium and Canada maintained their aid substantially above the average ODA/GNP ratios of DAC Members. Australia's and, to a lesser extent, Belgium's ODA have recorded more or less regular fluctuations around a modest upward trend; Canada's ODA, on the other hand, expanded rapidly until the second half of the 1970s, falling off in the latter part of the decade and recently showing a rising trend. In contrast, aid from Finland during the period 1970/71-1983/84 grew at a rate of almost 15 per cent per annum, the most rapid rate of growth among DAC countries. Aid from Austria and Switzerland has also expanded at a relatively sustained pace, but has not so far enabled either country to reach the DAC average ODA/GNP ratio....

3. FINANCIAL TERMS OF AID

Most Official Development Assistance by DAC Members is given at highly concessional terms. The average grant element of current DAC ODA exceeds 90 per cent. (For an explanation of the grant element concept see "The ODA and Resource Flow Concepts—Problems of Definition and Measurement" at the end of Part 2 of this Report.) About 80 per cent of all DAC ODA is in the form of outright grants. The average loan terms for DAC bilateral lending as a whole are roughly 3 per cent interest rate, 28 years maturity, of which an eight-year grace period, corresponding to an average grant element of close to 60 per cent.

Current terms performance of individual DAC Members is set out in Table III-4. ODA terms have improved over the years. In 1965-66, the first years for which the average grant element was calculated, it was considerably lower at 84 per cent. Trends in financial terms by individual DAC Members are shown in Table III-3.

Financial aid terms have been a major subject of DAC concern since its inception. The Committee has adopted a series of Terms Recommendations, starting in 1963, which dealt with terms in general and the criteria for "appropriate terms" for individual categories of developing countries.

Financial terms are one of the few areas in which the DAC has established quantitative norms. The Recommendation on Terms and Conditions of Aid currently in force is the one of 1972, slightly amended in 1978. The Recommendation comprises a single target for financial terms: at least 86 per cent grant element for each Member's total annual ODA programme. The Recommendation includes a special sub-target for the least developed countries (LLDCs): as a minimum, ODA commitments to the group of LLDCs by each DAC Member must have 90 per cent grant element annually, or 86 per cent grant element on a three-year average of aid committed to each of the LLDCs. In 1984 Austria, Germany and Japan failed to reach the concessionality target of 86 per cent. New Zealand and the United States as well as, exceptionally for 1984, Switzerland (as a result of erratic timing of multilateral contributions) and Austria (due to an unusual drop in official loan commitments) failed the "volume test" of the DAC Terms Recommendations because their ODA volume as a share of GNP was significantly below the DAC average. France and Japan failed to meet the sub-target for the least developed countries. Italy has not adhered to the current DAC Terms Recommendation. At the DAC Aid Review of Italy in May 1985, however, the Italian Delegation reported recent decisions to soften the terms of Italian aid loans and to increase the proportion of grants in aid to lower-income countries. Consequently, the Italian authorities except that all Italian aid soon will be in compliance with the DAC Recommendation, including aid to the least developed countries.

While setting quantitative norms for the average concessionality of aid programmes, the DAC Terms Recommendation also stresses the need to relate the terms of aid on a case-by-case basis to the circumstances of each developing country, taking into account such factors as the current position and prospects in income levels, development performance, balance-of-payments and debt burden. The Recommendation also exhorts Members to make concerted efforts to harmonize terms at the level of the recipient country. They should make use of consortia, consultative groups or other

Table III-3. FINANCIAL TERMS OF ODA COMMITMENTS OF DAC MEMBERS

	Grant element of total ODA (norm: 86%)[a]					Grant element of ODA to LLDC's (norm: 90%)[b]		
	1965-66	1970-71	1975-76	1980-81	1983-84	1975-76	1980-81	1983-84
Australia	100.0	95.5	100.0	100.0	100.0	100.0	100.0	100.0
Austria	38.0	67.0	95.0	61.4	69.0	89.5	93.6	99.7
Belgium	97.8	97.0	97.8	97.9	97.6	98.9	98.3	98.5
Canada	96.7	93.8	96.9	97.6	98.9	97.7	100.0	100.0
Denmark	83.6	94.7	96.3	96.6	97.2	91.4	94.1	99.7
Finland	..	85.1	91.2	96.5	97.2	86.3	97.5	100.0
France	87.7	83.7	90.9	89.9	88.9	96.4	83.9	(79.6)
Germany	67.7	82.1	87.6	86.7	86.5	90.1	98.9	99.5
Italy	49.6	56.5	97.8	94.0	90.9	100.0	60.3	84.4
Japan	55.4	67.6	72.6	74.7	76.8	78.1	82.7	88.0
Netherlands	86.5	86.0	89.3	93.0	94.2	94.5	99.0	99.5
New Zealand	..	95.0	98.3	100.0	100.0	100.0	100.0	100.0
Norway	99.0	99.4	100.0	99.8	98.8	100.0	100.0	98.8
Sweden	92.6	95.6	99.6	99.4	99.9	100.0	100.0	100.0
Switzerland	78.8	92.4	92.5	97.0	98.4	93.9	100.0	100.0
United Kingdom	79.6	80.9	97.4	96.8	98.9	99.3	99.8	100.0
United States	88.3	84.6	86.1	92.4	94.2	81.2	95.6	97.1
Total DAC countries	84.0	83.1	89.3	89.7	90.7	91.3	94.1	(94.4)

a) Excluding debt reorganisation.
b) 36 least-developed countries as presently defined by the United Nations.
c) 1971-1972.

Table III.4. DAC MEMBERS' COMPLIANCE WITH THE 1978 DAC TERMS RECOMMENDATION IN 1983 AND 1984

Countries	ODA commitments[a] $ million 1983	ODA commitments[a] $ million 1984	Grant element of ODA commitments (Norm: 86 per cent) 1983	Grant element of ODA commitments (Norm: 86 per cent) 1984	Volume test: ODA commitments as per cent of GNP[b] 1983	Volume test: ODA commitments as per cent of GNP[b] 1984	Grant element of ODA commitments to LLDC's Annually to all LLDC's (Norm: 90 per cent) 1983	Grant element of ODA commitments to LLDC's Annually to all LLDC's (Norm: 90 per cent) 1984	Grant element of ODA commitments to LLDC's 3 year average to each LLDC (Norm: 86 per cent) 1983	Grant element of ODA commitments to LLDC's 3 year average to each LLDC (Norm: 86 per cent) 1984
Australia	736	927	100.0	100.0	0.48	0.55	100.0	100.0	c	c
Austria	231	139	61.1	82.1	0.34	0.22	99.4	100.0	c	c
Belgium	569	(433)	97.3	(98.1)	0.70	(0.56)	98.2	98.8	c	c
Canada	1 739	2 279	99.3	98.6	0.55	0.70	100.0	100.0	c	c
Denmark	427	483	96.4	98.0	0.79	0.92	99.1	100.0	c	c
Finland	167	265	99.7	95.6	0.35	0.54	100.0	100.0	c	c
France	5 061	4 330	89.3	(88.4)	0.98	0.88	79.5	(79.7)	–	–
Germany	3 132	3 797	88.8	84.6	0.48	0.62	98.9	100.0	c	c
Italy[d]	1 784	2 007	90.7	91.2	0.51	0.58	89.4	79.6	–	–
Japan	5 364	5 231	79.8	73.7	0.46	0.42	87.3	88.6	–	–
Netherlands	1 225	1 273	95.1	93.4	0.93	1.03	99.0	100.0	c	c
New Zealand	51	53	100.0	100.0	0.23	0.24	100.0	100.0	c	c
Norway	532	641	98.1	99.4	1.00	1.21	99.9	97.9	c	c
Sweden	734	792	99.8	100.0	0.82	0.86	100.0	100.0	c	c
Switzerland	398	261	98.5	98.1	0.39	0.27	100.0	100.0	c	c
United Kingdom	1 612	1 616	98.3	(99.4)	0.35	0.38	100.0	100.0	c	c
United States	9 430	10 434	94.7	93.7	0.28	0.28	96.2	97.8	c	c
Total DAC countries	33 192	34 961	91.3	90.0	0.44	0.44	94.3	94.4	–	–

a) Excluding debt reorganisation.
b) Norm for 1984 = 0.33.
c) Compliance.
d) Italy has not subscribed to the DAC Terms Recommendation, and the figures shown are for information only.

Table III-5. DAC MEMBERS' ODA TERMS PARAMETERS[a] IN 1983 AND 1984

Countries	Grants as a share of ODA commitments[b] % 1983	1984	ODA loan terms Interest rate % 1983	1984	Maturity (years) 1983	1984	Grace period (years) 1983	1984
Australia	100.0	100.0	n.a.	n.a.	n.a.	n.a.	n.a.	n.a.
Austria	42.2	74.5	5.0	4.3	12.1	16.8	6.3	6.7
Belgium	84.9	(89.0)	0.4	0.3	30.0	30.0	10.0	10.0
Canada	92.4	85.3	0.0	0.0	50.0	50.0	10.0	10.0
Denmark	81.6	88.2	0.0	0.0	30.8	31.6	8.3	9.3
Finland	99.6	85.7	4.0	0.8	10.0	24.5	2.0	7.4
France	79.4	76.7	3.5	3.1	22.7	23.0	8.2	8.2
Germany	71.1	63.7	2.2	2.8	35.0	36.8	6.7	5.7
Italy	84.1	83.7	2.3	2.5	15.7	16.3	2.7	4.9
Japan	55.4	46.1	3.2	3.4	27.8	26.7	8.7	8.6
Netherlands	87.4	83.2	2.5	2.5	29.0	30.1	7.9	8.0
New Zealand	100.0	100.0	n.a.	n.a.	n.a.	n.a.	n.a.	n.a.
Norway	97.4	99.2	3.8	3.9	11.6	13.9	3.5	6.3
Sweden	99.6	100.0	2.0	n.a.	25.0	n.a.	10.0	n.a.
Switzerland	94.2	90.2	0.3	0.0	22.6	22.3	10.1	12.8
United Kingdom	97.0	98.5	3.7	1.4	23.4	20.3	5.6	6.3
United States	85.8	82.5	3.0	2.8	32.5	34.6	9.4	10.0
Total DAC countries	80.0	76.8	2.9	2.9	28.5	30.4	8.2	8.2

a) Excluding debt reorganisation.
b) Including grants and capital subscriptions to multilateral agencies, which have been subject to fluctuations as explained in Chapter IV of the Report.

concerted aid operations, where these exist, in co-operation as appropriate with the international bodies involved, in order to reach a common view as to the appropriate terms at which assistance should be provided to a particular country.

The original and continuing preoccupation of the DAC with financial terms was prompted by two factors. The first was concern with the debt-servicing burden resulting from hard loan terms of official bilateral flows (this category, including official export credits, was the basis of the first Terms Recommendations) for aid recipients which are primarily low-income countries. It must be remembered that during the early 1960s official bilateral flows constituted over 60 per cent of developing countries' total external financing, compared to only somewhat over a quarter now. The second factor concerned burden-sharing problems arising from marked differences in financial aid terms among donors.

Countries which initially extended their aid on relatively hard average terms included Austria, Italy, Japan and Germany, and to a lesser extent Switzerland and the United Kingdom.

The first DAC Chairman's Report, published in 1962, had the following observation:

The significant differences in the terms on which contributions are made available by the various DAC countries greatly affect their real contribution to development. The variations arise from the particular purposes for which public funds are made available to developing countries, ranging from budgetary support through social and economic infrastructure investment to profit-making projects in manufacturing industry. They also stem from the unequal economic and financial capability of the various DAC countries as well as from differences in the judgment of governments about the appropriateness of the terms from the point of view of the efficacy of the contributions.

A few countries, in particular Germany and the United Kingdom, have raised objections of principle against soft loans, especially with respect to interest rates. The German Government feels that loans at soft terms may impair the role of private capital, distort competitive positions and weaken the function of interest rates in allocating scarce capital among competing uses. Care must be taken, in the view of the German Government, to ensure that the granting of loans at soft terms does not constitute a substitute for monetary and financial discipline on the part of the recipient countries. The United Kingdom Government generally makes loans at the rate at which it can borrow plus a small management charge. It is concerned, in addition, that lending at soft rates might have repercussions on the terms of treasury lending to domestic borrowers, such as the nationalised industries.

Such objections of principle have given way over the years to recognition of the weak debt-servicing capapcity of many of the major recipients of aid. Considerable efforts have been made by all DAC Members to improve their aid terms. The only two countries which still have relatively hard terms are Austria and, to a lesser degree, Japan. This is the result of both a relatively small component of grants and less concessional loan terms. The relative hardness of the aid terms of some donor governments is related to the fact that, because of budgetary constraints, they still use capital market resources for aid financing, a practice abandoned by most other donor countries, which finance the bulk of their aid out of current budgets.

Current debt problems of developing countries are primarily the result of heavy borrowing at commercial terms rather than because of onerous ODA terms. For the least developed countries the debt burden of outstanding ODA debt has been further reduced. By the "Retroactive Terms Adjustment (RTA)" agreed at UNCTAD in 1978, DAC Member countries undertook to improve the ODA net flow to poorer developing countries, particularly the least developed countries, by adjusting the terms of past ODA, or through other equivalent measures, to bring them into line with the then prevailing softer ODA terms. Implementation of this Resolution has covered some $6 billion debt to the benefit of more than 45 countries. Over $3 billion of this debt was cancelled. Nearly all DAC creditors particiated in this action, though to differing degrees. Nevertheless, for low-income countries ODA from all sources still represented in 1984 53 per cent of their total long-term debt and about 24 per cent of their debt service; for the least developed coutnries the respective ratios were 66 and 44 per cent.

4. MAIN USES OF AID BY ECONOMIC AND SOCIAL SECTOR AND TYPES OF ASSISTANCE

Table III-6 gives a summary view of the major current uses of economic assistance. The data are shown separately for DAC bilateral official development assistance and for contributions from multilateral institutions. These latter are on the basis of "official development finance", i.e., they include not only concessional aid but also lending at market terms. (About 60 per cent of multilateral official development finance is at market terms.)

Almost half of total assistance is devoted to the long-term effort to build the basic development potential of developing countries. This is directed both at developing their human resources potential and at creating the required physical infrastructure. About 20 per cent of total aid is devoted to developing the basic social infrastructure and related services. Within the social infrastructure complex, a major effort is made to develop and maintain the educational systems of de-

Table III-6. THE MAJOR USES OF OFFICIAL DEVELOPMENT FINANCE

Percentages 1982/83 averages commitments

	Bilateral DAC ODA	Multilateral Finance[a]	Total
Social infrastructure and services	22.1	15.9	19.3
Education	12.0	5.1	8.8
Health	5.8	0.9	3.6
Other including water supply and sanitation and public administration	4.7	9.9	6.9
Economic infrastructure and services	21.3	33.3	26.8
Transport and communications	10.9	13.2	12.0
Energy	10.4	20.1	14.8
Production sectors	27.2	36.8	31.6
Agriculture	12.1	23.0	17.1
River development and other multisector	7.1	1.2	4.4
Industry and other productive sectors	8.0	12.6	10.2
Non-project assistance	20.4	14.0	17.3
Financial assistance	12.5	8.9	10.7
Debt relief	1.0	–	0.5
Food aid	6.9	5.1	6.1
Aid through NGOs	5.3	–	2.9
Administrative expenses	3.7	n.a.	2.1
Total	100.0	100.0	100.0
of which: Technical assistance	30.0		
Students and trainees	4.1		
Other technical assistance provided in donor country	2.6		
Experts (and related equipment)	19.5		
Other, including research	3.8		

a) Excluding UN agencies with the exception of WFP, but including non-concessional development finance.

veloping countries. About 9 per cent of total aid is devoted to this purpose. This includes substantial expenditures on student and trainee fellowships for study in the donor countries shown separately under technical assistance. Health is both a social service and an important aspect of human resources development. Other activities in the broad category of social infrastructure and services include water supply and sanitation, public administration, housing, community development and environmental protection. A substantial part of aid channelled through NGOs is used for human resources development. (See Chapter V.) Most of this effort is directed to the countries which still have the longest way to go in human resources development.

Building the basic economic infrastructure has always been a major field of economic assistance. Transport (including roads), communications and energy supply systems have been the sectoral fields of some 27 per cent of economic assistance. Aid for energy has been given increased priority since the oil price rises in the early 1970s and its share in total assistance has tended to increase.

Roughly one-third of total assistance is allocated to the development of the directly productive sectors: agriculture, manufacturing, mining, tourism, banking and other services. Agriculture has been the largest of these sectoral fields. (A special section of this Report, in Chapter IX, is devoted to a more detailed description of trends and issues in aid for agricultural and rural development.) Including the development of large river basins and other multi-purpose projects which usually also have an important basic infrastructure component which cannot be separately identified (energy and transport), agricultural development accounts for over 20 per cent of total assistance, i.e., twice as much as industry and other productive sectors together. Aid to agriculture has been one of the fastest growing categories of aid in the past decade.

A substantial part of aid has gone into general development support, including various types of non-project assistance, e.g., policy-related programme assistance, aid to finance current imports and budget support. A number of developing countries are in a position of administrative strength where the choice and implementation of projects can be left to them. Or they have already a substantial industrial base themselves and need current supplies for producing capital equipment, etc. In many other cases the provision of current supplies may be a very effective form of aid, especially assistance given to support sectoral recovery and broader adjustment and reform programmes.

Donors also face many situations, however, calling urgently for current sustenance aid. Most evident is urgent relief of famine, drought, other natural catastrophes, and the needs of refugees. A major part of, although by no means all, food aid is used for these purposes.

Finally, as has been remarked in other connections, substantial economic assistance is granted to help countries in carrying special burdens arising from political stability and security problems.

Some of the individual country patterns which stand out include:

— The large share of French aid devoted to "social infrastructure and services", including education and health;
— The large share of economic infrastructure (including transport and communications and energy) in the aid programmes of Germany, Japan, the Netherlands, the United Kingdom and Austria;
— The relatively large share of aid devoted to agricultural development by the Nordic countries, Canada, the Netherlands, New Zealand and Switzerland;
— Above the DAC average shares of aid for industrial development in the case of Germany, Japan and Sweden;
— The relatively large share of financial non-project assistance in the programmes of the United States, Australia (mainly to Papua New Guinea) and Sweden and Denmark, the latter two countries having traditionally followed very flexible aid approaches;
— The predominance of the United States, the EEC, Australia, Canada and Japan in the provision of food aid.

5. AID FROM NON-DAC DONORS

The bulk of international economic assistance has always come from Members of the DAC, which groups together the major industrial nations, but other countries are also significant sources of aid. These are the Arab/OPEC countries, the communist countries grouped in the Council for Mutual Economic Assistance (CMEA), OECD countries which are not members of the DAC (Iceland, Ireland, Luxembourg, Portugal and Spain), and a number of developing countries. The relative importance of the contributions from these sources and their evolution appears in Table III.1. Currently non-DAC countries account for about one quarter of total economic assistance to developing countries, of whcih the OPEC countries contribute some 12 per cent and the CMEA countries 8 per cent.

The quantitative role of non-DAC economic assistance has varied over time. It peaked in 1975 and again in 1980 due mainly to rapid growth of OPEC aid—in particular from the Gulf States—after the oil price rises. The subsequent decline has followed the fall in OPEC governments' oil revenues.

OPEC aid has many features in common with DAC aid, and DAC and OPEC aid agencies have met informally since 1978 to discuss the scope for expanded cofinancing and other matters of common interest. OPEC countries are also significant contributors to the multilateral development programmes. On the other hand, and understandably, their aid is much more concentrated geographically.

CMEA aid has remained small in absolute terms and in relation to GNP. The bulk of it is concentrated on the less developed communist countries, especially Vietnam, Cuba and Mongolia. Other significant recipients include Afghanistan, Kampuchea and India. The CMEA countries are not contributors to the major multilateral development programmes (with the exception of small non-convertible contributions to the UNDP and some other UN agencies) and there are no arrangements for co-ordinating CMEA aid with other international assistance sources.

The main features of non-DAC aid are summarised below by donor groups. It must be emphasized that the data shown for non-DAC aid sources are not, in most cases, based on reporting comparable to that of DAC countries. Reference is made to the more important problems of assessment and comparability below.

Aid from Non-DAC OECD Countries

Five OECD countries which are not Members of the Committee provide aid. They are Spain, Ireland, Portugal, Luxembourg and Iceland. They contribute to multilateral agencies and also have set up their own programmes of technical and financial assistance. Spain's aid is by far the largest, running in 1984 at $144 million or 0.10 per cent of its GNP. Bilateral Spanish aid goes mainly to Latin American and North African countries and to Equatorial Guinea. Spain is followed by Ireland, at $35 million or 0.22 per cent of its GNP. Irish bilateral aid, which consists exclusively of grants, goes mainly to four countries: Lesotho, Sudan, Tanzania and Zambia. Figures for current aid from Portugal are not available (but see Table III.1 for Portugal's earlier aid performance). Luxembourg's development assistance programme amounts to 0.2 per cent of GNP. Multilateral aid is directed mainly through the EEC/EDF. Bilateral aid is focused on a number of least developed countries (e.g., Rwanda, Burundi, Togo) and is untied. Iceland has a small development assistance programme running at about 0.1 per cent of its GNP. The main bilateral project has been a fisheries programme in Cape Verde.

Aid from Arab/OPEC Countries

A detailed description of Arab/OPEC aid programmes was published by the OECD in 1983 under the title "Aid from OPEC Countries".

In the early 1970s, when the OECD began to assemble data on OPEC aid trends, annual economic assistance from OPEC countries to developing countries was running at some $1 billion (in 1983 prices and exchange rates). The main donors were Saudi Arabia and Kuwait; their aid efforts corresponded to an aid/GNP ratio of the order of 5 per cent (see Table III-1) and were largely cash transfers to less advantaged and more populous Arab neighbours—Egypt, Jordan and Syria—and project aid from the Kuwait Fund.

After the major increases in oil prices and oil revenues in 1973-74 these two countries very substantially increased their economic assistance. Other OPEC countries, notably the United Arab Emirates and Iran, also joined the expanded aid effort. As a result OPEC aid in 1975 exceeded $9 billion (measured in 1983 prices and exchange rates).

OPEC aid reached another peak of over $9 billion in 1980 and has subsequently declined to a level of $5 billion in 1983-84. For Saudi Arabia and Kuwait it is still at a level of 3 to 4 per cent of their GNP.

The decline of OPEC aid in recent years can be attributed to such factors as the war between Iraq and Iran, which led to the virtual disappearance of the aid programmes of these two countries, and the decline in oil revenue, which resulted in a sharp reduction in the surplus and finally a deficit in the balance of payments of OPEC countries. Only Kuwait and Saudi Arabia remained important donors. Together they provided over 90 per cent of OPEC aid in 1984. The present situation, therefore, resembles the one prevailing before 1973 when the same two countries and Libya accounted for the bulk of Arab/OPEC aid.

A particularly useful element of economic assistance from Arab/OPEC countries is their contribution to multilateral institutions. Arab/OPEC country contributions to worldwide multilateral institutions, such as the World Bank family, UNDP and other UN programmes, IFAD (established at the initiative of OPEC countries) and the regional development banks in 1983-84 were $0.5 billion. For Saudi Arabia and Kuwait contributions to these programmes account for 7.5 and 8 per cent respectively of their total aid and for 0.25 and 0.31 per cent of their GNP (1983-84 average). The corresponding figures for DAC countries are $9.0 billion and 0.11 per cent of GNP.

The Arab/OPEC countries have also established their own multilateral institutions. These are (figures in brackets are average annual net disbursements and commitments respectively in 1983-84):

— The Islamic Development Bank ($135 million and $708 million);
— The OPEC Fund for International Development ($130 million and $158 million);
— The Arab Fund for Economic and Social Development ($69 million and $306 million);
— The Arab Bank for Economic Development in Africa ($28 million and $69 million).

Bilateral assistance from OPEC countries consists essentially of the operations of the national development funds, such as the Kuwait Fund, the Saudi Fund for Development and the Abu Dhabi Fund, and large amounts of non-project assistance extended directly by the finance ministries, the main source being Saudi Arabia. Of current bilateral Arab/OPEC assistance of $4 billion, $0.6 billion is project assistance extended through the development funds. Transport, storage and communications have been the leading sectors, followed by energy. More recently agricultural development has become a priority sector and, consequently, is receiving increased attention.

Bilateral Arab/OPEC aid is geographically highly concentrated, as emerges from Table III-7.

Aid by Developing Countries

Over the years an increasing number of developing countries have been extending some kind of development assistance, mainly in the form of technical assistance, food aid or emergency assistance. Some countries, such as Argentina, Brazil, China, India and Yugoslavia, have also extended development loans and grants and/or official export credits. Financial assistance from Argentina and Brazil has mainly been in the form of export credits, frequently at non-concessional terms.

India has been a source of technical and financial assistance now for three decades. Technical assistance was first provided under the Colombo Plan. In 1964 India initiated the Indian Technical Co-operation Programme, thus expanding its activities to a larger number of countries in Asia, Africa and Latin America. India also contributed to the Commonwealth Fund for Technical Co-operation and the Special Commonwealth African Assistance Programme. During 1981-83 about 900 students and 600 trainees were financed on average. India has been providing on average $100 million annually in development assistance, of which 60 per cent is in the form of grants, mainly to the neighbouring countries of Bhutan, Bangladesh and Nepal, followed by Vietnam and Sri Lanka.

China has provided the largest amounts of financial and technical assistance among the developing countries over the past thirty years, but the volume of its aid has been characterised by wide fluctuations. New disbursements, which had exceeded $1 billion in 1971 (in 1983 prices and exchange rates) following large commitments in 1970 to Pakistan, Tanzania and Zambia, declined to below $150 million in 1983, but were again on the increase in 1984 as a result of China's renewed interest in Sub-Saharan Africa. Following the change in government in 1978 there has been a profound reorganization of the Chinese aid programme, involving a reduction of the scale of individual projects and a more commercially oriented policy. The sectoral distribution has largely remained unchanged with emphasis being placed on agriculture, followed by transport and the health sector. The Chinese aid programme has usually been appreciated by the recipient countries, in particular the poorer countries in Sub-Saharan Africa, because its technologies were adapted to the needs of those countries, particularly in the field of small-scale industries, agriculture and health.

Yugoslavia's technical assistance programme dates back to 1954 and was complemented in 1975 by a "Solidarity Fund for Developing Countries", which finances scientific co-operation, preinvestment and feasibility studies and emergency assistance. Assistance has been extended in the form of loans at concessional terms or in grants. Disbursements peaked in 1976 at over $30 million but declined to just over $20 million in 1982, the last year for which data are available. There was also a sharp decline in the number of experts in recent years. Developing countries also make contributions to multilateral institutions, in particular the UNDP and some other UN organisations as well as the regional financial institutions.

Table III-7. MAIN RECIPIENTS OF BILATERAL ARAB/OPEC AID IN 1983-84

$ million

	Gross disbursements	
	1983	1984
Syria	922	834
Jordan	703	613
Bahrain	155	208
Yemen	201	183
Sudan	361	118
Other Arab countries	440	259
Kenya	7	53
Senegal	48	25
Tanzania	44	12
Other Non-Arab Africa	216	217
Bangladesh	114	28
Other Asia	224	237
America, Europe, Oceania	66	61
Unallocated[a]	1 369	1 392

a) Largely treasury grants and loans from Saudi Arabia, for which no breakdown is available.

While only two developing countries had contributed to the fourth and fifth IDA replenishments ($6 million and $9 million respectively) there were eight (Argentina, Brazil, Colombia, Greece, Korea, Mexico, Portugal and Yugoslavia, in addition to Kuwait, Saudi Arabia and the UAE) contributing to IDA-6, with total contributions amounting to $141 million. The same developing countries, except Korea, also contributed to the seventh IDA replenishment, but total commitments declined to $88 million. The number of developing countries contributing to the African Development fund increased from three in 1980 (Brazil, Korea and Yugoslavia) to seven in 1985 (Argentina, India and Portugal, which joined in 1982 and 1983, and China in 1985). Argentina, Brazil, India, Korea, Portugal and Yugoslavia also joined the African Development Bank in 1982, 1983 and 1985 as non-regional members, while Israel, Portugal and Yugoslavia contributed to the interregional capital and to the Fund for Special Operations of the Inter-American Development Bank.

TRENDS IN THE GEOGRAPHICAL DISTRIBUTION OF AID

The geographic distribution of aid is the cumulative result of the independent allocation decision of a large number of individual donors and multilateral agencies. These decisions in turn are based on a variety of factors, including bilateral donors' perceptions of their national political, economic, security and other interests and objectives, both short-term and long-term, and the mandates and governance of multilateral agencies. Donor countries have built up long-standing sustained aid relationships with their preferred sets of developing countries. But they have also responded to new needs as they arose. Multilateral agencies distribute resources more broadly, the development banks — especially the World Bank — being more selective in their distributive decisions than the UN technical agencies.

While there are no arrangements for systematic international evaluations of comparative aid needs and priorities, the resources situation of the major recipients of development-motivated aid is subject to regular review in international aid consultative arrangements. Through a variety of such discussions and contacts, and the operations of many independent channels of aid, the current priorities for development aid and relief are continually reassessed and substantially served.

This is not to say that the resultant pattern of aid distribution has normally corresponded closely to objective criteria of developmental need or efficiency. Some bilateral aid allocations are patently determined mainly by political, security or commercial considerations. Moreover, "needs" for developmental aid cannot be determined objectively. Assessments of aid needs imply judgments about feasible and desirable growth rates, about the domestic resource mobilisations and policy efforts that can reasonably be expected from recipient countries, and about the net influence of aid on these efforts. While economic and other technical analyses provide a useful, even dispensible basis, the final judgments and decisions are necessarily influenced in varying degree by political considerations. Recently such judgments have been made more complicated by the fact that many developing countries required support not only to finance long-term development efforts but also to maintain minimum levels of current imports and administrative and social services.

Table III-10 sets out the general pattern of the distribution of concessional assistance from bilateral DAC and OPEC donors and the multilateral agencies and its evolution since 1960-61.

The major concentration areas of recent aid distribution have corresponded to the areas of concentration of mass poverty: Sub-Saharan Africa (30 per cent of all aid) and the South Asian subcontinent (16 per cent). The Middle East (including Egypt), countries of major concentration of United States and Arab aid, received almost 20 per cent of all concessional assistance in 1982-83. For DAC bilateral aid the Middle East's share was some 16 per cent.

Table III-11 shows the major recipients of DAC bilateral aid. Similar material for individual donors is shown in the Annex tables. Current donor priorities emerge very clearly from these tables.
Geographic aid patterns have changed fundamentally over the past two or three decades, as emerges clearly from tables III-10 and III-11.

One of the most interesting features is the "graduation" of several developing countries out of the category of significant aid recipients. This is true especially of a number of Asian countries, such as Korea and Taiwan, which were major aid recipients in the 1960s. The same is true for a number of countries in Latin America, in particular Barzil and Chile. Algeria was a major aid recipient in the late 1950s and early 1960s (i.e., during the years immediately preceding and following that country's independence) because of a massive inflow of French aid. As aid from France (the sole source of aid before independence and still the largest one today) declined sharply, partly as a result of the improvement in Algeria's economic situation brought about by oil and natural gas exports, so did Algeria's aid receipts, which fell from some 10 per cent of total ODA in 1960-61 to less than 1 per cent in 1982-83. These countries have moved into the "upper middle-income country" category. In Europe, Yugoslavia and Greece have ceased to be recipients of official development assistance, but Turkey continues to receive substantial economic assistance under the auspices of the OECD Consortium.

Table III-10. TOTAL NET DISBURSEMENTS OF ODA TO DEVELOPING COUNTRIES FROM ALL SOURCES[a] BY REGION AND INCOME GROUP

Annual averages

	Percentage of total ODA			Percentage of GNP		
	1960/61	1970/71	1982/83	1960/61	1970/71	1982/83
ASIA	44.8	47.1	27.8	1.6	1.3	0.8
Low-income countries[b]	33.7	39.3	23.9	1.5	1.4	1.0
of which: Bangladesh	..	..	4.7	..	..	10.8
Sri Lanka	0.3	0.8	1.7	0.8	2.7	9.1
Burma	0.7	0.5	1.2	2.2	1.5	5.2
Indochina[c]	6.3	8.5	0.8	15.9	13.2	3.0
Pakistan	6.3	6.4	2.9	6.5	4.1	2.4
Indonesia	2.5	8.1	3.2	6.8	5.8	1.0
India	16.8	14.0	6.3	2.1	1.6	0.9
China	x	x	2.3	x	x	0.2
Lower middle-income countries	1.8	2.0	3.0	0.7	0.7	0.8
Thailand	0.9	1.1	1.6	1.4	1.0	1.1
Philippines	0.9	0.9	1.5	0.5	0.8	1.0
Upper middle-income countries	9.3	5.8	0.8	4.1	1.5	0.1
Malaysia	0.4	0.5	0.6	0.7	0.9	0.6
Singapore	x	0.5	0.1	x	1.4	0.1
Hong Kong	0.1	x	x	0.4	x	x
Korea	6.0	4.6	0.1	7.8	3.2	x
Taiwan	2.7	0.1	x	6.5	0.2	x
SUB-SAHARAN AFRICA	9.0	18.7	30.2	1.9	2.9	4.5
Low-income countries	7.8	13.0	25.2	2.5	3.6	9.7
of which: Somalia	0.6	0.4	1.5	12.0	9.0	24.3
Sahel group[d]	0.2	2.7	5.0	0.4	7.4	18.1
Lesotho	0.1	0.2	0.4	7.3	12.6	15.7
Tanzania	0.6	0.9	2.5	4.1	4.3	13.7
Sudan	0.5	0.1	3.3	1.8	0.4	10.8
Rwanda	0.2	0.4	0.6	6.1	10.5	10.0
Kenya	1.1	1.0	1.7	5.5	3.8	7.7
Zaire	2.2	1.5	1.3	7.3	5.3	7.0
Ethiopia	0.5	0.7	1.0	1.9	2.4	5.9
Ghana	0.1	0.9	0.5	0.3	2.9	3.0
Lower middle-income countries	1.0	3.7	3.0	0.6	1.4	0.8
of which: Congo	x	0.3	0.4	0.1	5.8	5.1
Cameroon	0.1	0.8	0.7	0.7	4.8	2.4
Ivory Coast	x	0.8	0.6	0.3	3.6	2.3
Nigeria	0.8	1.7	0.2	1.0	1.0	0.1
Upper middle-income countries	0.3	2.1	2.0	3.7	15.5	9.8
of which: Reunion	..	1.6	1.6	..	25.8	22.0
NORTH AFRICA & MIDDLE EAST	26.7	11.2	23.9	4.2	1.2	1.3
Low-income countries	4.1	2.7	7.4	4.6	2.1	5.6
of which: Egypt	3.7	2.3	5.5	4.5	1.9	4.8
Lower middle-income countries	4.0	3.4	3.1	6.4	3.9	3.5
of which: Morocco	2.1	1.7	2.2	4.2	2.6	4.1
Tunisia	1.8	1.7	0.8	8.5	7.1	2.6
Upper middle-income countries	18.7	5.1	13.4	3.9	0.7	0.8
of which: Jordan	2.3	1.0	3.1	27.6	12.7	20.1
Syria	0.4	0.3	3.7	1.8	0.8	5.9
Israel	2.7	1.0	4.2	3.9	1.1	5.3
Algeria	9.9	1.9	0.6	15.1	2.4	0.3

Another development of major significance is the sharp decline in the proportion of economic assistance directed to India and Pakistan.

During the 1960s and into the beginning of the 1970s India received between 10 and 12 per cent of DAC gross ODA, but by 1982-83 this proportion had fallen to some 3 per cent. Nearly all of this $1.35 billion decline is attributable to reduced aid from the United States, the United Kingdom and Canada, the three major bilateral donors to India in the early 1970s. United States aid, which had exceeded $1 billion (in present prices) and represented on average more than 50 per cent of DAC bilateral ODA at the turn of the decade, fell off after 1971. Concessional food aid loans (which had played a large part in United States ODA) were discontinued at the request of the Indian government and other programmes were scaled down: by 1982-83 United States ODA had fallen by some $900 million in present prices to about 13 per cent of its 1970-71 levels. Political factors played a part in these developments but improvements in the economic situation of India (particularly in agricultural production and food self-sufficiency) also contributed. Substantial declines also

Table III-10. (cont'd) TOTAL NET DISBURSEMENTS OF ODA TO DEVELOPING COUNTRIES FROM ALL SOURCES^a BY REGION AND INCOME GROUP

Annual averages

	Percentage of total ODA			Percentage of GNP		
	1960/61	1970/71	1982/83	1960/61	1970/71	1982/83
AMERICA	9.9	16.0	11.9	0.5	0.6	0.5
Low-income countries	1.1	1.1	2.0	3.1	2.6	6.3
of which: Haiti	0.3	0.1	0.5	4.3	1.7	8.5
Bolivia	0.4	0.5	0.6	2.8	2.3	4.5
Lower middle-income countries	0.5	2.2	4.2	0.3	0.9	2.3
of which: Jamaica	0.1	0.3	0.7	0.7	1.2	6.3
Nicaragua	0.2	0.3	0.5	1.9	2.1	4.8
Peru	–0.4	0.9	0.9	–0.6	0.8	1.3
Guatemala	0.4	0.3	0.3	1.4	1.1	0.8
Upper middle-income countries	8.3	12.6	5.8	0.5	0.5	0.3
of which: DOM/TOM	..	2.5	2.3	..	25.9	31.5
Suriname	0.2	0.4	0.2	9.7	10.0	4.2
Dominican Republic	x	0.6	0.5	x	2.4	1.5
Ecuador	0.2	0.4	0.2	0.9	1.6	0.5
Colombia	0.4	2.2	0.4	0.4	2.0	0.2
Mexico	0.8	0.9	0.5	0.3	0.2	0.1
Brazil	3.6	2.7	0.6	0.9	0.4	0.1
Chile	1.6	0.9	x	1.6	0.7	x
EUROPE	9.3	2.8	2.4	1.4	0.4	0.4
of which: Turkey	4.1	2.9	2.0	2.2	1.5	1.0
Greece	1.4	–0.1	0.1	1.5	x	x
Yugoslavia	2.9	–0.3	x	1.0	–0.2	x
OCEANIA	..	4.2	3.8	..	16.2	15.2
of which: Papua-New Guinea	..	2.2	1.2	..	22.3	14.1
TOTAL	100.0	100.0	100.0	1.7	1.2	1.1
Memo items:						
1. Least-developed countries	6.5	10.2	24.9	2.1	3.1	10.5
2. Low-income countries (excluding China)	46.5	56.2	56.1	2.8	2.9	3.3
3. Lower middle-income countries	11.8	17.4	17.5	1.3	1.6	1.4
4. Upper middle-income countries	41.5	26.2	23.7	1.5	0.7	0.5

a) Net ODA from bilateral DAC and OPEC sources; net concessional resources from multilateral programmes (i.e., excludes multilateral development bank non-concessional lending). For major recipients of CMEA aid (Viet Nam, Cuba, Mongolia and Afghanistan) no comparable data on net disbursements from that source are available.
b) Least-developed countries and all others with an average GNP per capita in 1983 of less than $700.
c) Comprises Kampuchea, Lao P.D.R. and Viet Nam.
d Comprises Burkina Faso, Cape Verde Islands, Chad, Gambia, Mali, Mauritania, Niger, Senegal.

took place in aid from the United Kingdom and Canada, the latter partly as a result of a temporary suspension. Increased bilateral aid from the Netherlands and the Nordic countries was insufficient to offset the major DAC donors' declining ODA flows. At the same time, CMEA (mostly Soviet) aid, which had taken on some importance in the 1960s, also declined by the early 1970s to very modest levels in the 1980s. Nearly two-thirds of this general falling-off in bilateral aid was compensated by substantially increased multilateral ODA, particularly from IDA. By 1982-83 IDA was by far the largest donor to India, accounting for nearly half of India's gross aid receipts.

India's current aid receipts account for less than 1 per cent of its GNP, the lowest among all low-income countries. On the occasion of the most recent meeting of the India Consortium, in June 1985, the Government announced its objectives for the Seventh Five-Year Plan, which include a higher growth rate of 5 per cent per annum. If this higher rate of growth is to be achieved the Government estimates that India's capital requirement will rise substantially and commerical market borrowing will have to increase. Enlarged concessional flows not only have a critical role to play in alleviating domestic resource constraints to growth acceleration and poverty reduction, but would also enable India to expand its commercial borrowing while maintaining a manageable debt service burden, which currently stands at 14 per cent of export earnings. The World Bank recommended that the Consortium increase concessional flows to India by between 5 to 10 per cent a year in real terms, and the meeting endorsed India's strong case for more ODA in the Seventh-Plan period.

Aid flows to South Asian subcontinent were also affected by the emergence of Bangladesh as an independent nation. Aid to Bangladesh rose rapidly after its secession from Pakistan and has since 1972 exceeded that extended to present-day Pakistan, reflecting both Bangladesh's low income levels (it is an LLDC) and the at times substantial amounts of emergency aid extended to help alleviate the ef-

Table III-11. MAJOR RECIPIENTS OF BILATERAL ODA FROM DAC COUNTRIES, ANNUAL AVERAGES

Gross disbursements   *Per cent of total ODA*

1960-61		1970-71		1982-83	
India	11.5	India	11.5	Egypt	4.4
Algeria	7.4	Indonesia	7.2	Israel	4.0
Pakistan	4.8	Viet Nam	4.8	India	3.0
Korea	4.5	Pakistan	4.6	Indonesia	3.0
Brazil	3.4	Korea, Rep.	3.4	Bangladesh	2.4
Viet Nam	3.3	Turkey	2.5	Turkey	1.7
Turkey	2.9	Brazil	2.0	China	1.6
Egypt	2.3	Papua New Guinea	1.8	Tanzania	1.6
Yugoslavia	2.3	Colombia	1.4	Pakistan	1.5
Israel	2.2	Algeria	1.4	Sudan	1.4
Taiwan	2.2	Reunion	1.4	Reunion	1.4
Indonesia	1.9	Morocco	1.4	Kenya	1.2
Morocco	1.6	Tunisia	1.3	Philippines	1.2
Iran	1.6	Nigeria	1.3	Sri Lanka	1.2
Chile	1.5	Israel	1.2	Thailand	1.1
Argentina	1.4	Martinique	1.0	Martinique	1.0
Tunisia	1.3	Zaire	1.0	Papua New Guinea	1.0
Jordan	1.3	Laos	0.9	Zaire	0.8
Zaire	1.2	Thailand	0.9	Morocco	0.8
Mexico	1.1	Guadeloupe	0.8	Burma	0.8
Greece	1.1	Philippines	0.8	El Salvador	0.7
Philippines	0.9	Egypt	0.8	Senegal	0.7
Colombia	0.8	Kenya	0.7	Peru	0.7
Laos	0.8	Ghana	0.7	Zambia	0.6
Libya	0.7	Chile	0.7	Tunisia	0.6
Kenya	0.6	Pacif. Isl. (Trust Tr.)	0.6	New Caledonia	0.6
Thailand	0.6	Sri Lanka	0.6	Polynesia (Fr.)	0.6
Burma	0.6	Tanzania	0.6	Brazil	0.6
Afghanistan	0.5			Guadeloupe	0.6
				Zimbabwe	0.6
Total above	66.0	Total above	56.3	Total above	40.6
Multilateral programmes	11.0	Multilateral programmes	12.5	Multilateral programmes	31.2
Unallocated[a]	12.5	Unallocated[a]	9.6	Unallocated[a]	8.3
Total ODA $ million	5 363	Total ODA $ million	7 884	Total ODA $ million	29 250

a) Including NGOs, administrative costs and central activities which cannot be allocated to specific geographic areas, such as research support.

fects of natural catastrophes. Aid to Pakistan (which lost both territory and population following Bangladesh's independence) declined substantially after 1970-71. Although ODA to Pakistan, largely from the United States and Japan, rose again after the Soviet intervention in Afghanistan (and its economic efficiency in using aid has recently been excellent), it never regained in real terms the levels reached in 1970-71. These developments cannot, however, be viewed as representing a reallocation to Bangladesh of aid previously extended to Pakistan since the aggregate aid volume extended to both countries has since 1972 exceeded by a substantial margin the volume of ODA Pakistan received prior to 1971.

Indochina, which absorbed a large portion of economic assistance until the middle of the 1970s, is no longer a major recipient region because of the cessation of aid from the United States with the end of the war in Vietnam early in 1975. Between 1974 and 1976 total ODA to Indochina fell by about $1 billion. Although aid to the region subsequently recovered to some extent, largely as a result of relief efforts for Kampuchea, it fell off again and by 1982-83 amounted to some $300 million, less than 15 per cent in real terms of the amount reached in the peak year of 1974.

Most of the substantial increases in aid over the past two decades have been directed to Sub-Saharan Africa.

The aid reliance of the Sub-Saharan low-income countries has increased on average from 3 per cent of their combined GNPs in the early 1960s to the current level of more than 10 per cent.

The sharp increase in aid to Sub-Saharan Africa reflects the recognition by donors of the heavy and intractable long-term development problems of the region as well as a response to pressing emergency situations arising from natural calamities and adverse international economic environment and refugee problems. The drought in the Sahel led to a major relief effort in 1972-74 which was followed by longer-range concerted actions undertaken under the aegis of the Club du Sahel establishd in 1976. In East Africa, emergency needs and improved prolitical relations with the West led to increased assistance. The 1970s also saw the rapid expansion of aid receipts of countries such as Tanzania, which enjoyed a high degree of priority in the rapidly expanding programmes of the Nordic countries. This group of donors increased its aid to Tanzania by about four-and-a-half times in real terms between 1970-71 and 1982-83 and currently contributes about 40 per cent of DAC bilateral ODA to that country. Multilateral flows also increased substantially. Aid to Knya followed a somewhat similar pattern. Sudan became a major recipient of aid from DAC countries, OPEC countries and multilateral institutions in the middle of the 1970s. Aid to Africa increased substantially further in 1984, for both emergency relief and development.

In Asia ther share of Thailand and of the Philippines in ODA increasesd in the 1970s. In the case of Thailand the major factors were the expansion of Japan's aid to the ASEAN countries, a traditional recipient region, and, more recently, aid from several donors to refugees from Kampuchea. The share of aid going to the Philippines increased as a result of an expansion of ODA flows from Japan, which has been the major donor for more than a decade, and of continued aid from the United States, which has historical links with the Philippines and keeps large-scale military facilities in that country.

A relatively recent phenomenon is the use by China of substantial amounts of concessional assistance. China assumed its seat in the World Bank in 1980 and was added to the DAC list of developing countries during the same year. ODA to China, which had amounted to less than $20 million in 1979, rose to almost $600 million in 1983. Three-quarters of the increase recorded since 1979 came from Japan, which currently provides about 60 per cent of China's ODA receipts, ther other significant donors being Germany and IDA.

Indonesia is another major recipient of DAC aid although its share in the total declined from 7 to 3 per cent between 1970-71 and 1982-83. Indonesia became a major aid recipient following, first, the resumption of aid from the Netherlands, and, in 1967, the establishment under Dutch chairmanship of the Inter-Governmental Group for Indonesia. ODA to Indonesia remained at a high level for most of the 1970s in spite of the improvement in the country's financial position following the 1973-74 oil price increase, in some measure because of the long gestation period of some of the projects financed by major donors (notably Japan). Aid declined in the wake of the 1978-79 oil shock but recovered in the early 1980s to about $1.1 billion. Its subsequent decline at a time of diminishing oil export receipts may in part be explained by a generally improved economic situation and a 140 per cent increase in real terms in non-concessional official flows, mainly from multilateral institutions.

The share in total ODA of the developing countries of Oceania—which range from small, widely scattered Pacific islands and archipelagos virtually devoid of natural resources to the much larger land mass of Papua New Guinea with a varied resource endowment—increased rapidly in the 1960s, and has since settled at around 4 per cent. The initial phase of expansion reflects the growth of the aid programmes of Australia and New Zealand, which have traditionally extended much of their aid to their neighbours in the South Pacific, as well as a substantial effort on the part of France in respect of the Pacific DOM/TOM and the United States in respect to Pacific Islands trust territories. The subsequent stabilization in Oceania's share of aid is to a considerable extent attributable to the growing diversification of Australia's aid, which led to a moderate decline in real terms in that country's aid to Papua New Guinea, and possibly also to absorptive capacity problems in the smaller islands.

Table III-12. TRENDS IN AID FROM MAJOR DONORS TO INDIA

	Gross disbursements $ million at 1983 prices and exchange rates	
	1970-71	1982-83
IDA	203	939
Germany	208	183
Other multilateral	84	179
United Kingdom	358	138
Japan	183	136
United States	1 040	134
Nordic countries	38	104
Netherlands	40	73
Other DAC	100	61
CMEA	102	58
Canada	257	45
Total	2 511	2 033
of which:		
DAC bilateral	2 224	874

In addition to the familiar geographic groupings, Table III-10 shows a number of sub-categories mainly related to different levels of average per capita income and development. The groups are defined as follows: *i)* the 36 "least developed countries" defined by the United Nations; *ii)* the remaining "low-income countries" (LICs), which comprises countries with a per capita income in 1983 under $700 as shown in the World Bank Atlas, including in particular the South Asian subcontinent, China, Indonesia, Vietnam and Egypt (which is on the borderline with the next group, and may move into it on the next review of these categories); *iii)* the "lower middle-income countries" defined as developing countries with a per capita income in 1983 exceeding $700 but below $1,300, including some countries in Latin America, two countries in South-East Asia (the Philippines and Thailand), two Mediterranean countries (Morocco and Tunisia) and a few Sub-Saharan Africa countries (e.g., Ivory Coast and Nigeria), as well as Turkey, which is very close to the next group.

"Upper middle-income countries" (UMICs) includes all countries with a per capita income in 1983 above $1,300. It includes such countries as Saudi Arabia and the newly industrialised countries in East Asia (Hong Kong, Taiwan, Korea, Singapore) and in Latin America (Mexico, Brazil, Argentina) as well as Greece and Portugal (now members of the European Economic Community) and Yugoslavia in Europe. Also included in this group are countries or dependencies with which a donor maintains a special relationship, such as Israel, the French DOM/TOM and the Netherlands Antilles. (For a comment on the list of developing countries used by the DAC, see "The ODA and Resource Flow Concepts—Problems of Definition and Measurement"

136 International Borrowing

Table III-13. TRENDS IN AID FROM MAJOR DONORS TO SUB-SAHARAN AFRICA

	Gross disbursements $ million at 1983 prices and exchange rates	
	1970/71	1982/83
France	1 063	1 476
OPEC countries	16	981
Multilateral other than IDA and WFP	242	917
United States	407	728
Germany	229	697
IDA	1 596	661
EEC	366	571
Nordic countries	110	550
United Kingdom	431	330
Japan	33	311
Netherlands	38	275
Canada	128	265
CMEA	54	228
WFP	64	201
Italy	33	196
Belgium	78	188
Other DAC	351	148
China	175	109
Total	5 185	8 554
of which: DAC bilateral	2 901	5 164

Table III-14. ODA NET DISBURSEMENTS BY MAJOR DONORS AND RECIPIENTS
1982-83 AVERAGE

Percentages

	Total DAC	U.S.A.	France	U.K.	Germany	Japan	Other DAC
LLDCs	20.5	14.6	14.2	31.3	25.2	14.6	31.1
China and India	6.7	0.8	1.0	12.2	10.6	19.4	7.0
Other LICs	29.1	33.8	13.1	31.6	27.8	33.8	32.5
LMICs	20.2	25.9	15.9	13.8	17.0	20.6	19.0
UMICs	23.6	25.0	55.7	11.1	19.4	11.6	10.4
Total	100.0	100.0	100.0	100.0	100.0	100.0	100.0

following Chapter VI of this Report.)

The trends described have produced a pattern of aid distribution in which low-income countries receive about 60 per cent of total aid while the proportion of upper middle-income countries (mainly the "special relationship" cases) is relatively high at about 23 per cent. For DAC bilateral aid, the corresponding figures are around 61 per cent and 28 per cent.

Aid to the "least developed countries" (LLDCs) has increased significantly in absolute terms as well as rising proportionally. The LLDCs' share in total ODA supplied by DAC Members, OPEC and multilateral sources rose from a little less than 20 per cent in the mid-1970s to about 25 per cent in 1982-83. In terms of present prices and exchange rates ODA net disbursements to these countries has increased by about 50 per cent since 1975—from $4.1 billion in that year to $6.3 billion in 1983. As a result DAC Members' ODA to the LLDCs (including Members' share of ODA channelled through multilateral organisations) rose from 0.07 per cent of aggregate DAC GNP in 1975 to 0.08 per cent in 1983. The reliance of the LLDC group on ODA as a percentage of their GNPs now averages about 10 per cent.

In addition to the "special relationship" cases, a number of other UMICs still suffer from serious problems of economic and social imbalance and some donors feel that the continued selective use of concessional assistance in such situations is justified. A significant proportion of such aid consists of student fellowship and similar cultural co-operation programmes. Financial and technical assistance is also given for socially oriented projects. The use of concessional assistance for major capital projects in UMICs is rare but has given rise to considerable controversy in sectors of intense international competition because of the possible trade-distoring effects.

Given the determinants of aid to most UMICs, the scope for a major reorientation of ODA from them to poorer countries is limited. Nevertheless, it is generally accepted that the bulk of scarce aid resources, especially future increments, should be increasing concentrated on the LICs and temporarily distressed LMICs, where the comparative needs are most pressing, with a gradual replacement of concessional aid to stronger developing countries by other forms of co-operation.

7. FACTORS DETERMINING COMPARATIVE AID LEVELS

Differences in Comparative Contributions to the International Aid Effort

The underlying trend in the total volume of DAC official development assistance (ODA) has been upwards. On the other

Table III-15. **PRINCIPAL AID RELIANT DEVELOPING COUNTRIES**

Net ODA receipts from all sources as percentage of GNP

	1982/83	1970/71
Cape Verde*	58.0	..
Guinea-Bissau*	40.8	0.2
Mauritania	25.3	7.0
Chad*	24.9	9.5
Somalia*	24.3	9.0
Gambia*	22.2	4.6
Mali*	21.0	9.1
Jordan	20.1	12.7
Djibouti*	18.6	32.6
Burkina Faso*	17.8	7.6
Pacific Islands	16.1	12.1
Lesotho*	15.7	12.6
Niger*	15.5	9.3
Papua New Guinea	14.1	22.3
Central African Republic*	13.9	8.1
Tanzania*	13.7	4.3
Botswana*	13.6	17.5
Burundi*	12.9	8.3
Togo*	12.6	6.9
Senegal	12.4	5.6
Dem. Yemen*	12.3	..
Liberia	11.9	3.9
Seychelles	11.5	29.2
Guyana	11.1	6.5
Bangladesh*	10.8	..
Sudan*	10.8	0.4
Rwanda*	10.0	10.5
Malawi*	9.3	10.6
Yemen*	9.2	6.5
Sri Lanka	9.1	2.7
Haiti*	8.5	1.7
Nepal*	8.4	2.7
Belize	8.3	11.0
Bhutan*	8.2	2.0
Benin*	8.0	8.4
Zambia	7.8	1.1
Madagascar	7.8	5.3
Kenya	7.7	3.8
El Salvador	7.1	1.3
Zaire	7.0	5.3
Costa Rica	6.9	1.6
Sierra Leone*	6.5	2.1
Honduras	6.5	2.5
Jamaica	6.3	1.2
Ethiopia*	5.9	2.4
Syria	5.9	0.8
Israel	5.3	1.1
Swaziland	5.3	3.3
Burma	5.2	1.5
Congo	5.1	5.8

Note: * denotes "least-developed country".

hand, the trends in proportion to total DAC GNP have been much less satisfactory. The ODA/GNP ratio for the DAC as a whole declined in the 1960s from the very high and, for the reasons explained above, exceptional levels of the late 1950s. Even in the 1970s, however, and after the adoption of the 0.7 per cent target by the United Nations in 1970, the aggregate ODA/GNP ratio has barely increased at all. For DAC Members as a group, strong growth in aid volume was matched by strong growth in GNP, and the ODA/GNP ratio ranged around 0.36 per cent of GNP, or just over half of the 0.7 per cent target. In addition there continued to be wide differences between the aid efforts of individual donor countries as measured by their ODA/GNP ratios.

Trends in the ODA/GNP ratios for individual donors are shown in Table III-1 and trends for major countries and groups of countries are depicted in Chart III-4. Chart III-3 ranks DAC countries according to their current ODA/GNP performance.

At present (1983-84 average) five DAC countries stand out with ODA/GNP ratios substantially exceeding the 0.7 per cent target: Norway, the Netherlands, Sweden, Denmark and France (including flows to its overseas departments and territories). Another four countries (Belgium, Canada, Australia and Germany) constitute an intermediate group with ODA/GNP ratios above the DAC average. The remaining DAC countries (the United Kingdom, Japan, Finland, Austria, New Zealand, Italy, Switzerland and the United States) are below that average.

Relative contributions as measured by the ODA/GNP ratio have changed considerably over time. In the early 1960s when the DAC started its work on systematically reviewing aid performance and encouraging improved aid "burden-

Table III-16. ODA AND GNP IN DAC COUNTRIES

Percentages

	Aid growth 1970/71-1983/84[a]	GNP growth 1970/71-1983/84[a]	ODA/GNP 1970-71	ODA/GNP 1983-84	GNP per capita 1983-84 $
Norway	13.3	3.8	0.33	1.04	13 070
Netherlands	6.2	2.4	0.60	0.96	8 880
Sweden	8.0	2.0	0.40	0.82	10 910
Denmark	7.5	2.0	0.40	0.79	10 480
France	3.7	2.9	0.68	0.75	9 190
Belgium	3.7	2.3	0.48	0.58	8 040
Canada	4.4	3.2	0.41	0.48	12 820
Australia	1.5	3.2	0.59	0.47	10 460
Germany	4.8	2.1	0.33	0.47	10 360
Finland	14.6	3.3	0.09	0.34	9 820
Japan	7.5	4.2	0.22	0.34	9 990
United Kingdom	0.3	1.8	0.42	0.34	7 860
Switzerland	7.8	0.5	0.12	0.31	15 270
Italy	7.2	2.3	0.16	0.28	6 110
New Zealand	3.9	2.7	0.12	0.27	6 800
Austria	13.5	3.0	0.07	0.26	8 660
United States	1.2	2.6	0.30	0.24	14 830
Total DAC	3.6	2.9	0.34	0.36	11 240

a) Annual rates in real terms.

sharing" the main aid donors, in relative terms, were France, the United States, the United Kingdom and Belgium, with quite high aid/GNP ratios. Among the other founding DAC Members Japan, Canada and Italy had at that time aid/GNP ratios of the order of 0.2 per cent. The Netherlands was at 0.4 per cent of GNP. The relatively high German aid share was affected by large indemnification payments to Israel and official refinancing of export credits.

Most of the other countries which joined the DAC only later—the Nordic countries, Switzerland and Austria—had comparatively limited aid activities at this time. Australia, on the other hand, had a large aid programme, mainly directed to Papua and New Guinea.

By the early 1970s the aid/GNP ratio of the main early donors had substantially fallen but France, the United Kingdom and Belgium continued to be considerably above the DAC average, while the United States had fallen somewhat below. Today's "front-runners" were on their way up and already in most cases well above the DAC average, especially the Netherlands, Sweden and Denmark.

The "problem countries" from an aid volume performance point of view in the early 1970s were Japan, Italy, Austria and Switzerland. Germany's aid/GNP ratio was around the DAC average. New Zealand and Finland joined the DAC only during the 1970s.

Three Arab donor countries had already in the early 1970s before the oil price increases very high aid/GNP ratios (Saudi Arabia, Kuwait and the UAE above 5 per cent). The average for the CMEA countries was 0.15 per cent.

Economic Situation and Aid Levels

The rapid increase in ODA in many DAC countries during much of the 1960s and 1970s was facilitated by sustained economic growth, rapidly expanding government revenue and a generally permissive budgetary climate. Even taking the recent recession years into account, DAC Members' GNP growth averaged 2.9 per cent during the 1970/71-1983/84 period, while DAC aid grew by 3.5 per cent per year. Japan, with the fastest GNP growth, contributed almost a quarter of total DAC aid growth during this period. On the other hand, the performances of individual DAC countries do not point to the existence of very close links between the rate of growth of GNP and that of aid. In fact, between 1970-71 and 1983-84 eight DAC countries (Belgium, Denmark, Germany, Italy, the Netherlands, New Zealand, Sweden and Switzerland), including three of the four "front runner" countries, whose aid grew very rapidly, recorded above average ODA increases in real terms while their GNPs expanded at a rate lower than the average for the DAC (see Table III-16). It should also be noted that ODA from France and Italy has more recently grown rapidly during a period of particularly slow GNP growth.

Table III-16 also shows the considerable differences between the per capita incomes of the industrialised countries, which can be taken as an approximation of their comparative aid-giving capacity. For some DAC countries there is a correlation between official aid efforts and relative wealth. This relationship is suggested by the fact that the relatively rich Scandinavian countries are at the top of the aid-giving list while Italy and New Zealand—which rank considerably below the OECD average per capita income level and have to master particularly acute economic and social problems—rank among the last with respect to aid (these considerations also applied to Japan in the 1960s and part of the 1970s). Differences in income levels, however, cannot explain the degree of diversity in aid performance. Thus, the countries which have exceeded the 0.7 per cent of GNP level include two with per capita incomes which are below the DAC average (France and the Netherlands), while the countries at the bottom of the aid-giving list comprise also two

Table III-17. **DAC MEMBER COUNTRIES' ODA/GNP RATIOS COMPARED WITH OTHER GOVERNMENT ACTIVITIES AS SHARES OF GNP**

Percentages

	ODA/GNP ratios (1983-1984)	Aid appropriations as % of national budgets (average for fiscal years 1982 to 1983)	Tax revenues of governments as % of GNP (1982-83)	Current expenditures of governments as % of GNP (1982-83)	Social expenditures of governments as % of GNP (1982-83)
Norway	1.04	2.3	49	47	28
Netherlands	0.96	3.1	49	59[b]	35
Sweden	0.82	2.4	53	64[b]	36
Denmark	0.79	2.0	48	60	33
France	0.75	3.3[a]	46	48	29
Belgium	0.58	1.4	48	54	35
Canada	0.48	2.1	33	44	22
Australia	0.47	1.5	32	35[b]	18
Germany	0.47	2.5	39	45	29
Finland	0.34	1.2	36	37	28
Japan	0.34	2.2[a]	26	28	14
United Kingdom	0.34	1.2	41	44	23
Switzerland	0.31	2.6	31	29	14
Italy	0.28	1.0	39	48	26
New Zealand	0.27	0.5[a]	36	..	20
Austria	0.26	0.5	42	46	25
United States	0.24	1.0	27	36	20
DAC average	0.36	(1.5)	32	39	22

[a] 1982 or 1982/83.
[b] 1982.

DAC countries with very high per capita incomes (Switzerland and the United States).

The Place of Aid in National Budgets

It is also of interest to look at the relationship between official development assistance and national budgets. Table III-17 indicates ODA appropriations as a percentage of the central government budgets of DAC Member countries and some other features of national budgetary activity by these countries. Not unexpectedly, given the wide range in ODA/GNP performance between DAC Members, Table III-17 shows considerable variations also in the percentage of central government budgets devoted to aid, ranging from above 3 per cent in the case of France and the Netherlands to 0.5 per cent in Austria and New Zealand. For most other DAC countries, however, the aid share in the national budget is in the range of 2-3 per cent: Canada, Denmark, Germany, Japan, Norway, Sweden and Switzerland—as well as France, excluding aid to the DOM/TOM. On the whole, the country diversity in aid performance tends to be somewhat narrower in relation to the share of national budgets devoted to aid than in the ODA/GNP ratio.

From the material in Table III-17 one also derives the general impression that ODA/GNP shares tend to be higher in countries where the role of govenment in economic life (as measured by government revenues or total government expenditures as a share of GNP) tends to be larger. There also appears to be a positive correlation between the political acceptability of large foreign aid programmes and relatively large domestic social expenditures.

A striking feature emerging from Table III-18, which shows trends over time, is the relative stability in the share of ODA appropriations in national budgets compared with the fluctuations over the same period in ODA/GNP ratios. Even with the "front-runner" countries Sweden, Denmark and Norway, which were late starters as aid-givers and whose ODA/GNP ratios grew rapidly during the 1970s, the percentage share of the national budget allocated to aid has not moved significantly upwards over the past ten years (in the case of Sweden it actually declined). The explanation undoubtedly lies in the finding of the 1985 OECD Study on "The Role of the Public Sector" that "the relative size of the general government budget has grown significantly over the past two decades in all OECD countries, though the degree to which government budget growth has outstripped the overall expansion of the economy differs widely between countries".

Aid appropriations as a percentage of national budgets have generally held up well also in recent years despite a general deterioration in the fiscal situation of virtually all DAC Members over this period, marked by almost universal policies of budgetary constraint as governments have striven to restrain government expenditure and rein back inflation. In fact, the expanding aid plans for such countries as Japan, Italy, Finland and Switzerland imply a steady increase of the share of aid in national budgets.

A factor which has been of direct relevance in sustaining aid volume performance despite budgetary restraint is the adoption by several DAC Members of either the 0.7 per cent target —with a date—or particular national aid volume targets. The evolution over time of the concept of aid volume targets and of their acceptance by DAC Members is summarised at the end of this chapter. Consideration of such targets and of other means by which Member countries could underpin sustained increases in their aid volume has been a marked feature of the work of the DAC over the years.

140 International Borrowing

Table III-18. ODA APPROPRIATIONS AS PERCENTAGE
OF CENTRAL GOVERNMENT BUDGET EXPENDITURES 1970-83

	Fiscal years (three year averages)			
	1970-72	1975-77	1978-80	1981-83
Australia	2.2	1.6	1.5	1.5
Austria	0.3	0.4	0.4	0.4
Belgium	1.9	1.9	1.7	1.4
Canada	2.8	2.3	2.3	2.1
Denmark	1.5	1.9	1.9	2.0
Finland	0.6	0.6	0.7	1.1
France	3.6	3.3	3.1	3.1[b]
Germany	2.3	2.1	2.4	2.5
Italy	..	..	0.6[a]	1.0
Japan	1.9	1.8	2.0	2.1[b]
Netherlands	2.6	2.7	3.1	3.0
New Zealand	0.7	0.9	0.7	0.6
Norway	1.4	2.5	2.7	2.4
Sweden	2.2	2.7	2.5	2.5
Switzerland	1.9	1.9	2.2	2.6
United Kingdom	1.8	1.5	1.4	1.2
United States	1.2	1.0	1.2	1.0

a) 1980.
b) 1981-1982.

Note: In making inter-country comparisons from this table it should be borne in mind that some Member countries fund part of their aid programmes from sources other than the central budget and that in the case of federal states the central budget is smaller than would have been the case if the Member country concerned was a unitary state.

Basic Attitudes to Aid

While economic strength is a significant factor in explaining comparative aid levels, the size and orientation of national aid programmes are determined by many complex factors. These include:

— Support for aid on the part of the political elites and broader public opinion, based on humanitarian concern and understanding of the need to contribute to international economic and social stability

— Traditional links with countries of the Third World;

— The importance of developing countries as economic partners (markets, suppliers of raw materials);

— Specific or global foreign policy, security and strategic interests and responsibilities;

— Particularities of the political/constitutional decision-making and budget processes.

The Nordic countries and the Netherlands clearly stand out for an extraordinary degree of public support for strong development assistance programmes. This reflects genuine sympathy for underprivileged people, the fact that a large part of the population is conscious of living in an affluent society and an optimism about the feasibility of promoting social justice through public programmes. It may be a matter of projecting on the international level the collective sense of responsibility for the less fortunate which seems to ba particularly developed in these countries at the national level. The sense of international solidarity may also be favoured by the stronger homogeneity of the population in these countries, which are largely free of social, racial, religious or language tensions, and by their relative insulation, as small countries, from international political conflicts that have affected public opinion toward particular developing countries in, for example, the United States.

It would be misleading, however, to assert that people in other countries lacked feelings of solidarity with the Thrid World. It is revealing in this context to compare official development assistance with the performance of voluntary non-governmental organisations (see Chapter V). A comparison of official development assistance as a percentage of GNP with privately collected grants by voluntary non-governmental organisations shows the leading role of Sweden, Norway and the Netherlands in both cases. With respect to private grants, however, these countries are joined at the top by Switzerland and the United States, whose official assistance is much smaller in relation to the GNP. The generous readiness of American people to help in emergencies is renowned. In Switzerland a traditional suspicion prevails against bureaucratic economic activity by the State (as witnessed also by the negative vote in the national referendum in 1976 on a possible Swiss contribution to IDA) in comparison with a strong public humanitarian concern for the problems of the Third World. In Germany too the readiness of the people to participate in direct actions through private organisations exceeds by far, in international comparative terms, the relative position of the FRG with respect to ODA.

In the Nordic countries and the Netherlands active public education has contributed to create a positive public opinion towards development assistance. Although causal conclusions in this field are difficult it is significant that the public authorities spend some 50 US cents per capita for public information on development issues in Sweden and Norway and some 20 cents in Denmark and the Netherlands, whilst the comparable figure in the United States and the United Kingdom is only about 1 cent.

The United States, because of its weight in the world economy, also plays a unique role in international development assistance. The United States aid programme remains the largest at 30 per cent of total DAC ODA in 1984, but its ODA/GNP ratio has now fallen to the lowest level among all DAC Members. At a recent DAC Aid Review of the United States, the Committee appreciated the recent increases in United States aid, which were due partly to a major and prompt emergency food aid response to drought-stricken African countries. But the Committee also reiterated its deep concern at the level of the United States aid effort as measured by the ratio of ODA to GNP.

Over the past twenty years there have been recurrent periods in which politicians and the press have talked of a climate of aid weariness. Contrary to what might have been feared, however, a careful review of the results of available polls shows that the recent recession and persistent high unemployment in many DAC Member countries have by and large had no adverse effect on public attitudes to aid, which often emerge as even more positive than in the 1970s.

6C. Comecon Connection

The 10-member Council for Mutual Economic Assistance (CMEA) or Comecon, assists 97 countries in the Third World, compared to 34 in 1962, when the decolonisation process was beginning to gain momentum.

Formed in 1949, Comecon was in many ways a precursor of the European Economic Community, its western counterpart. Its membership has since been enlarged to include Cuba and two countries from Asia — the Mongolian People's Republic and Vietnam. The seven original members, on which this report focuses, are the Soviet Union, the German Democratic Republic, Romania, Bulgaria, Czechoslovakia, Poland and Hungary. Comecon also cooperates with Yugoslavia, Finland, Iraq and Mexico.

In its June 1984 meeting in Moscow, the body reaffirmed its commitment to the Third World. The Soviet Union alone has helped build about 1,700 industrial plants, power station, hydroengineering, agricultural and other projects. About 1,400 more projects are under construction or planned to be built.

Apart from achieving an average overall growth of around 2 per cent in the first years of this decade, Comecon has had full employment and relatively stable prices. Many Third World countries find these features highly attractive and are increasingly favouring contacts with Comecon over those of the EEC, the United States and the rest of the Organisation of Economic Cooperation and Development.

However, the relative stability of Comecon economies is only one reason for maintaining trading links. There is, for example, considerable logic for Third World parastatals and large, nationally supported companies to deal with enterprises that share a similar management structure. Decisions are made at similar levels and are unlikely to be frustrated by 'third party' intervention. This compares with the time-consuming and often frustrating negotiations with western firms that founder because the US Treasury thinks the credit arrangements are too lax or because the UK Foreign Office thinks the recipient country might be friendly towards Argentina.

Then there is the question of technological level and access. Because technology employed by many socialist countries is often labour-intensive the West finds it inefficient. Western economists gauge improved productivity by successive technological 'leaps', which in the Third World are restricted to affiliates of western transnationals. These are not necessarily justifiable where improvements in employment opportunity are an essential part of the development process. The technological gap in most industries between the Socialist economies and the Third World is far less than that between the Third World and the West.

The other facet to this is the reluctance of western companies to allow access to technology, their predilection for surrounding all aspects of techniques and technology with rigid and wide-ranging patents and their opposition to the training of local personnel. Although advisors and technicians from some Comecon organisations are accused of being 'stand-offish', these criticisms usually hail from vested western interests.

Allied to these questions is the effect technology has in changing social structures. Much of the sophisticated equipment used by western companies can be operated by local personnel, only after major changes in the employment patterns. One example is that of the 'high-tech' tractor which may replace a number of agricultural and plantation workers but fully employs only one man, who may not be from the area of operation. Even after some years many West-South operations still employ large numbers of expatriate workers to do the most skilled jobs and often make demands on the local economy which can create problems.

Political questions, although sometimes overstated, cannot be ignored. The volume of trade between, for example, the US and the Third World is steered towards those countries that accept some, if not all, the tenets of the US view of the world. While trade patterns with the USSR are not substantially different, this has something to do with the differing levels of development. The socialist countries do not operate any schemes such as the political US PL480 Food for Peace programme.

A more conventional factor promoting Comecon-South trade is the substantial production bases from which companies in Comecon work. For example, the Hungarian bus builder, Icarus, and the Bulgarian mechanical handling equipment firm, Balkancor, are the world's largest operations in their sector. Similar examples apply to machine tools, heavy-duty trucks and some textile machinery. These are the capital goods that many Third World companies and state enterprises need to acquire. Subsidiary to this is longevity of type; a model will be in production in a Comecon-based concern far longer than in a western counterpart.

It was in the early 1960's that East-South links took and assumed new proportions. Colonies were achieving independence and when the former Portuguese colonies of Africa became independent in the second half of the 1970's, the pace of links accelerated. Bulgaria, Czechoslovakia, Hungary and Poland today extend preferential treatment in favour of the South, while the Soviet Union grants duty-free treatment. In addition, trade has been encouraged by the removal of discriminatory import licensing requirements for Comecon commodities.

While prices for mutually delivered commodities are pegged on world market prices, several Third World countries have been offered a higher price and more favourable terms for their exports.

The United Nations Conference on Trade and Development has recently completed a study of East-South economic links. In its report published in August 1984, it identified several areas which have encouraged such growth.

Geographical distribution of Soviet foreign trade: 1970, 1975, 1980 and 1981
(billion roubles)

	1970 Value	% of total	1975 Value	% of total	1980 Value	% of total	1981 Value	% of total
Socialist countries of Eastern Europe:								
Turnover	12.1	55	23.2	46	40.0	43	45.4	41
Exports	6.1	53	11.9	49	20.9	42	24.3	42
Imports	6.0	57	11.3	42	19.1	43	21.1	40
Balance	+0.1		+0.6		+1.8		+3.2	
Developing countries:								
Turnover	5.2	24	11.4	23	21.7	23	28.3	26
Exports	3.2	28	5.9	25	12.3	25	15.1	27
Imports	2.0	19	5.5	21	9.4	21	13.2	25
Balance	+1.2		+0.4		+2.9		+1.9	
Developed market-economy countries:								
Turnover	4.8	21	15.9	31	32.0	34	35.8	33
Exports	2.2	19	6.2	26	16.2	33	17.6	31
Imports	2.6	24	9.7	37	15.8	36	18.2	35
Balance	-0.4		-3.5		+0.4		-0.6	

Source: USSR Foreign Trade Statistical Yearbook for the years in question (in Russian only)
Note: US$1 = 0.73 roubles

Partner countries from each group have adopted measures at the national level through the provision of new laws and regulations to facilitate trade and economic links and the setting up of special institutions and bodies. Since 1979, for example, the Indonesian government's enterprise PT (Pesero) Panca Niaga has been functioning as coordinator and liaison office for expanding trade with Comecon.

Action on a bilateral basis by individual partners of both groups of countries also exist. They include:
☐ the conclusion of inter-governmental agreements and programmes on trade, economic, technical and scientific cooperation;
☐ cooperation agreements for implementing projects in specific sectors of the economy like industry and agriculture;
☐ credit and financial agreements for long-term contracts for the delivery of goods;
☐ cooperation agreements in planning; and
☐ agreements for joint ventures and cooperation in third countries.

There are also agreements to allow Third World countries to obtain technical expertise through sending experts and the funding of scholarships and educational institutions.

Governing all agreements between the South and Comecon's European members is the mutual granting of most-favoured nation treatment. Stipulated in these contracts is also the declaration that trade be conducted to mutual benefit on the basis of international law and on the principles of the sovereign equality of states.

Cooperation is mainly concentrated on the establishment and modernisation of new production capacities. In other cases, the socialist countries cooperate in implementing infrastructural projects such as road construction, dams, ports and basic industries.

The contribution made by Comecon in the development of the Third World is enormous. The Soviet Union, for instance, declared in 1982 that "In the USSR, provision of effective aid to the liberated countries in their struggle to overcome their economic backwardness has been elevated to the rank of State policy."

A recent Unctad study on the transfer of resources reveals that Bulgaria, for instance, gave US$900-million in various forms of economic assistance between 1976-81. This represented, on an average annual basis, 0.79 per cent of the value of its net material product. According to Unctad, in 1982 Czechoslovakia rendered assistance of US$620-million or 0.74 per cent of its national income. The German Democratic Republic gave US$480-million, 0.79 per cent of national income.

From 1976 to 1980, the net economic assistance of the Soviet Union to the Third World amounted to 30-billion roubles (US$35-billion), or about 1 per cent gross national product, Unctad calculates. In 1980 and 1981 it went up to 1.3 per cent, an increase over the 0.9 per cent figure of 1976. In 1981 alone, the amount equalled US$9.8-billion. Reports obtained show that in 1982 the level increased by 5 per cent to 1.27 per cent of GNP. In relation to the least developed countries, the total assistance given by the Soviet Union in 1981 equalled 0.18 per cent of GNP. This transfer of resources is not the same as aid measured in the West. As well as aid, the figures include loans on 'soft' terms as well as commercial credits.

What is significant between East-South trade is that, in 1965, turnover was US$5.8-billion, while it leapt to US$65-billion in 1983. This 14.3 per cent average annual increase is higher than the 13.4 per cent increase in world trade for the same period, the 11.5 per cent increase trade turnover of the socialist countries of Eastern Europe or the 14.1 per cent growth of East-West trade. There has been an acceleration over the past two decades. The period 1965-70 saw trade between the two groups increase by 10 per cent, contrasting with the 20 per cent from 1970-80. There are two factors for this leap: the arrival of independent countries and detente under the Brezhnev era.

Foreign trade of Czechoslovakia: 1970 and 1981

(million Czechoslovak crowns)

Geographical distribution	Exports 1970	Exports 1981	Imports 1970	Imports 1981
Total trade	27,305	87,689	26,605	86,276
of which:				
Developing countries	3,675	12,362	2,724	8,365
Developed market-economy countries	5,634	17,424	6,599	19,195
Socialist countries	17,994	57,903	17,278	58,716

Source: National statistics
Note: US$1 = 12.34 crowns

Foreign trade of the People's Republic of Bulgaria: 1970 and 1981

(million foreign exchange leva)

Geographical distribution	Exports 1970	Exports 1981	Imports 1970	Imports 1981
Total trade	2142.3	9838.2	2344.5	9914.9
of which:				
Developing countries	294.6	1927.3	162.5	736.7
Per cent of total	13.8	19.6	6.9	7.4
Developed market-economy countries	216.8	1424.6	542.9	1986.9
Per cent of total	10.1	14.5	23.2	20.1
Socialist countries of Eastern Europe	1630.9	6486.3	1639.1	7191.3
Per cent of total	76.1	65.9	69.9	72.5

Source: Bulgarian Chamber of Commerce and Industry, Economic Outlook 1982 (Sofia, 1982)
Note: US$1 = 0.85 leva

However, the down-turn in the global economy, or at least in the non-socialist world, has a ripple effect on East-South trade. In 1981 and 1982, turnover slowed to its lowest levels, 10.8 per cent and 4.2 per cent, respectively. The contraction of East-West trade recently and the absolute decline of Poland's volume of foreign trade, have also aggravated the decreasing growth rate of East-South trade.

The development of foreign trade varies significantly within Comecon's Eastern European members. Bulgaria and Romania recorded the highest annual average growth of 16.7 per cent and 21.5 per cent, respectively, compared with Czechoslovakia (9.9 per cent) and Poland (9.5 per cent).

The Soviet Union was the single largest trading partner of the South, accounting for about 60 per cent of Comecon's trade with the Third World. Apart from other Comecon members, Vietnam, Cuba and Mongolia, the major Third World trading partners of the Soviet Union are Afghanistan, Argentina, Brazil, North Korea, Egypt, India, Iraq, Iran, Libya, Malaysia, Nigeria and Syria. Yugoslavia, although not a Third World country, but a founding member of the Non-Aligned Movement, is also a major trading partner with the USSR. Recently, Argentina, Brazil and Malaysia have become net exporters to the Soviet Union, while the situation is reversed with Nigeria and Vietnam.

Socialist countries' imports from the Third World increased by an average of 13.7 per cent annually from 1965-83. This contrasts sharply with the 13.5 per cent growth of imports by the socialist countries from the West and the market-economies of the North. At the same time, socialist exports to the Third World increased during the same period at an annual rate of 14.9 per cent.

The rapid rise of two-way trade can be illustrated by the increasing share of Third World imports from Eastern Europe. They have risen from 13.6 per cent in 1965 to 17.1 per cent in 1983; their share in Comecon exports increased from 15.7 per cent to 21.7 per cent. These developments also vary from country to country. The share of the Third World in the Soviet Union's total imports went up from 18.7 per cent in 1965 to 21.9 per cent in 1983. For the rest of Eastern Europe, this did not exceed 13.6 per cent, although about a third of Romania's imports come from the Third World. The share of the Third World in the Soviet Union's total exports rose, during the same period, from 23.5 to 27.5 per cent. In the total exports of the other six European members of Comecon, the share of the Third World was under 20 per cent. In the case of Romania, the Third World absorbed about 30 per cent.

The trade links of the socialist countries of Eastern Europe and the Socialist countries of the South are more intensive as well as with those Third World countries which have special agreements and status with Comecon — Afghanistan, Angola, Ethiopia, Mozambique, South Yemen and Yugoslavia. This latter group was responsible for 10-12 per cent of the foreign trade of the socialist countries of Eastern Europe during the last decade.

The development strategy and industrialisation programme of Third World countries have received a boost from the Eastern European members of Comecon. By 1982, over 6,400 industrial enterprises and other projects have been completed or were in the process of completion. Many of these belong to the state sector of the economy and are concentrated on key projects. By January 1980, the tally was:

Power stations	23-million KwH
Coal	22-million tonnes
Pig iron	14-million tonnes

Steel	30-million tonnes
Oil extraction	67-million tonnes
Oil processing	50-million tonnes
Cement	7-million tonnes
Bauxite	2.5-million tonnes
Fertilisers	0.2-million tonnes
Irrigation, land reclamation	3-million tonnes
Railway network	3,000 km
Road network	2,700 km

The importance of this two-way link goes far beyond this. Traditional primary products still play the dominant role in Third World exports to the socialist countries. These commodities include sugar, textile fibres, grain, natural rubber and oil seeds while tropical fruits, coffee, cocoa and tea are increasingly important items. Fuel exports from the Third World, mainly crude oil, rose sharply until 1980.

At the same time, Third World countries are selling non-traditional manufactured goods such as iron and steel, machine tools, agricultural machinery, tractors, diesel generators, air compressors, electrical equipment, cables, chemicals, detergents, photographic and optical articles, road vehicle spare parts.

Exports and imports of the German Democratic Republic: 1970 and 1981

(million marks, at current prices)

Geographical distribution	Exports 1970	Exports 1981	Imports 1970	Imports 1981
Total trade of which				
Developing countries Per cent	7.4	9.8	6.0	6
Developed market-economy countries Per cent	21.9	27.4	26.7	29
Socialist countries of Eastern Europe Per cent	70.7	62.8	67.3	63

Note: US$1 = 2.45 marks

A WIDE RANGE OF PROJECT SECTORS
Geology

Assistance to 45 Third World countries in surveying for minerals:
- Bulgarian specialists have done geological surveys for oil, aluminum, tin and other minerals in Algeria, Congo, Libya, Somalia, Tunisia and other Third World countries.
- Hungary has participated in prospecting for bauxite deposits in Ghana, Guinea and India, and for oil in Iraq.
- East German specialists have surveyed coal deposits in Algeria, Mozambique and Syria.
- Poland has rendered assistance in prospecting for and developing coal deposits in Argentina, Colombia, India, Indonesia, Iran and Peru; phosphate deposits in Egypt and Syria; and copper, sulphur and potassium salts deposits in Algeria.
- Soviet geologists have helped to strike oil pools in Afghanistan, Algeria, India, Iran and Syria; gas deposits in Afghanistan and Pakistan; hard coal deposits in Nigeria; iron ore in Iran and Nigeria; bauxites in Guinea; copper in Algeria and Congo; gold in Afghanistan, Mali and Tanzania; phosphorites and tantalum in Egypt; mercury and antimony in Algeria; and barites in Afghanistan.
- Czechoslovak specialists are assisting in prospecting for coal in Algeria, have helped to discover hard coal, phosphate and copper deposits in Egypt, and carried out geological surveys in Burma, Ivory Coast, Morocco, Nigeria, Zambia and some Latin American countries.
- Soviet and other Comecon specialists have helped discover high-grade iron ore (with an iron content of more than 63 per cent), coal, gas, non-ferrous metals and gold in Afghanistan. There are 140 geological surveys for different minerals carried out in 42 Third World countries by Comecon and about 90 surveys are now in progress.

Power Engineering

More than 1,000 projects in the power industry and infrastructure have been built with Comecon participation in the Third World and more than 750 projects are under construction or planned. The beneficiaries include Afghanistan, Algeria, Bangladesh, Brazil, Congo, Egypt, Guinea, India, Iran, Libya, Morocco, Peru, Syria, Tanzania and Zambia. Some of the major projects are:
- The Aswan hydropower complex in Egypt, the largest power project in Africa.
- A hydropower complex built on the Euphrates River in Syria, which increased the generating capacity of the country by more than 2.5 times.
- About 20 power projects with an aggregate capacity of about 3.5 million kW in India. They include the Bhakra-Nangal hydropower station on the Sutlej River (600,000 kW); the Patratu hydropower station (400,000 kW); the Balimela hydropower station (400,000 kW); the Mettur-Tunnel hydropower station (200,000 kW); the Neweili thermal heat power station (600,000 kW); and the Korba thermal heat power station (200,000 kW).
- The installation of 210,000 kW generating unit at the Guddu heat power station power plant in Pakistan.
- The Ghorazal thermal power station in Bangladesh.
- A 55 MW thermal power plant in Annaba, Algeria, the Mansour-el-Dhahaby hydropower complex and the Moulay Yousef hydropower station in Morocco.

Exports and imports of Hungary: 1976 and 1981
(million forints)

Geographical distribution	Exports (f.o.b.) 1976	Exports (f.o.b.) 1981	Imports (c.i.f.) 1976	Imports (c.i.f.) 1981
Total trade	204,833	299,405	230,056	314,284
of which:				
Developing countries	24,074	46,663	27,427	38,108
Developed market-economy countries	64,450	90,341	84,012	126,104
Socialist countries of Eastern Europe	116,309	162,401	118,617	150,072

Source: National statistics
Note. US$1 = 35.58 forints.

Exports and Imports of Poland: 1970 and 1981
(million-zlotych)

Geographical distribution	Exports 1970	Exports 1981	Imports 1970	Imports 1981
Total trade	14,191	44,530	14,430	52,013
of which:				
Developing countries	1,305	5,822	1,042	4,204
Per cent	9.2	13.1	7.2	8.1
Developed market-economy countries	4,097	13,440	3,752	15,141
Per cent	28.9	30.2	26.0	29.1
Socialist countries of Eastern Europe	8,789	25,268	9,636	32,668
Per cent	61.9	56.7	66.8	62.8

Source: National statistics
Note. US$1 = 80 zlotych

Oil and Gas

The projects include:
- Helping Syria to develop an oil-extracting industry from scratch.
- An oil refinery built with Soviet assistance in Ethiopia, which produces 12 types of petroproducts, including petrol, kerosene, jet and diesel fuel, fuel oil and liquefied gas.
- An oil refinery built with Soviet assistance in Aliaga, Turkey, accounting for 27 per cent of Turkey's output.
- Iraq's first national oilfield, Northern Rumaila, built with Soviet assistance in 1972.
- More than 45 promising oil deposits have been struck in India with help from Comecon, generating about 70 per cent of the country's total output. Oil refineries have been built also in Baruni, Koyola and Mathura.

Ferrous and Non-Ferrous Metallurgy

Some of the assistance extended are:
- Steel plants in India, such as Bhilai and Bokaro, each with a capacity of 2.5-million tonnes a year, accounting for 40 per cent of India's steel output. A new steel works with a capacity of 3-million tonnes a year is planned for Vishakhapatnam.
- The construction of a 550,000 tonnes steelworks in Isfahan, Iran, with Soviet, East German and Czechoslovak assistance.
- A major project in Turkey between the government and the Soviet Union to increase Turkey's output. The project, at Iskenderun, will amount to 35 per cent of the country's steel production.
- A steel works near Ajaokuta, Nigeria between the government and East Germany, the Soviet Union and Czechoslovakia, with a full production capacity of 5-million tonnes to enable Nigeria to export steel.
- A steel works with Soviet assistance in Oruvel, Sri Lanka, now operating for 13 years.
- A government-owned mine in Guinea, which produces 2.5-million tonnes of bauxite a year.
- An aluminum plant in Seydisehir, Turkey, with a capacity of 400,000 tonnes of alumina, 120,000 tonnes of aluminum and 27,000 tonnes of rolled stock a year. It is the first aluminum plant in the country, saving Turkey up to US$50-million.
- An aluminum plant in Korba, India, with a capacity of 100,000 tonnes of aluminum a year.
- The Isael mining and smelting complex in Algeria, with a capacity of 317 tonnes of mercury a year, and also a lead enrichment plant in El Abed; a mining complex and an ore-dressing works, Kerzet Yousef, to process 100,000 tonnes of lead and zinc ore a year, built with Bulgarian assistance.
- The expansion of an aluminum plant in Nag Hammadi, Egypt, from 100,000 to 166,000 tonnes a year.
- The designing of a copper enrichment plant with a capacity of 100,000 to 120,000 tonnes of copper a year in Afghanistan.
- A gold mine being developed near Kalana in Mali.

Engineering

There are 149 engineering and metal-working plants in the Third World built with the assistance of Comecon member countries and more than 40 are under construction. They include:
- Plants built in India, including a heavy engineering plant in Ranchi — built with Soviet and Czechoslovak assistance — which produces sophisticated equipment for metallurgical, mining, power, and ship-building industries.

There is also a mining equipment plant in Dargapur, with a capacity of 45,000 tonnes of diverse equipment a year.

India's major industrial project is a heavy electric engineering plant, which makes 200 MW steam turbines and turbogenerators from components supplied by the USSR.
- A farm machinery plant built by Comecon member countries in Iskandariyah, Iraq, the largest in the Middle East.

The plant produces, in addition to farm machinery, automobile bodies, tractor engines and castings. A major role in the development of the Iraqi engineering industry is played by an electric engineering factory in Baghdad.
• An engineering plant producing 25,000 to 30,000 tonnes of machinery a year, including cranes, boilers and farm machines has been built with Soviet technical assistance in Arak, Iran.
• The Jengalak auto repairs works in Afghanistan, does repairs for the motor transport industry and produces a range of metal products, from spares for motor vehicles and looms to turbo-drills and metal-working machine tools.
• A number of engineering and metal-working plants built in Egypt, including a forging works and a machine-tool factory in Helwan, a files factory and workshops producing fittings and cutting tools. The Helwan machine tool factory is Egypt's largest engineering plant and is designed to produce more than 1,300 machine tools a year.
• A large industrial complex producing different industrial accessories, castings, and pumping equipment for water supply, oil, gas and chemical industries and other sectors of the economy, has been built with East German and Czechoslovak assistance near Berrouaghia, Algeria.
• A fittings factory has been built with East German assistance in Medea, Algeria. Hungary, Poland, the USSR and Czechoslovakia have also supplied machinery and equipment for that factory.

Building Materials Industry

More than 110 such projects have been built with more than 60 under construction. They include:
• A house-building integrated works in Kabul, Afghanistan.
• A large panel reinforced concrete components plant in Ghana.
• Several large panel house building integrated works in Iran.
• Cement plants in Iraq, the Yemen Arab Republic, Mali and Syria.
• Glass works in Algeria, Iran and Turkey.
• Reinforced concrete sleepers plants in Algeria and Iraq.

Light and Food Industries

About 1,000 projects in the light and food industries have been built or are under construction in the Third World, and include:
• Cotton mills built in Algeria, Bangladesh, Egypt, Indonesia, Pakistan, Syria, Turkey and Uganda; cotton and textile factories in Ethiopia, India, Iran, Iraq, Kenya, Sri Lanka and Turkey; shoe factories and tanneries in Afghanistan, Algeria, Burma, Ethiopia, Ghana, India, Iraq, Sri Lanka, Syria and Turkey.
• A cannery in Kerbela, Iraq, producing 40 varieties of tinned vegetables and fruit and another cannery in Mamou, Guinea, with a capacity of 5-million tins of meat, vegetables, fruit and juice a year.

• Grain elevators have been built with the assistance of Comecon in Egypt, Iran, Iraq and Sudan.
• A sugar mill built with Soviet assistance in Birganj, Nepal, which produces two-thirds of the country's sugar output.
• A flour mill built in Colombo, Sri Lanka, which meets 20 per cent of the country's flour needs.
• The largest slaughterhouse in the Middle East has been built and put into operation with East German help in Baghdad, Iraq.
• Industrialised fishing is rendered assistance to Algeria, Iran, Iraq, Mauritania, Mozambique, South Yemen, Egypt and Ethiopia by Bulgaria, Cuba, East Germany, Poland and the Soviet Union. These involve building modern fish-processing plants and canneries, improving fishing tackle, modernising ports and shipyards and equipping them with modern machinery, storage and refrigerating facilities, and training national personnel.

Agriculture

With agriculture being the leading economic sector in many Third World countries, Comecon pays great attention in rendering assistance. Their projects include:
• A crop-farming and livestock centre built in Suratgarh, India, on an area of 12,000 ha. It raises high-yield strains of wheat, rice, barley, oil crops and cotton and also livestock breeding. Five more government-owned farms have been set up in Hisar, Raichuru, Ladhoval, Kannanor and Jetsar.
• A hydro-engineering complex on the Araks River in Iran, irrigating 18,000 ha.
• The Aswan hydro-engineering scheme in Egypt, increasing the farmland area by 30 per cent.
• The construction of the Euphrates hydrocomplex in Syria, irrigating an additional 640,000 ha, doubling the area under irrigation.
• The irrigation complex Chemoltau built with Soviet assistance in Burma, bringing water to about 12,000 ha and the Mansour-el-Dhahaby hydroscheme built with Polish assistance in Morocco to 19,000 ha.
• The Jalalabad complex developed in Afghanistan incorporates a 70-km irrigation canal bringing water to 24,000 ha of virgin land in the Nangrahar province.
• Vaccination of more than a million head of cattle in Angola in 1980 and selective examination of livestock for different diseases.
• Twenty machine and tractor stations have been established and equipped with Soviet-made tractors and farm machinery in Burma.
• New cotton varieties being introduced in Algeria, Angola, Burma, Ethiopia, Ghana and Togo.
• New tobacco strains in Nepal and new vine varieties in India.

Transport and Communication

More than 300 projects have been put into operation and another 130 are under construction or planned. They include:

- Modernising and building railroads with a total length of 1,400 km in Syria and assisted by the Soviet Union, Bulgaria and East Germany.
- The Damascus-Homs railroad will stretch for 208 km to link the Syrian capital with the economically developed western parts of the country and the Tartus port. A 120 km railroad between Mehin and Palmira and a 65 km railroad between Homs and 'Akkari' will carry phosphates to Mediterranean ports.
- Railroads in Iraq to link Baghdad with Basra and Shu'aiba with Umm Qasr have increased the total length of the country's rails by 45 per cent.
- The USSR has helped to convert to electric traction the 146-km long Julfa-Tabriz rail in Iran.
- The 426 km Tuma Vaslala-Siuna road built with the assistance of Cuba in 1982 in Nicaragua, linking the Atlantic and Pacific coasts.
- The construction of a network of roads with Soviet aid in Afghanistan, including a 107 km long road with a 2.7 km tunnel at an altitude of 3,300 metres.
- The 230 km Hodeida-Ta'izz road in the Yemen Arab Republic, with 23 bridges.
- The 109 km Simra-Janakpur road in Nepal.
- Cuba and the Soviet Union have assisted Angola in the rehabilitation of its motor roads and bridges; about 300 bridges have been destroyed.
- Pipelines to transport gas and petroproducts are being built in Afghanistan, Iran, Iraq, Libya and Nigeria.
- Sea and river ports and airports are being built or modernised in Afghanistan, Angola, Bangladesh, Guinea, Syria and the Yemen Arab Republic.
- Various communications networks, mass communications facilities and multi-channel communication lines, radio stations, stations of the Intersputnick satellite-aided communications system, telecommunications systems, telephone exchanges and print shops are under construction in Afghanistan, Algeria, Bangladesh, India, Iraq, Pakistan and South Yemen.

Training of Personnel

Nearly 1.5-million engineers, technicians and skilled workers have been trained in every form of education and training by Comecon members. There are 240 occupational training schools and centres established for this purpose in the Third World. They include:
- A mining institute, an institute of oil, gas and chemicals and a national light industry institute in Algeria, the Kabul Polytechnical Institute and a mining/oil school in Afghanistan, a technological institute in India, a polytechnical institute in Ethiopia, and a national technical institute in Tunisia.
- The Rangoon Polytechnical Institute, built with Soviet assistance, has become Burma's first technical higher educational establishment with an enrollment of 1,000 students.
- A polytechnical institute built in Conakry, Guinea, in 1964, 1,500 students, is the largest in Western Africa.
- A higher managerial school in Mamako, Mali.
- More than 83,000 people from 121 Third World countries — excluding those from Vietnam, Cuba and Mongolia — study at higher and specialised secondary educational institutions in Comecon member countries. During the past 10 years, 50,000 specialists from the Third World trained in the Comecom countries in industry, agriculture, health care and education.

6D. Co-operation with Non-Government Organizations
OECD

The economic development and social welfare activities of private, voluntary, non-governmental organisations constitute a special feature of development co-operation between industrial and developing countries. The resources raised annually by the private organisations through various forms of voluntary collections run at a level of well over $2 billion: and for some countries they may well be substantially under-recorded. DAC official aid institutions are channelling roughly another billion dollars through these organisations, about 5 per cent of total ODA (Table V-1).

The volume of contributions collected by NGOs and the extraordinary effort by many thousands of individuals in running these operations in often the most difficult circumstances are a manifestation of the strong commitment of large numbers of people in OECD countries to the concept of solidarity with poor people in the Third World. As part of its general aid review activities, the DAC has followed the work of the NGOs and has examined operational experience and ways of improving their co-operation with official aid agencies.

Well over 2000 non-governmental organisations (NGOs) in OECD countries are active in development assistance, relief, and development education. NGOs are very diverse. Church-related groups still make up the largest number. Some of their aid is given to church-linked institutions in the recipient countries, but over the past two decades church-donated funds have increasingly been given to a wide variety of organisations, including non-denominational. A number of NGOs are partly, and in some cases even wholly, financed by governments, but most of them must raise the bulk of their funds from the public through voluntary contributions of individuals concerned with poverty alleviation. This helps to maintain the autonomy and credibility of NGOs; but it also renders them vulnerable to any falling-off of contributions. Furthermore, it keeps NGOs relatively small. It has been argued that this may in some ways be an advantage because it puts pressure on NGOs to do more with fewer resources. The continued pressure on resources may be central among the factors which incline NGOs to seek to work with local groups and individuals in ways which will make their contribution catalytic, by matching local effort, and this is one of the most appreciated features of their work.

The DAC started collecting information on grants by private voluntary agencies in 1970. By that time, a number of DAC Members had already established mechanisms for financial collaboration with NGOs. By 1979 virtually all DAC Members had adopted some system for cofinancing projects designed and presented by NGOs. The reasons for matching private efforts with official contributions included a wish by governments to encourage the interest and participation of the public in Member countries, as well as an appreciation of the distinguishing features of NGO activities in the field. Foremost among these are flexibility, since NGO projects tend to be small compared with official aid activities, and the ability to work directly with population groups in developing countries. NGOs strive to work at the grass-roots level, with the poorest people, fostering self-reliance by helping communities to help themselves. This implies the nurturing of local potential, the provision of training and the solving of often arduous technical, financial and marketing problems. NGOs do not succeed in these directions with all of their projects. But they at least often succeed in establishing models for the provision of services to previously uncovered areas and population groups.

In their cofinancing schemes, governments recognise the autonomy of NGOs, although some have established preferential criteria, such as a higher share of official funds for certain activities (for example, for the least developed countries, for family planning, for the promotion of the role of women).

In its original and classical form, cofinancing is done on a project-by-project basis, with cost-sharing guidelines varying from Member to Member. As a general rule, the percentage of official funding is currently as follows:

— 50 per cent: Australia, France, Italy, New Zealand, UK, US, CEC
— 50 to 66 per cent: Switzerland
— 60 per cent: Finland
— 75 per cent: Belgium, Germany
— 80 per cent: Norway, Sweden
— 100 per cent: Denmark, Netherlands
— No fixed percentage: Austria, Canada, Japan

Table V-1. RESOURCES FOR DEVELOPMENT AND RELIEF ACTIVITIES OF NON-GOVERNMENTAL ORGANISATIONS (1983)

	Private grants raised by NGOs[a]		DAC Member contributions to NGOs	
	US$ million equivalent	Percentage of GNP	US$ million equivalent	Percentage of total ODA
Australia	32	0.02	18[b]	2.4
Austria	12	0.02	n.a.	n.a.
Belgium	30	0.04	16	3.1
Canada	132	0.04	125	8.7
Denmark	13	0.02	18	4.6
Finland	16	0.03	2	1.1
France	36	0.01	14[b]	0.4
Germany	370	0.05	177	5.6
Italy	3	0.01	n.a.	n.a.
Japan	30	0.01	31	0.8
Netherlands	107	0.08	111[b]	6.6
New Zealand	5	0.03	1	2.3
Norway	43	0.08	24	4.1
Sweden	61	0.07	44	5.9
Switzerland	48	0.05	46	14.4
United Kingdom	83	0.02	11[b]	0.7
United States	1 320	0.04	595[b]	7.4
CEC			81	5.8
Total DAC Members	2 341	0.03	1 281	4.8

[a] Private grants by some countries may be understated due to incomplete recording.
[b] Including emergency aid channelled through NGOs and, in the case of France and the United Kingdom, the financing of volunteer schemes.

Financial collaboration practices, however, have evolved over time. In order to ease the administrative burden of scrutinising a great number of projects, many of which are small, and in recognition of the experience and standing of some NGOs, some Members also extend "block grants". Block grants cover the official share of a number of projects, with detailed assessments after their termination rather than in advance. This facilitates rapid funding of, for example, urgently needed spare parts, and permits, at times, so-called "umbrella organisations" to assume a financing intermediary position involving the appraisal, subsequent financing and monitoring of projects implemented by individual NGOs affiliated to them. Block grants have recently been extended by some Members to individual NGOs also to cover larger projects. In 1982, block grants accounted for 82 per cent of Dutch and 85 per cent of Swedish cofinancing.

In recent years, in response to activities for which the project framework, with its precise forecasts in terms of goals and duration, is less suited, some aid agencies have developed even more flexible cofinancing procedures. These include the "renewable programmes" and "flexible funding" methods used in some cases by, for example, Canada, Germany, the Netherlands and Switzerland. Norway may extend its official support for NGO projects over a ten-year period. Such flexible procedures are particularly valuable when external support aims at matching in timely fashion the efforts made by local groups, which contribute their labour and savings through their own organisations and for programmes of their own.

Multiple partnerships link DAC Members' aid agencies and NGOs with organisations in developing countries, such as farmers' associations, consumers' unions, credit unions, women's groups. Many official aid agencies are increasingly interested in providing direct or indirect support for such NGOs of developing countries, in particular those which stress income generation, self-help and the organisation of local groups. Some aid agencies have also started providing grants for the extension of two-step loans, revolving loans and other forms of credit to local groups, co-operatives, and small entrepreneurs. These developments may be of special interest should NGOs focus more closely, in low-income countries in Sub-Saharan Africa and elsewhere, on their potential contribution to the rehabilitation of rural populations, as is likely in view of the concern, in the wake of the African famine, for a better linkage between relief, rehabilitation and development assistance.

NGO activities have not been systematically recorded in a centralised manner. Their distribution by sector, therefore, can only be estimated, on the basis of data available for the cofinanced projects of some DAC Members. Probably more than one-third of NGO expenditures are for education, training and health, with perhaps somewhat below one-sixth for agriculture and rural development. Typically, another sixth may be for relief work, more than that recently, because of the situation in Africa. The remainder consists of other income-raising activities, water, appropriate technology and multidisciplinary projects.

In some sectors, NGOs have evolved pioneering approaches. The concept of "primary health care", for example, owes much to the experience of projects run by dedicated individuals with private support, from India to Indonesia to Guatemala, which gradually led initially medical projects to include health precursors in their scope of activities, e.g., clean water, improved sanitation, improved nutrition (hence, income-raising activities), health education and the training of community organisers. Findings from a major survey by the Club of Rome published in 1985 also indicate that NGOs, including NGOs from developing countries, have been pioneering rural development approaches in recent years with focus on self-help and have contributed significantly to the training of rural people within that context. The Club of Rome estimates that about 100 million people are benefitting directly or indirectly from these activities.[1]

Development education, addressed to the populations of OECD Member countries, is a growing activity of NGOs. On longer-term issues, NGOs in some countries lead the public debate on the volume of aid (petitions in Switzerland in 1983 to maintain the volume of ODA) or its quality (the "real aid" campaign in the United Kingdom). It has been repeatedly noted, in particular, that NGOs have constituted perhaps the strongest domestic constituency or lobby in industrialised countries to meet the aid volume targets of 0.7 per cent of GNP as ODA or more recently the 0.15 per cent of GNP for the least-developed countries. There is also a noticeable concern among NGOs not to divorce ODA from other issues such as trade patterns in the broad North-South context. Together with the aid agencies and educational authorities, many NGOs are also active in the introduction of development education in school curricula in DAC countries.

NGOs also have their problems and disadvantages. The diversity and lack of common ground rules among NGOs probably constitute the single largest problem for any government or group seeking aid from the private sector[2]. Traditionally, also, NGOs have often been found to operate in isolation from one another. The situation has been gradually evolving, with the constitution in many donor and recipient countries of national consultative councils of NGOs, allowing for regular exchange and contact and, in some countries, joint activities (e.g., for the up-grading of professional staff, joint appeals, etc.). These bodies also strengthen the "bargaining" position of NGOs vis-à-vis the government. Within DAC countries, recently formed umbrella organisations of this kind are INTERACTION, established in 1984 in the United States and grouping about one hundred develop-

mental private agencies, and the "Intercollectif", grouping NGO federations in France. An important role in getting NGOs to work more closely together has been played by the Commission of the European Communities, with its NGO Liaison Committee, and by the Geneva-based UN Non-governmental Liaison Service. In developing countries, associations grouping foreign and national NGOs have been growing in number, providing a focus for consultation at country level. In a number of cases, their role could be usefully strengthened if additional resources were devoted to tasks of common interest. In some cases, also, host-country governments could be made more aware of the potential role of voluntary agencies and the value of their autonomy. Canada is assisting an inter-regional network of NGOs, IRED (Innovations et Réseaux pour le Développement: Development Innovations and Networks), in particular for the circulation of information and the financing of South-South exchange visits. Inter-agency consultative bodies at international level include the International Council of Voluntary Agencies (ICVA), which now also includes affiliates from the South, and CIDSE, which is a network for some of the Catholic agencies in the ten European countries, Canada and the United States. Groupings and consortia have been formed for operational purposes such as EURO-ACTION/ACORD, which undertakes programmes in several African countries for its funding member agencies, e.g., a long-term rural development project in Northern Mali and activities for both refugees and local population groups in Sudan.

Since about 1980, there has been keener interest in the evaluation of NGO projects and programmes, whether by aid agencies or NGOs (or both, through joint evaluations). A forerunner was a study commissioned by USAID to document evidence of developmental impact of seventeen NGO projects in Kenya and Niger. An important conclusion was that high or moderate impact was associated with strategies where the foreign NGOs had a supplemental role in community self-help projects and the projects where key decisions were made by small groups at local level. Marginal impact was associated with a high degree of NGO involvement in decision-making and in support of projects initiated by the host government[3]. A study of NGO project documents by Judith Tendler has raised critical issues relative to the comparative advantages of NGOs in terms of reaching the poor, using participatory processes in project implementation, being innovative and experimental, and carrying out projects at low cost[4]. While some of the issues, such as costs, deserve further research both on NGO and official projects, this study has influenced subsequent evaluations and usefully clarified the perception of both achievements and shortcomings in particular situations. The summary report of a comparative joint evaluation of twenty-six cofinanced NGO projects in five countries, published by the European Economic Commission in June 1981, stressed positive results but also raised critical points which are currently of active concern to the NGO community. These mainly relate to a greater involvement of local population groups in project design; the temptation to duplicate host-country structures, with no prospect for continuity of services once the NGO withdraws; the need for in-country co-ordination mechanisms; and the need for more flexible funding procedures in support of self-help efforts. More recently, a number of DAC Members' aid agencies have undertaken evaluations which have a bearing on the latter point; they assess, among other questions, the adequacy of their own cofinancing procedures to enhance the flexibility of NGOs' responses to development programming by local groups.

The dedication of NGO personnel involved in relief work, from refugee camps to feeding centres or the rescue of victims of civil wars and international conflicts, is well known. The central pillars of humanitarian action, the International Committee and the League of Red Cross Societies, were established a century or so ago (1863 and 1919). New groups have been added more recently, from the Save the Children agencies to "Médecins sans Frontieres." Encouragingly, a major concern of the private agencies involved in relief is currently an improved meshing of emergency with development aid. Swift operations for the purchase, transportation and distribution of seed, several of which have been mounted by NGOs in famine-stricken areas of Africa, are examples. Analysis shows that the margin left for staged rational programming in emergency operations is often narrow, beyond immediate survival needs, due to pressure of public opinion for quick spending, not to mention political constraints.[5] Closer contact with the media is advocated on several sides to correct the imbalance between immediate emotion and longer-term commitment. This challenge requires and probably deserves more cohesive initiatives on the NGO and official sides together, within a broadened movement for development education in OECD countries.

NOTES

1. Bertrand Schneider, "La Révolution aux Pieds Nus — Rapport au Club de Rome", Fayard, Paris, 1985.
2. Sir Geoffrey Wilson, "The Role of Non-Governmental Organisations in Aid to the Least-Developed Countries", in "Liaison Bulletin between Development Research and Training Institutes", OECD Development Centre, 1983, No. 10, New Series (special issue on the role of non-governmental organisations in development co-operation).
3. A.H. Barclay, with M.W. Hoskins, W.K. Njenga and R.B. Tripp, "The Development Impact of Private Voluntary Organisations: Kenya and Niger", report to the Office of Private and Voluntary Co-operation, USAID, by Development Alternatives, Inc., Washington, 1979.
4. J. Tendler, "Turning Private Voluntary Organisations into Development Agencies; Questions for Evaluation", USAID Evaluation Publication Series, Discussion paper No. 12, Washington, 1982.
5. W. Shawcross, "The Quality of Mercy — Cambodia, Holocaust and Modern Conscience", André Deutsch, London, 1984.

Section II: Sources of Funds
Chapter 7: Export Credits

7A. What is Export Finance?
A. Dunn and M. Knight

All major exporting countries have arrangements to protect exporters, and the banks who provide them with funding support, from the risks of exporting. The arrangements are based upon insurance concepts and they also provide a bridge between the buyers and suppliers of internationally traded goods and services, and the banking systems which provide the funding necessary to support such trade. In all cases, governments have — inescapably — become intimately involved in a number of areas.

This first chapter describes the nature of these mechanisms, dealing first with the arrangements themselves, then with how they are funded, and finally with the role of government. The chapter is a general one, and is intended to provide an overview of the problems which will be useful as a basis from which to understand the export insurance and finance arrangements of any country.

WHAT EXPORT FINANCE MEANS

The expressions export credit and export finance in this book are taken to mean the set of facilities available to an exporter in any country to help him cover the risks of non-payment in his export business. It is, therefore, essentially an insurance concept. Since, however, there will be no risk if cash is received from the buyer with each order, this insurance is required only when deferred payment terms are offered to the buyer, or when specific financing facilities are made available to him. Export credit is, therefore, a mixture of insurance and banking mechanisms.

No two national export credit systems are identical. Each has evolved in its own pattern, and each operates in its own political and commercial environment. The structure of each economy, the nature of its major industries and of their markets, the sophistication of its banking sector and insurance industry, all play a part in determining the set of facilities available to the exporter of that country, and how they work.

The set of problems faced by exporters are, however, similar, so it is not surprising that many systems attack each problem in recognizably similar ways and that common concepts apply to many different systems. The greatest similarity is perhaps the universal involvement both of government through the export credit agency concerned, and of the commercial banking sector in the workings of the system. Common types of insurance policy and banking facility are generally available around the world.

Export credit agencies are both in competition and in communication with each other. Regular communication at a technical level has been taking place since the formation, in 1934, of the Berne Union of Export Credit Insurers. More recently, since 1973, a series of negotiations and agreements have been pursued under the auspices of the OECD, seeking to prevent harmful competition on credit terms. More recently still, within the EEC, where export credit falls within the competence of the EEC Commission, discussions among member countries have taken place both on the facilities that should exist for intra-Community trade and on the posture the Community should adopt in negotiation with third countries. The impact of competition between the agencies is most easily imagined in final discussions over a single prestigious deal, when all concerned will seek ways to make their financing look most attractive. But at a less obvious level, pressure exists permanently from exporters on agencies to persuade them to improve the facilities available, when the exporters perceive a case for doing so.

The world's export credit systems, therefore, evolve within common parameters. They meet particular needs of a common general nature; they have a particular history and a particular legal, banking and insurance tradition; they operate in a common environment, confront common problems, and propose particular (though perhaps very similar) solutions.

The following paragraphs describe facilities which are generally available and explain the common terminology used in this book.

Insurance

The fundamental *risk* covered is of non-payment. The event causing loss can either be of a *commercial* or a *political* nature. Commercial loss arises through the inability of the buyer to meet his obligations *vis-a-vis* the exporter, because of his insolvency or bankruptcy or other severe deterioration in his financial position. Political loss arises through the occurrence of some event in the buyer's country which hinders or prevents him from meeting his obligations towards the supplier. Political events can cover the whole spectrum from war or civil war to an inability to pay caused by the non-availability of foreign exchange.

Most systems will provide that the supplier and/or his bank should share a proportion of the risk, largely to give the supplier an interest in the safety of his own export business, and thus an incentive to screen for himself the creditworthiness of his own customers.

The form of the insurance policy is likely to be *global* or *specific* or some hybrid of the two. Under a global policy, the exporter will nominate all his export orders for cover (within the parameters set in his policy), paying premium on the amount outstanding in the appropriate time period. A specific policy is designed to cover a particular export contract; inevitably, this will be a more labour-intensive operation, and a specific policy will be appropriate if the size of the operation is large, the order unique, or the credit period substantial. Global and specific policies may cover *short-term* (usually up to two years' credit) or *medium-term* (usually over two years' credit) transactions under one policy, or separate policies may be needed.

Credit insurance must cover *post-shipment* risks. However, risks exist between the award of the contract and the shipment of the goods when the goods are manufactured to order, and thus *pre-shipment* cover is usually available in addition for contracts of this nature.

Many other peripheral insurance schemes are in operation. The more important additional risks covered under some systems include *bond support, escalation insurance* and *exchange rate fluctuation insurance*.

Typical contract conditions may require an exporter to provide a bank bond to assure the buyer:

1. that if awarded a contract on the lines of the tender, the exporter will accept that contract *(bid-bond)*;
2. that the down-payment and any progress payments will be returned in the event that the exporter does not complete the contract *(down-payment* and *progress payment bonds)*;
3. that if the export fails to perform to specification, the exporter will forfeit a penalty *(performance bond/retention bond)*.

Support may be available to indemnify the exporter against the unfair calling of any of these bonds *(unfair calling cover)*; or it may indemnify the bank putting up the bond, which therefore will not book the amount of the bond against its credit ceiling for the exporter, but with the agency maintaining limited or no recourse, in the event that the bonds are justifiably called if the fault lies elsewhere than with the supplier.

Escalation insurance has been introduced only by France, Finland and the United Kingdom. It was intended to help exporters to fix prices for long lead time contracts without the disadvantage of having to make substantial but unquantifiable provision for domestic inflation in their contract prices. The schemes are uniformly unpopular: internationally, because they are held to be unfair competition; with governments, because of their cost; and with exporters, because of their limitations. Nevertheless, they have proved impossible, so far, to remove.

Various forms of insurance can be conceived to help cover exchange risks. These risks arise for an exporter bidding for, or performing, a contract denominated in a currency other than his own, and even for one denominated in his own currency where there is a substantial third country element, if that is contracted for by the exporter in the currency of a third country. The risks lie from contract award until receipt by the supplier of the final receipt due to him. Another period of risk lies from the moment a tender is issued until a contract becomes effective. Certain protection is available through the forward exchange markets to cover the former period; the latter period, however, because of the uncertainty as to whether a contract will ensue, can only be covered by insurance.

Guarantees

The provision by agencies of clean financial *guarantees* to the banking sector is near universal in systems which rely on the banking sector to provide funds for export finance facilities, and common in systems which rely wholly or partially on an export bank for the provision of funds. As the systems have evolved, the common need to minimize the banking risk to facilitate the provision of credit led first to banks having assigned to them the benefit of the insurance policy held by the supplier. Such a mechanism still requires the banks to be satisfied with the credit risk on the supplier, for this can hinder the completion of a transaction which is acceptable to an agency, if the supplier is not accepted by the bank. Hence, it is efficient to leave both aspects of the choice (i.e. the risk assessment both on the buyer and on the supplier) with the agency, and for the bank to put up funds relying solely on the credit of the agency. Most systems offer guarantees to the bank for the full amount of the exposure, though under some systems a small element of risk on the buyer or recourse against the supplier will be left with the bank.

Most agencies are charged (in relation to insurance and guarantees at least) with acting commercially. Nevertheless, most systems have specifically reserved the right to support business which cannot be accepted by the agency on commercial grounds by resorting to some direct government intervention if that business meets their *national interest* criteria. Such criteria, and the mechanisms used to support the business, and to account for premium as well as subsequent losses, differ from system to system.

Finance

Finance is required to support export credit business. The second leg of an export credit system is the mechanism by which finance is made available.

Most agencies insist (and the OECD Arrangement requires) that the buyer makes a direct payment in cash of at least 15% of the contract value, by one or more payments between contract signature and shipment of the goods.[1] The *financed amount* of any supply contract will, therefore, be at most 85% of the value of the contract. Where a contract provides for more than simply the delivery of hardware, however, its value may include, in addition to the purchase of hardware, the provision of material and services on site (the *local element*). A contract can also include the provision of hardware, services, or technology (in the form of license fees) from a third country (the *third country element*). If the contract is for the provision of some complete new facility, an important cost as far as the buyer is concerned is the due *interest during construction*. A supplier may logically offer to finance this element of the buyer's costs also. Thus finance for a major contract may cover a substantial part of these other elements, as well as the financed amount of the value of the hardware supply.

Export credit support is applicable in principle for contracts of any nature. The broad common categories are contracts for the supply of equipment, for the provision of services, and for the performance of civil contract works in the buyer's country; or for some amalgam of these.

Finance can be made available as *supplier credit* or *buyer credit*; it can be short term or medium term; it can be made available by banks, by an export bank, or by both in tandem.

A supplier credit is an arrangement under which a supplier agrees to allow deferred payment by his customer of the financed amount of the contract. The supplier will nevertheless want to get his receivables as soon as he can after the performance of the work, and the supplier credit mechanism permits him to do this. The buyer's obligation to make extended payment to the supplier is documented by the issue by the buyer of a stream of promissory notes or the acceptance by the buyer of a stream of bill of exchange. The bills or notes may be interest-bearing (in which case, under certain legal systems, an additional stream of interest notes will also be required) or the interest may have been capitalized within the principal sum financed. Once the bills or notes have been received by the supplier, an arrangement can be made between him and his bank under which the bank buys or discounts them, thus effectively providing credit through the supplier to the buyer. The instruments will have been expressed to be "for value received" and thus will technically acknowledge that the supplier has already performed his obligations under the contract. In practice, however, the fact that the direct financial relationship is between the supplier and the buyer makes it more likely that the buyer will contest this if for some reason the goods do not "work". It is common, therefore, for a greater degree of recourse to be maintained by the agency (and by the bank if the agency's guarantee to the bank is for less than the whole of the financed amount plus interest) against the supplier under a supplier credit than might be the case if a direct financial relationship existed between the bank and the buyer.

Under a buyer credit, a specific loan is arranged between the lender and the buyer or some borrower in his country with whom he is connected. This is documented by a direct loan agreement between the lender and the borrower. Apart from appropriate cross references, the obligations of the parties are independent of the obligations of the parties to the commercial contract. The loan is usually drawn down and paid directly to the supplier when the supplier delivers to the lender the documents specified in the loan agreement and the commercial contract which show that the supplier is entitled to a payment under the terms of the contract. The *credit period* is defined, unlike the case under a commercial loan agreement, as the period following completion by the supplier of his contractual obligations until the date on which final repayment is due. Because of the separation in legal terms of the loan agreement from the commercial contract, complex arrangements will be needed in the supplier's country to document the obligations of the supplier, the agency, and the banks between themselves before the loan agreement can be signed.[2]

A *confirming house* transaction is a third possible form. The prime function of a confirming house in short-term credit arrangements is to confirm an irrevocable letter of credit issued in favour of the supplier by a bank in the buyer's country; some export credit systems make it possible for a confirming house to insure a part of the risk with the agency concerned. However, such an institution can also make a useful intervention in medium-term transactions which then assume some of the characteristics of both buyer and supplier credit. The supplier enters into a cash contract with the buyer, and the confirming house enters into a lending arrangement, documented by an agreement and notes, with the buyer. The confirming house is thus in a position to confirm the cash contract by signing a contract of confirmation with the supplier. To fund the arrangement, the confirming house will discount the notes with a bank, i.e. will get a supplier credit from the bank. The agency is likely to provide insurance support to both confirming house and bank.

The buyer credit mechanism lends itself to the concept of *lines of credit*. A line of credit is a single loan agreement which is set up to finance a number of separate contracts. It may be a *general purpose* (or shopping basket) *line*. In this case, the borrower is usually a bank in the foreign country which advertises the existence of the line to its domestic clients. When a contract consistent with the criteria is nominated to it, and through it to the lender and agency, and is acknowledged to be eligible for finance under that line, a mechanism in relation to that contract analagous to a buyer credit has been created. The supplier will be paid at the due time, creating an obligation from the borrowing bank to the lender, which is guaranteed by the agency in return for premium paid by the supplier. Simultaneously an obligation is created between the buyer and the borrower, and since the borrowing bank is accepting the credit risk on the buyer, it is usual for it to make a turn on the funds. Such a line may cover contracts for different types of goods, of different sizes, and for several buyers. Hence, the length of the repayment period and its starting date is usually fixed for each individual contract placed under the line.

Many systems also recognize the concept of a *project line of credit*. This is a similar mechanism but applied to a single project. The borrower is more likely to be the project itself, and not some intermediary, and the main difference is that the repayment period will probably be the same for all contracts placed under the line, with its starting date at the commissioning of the project.

France is held to be the inventor, and most enthusiastic user of, *credit mixte*. As a formal arrangement to assist projects in development aid-worthy countries, the mixture of an aid element with an export credit package must count as a proper use of development aid funds. *Credit mixte* is, however, a major irritant to those countries which are followers rather than leaders in its use, since it gives the aid and credit decision-makers in the donor country the ability, by clever and selective use, to make a major impact on the proportion of important capital goods contracts obtained by their exporters in the recipient countries. Attempts to limit its use in an unfairly competitive way have not been succesful and an increasing number of countries are taking steps to enable them to use *credit mixte,* at least to match offers from competing countries, and selectively to lead the race.

HOW IT IS FUNDED

Export finance must be funded. Such funding can be provided by an export bank or by commercial banks, and may come from the domestic capital market of the supplier's country, from the international markets, or from the domestic capital market of the buyer's country. Each possible source has implications for the various parties involved.

Two distinct approaches have been developed to meet the funding requirements of export finance. In some countries the export credit agency is structured as an export bank (e.g. the Export-Import Bank of the United States) as well as an underwriter of insurance risks. In other countries (e.g. the United Kingdom) the agency is an insurer only, and specific mechanisms have been devised to enable the agency or some other government body to intervene in support of the provision and cost of the funding required. Some systems use elements of both solutions.

The Export Bank

In many ways, the export bank route is the more efficient. An export bank, wholly owned by the government, will have a credit rating almost indistinguishable from that of its government. It will be able to fund the consolidated balance of its lending by borrowing in the capital markets in an aggressive and professional manner and obtaining the finest terms on offer. It will not be constrained to match amounts, maturities or drawing schedules to those of particular export transactions. It will be borrowing on its own name, negotiating the terms and conditions of each operation directly with its lenders.

The Triangular Route

The other main route can be described as the *triangular* route. The funds will be provided from capital markets, usually from banks, as a loan either direct to the buyer or to the supplier, to enable him to offer deferred payment terms to his customer. The agency will underwrite a part or all of the creidt risk, and may intervene to help procure the needed funds and to smooth or subsidize their cost. Such a system requires that funds be provided in support of each export transaction, on draw-down and repayment conditions which match those of the transaction. A third party, either the banker, buyer or the supplier, will need to be involved in the negotiation of the documentation. The agency, rather than borrowing in its own name, will either be guaranteeing the credit risk, or supporting it in a less direct manner. In comparison with an export bank's funding, therefore, operations become more complex and less direct, and more of them are required. These factors tend to increase the cost of the funding, and to increase the input required to complete the necessary operations.

The triangular route, however, has certain features which may offset the banking advantages of the export bank concept. First, a smaller agency is required to conduct a given volume of business, and it does not need the capital base which an export bank needs to support its banking book. Second, in national accounting terms, the funds used for export finance are contingent, rather than actual, liabilities of the agency and thus of the government concerned.

Some systems operate with elements of both models. EFIC (Export Finance and Insurance Corporation) in Australia, for example, acts as a pure insurer excpet when a direct subsidized lending facility is required. In this case, it acts as an export bank, borrowing the funds needed directly from the Australian trading banks and on-lending the funds in its own name. In France, the longer maturities of any transaction are lent directly by BFCE (Banque Francais du Commerce Exterieure) while the shorter maturities are lent by commercial banks. Most of the export banks, furthermore, seek the involvement of commercial banks in co-financing of export credits from time to time, and some of them do so on every occasion.

The funds themselves may be provided from the domestic capital market of the exporting country, from an international market, or on occasions from the domestic capital market of the buyer's country.

Domestic Capital Markets

The domestic capital market of the exporting country is in many ways the most natural source of the funds. It is still the major source for all developed country export finance systems and the only source for a number of the most important. Loans sourced from the domestic capital market of the exporting country will be denominated in the supplier's currency. The balance of payments effect of a loan funded in this way is neutral, since it is drawn-down and paid to the supplier without crossing the exchanges. Indeed, if a third country or local cost element is being financed, the immediate balance of payments effect of the financed portion of the contract is negative, as the supplier pays out across exchanges for these elements and is reimbursed from the loan in domestic currency. After draw-down, the current account of the balance of payments benefits as interest payments are received, either through the sale of foreign exchange to buy the necessary domestic currency, or through the use of domestic currency balances held externally. (In the former case, an inflow crosses the exchanges; in the latter case, a liability to an external holder is extinguished.) The capital account benefits (through the same mechanisms) only as repayment of the loan is received.

If the supplier's country experiences a period of high inflation during the life of the loan, the real value of the receipts generated by the export is correspondingly eroded. Hence, particularly when inflation exceeds the agreed interest rate, the economic value of exporting on extended credit funded in this way can be seriously questioned, whatever the cost of the interest rate subsidy involved.

External Capital Markets

These factors have been important considerations in the decisions of individual systems to seek partial reliance on funds sourced in external capital markets. The most readily available external market is the Eurocurrency market. Indeed this in many respects is a result of past international trade, and the finance of new international trade is an immediately obvious function for it to perform.

If an export credit is funded from any capital market external to the exporting country, its balance of payments benefits immediately the loan is drawn-down. Domestic currency is purchased by the supplier using the foreign currency received. Thereafter, during the life of the loan, interest received is neutral in its effect (except to the extent of any subsidy, which has a negative effect). The repayment is also neutral. A contingent foreign exchange liability is likely to be created to the extent that it is not possible to pass on to the buyer on a back-to-back basis certain funding risks conventionally carried by borrowers in the Euromarket. The burden of the contingent liability is no harsher than the remote risks that accelerated repayment would be called for if the agency or its government had itself borrowed the funds directly. Additionally, the insurance and any bank guarantees are themselves contingent liabilities on the capital account of the balance of payments, and any claim would have to be met by the sale of domestic currency to purchase the required foreign currency, or by a debit to the reserves. A decrease over time in the real value of the external currency reduces the real burden of these contingent liabilities.

The Buyer's Capital Market

Use of the buyer's currency to fund export credits is still rare. As far as the exporting country is concerned, the transaction is identical in balance of payments terms to one funded in any other external capital market. As far as the buyer's country is concerned, the balance of payments effect is identical to a cash purchase. It has proved relevant in certain cases where the buyer is creating a facility (e.g. a mass transit system) whose revenues will depend wholly upon domestic economic conditions rendering him unprepared to accept any degree of exchange risk.

Other Markets

Following the Wallen Report*, serious consideration has been given in the inter-governmental debate to the concept of opening the domestic capital markets of subscribers to the OECD Arrangement to fund export finance transactions between third countries. Certain national capital markets which are well developed, and operate with little government influence on commercial decisions, could relatively easily accommodate such a policy. Where government intervenes in a substantial way, however, this may prove to be more difficult. In any case, major exchange risks will emerge for the exporters, and considerable evolution of the forward exchange markets will be needed before these can be satisfactorily resolved. Underlying this suggestion is the idea that if export credit interest rates are to be more closely linked to the market rates applying to each currency, fair competition will prevail only if suppliers from rival countries are able to offer to the buyer alternative financing structures, based on contracts and credit denominated in the currencies of their competitors, and on terms identical to those their competitors offer.

The Role of Government

Governments play a number of roles in support of export finance and insurance. They can be insurers of export risks; they can provide finance to exporters or to their customers; or they can intervene in the cost of providing finance, i.e. they can subsidize. In theory, all these activities, except that of subsidizer, can be carried out by bodies which are not related to their governments. In practice, in every country in the world today which has an export credit system, the government plays some part in the workings of that system. In some, the role of government is all-pervasive; in others, it is more limited. But if there is a tendency, it is for the government's role to expand; where for a time governments have tried to reduce their involvement, the result has usually been to reduce the level of activity of that export insurance and finance system rather than to reduce the involvement of government in it.

The Government as Risk-Taker

Official support for the insurance of exports is almost universal. This support is provided by the export credit agency concerned, which is usually either government-owned or a department of the government. The agency, in return for premia paid to it, insures the ultimate beneficiary of its policies against losses arising from the export business. In spite of the fact that all the agencies are required to operate on a basis of no net cost to public funds, all agencies have in recent years had to meet substantial claims which in some instances have come close to, or exceeded, premium income. The cumulative effect of inflation in the last decade has also meant that new liabilities undertaken in recent years have risen steeply, even if, as is the case in some countries, the volume of export trade underwritten has remained relatively static. The ratio of accumulated reserves to current liabilities, in the absence of periodic topping up of reserves from budget funds, will inevitably worsen with inflation, and agencies will become more exposed to a situation in which claims over a number of years exceed premium income. Since all export credit agencies are regarded by the beneficiaries of their policies as effectively having the same credit standing as their own government, and bankruptcy of the agency is not an option that can be comtemplated from either side, governments effectively support export risks.

The Government as Provider of Finance

Export finance is funded on the basis that most or all of the credit risk on the buyer is underwritten by the supplier's export insurance agency. Thus, indirectly the government is supporting the provision of this finance and effectively allows credit lines to be used which would otherwise be available for the use of the government itself. Further support is given in some systems (e.g. France) under which export finance facilities within the domestic market are allowed to be outside aggregate financial limits on the banking sector. In some systems, direct refinancing facilities are available to lenders; to the extent that these are used, the government is not only supporting the provision of finance, but is actually making the finance available itself.

The Government as Subsidizer

Finally, the government may intervene in the provision of finance by affecting the cost of that finance. Such intervention has typically started as a smoothing operation, converting variable rate funding to a fixed rate which is expected to reflect some median level over the credit period of the cost of funds. In the past decade, however, the combined effects of high interest rates in the wake of high inflation, on the one hand, and the competitive pressures on exporters providing an incentive to keep export credit rates low while commercial rates have risen, on the other, have led inexorably to an acknowledged subsidy being provided in many countries for export credit interest rates.

Once in this position, it is difficult to escape. In the absence of any autonomous decline in rates in the markets in question, governments have only four options: they can stop their intervention in export finance; increase their own export credit rates unilaterally; continue their subsidy; or seek, through international discussion, a co-ordinated increase in all countries'

---

* Editor's note: The Wallen Report is a report on the effect of the structure of interest notes on export credits. This report was prepared by a commission headed by Axel Wallen of the Swedish Export Credit Agency for the OECD Secretariat in 1979-1980.

rates. In recent years, most countries have simultaneously followed the third and fourth of these options.

Some systems have at times been forced, by budgetary constraints, temporarily to discontinue such intervention. In the mid-1970s, the Italian system repeatedly found itself unable to provide new commitments; the U.S. Eximbank has for many years been chronically restricted by its need for congressional approval; in late 1976, the U.K. might very well have had to discontinue supporting export finance, had it not been able to switch to a Eurocurrency-funded scheme. In budgetary terms this was expected to be substantially cheaper, because the authorities had no immediate financing obligations, and because it was expected that Eurodollar interest rates would remain substantially below domestic sterling interest rates. In Singapore, the higher than anticipated cost of interest rate subsidy caused a temporary hiatus, in 1980, in the support given on finance for Singapore's exports, and by 1982 a complete cessation of fixed rate and subsidized financing.

The unattractiveness, in domestic political terms, of pulling out needs no emphasis. It puts an immediate competitive disadvantage upon domestic manufacturers of capital equipment. This would be reflected immediately in a sharp downturn in new export orders, leading in due course to a decline in workload. The complaints of U.S. exporters of the harshness of their exposed position, caused by Eximbank's initial shutdown in the first half of 1981, is evidence of fears, if not the reality, of this.

NOTES

[1] Editor's note: The OECD Arrangement, often termed the "Consensus" is a short-hand term for the "Arrangement on Guidelines for Officially Supported Export Credits," which was established in 1978 and is regularly reviewed by its OECD signatories.

The Consensus established standards for the terms of export credits. The standards, which are regularly reviewed and revised, apply to such terms as the minimum size of the requisite direct payment from the buyer (currently 15% of the contract value); the minimum interest rate; the maximum maturity of the credit, and rules governing the aid element of mixed credits.

The terms of the Consensus vary according to the identity of the importing countries. All importing countries are divided, on the basis of per capita income, into three categories, namely relatively rich, intermediate, and relatively poor countries. Below is a list of the countries belonging to those categories with category I being relatively rich countries and category III being relatively poor countries. It should be noted that the membership of each category is subject to review and countries can "graduate" from one category to another.

[2] Editor's note: Due to a quirk of the Gregorian calendar it is not possible for a loan to carry both equal daily interest charges and monthly interest charges. The need to choose between the two has resulted in three methods for calculating interest charges:

a. 365/365 Method — (also known as actual basis). This method is based on equal daily charges. According to this method the annual interest rate is divided by 365 and the result is the daily interest rate. To obtain the interest charge, this daily rate is multiplied by the outstanding principal amount and the number of days in the payment period. If the loan agreement is silent as to the method of calculating the interest charge it is assumed that the parties intended this method to apply.

b. 360/360 Method — (also known as bond basis). This method is based on equal monthly charges. It assumes that the year consists of twelve months, each having thirty days. To calculate the interest charges the annual interest is divided by twelve and the result is multiplied by the outstanding principal amount and the number of months in the payment period.

The same result can be obtained by dividing the annual interest rate by 360 and then multiplying the result by the principal outstanding and the number of assumed days (based on all months having 30 days) in the payment period. When this method is the intended method, the loan agreement will refer to interest being calculated on the basis of 12 months of 30 days each.

c. 365/360 Method — (also known as bank basis). In this method a year is considered to consist of 360 days. Consequently, interest charges are calculated by dividing the annual interest rate by 360 and then multiplying the result by the principal outstanding and the actual number of days in the payment period. When this method is the intended method for calculating interest charges, the loan agreement will refer to interest being calculated on the basis of "the actual number of days elapsed over a year of 360 days."

It should be noted that the first two methods both result in exact simple interest with no distortion of the nominal interest rate. The third method distorts the nominal interest by, in effect, adding another 5 days onto its year of 360 days. The result is to make the actual interest charge to the borrower 1/72 more than the nominal interest rate.

LIST AND CLASSIFICATION OF RECIPIENT COUNTRIES

Editor's Note: This list is subject to change and is included for illustrative purposes only.

CATEGORY I

American Samoa
American Virgin Islands
Andorra

Australia
Austria

Bahrain
Bermuda
Brunei

Canada
Czechoslovakia

European Community*

Faroe Islands
Finland
French Antarctic Territories
French Guiana
French Polynesia

German Democratic Republic
Gibraltar*
Greenland
Guadeloupe
Guam

Iceland
Israel

Japan

Kuwait

Libya
Liechtenstein

Martinique
Mayatte
Monaco

Nauru
New Caledonia
New Zealand
Norway

Puerto Rico

Qatar

Reunion
Ross Dependency

San Marino
Saudi Arabia
St. Pierre & Miquelon
Sweden
Switzerland

*United Arab Emirates
United States
USSR

Vatican

Wallis & Futuna

*Abu Dhabi, Ajman, Dubai, Fujairah, Ras al Khaimah, Sharjah, Umm al Qaiwan

*Interest rate support is not available for intra-EC business or business carried on between EC member states and Gibraltar.

CATEGORY II

Albania
Algeria
Anguilla

Antigua & Barbuda
Argentina
Azores

Bahamas
Barbados
Belize
Botswana
Brazil
British Antarctic Territories
British Indian Ocean Territory
British Virgin Islands
Bulgaria

Cayman Islands
Chile
Colombia
Cook Islands
Costa Rica
Cuba
Cyprus

Dominican Republic

Ecuador
Falkland Islands & Dependencies
Fiji

Gabon
Guatemala

Hong Kong
Hungary

Iraq
Iran
Ivory Coast

Jamaica
Jordan

Kiribati
Korea (North)
Korea (South)

Lebanon

Macao
Madeira
Malaysia
Malta
Mauritius
Mexico
Mongolia
Montserrat
Morocco

Namibia
Netherland Antilles
Nigeria
Niue

Oman

Panama
Papua—New Guinea
Paraguay
Peru
Poland
Portugal
Romania

Seychelles
Singapore
South Africa
St. Helena & Dependencies
St. Lucia
Surinam
Syria

Taiwan
Trinidad & Tobago
Tunisia
Turks & Caicos Islands
Turkey
Trust Territory of The Pacific Islands (US)*

Uruguay

Venezuela

West Indian Associated States
St. Kitts—Nevis
Yugoslavia

*Palau, Micronesia, Marshall Islands, North Marianas

CATEGORY III

Afghanistan
Angola

Bangladesh
Benin (ex Dahomey)
Bhutan
Bolivia
Burkina Faso (ex Upper Vo
Burma
Burundi

Cameroon
Cape Verde Islands
Central African Republic
Chad
China
Comoro Islands
Congo

Djibouti
Dominica

Egypt
El Salvador
Ethiopia

Gambia
Ghana
Grenada
Guinea-Bissau
Guinea-Equatorial
Guyana

Haiti
Honduras

India
Indonesia

Kampuchea (ex Cambodia)
Kenya

Laos
Lesotho
Liberia

Madagascar
Malawi
Maldives
Mali

Mauritania
Mozambique

Nepal
Nicaragua
Niger

Pakistan
Philippines
Pitcairn Islands

Rwanda

Sao Tome & Principe
Senegal
Sierra Leone
Solomon Islands
Somalia
Sri Lanka
St. Vincent & The Grenadines
Sudan
Swaziland

Tanzania
Thailand
Togo
Tokelau
Tonga
Tuvalue (ex Ellice)

Uganda

Vanuatu
Vietnam

Western Samoa

Yemen Arab Republic (Sanaa)
Yemen People's Democratic Republic (Aden)

Zaire
Zambia
Zimbabwe

Note: Transitional arrangements apply to countries underlines ie maximum credit period 10 years.

7B. The Role of Export Credits in Economic Development
The World Bank

Export credits have formed a key element of financial flows to developing countries in recent years, especially to the low-income countries for which sources of commercial bank finance are not readily available. Although their use has brought problems as well as benefits, it is clear that they will continue to play an important role in financing development. This World Bank paper complements an earlier paper prepared by the staff of the International Monetary Fund,[1] which addressed important issues affecting the flow of export credits to developing countries. The present paper focuses on the use made of these credits by the borrowing countries.

Two key issues for providers and users of export credits have been highlighted by the debt-servicing difficulties of many developing countries since 1982:

- How to ensure that export credit flows remain at levels broadly appropriate to the capacities and needs of the borrowing countries, and that abrupt changes in availability do not occur in a manner that is damaging to these countries

- How to ensure that export credits are used effectively by the recipient countries in a way that protects the position of creditors and helps to avoid repetition of the widespread losses suffered by export credit agencies over the period 1982-84

These issues are in fact closely interrelated and cannot be properly treated in isolation. Although export credits are normally seen as serving very different objectives for providers and users, the two groups have a strong mutual interest in looking broadly at the role and effectiveness of export credits as a source of development finance.

This paper provides a preliminary examination of the issues raised by the use of export credits in the development context. Existing data are limited in their coverage of the provision and use of export credits, and there is at present no body of case study analysis on which to base a systematic review. The method followed here has been to examine the record of export credit-financed projects by drawing on the experience of Bank staff and others active in the development field. A number of common features emerge, but the degree to which these can be attributed specifically to the use of export credits remains conjectural. More research is required before confident conclusions can be drawn.

Other restrictions on the coverage of this paper should be mentioned. The paper is primarily concerned with the use of export credits in developing countries and does not address issues relating to their use by the developing countries themselves in support of their own exports. The use of export credits for military expenditures and the mixing of official aid finance with export credits in the form of associated financing are also considered to lie outside its scope, though both raise important questions in the context of development.

The focus of the paper is a more limited one. Export credits have a number of basic characteristics which are not shared by other forms of development finance. It is believed that analysis of these, in the context of project experience in which export credits have been used, may suggest lines of enquiry that will be helpful in reviewing the policy issues faced by providers and users.

The first section gives basic definitions of export credits and examines trends in their provision since 1970 within the context of overall financial flows to the developing countries. The special characteristics of export credits are examined in the following section as an introduction to the main body of the paper, in which these characteristics are related to problems encountered in the use of export credit financing for projects. The experience of other, more successful, users is also reviewed. Tentative conclusions are drawn in the final section and ideas for strengthening the way the system operates are discussed.

EXPORT CREDITS AND THEIR CONTRIBUTION TO INTERNATIONAL FINANCIAL FLOWS

Export credit is financing tied directly to the cross-border purchase of specific goods. Export credit agencies (ECAs) exist either to provide such finance directly or to guarantee other providers. Their terms of reference require them to carry out that part of their governments' commercial or foreign policies that they have been established to implement; the common overriding objective is the promotion of national exports. They are normally also required to operate at a profit, or at least to break even over a period of years. To maintain safe lending standards, they also need to ensure, as far as they can, that the resources they provide contribute to the development of the recipient countries.

A basic distinction is made between export credits provided by the exporting company, called suppliers' credits, and those provided to the buyer by other than the exporter, which are called buyers' credits. The latter may be granted on an initially unspecified basis, a line of credit being established which can then be drawn upon over time against agreed purchases. Suppliers' credits may be financed by the exporter but are normally refinanced by discounting through the banking system. By their nature, buyers' credits require financing by a third party.

Where finance is supplied directly by government agencies, it is known as official export credit. It forms a relatively small proportion of total officially supported export credit flows, however (see table 3-1), because the majority of ECAs are limited in their function to the provision of guarantees for credits financed by the commercial banking sector or other financial intermediaries. Few of the major export credit-granting countries provide for direct export financing; those that do include Canada, the Federal Republic of Germany, Japan, and the United States.

Export credits are normally provided at fixed rates of interest on the basis of internationally agreed terms coordinated under the OECD's export credit "Consensus" arrangements.[2] Where financing is provided by commercial banks, the banks are compensated by the government for the difference between the market interest rate at which they fund themselves and the fixed rate of interest at which the export credit is formally provided, plus an agreed margin. The level of subsidy for export credits implicit in this arrangement is controlled through the Consensus, with minimum interest rates structured (in three categories) according to the per capita income level of the importing countries.

DATA

Statistical data on export credits are incomplete because of difficulties of identification. For trade with the developing

Table 3-1. *Export Credits Provided to Developing Countries, 1970–83*
(billions of U.S. dollars)

Item	1970–72 average	1977	1978	1979	1980	1981	1982	1983
Net disbursements from DAC countries								
Official export credits	0.84	1.44	2.22	1.73	2.46	2.01	2.66	2.10
Private export credits (guaranteed by ECAs)	1.92	8.84	9.70	8.85	11.12	11.30	7.09	5.50
Total	2.76	10.28	11.92	10.58	13.58	13.31	9.75	7.60
Total receipts of developing countries (from all sources[a])	17.82	66.44	86.51	85.78	99.15	109.76	97.41	99.75
Total export credits as percentage of total receipts	15	15	14	12	14	12	10	8
Gross disbursements from DAC countries								
Official export credits	2.01	4.70	5.97	5.83	7.14	6.87	6.85	6.54
Private export credits	5.72	18.15	21.77	22.93	27.77	29.36	26.01	23.34
Total	7.73	22.85	27.74	28.76	34.91	36.23	32.86	29.88

a. DAC definition.
Source: OECD, *Development Cooperation* (Paris, 1981 and 1984).

countries, however, two statistical series provide important information on past trends. These are compiled by the OECD, which collects data of officially supported medium- and long-term export credits from creditor countries under its Creditor Reporting System (CRS), and the World Bank, whose Debtor Reporting System (DRS) captures credit commitments undertaken by the debtor countries. The identification of export credits from DRS data is more detailed but is partly derived with the use of proxies and must be interpreted with caution. The two series cannot be fully reconciled (see appendix A); references in this paper are therefore carefully identified.[3]

RECENT TRENDS

Export credits grew substantially in the 1950s and 1960s. By 1970 they accounted for 25 percent of all outstanding debt owed by developing countries.[4] Through the 1970s, as commercial bank lending became more prominent in international capital movements, the share of export credits in total lending experienced a decline. For the period 1970-78, however, this was relatively modest. The total debt of the developing countries grew by 22 percent a year over this period, while export credits (DRS data) rose by 20 percent. After 1978 the pace of export credit growth slackened and then fell sharply as debt-servicing difficulties emerged in 1982 and 1983.

One reason for this break in the growth trend was the decline in new suppliers' credits after 1978. The net flow of suppliers' credits declined from $2.45 billion in 1978 to below $800 million in 1979, and thereafter remained a generally weak element in export credit flows. Total suppliers' credits outstanding at the end of 1983, at $22.37 billion, were only $1 billion above the 1978 level.

The causes of this reduced flow of suppliers' credits are unclear. In part, the slowdown in net flow reflects the effect of rising amortization payments. The DRS data also show it to have been especially pronounced in North Africa and the Middle East, pointing to a relationship with the 1979-80 OPEC oil price increases; it may be assumed that these reduced the demand for credit on capital goods imports to the region. Nevertheless, the weaker trend in new suppliers' credits affected all regions to some degree after 1978. Earlier lending in this form may have included a greater element of credit provided directly by exporters without ECA cover. If so, a source of additional export finance may have been lost, at least temporarily, after 1978, as conditions in international lending markets became more volatile.

With regard to the direction of export credit flows, the most pronounced change shown by DRS data has been the sharp fall in the share going to Europe and the Mediterranean.[5]

Whereas this ranged between 15 percent and 20 percent of total export credits in the early 1970s, it has remained at below 10 percent in the period 1980-84. The decline may reflect the stiffening of interest rate terms against more developed importing countries introduced by the OECD's export credit Consensus arrangements after 1978. It no doubt also points to a greater volume of import trade to these countries being conducted on an uninsured basis.

The corresponding increase in export credit shares has been taken by Asian countries, including those in South Asia, and by countries in Sub-Saharan Africa. Export credits to the latter group rose strongly in the 1970s to a peak of over 20 percent of the total in 1980, before falling back as debt-servicing difficulties emerged. Latin American and other developing countries in the Western Hemisphere have consistently taken the largest share of export credits, at around 40 percent, but this has shown relatively little change over the period monitored.

For individual countries, the incompleteness of present data and the general lack of earlier analysis to draw upon mean that only preliminary discussion of the pattern of export credit flows is possible. OECD data point to a significant degree of concentration among recipients of export credits, with the twelve largest net recipients attracting between 46 percent and 61 percent of all such flows in the years 1979-82. As might be expected, however, this pattern shows a significant degree of correlation with trade movements to the developing countries over the same period[6] and in this sense is a natural reflection of the close link between export credits and physical trade, especially trade in capital goods.

A more instructive measure of the degree of concentration is to compare the pattern of export credit flows with that of commercial bank lending. In the same four-year period examined above, the twelve largest developing-country borrowers from the international syndicated loan market typically accounted for 75 percent to 80 percent of the total. Export credits thus show a significantly broader distribution than commercial lending and represent an important source of development finance for many countries.

This importance appears more clearly from an analysis of the sources of external debt for different country income groups among developing countries, as in table 3-2. In all groups, export credits provided by OECD countries form an important, and not dissimilar, proportion of total debt. For the low-income countries, however, they are substantially greater than private debt (almost twice as large) and thus represent the major source of commercial, or quasi-commercial, finance.

The low-income countries may, however, also be more vulnerable to discontinuities in the flow of export credits.

The effect of the sharp reduction in new export credits after 1981 was particularly severe on the low-income countries of Sub-Saharan Africa. Disbursements of medium- and long-term credits to these countries (DRS data) fell from $1.28 billion in 1980 to $250 million in 1983. In part, this fall was accounted for by reduced demand as debtor countries adjusted to balance of payments pressures by reducing investment. As the Fund paper has identified, however, it also resulted from the retrenchment measures taken by the ECAs themselves; many faced mounting losses and sought to curtail them by limiting further exposure to countries of reduced creditworthiness.

THE CHARACTERISTICS OF EXPORT CREDITS

The risk of discontinuities in the provision of export credits arises from the terms of reference under which the ECAs operate. These relate to the commercial and political priorities of government and to the requirement that most ECAs operate at no cost to the public purse (averaged over a number of years). They do not relate directly to the market's need for export insurance or to the importing countries' development needs.

There is thus an essential paradox to recognize in considering the role of export credits in economic development. Promoting development is not a defined objective of export credits or of the ECAs, and at times their primary objective (export promotion) may be at variance with it. This makes it important to look carefully at the characteristics of export credits before attempting to assess, or seek means of strengthening, their contribution to development; otherwise the enquiry risks being falsely based and reaching unrealistic conclusions.

Operationally, export credits have a number of characteristics that make them well suited to financing investment and often superior to alternative sources of commercial finance to which the recipient countries may have access. The principal characteristic is the fixed rate of interest that export credits offer (this is no longer the invariable rule, but remains typical). The availability of fixed interest rates has protected borrowers against the volatility of market rates in recent years and has facilitated project appraisal on the basis of an effective financial rate of return.

A second attractive feature of export credits is their longer maturity term than most commercial loans. For export credits committed in 1983 the average term was close to ten years, against an average of less than eight years for new financial market lending to developing countries in the same year (DRS data). The credit period for export credits, moreover, usually commences six months after the buyer takes responsibility for the goods. In the case of equipment commissioned by the supplier, this frequently means when the project incorporating the goods commences production, which can render the terms of some loans (for example, for power generators) closer to those of fifteen-year loans from development financing institutions.

The credit guarantee provided by ECAs is also a positive feature in the global development context, since it has encouraged a wider distribution of export credits—as was shown under "Recent Trends," above—than would have occurred naturally through private capital markets at this

Table 3-2. Developing Countries' Long-Term Debt, by Country Group, 1983

	Low-income countries		Lower-middle-income countries		Upper-middle-income countries	
	Billions of dollars	Percent	Billions of dollars	Percent	Billions of dollars	Percent
Official development assistance (ODA)	36	26.7	9	9.9	17	4.5
Export credits	24	17.8	20	22.0	83	21.8
Private	13	9.6	30	33.0	224	58.8
Multilateral	35	25.9	16	17.6	32	8.4
Other[a]	27	20.0	16	17.6	25	6.6
Total	135		91		381	

Note: The income classifications are based on 1980 per capita GNP as shown in the 1981 World Bank Atlas (Washington, D.C.: World Bank, 1981). Low-income countries are those with per capita GNP below $600; lower-middle-income countries, between $600 and $1,200; upper-middle-income countries, above $1,200. These definitions differ from the World Bank's own definitions, which classify low-income countries on 1980 data, for example, as those with per capita GNP of $410 or less.

a. Includes lending by OPEC and the Council for Mutual Economic Assistance.

Source: OECD, "External Debt of Developing Countries," 1983 Survey (Paris, 1984).

stage. Moreover, the shifting importance of financial sources shown in table 3-2 for the different country income groups suggests that export credits may act as an important dynamic in the process of graduation from official concessional finance to market borrowing.

Finally, but more ambiguously, there is the element of interest rate subsidy carried by most medium- and long-term export credits to developing-country purchasers. The availability of subsidized credit offers the possibility of financing investment that would not otherwise be financially viable.

In any transaction, however, it is inadvisable to consider the cost of credit in isolation from the cost and quality of the goods being financed. The characteristic feature of export credit subsidies is that they are employed according to the needs of the exporter and not those of the importer. Their function is to promote sales, not to monitor the appropriateness of purchases. They may, therefore, encourage purchases that have limited or low priority in the development program of the importing country, if proper controls in the developing country are lacking. In this sense they are potentially wasteful as a development source.

This export-promoting function is reinforced by a further characteristic of export credits—that they are provided only for purchases of goods made from the country offering the credit.[7] Although this is an entirely logical feature of a system designed to promote exports, it clearly places a constraint on the development-financing value of export credits. Countries that organize themselves well can arrange competitive bidding for contracts without losing access to export credit finance, but the rational purpose of export credits is to establish a relationship between buyer and seller that reduces the scope for international competition in this form.

The subject of subsidies is a complex one. They have been associated with the provision of export credits for so long that they are regarded as one of the characteristic features of export credit. This results from custom rather than necessity, however, as the rationale of export credit support through ECAs does not depend on the provision of subsidies. Credit insurance is the primary function of ECAs: their economic purpose is to supplement the market mechanism when the absence of official support would result in lost trading opportunities because of the exporter's (not the importer's) reluctance to complete the transaction—that is, when the exporter has limited ability to assess the risks involved and limited capacity to sustain losses. When private market agents are unwilling to provide insurance on an adequate scale, official guarantees are a legitimate and desirable activity in support of international trade and contribute significantly to world economic growth. What may be asked in this context is whether the de facto link between subsidies and export credit guarantees has not been restrictive, serving to preserve export insurance within the public sector and to inhibit the development of market alternatives.

EXPORT CREDITS IN DEVELOPMENT

Among providers of international finance, only the development institutions (including aid agencies) have an explicit mandate to take full account of the economic and social merits of the projects to be financed by their lending. This often entails close involvement in the planning, procurement, and implementation stages of projects and brings into play the development and project expertise of the financing institution.

Other lenders are primarily concerned to ensure that the terms of their lending are honored by the borrower so that their own commercial or (in the case of many ECAs) statutory operating objectives are achieved. Given the special character of soverign risk, this implies a greater interest in the borrower's overall debt-servicing capacity than in the purpose for which the additional loan is raised, its economic merits, and the likely financial return. Where these are seen as marginal to debt-servicing prospects, other lending considerations may claim priority—the importance of the client relationship with a lending bank or the promotion of national exports with an ECA.

Availability by itself, however, does not guarantee that foreign borrowing will contribute positively to the development goals of the debtor country. How the borrowing is used is of critical importance. Except when shared with a development institution, responsibility for this rests with the borrower. Since it is the borrower who undertakes the commitment to service and eventually repays the debt, this may be seen as appropriate. In principle, it ensures that long-term self-interest is effectively harnessed to investment decisions. In practice, however, the link may be frustrated in many ways, and then problems arise for both borrowers and lenders.

Project problems can arise for many reasons, which often have little direct connection with the form of financing used. When governments are pursuing inappropriate macroeconomic policies, for example, the signals given within the economy may lead to inefficient sectoral investment, however carefully an individual project is planned. Care is therefore needed in drawing a linkage between project difficulties and export credits; but characteristic problems have arisen sufficiently often in projects financed by export credits to raise concern. These problems are analyzed here on the basis of examples from several countries in preliminary reviews by Bank staff and by others active in the development field. They focus on four issues: project priorities, project design, pricing, and the broader question of credit availability.

Project Priorities

The review undertaken by Bank staff identified several export credit-financed projects which were low in development priority but were supported in the developing country for essentially noneconomic reasons. The problem arises in acute form when a project has been turned down by bilateral and multilateral agencies but is then financed by ECA-supported credits because it satisfied particular objectives of the agency's government. This can occur even when the recipient country is technically off-cover with the ECA if the project results in orders for a company or industrial region identified as requiring official support or if critical considerations of market share arise.

Examples include the construction of a new capital city in one developing country and a new metro system in another. These would—in the view of the Bank's regional offices—have very low priorities on developmental grounds. The construction and construction supply sectors, however, are among the sectors most seriously affected by the recession in OECD countries, and both projects were able to obtain export credit financing without difficulty. Nuclear power stations provide other examples of projects which, in the view of development and aid agencies, are of low priority or are even inappropriate to the stage of development of certain developing countries, but which fairly readily find support from ECAs in the major nuclear construction countries.

Projects of this type raise large judgmental issues on which there is unlikely to be complete agreement at any time. Nevertheless, the present requirement for carefully phased adjustment programs for many countries emerging from debt-servicing difficulties, and for others with very limited access to external finance, implies that such issues deserve attention. Better communication between development agencies and the ECAs is one aspect for consideration.

PROJECT DESIGN

Appropriate projects may be rendered inefficient in practice by poor design specifications, including inappropriate siting and technology. These are areas in which the authorizing ECA is unlikely to have expertise. Suppliers and contractors have an active self-interest in seeking the success of projects in which their own reputations are concerned, and this is an important safeguard. Nevertheless, they may lack sufficient knowledge of local operating conditions to ensure that the design and technology are appropriate—and their protected financial position, as a result of ECA guarantees, may redue their concern. This is a particular problem for poorer countries with limited domestic expertise for evaluating suppliers' bids and monitoring project implementation. Where differential subsidies are available and are tied to packages of equipment, the risk of poor decisionmaking will be increased.

In a recent example of unsatisfactory design, the specifications for a water treatment project did not take account of the reticulation system into which the pipeline would feed and thus prevented the treatment plant from operating at full efficiency. In another case, the advanced technology for a fertilizer project proved unsuited to the country, and delays in preparing the infrastructure for the oversophisticated design led to construction delays at the implementation stage. As a result, some equipment lay idle for so long after delivery that it was out of warranty by the time it was installed. Subsequent maintenance problems and the restricted availability of foreign exchange for spare parts have prevented the plant from ever running at more than 50 percent capacity.

An example of a different kind is provided by the inland petroleum refinery commissioned in one oil-exporting country which was technologically unable to refine the nationally produced crude. The required feedstock therefore has to be imported, on a swap basis, from another oil-producing state. In a second country, an alumina processing plant was built, with the support of export credits, far away from the port through which its raw material is imported, with the result that alumina has to be shipped long distances for processing and aluminum shipped back for export.

Design problems are a serious and common area of waste—and they are not, of course, restricted to developing countries or to export credit projects. Export credits, however, have a potential for increasing the incidence of design problems if the financial inducement of subsidized loans leads to inefficient buying decisions. The main issue, however, is to ensure the appropriateness of technology to the operating conditions and the level of the managerial and technical skill in the importing countries. When a development agency is involved in the project, the risk of inappropriate technology may be reduced. Nevertheless, under present export credit arrangements there remains a risk that the issue will be neglected.

PRICING

As with all financing involving tied procurement, the use of export credits raises questions about the pricing of goods financed in this way. Lines of credit can increase potential problems, especially when time limits are involved, since the position of the buyer will be known to the exporter. In such circumstances exporters will be tempted to raise prices to what they see as a captive buyer. The problem is not unavoidable, but it does expose developing-country purchasers to pressures they may have difficulty dealing with, especially with respect to goods for which export credits are not commonly provided and price information is therefore less readily available.

Overpricing is difficult to document, since it is most likely to occur when orders have not been subject to competitive bidding. Reliable alternative pricing is therefore hard to obtain. Differences in the price of suppliers' goods to different markets may or may not be validly accounted for by differences in local conditions or in certain aspects of the services provided. A theoretical study of export credit programs undertaken by World Bank staff[8] concluded that, under the assumptions about market structure made in the study, purchasers making use of subsidized export credits may receive between 50 and 100 percent of the subsidy, with the exporter capturing the balance. The observation of Bank staff, however, has been that importing countries on occasion fare significantly worse than this in practice.

CREDIT AVAILABILITY

The concept of appropriate credit levels is a difficult one and must be treated cautiously. Market forces can normally be expected to operate in a manner that will preclude excessive flows—through the continued provision of export credits to countries approaching serious balance of payments problems in the late 1970s and early 1980s raised obvious questions in this context. For ECAS, as the IMF paper demonstrates, pressures of a nonfinancial character may supervene, contributing to flows which cannot be strictly justified on the basis of assessed creditworthiness.

Situations have been identified by Bank staff in which ECAs continued to guarantee credits even when the evidence clearly suggested that the recipient country could not use the additional resources productively. The extension of new credits to some oil-exporting countries whose transport infrastructures were already hopelessly overloaded exemplified this. In one well-known instance, goods had to wait several months to be unloaded from ships, only to lie unused on the dockside.

A more recent example was the provision, financed by export credits, of telephone exchange equipment two years before installation was feasible. The ECA involved was aware of the situation, since the World Bank had so advised it. Given the competition in the international telecommunications industry, however, it took the view that if it did not provide the credtis another agency would.

These and similar examples raise questions about the adequacy of information flows to the ECAs. More obviously, prehaps, they illustrate how the interpretation of national interest in the exporting country may override other considerations. The merit of the argument is not clear-cut, given the responsibility of the importing country government for loans whose repayment it is guaranteeing. Especially when finance is being provided with a significant subsidy element, the probability of supporting potentially wasteful resource flows to low-income countries must raise questions about the collaborative efforts between ECA, and between these agencies and the international development institutions.

The frequency with which the above problems arise for many developing countries marks them as being important. Nevertheless, few of the situations described constitute problems—at least, not problems of the same magnitude—to all users of export credits. Among more advanced developing countries, many have organized their use of credits in a way that maximizes benefits within the constraints of the system as it currently operates. To such countries, in particular, the availability of export credit has represented a very valuable additional source of development finance, adding flexibility to financing arrangements and frequently reducing cost. Projects planned in association with the Bank have, on occasion, ultimately been financed by export credits rather than the Bank loans because the export credits were available more cheaply.

With the exception of countries that are able to rely on effective incentive structures to allocate credit efficiently in their economies, this more sophisticated use of export credits is usually dependent on the existence of a well-ordered, formal development program. Such programs have two common features: controlled planning of investment projects within the public sector, and a significant degree of centralization over purchasing decisions involving use of export credits.

Proper investment planning enables purchasing agencies to identify plant and equipment requirements well in advance of need and to invite competitive tendering from the major international suppliers. This may be asked for on an inclusive financing basis (as is customary, for example, in Indonesia) or it may exclude financing initially (as happens in the Republic of Korea). Flexibility can be further increased by breaking project needs down into small packages of equipment and putting these out for separate tender. In doing so, however, the country must assure itself that no serious loss of design efficiency will result to offset the competitive benefits gained at contract stage.

By organizing bidding in this way, countries rarely exclude themselves from access to the favorable financing terms of export credits, but they do ensure that contract prices for equipment reflect competitive market forces. The reverse may be true of the financing terms. The knowledge of competitive bidding may cause ECAs to review the possibility for improving terms through the use of associated financing or other available means.

By centralizing the sanctioning authority for use of export credits in investment projects, governments can reinforce the discipline of the planning process and, when necessary, extend its priorities to the private sector. Such sanctioning is an aspect of a country's overall procedures for managing its foreign debt and normally involves cooperation between several departments of government. Turkey, for example, has two multi-agency screening systems, one for the public sector and a second for the private, both of which come ultimately under the authority of the Treasury.

The object of such systems is to ensure that the availability of export credit financing is treated as a scarce national resource and used efficiently. In some instances this involves official limits on the volume of export credits used by a single project or by a particular agency in a given year. A division of government may also monitor the condition of international capital markets in order to optimize the timing of international borrowing, including export credits, and to influence investment project decisions accordingly.

To operate the system well, a country needs an efficient administration and the technical competence to implement and monitor its investment programs. Export credits are thus more likely to prove a cheap, flexible, and efficient financing tool for countries already well advanced along the development path than for those in its earlier stages. But even when more elaborate control structures are not in place, a timely initiative can frequently bring improvement. The cost of a Tanzanian textile project, for example, was lowered significantly simply through the dispatch of telexes to a number of ECAs prior to final contract signing on the originally proposed deal.

When appropriately used, therefore, export credits clearly have a positive contribution to make to development, and poorer developing countries can learn to use them to their own advantage within the system as it operates at present. Nevertheless, for these countries the problems identified earlier arise from basic features of export credit finance:

- The role and objectives of the ECAs, as currently defined, mean there is no automatic consideration of development priorities in export credit procedures. Caveat emptor generally applies.

- The limited recourse to which the exporting company is subject once guaranteed financing has been arranged may expose developing countries to pressurized selling techniques, especially when the exporter is able to offer the inducement of a significant element of subsidy in the financing terms.

- The implied risk (of buying the wrong goods at the wrong price) is increased by the tied nature of export credits. This discourages buyers from seeking competitive tenders for purchases—though it does not (as discussed above) prevent it.

These features impart a bias toward weak investment decisionmaking in countries whose development priorities are inappropriately defined or which lack the necessary technical and administrative skills to implement effective program and project planning.

CONCLUSIONS

As indicated at the beginning of this paper, developed and developing countries have a strong mutual interest in raising the effectiveness of development financing. The heavy losses sustained by ECAs show the cost of narrowly focused export credit policies from the point of view of providers, while the continuing debt-servicing difficulties of many debtor countries emphasize their need to raise the productivity of future investment.

Export credits have limitations in the development context arising out of their primary function of promoting exports. To counter these limitations directly would require agreements among sponsoring governments to alter the priorities under which the ECAs operate. But greater recognition of the limitations would in any case reduce their negative effects and help to avoid a repetition of past problems. The foregoing analysis suggests that attention to the following issues could serve to improve the way export credits assist development objectives:

- Making development priorities more explicit
- Improving the quality and flow of project information
- Strengthening screening arrangements for project approval.

Development Priorities

Export credits are not an aid instrument, nor could they easily accommodate a wide range of development objectives without running into conflict with their export support function and creating serious operational problems for ECAs. Nevertheless, it may be possible to bring development priorities more explicitly under consideration with regard to low-income countries.

Where consultative groups or aid consortia have been established to assist countries in this group, some governments have sought to involve their ECA staff in discussions. This has proved generally helpful, and it is for consideration whether the practice could be extended in the future to include a somewhat more formalized role for the ECAs. The usefulness of this would depend on the willingness of governments and ECAs to commit resources in support of the priorities established by the consultative gourp and to amend authorization and allocation procedures in a manner compatible with these priorities.

Information

The need for improved information is clear both from the failure of individual projects supported by export credits and from the losses suffered by the ECAs.

ECAs need information that will improve judgment in credit sanctioning policy. ECAs cannot realistically improve their skills in project appraisal to the extent required to form detailed technical judgments on the merits of individual proposals. Nevertheless, the quality of individual projects in the aggregate is a critical determinant of a country's debt-servicing capacity, and lenders are concerned to ensure that new investments contribute positively to the overall performance. There are no easy prescriptions for achieving this, but greater knowledge of the development priorities within countries, especially low- and lower-middle-income developing countries, would assist decisionmaking. How this might be achieved in practice is discussed under "Screening Arrangements," below.

Developing-country users of export credits need more project-specific information relating to technical specification, performance, and pricing. Improvement in this area may largely be a matter of more self-disciplined use of available export credits—giving priority to the economic merits of particular investment projects over the terms of the accompanying finance, and making the effort required to examine alternative proposals. ECAs can assist in this regard by indicating in advance their willingness to offer best Consensus terms for projects put up for competitive international tender should their national firms win the contract. The international and regional development agencies already provide important assistance through their role in identifying investment priorities and supplying technical project support. Ways in which this assistance can be strengthened and used more effectively will continue to be examined. One area of major importance is that of cofinancing, in which projects approved by the World Bank can be financed in association with ECAs (discussed below).

More generally in the area of information, it is clear that existing data sources do not yet provide an accurate picture of the role of export credits in development. The new statistical series prepared by the OECD and BIS (see note 3 above) represents an important improvement and is being supported by work among the major statistical reporting groups to reconcile and integrate data series. Progress would be assisted by improvements in the reporting arrangements of DAC members and in the provision of timely and accurate debt information by the borrowing countries. More documentation of the use of export credits in project financing could also lead to better understanding and improved practices by both providers and users.

Screening Arrangements

The most effective screening processes for project approval will, in the long run, be those developed by the importing countries themselves to ensure effective use of limited investment resources. Examples of such processes already in place have been given earlier in this paper, and it must be an objective of the development agencies, ECAs, and other providers of international loans to encourage the spread of similar arrangements to all developing countries, compatible with individual countries' ability to operate them effectively.

In the shorter term, however, governments might usefully consider the case for more explicit guidance on the suitability of projects that cannot be met in this way. Renewed investment flows are important to the prospects of debtor countries' pursuing adjustment policies in order to restore economic growth as quickly as possible, consistent with continuing financial soundness. Investment projects which contribute directly to this process should enjoy priority, both in the recovery programs pursued by the countries themselves and in the provision of new finance by official and private creditors. The low level of confidence prevailing among international lenders since the generalized onset of debt-servicing difficulties, however, implies a serious risk that the appropriate level of new financial flows will not materialize—unless means are found to bridge the confidence gap.

Project screening by the international development agencies may have a role to play in this context. The World Bank can bring to bear a wide knowledge of developing countries' circumstances, experience in debt management, and expertise in project appraisal for this purpose. The Bank does not have the staff resources for, nor would it be appropriate for it to accept, a broad supervisory role. The following, more limited, alternatives, however, have practical merits.

Expanded use of Cofinancing With the ECAs

The Bank has carefully reviewed its cofinancing programs, believing them an important and effective means of encouraging increased financial flows. At present, less than 10 percent of OECD long-term export credits (more than five years' maturity) committed to developing countries are used in cofinancing projects. Detailed discussions have been held with the ECAs with a view to increasing this proportion. Several areas for improvement, operating to the benefit of lending agencies and borrowers, have been identified. These are now being—or have been—put into effect.

Increased Information Flows and Support in Development Programs and Debt Planning

The Bank already supports developing countries in

establishing appropriate investment priorities. Within the constraints of its staff resources, and if requested, the Bank could make available to ECAs its knowledge of sectoral and project priorities in developing countries to assist ECAs in their project choices. The Bank could increase its informal contacts with ECAs and increase its exchange of information on countries' development programs, economic policies, and resource capabilities, either bilaterally or in the context of multilateral fora. Where a project is seen as having particular importance within a country's investment program but does not involve official development agency financing, an analysis of its cost-effectiveness by the World Bank could be helpful, if so desired by the governments. The Bank could also increase its assistance for developing countries seeking to improve administrative procedures for managing their external debt.

NOTES

1. "Export Credit Cover Policies and payments Difficulties," December 1984.

2. OECD, "An Arrangement on Guidelines for Officially Supported Export Credits provided by participating countries, including minimum permitted interest rates and maximum maturities. The arrangement provides that any participant who intends to offer a credit that exceeds the maximum degree of permitted concessionality (for example, by a lower interest rate or a longer maturity) should notify other participants of his intention beforehand and explain the reason for his intended action. Special notification rules apply to the use of tied aid credits.

3. The new statistical series "Statistics on External Indebtedness: Bank and Trade-Related Non-Bank External Claims in Individual Borrowing Countries and Territories," produced jointly by the OECD and the Bank for International Settlements(BIS), will improve the basis of future analysis. This covers official and officially guaranteed or insured trade-related claims of banks and nonbanks in twenty OECD countries, including both short- and long-term claims. This series began only in mid-1983, however, and covers little of the period reviewed in this paper.

4. This percentage is common to both the OECD and the DRS series. Appendix A discusses the difference between the two series and also describes in detail the basis on which the DRS data on export credits have been compiled.

5. European and Meditteranean countries covered by the DRS include Cyprus, Greece, Hungary, Israel, Malta, Portugal, Turkey, and Yugoslavia.

6. The twelve countries accounted for between 35 percent and 40 percent of all imports into developing countries in the period 1979-82.

7. Export credits may, however, assist with the financing of local costs or other minor purchases when the major item of project cost is purchased from the issuing country.

8. Heywood Fleisig and Catharine Hill, *The Benefits and Costs of Official Export Credit Programs of Industrialized Countries,* World Bank Staff Working Paper no. 659 (Washington, D.C., October 1984).

7C. Export Credit Agencies*

Argentina
Compania Argentina de Seguros de Credito a la
Exportacion SA
et de
Sarmiento 440
4 Piso
1347 Buenos Aires
Tel: 49 0095, 49 1905
Telex: 21167

Australia
Export Finance and Insurance Corporation
Export House
22 Pitt Street
Sydney, NSW 2000
Tel: 231 2655
Telex: AA 21224

Austria
Oesterreichische Exportsfond
Gottfried Kellergasse 1
1030 Vienna
Tel: 731213

Oesterreichische Kontrolbank A.G.
A.M. Hoff 4
1010 Vienna
Tel: 66270
Telex: 13-2747

Oesterreichische Nationalbank
Postfach 61
A-1011 Vienna
Tel: 531633
Telex: 75420

Belgium
Compromex
Ministére des Affaires Etrangeres
Rue des Quatre-Bras 2
B-1000 Brussels

Credit Export
Institut de Reescompte Garantie
Rue du Commerce 78
B-1040 Brussels
Tel: 511 7330

Brazil
FINEX
Banco de Brasil
Cateria de Commércio Exterior
Avenida Rio Branco 65

CEP 20090, C.P. 1.150
Rio de Janeiro (RJ)
Tel: 253 0077/0280
Telex: 2151109 BBSA

Brazilian Reinsurance Institute (IRB)
SEDE (Brasil)
Avenida Mareshall Camara 171
Rio de Janeiro (RJ)
Tel: 297 1212
Telex: 2121237/2121019

Canada
Canadian International Development Agency
200 Promenade du Portage
Hull
Quebec K1A 0G4
Tel: (819) 997 5456
Telex: 053 4140

Export Development Corporation
110 O'Connor Street
Box 655
Ottawa
Ontario K1P 5T9
Tel: (613) 237 2570
Telex: 053 4136

*This list is compiled from:
a) *List of Members of International Union of Credit and Investment + Insurers* (Berne Union).

b) *Export Finance,* Angus Dunn and Martin Knight (Euromoney 1982).

Cyprus

Export Credit Insurance Services
Ministry of Commerce and Industry
Nicosea
Tel: (35721) 40-3441-8
Telex: 2283 MINCOMIND

Denmark

Dansk Eksportfinansieringsfond
Nyropsgade 17-19
DK-1602
Copenhagen V
Tel: (01) 131321
Telex: 15070

Eksportkreditradet
Codanhus
Gl. Kongevej 60
DK-1850
Copenhagen V
Tel: (01) 313825
Telex: 22910

Finland

Finnish Export Credit Ltd.
Etelaesplanadi 8
P.O. Box 123
SF 00131 Helsinki 13
Tel: 177171
Telex: 121893 EXCRE SF

Vientitakuulaitos (VTL)
Etelaranta 6
00130 Helsinki 13
Tel: 661 881
Telex: 12 1778 VTL SF

France

Banque Francaise du Commerce Extérieur
21 Boulevard Haussmann
Paris Cedex 09
Tel: 247 47 47
Telex: 660370

Compagnie Francaise d'Assurance pour le Commerce
 Extérieur (COFACE)
32 Rue Marbeuf
75008 Paris
Tel: 256 60 20
Telex: 650 342

Germany, Federal Republic

AKA
Gross Gallustrasse 1
D-6000 Frankfurt/Main 1
Tel: (611) (20601)
Telex: 212631-90 HK D

Kreditansalt fur Wiederaufbau
P.O. Box 111141
D-6000 Frankfurt/Main
Tel: (611) 20601
Telex: 411352

Treuarbeit AG
Bockenheimer Anlage 15
D-6000 Frankfurt/Main 1
Tel: (611) 71231
Telex: 411492

Hong Kong

Hong Kong Export Credit Insurance Corporation
International Building
23rd Floor
141 Des Voeux Road
Box 939, GPO
Central Hong Kong
Tel: 4 451192
Telex: 86200 HKXC HX

India

Export Credit and Guarantee Corporation Ltd.
Express Towers, 10th Floor
Nariman Point
Bombay 400 021
Tel: 230 233023, 230 233046
Telex: 11 3231

Italy

Instituto Mobiliare Italiano
Viale Dell'Arte 25
00144 Rome
Tel: 54501
Telex: 610256 IMIROM, 611311 IMISFE

Sezione Speciale per l'Assicurazione del Credito
 all' Esportazione (SACE)
Piazza Poli 37
00100 Rome
Tel: 67367
613160 SACE

Iceland

Export Credit Fund of Iceland
Landsbanki Islands (National Bank of Iceland)
Austurstraeti 11
101 Reykjavik
Tel: 27722
Telex: 30

Ireland

The Industrial Credit Ltd.
32/34 Harcourt Street
Dublin 2
Tel: 720055
Telex: 4140

Israel
Israel Foreign Trade Risks Insurance Corp.
74 Petach Tikra Road
Tel Aviv 67215
Tel: 337220
Telex: 341179

Japan
Export-Import Bank of Japan
4-1 Ohtemachi 1-cho-me
Chiyoda-ku
Tokyo 100
Tel: 287 1211
Telex: 222 3728

Ministry of International Trade and Industry (MITI)
Export Insurance Division
1-3-1 Kasumigaseki
Chiyoda-ku
Tokyo 100
Tel: 501 1511
Telex: 28576 EIDMITI

Korea
The Export-Import Bank of Korea
541 5-ka Namdaemun-Ro
Chung-ku
Seoul 100
Tel: 778 3951/9
Telex: K26595

Luxembourg
Office National du Ducroire
Chambre du Commerce
B.P. 1503, Luxembourg
Tel: 435853
Telex: 2784

Malaysia
Malaysia Export Credit Insurance Berhad
2nd floor, Wisma Damansara
Jalan Semantan
P.O. Box 1048
Kuala Lumpur 01-02
Tel: 949366, 949458
Telex: MA 31190

Mexico
Fondo para el Formento de las Exportaciones de
   Productos Manufacturados
Banco de Mexica S.A.
Insurgentes sur 1106
Piso 8-12
Mexico 12 D.F.
Telex: 1771989 DMFXME

Netherlands
Export Financiering Maatschappij
Prins Mauritslaan 6
2582 LR The Hague
Tel: (70) 558900
Telex: 31121

Nederlansche Credietverzekering Maatschappij
P.O. Box 473
1000 AL Amsterdam
Tel: (20) 520 2911
Telex: 11496

New Zealand
Exports Guarantee Office
P.O. Box 5037
Wellington
Tel: 720265
Telex: NZ 31239 STATINS

Norway
Eksportfinans AS
Dronning Maudsgt 15
Oslo 2
Tel: 02 425960
Telex: 18213

Garanti-Instituttet for Eksportkreditt (GIEK)
Dronning Maudsgt 15
P.O. Box 1756
Vika
Oslo 1
Tel: 02 205140
Telex: 16783 GIEK N

Norwegian Agency for International Development
   (NORAD)
Victoria Terrase 5-7
Oslo 2
Tel: 314055
Telex: 16548

Spain
Banco Exterior de Espana
Carrera de San Jeronimo 36
Madrid 14
Tel: 429 4477
Telex: 22033, 27741 EXTBK E

Compania Espanola de Seguros de Crédito
   a la Exportacion SA (CESCE)
Pasco de la Castellana 147
Madrid
Tel: 279 5900, 279 4900
Telex: 23577, 45369

Sweden
Exportkreditnamnden (EKN)
Norrl. g. 15
P.O. Box 7334
S-10390 Stockholm
Tel: (8) 235 830
Telex: 17657

Svenska Export Kredit
Birg. Jarlsg. 37
P.O. Box 7535
S-10393 Stockholm
Tel: (8) 143 780
Telex: 12166

Pakistan
Export Credits Guarantees Scheme
Pakistan Insurance Corp.
Pakistan Insurance Bldg.
M.A. Jinnah Road (opp. Mereweather Tower)
P.O. Box 4777
Karachi-2
Tel: 516840, 516849
Telex: 2829 PAKRE

Portugal
Companhia de Seguro de Créditos EP
Av. Republica 58
1094 Lisbon Codex
Tel: 76 01 31 76 70 75
Telex: 12885 COSEC P

Singapore
Export Credit Insurance Corporation of Singapore Ltd.
3702-3, Tower Block,
Shenton Building
6 Shenton Way
Singapore 0106
Tel: 2208344
Telex: RS 21523 ECICS

Switzerland
Geschaftsselle fur die Exportrisikogarantie (ERG)
Kirchenweg 8
CH-8032 Zurich
Tel: 47 66 54
Telex: 54924 VSM

South Africa
Credit Guarantee Insurance Corporation of Africa Ltd.
P.O. Box 9244
Johannesburg 2000
Tel: 21 3385
Telex: 8-7005

Industrial Development Corporation of South Africa
P.O. Box 6905
Johannesburg
Tel: 833 3711
Telex: 87715

United Kingdom
Export Credits Guarantee Department
P.O. Box 272
Aldermanbury House
Aldermanbury
London EC2P 2EL
Tel: 606 6699
Telex: 883601

United States of America
Export-Import Bank of the United States
811 Vermont Ave. NW
Washington, DC 20571
Tel: (202) 566 8990
Telex: ITT 440296 EXIM UI, RCA 248460 EXBK UR, WUI 64319 EXIBANK

Taiwan
Export-Import Bank of China
8th floor
100 Chin Lin Road
P.O. Box 67-696
Taipei
Tel: 563 6363
Telex: 26044

Venezuela
Fondo de Financiamento de la Exportaciones (FINEXPO)
Torre Financiera del Banco Central de Venezuela
Av. Urdaneta
Esq. Sta. Capilla
Piso 9
Caracas

Yugoslavia
Yugoslavia Bank for International Economic Co-operation
Bulevar Revolucije 84
P.O. Box 294
Belgrade
Tel: 436122
Telex: 11710 YU INTBANK

Section II: Sources of Funds
Chapter 8: Commercial Sources

8A. International Capital Markets
David K. Eiteman

THE EUROCURRENCY MARKET

The Eurocurrency market is a financial intermediation market. In other words, deposits are accepted by banks, funds are commingled before being reloaned, and the supplier of the funds, the depositor, look to the bank rather than to a downstream end user for return of capital.

A Eurocurrency is any currency deposited in a bank outside the country where that currency is the unit of account. The most common Eurocurrency, the Eurodollar, is thus a U.S. dollar deposited in a bank outside the United States. Eurosterling deposits are pounds sterling deposited in banks outside the United Kingdom, and Euromarks are deutsche marks deposited in banks outside West Germany. Each Eurocurrency deposit is a large amount of money, usually increments of half a million U.S. dollars, and is in the form of a time deposit, at times including a negotiable certificate of deposit on which interest is paid. Eurocurrency deposits are not demand deposits as that term is understood in the United States.

Eurodollar deposits are held in European banks as well as in banks outside of Europe, since the prefix "Euro-" springs from the function performed rather than from an inherent need for a European location. A market in foreign currency deposits exists in Singapore, where it is commonly referred to as the Asiadollar market, and similar markets exist in other non-European financial centers.

History of the Eurodollar Market

The modern Eurodollar market arose shortly after World War II, when the Soviet Union and East European holders of dollars were afraid to deposit their dollar balances in the United States because those deposits might be attached by U.S. residents with claims against Communist governments. European banks had accepted limited amounts of dollar deposits before the war, and in the post war period dollars were again deposited in such banks. As the postwar market grew, additional funds came from banks and central banks seeking higher yields than were available in the United States. Still more deposits came from European insurance companies and from holders of international refugee funds.

In the 1960s the United States responded to the growing weakness of the U.S. dollar by segmenting its capital market from the rest of the world, a step that enhanced the attractiveness of offshore financing and boosted the Eurodollar share of short-term international dollar financing. When the restrictions were moved in the early 1980s, the market continued to thrive, primarily because it had become highly efficient at attracting both depositors and borrowers away from purely domestic financial intermediaries, an ability fostered by the accumulated experience in international money matters available in London.

The key factor attracting both depositors and borrowers to the Eurodollar market has been, and remains, the availability of a narrower interest rate spread between deposit rates and lending rates than is available in the United States...the effective lending rate in the United States tends to be higher than that in the Eurodollar market, while simultaneously the effective deposit rate in the United States is below that usually available in the Eurodollar market.

The narrower spread in the Eurodollar market arises for a number of reasons. The Eurodollar market is to a large extent an interbank market with a large portion of the depositing and lending between banks, a process referred to as "chaining." An additional reason is that market activity is in fairly large amounts — half a million dollars or more — and is usually conducted on an unsecured basis. Nonbank borrowers are generally large corporations or government entities that qualify for low rates because their risk is perceived to be low. Finally, the Eurodollar operation does not carry much of the overhead of the banks in the market.

Interest rates in the Eurodollar market are normally quoted as premiums above the London Interbank Offered Rate (LIBOR), which is the deposit rate offered by London banks to other banks. The premium over LIBOR reflects adjustments for maturity and for additional credit risks. Many Eurodollar credits are extended on a floating rate basis, meaning that the rate for a maturity longer than three or six months is set at the short-term LIBOR rate and then adjusted (or "rolled over") at the new rate every three or six months. This process assures borrowers of funds for longer periods of time while simultaneously protecting the bank from a squeeze if short-term rates rise while the bank is committed to a longer-term loan. When U.S. interest rates rose substantially above European rates in 1980 and 1981, some Eurodollar rates were quoted as a premium over the U.S. prime rate rather than over LIBOR. Compromise rates also have been used.

Asian Currency Market

An Asian version of the Eurocurrency market was created in 1969 when commercial banks in Singapore were allowed to accept foreign currency deposits. The idea for this Asiadollar market, as it is sometimes called, arose from the observation that many Asian residents, including both multinational firms and overseas Chinese, had dollars or other foreign currencies that were being loaned or deposited in Europe and the United States rather than being put to use closer to home. A regional version of the Eurocurrency market would serve both investors and entities that wanted to borrow American or European funds by providing a mechanism to reinvest in Aisan projects.

The Asian currency market has grown rapidly, and by March of 1983 some 108 banks or other financial institutions were licensed by the Monetary Authority of Singapore to operate Asian currency units (ACUs). An ACU is a section within a bank having authority and separate accountability for Asian currency market operations.

Creation of Eurodollars

The process of creating a Eurocurrency is best illustrated with a U.S. dollar example. As has already been explained, a Eurodollar is a U.S. dollar-denominated time deposit held in a bank outside the United States. Beginning in December 1981, U.S. banks within the United States were allowed to establish special "international banking facilities" to accept Eurocurrency deposits and make Eurocurrency loans. Although physically within the United States, these new facilities operate separately and keep their books separate from normal domestic banking. For our example, we will use a traditional Europe-based bank.

Assume that a Danish corporation has a $1 million time deposit with a New York bank, possibly in the form of a negotiable certificate of deposit, on which it is earning 8 percent. The balance sheet of the New York bank and the Danish corporation would appear as shown below.

NEW YORK BANK

Time deposit due
Danish corporation
(costing 8%) $1,000,000

DANISH CORPORATION

Time deposit in
New York bank
(earning 8%) $1,000,000

The Danish corporation learns that a bank in London will pay 8.25 percent on a dollar-denominated time deposit. When the New York deposit matures, the Danish corporation redeposits the funds in the London bank. The physical transfer is effected by wire, and the net result leaves the three parties as shown below.

NEW YORK BANK

Demand deposit due
London bank (costing no
interest) $1,000,000

DANISH CORPORATION

Time deposit in
London Bank (earning
8.25%) $1,000,000

LONDON BANK

Demand deposit in
New York bank (earning
no interest) $1,000,000

Time deposit due
Danish corporation (cost-
ing 8.25%) $1,000,000

Redeposit of the dollar funds in the London bank has created a Eurodollar deposit, for now a bank outside the United States (in London) has a liability denominated in dollars.

In New York, the New York bank created a demand deposit for the Danish corporation when the time deposit matured. If the time deposit had been in the form of a negotiable certificate of deposit, the Danish corporation could have sold it at any time rather than waiting for maturity. In either case the Danish corporation initially acquired a demand deposit, which is then transferred to the London bank. This transfer, one must note, did not result in a reduction in dollar deposit liabilities of U.S. banks or in the quantity of money in the United States. The transfer just meant that on the books of the New York bank, funds were now owed to a London bank rather than to a Danish corporation.

The Danish corporation previously had $1 million on which it was earning 8 percent per annum. After the transfer it has $1 million in a London bank on which it is earning 8.25 percent. Because the deposit remains a bank obligation denominated in U.S. dollars, the Danish corporation has not changed its foreign exchange risk vis-a-vis Danish kroner, nor has it changed the potential purchasing power of the dollar principal of the deposit.

The London bank acquires a demand deposit in a New York bank, on which it presumably earns nothing, and simultaneously incurs a liability denominated in dollars on which it must pay 8.25 percent interest. The London bank has no foreign exchange risks because it has a dollar asset equal in value to its dollar liability, but for the moment the bank is in a disadvantageous earnings position, in that the cost (interest paid) on its deposit liability exceeds the earnings (nothing) on the demand deposit in New York that it acquired.

This profit dilemma is quickly resolved by the London bank's making a dollar loan at a rate greater than 8.25 percent. In fact, if the London bank did not know that it could reloan the funds at a rate greater than 8.25 percent, it would not have agreed to pay the Danish corporation 8.25 percent for the deposit. Assume that the London bank reloans the dollars to an Italian bank at 8.375 percent per annum. Such a very narrow spread would be normal, because the Eurodollar market is very competitive and transaction sizes are very large. The balance sheet of the Danish corporation would not change; in fact, since the Danish corporation looks only to the London bank, a financial intermediary, it would not know that its funds had been reloaned. (In practice, of course, funds are commingled and the London bank would think only of lending its free U.S. dollar balances, not the particular funds acquired from the Danish corporation.)

After the London bank loaned and transferred the funds to the Italian bank, the balance sheets would appear as shown below.

NEW YORK BANK

Demand deposit due Italian bank (costing no interest) $1,000,000

LONDON

Loan to Italian bank (earning 8.375%) $1,000,000

Time deposit due Danish corporation (costing 8.25%) $1,000,000

ITALIAN BANK

Demand deposit in New York bank (earning no interest) $1,000,000

Time deposit due London bank (costing 7.375%) $1,000,000

After clearing the day's cable transfers, the New York bank now finds that it owes $1 million more to an Italian bank and $1 million less to a London bank. The London bank is paying 8.25 percent interest to the Danish corporation on funds that it has loaned to an Italian bank at 8.375 percent, for a gross spread of 0.125 percent. The Italian bank now owns the noninterest-earning demand deposit, and at the same time is obligated to pay the London bank 8.375 percent interest on the fund acquired.

At this moment the Italian bank is in a disadvantageous profit position. It would reloan the funds at another small increment in interest rate to yet another bank, which in turn could lend them to still another bank, creating a chain of interbank deposits at ever slightly higher interest rates. Although such chains of interbank deposits do occur, the ultimate purpose is to make a loan at the end of the chain to a user that needs the funds for productive business purposes.

For simplicity, let us assume that the Italian bank is the last in the chain of interbank deposits. The Italian bank loans the funds at 8.5 percent interest to Alitalia, the Italian state airline, which plans to purchase spare aircraft parts from McDonnell Douglas Corporation in California. After the loan to Alitalia, but before the purchase of the spare parts, the balance sheets that change because of the transaction would be as shown below.

NEW YORK BANK

Demand deposit due Alitalia (costing no interest) $1,000,000

ITALIAN BANK

Loan to Alitalia (earning 8.5%) $1,000,000

Time deposit due London bank (costing 8.375%) $1,000,000

ALITALIA

Demand deposit in New York bank (earning no interest) $1,000,000

Note payable to Italian bank (costing 9.5%) $1,000,000

When Alitalia actually pays McDonnell Douglas, the following accounts would result:

NEW YORK BANK

Demand deposit due McDonnell Douglas (costing no interest) $1,000,000

ALITALIA

Inventory of spare parts $1,000,000	Note payable to Italian bank (costing 8.5%) $1,000,000

McDONNELL DOUGLAS CORPORATION

Demand deposit in
New York bank
$1,000,000

At the end of this series of transactions, the New York bank has a demand deposit liability to McDonnell Douglas Corporation. From the point of view of the New York bank, the deposit has simply been transferred from one customer to another. Some customers will be commercial firms, and some will be banks. Some will be U.S. entities, and some will be foreign entities. During the entire series of transactions, a demand deposit liability has always existed on the books of the New York bank.

In reality the focus of the underlying dollar demand deposit could have shifted within the United States. The Danish corporation could have kept its dollar funds at Morgan Guaranty Bank, the London bank could have kept its correspondent account at Chase Manhattan Bank, the Italian bank could have kept its correspondent account at Bank of America in San Francisco, and Alitalia could have kept its dollar balance at Citibank in New York. McDonnell Douglas might keep its funds at Wells Fargo Bank in California. However, this possibility for the transfer of funds among U.S. banks does not differ from what would occur in any series of domestic banking transactions.

Behind the transfer of the dollar deposit in a U.S. bank are a series of Eurodollar transactions. If European banks were asked to report their total dollar liabilities, as they are in fact asked by the Bank for International Settlements, both the London bank and the Italian bank would report a liability of $1 million, for a total Eurodollar liability of $2 million. Thus, it can be seen that "chaining" of deposits causes the statistical measure of Eurodollar liabilities to rise to a multiple of the underlying deposit maintained in the United States.

During the course of events in the example above, another type of transaction could have occurred. Any sequential holder of the Eurodollar deposit could reinvest the funds in the U.S. money market rather than loan them to someone else. If, for example, the Italian bank chose to purchase $1 million of U.S. Treasury bills, the New York bank would be instructed to make payment to the Federal Reserve Bank of New York for credit to the account of the U.S. Treasury. This would cause a loss of reserves to the U.S. banking system. (However, if the Treasury bills were purchased in the secondary market, the New York bank would simply transfer the funds to the seller.)

In the original example above, both the London and the Italian bank eventually possessed a dollar-denominated asset that earned more than the cost of the matching liability. The Danish corporation earned what it perceived to be the highest rate of interest available on its dollar balances. One might ask why the Danish Corporation did not deposit its funds directly in the Italian bank at 8.375 percent — or, for that matter, why it did not make a loan directly to Alitalia. The Danish firm might not know of these options and might not find it worthwhile to engage in the systematic search and analysis that would be required. Or it might simply perceive that the risk of dealing with other than a London or New York bank is too great.

Alitalia alone remains "exposed," in that it has a dollar-denominated debt and no dollar-denominated assets. Between the time when the loan is taken down and when it is repaid, Alitalia either will have to earn dollars (presumably by selling tickets to passengers who will pay with dollars) or to purchase dollars (with lire or other currencies that Alitalia accepts). By maturity, Alitalia must acquire sufficient dollars to repay the loan plus interest. When the chain of loans and deposits matures, each participant in the chain will retain that portion of the interest that is its spread, and repay principal and interest to the next party in line. At the end of the chain, the Danish corporation will receive its principal plus interest at 8.25 percent.

Depending on its business needs, the Danish corporation might redeposit the dollars for another interval of time wherever it finds the best rate, use the dollars to pay dollar-denominated expenses (such as the purchase of raw material acquired outside of Denmark), or exchange them for Danish kroner to pay domestic expenses. If the dollars were exchanged for Danish kroner at a Copenhagen bank, that bank would then acquire a dollar deposit in New York and would have to decide if it wanted to make a Eurodollar loan or sell the dollars for some other currency...

THE INTERNATIONAL BOND MARKET

An international bond issue is sold to investors in countries other than the country of the issuing entity. All international bonds are either foreign bonds or Eurobonds. A foreign bond is issued by a foreign borrower, underwritten by a syndicate composed of members from within a single country other than the country of the borrower, sold principally and denominated in the currency of that country. Foreign bonds sold in the United States are often called "Yankee bonds," and foreign bonds sold in Japan are sometimes called "samurai bonds."

In comparison, a Eurobond is underwritten by a multinational syndicate of banks and other securities firms, and is sold to investors in a number of countries other than the country of the issuing entity. The Eurobond may be denominated in the currency of the country of the issuing entity — for example, U.S. companies that seek Eurobonds in Europe typically denominate them in U.S. dollars. Or it may be denominated in some other major currency, as would occur if a British firm issued a Eurobond denominated in Swiss francs or Eurodollars. Some Eurobonds have been denominated in Special Drawing Rights (SDRs).

In some respects the Eurobond market is similar to the Eurocurrency market. Both markets are "external," in that obligations in a particular currency are written or carried out in a country other than the country whose currency is used. However, the Eurocurrency market is a financial intermediation market, with major world banks operating as intermediaries between depositors (suppliers) and borrowers (users) of Eurocurrencies. By contrast, the Eurobond market is a direct market in which investors hold the securities issued by final borrowers. Institutions in the Eurobond market carry out an underwriting and direct marketing function. These functions are performed by departments of banks, the same banks that conduct a Eurocurrency business. However, underwriting and marketing groups for Eurobonds include many types of securities firms in addition to banks. Eurobonds are debt obligations of leading multinational firms, of governments, or of government enterprises. Most Eurobonds are issued in bearer form and have call provisions and sinking funds.

The Eurobond market owes its existence to several unique factors. National governments sometimes impose tight controls on foreign issuers of securities denominated in their local currency and sold within their national boundaries. However, such governments are often much more flexible about securities denominated in foreign currencies and sold to local residents already possessing those foreign currencies.

Other reasons for the popularity of the Eurobond market are its freedom from the stringent and time-consuming registration requirements of domestic agencies such as, in the United States, the Securities and Exchange Commission. This freedom saves both time and money. The fact that Eurobonds appear in bearer form is also an attraction, since the country of residence of the investor is not a matter of public record and interest paid is generally not subject to a withholding tax. (By comparison, foreign residents who hold bonds issued in the United States are subject to a 30 percent withholding tax by U.S. authorities.)

Currency Cocktail Bonds

Fluctuating exchange rates have increased the sensitivity of financial executives to the potential for unexpected changes in the cost of servicing bonds denominated in foreign currencies. One response has been to issue bonds denominated in one of several multicurrency units or "currency cocktails," composed of a weighted average of several currencies.

Actual subscription to the bonds, and interest and principal payments, are not made in the currency cocktail, since the unit is not a means of payment or an instrument of exchange. Rather, payments are made in any of the component currencies in an amount sufficient to "buy" other components of the unit at current exchange rates and in the proportion defined by the unit. The underlying logic of a currency cocktail bond is that, because of the effects of diversification, the cost of service will be more stable than the cost of servicing a single-currency bond. Portfolio theory has shown that a portfolio of securities will have a lower standard deviation of expected returns than the standard deviation of expected returns from a single security within that portfolio. The same reasoning has been applied to the portfolio of currencies used in a currency cocktail.

Three currency cocktails are in general use. The Special Drawing Rights (SDRs) are defined by the International Monetary Fund as the value of a basket of five currencies. The quantities of each of the five are shown in Table 3.6, along with the implicit weighting. The definition became effective January 2, 1981, and replaced an earlier definition based on 16 currencies.

The European Currency Unit (ECU) was created in March 1979 by the countries of the European Economic Community, and consists of the amounts of each of the nine member countries' currencies shown in Table 3.6. The ECU was set equal to another currency cocktail, the European Unit of Account (EUA) had been originally intended as a legal standard of value for settlement between members of the European Economic Community. At present both the ECU and the EUA have the same composition.

TABLE 3.6. Composition and Weighting of Multicurrency Units

	Special Drawing Rights (SDR)		European Currency Unit (ECU) and European Unit of Account (EUA)	
	Composition	1/2/81 Weighting	Composition	3/1/79 Weighting
U.S. Dollar	0.540	42.5%	-	-
Deutsche mark	0.460	18.3	0.828	33.02%
Pound sterling	0.071	13.3	0.0885	13.15
French franc	0.740	12.8	1.15	19.89
Japanese yen	34.000	13.2	-	-
Italian lira	-	-	109.0	9.58
Dutch guilder	-	-	0.286	10.56
Belgian franc	-	-	3.66	9.23
Luxembourg franc	-	-	0.14	0.35
Danish krone	-	-	0.217	3.10
Irish pound	-	-	0.00759	0.11
		100.00%		100.00%

Note: Items do not add totals due to rounding.

Source: SDR composition described in International Monetary Fund, IMF Survey, January 12, 1981, p. 6; EUA and ECU components in European Investment Bank,. Annual Report 1980, p. 8.

8B. Arranging and Marketing Syndicated Eurocurrency Loans
Henry S. Terrell and Michael G. Martinson

In recent years, the syndicated Eurocurrency bank loan has become one of the most important techniques in international lending through which banks have provided large amounts of credit to governments and other borrowers. It is estimated that publicized syndicated Eurocurrency amounted to about $28 billion in 1976, and $34 billion in 1977. The emergence of the syndicated Eurocurrency bank loan has also contributed to a major institutional development, the establishment of a number of new "merchant banks." These merchant banks are generally subsidiaries or affiliates of large banks, located in London or other banking centers. Often the primary purpose of the merchant bank subsidiaries is to market syndicated credits.

ARRANGING A SYNDICATED CREDIT

Syndicated loans are often led by a single large bank. This lead bank is responsible for developing contacts with the prospective borrower and obtaining a mandate to raise funds. Often, several major multinational banks will compete for a mandate from the same borrower.

The business development aspects of syndicated credits are generally similar to other large credits. A bank's credit officers are responsible for contacting and seeking lending business from potential borrowers. Credits to foreign sovereign borrowers are usually negotiated by the bank's officers in charge of that country or geographic area. Negotiating credits for major multinational corporations is usually the responsibility of the account officer assigned to that corporate borrower.

Because of the size of the funds for which a bank generally commits itself in a syndicated loan, responsibility for credit analysis and final approval for both sovereign and corporate borrowers often resides at the bank's head office or, for decentralized banks, with officers in regional centers. In addition to analysis for commercial and country risks, the bank's credit committee must also determine whether the amount of credit that might be provided by the bank is consistent with the bank's diversification policy and country exposure limits.

Editors' Note: This article provides a clear description of the loan syndication process. The fact that it was written in 1978 means that its description of market characteristics should be treated as illustrative rather than accurate.

Since the loan is to be syndicated, the loan officer also needs to consult with the bank's loan syndication office. This office, often a part of a merchant bank subsidiary in London, is in close contact with other major lenders in the market to determine the interest rates, maturities, and other terms on which credits for particular borrowers can be marketed. The assessment of the marketability of any credit by the loan syndication office will play an important role in the terms and conditions offered to the potential borrower and in determining the amount of credit that will be provided.

THE MANAGEMENT GROUP

While negotiating with a potential borrower, a lead bank attempts to establish a group of managing banks.[1] In drawing together this management group, the lead bank seeks to determine precisely the terms and conditions on which these banks would be willing to underwrite, in large part, a particular credit. In selecting its managing group, a lead bank looks for banks with the ability to take a significant proportion of the loan into their own portfolios and with the ability to place the loan with potential participants. In this phase of the negotiations, the lead bank may need to renegotiate the terms and conditions of the loan with the borrower if it encounters difficulties in arranging its management group. Once the lead bank has established its group of managing banks, it then commits the group to raise the funds for the borrower.[2] The lead bank then prepares a placing memorandum, based primarily on information supplied by the borrower. This assists the management group in marketing the credit to a wider group of banks.

In the past, a lead bank negotiated a credit with a borrower and agreed to market the credit on a "best efforts" basis. With this type of situation, the borrower could not be certain that a lead bank would arrange a syndicate that would deliver the entire amount of credit, and borrowers had little recourse, since the term "best efforts" was difficult to define. In more recent years, competitive pressures generated from the existence of a number of banks willing and able to lead syndications have resulted in borrowers demanding that any lead bank issue a firm commitment to provide the funds before any mandate to syndicate the loan is issued. The banks' leading syndications have adjusted to this requirement by establishing a management group of banks willing to take the entire issue into portfolio in the event it cannot be successfully marketed to a wider group of banks.

The lead bank and the group of managing banks generally must have extensive resources because they often commit themselves to provide extremely large sums to the borrower.[3] This requirement limits participation as a lead or managing bank for major credits to the largest banks. The importance of a lender being able to guarantee the borrower a successful placement has given the commercial banks, with their extensive ability to take a share of the credit into their portfolios, a considerable competitive advantage over the investment banks, which have to market the entire amount of the credit. Lacking their own financial resources, the major investment banks are finding it increasingly difficult to compete in leading loan syndications, and their share of the market has diminished substantially in the last two years. The need to be able to commit large amounts of funds also makes it unlikely that regional U.S. banks will play an important role in leading major syndicated credits.

Several other factors lead borrowers to prefer one bank over another as a manager: (1) historical relationships, i.e., some banks are simply the bankers for certain countries or companies, (2) the borrower's assessment of the professional capabilities of the bank and the bank's track record in raising funds, or (3) competition in price and terms, where a borrower solicits bids from several major banks and selects the lead bank on the basis of the most attractive bid. Some major borrowers have a policy of rotating management of their loans among banks to form continuing relationships with a number of banks.

MARKETING A SYNDICATED CREDIT

Once a bank has received a mandate from a borrower and established a management group, the group attempts to market the loan. If the group has already committed the full amount to the borrower, the main purpose of the marketing effort is to reduce the portion of the loan that will be taken by the lead bank and others in the managing group.

General market practice is for a lead bank to take into portfolio a portion of a syndicated credit that is at least as large as that of any other participating bank. A current "rule of thumb" seems to be that for all but the larger credits the lead bank's share will amount to 10 percent or more of the total. It is currently an unaccpetable practice for a bank to arrange a loan, receive a fee, and then not take any portion into its own portfolio. The other banks in the management group are also expected to retain a large portion of the loan to ensure their long-term interest in the credit.

The lead bank bears primary responsibility for marketing the loan, although all the banks in the managing group participate in the effort. Often, other banks have contacted the borrower expressing an interest in participating in credits, and these banks' names may be provided to the lead manager. Sometimes the borrower even specifies that certain banks should be given the opportunity to participate. In addition, each major bank's loan syndication office in London maintains files on the syndicated lending activity of as many as 500 other banks. The filing systems vary in sophistication and content, but the files generally contain lists of banks which have joined various syndications. These data assist the loan syndication office in identifying which banks may be interested in which borrowers. The files are also augmented by market information obtained through contacts with other bankers in the London market.

This information, developed through informal contacts, indicates which banks are interested in expanding their portfolios, and on what terms, and which banks are unwilling to increase their credit exposure to particular countries. If the credit is attractive, a small number of banks may be contacted. Some credits are obviously harder to place and require greater effort.

Potential participating banks generally base their decision to participate on their assessment of the merits of the credit as an investment, i.e., on considerations of risk (creditworthiness) and yield, and whether their participation falls within their internally established country limits. Participation in joint ventures and correspondent relationships with the lead bank or other banks in the managing group have very little impact on the decision of banks to participate in a credit.

In deciding whether to lead or participate in a Eurocurrency loan, some banks try to take into consideration collateral benefits, such as expansion in other activities with borrowers, as well as risk and yield. In syndicated Eurocurrency lending, just as in domestic lending, these collateral benefits are extremely difficult to quantify in advance and are usually analyzed at most banks in qualitative terms. It is generally believed that most of the collateral benefits in terms of additional banking business from the borrower accrue to the bank leading the syndication.

The banks invited to participate in syndicated credits are usually larger banks more active in international finance. U.S. regional banks are not generally considered major market participants, although they are somewhat more active in 1976 and 1977 than in 1975; but not nearly as active as in 1973 and early 1974. Regional U.S. banks will probably withdraw further from the market if their local loan demand increases.

Potential participants are given the terms and conditions of a particular loan on essentially a take-it-or-leave-it basis to minimize the negotiation process and to expedite placement. After a loan has been fully subscribed, participating banks may suggest some modifications in the language of the loan documents, but these are invariably of a minor nature.

Most loan agreements contain provisions prohibiting participating banks from assigning their rights and obligations without the consent of the borrower, and in some cases, the lead bank. The reason for restricting the participating banks is that there may be complicated negotiations between the borrower and the lending banks over the course of the loan, possibly concerning rescheduling of payments or other adjustments in terms and conditions. Both the borrower and the lead bank want to be able to exercise some control over which banks might be party to these negotiations. There is usually no limit, however, on a participating bank selling a subparticipation.

THE ROLE OF THE LEAD BANK

The role and especially the responsibility of the lead bank are currently topics of active discussion. The lead bank is generally the only bank that negotiates directly with the borrower, although in some of the largest syndicated credits the borrower may deal with more than one bank. The lead bank also is responsible for circulating a memorandum of information describing the transaction and providing all available information about the borrower. The information memorandum may be prepared either by the lead bank or by the borrower. In virtually all cases, the borrower, rather than the lead bank, certifies that the information memorandum is accurate.

Lead banks carefully review these memoranda to be certain they contain factual and statistical information useful to a potential lender. The memoranda contain various statements suggesting that they should not substitute for independent credit review by potential participants.[4] In addition, loan agreements often carry explicit clauses where participating banks certify they have performed an independent analysis of the credit.

The clauses in the placing memoranda indicating their informational rather than analytical nature and the clauses in the loan agreements, where each participating bank agrees it has performed an independent analysis of the credit, were the general practice well before the *European-American-Colocotronis* case. The effect of that case has been that bank lawyers are reviewing the disclaimer clauses more carefully; and bank officers responsible for distributing the memoranda are reviewing them to remove independent analysis. At least one major bank is currently drafting a statement setting forth what it considers its responsibility to be when managing a syndicated Eurocurrency loan.

A lead bank will also prepare separate internal analytical material for its own loan review committee. Much of this information and internal analysis is done prior to the decision to compete for the position of syndicate leader. This material will generally provide an assessment of the borrower and some quantitative estimates of the longer-run benefits that might result from leading the syndication.

THE AGENT BANK

Aside from the lead bank which has negotiated a credit, there is also an agent bank in a syndicated loan. The agent bank usually is the lead bank, but in some loans the management group may agree that a different bank will serve as agent.

The role of the agent bank is well-defined in the loan agreement. It consists of making disbursements, receiving payments, computing the appropriate interest rates, and making certain that the borrower adheres to the various pledges in the loan agreement. The agent bank is responsible for notifying the participants of any problems with the loan and making other information relevant to the condition of the loan available to the participating banks. Banks generally receive relatively little remuneration for serving as agent. However, the agent bank's responsibilities keep it in close contact with the borrower, which makes the role attractive.

PRICING A SYNDICATED CREDIT

Syndicated credits are almost invariably priced to yield a spread over the London Interbank Offer Rate (LIBOR). In most cases, various management, participation, and commitment fees increase the spreads to the banks and are sometimes used to conceal spreads. But the spread over LIBOR provides the bulk of the net revenue to the banks.

The base LIBOR rate to which the spread is added is calculated by averaging the offer rate on a prespecified deposit maturity (usually six months) of a reference group of three to five banks that are chosen as representative of the banks providing the credit. The list of specific reference banks is generally contained in the loan agreement, and adjustments are not made to assist banks which may have to pay a premium over the reference rate to obtain funds in the market.

Borrowers also have to pay fees which provide the lending banks with income in addition to the gross spread, fees often amounting to 0.5 to .75 percent of the total credit are often negotiated with the borrower by the lead bank.[5] Fees may be higher if they are used to make the loan acceptable to the market.

The lead bank then determines to a large extent how that fee income is distributed among the various participants in the loan. Fee income is commonly broken down into two components: participation fees and management fees. Participation fees are given to all participants in a loan and are a percentage of the amount lent by each participant. They may be the same percentage for all participants, or larger participants may receive a higher fee. In the latter case, the fee differential is a means for rewarding the management group, since the managers almost always take the largest participations.

In most cases, the lead bank does not distribute all of the fee income as participation fees; the remainder is termed the management fee. The management fee component is distributed among the managers, usually in proportion to the amount of the loan each agreed to provide prior to syndication (i.e., the underwritten portion). Any income left after this distribution is retained by the lead manager as additional compensation. The proportion of the fee income retained by the manager is determined by competitive and marketing pressures—the lead bank may need to share it more evenly in order to attract other banks into the management group.

FEES AND DISTRIBUTION

This is how fee income might be distributed:

A $100 million syndicated credit has been arranged with a managing group (including the lead bank) of five banks, and ten other participating banks. Each managing bank prior to syndication committed to provide up to 20 percent of the loan. After syndication, each managing bank provided 10 percent of the loan. Other participating banks each provided 5 percent of the loan. Total fee income was 0.5 percent of the loan. Each bank received a .25 percent participation fee on the amount provided, and each managing bank received an additional .125 percent on the portion initially committed for. The remainder of the fee income, .125 percent of the total loan, was retained by the lead bank.

Fee income would be:

	Participating Bank (But not Part of Managing Group)	Managing Bank (Other than Lead Bank)	Lead Bank
Participation fee (1/4%)	$12,500	$25,000	$ 25,000
Management fee (1/8%)	—	—	$ 25,000
Retained by lead bank (1/8%)	—	—	$125,000
Total	$12,500	$50,000	$175,000

Besides these fees, it is also common for commitment fees to be charged on syndicated Eurocredits. Such fees are similar to fees charged on domestic lines of credit and are a flat rate paid to each participant for the undrawn portion of the credit.

Different borrowers pay different interest spreads to borrow funds. In theory, differences in interest spreads should, in large part, reflect differences in the creditworthiness of difference borrowers. Determining the difference in creditworthiness of different borrowers is a very imprecise exercise at most banks, since there is limited historical information on which to predict the probability of nonpayment on foreign loans. Competitive factors also play a role because some borrowers are well-known to a large number of banks and can seek competitive bids, while other borrowers are less well-known and have fewer alternatives.

Aside from calculations of expected risk and competitive factors, another determinant of interest spreads is the extent to which some potential participants have borrowed in the market. In some cases, potential participating banks have reached their internally established limits on loans to particular borrowers. So, to raise additional credits, large borrowers have to offer a higher yield, either to convince banks to raise their internal limits for that borrower or to make the loan attractive to banks that might not otherwise lend to that borrower. If two borrowers are judged to be equivalent risks, a borrower with the larger amount of outstanding loans may have to pay a higher spread because lenders are unwilling to increase their exposure to that borrower without additional compensation. At the other extreme, some borrowers who are completely new to the market may have to pay a somewhat wider spread.

Overall bank liquidity and loan demand seem to affect both the general level of spreads and differences in spreads to different borrowers. Under situations where domestic loan demand in the United States and other industrial countries is weak relative to the liquidity of the banks, competition among banks will reduce the overall spreads on Eurocurrency lending. When banks are relatively liquid with limited credit demands from prime borrowers, banks seem willing to expand their credits to nonprime borrowers, and consequently the differential between prime and nonprime borrowers narrows. Conversely, if loan demand increases, the average spreads on syndicated Eurocurrency lending would rise, differentiation in costs to borrowers of varying quality would widen, and some marginal borrowers might be unwilling to borrow on unfavorable terms.

IN PERSPECTIVE

The syndicated Eurocurrency bank loan has proven to be a flexible technique for raising large amounts of credit for a wide variety of borrowers. The market in syndicated loans operates within a framework of a set of well-understood but unwritten rules of behavior, that are adapted to meet changing circumstances.

Through the mechanism of syndicated loans, banks are able to provide large sums of credit in a brief period of time. Two factors account for this flexibility. First, the syndicated loan market operates largely on the basis of close personal contacts between London-based officers of the major participating banks. This contact permits timely interaction between likely participants in a loan. Second, it seems that senior management of major banks have developed predetermined guidelines concerning lending policy toward major borrowers in the market and the minimum spreads desired that permit syndication officers and other bank officials to make rapid decisions to help co-manage or otherwise participate in a syndicated loan.

In addition to its flexibility, an important benefit of the market is that it affords banks without worldwide networks an opportunity to diversify their portfolios through participations in syndications to borrowers with whom they might not have been able to establish contact on their own. Of course, there is the possibility that this opportunity for portfolio diversification may lead banks to extend credit to borrowers about whom they have insufficient information.

NOTES

1. Some credits only distinguish between the managing group and other banks providing funds. In larger credits, a separate designation of co-manager may be made for banks which have provided more than a prespecified amount of funds.

2. The extent of simultaneity of negotiations with the borrower and prospective members of the management group can vary from transaction to transaction. In some cases, a lead bank will have its management group firmly in place before it obtains a definitive mandate from a borrower; in other cases the receipt of the mandate may actually precede any firm commitment from the members of the managing group of banks.

3. See Liddel, *Syndicated Euro-Credits: The Drift Toward Big Banks,* The Banker, November 1976 at 1221-1223.

4. A typical statement might read as follows: "This presentation is being distributed to a limited number of banks. The contents have been checked by [name of borrower] and in their opinion provide as accurate and representative account of the present and future economy of [name of borrower]. Neither the managing banks nor their affiliates make any representation of warranty, express or implied, as to accuracy and completeness and banks should make their own independent assessment of the credit in question."

5. For example, on a five year credit with interest spread of 1.5 percent over LIBOR, a .75 percent fee package will raise the yield by nineteen basis points, which is equivalent to a 13 percent increase in net income.

8C. Guide for Private Corporations from Developing Countries to Doing a Eurobond or Foreign Bond Issue
International Finance Corporation

TYPES OF EXTERNAL BOND ISSUES
1. Foreign vs. international bonds
2. Public offering vs. private placement
3. Fixed vs. floating rate
4. Straight vs. convertible
5. Drop-lock bond/floating rate notes convertible into fixed rate bonds.

Foreign vs. international bonds. Generally, a distinction is made between international bonds (or Eurobonds) and foreign bonds. International bonds are issued in one of the Eurocurrencies and underwritten by an international underwriting syndicate of (investment) banks while foreign bonds are defined as issues by foreign borrowers in the domestic bond market of another country which are underwritten by an exclusively domestic group of (investment) banks. The first Euro-dollar bond issue was done in 1963, followed in 1964 by a Euro-DM issue, and in 1965 by Euro-issues in French francs and Dutch guilders. Euro-issues in Canadian dollars became popular in the 1970's while the first SDR or "currency cocktail" Eurobond was launched. The most important domestic markets for foreign bond issues are the Swiss Franc market, the US ("Yankee") bond market, the Deutsche market (DM) market, and the Yen ("Samurai") market. Other markets are the Dutch guilder, Canadian dollar, French franc, Hongkong dollar, Kuwaiti dinar, Saudi riyal and Bahrain dinar markets.

Public offering vs. private placement. A public issue is offered to the general public through a group of international (investment) banks which market the securities to their clients. A private placement is made to a small number of institutional investors or even a single investor (such as a central bank). Private placements are generally not listed on a securities exchange whereas public offerings are. A public offering in the US, Japanese and French market is subject to registration with regulatory authorities (in the United States, the Securities and Exchange Commission) whereas private placements are not. In some bond markets such as Switzerland, public offerings are subject to "queuing" for access while private placements have a shorter waiting period.

Fixed vs. floating rate. Bond issues generally have a fixed rate, but in 1970, during a period of high short-term interest rates, the first dollar-denominated floating rate note issue (FRN) was done. FRN's are a type of Eurobonds in some way similar to syndicated loans because their rate of interest is tied to the London (or Singapore) interbank rate (LIBOR or SIBOR) and is adjusted each six months. However, in contrast to syndicated Euro-credits, FRN's typically have a minimum interest rate. Also, the minimum participation in a syndicated loan is generally not smaller than $100,000 while FRN's are available to the general public in denominations of $1,000-$10,000. As a result, FRN's are actively traded in a secondary market maintained by a number of investment banks which are also active in the new FRN issue market. This provides a liquidity which participations in a syndicated loan do not possess.

Traditionally, most of the issuers in the floating rate note market have been financial institutions. Many of them are prime international names but, more recently, several major banks from Latin American and Asian nations have issued FRN's. In recent months, several Mexican industrial groups have also entered the floating rate note market thus becoming among the first private industrial corporations from the developing world to successfully enter the international bond markets. In addition, some countries (Panama and Thailand) have issued FRN's. A floating rate note is often considered as "second step" toward a fixed rate bond issue with a Euro-dollar syndicated loan being the first step. The reason is that many investors in FRN's (especially those of less well-known names) are major international banks who may find this instrument, on the basis of total yield, more attractive than syndicated loans. However, from the point of view of the borrower, this means that he may not attain his objective of diversifying his sources of funds as well as through a fixed rate issue.

Editor's Note: While this article is designed for private corporations, its description of Eurobonds, foreign bonds and the process of their issuance are of relevance to sovereign debtors. Since this article was written in 1981 its description of market characteristics should be treated as illustrative rather than accurate. Its description of the bond issuing process, however, is still accurate.

"Straight" bonds vs. convertibles. In addition to "straight" Eurobonds there are equity convertibles, convertible FRN's, warrants, and currency convertibles. All of these special bond types have in common that they may be converted at some future date, at the option of the investor, into common stock of the corporate issuer. They are generally sold at a lower coupon rate than "straight" debt and permit an issuer to sell equity at a time market conditions are less than favorable. Warrants may be detached from their bonds and traded freely in the secondary market. In the case of currency convertibles, bonds can usually be converted into common stock at the rate of exchange prevailing at the time of the bond offering.

Drop-lock bonds and FRN's convertible into fixed rate bonds. In 1981, during a period of high interest rates, a new concept was introduced which is a variant on the FRN. Instead of having a floating rate for the entire life of the issue, the drop-lock bond converts automatically into a fixed rate bond as soon as LIBOR "drops" to a predetermined percentage. Both issuer and investor are then "locked" into the new rate for the remaining life of the issue. This concept works to the advantage of the issuer if rates increase again subsequently whereas the investor gains if rates subsequently drop even lower and on average, remain lower. FRN's may also be convertible into fixed rate bonds at the *option* of the investor.

PARTIES INVOLVED IN AN OFF-SHORE BOND ISSUE

a. Issuer
b. Lead manager
c. Co-managers
d. Underwriters
e. Selling group
f. Legal counsel
g. Investors
h. Regulatory agencies
i. Trustee, fiscal or principal paying agent
j. Rating agencies

Frequently, the issuer only deals with the lead manager who, in turn, deals with the various other parties. In some cases, however, the issuer has direct contact with some of those parties.

Issuer (or borrower)

The issuer of a bond can be a government, a government agency, an international organization (such as the World Bank), a regional development bank (such as the Asian Development Bank), a commercial bank, development finance institution or a private corporation. Issuers of external bonds tend to be leading institutions in their countries of domicile and usually have had prior experience in the syndicated Eurodollar credit market. During the 1977-80 period, the share of non-OPEC developing countries in the total amount of external bonds issued was 8%. Eighteen LDC's did at least five bond issues during the 1976-1981 period. Virtually all of the developing country borrowers have been governments or government agencies. Only a handful of fixed rate bond issues, mostly privately placed, by developing country corporations have been done. However, recently a number of commercial banks and industrial groups from selected LDC's have been able to do floating rate note issues.

Normally, the issuer wants to receive a fixed amount of proceeds (and, does not want to take the risk of receiving only a portion of the amount he needs) nor is the issuer a specialist in the distribution of securities. For these reasons he turns to underwriters, who are the intermediaries between the issuer and the ultimate investors.

Lead Manager

The lead manager (also called "manager" or "managing underwriter") plays the key role in an underwriting, working usually with a small group of co-managers, a larger group of underwriters, and a selling group of many members. Whether an underwriting succeeds or fails largely depends on the manager. How the lead manager is selected by the issuer differs from case to case. Sometimes, the investment bank has built up a close relationship with the issuer over a period of years. In other cases, the issuer negotiates with several investment banks before selecting the one who appears to offer the best package. In the latter case the issuer negotiates point by point aspects such as (i) the coupon rate, issue price, and years to maturity; (ii) fees and other expenses charged by the manager, underwriters, and sellers of the issue; (iii) support the manager promises to give with respect to demand for the price of the issue after the offering; and (iv) other terms and conditions. In rare cases, the lead manager is selected through competitive bidding.

The tasks of the lead manager include the following:

(a) to evaluate the creditworthiness of the potential issuer[2] and give him a professional opinion about his chances of being accepted by the "market," the collective judgment of the financial community and investors;
(b) to present financing alternatives to the issuer;
(c) to suggest the optimal terms and conditions;
(d) to negotiate the amount, fees, other terms and conditions and timing of the issue;
(e) to form a management group (co-managers), an underwriting syndicate, and a group of selling agents through which the issue will be distributed ("placed" or "sold") and to allot subscriptions;
(f) to assist an issuer in preparing a prospectus containing the required and/or customary disclosure of information;
(g) to maintain contact with the various regulatory bodies on behalf of the issuer;

(h) to prepare, with his legal counsel, legal documents, such as the underwriting agreement (or "subscription agreement") and agreement among underwriters (or "sub-underwriting agreement");
(i) to handle all paperwork connected with payment and delivery of securities, press releases, and technical details such as contacts with the printer, etc.;
(j) to continually maintain liaison with the issuer, members of the syndicate, and other interested parties; and,
(k) to stabilize the price of the issue for a number of days after the securities are offered to the investors.

In preparing the prospectus and other legal documents as well as his contacts with the regulatory authorities, the lead manager normally relies heavily on his legal counsel. Accountants and engineers frequently play an important role in the due diligence review.

In making his decision about the choice of a lead manager, the potential issuer usually considers not only the terms of the various proposals received but also such factors as the reputation of the investment bank, its past experience in doing issues for companies similar to the borrower, and, most importantly, its placement power, i.e., its ability to successfully distribute the issue on the basis of the price and other conditions agreed upon. Both *Euromoney Magazine* and the *Institutional Investor* regularly publish "league tables" indicating the ranking of various banks and investment banks in lead managing, co-managing and underwriting new issues.

It should be pointed out that investment banks are normally at least as selective in choosing clients as the clients are in choosing them because one of the prime assets of an investment bank is its reputation, and the clients of an investment bank are a major factor affecting that reputation. Obviously, an unsuccessful underwriting damages the reputation of the investment bank.

For his efforts the lead manager receives a management fee on the entire amount of the issue. Since a lead manager usually acts also as underwriter and selling group member, he also receives an underwriting commission and selling concession of the portions of the issue which he underwrites and sells. The management fee is usually about 9.375% of the gross spread and is shared between the lead manager(s) and co-managers.

Co-managers

The lead manager (who initiates the bond issue or has received a mandate from the borrower) usually joins with several of the major underwriters (see below) to form a management group. The lead manager (or one of the lead managers) "runs the books" but some of the work may be divided among the co-managers. For example, one may be more involved in preparing the prospectus whereas another may prepare the subscription (or underwriting) agreement, and still another other documents.

Under the system most commonly used in the Eurobond market, the managers are committed jointly and severally to buy the entire issue although an agreement among managers usually limtis the extent of the exposure of each individual manager. In other words, the managers act as principals rather than as representatives of the underwriters although the managers are of course careful not to legally bind themselves until they have found enough underwriters to underwrite the whole issue.[3]

Underwriters

Underwriters earn their "underwriting fee"[4] for their commitment to pay for the issue. Their key function is to accept the market risk or, in other words, to guarantee the issuer that he will receive the agreed upon amount whether or not they are able to sell the securities issued to the invested public. This risk can be substantial in volatile markets or in cases where the issuer is not well-known in the market. If an issue is not completely sold, the underwriters are obligated to buy the remaining securities on a pro-rata basis and keep them in their own portfolio until they can be sold at a later date, frequently at a loss. An underwriter who is in the syndicate usually works also as a selling group member and he receives a selling concession on the portion he could sell to the investors — whatever his underwriting portion is. Underwriting commission is usually around 3.8% of the principal amount of the bonds.

A first-time issuer soon learns that the decisions on how many underwriters should be invited and what percentage of the underwriting each gets allocated are subject to considerable negotiation. For public issues, the managers generally commit themselves to underwrite about 40% or more of the total issue. Next in line (and listed next on the "tombstone" advertisement published in connection with the issue) are the "special bracket" underwriters who receive 1.5-2% each. Because investment bankers are proud of their "place on the tombstone" and easily offended if they are not invited in the special bracket while one of their major competitors is, this bracket is often avoided in smaller underwritings. Other categories of underwriters include "majors" (about 0.75%), sub-majors (about 0.375%) and minors (about 0.1%).

In the United States, the underwriters are investment banks or brokers but in other countries, such as Germany, France, and Holland, commercial banks can also act as managers and underwriters.[5] However, merchant banking subsidiaries of the U.S. banks in London, Hongkong and elsewhere overseas may act as underwriters.

Selling Group

The members of the selling group do not take any underwriting risks[6] but simply receive a commission for bonds they sell. It could be said that they serve as antennas on the market. In practice, however, a major part of the total issue is sold by the lead manager and other underwriters themselves, while each of the members of the selling group receives only a very small allotment, often less than 0.5% of the total issue. Sometimes there is no separate selling group at all because the managers and underwriters function as selling group members.

Legal Counsel

Legal counsel plays an important role in bond issues. Normally more than one legal counsel is involved. In the case of a foreign or Eurobond issue, four lawyers are usually involved.

The issuer appoints two legal counsels for the issue. One is a legal counsel in the issuer's country ("local counsel") who gives legal advice to the issuer on whether the issue is in conformity with the laws of the issuer's country. The other is a legal counsel in the country of issue who provides the legal advice for the issue to satisfy the legal requirements in the country of issue. He will help the issuer in the preparation of a registration statement or prospectus, and other legal documents required to obtain an authorization of the issue in the country. Most importantly, especially for first-time issuers, he will also assist the issuer in his negotiations with the lead manager and other underwriters.

A lead manager also appoints two legal counsels, one in the country of issue and the other in the issuer's country. One of the important duties of the former is to prepare the drafts of all the agreements and other necessary documents. The counsel also carefully watches the issue process from the legal point of view and may maintain contacts, on behalf of the issuer, with regulatory agencies. The legal counsel to the lead manager in the issuer's country plays a less important role, only giving a comfort letter concerning legitimacy of the lead manager's legal action for the issue in light of the laws of the issuer's country.

In the case of the Eurodollar bond issue, there is no regulatory agency and procedures are, to a large extent, subject to the market practices which are much simpler than those in any particular domestic market. Sometimes only one counsel to the issuer, who covers the legal matter in the issuer's country, and one legal counsel to the managers who prepares the agreements as well as other documents and gives advice to managers, are involved. In some cases, the role of the issuer's counsel is played by a legal department or an in-house attorney of the issuing company.

Investors (Buyers)

The main groups investing in bonds are private individuals and institutional investors such as insurance companies, investment trusts, pension funds, central banks, commercial banks and corporations. It is estimated that three quarters of all Eurobonds are held by private individuals with the remainder held by institutional investors.[7] Individuals often invest through trust departments of Swiss or other banks which manage their money. On the whole, bond investors tend to be more conservative than the international banks which are active in the syndicated Eurocurrency market. For this reason, it is usually easier to obtain funds through a syndicated credit than to do a successful bond issue. Bond issues are sometimes "tailor-made" for a specific group of investors. One of the roles of the lead manager is to identify such groups and bring them together with a specific borrower.

Many institutional investors, especially pension funds and insurance companies, are strictly regulated as to the amounts they may invest abroad and the quality of the bonds they may buy. In the United States, these regulations were recently relaxed which bodes well for the future. Many U.S. institutional investors have thus far had little experience with overseas names which presented another obstacle in selling them bonds of foreign issuers (especially from developing nations). However, portfolio managers and rating agencies have recently become more interested in foreign borrowers as a result of the fluctuating value of the dollar.

Regulatory Agencies

Offshore bond issues are regulated by (i) domestic authorities of the country of the issuer, (ii) agencies in the country whose currency is used for issue, and (iii) listing requirements of the securities exchanges on which the issues are listed.

Local Regulatory Agencies

Before doing a bond issue abroad the borrower frequently has to obtain permission from the ministry of finance or central bank of his own country. Local regulators normally keep a close watch on the country's debt burden and balance of payments in order to protect the country's creditworthiness and standing in the international financial markets. In some cases, they may even intervene in actual negotiations or, alternatively, establish general guidelines in order to obtain the best possible terms and conditions. In other cases, local securities commissions require listed companies to register with them any offshore bond issues.

Offshore Regulations.

Eurobonds. A main reason for the rapid growth of the Eurodollar bond has been its relative freedom from government regulations. In the final analysis, the attitudes of the investors and the investment banking community determine which issues can be sold. Public issues in other currencies than the dollar — Euro as well as domestic — are usually subject to authorization, registration requirements or an issue calendar ("queuing"). On the other hand, private placements are mostly unregulated. Regulations for public issues are not always written or formal but the authorities in Germany, Japan, France and the Netherlands keep a close watch on Euro-issues as well as domestic issues in their currencies.[8] Although they usually act through "voluntary" guidelines or "gentlemen's agreements" on prior consultation, they can effectively close their markets for certain periods for balance of payments or interest rate policy reasons. They can also bar certain borrowers in an effort to protect domestic institutions or individuals. Furthermore, Euro-issues in currencies other than the dollar are always lead-managed by major banks or investment banks headquartered in those countries.

United States. The Securities and Exchange Commission (SEC), created in 1934, regulates the disclosure required at the time of an underwriting and, later through regular reporting while it also keeps a close eye on the activities of underwriters and brokers; the New York Stock Exchange and the American Stock Exchange have listing requirements for new issues. Since 1974, there have been no special restrictions for foreign borrowers in the U.S. bondmarket. Even during the 1963-74 period when most foreign issues were effectively barred by the so-called Interest Equalization Tax, developing country borrowers were allowed, although few actually issued bonds. However the "Yankee bond" market has been selective in its acceptance of private corporations from developing countries because of the stringent disclosure requirements of the SEC combined with unfamiliarity of American institutional and private investors with developing country names.[9]

Other foreign markets. The share of foreign bonds in most domestic bond markets has not surpassed 2-3% of all issues except for Switzerland and Luxembourg where more than half of all issues are by foreign borrowers.

Listing

The second market for Eurobonds is mostly an "over-the-counter" market handled by professional bond dealers, but it is common practice to list public Eurobond issues on one or more stock exchanges. The Luxembourg Stock Exchange is most popular but a growing number of issues is also listed in London. For issues which are widely bought in Asia ("Asian dollar" issues), an additional listing on the Singapore Stock Exchange is usually sought. The main reason for listing is to make the issue eligible for the widest possible range of investors. Many institutions only buy listed securities because of legal restrictions. An additional advantage is that regular quotations of listed bonds in financial newspapers remind potential investors of the issuer's existence which may be helpful in subsequent bond issues. Listing requires disclosure of essential financial information in a prospectus and the printing of annual reports but these documents are needed in any case for the financial community and the investors and, thus, the extra work involved is not onerous. Procedures in London and Luxembourg are uncomplicated and the review is fast. Compliance with Stock Exchange regulations in Singapore takes a few weeks and usually necessitates additional disclosure and paperwork.

Trustee, Principal Paying Agent or Fiscal Agent

The trustee is usually a bank, independent from the underwriters, which is appointed by the issuer under a trust deed (or trust indenture). His principal task is to protect the rights of the investors (who are legally the beneficiaries of the trust) especially in case of a default by the borrowers. The trustee also assumes the administrative responsibility of keeping track of bonds and interest coupons which have been presented for payment. In addition, the trust deed spells out the mechanics of interest and principal payments and makes provisions for the appointment of paying agents, usually commercial banks in the major financial centers. In Eurobonds, the lead manager often acts as principal paying agent and no trustee is appointed. In those cases a fiscal agent sometimes takes the place of the trustee under a paying agency agreement to perform the administrative tasks of payments and cancellation or replacement of coupons and bonds although his function does not fully include the protection of bondholders in case of default.

Rating Agencies

A rating is not required in the Euro-markets. However a rating, preferably by one of the two major rating agencies (Moody's and Standard & Poor's), is essential for the success of any Yankee bond issue. Only 3% of all foreign issues were not rated. Many institutional investors in the United States are allowed to buy only securities which have a rating of one of the top four letter grades (AAA, AA, A, or BBB or their equivalent). Private investors, not only in the Yankee bond market but also in the Eurodollar bond market and other markets, are also — although much less — influenced by such ratings. Thus far, only one private institution from one of the developing countries has been rated but more are expected to follow. Countries have sometimes been deterred from seeking a rating out of fear of receiving anything less than the highest rating, but for corporations it should be easier to accept a lower rating as long as the rating will help them to sell their securities.

MAJOR TERMS AND CONDITIONS

1. Amount of issue
2. Maturity (life)
3. Redemption schedule and average life
4. Coupon rate
5. Currency
6. Gross spread and other expenses
7. Issue price
8. Overall cost

Amount of issue. A borrower who does his first bond issue is generally well advised not to aim for too large an amount because it is damaging to the reputation of a first-time borrower if it becomes known in the market that the issue was not fully subscribed. Borrowers with experience in the syndicated Eurodollar market might be surprised to learn that the size of a typical Eurobond issue is well under $100 million or its equivalent in other currencies. Issues by developing country governments have usually not exceeded $50 million and first issues by corporate borrowers probably should not be larger than $15-30 million (or its equivalent in other currencies). A small issue, of course, increases the overall cost of borrowing because legal and other similar expenses are more or less fixed.

Maturity. The maximum final maturity (or "life") of bonds depends on market and currency chosen, market conditions at the time of the issue, and, of course, the credit standing of the issuer. In recent years, bond issues for developing countries have had final maturities of as long as 10 years in the Eurodollar bond market, 15 years in the Yankee bond market, 8 years in the DM market, 15 years in the Swiss Franc market (for private placements mostly), 15 years in the Yen market, 10 years in the Kuwaiti Dinar market and 8 years in the French franc market. On the whole, the length of maturities has declined since 1972 when the best borrowers in the Eurodollar bond market could obtain maturities of 15 years. They have declined further since the tightening of credit in the United States in October 1979. Annex 8 summarizes the approximate terms and conditions a first class institution from a major developing country may possibly be able to obtain in the various bond markets under present conditions. Of course, such terms and conditions are subject to frequent and constant change. Obviously, they should not be taken as more than a very approximate indication of what may be achieved.

Repayment and Average Life. Sometimes bond issues are repaid in full at the end of the life of the bond ("bullet maturity") but, more commonly, repayments ("amortization" or "redemption") begin after a "grace" period of several years. Repayments can take place through a sinking fund, a purchase fund or a combination of these two. A sinking fund resembles the practice in the syndicated Eurocurrency market of repayments at stated and regular intervals, usually of one year. It is generally more advantageous to the borrower to have a purchase fund arrangement. The difference with a sinking fund is that the issuer undertakes to buy back (i.e. repay) a specified number of bonds at regular intervals *only* if the issue is trading below a set price. Such an arrangement not only helps to support the price of the issue but also makes it possible that repayments may not have to take place at all before final maturity, thus lengthening the "average life" of the issue. The average life of an issue is the weighted average of the maturities of all bonds and is determined by the final maturity, the repayment schedule, and the grace period. For example, an issue with a final maturity of ten years, a four-year grace period and annual repayments has an average life of seven years.

Coupon Rate. The stated rate of interest on a bond is called the coupon rate. A coupon is one of the actual certificates attached to the bond (and "clipped" by the investor before the age of computerized custody and clearing of securities). It should be noted that the coupon rate is only part of the overall cost to the issuer (see "overall cost"). In comparing the cost of U.S. and Eurobonds, the issuer should keep in mind that annual interest payments, resulting in a slightly lower cost, are standard pratice in the Euromarket[10] whereas a semi-annual coupon is used in the Yankee bond market. Interest rates are more sensitive than any other terms (except the price) to changes in market conditions which may be quite abrupt. In general, interest rates in the Euro and foreign bond markets depend on such factors as the interest rate policy of the world's major central banks, inflationary trends, exchange rate stability, and the general feeling of optimism or uncertainty about the world political situation.

Choice of Currency. As a general rule, countries with strong currencies have lower interest rates than those with currencies which are perceived as weak. Balance of payments surpluses and recent revaluations generally lead to an expectation of future currency strength. In choosing the currency of issue, the issuer should weigh the benefit of interest differential against the risk (and, thus, cost) of revaluation and resulting foreign exchange losses. In recent years, dollar rates have been higher than those of other major issue-currencies such as the Deutsche mark, Japanese yen and Swiss franc. The differential has been as high as 5% or more.

Gross spread and other expenses. The fees for underwriting and placing an issue in the Eurobond market are fairly standard and usually expressed as a percentage of the amount of the issue. Fees increase with maturities to compensate for the greater risk involved and to a lesser extent with the credit standing of the issuer. Fees are divided into three parts:

(a) Management fee   0.375 – 0.5%;
(b) Underwriting fee   0.375 – 0.5%; and
(c) Selling concession   **1.250 – 1.5%**
     Total gross spread   **2.0 – 2.5%**

Unlike interest (which is paid over the life of the loan), underwriting fees are one-time fees immediately subtracted from the proceeds of the bond issue ("front end fees"). The lead manager divides the management fee between himself and the co-managers, often after first taking an initial share (or "praecipium") for himself. The underwriting fee is split among the underwriters in proportion to their commitments. Similarly, the selling commission is divided on the basis of actual sales among the lead manager, co-managers, underwriters and selling agents. A substantial part of the selling commission (0.5-1.25%) is often given away in the form of a "re-allowance" to institutional investors and large private clients. The gross spread is usually much lower (1-1.5%) for private placements. A prospective issuer should always ask the lead manager for an estimate of additional expenses and preferably agree in advance on a ceiling for such expenses. Expenses vary greatly but for a first-time (Eurobond) issue done in London, the following expenses are usually paid by or passed on to the issuer:

Expenses (Front End)	**Estimate** ($)
Printing (prospectus, certificates, agreements, etc.)	$60,000–80,000
Legal Counsel of Issuer (London/local)	$40,000–100,000
Tombstone Advertising	$10,000–20,000
Stock Exchange Listing Fee (Luxembourg)	$10,000
Authenticiation of Bonds	$7,000
Fiscal Agency Acceptance Fee or Trustee Fee	$3,000–6,000
Underwriters Expense Reimbursement	$70,000–140,000
	$200,000–363,000
As percentage of $25,000,000	0.8–1.42
$50,000,000	0.4–0.71

The underwriters expense reimbursement includes such items as legal expenses (of counsel to the underwriters), travel, telephone and telex, delivery of bonds and entertainment expenses. Certain expenses (e.g. printing, advertising) are sometimes paid by the underwriter and then included in the estimate for the reimbursement, while the isuser pays these expenses directly in other cases. In addition, there are *annual* expenses for the trustee or fiscal agent, paying agents, stock exchange, etc., totalling usually not more than $20,000 per year. Finally, there are usually expenses connected with the redemption of the bonds totalling $5-10,000. Not yet included in these estimates are the issuer's own expenses for accountants, travel and communications.[11]

Issue Price. The issue price is usually decided upon during a last minute pricing meeting the day before the "offering day."[12] The offering day is usually about 12 days after the initial announcement of the issue to the press and sending of invitations to the underwriters. On the offering day, telexes must be received from the selling group indicating the amount of their participation. It is not common practice to revise terms (other than the price) after the announcement unless there has been a dramatic change in market conditions. Traditionally, the fine-tuning of the issue terms is done through an adjustment to the par pricing. Obviously, a price above a par ("at a premium") gives a lower yield than the stated coupon rate while a price below par ("at a discount") give a higher yield. The final pricing decision is made on the basis of (i) prevailing market conditions and (ii) an assessment of the amount and quality of the orders which are recorded in the syndicate book ("book"). This assessment is an art rather than a science because some investment banks tend to overestimate their demand or ask for more bonds than they can sell (this exaggeration is called "fluff" or "air").

Overall Cost. The overall cost depends on:

(a) the coupon rate;
(b) the average life of the issue;
(c) the issue price;
(d) the annualized cost of front end fees (gross spread and other expenses); and
(e) annual expenses.

In order to compute the "overall cost" of a bond issue, for example, for comparison with the terms of a syndicated Euro credit, it is necessary to "annualize" the cost of front-end fees and add other expenses. Because of the present value effect, we cannot simply divide the front-end fees over the average life of the loan but need bond yield tables or a calculator to compute the overall cost accurately. For example, a $25 million issue with a coupon rate of 14%, annual interest payments, a gross spread of 2.25%, other expenses of $200,000; no sinking fund and a final maturity of eight years issued at 100% would have an overall cost to average life of 14.67% per year. In other words, the annualized cost of the front-end fees amounts in this case to 0.67%.

PROCESS OF UNDERWRITING
Origination

When a company needs new long-term financing through bonds it will look to an investment bank for help.[13] The main reason is that underwriting is a specialized business. It requires not only contacts with other underwriters and a feeling for the market which can only result from daily and close contact, but also a knowledge of finance and relevant securities and other legislation. Sometimes, it is the investment banker who takes the first initiative in an underwriting. From his knowledge of the country, the corporate sector in general or the company, he may know or sense that a particular company needs long-term financing and he may present a proposal to the company on how, when, and at what price funds can be raised.

Market conditions have an important impact on how much underwriting business can be done. In a period of stable or dropping interest rates (and, thus, stable or rising prices) or after several successful underwritings, the market is usually receptive to new underwritings and investment bankers are eager to undertake them. When market activities are slow and prices depressed, it tends to be more difficult to sell new bonds. At such a time, investment banks as well as potential issuers will be less enthusiastic to come to the market because it may not only be difficult to sell bonds, but the interest rate, issue price and other terms of the underwriting will be less attractive. Long-term debt underwritings are rarely done when interest rates are rising rapidly, volatile or at unprecedentedly high levels.

Evaluation and Mandate

As soon as an investment bank has been approached by a potential issuer or has identified a potential candidate for a new issue, its corporate finance department will do an investigation of the prospective client. If the client measures up to the criteria of the investment banker, the proposed financing will be subject to detailed analysis. Assuming that the client and the underwriter agree in principle on the type of financing, size and timing on the issue, approximate pricing, fees and expenses, and assuming also that market conditions have not deteriorated, the investment banker will then expect to receive a "mandate" from the issuer describing the issuer's intentions with respect to the proposed offering in general terms. This letter is not binding although it may specify fees to be paid if the underwriting effort is terminated before completion. Without receiving a written mandate, the investment banker might be reluctant to make any further steps because of the time and money involved in a professional underwriting.

Upon receipt of the mandate, the underwriter conducts an in-depth investigation of the issuing company (see Annex 9). Usually, legal, auditing and engineering experts are brought in to complete the analysis. This examination provides much of the information needed at a later time to prepare the prospectus and other documentation required by the regulatory or listing authorities.

Syndication

If the amount of the underwriting is small in relation to the capital of the investment banker, he may choose to take the entire risk of selling the issue himself. Normally, however, an "underwriting syndicate" is formed. This way, the investment bank not only shares the risk (and expected profits) with other underwriters but also knows that he will be asked to participate in other underwriting led by his colleagues/competitors in the investment banking industry. Each investment banker is keenly aware of the importance of reciprocity in his relationship with other underwriters. In most cases, the managing underwriter has a relatively free hand in selecting the members of the syndicate but sometimes the issuer will insist on the inclusion of particular firms. Custom and "quid pro quo" arrangements typically affect the selection of syndicate members and their allotments (i.e., the amount to be underwritten or sold by a particular firm).

Before final negotiations with the issuer, a draft *Subscription Agreement* is sent to co-managers.[14] This document defines the relationship between the issuer and the management group (as well as the underwriters in case of an Underwriting Agreement) and is signed after both sides have agreed on the final details of the underwriting including the issue price. Besides setting out on the basic terms and conditions of the underwriting and defining the "closing date" at which the issuer will receive the net proceeds of the underwriting, this agreement usually protects the underwriters against any legal action in case the company has provided them with wrong information on its financial and operation conditions.

Another major document is the *Sub-underwriting Agreement* which is distributed to the underwriters.[15] It is usually negotiated in the weeks before the offering, but not signed until just before the beginning of the actual offering. The agreement deals with such aspects as names and allotments of each underwriter, price, size and type of underwriting; shares served by the lead manager for direct sales delivery and payment, stabilizaton and trading in the after-market, closing date, settlement, management fee, and various indemnifications protecting the lead manager. Finally, there may be a special *selling group agreement* for the members of the selling group.

Most underwriting (or subscription) agreements are "firm commitments" under which the underwriters agree to buy the whole issue outright at a particular price for resale to the public. Sometimes, the underwriters only give a "best efforts commitment" to distribute the issue to the public at a predetermined "gross spread" while the issuer only receives the residual, or sometimes a fixed price but no guarantee on the quantity to be sold.

Usually, the investment bankers insist on "market-out" or "disaster" clauses which relieve the underwriters of their obligations under certain circumstances beyond their control, such as a material change in the economic, political or financial environment. This protects the underwriter against a sudden and unexpected change in the stock market or sudden negative developments related to the issuer. Such a clause is important because of the small capital base of most underwriters. Although the determination of what is "material" usually rests solely with the investment bankers, they will generally try to avoid using this clause in order to preserve their reputation.

Regulation

Regulation differs from country to country. However, in nearly all cases an effort is made to protect the public (i.e., the investors who are not major stockholders, directors, management or other insiders). Providing the investor with sufficient, understandable and reliable information to make an informed judgment is of crucial importance in preventing speculative excesses leading to a breakdown of investors' confidence.

A *prospectus* reviewed (or approved) by the Securities Commission, stock exchange, or other regulatory agency before the public can buy a new issue and/or the bond can be listed on a securities exchange is one of the main and most effective ways to provide the investor with information. Although formally the company is responsible for most of the information provided in the prospectus, the bulk of the actual work is usually done by the lead manager and his lawyers who must carefully check all information provided by the issuer in order to protect themselves against shareholder suits or damage to their reputation.

Pricing

In all mature securities markets, the price of an issue is determined freely (without interference from governmental authorities) by the underwriter together with the issuer. Pricing of an issue is the most difficult part of an underwriting. Too high a price can cause losses to the underwriter and difficulties for the issuer the next time he comes to the market. A low price may damage the reputation of the underwriter and may cause him to lose the issuer as client. The managing underwriter will therefore thoroughly study the pricing issue on the basis of the pricing of other recent issues, recent and expected interest rate trends and any new developments regarding the country of domicile of the issuer and the issuer itself.

Distribution

After all terms of the issue are approved, investment banks contact those investors who initially indicated interest to decide upon the actual size of purchases by the investors. If a portion of the underwriting remains unsold after contacting all investors who initially expressed interest, the underwriters must take securities into their own inventories until the syndicate is terminated.

Depending upon how well the underwriting has been received, the syndicate may be held together for an indefinite period or as little as one hour. Usually, after receiving "all sold" notices from the selling group members, the manager will lift all price and trading restrictions on the issue. However, termination of the syndicate does not always mean that all the securities have been sold. Selling groups are unlikely to be able to distribute entire issues at offering prices during pronounced downward trends of the general market. If such a situation were to be encountered during the agreement period and if it is decided that this is the best way to protect the interest of the underwriters, the manager may immediately permit selling at the best possible price.

Settlement

At the conclusion of the public offering the manager is responsible for all the details of the final settlement. In conjunction with his counsel he will determine whether all conditions of the Underwriting Agreement have been met by all parties. If all requirements are satisfied, the underwriter and selling group members make their payments (usually by cashier's check) to the issuer to return for the delivery of temporary share certificates. The manager then makes payment to selling group members to compensate them for their service. The final task of the manager is to divide those expenses which are borne by the underwriters (and not reimbursed by the issuer), such as transfer taxes, carrying charges advertising, sales expenses, postage, printing, etc. after subtracting those expenses, the underwriting spread is split on a pro rata basis with the other syndicate members...

NOTES

2. Sometimes called "Due diligence review": Securities legislation in the United States requires that the lead manager, his legal counsel, and various experts used to provide opinions are very careful about any possible misstatements in the prospectus otherwise the investor (and the SEC) may sue them.

3. Under the U.S. system, the management group signs an underwriting agreement on behalf of the underwriters. Each manager and other underwriter is severally but not jointly responsible for his own underwriting commitment. The management group is appointed and vested with specific powers as agents under the Agreement among Underwriters.

4. In the Euromarket separate management and underwriting fees are usual. Whereas in the United States, the underwriters give up part of this fee to the lead manager.

5. The separation of commercial banking (deposit taking and lending) and investment banking (specifically underwriting) in the United States dates from the Glass-Steagall Act (also referred to as the Banking Act) of 1933.

6. At least not in a legal sense. Of course they have a moral commitment to sell the number of shares they have committed to, otherwise they run the risk of not being included in subsequent underwritings.

7. However, in the Yankee bond market about two-thirds of the investors are institutions.

8. Thus far, no Euro-issues have been offered in Swiss francs.

9. Recently, the SEC has relaxed several disclosure and reporting requirements; several more changes (including "shelf registration," less stringent reconciliation of U.S. and foreign accounting principles, and less detailed annual reporting requirements) are under discussion.

10. Except for floating rate notes.

11. Total costs connected with a Yankee bond issue, including substantial fees usually required by the company's auditing firm for conforming to the company's accounting system and reporting to SEC standards may be as high as $1 million for a first-time borrower or issuer of equity. However, this is largely a one-time cost. Expenses connected with a second or subsequent issue are considerably lower.

12. In the Eurobond market, the practice of the "bought deal" whereby the underwriters commit themselves to a firm price well in advance has become more prevalent although, as a result of recent mis-pricings due to interest rate fluctuations, this method of pricing has come under severe attack in recent months.

13. See also Section VII on services IFC can provide.

14. In the U.S. market (and by some U.S. investment banks in London), this document is called an *Underwriting Agreement*. It is sent to both managers and underwriters because both are party to this type of agreement while only the management group signs the subscription agreement.

15. Some U.S. investment banks operating in the Eurobond market follow the U.S. practice of an *Agreement among Underwriters* which is signed by all underwriters (including the lead manager and co-managers) and appoints the lead manager as agent for all the underwriters.

8D. Direct and Portfolio Investments: Their Role in Economic Development
The World Bank

Through most of the twentieth century, direct investment has been an important source of capital, technology, and expertise for countries in the process of development. Portfolio investment, in contrast, is a relatively new phenomenon which has assumed significance only with the growth of large public companies and the emergence of share or stock markets in developing countries.

The recent decline in voluntary bank lending to developing countries, coupled with a virtual stagnation in official financing, has raised concerns about how efficient capital flows might be restored. Expanded equity and portfolio investments are seen as possibilities for providing additional capital. Such forms of capital have advantages for developing countries in that they provide for the sharing of commercial risks with foreign investors and also contain a package of capital, technology, and expertise.

In the 1980s the combination of higher real interest rates and more receptive attitudes in host countries may set the stage for foreign direct investment to play a greater role in development. The liberal availability of commercial bank lending at low interest rates had made these investments less attractive in the previous decade. This paper analyzes the nature and the role of equity forms of investments in development, the factors that affect their growth, and the role they can play in providing a higher proportion of the external financing required by developing countries in the future. The last section discusses the role the World Bank Group can play in support of efforts by developing countries to take greater advantage of the opportunity equity forms of investment offer for their development.

THE NATURE AND ROLE OF DIRECT INVESTMENT

Direct investment is a unique form of capital flow in that, unlike commercial lending, the funds provided are always part of a package of technology and management, both of which can enhance the productivity of the capital transfer. In addition, like portfolio investment, direct investment shares in both the risks and rewards associated with the project financed. It is these two qualities—the combination of technology, management, and capital with risk sharing—which give direct investment a special role in financing in developing countries. Accordingly, the measured volume of direct investment will normally significantly understate the importance of this type of capital to the recipient country.

The substitutability between direct investment and bank finance is circumscribed by the fact that the former always finances specific investments while the latter is often general purpose finance. But there are important complementarities between direct investment and other types of capital flows, especially commercial bank loans. Complementary flows are needed both to help create investment opportunities and to complete the financing of direct investment enterprises and to complete the financing of direct investment enterprises. For example, U.S. parent firms have supplied only about 60 percent of the resources external to their subsidiaries in Latin America. The remainder has come from commercial banks (both local and foreign) and trade credit. Trade credit has been a major source of complementary funds, supplying on average 75 percent of the borrowing by subsidiaries. Without this external borrowing, many of the subsidiaries would not have been established.

Other forms of international capital—such as bilateral and multilateral aid—have also facilitated direct investment by helping to finance essential infrastructure and to create investment opportunities for both domestic and foreign private investors.

Direct investment is normally undertaken by a relatively small number of large firms. The firms themselves take the initiative to invest, attracted in many instances by the existence of a natural resource, a favorable cost environment, and occasionally special inducements offered by host countries.

Traditionally, foreign direct investment in developing countries was attracted by the development of natural resources, including petroleum, minerals, and tropical foodstuffs. A great deal of such investment was for export. The trend toward nationalization and other actions by host countries reduced profitability in these sectors during the 1960s and early 1970s and thus diminished the attraction of these traditional forms of investment in recent periods.

Direct investments in manufacturing and services are often made by firms with some kind of special advantage that is best utilized by maintaining management control of operations in foreign countries. Such advantages may be a superior product or production process, or a product that the foreign company can, through advertising, differentiate from those of its competitors.

It is a few of the largest firms in concentrated industrial sectors in major industrial countries that make the majority of direct investments. The foreign sales of the 380 largest transnational corporations were approximately $1,000 billion in 1980, or an average of nearly $3 billion per firm.

Firms choose to exploit their technical, marketing, and other advantages through the establishment of a direct investment, rather than through exports or licensing, when external markets for these advantages are imperfect or nonexistent. One common motivation for foreign investment is a threat to an existing export market. The threat might come either from the actions of a competitor or from new policy measures of the host government which restrict the market to local producers. Whatever the source, the company is forced to search for solutions to the new competitive conditions. The need to consider alternative strategies might also be stimulated by import competition, which drives managers to consider possible ways to reduce costs of production. One alternative could be operations abroad where costs are attractive.

Growth and Concentration

In establishing an enterprise in a developing country, a direct investor provides a package of management and technological expertise as well as capital. These important ingredients in the economic growth process are scarce in developing countries. The potential of this type of capital flow, however, was not realized during the 1970s.

Although the nominal value of direct investment resource flows to developing countries increased by 10 percent a year, the real value hardly increased at all between 1967 and 1982. A substantial share of the measured direct investment flows was reinvested earnings in existing investments. It is estimated that reinvested earnings now constitute over half of the measured flows of direct investment in developing countries. Although the real value of direct investment resource flows has hardly changed since 1970, the amount of medium- and long-term flows to developing countries from private creditors increased by 9.5 percent in real terms between 1970 and 1982. In the meantime, the share of direct investment resource flows in the total net flow of financial resources from developed countries to developing countries declined from an average of about 22 percent at the beginning of the 1970s to close to 13 percent in the early years of the 1980s. Private bank lending as a share of total net flow of financial resources from developed to developing countries increased from 15 percent in 1970 to an average of about 30 percent in the early 1980s. Private bank lending thus grew by 21 percent a year during this period.

The direct investment that has flowed to developing countries has been highly concentrated in relatively few countries. Table 2-1 shows that most foreign direct investmet has gone to developed countries—about three-quarters of the total in the past decade. The flows to developing countries, like commercial bank lending, have gone mainly to the higher-income countries in Asia and Latin America. Brazil and Mexico in particular have received large volumes of direct investment. Within Asia, Hong Kong, Malaysia, the Philippines, and Singapore were the major recipients; Singapore alone accounts for nearly one-half of total Asian receipts of foreign direct investment in recent years. Direct investment has played a minor role in providing capital for low-income developing countries. This reflects among other things the relatively small size of domestic markets in these countries, the lack of skilled manpower, and industrialization policies with a strong bias in favor of the public sector.

Direct investment financing for developing countries comes almost entirely from industrial countries. Companies from the United States and the United Kingdom continue to maintain the largest investment positions in developing regions. However, the growth rate of their new investment has been exceeded by a number of other countries. Companies in the Federal Republic of Germany and especially in Japan, for instance, have become significant suppliers of direct investment capital to developing countries. Together, these four countries have supplied more than three-quarters of the direct investment in developing countries, the United States alone accounting for nearly half of the total.

In the allocation of investment among developing countries, regional concentration is typical for almost all investing countries. U.S. investment tends, for example, to be heavily concentrated in Latin America, while Japan's investment is concentrated in Asian countries. Similarly, United Kingdom investment goes to British Commonwealth nations, with France focusing on countries in Africa and elsewhere with which it had colonial ties.

Direct investment is also relatively heavily concentrated in certain economic sectors. Table 2-2 shows that direct investment by United Kingdom firms and in particular by German firms has been heavily concentrated in manufacturing; U.S. and Japanese investment, although more evenly spread over the major economic sectors, has a decided bias in favor of manufacturing and the extractive sectors. Even within the major sectors, direct investment has been highly concentrated in a few industries. Within manufacturing, for example, direct investment has been mainly in transport equipment, chemicals, and machinery (which includes electronics).

Causes of Stagnation in Flows

The flow of private direct investment in the 1970s was influenced by the shift in financial surpluses to OPEC countries, by the preferences of developing countries, and by the fundamental nature of the direct investment process.

To some extent the slow real growth of direct investment was due to the shift in world savings to oil-exporting countries after the first oil price increases in late 1973. The OPEC countries initially had a preference for bank deposits and other liquid assets. Unlike the industrial countries, OPEC countries did not have the expertise or domestic industrial base to establish and operate enterprises abroad. They did acquire controlling interests in some enterprises, mainly in industrial countries, but in most cases these were portfolio investments or investments made to acquire expertise.

The increased availability of commercial loans may have induced some capital-importing countries to favor sovereign borrowings over direct investment capital. Many developing countries took a more restrictive approach to foreign direct investment, reducing the range of industries in which they could invest, raising local ownership requirements, and increasing performance requirements (for example, export requirements).

Apart from the availablity of an alternative cheaper source of funding, some policymakers in developing countries questioned the contribution of direct investment to economic development. A paramount concern has been the political implications of control of domestic resources by multinational corporations (MNCs) based in foreign countries. Developing countries frequently charge that production technologies employed by MNCs are inappropriate and that centralized management, characteristic of MNCs, promotes dependence and retards independent managerial development. They also point to the fact that funding includes locally raised capital, which may crowd out potential domestic borrowers. Finally, they have suggested that direct investors use transfer prices, royalty and interest payments, management fees, and other means to avoid limits on profit remittances, circumvent price controls, avoid foreign exchange regulations, and escape local taxes. Thus, it is frequently alleged that any gains from foreign investment are distributed disproportionately in favor of the companies.

These charges were made particularly in countries where import restrictions were established to encourage local production of goods previously imported. Inappropriate trade regimes (as discussed below) sometimes provide investors, whether domestic or foreign, with financial rates of return which are markedly higher than economic returns to the host country. Governments, however, attempt to control such profits in the case of foreign enterprises. This leads to the creation of incentives for foreign firms to engage in a variety of the practices listed above. Open trade regimes increase the benefits to developing countries of foreign private direct investment and reduce problems associated with it.

Past skepticism in developing countries was matched by skepticism among potential investors. Faced with unreceptive host countries, volatile economic policy environments, and confusing combinations of inducements to and constraints on investment, investors were wary of committing capital to developing countries.

Through the period of the 1970s there was increased emphasis on unbundling the management, technology, and financial components of private direct investment. Licensing and other contractual arrangements permitted developing countries to obtain some of the benefits of private direct investment without incurring some of the perceived costs resulting from foreign equity ownership. Ready access to commercial bank lending at low interest rates also reduced the need for private direct investment as a means of obtaining finance. There has recently been a positive shift in the receptivity of developing countries to private direct investment. It remains to be seen whether this will generate larger direct investment flows and in what forms and under what arrangements such investments will be made.

IMPROVING THE ENVIRONMENT FOR DIRECT INVESTMENT

Countries with large internal markets that have generally followed an import-substitution developement strategy are among those which have received the largest amount of direct investment. Sometimes these are the same countries in which prices have been distorted and complaints about the development contribution of direct investment have been most frequent.

Countries that have followed a more open development strategy have had fewer problems with direct investment. Such a strategy makes production for both domestic and export markets equally attractive and requires for its implementation market prices (including both factor and product market prices) which more accurately reflect resource scarcities. In countries that have followed this approach, tariffs have been lowered, prices of local resources have been allowed to conform to opportunity costs, and real interest rates have been positive. As a result, the investment that has taken place has been geared more closely to the country's comparative advantage. The contribution of direct investment to the development process depends heavily, therefore, on the policy framework within which the investment takes place.

Against this background the question arises as to how the policy environment can be improved so that the contribution of direct investment to development can be enhanced and the resource flow increased. There is also the question of what role the World Bank Group—and in particular the International Finance Corporation (IFC)—can play in this area.

Policies of Host Developing Countries

Most developing countries provide incentives to direct investment while simultaneously imposing regulations designed to minimize the perceived adverse effects of this type of flow. Specific policies have been tailored to encourage or discourage direct investment inflows. But the stability of the general economic and political environment in a country, as well as the financial and exchange rate policies pursued, have been of greater significance in shaping the flow of direct investment than specific incentive policies.

A number of factors affect a country's policies with respect to direct investment. Its development strategy, its market philosophy, and its underlying attractiveness as an investment location are all important. The size and growth of the domestic market, the suitability for export-oriented production, and the natural resource endowment are all factors which influence location. Countries have differed widely with regard to the policies pursued and the results obtained. Despite offering substantial incentives to potential investors, countries in Africa and the Caribbean with small domestic markets and limited natural resources were unable to attract significant inflows of direct investment. Some of the faster growing newly industrializing countries in Southeast Asia—Malaysia and Singapore, for instance—have been able to attract direct investment on the basis of their export-oriented development policies without significant incentives.

India, Nigeria, and a number of Latin American countries have had considerable potential for attracting direct investment for import-substitution purposes, but chose to impose restrictions and specific performance requirements so as to extract greater benefits from this form of capital inflow. Incentives were sometimes mixed with restrictions, which created a complex mix of signals for potential investors.

The policies of the Southeast Asian countries during the 1970s point the direction that the general economic policies of host countries could take to increase the flow and enhance the contribution of direct investment. These are the policies of an open development strategy described earlier, in which price distortions are held to a minimum. Such policies provide appropriate economic signals for investors, while establishing the stable environment necessary to induce foreign enterprises to consider investment opportunities. An important maxim which arises from the experience of Southeast Asian countries is that what is good policy for domestic investors is also good for foreign investors.

Although the general policy environment is of prime importance, the policies for specific sectors and industries will also affect whether investments are actually made. If policy constraints are identified clearly and acted upon, new direct foreign investment can take place.

All developing countries have a number of policies and institutions that are specifically for direct investments. These include the incentives (or disincentives) offered and the services and infrastructure provided. The ways in which these policies are administered, their variety, selectivity, and transparency, define the country's strategy toward direct investment.

If more direct investment is to be fostered, developing countries must critically review the necessity for various types of restrictions imposed on such investment. Restrictions have sometimes taken the form of limitations on the degree of foreign participation or prohibitions on entry into particularly sensitive industries. Key industries are reserved for state-owned enterprises, and thus the scope for the domestic private sector is also circumscribed in countries such as Brazil, Egypt, India, and Mexico. In some countries, India, Mexico, and the Philippines, for instance, only minority equity participation is permitted by a foreign investor. The only exceptions would be in the case of an industry with high priority or whose production is mainly for export. In other countries, some in Latin America, foreign companies are required to release ownership and control gradually through the sale of shares to residents over a specified period.

Remittances of interest and dividends on direct investment are subject to restrictions in some developing countries. These have often been major disincentives to investment and have encouraged such practices as the manipulation of transfer pricing.

Performance regulations have also been used (in Latin America, for example) to dictate a required level of exports or a given domestic content in total output from an investment. Some countries such as Argentina, Kenya, Peru, and Turkey have limited the access of foreign investors to domestic currency financing. The debt-servicing difficulties encountered by many developing countries have led to some liberalization of regulations limiting equity investment in recent years.

Investment incentives should also be handled with care if foreign investment is to be encouraged. These incentives are designed to improve the terms under which investment would otherwise take place. Typically they either enhance revenues or reduce costs for foreign firms contemplating investment. Revenue enhancing incentives include import tariffs or quotas on the product concerned, tax breaks, and preferential treatments of various kinds. Among these, none has been more important than tariffs or other forms of protection covering products to be manufactured for local sale. But these, as noted earlier, reduce the contribution made to development, especially if the protection is maintained beyond the infant-industry stage. On the cost-reduction side are such incentives as reduced tariffs on needed imports and exemptions from taxes on inputs.

The type and size of incentive offered by a country depend on the market orientation of the investment it wishes to attract and on the degree of competition it faces from other countries in attracting that type of investment. There are indications that incentives become less effective the greater their complexity and the more frequently they are altered.

The impact of these specific incentives for direct investment is uncertain. Numerous studies have suggested that business executives tend to ignore or downplay the impact of these specific incentives on their own investment decisionmaking. What the government gives, the government can take back. A study undertaken by the IFC, however, concluded that the choice of country location usually takes incentives into account.[1] Performance requirements, including forced exports, local content requirements, and ownership sharing, are also likely to be analyzed quite carefully in the investment decision. The conclusions arising from these studies support the view that once the host country's environment is made less satisfactory through regulation, no specific incentives can encourage foreign investment.

Because of the uncertainty about the impact of direct investment incentives and regulations, each country will have to formulate its own strategy in light of its own specific circumstances. Such a strategy would include a set of policies that define the terms and conditions under which direct investments may be made in the country. The more transparent and more stable are these terms and conditions, the more successful they are likely to be in securing investment.

Policies of Industrial Countries

The general economic policies of the industrial countries influence the supply of direct investment in developing countries. Some industrial countries have developed specific programs to encourage direct investment in developing countries. These programs have included the following instruments:

- Provision of low-cost credits
- Provision of information about opportunities
- Tax benefits
- Dispute settlement mechanisms
- Investment insurance.

At the same time, their own efforts to encourage and protect production at home have in some instances discouraged such investment. Some industrial countries provide attractive concessions in an effort to foster inward foreign investment. Although these incentives are in many cases specifically directed toward certain industrial sectors, they can be directly competitive with similar incentives being offered by developing countries. Direct and indirect subsidies in industrial countries to ailing industries have also reduced the incentives for firms in these industries to consider investment in developing countries. Restrictions on trade flows are an example of such measures. The recent restrictions on Japanese automobile exports to the United States, for instance, lessen the motivation for U.S. producers to seek lower-cost manufacturing locales in developing countries to produce parts and components. To increase investment in developing countries, it would clearly be desirable to remove subsidies and import controls which protect domestic industry in the industrial economies.

Some policy initiatives in industrial countries have had positive effects on investment in developing countries. Trade liberalization, for instance, has given powerful encouragement to direct investment in developing countries aimed at export markets. Competition from imports following the lowering of trade restrictions was an important factor in motivating U.S. firms to search for investment opportunities in Asia and elsewhere to produce for the U.S. market. Japanese textile firms also made direct investments in developing countries in Asia in order to remain competitive in export markets.

Some domestic policies in industrial economies can also have, as a by-product, benefits for direct investment in developing countries. Corporate income tax policy can, by favorable treatment of profits on earnings abroad, create an incentive for domestic companies to move plants overseas. Many industrial countries have also developed specific programs to encourage private direct investment in developing countries.

Investment Protection and Insurance

Some industrial countries have active programs of negotiating bilateral investment treaties with host countries in order to establish a stable legal and economic framework for direct investment. The establishment of mechanisms for the insurance of direct investment has been another means by which industrial countries have sought to improve the framework for direct investment.

Since direct investment is long term and usually takes the form of plant and machinery situated in developing countries, this type of capital is highly exposed to political risk—the threat of expropriation, blocked currency, war, revolution, or insurrection. By diminishing the flow of foreign direct investment to developing countries and boosting the rate of return required by investors to undertake investment in these countries, political risk impedes economic development and distorts the international allocation of resources. Two approaches have been adopted to diminish perceptions of political risk: reduction of the risks through legal protection, and alleviation of losses from such risks through investment insurance. The two approaches are mutually supportive.

Many developing countries have adopted legislation assuring foreign investors protection against expropriation; in a number of countries such assurances are embodied in their constitutions. Home countries and host countries have concluded some 200 bilateral investment protection treaties, which cover, among other things, transfer and expropriation risks.

With regard to insurance, twenty-two capital-exporting countries, including almost all industrial countries, as well as India and the Republic of Korea, have set up national investment guarantee schemes. These offer guarantees for new investments against political risks abroad to nationals or residents of the guaranteeing country. National schemes differ appreciably in their terms and conditions, scope of coverage, and administrative practices. Accordingly, they are utilized by investors to very different extents, with the share of foreign direct investment to developing countries covered under the respective schemes ranging from more than 50 percent to less than 5 percent. It is estimated that from 1977 to 1981 between 10 and 15 percent of foreign direct investment to developing countries from countries with national schemes was guaranteed. About 9 percent of the existing stock of foreign direct investment was covered by the end of 1981.

Moreover, in the early 1970s underwriters and brokers of Lloyd's of London pioneered a private political risk insurance market to provide such insurance for overseas investments and export contracts. Since then, the private political risk insurance business has grown substantially; it is now a large international business. In 1973 private insurers earned about $2 million to $3 million from political risk underwriting premiums; the underwriting capacity for a project did not exceed $8 million. In 1982 total premium revenues from private political risk insurance reached an estimated $95 million, the underwriting capacity for a single project soared to $450 million, and the aggregate liability under all political risk policies was estimated to be around $8 billion.

Despite the growth of national and private investment insurance schemes, there are opportunities to further stimulate private direct investment and other forms of private capital flows by means of multilateral insurance. Such a proposal has been put forth by the World Bank and is discussed below.

THE EMERGENCE OF FOREIGN PORTFOLIO INVESTMENT

Foreign portfolio investment has not to date been a significant source of funds for developing countries, but it is a growing one. Its slowness to emerge as a source of foreign capital reflects in part a skepticism in many developing countries about the potential benefits of such flows. As a result, restrictions and regulations have been instituted in a number of countries. The slow growth of portfolio investment reflects a lack of knowledge of the securities markets in developing countries by investors in the industrial countries and a concern about the risks inherent in such investment. Portfolio investment can, however, provide developing countries with equity financing without raising many of the concerns associated with foreign control in the case of direct investment.

The Perspective of Host Countries

Portfolio investment tends to be diversified over many companies and industries. It offers the investor long-term return and risk diversification and (unlike direct investment) does not involve management and control. As with direct investment, however, portfolio investment represents an alternative source of finance which does not create debt.

The potential benefits of portfolio investment work primarily through the strengthening of the fabric of domestic financial systems. Many indigenous corporations in developing countries have outgrown their domestic capital markets and would benefit from access to foreign portfolio investment. By the same token, interest from foreign investors would increase the demand for stocks in domestic capital markets. More market activity could ultimately lead to new stock issues and perhaps new investment. At a technical level purchases and sales of stock by foreigners may well counterbalance cyclical behavior of domestic investors, thus providing the secondary market with much-needed stability. If developing countries are to attract portfolio capital, they must provide a policy environment which is conductive to such flows.

At present a number of barriers in developing countries restrict the flows of portfolio investment. These exist in varying degrees in different developing countries. Modification or removal of these barriers could facilitate growth in portfolio investment. Such barriers include:

- Capital gains taxes and unduly high withholding taxes on dividend income

- Minimum periods during which foreign portfolio funds must remain invested

- Foreign exchange restrictions relating to foreign portfolio investment

- Restrictions on the types of share which can be purchased or held by foreign portfolio investors

- Discriminatory treatment of foreign investors compared with domestic investors.

The Perspective of International Investors

Almost all of the foreign portfolio investment by American and European investors has been in the markets of the major industrial economies or of developing economies with strong financial systems, such as Singapore. During the past five years, however, some developing countries have emerged as potential markets for portfolio investment, albeit on a limited scale. The IFC has taken the initiative in fostering the development of these markets through the support it has given to the formation of several national investment funds. Such funds have been organized in India, Korea, and Mexico.

In general, developing countries have a reputation as high-risk options for portfolio investors from industrial countries. However, such investment would allow investors to hold a broad range of international assets. Significantly, the returns from investing in the stock markets of the United States and other big industrial countries have not been synchronized with the returns from developing-country markets, so the widest spread of assets has been the least risky. Furthermore, in dollar terms on a cumulative basis over the past eight years, the returns obtainable from the emerging developing-country markets (excluding Hong Kong and Singapore) have recently been more than double those from the world's major equity markets. However, devaluations and major economic changes in the developing countries mean that returns have been volatile.

As a result of rapid growth during the past decade, total market capitalization of the emerging equity markets amounted to $133 billion in 1983. This represents more than one-quarter of the European market capitalization and 10 percent of all stocks traded outside of the United States. Excluding Hong Kong and Singapore, the total capitalization amounts to $75 billion.

For portfolio investment to become a significant source of capital for developing countries, an acceptance of its usefulness in the host countries is required. Also required is a change in perceptions among potential investors. As portfolio investors tend to follow a relatively cautions strategy of diversification, the necessary behavioral changes are likely to be slow in coming.

THE ROLE OF THE WORLD BANK GROUP

The World Bank Group plays an important role in the effort to improve the environment for private equity investment. It does this in several distinct yet interrelated ways.

First, through its lending program the World Bank helps to build up domestic infrastructure. This contributes to increasing the profitability of private sector and foreign private direct investment in developing countries.

Second, at the microeconomic level, the World Bank Group strengthens direct foreign private investment through the direct participation of the IFC in individual project financing. The recent expansion in IFC capital will permit it to play an expanded role in this area.

Third, at the sectoral level, the Bank and the IFC are uniquely qualified to identify policies that are inhibiting private investment. The IFC in particular is well placed to advise governments on the formulation of specific direct investment strategies, since the IFC, from its experience with its own investments, knows how existing policies have affected actual investment projects. Furthermore, in its sector work the IFC acts as a neutral partner in structuring project arrangements so as to ensure equitable sharing of benefits between the host country and the investor. Examples of recent areas of emphasis by the IFC include:

- Definition of project technology arrangements in such a fashion that the foreign technology suppliers bear the major risk in the case of unproven technologies

- Promotion of an approach to management agreements which insists that management fees be structured so as to be related more to performance and profitability than to the total value of sales or other such indicators

- Support of the development of capital markets, in part with a view toward helping to increase portfolio investment

- Discouragement of the use of performance criteria or other restrictions on the operators of foreign enterprises which might restrict the ability of a venture to generate maximum economic benefits.

Fourth, at the macroeconomic level, through its country policy dialogue, the Bank promotes general economic policies that are conducive to domestic and foreign direct investment. By way of example, the focus of the Bank's structural adjustment efforts is to gradually reduce the level of economic distortions prevailing in an economy through the reduction of effective protection and other market price distortions and, where appropriate, the strengthening of the private sector as a means of improving allocative efficiencies.

The Bank has also taken initiatives on an international level. With the establishment of the International Centre for the Settlement of Investment Disputes (ICSID) in 1965, the Bank has made a contribution to the improvement of the international environment for direct investment.

A proposed Multilateral Investment Guarantee Agency (MIGA)* is another important new initiative. MIGA would complement the insurance coverage provided by national insurance schemes and thus would help to reduce the risks accompanying direct investment in developing countries. MIGA would attempt to improve the investment climate in developing countries by (1) issuing guarantees against noncommercial risks for foreign private investments from member countries in its developing member countries, and (2) promoting such investments by carrying out research, providing information, rendering advice, and facilitating policy cooperation.

As a globally operating guarantee facility, the agency would complement national programs by enhancing risk diversification, contributing additional appraisal capacity, and working to overcome gaps resulting from different terms and conditions as well as administrative practices of the various national agencies.

While focusing on direct investments, the agency would be endowed with sufficient flexibility to gradually expand coverage to other forms of medium- and long-term transfer of resources for productive purposes, such as management and service contracts, licensing and franchising agreements, and, ultimately, project loans.

By combining these financing, policy, and institutional initiatives, the Bank could become the focus of an international effort to expand direct investment. This effort would be directed toward specific countries. It would recognize that it is not possible to promote direct investment in all countries and industries. Yet it would also recognize that beneficial direct investment can make a greater contribution to growth in the developing countries than it has done recently.

Bank management has been engaged in a series of consultations with potential members of such an agency and has been encouraged by the favorable reactions to the proposal in many countries.

CONCLUSIONS AND ISSUES FOR DISCUSSION

The following principal conclusions emerge from the preceding review.

- Equity forms of investment can clearly be beneficial to developing countries, and it is desirable that they be increased. Developing countries can reduce the level of risk attached to external capital inflows and secure the benefits of transfers of technology and expertise by expanding the amount of direct investment in total external financing.

- Given that equity investment is desirable, there is a question of how developing countries might attract it and use it efficiently. Experience over the past decade suggests that countries with stable economic and political environments and a system of relative prices that reflects opportunity costs are the most successful in this regard. Some countries have succeeded in attracting direct investment by offering inducements of various kinds, but these normally encourage inefficient investment and malpractices in investing firms. Special incentives can be costly for individual developing countries and offsetting within developing countries as a group. In general, developing countries benefit most from equity forms of investment when the overall policy environment is favorable and when the policies toward foreign investors are the same as those under which domestic investors operate.

- Policies in industrial countries are also important for encouraging equity flows; liberal trade and industrial policies are most conducive to direct investment in developing countries. Bilateral understandings and insurance schemes have also proved useful in mitigating some of the risks inherent in direct investment.

- Although all of the above factors could encourage a greater flow, direct investment, which is undertaken by relatively few companies in a narrow range of countries and industries, is likely to be relatively slow to respond. The evolution of indigenous stock markets and their acceptability among portfolio investors is also likely to be a slow process.

- Both direct and portfolio investments have the potential for covering a higher proportion of the funding needs of developing countries than they have in the past. To realize this potential, however, requires a significant reassessment of the benefits of those types of investment in host and investing countries alike. The relative size of private direct investment by comparison with commercial bank and other private capital flows suggests, however, that while equity flows can be an increasing proportion of total capital flows, they cannot by themselves substitute in the medium term for a significant decline in other private capital flows to developing countries. But given the complementary relationship between equity flows and other capital flows, an improved environment toward the former might help stimulate the latter.

- The World Bank Group has played an important catalytic role in fostering both direct and portfolio investment and in some instances has provided needed complementary finance to direct investment projects. The Bank can help create a more attractive environment for private direct investment through the establishment of MIGA. An important issue for consideration at the Development Committee meeting is governments' views about MIGA and their attitudes toward its potential establishment in the near future.

Note: This paper was prepared by Alex Fleming (World Development Report Staff) on the basis of material supplied by Dale Weigel (Finance Staff), Antoine Van Agtmael (Finance Staff), and Jurgen Voss (Legal Staff). Isaiah Frank (consultant to the Bank from Johns Hopkins University) provided helpful comments on the drafts. A revised version of this paper appeared as chapter 9 of the *World Development Report 1985* (New York: Oxford University Press, 1985).

NOTES

1. Stephen Guisinger, "Investment Incentives and Performance Requirements: A Comparative Analysis of Country Foreign Investment Strategies" (Washington, D.C.: International Finance Corporation, July 1983; processed).

---

*Editor's Note: MIGA was adopted by the Board of Governors of the World Bank at their meeting in Seoul, Republic of Korea in 1985 and has been opened for signature to all member states. MIGA will become operational when the requisite number of member states ratify their signing the MIGA.

Section III:
Selected Financing Techniques
Chapter 9: Project Financing

9A. The Project Cycle
Warren C. Baum

If the question, "What does the World Bank do?" had to be answered in a few words, those words would be: "It lends for development projects." The Bank's main business is to lend for specific projects, carefully selected and prepared, thoroughly appraised, closely supervised, and systematically evaluated. Since opening its doors in 1946, the Bank — in the context of this pamphlet, the International Bank for Reconstruction and Development and its soft-loan affiliate, the International Development Association (IDA), which began operations in 1961 — has made some 3,094 development loans and credits for a total of more than $92 billion. Of these, the overwhelming majority, over 90 per cent, have been for specific projects such as schools, crop production programs, hydroelectric power dams, roads, and fertilizer plants.

This concentration on project lending is directed at ensuring that Bank funds are invested in sound, productive projects that contribute to the development of a borrowing country's economy as well as to its capacity to repay the loan. The Bank is both a developmental and a financial institution, and each project for which it lends must satisfy both features of the institution.

The numbers of projects and the amounts loaned have grown markedly over recent years. In the early 1950s, the Bank was making fewer than twenty loans a year, mostly in Europe and Latin America, totaling about $400 million. In fiscal year 1967, there were sixty-seven loans, more widely spread geographically, totaling $1.1 billion. In the fiscal year ending in June 1981, 246 loans, totaling $12.3 billion, were approved for ninety countries.

There has been no less a change in the character of projects. Bank lending has become increasingly development oriented in terms of borrowing countries, development strategy, sectors of lending, and project design.

— In terms of *countries:* Lending has been directed increasingly toward the poor and less developed countries in Asia, Africa, and Latin America.

— In terms of *development strategy:* The so-called trickle-down theory, which assumes that the benefits of growth will eventually reach the masses of the poor, has been replaced in the Bank by a more balanced approach, combining accelerated growth with a direct attack on poverty through programs to raise the productivity and living standards of the rural and urban poor.

— In terms of *sectors:* The emphasis has shifted from basic infrastructure (roads, railways, power) and industry to more comprehensive programs aimed at growth, provision of basic services, and improvement of income distribution. While infrastructure continues to be important, lending for agriculture and rural development, oil and gas, urban sites and services, water supply and sanitation, small-scale enterprises, education, health, population, and nutrition has been introduced or greatly expanded.

— In terms of *project design:* Greater attention is given in all sectors, both new and traditional, to income distribution and employment, development of local resources and institutions, training of local personnel, impact on environment, and overcoming social and cultural constraints. The Bank has not diminished, however, the attention that it has always paid to market forces, realistic pricing, good management, and the recovery, where feasible, of project costs to permit adequate maintenance and replication.

This evolution in the development orientation — and in the quality — of Bank lending can be illustrated, at the risk of oversimplification, by comparing a "typical" loan of the 1950s with a "typical" loan of the 1970s.

The 1950s loan might be for power generation in a middle-income developing country. In a sense it would be an "enclave" project, designed and supervised by foreign consultants, executed by foreign contractors and suppliers, and managed with the help of expatriates. The technical and financial viability of the project would be analyzed, as would its organization and management, but little attention would be paid to its setting within the energy sector, to how the electricity would be distributed, and to the impact of the level and structure of tariffs on power consumption.

The loan of the 1970s would be for rural devlopment in a low-income developing country. It would provide an integrated package of goods and services (extension, credit, marketing, storage, infrastructure, research) to raise the productivity and living standards of farmers. Existing local institutions would be strengthened or new ones established; local staff would be used as much as possible, with the help of extensive training programs; low-cost design and appropriate technology would be emphasized, giving greater opportunities for local contractors and sources of supply; a system of monitoring and evaluation would be built in to help adjust the project as it went forward and to draw lessons for future projects; and attention would be paid to cost recovery from beneficiaries so that the project would be replicable.

Notwithstanding this record of growth and change, the Bank is still dealing with a relatively small number of quite large projects; the average loan is now about $50 million for a total project investment of $140 million. Bank-assisted projects can have an important demonstration effect and can encourage other investors to supplement Bank lending with their own, as cofinancers or separately; approximately one-third of Bank assisted projects in 1981 had cofinancing from foreign sources.

Every Bank-assisted project must contribute substantially to development objectives and be economically, technically, and financially sound. No two projects are alike; each has its own history, and lending has to be tailored to its circumstances. On the other hand, each project passes through a cycle that, with some variations, is common to all. This pamphlet will discuss the phases of the project cycle—identification, preparation, appraisal, negotiation and presentation to the Executive Directors, implementation and supervision, and evaluation — and the Bank's role in each of them. Each phase leads to the next, and the last phases, in turn, produce new project approaches and ideas and lead to the identification of new projects, making the cycle self-renewing.

The Bank's role in the project cycle is performed largely by its projects staff, who now number about 1,300 drawn from 100 nationalities. Projects staff comprise almost three-quarters of all operational staff employed by the Bank and nearly half of all professional staff. Though there are substantial groups of economists, financial analysts, and various kinds of engineers, an extraordinary variety of other disciplines is also represented: agronomists, specialists in tropical agriculture, groundwater, agricultural credit or livestock, demographers, architects, rural and urban sociologists, public health experts, environmentalists, educators, energy specialists, and physical planners. Typically, technical specialists come to the Bank in mid-career, after extensive experience in their field, sometimes as managers. Most have worked in developing countries. Projects staff are expected to have a broad understanding of development issues and the capacity and maturity to make sound, independent judgments. It is safe to say that, in terms of size and national and professional diversity, the Bank's projects staff is unique.

IDENTIFICATION

The first phase of the cycle is concerned with identifying projects that have a high priority, that appear suitable for Bank support, and that the Bank, the government, and the borrower are interested in considering (see box for the definition of a borrower). In earlier years, project identification was done *ad hoc,* largely in response to proposals by governments and borrowers. Over the years, the Bank has encouraged and helped borrowing countries to develop their own planning capabilities and has also strengthened its own methods of project generation. Economic and sector analyses carried out by the Bank provide a framework for evaluating national and sectoral policies and problems and an understanding of the development potential of the country. They also assess a country's "creditworthiness" for Bank or IDA lending. This analysis provides the basis for a continuing dialogue between the Bank and a country on an appropriate development strategy, including policy and institutional changes for the economy as a whole and for its major sectors. It is then possible to identify projects that fit into and support a coherent development strategy, that meet sectoral objectives, and that both the government and the Bank consider suitable. These projects must also meet a *prima facie* test of feasibility — that technical and institutional solutions are likely to be found at costs commensurate with expected benefits.

Identifying a project that meets these requirements is not easy. Knowlege required for reaching sound judgments may be lacking. The government and other lending agencies may not share the Bank's views on development objectives or sector priorities. There may be difficult choices regarding the scope of the project (Should it start with a pilot/experimental phase or with a larger but possibly more risky investment?). Differences may quickly surface over the need for policy or institutional reforms to achieve the project's objectives. Work on resolving some of these issues may extend well into the preparation stage.

In practice, how are the projects identified within this context? Both the Bank and the government are involved, making the process complex, and this complexity is compounded by the differing capabilities of governments for handling economic planning and project generation. The Bank's economic analysis of a country is affected by the extent and quality of the country's data base and its own economic work. Sector analysis might be done by the country itself, or might be carried out by the Bank or through one of the Bank's cooperative programs with a specialized UN agency, or through studies financed by the United Nations Development Programme (UNDP), bilateral aid programs, or a specific provision for studies in a previous Bank loan.

Finally, some projects are brought forward by private sponsors, such as mining and petroleum enterprises, seeking to develop new resources. These projects have to meet the standards described previously before being regarded as "identified" from the Bank's point of view.

Once identified, projects are incorporated into a multi-year lending program for each country that forms the basis for the Bank's future work in the country. Country programs are used for programming and budgeting the Bank's operations and for assuring that the resources necessary to bring each project forward through the successive phases of its cycle are available.

PREPARATION

After a project has been incorporated into the lending program, it enters the project pipeline, and an extensive period — normally one or two years — of close collaboration between the Bank and the eventual borrower begins. A "project brief" is prepared for each project, describing its objectives, identifying principal issues, and establishing the timetable for its further processing. It is difficult to generalize about the preparation phase because of the variables that abound: the nature of the project, the experience and capability of the borrower, the knowledge currently available (Is it the first loan to the sector/borrower or a "repeater"?), the sources and availability of financing for preparation, and the nature of the relationships between the Bank, the government, cofinancers, and other donors that may be involved in the sector or project.

Formal responsibility for preparation rests with the borrower. At one time, the Bank was reluctant to assist in project preparation, on the banker's principle that such involvement might prejudice its objectivity at appraisal. But experience has shown that the Bank must have an active role in ensuring a timely flow of well-prepared projects. That role has a number of aspects: making sure that borrowers with the capacity and resources to prepare projects themselves understand the Bank's requirements and standards; helping other borrowers to find the financing or technical assistance necessary for preparatory work; and filling gaps in projects that have been incompletely or inadequately prepared. There are even exceptional circumstances in which the Bank itself does preparatory work. The Bank's regional missions in Eastern and Western Africa were established primarily to supplement the limited capabilities of governments in those regions to identify and prepare sound projects.

Financial and technical assistance for project preparation can be extended in a number of ways. The Bank can provide special loans for technical assistance or detailed engineering, make advances from its Project Preparation Facility, reimburse the borrower under the loan in question for preparatory work done earlier, or include funds for preparatory work in a loan for another project in the sector. Cooperative programs between the Bank and the Food and Agriculture Organization of the United Nations (FAO), the United Nations Educational, Scientific, and Cultural Organization (Unesco), the World Health Organization (WHO), and the United Nations Industrial Development Organization (UNIDO) are also an important source of support, as are the UNDP and bilateral aid programs.

While most other assistance for project preparation is provided on a grant basis, and hence is especially attractive, Bank financing must be repaid by the borrower. In providing this help, care must be taken that the project is not perceived at this stage as "the Bank's project" and that the government and the borrower are fully committed to the project and deeply involved in its preparation. This care is more relevant to the "new-style" projects than to traditional infrastructure projects that involve well-established entities whose objectives, and ways of achieving them, are reasonably clear. In new-style projects, such conditions often do not exist, so the commitment of the government and the borrower is essential not only for preparation, but, even more, for successful implementation.

Preparation must cover the full range of technical, institutional, economic, and financial conditions necessary to achieve the project's objectives. For example, a resettlement project might require studies based on remote sensing data to locate arable land, transportation corridors, and the population living in the area proposed for resettlement. Verification on the ground would be followed by a more detailed investigation of soils and water resources; determination of appropriate cropping patterns on the basis of available resources and research knowledge; selection of the technical package necessary for increasing crop yields; and economic and sociological studies of the people being settled to determine appropriate systems of land tenure, extension services, marketing systems, project management, and other institutional arrangements. Government policies with respect to the costs of inputs and the prices of farm products would be studied, as well as levels and methods of cost recovery and their impact on the financial position of the beneficiaries and the government. The role of the private sector in relation to the project would be yet another subject to be examined.

A critical element of preparation is identifying and comparing technical and institutional alternatives for achieving the project's objectives. Most developing countries are characterized by abundant, inexpensive labor and scarce capital. The Bank, therefore, is not looking for the most advanced technological solutions, but for those that are most appropriate to the country's resource endowment and stage of development. Though the Bank has financed advanced telecommunications equipment and modern container-port facilities, project officers nevertheless must consider such questions as whether oxen are more economical than tractors for crop cultivation; whether slum upgrading or sites and services are more suitable than conventional housing as minimal accommodation for the urban poor; or whether public standpipes are more appropriate than house connections for water supply. Preparation thus requires feasibility studies that identify and prepare preliminary designs of technical and institutional alternatives, compare their respective costs and benefits, and investigate in more detail the more promising alternatives until the most satisfactory solution is finally worked out.

All this takes time, and the Bank is sometimes criticized for the length of time required to make a loan. But for the countries concerned, each project represents a major investment with a long economic life, and the time spent in arriving at the best technical solution, in setting up the proper organization, and in anticipating and dealing in advance with marketing and other problems, usually pays for itself several times over.

APPRAISAL

As the project takes shape and studies near completion, the project is scheduled for appraisal. Appraisal, perhaps the best known phase of project work, (in part, because it is the culmination of preparatory work) provides a comprehensive review of all aspects of the project and lays the foundation for implementing the project and evaluating it when completed.

Appraisal is solely the Bank's responsibility. It is conducted by Bank staff, sometimes supplemented by individual consultants, who usually spend three to four weeks in the field. If preparation has been done well, appraisal can be relatively straighforward; if not, a subsequent mission, or missions, to the country may be necessary to complete the job. Appraisal covers four major aspects of the project — technical, institutional, economic, and financial.

Technical

The Bank has to ensure that projects are soundly designed, appropriately engineered, and follow accepted agronomic, educational, or other standards. The appraisal mission looks into technical alternatives considered, solutions proposed, and expected results.

More concretely, technical appraisal is concerned with questions of physical scale, layout, and location of facilities; what technology is to be used, including types of equipment or processes and their appropriateness to local conditions; what approach will be followed for the provision of services; how realistic implementation schedules are; and what the likelihood is of achieving expected levels of output. In a family planning project, the technical appraisal might be concerned with the number, design and location of maternal and child health clinics and the appropriateness of the services offered to the needs of the population being served; in highways, with the width and pavement of the roads in relation to expected traffic and the trade-offs between initial construction costs and recurrent costs for maintenance, and between more or less labor-intensive methods of construction; in education, with whether the proposed curriculum and the number and layout of classrooms, laboratories, and other facilities are suited to the country's educational needs.

A critical part of technical appraisal is a review of the cost estimates and the engineering or other data on which they are based to determine whether they are accurate within an acceptable margin and whether allowances for physical contingencies and expected price increases during implementation are adequate. The technical appraisal also reviews proposed procurement arrangements to make sure that the Bank's requirements are met. Procedures for obtaining engineering, architectural, or other professional services are examined. In addition, technical appraisal is concerned with estimating the costs of operating project facilities and services and with the availability of necessary raw materials or other inputs. The potential impact of the project on the human and physical environment is examined to make sure that any adverse effects will be controlled or minimized.

Institutional

In the Bank's current terminology, "institution building" has become perhaps the most important purpose of Bank lending. This means that the transfer of financial resources and the construction of physical facilities, however valuable in their own right, are less important in the long run than the creation of a sound and viable local "institution," interpreted in its broadest sense to cover not only the borrowing entity itself, its organization, management, staffing, policies, and procedures, but also the whole array of government policies that conditions the environment in which the institution operates.

Experience indicates that insufficient attention to the institutional aspects of a project leads to problems during its implementation and operation. Institutional appraisal is concerned with a host of questions, such as whether the entity is properly organized and its management adequate to do the job, whether local capabilities and initiative are being used effectively, and whether policy or institutional changes are required outside the entity to achieve project objectives.

These questions are important for traditional project entities; they are even more important (and difficult to answer) for the entities charged with preparing and carrying out the new-style projects intended to benefit the rural and urban poor, where there may be no established institutional pattern to follow. The Bank's experience to date has not yielded any ready-made solutions for putting together an institution that can effectively and economically deliver goods and services to large numbers of people — often in remote areas and outside the ordinary ambit of government — and that can motivate them and change their behavior.

Of all the aspects of a project, institution building is perhaps the most difficult to come to grips with. In part, this is because its success depends so much on an understanding of the cultural environment. The Bank has come to recognize the need for a continuing re-examination of institutional arrangements, an openness to new ideas, and a willingness to adopt a long-term approach that may extend over several projects.

Economic

Through cost-benefit analysis of alternative project designs, the one that contributes most to the development objectives of the country may be selected. This analysis is normally done in successive stages during project preparation, but appraisal is the point at which final review and assessment are made.

During economic appraisal, the project is studied in its sectoral setting. The investment program for the sector, the strengths and weaknesses of public and private sectoral institutions, and key government policies are all examined.

In transportation, each appraisal considers the transportation system as a whole and its contribution to the country's economic development. A highway appraisal examines the relationship with competing modes of transport such as railways. Transport policies throughout the sector are reviewed and changes recommended, for example, in any regulatory practices that distort the allocation of traffic. In education, power, and telecommunications, the "project" as defined by the Bank may embrace the investment program of the whole sector. In agriculture, which is more diversified and accounts for a much larger share of a developing country's economic activity, it is more difficult to formulate a comprehensive strategy for the sector; attention is given to sectoral issues such as land tenure, the adequacy of incentives for farmers, marketing arrangements, availability of public services, and governmental tax, pricing, and subsidy policies.

Whenever the current state of the art permits, projects are subjected to a detailed analysis of their costs and benefits to the country, the result of which is usually expressed as an economic rate of return. This analysis often requires the solution of difficult problems, such as how to determine the physical consequences of the project and how to value them in terms of the development objectives of the country.

Over the years, the Bank has kept in close touch with progress in the methodology of economic appraisal. "Shadow" prices are used routinely when true economic values of costs are not reflected in market prices as a result of various distortions, such as trade restrictions, taxes, or subsidies. These shadow price adjustments are made most frequently in the exchange rate and labor costs used in the calculations. The distribution of the benefits of a project and its fiscal impact are considered carefully, and the use of "social" prices to give proper weight in the cost-benefit analysis to the government's objectives of improved income distribution and increased public savings is passing through an experimental phase. Since the estimates of future costs and benefits are subject to substantial margins of error, an analysis is always made of the sensitivity of the return on the project to variations in some of the key assumptions.

Less frequently, in cases of major uncertainty, a risk/probability analysis is also carried out. The optimal timing of the investment is tested in relation to the first year's benefits. When the Bank provides funds to intermediate agencies (development finance companies, agricultural credit institutions) for relending to smaller operations, or in the case of sector lending, those agencies' own appraisal methods must be acceptable.

Some of the elements of project costs and benefits, such as pollution control, better health or education, or manpower training, may defy quantification; in other projects, for example electric power or telecommunications, it may be necessary to use proxies, such as revenues, that do not fully measure the value of service to the economy. In some cases, it is possible to assess alternative solutions that have the same benefits and to select the least-cost solution. In other cases, for example education, alternatives are likely to involve different benefits as well as different costs, and a qualitative assessment must suffice.

Whether qualitative or quantitative, the economic analysis always aims at assessing the contribution of the project to the development objectives of the country; this remains the basic criterion for project selection and appraisal. And while greater concern with the distributional effects of projects reflects broader objectives of development, it does not mean that the Bank has lowered its standards of appraisal. Whether "old" style or "new," every project must have a satisfactory economic return, a standard that the Bank believes serves the best interests of both the country and the Bank itself.

Financial.

Financial appraisal has several purposes. One is to ensure that there are sufficient funds to cover the costs of implementing the project. The Bank does not normally lend for all project costs; typically, it finances foreign exchange costs and expects the borrower or the government to meet some or all of the local costs. In addition, other cofinancers, such as the European Development Fund, the several Arab funds, the regional development banks, bilateral aid agencies, and a growing number of commercial banks, are joining to an increasing extent in cofinancing projects that, in many instances, are appraised and supervised by the Bank. Therefore, an important aspect of appraisal is to ensure that there is a financing plan that will make funds available to implement the project on schedule. When funds are to be provided by a government known to have difficulty in raising local revenues, special arrangements may be proposed, such as advance appropriations to a revolving fund or the earmarking of tax proceeds.

For a revenue-producing enterprise, financial appraisal is also concerned with financial viability. Will it be able to meet all its financial obligations, including debt service to the Bank? Will it be able to generate enough funds from internal resources to earn a reasonable rate of return on its assets and make a satisfactory contribution to its future capital requirements? The finances of the are closely reviewed through projections of the balance sheet, income statement, and cash flow. Where financial accounts are inadequate, a new accounting system may be established with technical assistance financed out of the loan. Additional safeguards of financial integrity may include establishing suitable debt-to-equity ratios or limitations on additional long-term borrowing.

The financial review often highlights the need to adjust the level and structure of prices charged by the enterprise. Whether or not they are publicly owned, enterprises assisted by the Bank generally provide basic services and come under close public scrutiny. Because the government may wish to subsidize such services to the consuming public as a matter of policy, or perhaps simply as the line of least resistance, it may be reluctant to approve the price increases necessary to ensure efficient use of the output of the enterprise and to meet its financial objectives. But adequate prices are a *sine qua non* of Bank lending to revenue-earning enterprises, and the question of rate adjustments may be critical to the appraisal and subsequent implementation of a project.

Financial appraisal is also concerned with recovering investment and operating costs from project beneficiaries. The Bank normally expects farmers to pay, over time and out of their increased production, all of the operating costs and at least a substantial part of the capital costs of, say, an irrigation project. Actual recovery in each case takes account of the income position of the beneficiaries and of practical problems such as the difficulties of administering a particular system of charges or of levying higher charges on Bank-assisted projects than are collected elsewhere. The Bank's policy thus tries to strike a balance between considerations of equity, the need to use scarce resources efficiently, and the need to generate additional funds to replicate the project and reach larger numbers of potential beneficiaries.

Costs can be recovered in a variety of ways—by charges for irrigation water, through general taxation, or by requiring farmers to sell their crops to a government marketing agency at controlled prices. Some countries apply lower standards of cost recovery than those recommended by the Bank; thus, arriving at a common judgment on what is desirable and practicable can be one of the more difficult aspects of the appraisal and subsequent negotiation.

To ensure the efficient use of scarce capital, the Bank believes that interest charges to the ultimate beneficiaries should generally reflect the opportunity cost of money in the economy (indicating the cost of foregone alternatives). But interest rates are often subsidized, and the rate of inflation may even exceed the interest rate. In countries with high rates of inflation, a system of indexed rates is sometimes followed. As in the case of cost recovery, the appropriate level of interest rates may be a contentious issue. The Bank may have to set its sights on a long-term goal, recognizing that it will take time to bring about what may be far-reaching changes in financial policy. This may be particularly so when the government is seeking to control interest rates and other prices as part of an anti-inflation program.

The appraisal mission prepares a report that sets forth its findings and recommends terms and conditions of the loan. This report is drafted and redrafted and carefully reviewed before the loan is approved by the management of the Bank for negotiations with the borrower. Because of the Bank's close involvement in identification and preparation, appraisal rarely results in rejection of a project; but it may be extensively modified or redesigned during this process to correct flaws that otherwise might have led to its rejection.

NEGOTIATIONS, BOARD PRESENTATION

Negotiation is the stage at which the Bank and the borrower endeavor to agree on the measures necessary to assure the success of the project. These agreements are then converted into legal obligations, set out in the loan documents. The Bank may have agreed with a public utility borrower that, to earn an adequate rate of return and finance a reasonable proportion of its investments, prices are to be increased by, say, 20 percent immediately and 10 percent in two years' time. A financial covenant to be agreed upon during negotiation will define the overall financial objectives and specify the necessary rate of return and the timing of the initial rate increase. If a new project unit must be set up to administer the project or to coordinate the activities of the various ministries involved, the loan documents will specify when and how it is to be established and staffed. In fact, all of the principal issues that have been raised prior to and during appraisal are dealt with in the loan documents. Thus, the drafting and negotiation of the legal documents are an essential part of the process of ensuring that the borrower and the Bank are in agreement, not only on the broad objectives of the project, but also on the specific actions necessary to achieve them and the detailed schedule for project implementation.

Negotiations are a process of give and take on both sides of the table. The Bank, for its part, must learn to adapt its general policies to what can be reasonably accomplished in the country, the sector, and the particular setting of the project. The borrower, for its part, must recognize that the Bank's advice is generally based on professional expertise and worldwide experience, and that the Bank's requirement that its funds be invested wisely is compatible with the best interests of the project. Despite differences that inevitably arise when difficult issues must be resolved, the relations that have developed over time between the Bank and its borrowers at this and other stages of the project cycle are generally very good. Bank staff have become more aware of, and sensitive to, local conditions that are critical to the success of a project. Borrowers have come to appreciate that the Bank's approach is professional and objective, that it is in business to lend for well-conceived and well-executed projects, and that this is indeed the Bank's only interest in project work.

After negotiations, the appraisal report, amended to reflect the agreements reached, together with the President's report and the loan documents, is presented to the Bank's Executive Directors. If the Executive Directors approve the operation, the loan is then signed in a simple ceremony that marks the end of one stage of the cycle and the beginning of another.

IMPLEMENTATION AND SUPERVISION

The next stage in the life of a project is its actual implementation over the period of construction and subsequent operation. Implementation, of course, is the responsibility of the borrower, with whatever assistance has been agreed upon with the Bank in such forms as organizational studies, training of staff, expatriate managers, or consultants to help supervise construction. The Bank's role is to supervise the project as it is implemented.

Supervision is the least glamourous part of project work, but in several respects it is the most important. Once the loan for a particular project is signed, attention in the borrowing country shifts to new projects that are coming along; this attitude is understandable and it is reinforced by the fact that many months or years may elapse before the "old" project begins to yield tangible results. Nevertheless, it is obvious that no matter how well a project has been identified, prepared, and appraised, its development benefits can be realized only when it has been properly executed. All projects face implementation problems, some of which cannot be foreseen. These problems may stem from difficulties inherent in the development process or form more specific causes such as changes in the economic and political situation, in project management, or even in the weather. As a result, although the development objectives of a project generally remain constant, its implementation path often varies from that which was envisaged.

It is for these reasons that the Bank has decided that adequate supervision should be the first priority in the assignment of project staff. In practice, the resources devoted to supervision have increased substantially over the years, both absolutely and relative to other project tasks.

The Bank is required by its Articles of Agreement to make arrangements to "ensure that the proceeds of any loan are used only for the purposes for which the loan was granted." While this "watchdog" function has been and remains important, the main purpose of supervision is to help ensure that projects achieve their development objectives and, in particular, to work with the borrowers in identifying and dealing with problems that arise during implementation. Supervision, therefore, is primarily an exercise in collective problem solving, and, as such, is one of the most effective ways in which the Bank provides technical assistance to its member countries.

Over the years another central objective of supervision has emerged: gathering the accumulated experience to "feed back" into the design and preparation of future projects and into the improvement of policies and procedures. Monitoring and evaluation units are now frequently incorporated, particularly in the new-style projects, to gather information for this purpose. An annual review of the supervision portfolio as a whole is conducted to identify major issues of implementation and recommend appropriate changes in Bank policies and procedures.

Supervision takes place in a variety of ways. During negotiation, agreement will have been reached on a schedule of progress reports to be submitted by the borrower. These reports cover the physical execution of the project, its costs, the financial status of revenue-earning enterprises, and information on the evolution of project benefits.

Progress reports are reviewed at headquarters. Problems that surface are dealt with by correspondence or in the course of the field missions that are sent to every project. The frequency of these missions is closely tailored to the complexity of the project, the status of its implementation, and the number and nature of problems encountered. In the periodic internal reviews of projects under supervision, currently numbering about 1,600, some projects are classified as belonging to a special "problem" category. These projects, usually about 10 percent of the total, are watched with particular care and may be visited three or four times a year.

An important element of project supervision concerns procurement of goods and works financed under the loan. Procurement is carried out in accordance with guidelines, incorporated into every loan agreement, that are designed to ensure that the requisite goods and works are procured in the most efficient and economical manner. In most cases, this objective can best be achieved through international competitive bidding open to qualified contractors or manufacturers from all of the Bank's member countries and Switzerland and Taiwan, China. To foster the development of local capabilities, a degree of preference is accorded to domestic suppliers and, under certain conditions, to domestic contractors. Local competitive bidding, or even construction by the borrower's own forces, may be more economic and efficient in some projects for which the works are too small for international tendering to be appropriate.

Seeing that the agreed-upon procurement rules are observed in practice—a single loan may involve anywhere from a few individual contracts to several hundred— is a time-consuming job and one that the Bank takes very seriously. Sometimes the job is relatively straightforward and routine; on other occasions, major issues arise, as, for example, in a telecommunications or power project when there may be a very close choice among several international suppliers as to which has made the lowest evaluated bid on a multimillion dollar contract. The borrower, not the Bank, is responsible for preparing the specifications and tender documents and evaluating bids. The Bank's role is to make sure that the borrower's work is done properly and the guidelines are observed so that Bank funds may be disbursed for the contract. Any controversy concerning the proposed award is sure to be called promptly to the Bank's attention.

Consultant services in such fields as economics, management, finance, architecture, and engineering also must be contracted for by borrowers. Because the quality of these services is usually of overriding importance and can vary widely among firms, consideration of price, as applied to goods and works, is normally not appropriate, although it may be used in special circumstances. With respect to such contracting by borrowers, the Bank's role—as outlined in recently published guidelines—is to ensure that the firms considered for selection are treated equitably and that the firm selected is able to provide services of appropriate quality. For this work, too, the Bank encourages consideration of qualified firms from the borrowing country—either alone or in joint ventures— as well as firms from other developing countries.

EVALUATION

While supervision is, in part, a process of learning through experience, it is primarily concerned with that period in the project's life when physical components are being constructed, equipment purchased and installed, and new institutions, programs, and policies put in place. Once these stages are complete, and Bank funds fully disbursed, the level of supervision declines sharply. During the period of active supervision, attention tends to be focused on the problems of the moment. While projects may be subject to ongoing monitoring and evaluation, the need for a more comprehensive approach to evaluating project results has become apparent. In 1970, an evaluation system was established as the final stage in the project cycle.

All Bank-assisted projects are now subject to an *ex post* audit. To ensure its independence and objectivity, this audit is the responsibility of the Operations Evaluation Department (OED), which is entirely separate from the operating staff of the Bank and which reports directly to the Executive Directors. While this system ensures full accountability, it is also designed to mesh closely with, and take advantage of, the supervision activity of the operating staff.

As the final step in supervision, regular projects staff—or the borrower— prepare a completion report on each project at the end of the disbursement period. These reports are, in part, an exercise in self-evaluation—which has not prevented them from being frank and often critical. Each report is reviewed by the OED, which then prepares a separate audit report; both reports are sent to the Executive Directors. Most audits are based on a desk review of all materials pertaining to the project, but, whenever necessary, the audit staff undertakes a field review, sometimes as comprehensive as the original appraisal. Borrowers are asked to comment on the OED audits and are requested to prepare their own completion reports. Furthermore, the Bank encourages borrowers to establish evaluation systems to review all their development investments.

Each audit and completion report re-estimates the economic rate of return on the basis of actual implementation costs and updated information on operating costs and expected benefits. It cannot, however, pass a final judgment on the success or failure of some projects whose economic lives, with their attendant operating costs and benefits, extend well beyond the end of the disbursement period. To meet this need, OED prepares "impact evaluation reports" at least five years after the last disbursement for a small number of carefuly selected projects. Borrowers play an active role in this process, too.

In addition, an annual OED report reviews all project audits. Studies are made in greater depth of groups of projects (such as all loans to development finance companies), special problems (such as delays in loan effectiveness), or a sector in a particular country (such as agricultural projects in Indonesia).

The evaluation system is a gold mine of information, supplementing and complementing that provided by the broader stream of project supervision reports. Some of the findings are sobering; many are reassuring. Experience indicates, for example, that the Bank still has much to learn about technologies necessary to bring about sustained increases in yields of small farmers in rainfed areas, most notably in sub-Saharan Africa. Problems of cost overruns and delayed completion have plagued the implementation of a number of projects, particularly in the period following the oil price rises and ensuing worldwide inflation. Many projects change in scope during their implementation. Nevertheless, the most recent* annual review of the OED audits, comprising eighty-seven projects, indicates that over 93 percent of the investments remain worthwhile, and that a number of them had expected economic returns better than those estimated at appraisal.

Particularly gratifying is the indication that the Bank's response to the lessons of experience is generally positive. Mistakes, of which the Bank has had its share, are not often repeated. Subsequent projects build on earlier ones in the same sector. New approaches, policies, and procedures have been adopted to improve project performance: For example, the project brief system is helping to secure government agreement and commitment to project objectives at an earlier stage of project design; rural development projects now integrate the provision of all the services, inputs, and basic infrastructure necessary to bring about a sustained increase in small farmers' yields; lending for projects that are at a more advanced stage of preparation is being introduced to provide more accurate cost estimates and reduce the likelihood of cost overruns and implementation delays.

The lessons of experience are thus being built into the design and preparation of future projects. In other words, the project cycle is working as intended.

*Seventh Annual Review of Project Performance Audit Results. (Washington: World Bank). December 1981.

9B. An Introduction to International Project Financing
John M. Niehuss

I. NATURE OF PROJECT FINANCE

In recent years, there has been a dramatic increase in what bankers loosely refer to as "project lending" or "project finance." Unfortunately, it is difficult to get bankers or lawyers to agree on precisely what is meant by "project finance" as each seems to have his own way of defining or describing the concept. However, a few generalizations on the nature of project finance is possible.

A. General Characteristics

First, in a pure project financing, a separate project entity is usually created to raise funds and hold the project assets. Because the new entity has no operating history and no non-project assets, the funds are raised solely on the strength of the economics of the particular project. This contrasts with the more conventional, traditional methods of finance where funds are raised on the basis of the general credit-worthiness and past and expected financial strength of the sponsors of the project. In other words, in a project financing, the basic security for the lenders is provided by the expected cash flow and assets of the project rather than the historical financial strength and assets of the project sponsors. Consequently, the securities issued by the project entity are designed to be self-liquidating from the revenues received from the operation of the project facilities.

Second, since most major projects take several years to complete, project financing generally involves raising funds over a period of years in stages as the project progresses. This phase financing enables the type of finance to be tailored to meet the needs of each stage of the project and, if the finance plan is sufficiently flexible, to tap the world's capital markets at the most appropriate times. Third, project financing is generally "off-balance sheet" for the major sponsors of the project. This means that debt raised for the project does *not* appear as a liability on the sponsor's balance sheet or come within borrwoing limitations or debt service tests contained in the sponsor's outstanding loan agreements or indentures.

Fourth, project financings tend to be complicated and involve extensive legal documentation designed to ensure (1) that the cash flow from the project will be sufficient to repay the debt raised for the project or (2) that debt will be serviced by some creditworthy party even if the cash flow is inadequate or is interrupted.

Fifty, project financings most often occur in the context of very high, capital cost projects undertaken in three sectors: (1) extractive industries (for example, oil, natural gas and mining); (2) chemical and process plants (oil and petrochemical refineries, steel mills, cement, fertilizer and power plants, etceters); and (3) transportation (oil and gas piplines, shipping, etcetera.)

B. Reasons for Project Financing

Reasons for project financing vary from project to project and from industry to industry. Prime reasons for such financing include:

(1) the cost of the project is beyond the capacity of the individual sponsor (or sponsors) and the only way to arrange finance is on the basis of project economics and/or the creditworthiness of other parties who may become involved with the project (e.g. purchasers of project output);

(2) conventional financing is precluded by indenture or loan agreement restrictions;

(3) the sponsor may be creditworthy but want to do the debt financing off-balance sheet so as not to impact negatively on certain financial ratios; or

(4) tax and/or accouting considerations.

For a combination of these reasons, project financing is increasing throughout the world. Companies and governments have turned to project financing to meet their needs as the cheapest and most effective means and most major financial institutions now have project finance departments and specialists in strucutring large projects. Major projects are generally very complex involving several lenders, a number or related loan documents and contracts, and several interlocking corporations. While the structure of many projects may seem over complex, such complexity often results from the need to

(1) satisfy the host country's investment laws, (2) provide the lenders with the security they need (e.g. trust arrangements guarantees; or take-or-pay purchase contracts), or (3) satisfy the tax or accounting needs of the foreign corporations participating in the project (e.g. lease arrangements, advance payments; construction trust financings).

The ramainder of this essay outlines the nature and problems of various types of project financings with particular reference to the factors which a host government involved in such financing should consider. In reading this paper, one should keep in mind that each project is different and that as if progresses, it tends to acquire a distinct character and personality of its own. A project financing is, in essence, a process in which the parties seek the most effective way to accomplish the economic and developmental objectives of the host country and the financial, tax and accounting needs of the lenders and project participants. This means that generalizations are difficult and that the methods outlined herin will, therefore, need to be modified or adapted to meet the needs of a particular country or a particular project.

II. TYPES OF FINANCE

In complex project financing it is common to use different types of financing to fund different stages or components of the project. For example, equity funds may be used to finance feasibility studies and preliminary design and engineering; short-term revolving bank credit is often used during the construction period; export credits often finance major equipment; and development bank funds are used for longer term financing. In short, most project finance involves a blend of several different types of funding and one of the major challenges in any project financing is to combine them into a package which provides the lowest cost for the project. The purpose of this section is to outline briefly some of the most common types of finance.

A. Equity vs. Debt Finance

The basic distinction is, of course, between equity and debt funds. Equity is frequently referred to as the ownership interest in a project as it generally determines how ultimate control over a project is divided. Equity is also the risk element of any finance package since the providers of equity funds have no assurance that they will ever be able to recoup their invested funds. In this regard, it should be pointed out that equity contributions to a financing can be in kind as well as cash. Because they want to minimize the amount of cash at risk, corporations involved in international projects often try to make their equity contributions in the form of equipment, technology, patents or know-how.

Debt financing is based on contract (i.e. a loan agreement, a note agreement or an indenture) which spells out the terms and conditions under which funds are advanced. The providers of debt funds generally receive interest periodically and are entitled to receive repayment of the funds they advance in accordance with a schedule for repayment.

B. Types of Debt Finance

Project financings generally have high debt to equity ratios which means that the vast bulk of funds for any major project will be in the form of debt. Debt can be calssified in several different ways. Some of the more important methods are: maturity (short-term, medium-term or long-term), type of interest (fixed versus floating rates, market rates versus concessional rates), and basic sources (official or semi-official sources versus private sources). These basic sources of finance can be broken down into further categories. For example, official finance may be in the form of bilateral aid, multilateral aid (e.g. the World Bank, Inter-American Development Bank, the official export credits. Private sources include bank finance (term loans, syndicated bank loans and revolving credit), public markets (bonds and notes) and private placements (including commercial paper). In addition, debt can be classified according to the type of instrument (e.g. commercial paper, notes, bonds, mortgage bonds or debentures).

C. Methods or Structure of Finance

Another way of classifying types of finance is by the method or structure of the financing. Methods commonly used include: contract-based financing; production payment financings; advance-payment financing; compensatory financing arrangements; leveraged lease financing; and construction trust financing. These methods are summarized briefly.

1. Contract-Based financing. In a contract-based project financing, lenders advance funds to the project on the basis of a contractual commitment by clearly creditworthy parties to use the project facilities. These contractual commitments generally involve agreement to supply throughput to the project or to purchase output from the project. (See Section V-B-1 for further details).

2. Production payment. A production-payment financing is a specialized method of financing which has been commonly used in the United States and elsewhere in petroleum-related project financing. There are a number of types of production payment financing but its essence is that the actual physical product produced (e.g. petroleum or a mineral) is assigned to, or for the benefit of, the lender; and debt service is provided out of the proceeds from the sale of production. Thus, the lender obtains an interest in the output of the project and, essentially, uses this interest as the means to ensure repayment of its loan.

3. Advance payment financing. A relatively new method of finance related to production-payment finance is the so-called "advance-payment financing." This type of finance has been used in the United States since the energy crisis has forced companies to compete to obtain new energy sources—mainly natrual gas. In this type of financing, a company (often a natural gas utility) makes advance payments to subsidize exploration and development with the loan repaid out of production if the venture is successful. Of course, if the venture is unsuccessful, the company making the advance payment assumes the risk of non-payment. Advance payments are also used in other sectors where a creditworthy parent or sponsor company makes an advance payment to a newly-created project entity which constructs the project and reduces the advance payment account by supplying output from the project.

4. Compensatory financing arrangements. Compensatory financing is a type of finance which is growing in importance in financing East-West trade and investment. It is used as a tool for generating hard currency needed for projects in Eastern bloc countries and generally involves a contractual obligation by a Western credit. In essence, this contractual obligation is designed to generate the hard currency to repay loans made to finance the project.

5. Leveraged Lease Financings. Leveraged lease financing is a method of project financing in which the ultimate user of a project facility leases the facility during the period of its useful life rather than owning the facility in its own name. From an operational standpoint, the lessee treats the facility as if it were a part of its system. Lease financing is often used to finance power plants or industrial facilities in the U.S.

The advantages of leveraged leasing include:

(a) the fact that lease payments may be lower than the overall cost of capital if the lessee financed the plant itself;

(b) the lease payments can be structured to accommodate the lessee's cash flow over the life of the lease; and

(c) the lease arrangement will be a footnoted obligation on the lessee's balance sheet as opposed to an on-balance sheet obligation if the lessee financed the plant directly.

While these advantages can be important, they will need to be weighed against the fact that under U.S. law, the lessee will (1) lose tax benefits (e.g. the investment tax credit and accelerated depreciation) which could make leasing more costly than if they could be fully utilized by the lessee and (2) give up all rights to the plant's residual value which means that it may have to pay a substantial amount if it wishes to continue to operate the plant after its "useful life" for tax and lease purposes. Whether leveraged leasing would be possible or beneficial in a given project can only be determined after a careful analysis of legal, tax and financial considerations.

6. Construction trust financing. In a construction trust financing a party other than the ultimate user of a facility arranges for financing and has title to project assets during the construction period. At the end of the construction period the facilities are sold to the ultimate user. The benefits of this method of project financing include:

(a) increased financing flexibility and possibly lowers financing costs during the construction period; and

(b) the ability to defer long-term financing until later in the construction period.

The entity which owns the project assets during construction is able to raise funds because its creditworthiness is established by an agreement with the ultimate user of the facility in which such user agrees to purchase (or repurchase) the project facilities at the completion of construction, or, to assume all financial obligations of the entity if it chooses not to pay an amount sufficient to retire such obligations. The creditworthiness created by this agreement enables the construction phase entity to obtain capital from a variety of sources including revolving-credit facilities from commercial banks, fixed-rate intermediate credit loans and commercial paper.

III. SOURCES OF FINANCE FOR INTERNATIONAL PROJECTS*

One of the major problems in assembling any financial package is to determine the source of funds for the project, that is, which institutions and which countries will provide the finance. Complex projects are often financed by piecing together funds from many different sources, and the purpose of this section is to outline some of the more important sources of finance for any major international project.

While there is no established sourcing pattern, one generalization is, however, possible. Supply and construction contracts are often won by a supplier's ability to arrange finance. This means that the source of supply of finance is often the same as the source of major goods and services used on the project. In short, the reason a particular supplier is choosen may be due to financial assistance from its government (e.g. export credit finance or tied bilateral aid) or from commercial banks in its country.

A. Distinction between Local Costs and Foreign Exchange Costs

In considering sources of finance, one needs to distinguish between funding *local-currency costs* and funding foreign-exchange costs. In many projects a substantial amount of the local currency funding is paid out of the host country's own

*Editors Note: For more information on Sources of Finances, readers may refer to Section II (Chapter 2-8) in this volume.

budget. This is particularly true for the costs of providing essential infra-structure for the project. Depending on the country, there may be a local capital market which can provide funds; and the local banking system may be sufficiently developed to help provide finance. In addition, the international development banks occasionally provide some local-cost financing for projects in which they are involved. Finally, funds which are raised on foreign capital markets, can, of course, always be used to help fund local costs.

Generally, meeting the *foreign exchange requirements* of a major project is more difficult than raising funds in local currency. The previous section listed a number of the major sources of finance for foreign-exchange costs, pointing out the distinction between official and private sources and noting the differences among the various categories. This section considers these sources in further detail.

IV. THE FOREIGN INVESTOR'S PERSPECTIVE: FACTORS AFFECTING ITS ATTITUDE TOWARD THE PROJECT

On any major project financing there will usually be one or two private corporations involved as joint-venture partners and/or providers of technical or managerial assistance. Typically, these private corporations will be large multinational companies. While the foreign investor must comply with all host-country laws, it will also be subject to a number of constraints imposed by its own legal and financial system which will influence its attitude towards the structure and operation of the project. For example, U.S. tax laws and/or accounting considerations may affect the form of the legal entity the U.S. partner uses to participate in the venture, the nature of its capital contribution and the form in which it receives its return on invested resources. In addition, loan agreements and indentures relating to previous borrowings may place restrictions on a foreign partner. Moreover, its lawyers may insist on certain types of choice of law, arbitration and dispute settlement clauses. The purpose of this section is to look at some of these factors which may constrain a foreign investor and influence its attitude toward the project.

A. Accounting Considerations

Accounting considerations are often the reason that companies seek off-balance sheet project financing. These considerations also lie behind the precise form of project financing. As the finance plan for any major project begins to take shape, it will be necessary to consult with auditors to ensure that the accounting objectives of all parties are being met. The following are a few of the key accounting concepts and the reasons why they can be important in determining the shape of a project financing.

1. Consolidated financial statements. A common objective of project financing is to keep debt raised to construct project facilities off a company's balance sheet so that there will be no negative impact on financial ratios. If a project is structured in such a way that the debt of the project entity is consolidated with the project sponsor's debt, the objective of off-balance sheet financing will be defeated. Thus, it is often important to ensure that the financial statements of any project entity used for a project will not be consolidated with those of the parent company of the foreign investor.

2. Off-Balance sheet. Even if the financials of the project vehicle are not consolidated with those of the main project sponsor (or sponsors), the form of the project financing or the nature of the contractual commitments may require some speical reference in the sponsor's financials. For example, in the case of construction trust financing, the purchase obligation of the project user must be shown as a special liability on the balance sheet under a heading entitled "Construction Trust Financing" and footnoted. As funds are disbursed by the construction financing entity, the user records the construction in progress on its balance sheet and credits long-term debt liability.

On the other hand, leveraged-lease financing and contract-based financing are generally considered to be off-balance sheet. Lease obligations and major pruchase contract obligations in the United States are often discussed in footnotes to the financial statements.

3. Accounting factors. Special accounting rules and procedures that often apply to specific industries may also be a constraint on a foreign investor. For example, special rules which apply to the utility, natural gas or mining industries may affect the way a foreign investor prefers to structure a project. Furthermore, negotiations may be complicated if foreign investors from different countries with differnt accounting systems are involved. What is acceptable to one foreign partner may be unacceptable to another.

B. Tax Considerations

Tax factors, like accounting and indenture considerations, can determine the feasibility and/or form of a project financing. Each project will have its own unique tax problems, difficult to generalize. However, it is clear that every proposed project financing plan must be carefully reviewed by tax counsel to ensure that it satisfies the host country's revenue objectives, meets the needs of the project sponsors, and does not prejudice the tax needs of the lenders to the project.

C. Nature of the Project Entity

The private corporation participant is, because of legal, tax and accounting considerations, often very concerned about the nature of the project entity. There are a number of legal entities which are used as the financing vehicle in off-balance sheet project financings. These include corporations, partnerships, trusts, and unincorporated joint ventures. The most appropriate form will vary from project to project, and it is impossible to recommend a form of project entity for a project without an extensive review of several key factors. These areas include:

(a) the tax and accounting objectives of parties;

(b) the loan agreement and indenture restrictions that are applicable to the various parties to the contract;

(c) the nature of the financing being contemplated (e.g., leveraged lease, construction trust or contract backed financing), and

(d) the legal investment and securities laws governing the issuance of the entity's securities.

It is likely that the precise legal form of the financing vehicle will not be determined until several other pieces of the financing package have fallen in place. However, it is important to keep in mind that some flexibility will be needed in order to devise an off-balance sheet financing which meets the needs of all the parties.

V. THE LENDER'S PERSPECTIVE: BASIC CONCERNS OF LENDERS IN PROJECT FINANCING

Project financings typically have a high debt-equity ratio which means that the most critical sources of funding are the lenders who provide debt funds. This group is generally sophisticated but conservative. As a result, in conventional on-balance sheet financing, lenders insist on extensive covenants, debt issuance tests and maintenance ratios to help ensure the continuing creditworthiness of the borrowing company.

In project financings, institutional lenders always ensure that they are adequately protected from the risks of project financing. Since the basic protection is provided by the cash flow and assets of the project, lenders are sensitive to any fact that might interrupt the cash flow or reduce the value of project assets. This section outlines the basic risks in any project financing and the methods that are commonly used to protect against them.

A. Typical Project Risks

1. Cost-Overrun and completion risks. In every project, no matter how carefully conceived and carried out, it is always possible that actual project costs will exceed estimated costs due to a variety of factors, including construction problems, inflation, environmental or technical problems, government regulation, or currency fluctuations. To satisfy lenders, every plan for a project financing must contain some mechanisms which assures the ultimate funding of cost over-runs so that the project is not abandoned prior to the completion because of lack of funds.

Overrun funding can be provided from a variety of sources For example, it is often provided by (1) the project sponsors if they are financially able to enter into open-ended overrun funding commitments; (2) the lenders to the project who agree to provide some additional funding up to a fixed amount; (3) a group of banks who open a stand-by line of credit to cover overruns; (4) the purchasers of output from this project; or (5) governments interested in having the project completed.

Even if capital is available to fund completion, there may be some technical or economic development which prevents the project from being completed. In the event of non-completion, the cash flow on which lenders rely for debt service will not be forthcoming. The project becomes, in the terminology of project finance experts, a "dead horse". To protect against this contingency, lenders will require some assurance that the funds they have advanced for the project will be repaid even if the project is not completed. Any finance plan for a major project funded on a project-financing basis must provide some mechanism to give lenders this assurance.

While generally a remote risk, the risk of non-completion is often difficult to protect against because the contingent liabilities are so large. The risk is frequently mitigated by requiring entity participants to advance their funds before any laons are disbursed. Sponsors sometimes have sufficient resources to give adequate assurances of debt repayment to lenders but, in larger projects, the purchasers of project output or other clearly creditworthy parties (e.g., host governments) are often called upon by lenders to assume the non-completion risk.

2. Market risks. Lenders look carefully at basic project economics when they engage in off-balance sheet, non-recourse financing. In particular, they need to be assured that demand for project output exists, and will continue to exist, at satisfactory price levels for the duration of their loan. In recent years, a number of major mineral projects have had to be postponed because of soft-market forecasts for the project output. Although the problem may be less acute in other areas (e.g., energy), lenders still need assurance that adequate demand will exist for the output produced. In addition, they will often insist on study of existing and planned competing sources of supply to make sure that the project in question will not, when aggregated with other projects underway, lead to a problem of overcapacity.

At a minimum, the lenders will insist on seeing the demand projections and other market studies that have been done in connection with the project. In addition, many of the major financial institutions have their own research groups who will do independent market studies of the project. Finally, in cases where there may be some doubt, lenders may insist on a third-party feasibility study as a pre-condition to any lending.

3. Resource risk. In major energy or natural-resource projects, lenders must be satisfied that the basic resource around which the project is built will be available for the duration of their loan. Ultimately the security for any loan to a nautral resource project is the recoverable reserve in the ground. The project may not be able to produce or deliver as much ore or oil or gas as anticipated because the recoverable reserves have been overestimated or construction or production difficulties are encountered. When this happens, the revenue from the project may be insufficient to service project debt.

In order to protect against this risk, lenders routinely insist on extensive geological surveys and opinions as to the size and nature of the reserve before advancing funds. Other methods to minimize the reserve risk include: (1) requiring the producers to make up any shortfall in estimated production from other sources (e.g. from other mines or wells or through open market purchases) or (2) a type of "throughput and deficiency" agreement in which the producer agrees to supply a certain minimum amount or make direct cash payments to purchasers and/or lenders.

In addition, in cases where supply of a key resource is essential to a project (e.g., coal for a power plan project) lenders generally insist that the project sponsors make adequate provision for a substitute supply source in the event that the basic supply is interrupted or discontinued. Sometimes suppliers will agree to supply products of the same quality from alternative sources.

For example, if a loan were being arranged for a coal fired plant, lenders would look carefully at:

(a) the amount and quality of coal source for the project;

(b) the expected continuity of coal supply for the life of the project;

(c) the reliability of the company supplying the coal, and

(d) the basic terms and conditions of the coal supply contract.

The interest of lenders in the supply source underscores the critical importance of supply arrangements for the successful financing of many projects.

4. Regulatory risk. In many project financings, the level and continuity of the cash flow may depend on the existence of a particular regulatory treatment of the project. The most common examples are found in the areas of taxation and public utility rates. For example, changes in accounting treatment host-country taxation of a project may determine whether or not it is profitable. In addition, many project financings of energy projects are dependent on tariff arrangements which ensure cash flow by requiring the end users of the energy to make payments whether or not they receive any energy. In such cases, lenders will be hesitant to advance funds if they are not convinced that regulatory approval will be given to the tariff arrangements and maintained in force for the duration of their loan.

5. Post-Completion risks. Once a project is completed and operating according to design specifications, the risks to lenders diminish substantially. However, it is always possible that through a technical difficulty, a natural disaster (e.g., a flood or earthquake), a change in host-government, or lack of a critical input for the project, there will be an interruption or diminution in production or transportation after a project has reached the fully operational stage. In such a case, the revenue flow from the project would be interrupted and debt repayment jeopardized. In cases of short interruptions, lenders would not be especially concerned. However, prolonged interruption would be of concern, and every project financing must have some method to assure lenders that their debt service will be met on a regular basis while repairs to the system are being made.

6. Political risks. A major concern of lenders is that a politically motivated act by the government of the territory in which the project is located will jeopardized the project. The most extreme examples are war, revolution or nationalization but other factors (e.g., foreign exchange controls; denial of export or import permits; denial of work permits; insistence on local sourcing or local participation) can also have a significant effect on a project's overall viability.

Political types of risks are of major concern in projects in both developed and developing countries. For example, the experience in Australia in the mid-1970s illustrates that political uncertainty can affect the flow of funds to projects in developed countries and the recent events in Iran illustrate the problem in the less developed nations.

It is virtually impossible to protect against these risks by contractual arrangements or covenants in loan agreements. Therefore, to help lenders overcome their hesitation to advance funds n the face of political uncertainty, governments have developed insurance schemes to protect against political risks and/or currency inconvertibility.

B. Methods of Protecting Lenders Against Project Risk.

Because of the various risks outlined above, potential lenders insist on ironclad assurances that any funds they advance for the project will be repaid even if the project runs into difficulties. Various contractual and other arrangements have been devised which help provide the lenders with the protection they need. This section briefly discusses some of the more common methods of protecting against project risk.

1. Contractual credit support. In a contract-based project financing, lenders advance funds to the project on the basis of aa contractual commitment by clearly creditworthy parties to use the project facilities. These contractual commitments generally involve agreement to supply throughput to the project (e.g., in the case of a pipeline or a refinery) or to purchase output from the project (e.g., in the case of a mine or a power station). In most cases, a separate project entity is created with the equity supplied by the sponsors of the project and the debt supplied by institutional lenders on the basis of the contractual commitments. The lenders also generally require a completion guarantee or an agreement to provide overrun financing from a creditworthy party—often the project sponsors.

The advantages of this type of financing include:

(a) the fact that it may enable the foreign sponsors to avoid restrictive indenture provisions which would prohibit them from issuing new debt; and

(b) the entire transaction would be off-balance sheet and reflected only as a contingent liability in a footnote to the financial statements.

(c) it enables the credit and financial strength of the users of the project (e.g., purchases of mine output or the shipper in the case of a pipeline) to be used to attract debt to the project.

There are a number of different types of contractual arrangements which are used to provide credit support to a project. Perhaps the most common is referred to as a *take or pay contract*. Under this type of arrangement, the purchaser of a project's output is required to make minimum payments (generally sufficient to service debt) even if output is not available or even if the project shuts down due to a natural disaster, interruption of transport, etc. Such contracts are, in effect, indirect guarantees of debt service by the purchaser and are sometimes called *"hell or high water" contracts* because the purchaser must pay even under the most extreme circumstances. In other words, they must, to use the American slang expression, pay "come hell or high water". In power or pipeline projects where it is common to negotiate tariff agreements, an arrangement in which the purchasers assume an unconditional obligation to pay under all circumstances is often referred to as *all-events-full-cost-of-service-tarriff*.

In some cases purchasers may resist assuming the extreme obligation to pay "in all events" or "come hell or high water". In such cases, the contract is generally referred to as a *take and pay* contract which means that the purchaser is only obligated to take and pay when the product is available. The purchaser's obligation then become contingent on the existence of the successful operation of the project to produce output in sufficient quantities to fulfill the contract.

Another type of credit support is provided by *throughput and deficiency agreements*. There are a number of variations of throughput agreements but perhaps the most common is illustrated by a pipeline project where the potential users of the pipeline agree to put a sufficient volume through the pipeline to generate revenues adequate to cover debt service or to make up any difference in such revenues through direct cash payments either to the project or to the lenders. In such cases it is the credit of the user of the facility which provides the security for loans to the project.

Another type of contractual support for a project financing is provided through *rental or use contracts* which provide for the use of a piece of equipment or a facility at rental rates calculated to cover debt service. For example, offshore drilling rigs are sometimes financed through such contracts so that the credit of the oil company user provides the ultimate basis for loans to the project.

2. Trust devices. In complicated project financings, especially those based on contractual credit support, it is common for the lenders to insist on trust arrangements designed to isolate the cash flow of the project in such a way that it is available for debt repayment on a priority basis. For example, in the case of a mining project in a developing country in which the output was sold to purchasers in Western Europe, the lenders might require the creation of trust based in London and require the purchasers to make payment to the trustee rather than the owners of the project. The trustee would then segregate in a trust account sufficient amounts to service debt and meet other essential obligations of the project. Only if such obligations were satisfied would funds be released to the owners of the project. The trust arrangements does not provide any additional credit support or financial backing for the project but is, rather, a payment mechanism designed to provide additional security to the lenders.

3. Guarantees. Another very common device used to protect lenders against project risk is a parent company or host government guarantees of their loans. Such guarantees are particularly important prior to completion and commencement of commercial operation of the project because contract credit support is generally not effective until the project begins operating. Therefore, to cover the cost overrun and commpletion risks discussed above, lenders frequently insist on guarantees by creditworthy parties (often host governments) that sufficient funds will be available to complete the project or that debt will be repaid in the event the project is abandoned prior to completion.

VI. HOST COUNTRY CONSIDERATIONS: EVALUATION OF FINANCIAL PROPOSALS

A major consideration for the host government or agency sponsoring a project, is whether a particular financial proposal is the one that is most appropriate for the project and most beneficial for the country. Any evaluation of financial packages inevitably involves trade-offs and the balancing of various interests. The purpose of this section is to look at some of the key factors to consider when evaluating an offer of finance and to discuss some of the trade-offs which may need to be made by the host government.

A. Interest Rate Consideration

1. Level. The interest rate is usually the first factor that any prospective borrower considers in evaluating a financing. The key factor is, of course, the absolute level of the rate. Interest rates in development projects could run from zero in the case of IDA financing to well over 10% for longer-term fixed-rate funds from the private capital markets.

2. Fixed vs. floating rates. A second major consideration is whether the rate is fixed or floating. A fixed rate is one that is established at a specified level at the time the loan is made and does not vary during the period that the loan is outstanding. World Bank loans, most bond and note issues, and most export credit financing provide examples of fixed interest rate sources of financing. Floating rates are, as their name implies, subject to variation during the period the loans are outstanding. Floating rates are generally set on the basis of a spread above a specified generally accepted interest rate. The most common method of determining floating rates is to have a spread above the London Inter-Bank Offered Rate (LIBOR). For example, interest on a particular loan may be set at 1% above LIBOR and then recalculated periodically as the LIBOR rate changes in accordance with supply and demand factors on the London market.

Fixed interest rates are obviously better for planning purposes, for they enable those involved in the project to predict accurately the cost of capital. On the other hand, fixed rates may be slightly higher at any given moment than floating rates for the same maturity. This is primarily because floating rates provide somewhat greater protection for lenders in that they have an assured spread above the funds that they borrowed to fund the project. Any potential borrower must, therefore, consider the trade-off between fixed rates, which are better for planning purposes but somewhat higher in cost, and floating rates, which are more readily available, potentially lower in cost, but less desirable from a planning standpoint.

3. Additional fees. In addition to the specified or coupon rate of interest, commitment fees and/or requirements for compensating balances (e.g., a requirement by a lending bank that a borrower keep a certain percentage of the funds on deposit in that bank) may raise the overall cost of borrowing and should be considered along with the interest rate.

4. Timing of interest payments. Another factor to consider in evaluating interest-rate proposals is the time at which the borrower is required to begin interest payments. In most cases, interest will accrue from the time when funds are dispersed pursuant to the loan agreement and the borrower will be required to make interest payments on a periodic basis thereafter. In the case of a project with a long construction time, this means that there will be a net drain on the borrower's cash resources until such time as the project actually begins to produce revenue. To alleviate this problem it may be possible to capitalize interest during the construction period so that there is no draw-down of cash flow from traditional sources. In other words, interest which accrues during construction is treated as a part of the capital cost of the project and funded by the same people who fund the project itself. In this way no immediate cash payments are required for interest during the construction period.

B. Currency Considerations

Another major factor for consideration in evaluating a financing offer is the currency in which the loan must be repaid. In general, expected changes in exchange rates must be considered as a part of the cost of borrowing. In other words, how much local currency does the project have to generate to buy the foreign exchange to repay the loan or, alternatively, how much foreign exchange do you have to earn to repay the loan?

Because of exchange rate factors, a low-interest rate in a currency that may appreciate may be less advantageous than a higher rate in a weaker currency. For example, assume that five years ago you had a choice of borrowing U.S. $100 million equivalent at 3½% in Swiss Francs, or 4½% in Deutschemarks or 5% in yen or 8% in U.S. dollars. Which offer should you have accepted/ You would probably have been better off to borrow dollars even though the interest rate was substantially higher than that of the other currencies. U.S. firms, for example, borrowed Swiss Francs at low interst rates and found that they were paying 15-20% effective interest when they considered the effect of exchange rate changes.

It is true that the interest rate differentials on loans in various currencies reflect, in part, the market's judgment as to the relative strengths of the currencies. However, the interest rate differential does not always accurately measure future currency movements and any borrower is generally faced with a choice of borrowing strong currencies at lower interest rates or weaker currencies at higher interest rates. This means that choice of sources of financing must be based on an assessment of future exchange rate developments. Use of various composite currency units to minimize exchange exposure is, of course, possible (e.g. ECU; SDR; EUA; etc.).

There are no basic differences in the way one evaluates public and private sources of finance when considering the currency aspects. However, there is a special problem with development banks in that the borrower's repayment obligation is in the currency actually disbursed for the project (or the currency used to buy the currency which is disbursed). In addition, the World Bank bears no exchange risk and all of the risk is placed on the borrower.

To summarize, the borrower should not be fooled by a low interest rate in a currency which is expected to appreciate against his own currency or the majority of the currencies' he earns. It may not always be best to accept the lowest interest rate loans as there will be a trade-off between interest rate level and currency strength. In addition, it is best for a borrower to know at the time of the loan what his ultimate currency obligation will be. This is one of the disadvantages with development bank lending and some composite currency units which give the lender some flexibility to designate the currency in which he will be repaid.

C. Maturity Considerations

The maturity of a given loan can have a major effect on the size of annual debt service payments and on cash flow. In some cases, it may even be a difference between an unprofitable and a profitable project. Total debt service over the life of a laon is generally greater with longer maturities because the borrower pays interest for a longer period of time. However, each annual payment on a level-payment basis may be less than in the case of shorter maturities and provide significant financial benefits for the project. In addition, longer maturities permit more flexibility to structure a payment schedule to provide for lower payments in the early years when a project is starting up and larger payments in later years when a project reaches its per revenue-producing capacity.

In addition to the absolute maturity of a loan there are a number of factors which can affect the average life and/or level of debt service repayments: (1), a borrower may be able to negotiate a grace period with respect to the payment of principal so that repayment of principal repayments is deferred until after the construction of a project; (2), Sinking funds, purchase funds, and other mechanisms for return of principal prior to maturity need to be analyzed carefully as these devices are used to shorten the average life (and hence increase the yield) on a given loan. (3), It may be possible to provide for a ballooning of payments with smaller payments in the initial years and larger payments in the later years.

Maturity therefore, is an important element of the evaluation of an offer of finance. Shorter maturities are generally more readily available than longer maturities, particularly in developing countries to which lenders are often reluctant to commit funds for substantial periods into the future. This is particularly ture with private-sector lenders who are extremely reluctant to make long-term loans. This means that the major source of longer-maturity finance will be official sources of finance like the development banks, bilateral aid and export credits. There are, therefore, some trade-offs between the maturity of a loan and the availability of funds. Long-term funds for development projects can rarely be obtained from private sources and, while short-term money may be available, this may not be the best way to finance the project in question. In addition, there is often a trade-off between interest rate level and maturity. With a normal yield curve, one would expect lower interest for shorter maturities and higher interest for longer maturities. Thus one is often forced to choose between rate and maturity-generally paying more for the longer-term money. (It should be noted, however, that there are times when a "reverse yield curve" prevails and one actually pays a higher interest rate for shorter-term money than for long-term money).

D. Considerations Concerning Methods of Payment

There are a number of different methods of repaying loans. For example, the level-payment method is designed to assure equal annual payments during the life of the loan which include repayments of principal and interest. At the other extreme, some loans are structured so that the entire amount of principal is repaid in one lump sum at the maturity date with interest being paid periodically during the years prior to maturity. In addition, borrowers are often able to negotiate balloon payments with higher overall debt service requirements in the later years when the project is more profitable. In some cases, borrowers will be able to negotiate grace periods whereby there is no payment on principal and/or interest for a period of time. Lastly, interest during the construction period is sometimes capitalized, paid out of loan proceeds and included in the capital costs of the project. All of these different methods of payment result in a different pattern of debt service obligations and have dramatically different effects on a project's cash flow.

The frequency of interest payments is also a factor affecting cost of capital and project economics. For example, interest on loans in Europe is customarily paid on an annual basis and interest in the United States is generally paid semi-annually. The U.S. system means that the coupon rate on a semi-annual basis can be slightly (a few basis points) lower than on an annual basis because of the time value of money.

In evaluating an offer of finance, the borroweer needs to consider the effect of the method of loan repayment on a project's cash flow and negotiate the pattern of debt service payments most appropriate for the project.

E. Overall Cost of Money

The previous paragraphs of this section have implied that there are a number of factors in addition to interest rate considerations which must be included to obtain the true cost of borrowing. These include currency fluctuations, commitment fees, compensating balance arrangements, and the timing of interest and principal repayment. In addition, one must include as a cost of borrowing various "front end" fees including a management fee paid to the lead bank or underwriter for arranging syndication and handling other procedural aspects of a transaction; a participation fee sometimes paid in order to induce banks to take part in a syndicated loan; underwriting fees paid to compensate investment and merchant banks for risks that they assume, and selling fees which must be paid to securities salesmen. In addition, there will be legal fees, accounting fees, advertising costs and other expenses (including travel and entertainment) of the managers.

In evaluating an offer of finance the potential borrower should be sure that he has a clear understanding of all of the fees that will be charged and to make sure that these fees are reasonable and consistent with the fees charged similar borrowers.

F. Availability of Funds from the Various Sources

In Section III above, a distinction was made between public and private sectors of funds and various alternatives within each of these categories were discussed. One of the major considerations in selecting a source of funds is, of course, the availability of finance from that source. Not all sources are equally accessible for the financing for international projects, and the purpose of this section is to provide a general overview of the availability of funds from various sources. In other words, can you get the amounts you need, when you need them, from the source that is most beneficial to your project?

Private Sector—The major types of private finance for international projects are bank loans, the international bond markets and private placements from institutional investors. Commercial bank loans are the most readily available to LDC borrowers, the international bond market is the next most accessible source and the international private placement market is just opening to a select group of LDC borrowers.

Unfortunately, these private sector sources are completely closed to some LDC borrowers. Many of the lower income developing countries are simply not sufficiently creditworthy in the eyes of potential lenders to be able to tap any of these sources. Moreover, another group of developing countries may be sufficient creditworthy to receive bank loan funding but not able to float successfully an issue on the international bond markets but still unable to attract substantial funds in the form of international private placement.

As discussed in other sections, these various sources of finance have different interest rates, maturity and documentation requirements which might make one source more attractive than another for a particular project. However, because some sources will be closed to a particular country or for a particular project, it may be necessary to make a trade-off between availability of funds (i.e. receiving any finance at all) and acceptance of a less desirable form of finance.

Public Sources—The major sources of public financing are the development banks, bilateral aid and official export credit financing. Collectively, these sources provide huge amounts of funds for developing countries. For many nations not able to tap the world's private capital markets, development bank funding and bilateral aid may be the only sources of foreign financing available. There are, however, definite limits to funding from these sources. As a matter of policy, the development banks cut back on loans to given country as it moves up the development ladder. This means that funds (particularly concessional funds) from the development banks become a less readily available source of finance the wealthier a country is. In addition, highly concessional aid (e.g. IDA financing or most bilateral aid) is limited because its availability depends upon approval of national legislatures and parliaments which are becoming increasingly reluctant to fund development. This means that even the lower-income developing countries will face limits in the amount of funds they can obtain from these sources.

While there is great competition among the industrialized countries to finance exports, there are also limits on the availability of export credit financing. Most export credit agencies have creditworthiness criteria which prevent or severly limit funding to some countries. In addition, interest rates on export credit financing tend to be substantially higher than those available from development bank and bilateral aid. Even when available, official funding is generally done on a project-by-project basis with funds allocated for a specific project and not available for more general use.

Trade-Offs. It is nard to evaluate in advance which sources of financing will be the best for a particular project. Commercial bank financing may be more readily available than financing from official sources but that availability has to be weighed against floating interest rates which are generally higher than rates of official sources. In addition, the various commitment fees, front-end fees and compensating balance requirements will add to the overall cost of money from commercial sources. And, banks will be less likely to capitalize interst during construction.

Official financing generally has a substantial subsidy or grant element which benefits the borrower by giving him a lower interest rate. Interst rates are generally fixed thereby improving the ability to plan for future foreign-exchange requirements needed to service the debt. Commitment fees are often required but tend to be less than on commercial bank money, and ther are no management, participation, or front-end fees. lastly, interest druing construction is often capitalized as a part of official funding.

G. Procurement Considerations

Often an offer of finance is made conditional on the purchase of goods or services from the supplier offering the finance or from the country supplying the finance. This is particularly true with bilateral aid and export credit payment where such aid and finance are generally tied. This means that the borrower loses the freedom to conduct unlimited international competitive bidding with the result that the price he pays in a tied aid situation may be higher than he would otherwise pay.

For example a 5% export credit loan which is conditioned on purchases from a supplier of the country offering the finance may be less advantageous to the borrower than a loan at a much higher interest rate which permits international competitive bidding. Therefore, in evaluating an offer of finance conditioned on purchase from the source of finance, a potential borrower should always estimate the additional price, if any, that he will pay by accepting tied finance and evaluate the total overall cost under tied and untied financing.

H. Conditions Imposed in Connection with Lending

Lenders commonly impose conditions on the granting of loans to ensure their repayment. In the case of loans to private coroporations such conditions include: limitations on the amount of debt which can be incurred; debt service coverage tests; certain minimum amount of liquid assets; ratio maintenance tests, etc.

In the case of loans to governments, private-sector lenders generally do not impose conditions as to conduct of economic policy or balance-of-payments policy except in rare cases. On the other hand, loans from official sources sometimes attempt to impose conditions on the conduct of economic policy, on the operation of a particular industry or sector of the industry, or on how a project is carried out. The World Bank often imposes conditions on a project or on industry structure (e.g. tariff rate levels for utilities in a particular country).

In the case of loans to projects or a project entity, lenders often require complex contractual and legal arrangements to be entered into to ensure debt repayment. In addition, they may impose conditions on how a project is carried out and require that the contractual arrangements which serve as a basis for their loan remain in place as long as loans are outstanding.

It is often inevitable that a borrower must accept certain conditions in order to obtain needed finance. However, any borrower should carefully evaluate the conditions imposed upon it to ensure that it can live with them and that they do not impose unreasonable burdens. For example, the borrower should be certain that the restrictions imposed do not limit its ability to borrower in the future. Otherwise, it may find that it will have financed the immediate project on terms that may pervent it from carrying out other high-priority projects in the future. For example, if a parastatal corporation accepts restrictions on the amount of debt it may have outstanding in order to secure finance *now*, these restrictions may prevent the raising of funds for future projects.

I. Sources of Information

In order to evaluate adequately financial proposals from potential lenders and to negotiate generally project financing arrangements, it is useful to have information on the terms, conditions and structure of similar projects. Often this information is difficult to assemble because the most relevant project may have been undertaken in a different part of the world in a country with a different language and legal system. However, in recent years there have been efforts to collect data on international financing and investment in a form and locale which would be useful to developing countries in their negotiations with foreign investors. The best known is the United Nations Center for Transnational Corporations in New York which has estblished a data center to provide information on foreign investment. This center plans to collect and serve as a repository for concession agreements, joint venture agreements, etc. A similar repository is found in the Sussex University Institute of Development Studies in England which collects agreements from around the world. In addition, the U.N. Mineral Adviser gathers documents pertaining to major projects.

For information on the actual terms and conditions of financing, the best sources are commercial banks and investment banks. The international finance business is very competitive and a potential borrower can always get a commerical bank or investment bank to give advice on the financing terms which have been proposed by one of their competitors. If a borrower has the opportunity, it is always wise to solicit several offers of finance so that it can get competitive bids for the various fees and other terms and conditions associated with the transaction. In addition, competing proposals provide a data base against which a borrower can evaluate the terms and conditions of each offer.

J. Role of Financial Adviser

In larger complex project finances, expert financial advisers are often hired to assist in negotiating and implementing the project. In some cases, a developing country government may have sufficient expertise of its own in its Ministry of Finance, Central Bank or elsewhere to negotiate effectively a major project financing. In other cases, one of the development banks may be involved in the project and might serve as an informal financial adviser for the government. However, if the project is large and complex and the government concludes it wants additional advice, it should consider hiring and independent financial adviser. Although the fees tend to be high, sound advice and assistance in negotiating financial terms often save a borrower many times the cost of the adviser.

There are three main functions which the adviser could perform. First, he would advise on how best to structure a project financing. This would include: the type of security devices which might be required by lenders; how to comply with restrictions in prior loan agreements, and the appropriate corporate structure for raising the financing. In addition, the adviser might perform some of the economic and financial-feasibility analysis which needs to be done in connection with every major project. Second, the adviser could play a major role in assembling the financing for the project. His experience in international capital markets would enable him to advise on the best sources of finance for the project and he would be able to contact them on the government's behalf. In addition, a commercial bank which acted as financial adviser might also make a substantial loan for the project and negotiate with other banks to put together an appropriate banking syndicate. Third, the financial adviser could provide guidance on the best terms and conditions which could be obtained for the project. He would keep the borrower informed of conditions on the world capital markets; advise it on the appropriate time to tap the relevant markets; and help it decide on what currency would be best for the project. In addition, he would be able to advise on the specific terms and conditions (including various financing fees) which will be proposed. Fourth, the adviser could assist in negotiating with financial institutions which were ultimately selected as the sources of finance for the project.

In some cases a borrower may be able to get the type of financial advice that it needs from one of the banks which is planning to be a substantial lender to the project. However, there may be instances in which such a bnak may have a conflict of interest in that it would give advice on the acceptability of terms and conditions which it proposes. In such cases, it may be better for the borrower to consider hiring another bank or an investment or merchant bank to act on its behalf and provide advice.

K. Scope for Negotiation

The old adage "everything is negotiable" is not always applicable to complex project financing. Most projects are dependent on foreign lenders for large amounts of finance. These lenders are generally a conservative and cautious group and they will insist on adequate security for their loans—especially on overseas projects. They will insist that some mechanism be established to ensure the repayment of their loans under all circumstances, even in the case of a project failure or in the event of an act of god. Since they provide the necessary finance, lenders have a great bargaining advantage and there may be little room to negotiate on their basic demands for ironclad protection. However, such protection can be provided in many ways (e.g. guarantees, investment insurance and various types of contractual protection discussed above). Therefore, a foreign borrower may be able to negotiate the particular method of providing protection to lenders.

Similarly, the scope for negotiation on the basic structure of the project may be limited. The foreign sponsors or partners in a project may have to structure the project in a particular way in order to meet the tax and/or accounting considerations which determine the profitability of the project for them. If their desired structure is not used, it may prevent them from obtaining tax or accounting benefits which they need to participate in the project. Thus, it may be a choice between accepting their structure or having no project at all.

On most of the more specific terms and conditions of finance, there is some scope for negotiation. Of course, the quality and creditworthiness of a governmental borrower will determine the limits of its ability to negotiate. A country with a strong economic program and good balance-of-payments position is often besieged with offers of finance. On the other hand, less fortunate countries may find it difficult to obtain finance from any source and be forced to accept a lender's proposed terms on a take-it-or-leave-it basis. In addition, supply and demand on the international capital markets will determine how liquid the banks and other capital sources are. If funds are scarce, they will be less willion to negotiate. During periods of high liquidity, they will compete to make loans by showing extreme flexibility on many of the terms of the financing.

In examining the negotiability of various specific loan terms, one finds some differences in the general latitude, to negotiate with lenders. With respect to interest rate, market conditions determine the general rate levels and the scope for negotiation is relatively limited. However, in every financing there is some room for negotiating at the margin and this latitude may be somewhat greater in the case of syndicated bank loans than it is on fixed-rate public issues which must be issued on the public market. There is also some room for negotiation in the maturity of a loan but this will also be dependent primarily on market conditions. Also, some markets are simply not long-term markets and there is a definite limit on the maturity one can achieve through issues in such markets.

With respect to financing fees, there is also room for negotiation. Although bankers will quote standard fees, a high-quality credit borrower may be able to negotiate a slight reduction in fees payable. The scope for negotiation is even greater in the area of the convenants and restrictions lenders often seek to impose. In this area, market conditions are less of a constraint and the individual lender has more discretion and ability to negotiate with its borrowers.

Most of the other key areas discussed in previous sections (e.g. currency considerations, tied procurements and availability of finance) are not really negotiable matters. They are generally offered on a take-it-or-leave-it basis, and it is up to the potential borrower to decide whether it is in its interest to accept. For example, it is really a matter of the borrower's choice as to which currency it chooses to borrow or whether it will accept tied aid.

Lastly, in deciding how hard to press lenders on specific terms and conditions, a borrower should remember that if it drives too hard a bargain, it may cool investor interest in participating in subsequent loans. Thus, the borrower may be forced to pay a higher rate the next time it wants to borrow. For example, in recent years some sovereign borrowers with large capital requirements did not press as hard as they might have for the tightest possible terms because of their need to return between how hard a borrower pushed lenders on interest rates and other terms and conditions of the financing and how often it needs to come to the capital markets.

Annex 1
POTENTIAL PARTICIPANTS IN A PROJECT FINANCING

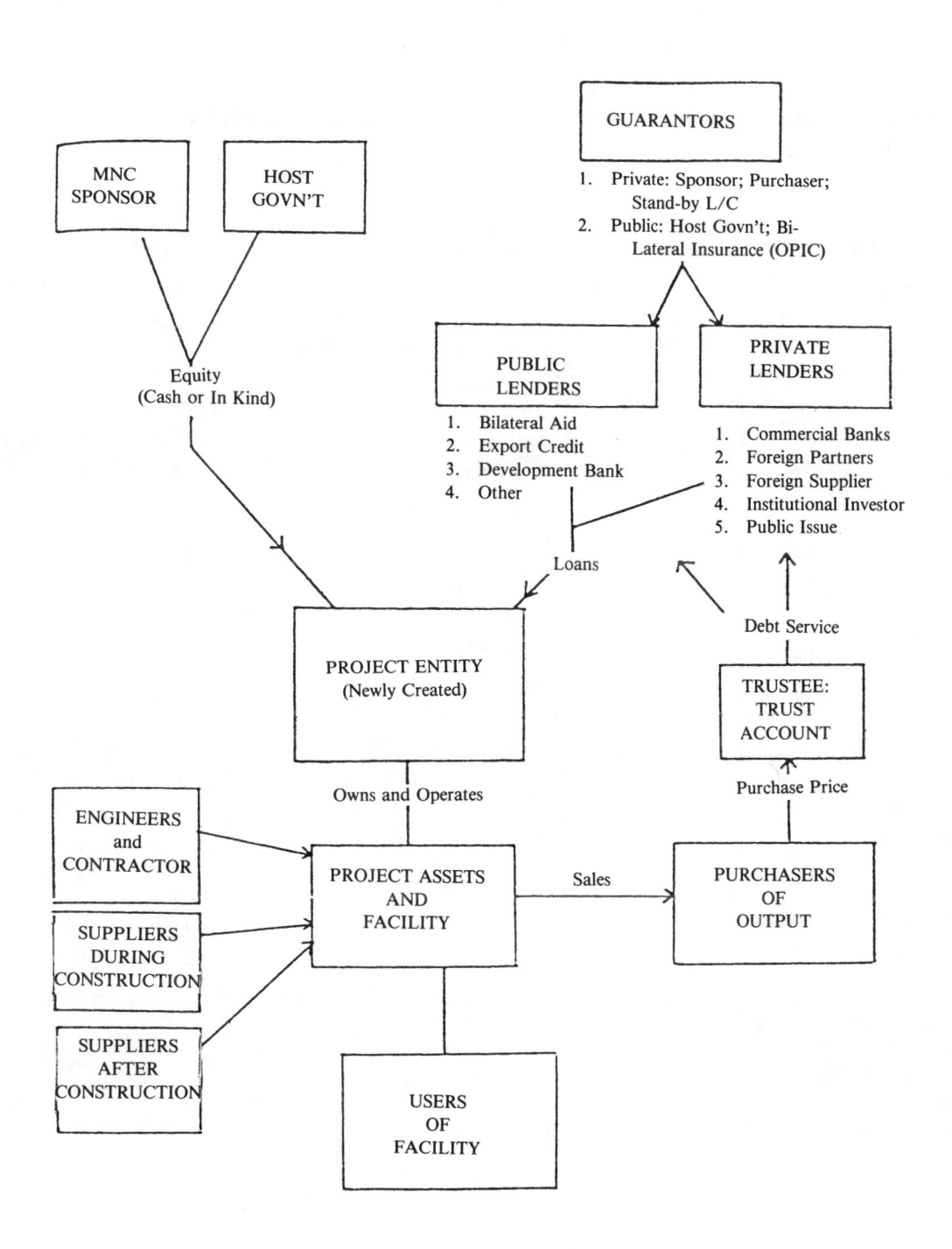

GUARANTORS
1. Private: Sponsor; Purchaser; Stand-by L/C
2. Public: Host Gov'n't; Bi-Lateral Insurance (OPIC)

MNC SPONSOR — **HOST GOV'N'T**

Equity (Cash or In Kind)

PUBLIC LENDERS
1. Bilateral Aid
2. Export Credit
3. Development Bank
4. Other

PRIVATE LENDERS
1. Commercial Banks
2. Foreign Partners
3. Foreign Supplier
4. Institutional Investor
5. Public Issue

Loans

PROJECT ENTITY (Newly Created)

Debt Service

TRUSTEE: TRUST ACCOUNT

Purchase Price

Owns and Operates

ENGINEERS and CONTRACTOR

SUPPLIERS DURING CONSTRUCTION

SUPPLIERS AFTER CONSTRUCTION

PROJECT ASSETS AND FACILITY — Sales → **PURCHASERS OF OUTPUT**

USERS OF FACILITY

Annex 2
RISK PROTECTION FOR LENDERS

General Risks All Phases

1. *All Risks*
   a. Debt guarantees
   b. Insurance

2. *Resource Risk*
   a. Independent evaluation
   b. Producer makes up shortfall from another source

3. *Market Risk*
   a. Independent survey
   b. Long-term purchase contract at fixed price

4. *Technical Risks*
   a. Independent analysis
   b. Guarantee of technology

5. *Currency Risks*
   a. Hedging
   b. Match debt service with currency

6. *Political Risks*
   a. Political risk insurance
   b. Multilateral Consortia
   c. World Bank Co-Finance or IDB Complementary Finance
   d. Advance exchange control approval

Construction Phase

1. *Cost Overruns*
   a. Fixed Price contract
   b. Turnkey Contract
   c. Independent expert check on cost estimates and technology
   d. "Over-Finance" - (i.e. Finance Plan covers 20% over the estimate)
   e. Forward Currency Contracts
   f. Overrun Funding Agreement

2. *Completion of Project*
   a. Drawdown equity first
   b. Performance bonds for contractor
   c. Tough "Completion Test"
   d. Completion & Guaranty Agreement - (i.e. fund completion or repay outstanding debt)

Operational Phase

1. *Interruption of Revenue*
   a. "All-events, take-or pay" contracts with supplier, user or purchaser
   b. Alternative source arrangement for key inputs
   c. Insurance
   d. Trust (Sponsor or host government "tops" the trust)

2. *Abandonment*
   a. All-event contractual relationship where debt service assumed by supplier, user or purchaser
   b. Debt guarantees
   c. Insurance

3. *Lack of Working Capital*
   a. Include initial working capital requirements in finance plan
   b. Commitments to supply working capital from sponsors
   c. Stand-by line of credit from banks

---

1. LIBOR is the abbreviation for London interbank offered rate. See Annex 3 for more detailed definition.

2. Counter trade is a concept commonly used in East-West trade and occurs when the Western participant agrees to purchase goods from the Eastern country to help provide needed foreign exchange.

**John M. Niehuss is Vice President, Merrill Lynch Pierce, Fenner and Smith, Inc.

Section III:
Selected Financing Techniques
Chapter 10: Lease Financing

Leasing
Charles J. Gmur

1. Introduction

Leasing as a means of trade financing is being increasingly stressed by leasing companies operating nationally and internationally. This has come about because producers of capital goods find that the financing assistance they can offer clients helps in the marketing of their products *vis-à-vis* those of their competitiors. However, companies with a high technical know-how frequently do not have staff experienced in financial matters. It would, therefore, be a difficult and risky undertaking for them to offer their clients financing by themselves. This is the role for leasing companies.

2. Definitions

2.1 What is leasing?

In a leasing arrangement, an investor (the user) does not buy a product himself, but buys the use of it against payment of a monthly rental fee to a leasing company (the lessor), which owns the product. Leasing substitutes an actual investment by a simple rental relationship over a fixed period of time.

The supplier of the good, i.e., the producer or trader, can be, but does not necessarily have to be, the lessor. In *operating leasing* it will normally by the producer who himself offers his product for lease, together with his technical services and possibly continuous replacement by up-dated products. In *capital leasing,* or *finance leasing*, a triangular relationship is set up between the seller of the article, the buyer who becomes the lessor, and the leasing party, the lessee. It is this kind of leasing which is most commonly discussed in trade financing. It is solely a financial set-up with no technical obligations of the lessor towards the lessee, as in operating leasing.

As an example to explain the three-party relationship, consider company ABC Ltd. which produces a specific machine tool which is of interest to XYZ-Works Ltd. Instead of selling the equipment on credit to XYZ-Works Ltd., who are short of liquid funds, ABC Ltd. will sell the machine tool to a leasing company on a cash basis. This company will lease the equipment to the user of the machine tool, in this instance XYZ-Works Ltd., and be repaid by rental payments, including amortization, interest and a leasing contract fee.

2.2 Domestic leasing

The most common type of leasing is domestic leasing, where the lessor and lessee are domiciled in the same country. It may be a company seeking finance for its investment programme which contacts its bankers and is directed by them to a leasing company. Or it may be a seller, using his existing contacts with a leasing company, who initiates a new lease.

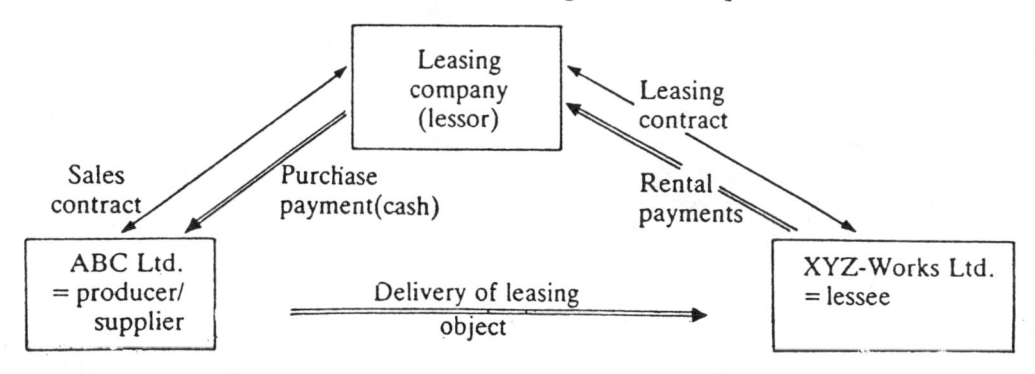

Exhibit 701: A leasing relationship

Domestic leasing occurs in the *long-life consumer goods* industry as well as in the *capital goods* industry. However, the most commonly leased item is a capital good, which thereby generates an income to pay for itself over its economic life. During the past 10 years, the leasing of *real estate*, mostly factory, service or administration buildings and warehouses, has also become popular. This leasing of immovables is often done in the form of *sale-and-lease-back*. The future lessee constructs the building, sells it to the leasing company and leases it back. In addition to industry and business, *communities* have also started to use leasing for investments. Depending on national legislation, this clientele should become of growing importance in the leasing business.

In Europe, leasing experienced a rapid expansion during the 1970s, particularly during the last three years of the decade. It has found broadest acceptance, however, in the U.S. where between 18 and 20% of investments, including construction, have been financed by leasing. In Europe, the role of leasing is more modest. Whereas in the U.K. leasing is used in about 11% of all domestic investments, continental Europe shows the following estimated percentages: France 9%, West Germany 5%, Switzerland 3-4% and Austria 2-3%.

The high percentage of leasing in the United States is explained by the tax system of the country. *Leveraged capital leasing* makes use of an investment tax credit and involves banks in the leasing business. In leveraged leasing the simple triangular relationship is considerably enlarged. A lease underwriter will initiate and structure the transaction, and the lessee will order the leasing object, leased to him by the owner/lessor. The latter will invest only about 25 to 40% of the cost of the equipment and take up a non-recourse loan for the remaining 60 to 75% from a lender, who will receive in return a charge on both the leasing object and on the rent payments due from the lessee. Since the owner/lesor has all of the tax benefits associated with ownership of the equipment, he can offer his lessee cheaper leasing conditions than his own refinancing costs. Both owner and lender will use trustees, normally commercial banks, as intermediaries. Additional parties in the relationship are the vendor of the equipment and legal counsels to the parties involved. Leveraged leasing allows marginally profitable, capital-intensive companies to enter the capital markets for medium-to long-term, fixed-rate 100% financing at an effective cost well below that which a company would have to pay on a straight-debt issue of similar terms. Attempts have been made to introduce leveraged leasing in a simpler form to the U.K. and Germany, but tax regulations make this kind of domestic leasing less interesting than in the U.S.

2.3 Leasing of international goods

The object to be leased does not necessarily have to be used within national borders. This would be the case, for instance, with means of transportation such as containers, trucks, railway carriages, ships and aircraft, but could also occur with construction machinery, or, more important nowadays, oil prospect drilling rigs and platforms. This poses an additional risk for the leasing company, who might find it more difficult to establish its rights of ownership in the case of non-fulfillment of the leasing contract by the lessee. However, if the equipment can be internationally registered, as in the case of aeroplanes (in the national air traffic register), or ships (through Lloyds insurance register), such leasing does not pose too many problems.

One common problem is that of owner's liability. If, for example, an aeroplane has been leased, the lessor as owner of the plane could be made responsible for any damages caused by an accident. Imagine the plane crashing on Wall Street, New York. There would be a flood of claims against its owner by individuals, companies, the city and the state. To avoid the accumulation of such risks, the lessor forms individuals companies for each item of leased equipment, thereby limiting possible claims to that particular firm. This is already practised in the leasing of aeroplanes, tankers and nuclear power-stations, for example.

2.4 Cross-border leasing

In domestic leasing, at least two parties in the leasing triangle belong to the same country, the lessor and the lessee. However, should a British exporter sell his product to a British leasing company, which then leases the equipment to a foreign lessee, leasing is done across borders: lessor and lessee come from different countries.

Cross-border leasing takes the place of an export transaction. The goods are shipped to the foreign country but remain the property of the domestic leasing company. This creates many legal and tax problems. In most cases, at the end of a leasing period, the equipment is bought by the lessee at a low price. The item is thus finally exported, although it has been in the possession of the importer for some time. The question of when custom duties have to be paid, and on what value, is one of the inherent problems of cross-border leasing. Another one is tax payment. If there are tax agreements between the two countries of the lessor and lessee, the lessor can probably avoid double taxation. Further complications arise in connection with value-added taxes which are deductable within the national tax system but not across borders. Other problems could arise, for instance, out of fiscal schemes for permitted depreciations. The leasing company has to take into consideration all such foreign regulations when calculating its rental fees.

In addition to all these fiscal problems, cross-border leasing may be hampered by legal uncertainties. Will the rights of ownership of the leasing company be honoured in the case of the lessee's default or bankruptcy? Some countries still consider leasing as a special way of purchasing on credit. The leasing company, therefore, would have only the same legal status as other lenders to the company. Moreover, cross-border leasing to socialist countries, though frequently discussed, founders on the regulations governing ownership of the means of production.

Even if all the legal and fiscal problems can be solved, there still remain currency problems. In which currency should the rental payments be effected? If the leasing contract provides for payment in the foreign currency, it is the leasing company which has to cover the currency risk by equivalent refinancing. Then there is the additional risk of interest fluctuations. If the leasing payments are made in the lessor's domestic currency, the lessee runs the risk that his leasing payments might become more expensive following a devaluation of his national currency against the foreign one.

Last but not least, cross-border leasing makes it difficult to monitor the foreign lessee. Before any leasing contract can be signed, a thorough investigation of the foreign customer will be made. And during the leasing period, economic and financial changes in the foreign country should be carefully monitored.

Cross-border leasing incurs large costs and encounters strong competition from local leasing companies, which can operate with all the advantages of the simpler domestic leasing. As a result, there are few cross-border contracts. There is a simpler way to perform an international leasing transaction.

2.5 International leasing

International leasing is leasing used in international trade but is not exactly the same as cross-border leasing. The difficulties inherent in the differing national fiscal and legal systems for lessor and lessee, characteristic of cross-border leasing, are avoided in international leasing. An internationally operating leasing company is a member of an international association of leasing companies, or has its own subsidiaries abroad.

An international leasing arrangement can be initiated by exporter or importer. An importer, for instance, contacts his leasing company which finds, with the help of its foreign associate, an exporter willing to supply the equipment. This exporter might sell the goods directly to the foreign leasing company, or he might sell them to his national leasing company which would then sell them on to its partner company in the lessee's country. Associates in an international chain of leasing companies may arrange with their partners for a commission to be paid for their assistance; but some also cooperate for free.

Within the European Economic Community, legal and fiscal systems will probably converge to a large degree, and encourage the creation of more international leasing companies, with their own subsidiaries in different countries.

3. APPLICATION

Leasing requires a contract. The first step towards setting up a contract will be made by:

a. The supplier: he wishes to sell his product and sees in leasing the means of achieving this with more certainty and speed.

b. The lessee: he wants to buy certain equipment and sees in leasing the means to do this with few financial pressures.

c. The bank of the lessee: the former is interested in the commercial success of the latter. Where it considers leasing to be the most advantageous possibility, it will advise the customer accordingly, and put him into contact with a leasing company.

d. The leasing company: it knows the requirements of its customers and keeps in close contact with them.

A leasing company will need to examine the solvency of any future lessee, the reliability of the supplier and the risk on the leased product. The lessee will be asked to fill in a leasing application. The leasing company will also need to know whether the leased product will help the lessee to increase his cash flow, etc.

In the process of investigating the lessee, the leasing company will have to find out whether its customer will be able to make the contractal rental payments. Besides analysing his actual financial situation, it will also make some estimates about his future position. The lessee will, therefore, be asked to submit his balance sheet and his profit and loss accounts for the past three years, in addition to his budget plans for the years to come. He may also be asked whether he has already contracted other leasing arrangements, because in many countries leasing obligations do not show in the balance sheet or profit and loss account. The most advantageous leases are offered when the leased equipment finances itself through its productive use.

The leasing company will also need to have details of the kind of equipment being asked for. Whereas in the English-speaking countries many leasing companies specialize in, and buy, certain products, in continental Europe the goods to be leased are normally not in stock at the leasing company and have to be bought from a supplier. In most cases, supplier and lessee have already agreed on all details of the equipment, including delivery and installation. The leasing company will have to check whether the supplier can fulfil his obligations regarding quality, delivery and service, and whether and for how long the equipment will increase productivity in the customer's company. Having been told the purchase price and the desired period for a lease, the lessor can calculate the cost of the lease, and submit an offer to his customer. In continental Europe, leasing is usually based on a 95-100% amortization of the leased object, though non-full pay-out contracts also exist. The rental payments will depend on the length of the lease—in Switzerland many contracts are signed for five years—and on the amortization percentage.

If the customer agrees to the leasing conditions offered to him, lessor and lessee will sign the leasing contract which is done by way of sending back a signed copy of the offer.

4. COSTS

In finance leasing, the lessee will be asked to insure the leasing object and to cede all rights to the lessor. It is the rule in finance leasing that the lessee pays for service, maintenance and repair. The actual leasing costs consist of:

a. a small fee due when signing the contract, calculated as a percentage of the purchase value; and

b. the monthly lease instalments.

The *fee* at the beginning of the lease is a commitment fee. It is also intended to cover the costs of a leasing contract, and it is the first payment from the lessee. In the early days of leasing, the leasing charge or fee was a few per cent of the leased equipment. Leasing companies engaged in financial leasing nowadays demand a very small charge of about 0.5-1%, and many of them have abolished the charge altogether.

The calculation of the *monthly leasing payments* is based on the refinancing costs to the lessor and a spread covering the amortization, his cost of administration and collection, a management fee and a risk premium. Depending on whether the payment is payable at the beginning or the end of the month, the percentage is lower or higher for the same interest rate. Such tables are of interest to every lessee who wants to compare his leasing cost with the cost of other forms of financing.

5. ADVANTAGES OF LEASING

5.1 General remarks

Leasing is a medium- to long-term means of financing. It is an alternative to financing out of equity. It is probably somewhat more expensive than a simple purchase, but has the advantage that payments are due only with the return on the investment. Leasing can be tailored to the needs of the lessee, by making the rental payments progressive or declining, by adjusting the leasing period, and by agreeing on full or only partial amortization (non-full pay-out) leasing. Leasing combines early investment with late payment.

When leasing, there is no risk that the leasing contract could be cancelled by the financing party as, for instance, in short-term credits (on a current account basis). There is also no risk for the lessee that interest rates' rise, rising costs or inflation could alter the leasing terms. Cost calculation and budgeting can thus be based on solid evidence.

5.2. Balance sheet considerations

In many countries, since the leased machines and equipment are not capitalized in the balance sheet, and corresponding rental obligations do not appear on the liabilities side, the balance sheet of a company obtaining its equipment through leasing looks very different from that of a company which purchases the product and takes up corresponding finance.

Since the balance sheet of a lessee is lighter than that of a company which has purchased with borrowed funds, the lessee has a higher borrowing capacity. Leasing is therefore different to equipment purchase on credit (supplier credit) or to drawing a bank loan. Leasing encroaches only slightly upon existing credit limits, and represents in effect a broadening of the avenues available to a company seeking external finance.

In contrast to the traditional bank loan, leasing procures 100% finance. It thereby helps to conserve liquidity which can be put to other uses, for example, into development and marketing.

5.3. Tax considerations

The tax advantages of leasing depend on the country's national tax system. When the investor buys the equipment, he will be allowed, in most cases, to deduct the interest on loans and the depreciation from his taxable income in accordance with tax allowance schemes. When leasing he may be allowed to deduct the total rental payments. So, there might be an interesting shift in the timing of these deductions.

5.4. Valuable alternative

Leasing is a new means of trade financing, and is therefore a sometimes difficult alternative to more traditional avenues. However, it provides a useful alternative approach.

6. AN EXAMPLE OF A LEASING CONTRACT

The text of a leasing contract used by a U.K. company is shown in Exhibit 709.

Exhibit 709: A U.K. leasing contract

BOWMAKER LEASING PLAN

ORIGINAL
THE COPYRIGHT OF THIS DOCUMENT IS RESERVED

L 1. L (Amd. 17)

NAME AND ADDRESS OF HIRER (In block letters please)
Firms please state (1) trading style and
(2) full names of proprietors/partners

Br. No. | Office use only—Agmt. No. | LL

Postcode .... Tel. No. ....

THE SCHEDULE

FULL PARTICULARS OF GOODS:
(Serial Nos. and Regn. Nos. and accessories must be stated)

Primary hiring period [ ] months
Total rentals payable during primary hiring period (exc. VAT) .. .. £

[ ] rental(s) paid prior to signing this Agreement (exc. VAT) totalling .. .. £

followed by [ ] rentals (exc. VAT) of .. £ payable in advance the first due on
.... 19......
(being ONE MONTH after the date of this Agreement) and thereafter on the same day of each succeeding month.

MOTOR VEHICLES

Date first Reg.	Make and Model	Regn. No.	Chassis No.

Secondary hiring period
Yearly rentals (exc. VAT) of .. .. £ the first due on
.... 19......

VAT is payable on all rentals at the rate from time to time in force.
Assuming that VAT remains at the rate of [ ] %:

(i) the total rentals payable prior to signing including VAT will be £

(ii) the total Primary hiring period rentals including VAT will be .. £

SITING ADDRESS(ES) OF GOODS (see clause 3(a) below)

Mark selected method of payment with X: through post [ ]   over bank counter [ ]   by Direct Debiting Mandate [ ]

Refund percentage............ (see clause 10 below)

SIGNATURES TO AGREEMENT

(1) Witness to signature of Hirer..............
Address..............
Occupation..............

NOTE: My/Our attention was drawn to Clause 11 below

SIGNATURE OF HIRER..............

(2) Witness to (Second witness required in Scotland only)
signature of Hirer..............
Address..............
Occupation..............

Signature for and on behalf of Bowmaker Leasing Limited
.... Date..............

TERMS OF AGREEMENT

This Agreement is made between BOWMAKER LEASING LIMITED of Bowmaker House, Christchurch Road, Bournemouth, BH1 3LG (hereinafter called "the Owner") of the one part and the Hirer named above of the other part whereby the Owner agrees to let and the Hirer agrees to hire the goods specified in the Schedule above (hereinafter called "the goods" which expression shall also include any accessories replacements renewals or additions thereto and in the event of more than one item of goods being the subject of this Agreement shall where the context so admits include each and any of such item of goods) for the Primary period stated in the said Schedule and on the terms set out below.

1. The hiring shall commence on the date on which this Agreement is signed by or on behalf of the Owner and unless determined by the Hirer or the Owner in accordance with the provisions hereof shall continue for the Primary hiring period specified in the Schedule above and thereafter in accordance with Clause 9 hereof.

2. (a) The Hirer having before the signing of this Agreement paid the rental(s) referred to in the Schedule above together with the appropriate VAT thereon shall unless the hiring shall in the meantime have been duly determined in accordance with the provisions hereof pay the rentals for the remainder of the Primary hiring period as set out in the Schedule above
(b) The Hirer shall with each rental or other payment payable hereunder pay to the Owner VAT on the amount of such rental or other payment at the rate from time to time in force
(c) All rentals and other payments hereunder are to be paid to the Owner at Bowmaker House, Christchurch Road, Bournemouth, BH1 3LG but should the Hirer make any payments by post or to any other person for transmission to the Owner they shall be at the risk of the Hirer and shall only be credited to the Hirer as and when received by the Owner. In default of punctual payment (but without prejudice to the Owner's rights hereunder) the Hirer shall on demand pay interest on any overdue rentals or other payments at the rate of 4 per cent. per annum over Finance House Base Rate from time to time.

Exhibit 709: A U.K. leasing contract (continued)

Terms of Agreement—*continued*

3. The Hirer shall

(a) keep the goods in good order repair and condition at the siting address(es) specified in the Schedule above or at such other address(es) as shall be agreed in writing by the Owner and be responsible for all risks of whatsoever kind fire included and in the case of a motor vehicle the Hirer shall ensure that the same has the routine maintenance and service called for by the manufacturer's recommendations at the intervals recommended by the manufacturer. If and whenever any service maintenance repair or replacement of parts is required it shall be carried out at the expense of the Hirer and in the case of a motor vehicle such service maintenance repair or replacement of parts shall be carried out by an authorised agent of the manufacturer of such motor vehicle provided that the Hirer shall not have or be deemed to have any authority to pledge the Owner's credit for the repair of the goods or to create a lien thereon in respect of such repairs or for any other purpose or thing whatsoever

(b) pay any licence duties fees insurance premiums road tax and registration charges payable in respect of the goods and if any such duties fees premiums road tax or charges shall be paid by the Owner (the Owner being hereby authorised to pay the same on behalf of the Hirer) the Hirer shall repay the same to the Owner forthwith

(c) neither use nor permit the goods to be used for any purpose for which they are not designed or reasonably suitable nor permit them to be used in contravention of any statute or statutory regulations for the time being in force, nor during the hiring take or send or permit to be taken or sent the goods out of the British Isles (save with the previous written consent of the Owner) and in the case of a motor vehicle not use the same for racing or pacemaking nor for competing in any rally

(d) allow the Owner or its duly authorised representative at all times to have access to the goods to inspect the condition thereof and within ten days after notice in writing from the Owner of any want of repair or injury in or to the goods to make good the same to the satisfaction of the Owner

(e) repay to the Owner forthwith on demand all expenses costs or charges incurred in ascertaining the whereabouts of the Hirer or the goods or in recovering or endeavouring to recover possession of the goods from the Hirer or any other person firm or company

(f) forthwith (unless otherwise agreed in writing by the Owner) insure the goods and during the currency of this Agreement keep them insured in their full replacement value against all insurable risks and without any excess or restriction (and in the case of a motor vehicle shall insure and keep insured the same comprehensively) under a policy issued by a reputable insurer and notify the insurer of the interest of the Owner in the goods and produce such policy and the latest premium receipt to the Owner upon demand. In the event of the Hirer returning the goods to the Owner or the Owner recovering possession of the same the interest of the Hirer in any insurance effected hereunder shall absolutely vest in the Owner who shall be entitled to the full benefit of such insurance including any claims thereunder which may be outstanding at the time of such return or recovery of possession

(g) in the case of a motor vehicle hold the registration document(s) to the Owner's order and on the expiry or termination for whatever reason of the hiring deliver up such registration document(s) to the Owner or such other person as the Owner may stipulate

(h) in the case of a motor vehicle pay all parking fines and other penalties in respect of the same and in the event of the Owner being required for whatever reason to pay such fines or other penalties on demand reimburse the Owner for all such amounts that it shall have been required to pay

(i) fully indemnify the Owner against any claims loss or costs arising out of any breach of the obligations of the Hirer under this Agreement (whether under this Clause 3 or otherwise).

4. The Hirer shall not agree the settlement of any claim under any insurance effected under Clause 3(f) hereof in respect of the goods without the concurrence of the Owner. The Hirer shall instruct the Insurer that any moneys receivable under any such insurance pursuant to a total loss claim shall be paid by the Insurer to the Owner and the Hirer hereby irrevocably appoints the Owner as its agent for claiming and/or receiving such moneys and authorises the Owner to give a good discharge to the Insurer for such moneys. In the event of all the goods being so damaged as to give rise to a claim under such insurance upon a total loss basis then the Hirer shall be entitled to terminate the hiring created hereby on payment to the Owner of such sum as will together with the amount received by the Owner from the Insurer equal the balance of the rentals which remain to be paid during the balance of the Primary hiring period (less an allowance as referred to in Clause 7 on any rentals not accrued due at the date of payment by the Hirer). In the event of some or one item only of the goods being so damaged as to give rise to a claim under such insurance upon a total loss basis then the rentals payable during the balance of the Primary hiring period shall be reduced by such amount as the Owner shall, in its absolute discretion, consider appropriate after taking into consideration any moneys received by the Owner from the Insurer in respect of such total loss.

5. Except with the previous consent in writing of the Owner the Hirer shall not attempt to assign sub-let pledge mortgage or charge the goods nor part with the possession or the control of the goods or the benefit of this Agreement nor allow any other person or persons to obtain any lien or charge upon the goods nor do or allow to be done any other thing which will tend prejudicially to affect the ownership of the Owner and the goods shall at all times remain the property of the Owner and nothing herein contained shall be construed to imply that ownership of the goods will or may pass at any time to the Hirer.

6. If the Hirer shall

(a) make default in punctually paying any of the rentals or

(b) commit any act of bankruptcy or have a receiving order made against him or if a judicial factor, liquidator or trustee shall be appointed on any portion of his estate or effects, or if he shall convene any meeting of creditors or make a deed of assignment or arrangement or compound with his creditors or (being a company) shall pass a resolution for winding-up or have a petition for winding-up presented or have a receiver appointed or suffer an execution of any legal diligence or

(c) have any execution or distress levied or allow the goods to be poinded or seized under any distress execution or other process or

(d) fail to observe and perform any of the terms conditions and stipulations on his part herein contained or

(e) do any act or thing which in the Owner's opinion may prejudice or jeopardise its rights of ownership of the goods

then it shall be lawful for the Owner (but without prejudice to any other rights it may have hereunder) forthwith to terminate the hiring and thereupon any consent by the Owner to possession of the goods by the Hirer shall forthwith cease. A demand by the Owner for the return of the goods or a notice by it terminating the hiring hereunder shall be sufficiently made if given orally to the Hirer by a duly authorised representative of the Owner or in writing left at or sent by prepaid post addressed to the Hirer's last known address or to his address shown in the Schedule above. For the purpose of retaking possession of the goods the Owner may enter any premises occupied by or under the control of the Hirer where the goods may be or be supposed to be and this clause shall be construed as a licence to enter in a lawful manner any premises of the Hirer and to remove the goods the Owner making good any damage occasioned by such entry and removal.

7. Should the hiring be terminated by the Owner in accordance with the provisions of Clause 6 hereof then the Hirer shall remain liable to pay to the Owner (i) all arrears of hire rent (ii) any other sums due hereunder up to the date of the receipt of the goods by the Owner (iii) by way of liquidated damages for breach of the provisions of this Agreement such further sum (if any) as shall be necessary to make the amount paid by way of rentals plus the arrears of hire rent due under (i) above equal to the full amount of the rentals that would have been payable if the hiring had continued for the Primary hiring period specified in the Schedule above, less a rebate calculated at the rate of 4 per cent. per annum on such rentals that would not at the date of payment have accrued due (iv) all sums payable under Clause 3(i) above.

8. The Hirer may terminate the hiring by giving not less than one month's notice in writing to expire on or at any time after the expiration of the Primary hiring period specified in the Schedule above and upon such termination the Hirer shall return the goods to the Owner to such place as the Owner shall reasonably appoint in good order, repair and condition (fair wear and tear excepted). Such termination shall be without prejudice to the rights of the Owner in respect of the agreements on the part of the Hirer herein contained.

9. If the hiring shall not have been terminated at the expiration of the Primary hiring period by the Owner or by the Hirer in accordance with the provisions hereof then it shall continue for a Secondary hiring period from year to year upon the terms and conditions herein contained and subject to any statutes and regulations for the time being in force and the Hirer shall pay to the Owner in advance the yearly rentals specified in the Schedule above applicable during the Secondary hiring period the first such rental being payable on the day following the expiration of the Primary hiring period and subsequent rentals on the same day in each succeeding year.

10. If the Hirer terminates the hiring in accordance with Clause 8 above the Owner shall upon sale of the goods make a cash allowance by way of refund of rentals equivalent to the percentage specified in the Schedule above of the net proceeds of sale of such goods exclusive of VAT received by the Owner. The decision whether a sale can reasonably be effected and the terms of any such sale shall be entirely at the discretion of the Owner and the granting of any such allowance will be conditional upon (a) there being no change in existing relevant legislation and (b) the Hirer having strictly performed and observed all agreements on the part of the Hirer contained in this Agreement and any document ancillary hereto and also any other agreement made by the Hirer with Bowmaker Limited or any subsidiary company of Bowmaker Limited.

11. The Hirer acknowledges that the Owner is not a dealer or expert in the goods. The Owner does not give make or agree to any condition warranty term stipulation or representation express or implied (whether by statute or otherwise) or in any other way arising as to the state condition quality or (if not new) the age of the goods or as to their fitness for any purpose (whether of the Hirer or any other) and any such condition warranty term or stipulation is hereby excluded.

12. In the event of two or more persons constituting the Hirer the obligations of such persons shall be joint and several.

13. Any dealer or manufacturer by or through whom this transaction may have been introduced negotiated or conducted is not an authorised agent of the Owner except insofar as he is deemed to be an agent of the Owner by virtue of the provisions of the Consumer Credit Act 1974 and except as aforesaid should the word "agent" have been or be used in connection with this transaction it shall be construed in a descriptive sense only and not as implying any legal relationship.

Section III: Selected Financing Techniques
Chapter 11: Documentary Credits

Documentary Collection and Letters of Credit
Paul O'Hanlon

1. INTRODUCTION

In the days when barter was the exchange mechanism, when goods and property were portable, or leadable in the case of livestock, and traded on the spot, the concept of credit did not exist, and it was unnecessary for buyers and sellers to employ documentation evidencing and accompanying transactions.

In the modern economy, the complexity of goods, and even staples which are increasingly differentiated to suit particular tasks, the regulations surrounding their production and distribution, and the universal extension of credit enabling their immediate consuption, have led to a different exchange system. In modern trade, goods are represented by documents, which are exchanged for cash or some kind of promise to pay. Unlike the days of primitive barter, it is not always possible for the buyer in the modern international trade economy to know for certain what he is buying, and the seller does not always know for certain whether he will be paid in full on time.

In primitive barter, the objectives of buyers and sellers were the same: to exchange one kind of good on the spot for another. The only problems, solved later by specie money, were comparability of value and convenience. Modern buyers and sellers, separated geographically and living in a world of financial uncertainty, have less convergent objectives.

The buyers objectives are:

i. to receive goods of the correct quality and quantity, on time at the right place; and

ii. to pay as late as possible.

The seller's objectives are:

i. to receive payment of the correct amount of money in the right currency; and

ii. to be paid as soon as possible.

There are four major alternatives available to the trade partners in resolving the conflicts in their objectives:

i.   pre-payment by the buyer;

ii. open account terms;

iii. a bank collection; and

iv. a bank letter of credit.

Prepayment obviously suits the seller's objectives but not the buyer's. The purchase order and payment will go out together, and at a later date the goods will be shipped by the seller. All the onus of trust is on the buyer, and he will need to have considerable confidence in the seller, based on either the seller's reputation or, much more likely, past experience. Prepayment, therefore, will usually not satisfy a new buyer's objectives.

Open account is the usual basis of sale for domestic trade. All that happens is that the seller ships the goods with an invoice, which gives the buyer time to pay. Here the onus of trust is on the seller, so that the new seller will probably find such terms unsatisfactory.

This chapter examines two methods of payment, the first a compromise in trust which on balance favours the buyer and the second which favours the seller. Both, however, have safeguards for the other party not present in open account or prepayment.

It is possible for export sellers to avoid the difficulty of reconciling their objectives with import buyers themselves, by using export or confirming houses as agents. For anything other than small export volumes, this is inefficient and expensive, and raises its own problems.

2. DEFINITION OF A BANK COLLECTION

A bank collection is a method of settlement of payment by a

buyer in one country to a seller in another country through bank channels at low cost. It is called a collection because the seller uses the bank system to collect payment from the buyer; the bank acting for the seller is called the remitting bank, since it remits documents to the buyer's country, and the remitting bank's correspondent or agent in the buyer's country is called the collecting bank. The collecting bank need not necessarily have a banking relationship with the buyer. There are two kinds of collection, and in both, documents are moved by banks from seller to buyer.

2.1. Clean collection

A clean collection consists exclusively of documents for payment of money, such as bills of exchange, promissory notes or cheques. The seller sends the payment instrument without any other trade documents such as invoices or bills of lading, to the seller, through banks channels.

2.2 Documentary collection

A documentary collection consists, like a clean collection, of a payment instrument but also has commercial or transport documents included for completing the transaction. Usually, these documents confer, fully or partially, title to the goods on the holder, and typically they would be bills of lading. In a clean collection, banks do not control title to the goods whereas in a documentary collection banks do have control. The documentary collection, therefore, safer for the seller than the clean collection, which is only slightly removed from open account.

2.2.1. Documents included in a documentary collection

The usual payment instrument in a collection is the bill of exchange. In the case of a sight bill, acceptance and payment occur at the same time, which is when the documents are presented by the collecting bank. Term bills requiring payment at a future date are a method for the seller to allow credit or time to pay to the buyer.

There are two ways in which the remitting bank can send a term bill to the collecting bank. The first is for acceptance by the buyer and return to the remitting bank for eventual return to the seller. This is called *acceptance and return*. When the seller returns the accepted bill, close to maturity, back to the buyer through the banking system, the collection is a clean collection, and this is how most clean collections arise.

By far and away the great majority of collections are not on acceptance and return, but completed by the simpler route of the collecting bank retaining accepted bills until payment.

Usual trade documents included in the collection are transport documents, such as bills of lading or warehouse receipts, giving title to stored goods.

Bills of lading (usually prepared in sets of two or more originals) are a combined receipt from the shipping company for the goods, a contract between the seller and shipping company as a common carrier specifying the latter's obligations, and thirdly and most importantly, a negotiable document of title. Negotiability, in this context, is the quality of being transferable by endorsement free from prior claims. This quality is essential in ensuring simplicity in commercial transactions and permitting straightforward financing of international trade, as it enables bills of lading and other such negotiable instruments to be used as security for finance.

Warehouse receipts are given by warehousers in exchange for the goods after unloading. In certain cases these receipts are negotiable but such cases are limited mainly to primary commodities stored by Western European and North American warehouses.

2.3. Purpose of collections

Since the valuable documents of title to the goods being traded are held by banks during a collection, the seller has a greater degree of security than with open account. Using the banking system as an intermediary, the seller can specify that the buyer will not get title until he has paid cash or accepted a bill drawn on him. The buyer can inspect documents before payment or acceptance and so long as the documents are satisfactory, he partially satisfies his objectives of assurance in quality and quantity.

Collections are, therefore, intended as a compromise mechanism somewhere between open account and prepayment, facilitated by the action of the banking system as a reliable intermediary.

2.4. Practical mechanics

Exhibit 301 shows the flows of documents and payment in an open account transaction, and Exhibit 302, those in a straightforward documentary collection against payment. If the two exhibits are compared, it will be seen that in the collection the buyer is still trusting the seller along the purchase order limb, but the seller is no longer trusting the buyer along the payment limb.

The buyer still has to trust the seller to perform quickly in processing the purchase order and also not to produce fraudulent or completely spurious documents. This is because the intermediary role of the banking system does not extend to providing guarantees of documents or enforce-

Exhibit 301: Open account transaction

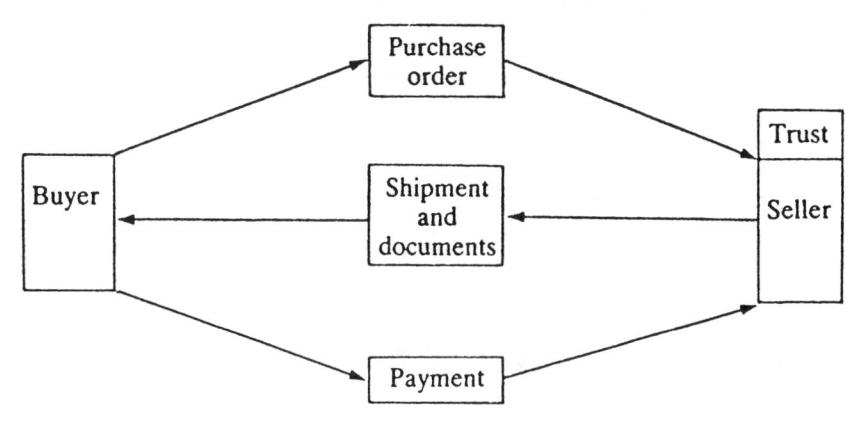

```
                    Purchase
                     order
                   ┌─────────┐
    ┌──────┐   ──▶ └─────────┘ ──▶  ┌──────┐
    │      │                        │ Trust│
    │      │       Shipment         ├──────┤
    │Buyer │        and             │Seller│
    │      │      documents         │      │
    │      │   ◀── ┌─────────┐ ◀──  │      │
    └──────┘       └─────────┘      └──────┘
                    Payment
                   ┌─────────┐
                ◀─ └─────────┘ ──
```

Exhibit 302: Documentary collection

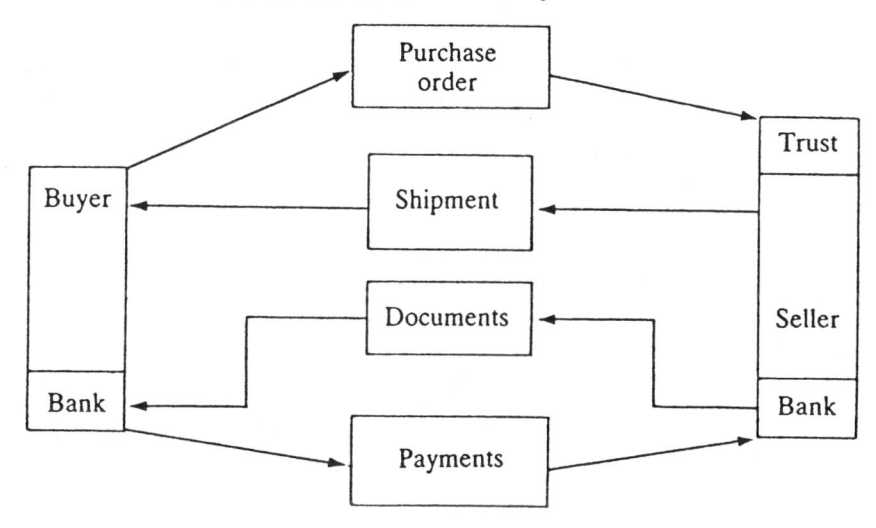

```
                    Purchase
                     order
    ┌──────┐                        ┌──────┐
    │Buyer │                        │ Trust│
    │      │       Shipment         │      │
    │      │                        │Seller│
    ├──────┤                        ├──────┤
    │ Bank │       Documents        │ Bank │
    │      │                        │      │
    │      │       Payments         │      │
    └──────┘                        └──────┘
```

Notes: 1. Bank acts as a collection intermediary, keeping documents from the buyer until payment or acceptance of draft.
2. Bank neither provides guarantee of payment nor enforces collection.
3. Title to goods passes to buyer only upon payment or upon acceptance of draft.

---

ment of responsibilities on either the buyer or seller's part under the sale contract.

Collection procedure is simple throuout (see Exhibits 303a and b). What happens is that, shortly after shipment by the seller, the remitting bank will receive from the seller the documents, including a bill of exchange if one is being used, together with instructions for payment (either cash or against a sight or time bill). The remitting bank sends all these to the collecting bank. Practice amongst collecting banks for presentation of the documents to the buyer varies considerably. Some banks will require the buyer to come to the bank's office to inspect, others release the documents with or without receipt. Practice also varies amongst branches of banks depending on local business procedures in different countries.

2.5. Obligations of the banks

The International Chamber of Commerce (ICC) publishes a wide range of documents for the assistance of importers and exporters, which taken together comprise an informal code or set of guidelines used by both commercial corporations and banks. These documents do not have the force of law, but describe current commercial practice. ICC Publication No. 322 of 1978 describes uniform rules for collections generally adhered to by all major international banks, and these are reproduced in Appendix I.

Exhibit 303a: Collection procedure

```
                    CITIBANK NA
                    WORLD CORPORATION GROUP
                    COLLECTION OPERATION
                    PO BOX 2003 GRAND CENTRAL STATION
                    NEW YORK NY 10017
                    (212 558 5770)

AIRMAIL TO COLLECTING BANK                      DATE 08/09/77
DEUICHE BANK AG
MUNICH, GERMANY


REF: OUR COLLECTION NO. 165288W
     IN AMOUNT OF    200,000.00 TO BE PAID AT SIGHT
     DRAWER
     DRAWEE B.BUYER

GENTLEMEN:
     THIS ITEM IS SENT FOR COLLECTION AND REMITTANCE IN NEW YORK
FUNDS AFTER FINAL PAYMENT. ADVICES OF PAYMENT, ACCEPTANCE AND
DISHONOR SHOULD BE SENT BY AIRMAIL UNLESS OTHERWISE SPECIFIED BELOW.
IF DRAWN IN YOUR CURRENCY, PLEASE CREDIT OUR ACCOUNT AFTER FINAL
PAYMENT, ONLY UNDER ADVISE TO US.

     IF DOLLAR EXCHANGE IS NOT IMMEDIATELY AVAILABLE AT MATURITY
(OR ON PRESENTATION IF DRAWN AT SIGHT) AND IT IS NECESSARY TO
PROVISIONALLY ACCEPT LOCAL CURRENCY PENDING AVAILABILITY OF DOLLAR
EXCHANGE, IT MUST BE DISTINCTLY UNDERSTOOD THAT THE DRAWEE SHALL
REMAIN LIABLE FOR ALL EXCHANGE DIFFERENCES. AT THE TIME OF DEPOSIT
OF LOCAL CURRENCY, OBTAIN FROM DRAWEES THEIR WRITTEN UNDERTAKING TO
BE RESPONSIBLE FOR ANY EXCHANGE DIFFERENCES. THE DRAFT MUST NOT BE
SURRENDERED TO DRAWEES UNTIL FINAL PAYMENT FOR FACE AMOUNT IN
U.S. DOLLAR EXCHANGE.


   ┌─────────────────────────────────────────────────────────────┐
   │ COLLECTION INSTRUCTIONS:                                    │
   │     DELIVER DOCUMENTS AGAINST PAYMENT.                      │
   │     ADVISE NON-PAYMENT BY CABLE.                            │
   │     REMIT PROCEEDS BY CABLE AT DRAWER'S EXPENSE.            │
   │     DO NOT PROTEST.                                         │
   │     COLLECTING BANK CHARGES ARE AT DRAWEE'S EXPENSE.        │
   │     IN CASE OF NEED REFER TO KURT SCHMIDT, AGENT, 14 BACHSTRASSE │
   │     MUNICH, WHO MAY ASSIST IN OBTAINING PAYMENT OF DRAFT, BUT IS │
   │     NOT TO ALTER ITS TERMS IN ANY WAY.                      │
   └─────────────────────────────────────────────────────────────┘

     THIS COLLECTION IS SUBJECT TO  UNIFORM RULES FOR THE COLLECTION
OF COMMERCIAL PAPER, INTERNATIONAL CHAMBER OF COMMERCE BROCHURE
NO.322 PLEASE USE OUR REFERENCE NUMBER 1652884 IN ALL CORRESPONDENCE.
THANK YOU.

   HR                                    WCG COLLECTION OPERATIONS
                                              COLLECTION LETTER
```

Exhibit 303b: Customer acknowledgement

```
                    CITIBANK NA
                    WORLD CORPORATION GROUP
                    COLLECTION OPERATION
                    P O BOX 2003 GRAND CENTRAL STATION
                    NEW YORK NY 10017
                    (212 558 5770)

                                                    DATE 08/09/77
A. SELLER                      EXP CODE 884    OUR REF. 165288W
1000 BROAD STREET
NEW YORK, NEW YORK 10005



            REF: YOUR COLLECTION ITEM LBIC 1/500 OF 06/24/77
                 IN AMOUNT OF   200,000.00 AT SIGHT

            DRAWER

            DRAWEE B. BUYER



GENTLEMEN:
      WE HAVE ENTERED THIS ITEM FOR COLLECTION, WITH THE FOLLOWING
INSTRUCTION

       ┌──────────────────────────────────────────────────────────┐
       │  DELIVER DOCUMENTS AGAINST PAYMENT.                      │
       │  ADVISE NON-PAYMENT BY CABLE.                            │
       │  REMIT PROCEEDS BY CABLE AT DRAWER'S EXPENSE.            │
       │  DO NOT PROTEST.                                         │
       │  COLLECTING BANK CHARGES ARE AT DRAWEE'S EXPENSE.        │
       │  IN CASE OF NEED REFER TO KURT SCHMIDT, AGENT, 14 BACHSTRASSE │
       │  MUNICH, WHO MAY ASSIST IN OBTAINING PAYMENT OF DRAFT, BUT │
       │  IS NOT TO ALTER ITS TERMS IN ANY WAY.                   │
       └──────────────────────────────────────────────────────────┘


      PAYMENT OR NON-PAYMENT WILL BE ADVISED AFTER PRESENTATION TO THE
DRAWEE OR OTHER PAYOR.

      OUR HANDLING OF THIS COLLECTION IS SUBJECT TO UNIFORM RULES FOR
THE COLLECTION OF COMMERCIAL PAPER, INTERNATIONAL CHAMBER OF
COMMERCE BROCHURE NO. 254 . PLEASE USE OUR REFERENCE NUMBER 165288W
IN ALL CORRESPONDENCE. THANK YOU.

                                        WCG COLLECTION OPERATIONS

HR                                      ACKNOWLEDGEMENT ONLY
+
NNNNJ
```

Obligations of the collecting and remitting bank in accordance with these rules may be summarized as follows:

i. To follow exactly the instructions of the seller or of his bank.

ii. At all times to control and ensure the safety of documents in the collection while in the bank's possession.

iii. To act promptly both in executing instructions and in advising the seller or his bank of all developments.

iv. Banks are not responsible for the actions of their agents, or in general for anything not directly attributable to their own negligence or that of their own employees. In particular, banks are not responsible for the validity or efficacy of any documents.

2.6. Problem/danger areas

Whilst the collection process adds a measure of commercial safety to the seller's dealings, problems may arise with delays caused by international postage or slowness on the part of the banks being used, or on the part of the buyer in paying.

Sometimes the collecting bank has the buyer as a general customer and may not be inclined to exert pressure to obtain quick payment or return of the documents, although a good bank will always exert pressure for prompt payment. Claims for interest where there is unreasonable delay may not be an entirely satisfactory remedy, as recoverable amounts may be small and difficult to collect without expense.

Slowness in postal transmission is mainly a problem on short voyages, where the vessel may well arrive before the documents of title to the goods. Not only can this create problems in unloading, but it can occasion warehousing charges when the goods are unloaded. Additionally, there may be difficulties in the collection itself if the title documents specified are bills of lading, and these have now been replaced by warehouse receipts or other documents.

Problems with documents, or in the collection, are most speedily dealt with by the seller nominating an agent in the buyer's country. Such an agent effectively replaces the seller in the collection, and is called the *case of need*. Because he has title to the goods, he can arrange storage or decide, if necessary, on legal action.

In a clean collection, if the bill is unpaid at presentation or on maturity, i.e., the bill is dishonoured after it has been accepted, there is an established legal procedure called noting or protest. This procedure is designed to establish sufficient evidence of the dishonour for a subsequent legal action.

Noting is a cheaper process than protesting, and consists of initialling of the bill by a notary public (a specialist lawyer) who under international law has credibility everywhere. Protesting involves the notary making out a formal certificate. Generally speaking, protesting is to be preferred to noting, as the law of most foreign countries requies it and it is therefore necessary on bills drawn under an export sale.

2.7. Costs

Collections are cheap, and a bank's commission rate is usually *ad valorem* and less than 1/5 of 1% with a ceiling of $100 or so. The buyer and seller reach agrement on which one of them bears charges, but in general it is the buyer who pays.

2.8. Recent developments in collections: direct collection

Many banks now offer a service called direct collection, designed to speed up the movement of documents between themselves acting as remitting bank, and their customer as seller. The seller is given a supply of special bank stationery (see Exhibit 304) which is completed and sent directly to the collecting bank together with the documents. Time is saved because the remitting bank does not have to duplicate the information on the collection letter.

2.9. Advantages and disadvantages

Advantages for seller

i. Collections are simple and usually cheap.

ii. Control of the valuable title documents is retained.

iii. In some cases, a collection may facilitate financing the sale.

iv. Communications with the foreign country of the buyer are usually simplified.

Disadvantages for seller

i. If the goods are refused by the buyer, unquantifiable demurrage, storage, insurance and agents' costs may well be incurred.

ii. If the shipping vessel docks late, or there is a delay in a government import license, the seller will not be paid until funds are received by the remitting bank.

iii. The ICC Code is not legally enforceable.

Exhibit 304: Direct collection form

London Direct Collection — Original | CITIBANK

Citibank N.A.
P.O. Box 78
336 Strand
London WC2R 1HB

Date: JUNE 24, (CURRENT YEAR)

Subject to "Uniform Rules for Collection" as provided in the International Chamber of Commerce brochure No 322

Mail to:
DEUTSCHE BANK,
2, LINDENSTRASSE,
MUNICH,
GERMANY

Mailed by:
A. SELLER,
1000 BROAD STREET,
NEW YORK   NY 10005,
U.S.A.

Drawers ref no.

We enclose the following draft and documents for collection and disposal of proceeds as instructed below. This collection is to be handled by you as if received direct from Citibank N.A. London, who will confirm by follow copy.

Citibank N.A. Reference	Amount	Drawee and address	Date of Draft	Tenor
NBG/DC	$200,000.00	B. BUYER, 2, LINDENSTRASSE, MUNICH	6/24/ CURRENT YEAR	SIGHT

Documents	Draft	Inv	Con. Inv.	CVO	Ins	B/L	PPR	Miscellaneous Documents	Vessel
Attached									
Duplicates to follow									

Please follow instructions marked X

X	Deliver documents against		If necessary warehouse and insure
X	Payment/acceptance may be deferred pending arrival of shipment		Do not insure
	Protest non-payment	X	Advise acceptance promptly by airmail/cable
	Protest non-acceptance		Advise dishonour promptly by airmail/cable
X	Do not protest non-payment		Collect interest at % p.a. from date of draft to approx. date of receipt of proceeds in London
X	Do not protest non-acceptance		Waive charges if refused

Collect Citibank N.A. charge of 1% min £5 max £20	Plus all other charges
Accept local currency deposit and written exchange undertaking	

In case of need refer to:

	Who will endeavour to obtain honour of draft as drawn	KURT SCHMIDT, 14 BACH STRASSE, MUNICH
X	Whose instructions regarding disposal of goods and/or documents may be followed unconditionally	

Payment Instructions

Place adhesive label here

Special Instructions

This collection is to be handled as if received by you from Citibank N.A. P.O. Box 78, 336 Strand, London WC2R 1HB to whom please acknowledge receipt and send all communications quoting Citibank N.A. (London) DC Number

SPECIMEN ONLY

A. SELLER CORP   Sender's signature

Incorporated with limited liability under the National Bank Act of the United States of America
A Subsidiary of Citicorp New York USA

252 International Borrowing

Advantages for buyer

i. Collections usually favour the buyer rather than the seller, since the buyer basically has time to inspect the goods (or the documents of title to them) before paying. This is particularly so with a clean collection, which is effectively the same as open account.

ii. Payment is deferred until the goods arrive, or later under a term bill.

Disadvantages for buyer

i. The use of a bill of exchange makes the buyer legally liable for his default in payment after acceptance, regardless of the underlying contract for sale of the goods.

ii. If the bill is unpaid in error, or protested in error by the seller, the buyer's trade reputation may be seriously damaged.

3. DEFINITION OF A LETTER OF CREDIT

A letter of credit is a written undertaking by a bank, the *issuing bank,* to the seller, *the beneficiary* in accordance with the instructions of the buyer, *the applicant*, to effect payment up to a prescribed amount within a prescribed time period against prescribed documents, provided these are correct and in order, i.e., they conform with the instructions of the applicant.

The documents include those required for the commercial purpose of effecting the sale, insurance and transport (usually bills of lading). Payment is made either against presentation of the documents on their own, or against the documents together with a bill (usually called a *draft*) drawn against the bank where the letter of credit is available. The draft may be a sight draft, or a time draft payable a specified number of days after a specific date, commonly the bill of lading date.

There are usually at least two banks involved in a letter of credit: the issuing banks is the buyer's bank, the second bank, called the *advising bank*, is a bank in the seller's country and is usually the seller's bank. The advising bank undertakes transmission of the credit, and authenticates the validity of issuing bank's execution, but undertakes no commitment to pay the seller.

In a case where the issuing bank is too small for the seller to trust it to pay, or where the seller feels that there is a political risk in dealing with banks in a certain country, the beneficiary will ask the advising bank to *confirm* the credit. The effect of this is for the advising (and now confirming) bank to substitute itself for the issuing bank in meeting obligations to the beneficiary to make payment.

A third bank comes into the picture if the currency of settlement of the transaction is not that of the country of the issuing bank. It would be unsatisfactory for an issuing bank in London to undertake to pay a credit in Malay dollars on a specific date, as that bank might not have Malay dollars available on that date, and to purchase them might be unnecessarily expensive against sterling. Therefore, a bank, called the *paying bank* is nominated in the country of the currency. The paying bank is either a branch or correspondent of the issuing bank, holding the latter's account in the currency, so that after payment the paying bank may obtain re-imbursement.

Merely acting as paying bank imposes no obligation on the bank to pay. Indeed, it is more prudent for the paying bank to send documents to the issuing bank for checking before payment. If this should inconvenience the beneficiary, his solution is to require the paying bank to act as confirming bank.

3.1. Purpose of a letter of credit

A letter of credit guarantees payment to the seller on the simple condition that he presents the correct documents, and does so independently of the underlying contract of sale or the financial condition of the buyer at the time of presentation. All the financial risk is passed to the issuing bank, and this security for the seller is the fundamental purpose of a letter of credit. The necessity for the seller to trust the buyer is entirely obviated—the seller is sure of payment and the buyer, for his part, is sure of receiving the correct documents.

3.2. Types of letter of credit

The letter of credit is a versatile and adaptable instrument. All letters of credit stem from two basic varieties, revocable and irrevocable.

3.2.1 Revocable letters of credit

A revocable letter of credit can be amended or cancelled at any time without prior notice to the beneficiary. It provides the seller with no greater security than a documentary collection or order to pay, and is therefore generally unsatisfactory, since the seller is in the same position of trust as he is without the credit.

3.2.2. Irrevocable letters of credit

An irrevocable credit cannot be amended or cancelled

without the beneficiary's consent. It is the only true kind of letter of credit. For the remainder of this chapter, all discussion of letters of credit will assume irrevocability.

Letters of credit are either *straight* or *negotiation* credits.

3.3. Straight and negotiation credits

The beneficiary may well not be close to the paying bank. In order for him to save time by presenting documents to his local bank, he will ask for the credit to be opened as a negotiation credit in which the issuing bank agrees to pay not just the beneficiary, but also any bona fide holders of drafts presented with the documents.

A negotiation credit enables either a specifically nominated bank (or any bank, if the words "feely negotiable by any bank" are used in the credit) to check the documents and, if they are in order, to pay them less interest for the time it will take to obtain re-imbursement from the issuing bank. Sellers should require negotiation credits where the currency of the credit is not their own currency, or where the seller's local bank offers preferential rates or service.

Generally, a negotiating bank pays with recourse to the beneficiary if anything goes wrong, but the legal position is by no means settled. This is a very important point for the beneficiary, as under every other kind of letter of credit, there is no recourse to him. All beneficiaries under negotiation credits should settle with the negotiating bank at payment, whether recourse to the beneficiary is reserved or not.

Straight and negotiation credits distinguish methods of settlement. Such settlement can be either at sight or by acceptance.

3.3.1. Sight credits

Sight credits are payable against drafts drawn on the paying bank at sight, i.e., payable immediately the documents are checked and found to be in order.

3.3.2. Acceptance credits

These are payable by acceptance of the paying bank of a term bill or draft drawn on it, payable at a specified date in the future. The paying bank must be specifically nominated as accepting bank under the credit.

The value of an acceptance credit is that the seller can extend time to pay to the buyer, who will not have to pay the face amount until maturity, and at the same time obtain a negotiable document, the bank acceptance, readily discountable for cash.

3.4. Less-usual forms of credit

There are four types of less-usual credit, adaptable to specific situations:

3.4.1 Revolving credits

A revolving credit is for a specific amount which stays the same without amendment, despite drawings under the credit. Such credits revolve either in time or value.

A credit revolving in time is available for a specific amount every week or month or year until expiry, regardless of whether any amount was drawn in the preceding time period. A credit revolving in time can be cumulative or non-cumulative, cumulative meaning that unused portions are carried forward for availability in the next period.

Revolving credits are useful where a seller has a long-term contract to supply a fixed quantity and value of merchandise over a specific time period.

3.4.2. Red clause credits

Red clause credits contain an authorization by the issuing bank to the advising or confirming bank to make advances to the beneficiary before presentation of documents. The description red clause arises from the colour of the ink that is used to draw attention to the credit's special condition.

The purpose of these credits is to provide pre-shipment finance to the seller, who might not be otherwise capable of raising the finance to produce the merchandise desired by the buyer. It is a method of financing between the buyer and seller; in the event of the seller not shipping the merchandise, the advising or confirming bank recovers the advances plus interest from the issuing bank, which in turn recovers from the applicant.

Red clause credits were once very common, particularly in the Australian wool trade with London. Woolbrokers in England used them as a way of financing Australian farmers' working capital needed to mature sheep for shearing. There were also blue-clause credits (only the ink was differnet) for New Zealand. Nowadays these credits are rare.

3.4.3 Transferable credits

A transferable credit enables the original beneficiary to transfer to one or more second beneficiaries. The transfer must be made by means of an advice given by a named bank, effecting the transfer to the second beneficiary in exactly the same wording as the original credit, with only three possible changes:

i. the transferee's name and address is substituted for the beneficiary's;

ii. the amount of credit may be reduced to allow for the first beneficiary's profit;

iii. the expiry date may be brought forward to allow for movement of documents from the bank effecting the transfer to the issuing bank.

Transferable credits are generally used by middlemen desiring to keep their identity secret from the seller, so as to protect their trade connections from becoming known. Normally, they work well and are not as complicated as they might seem at first sight, particularly if partial transfers are permissible. However, to ensure his profit under a partial transfer the first beneficiary must make certain that he presents on time his invoice for the full amount of the original credit to the bank effecting the transfer. If he fails to do so, the bank will present the second beneficiary's invoice direct to the issuing bank, and obviously this invoice will not include the first beneficiary's profit.

A transferable credit may be transferred once only.

3.4.4. Back-to-back credits

The idea of a back-to-back credit sounds simple, but in practice such credits are difficult to structure satisfactorily from the point of view of the issuing bank. The principle of a back-to-back credit is that the seller, as beneficiary of the first credit, offers it as security to the advising bank for it to open a second credit in favour of the seller's own supplier.

A back-to-back would be useful in the same circumstances as a transferable credit, and particularly useful to a more remote beneficiary than the second beneficiary who, under the provision that a transferable credit is only transferable once, cannot himself transfer a credit on. The back-to-back would enable him to use the transferred credit as security for a credit in his supplier's favour.

Many banks are reluctant to open back-to-back credits without other security, because they are required to pay the beneficiary regardless of whether the applicant is paid himself. There are two difficulties:

i. The back-to-back must match the wording of the first credit exactly, with only the amount and shipping dates changed to reflect the applicant's profit and earlier shipment.

ii. The applicant might agree to amendments to the first credit detrimental to the interests of the issuing bank of the back-to-back without informing it.

One way out of this is for the issuing bank of the back-to-back to become the confirming bank of the first credit, but this may be difficult where the issuing bank is weak or objects to its credits being confirmed. Generally speaking, banks confine issue of back-to-backs to situations where they know there is an alternative source of repayment than the first credit, usually the applicant's general financial resources.

3.5. Practical mechanics

The general procedure in a letter of credit usually follows the sequence below:

i. The buyer and seller agree terms of sale, including payment by letter of credit.

ii. The buyer completes an instruction to the issuing bank to issue the credit (Exhibit 305). The buyer will have needed to obtain a credit line from the issuing bank specifying the total amount of credits that the bank will issue on his behalf, and he will need availability under this line.

iii. The issuing bank instructs the advising or confirming bank, including specifications of documents.

iv. The advising bank informs the beneficiary.

v. The beneficiary, if he accepts the advice and is happy with it, arranges shipment.

vi. The seller obtains the bills of lading from the shipping company, origin certificates and whatever else is required and delivers them to the issuing, paying, acceptng or negotiating bank, whichever is the appropriate one for the settlement.

vii. The bank checks the documents and, if they are in accordance with the instructions from the issuing bank, or the applicant if the issuing bank is the paying bank, effects payment as appropriate, the paying or negotiating bank re-imbursing itself as appropriate.

viii. If the paying bank is not the issuing bank, it sends the documents to the issuing bank, which checks them and, if they are correct, releases them to the buyer upon payment of the amount of the credit or on such other terms, including a loan to the buyer, as may have been previously agreed.

ix. The buyer uses the documents to obtain possession of the goods.

Exhibit 305: Application and agreement for commercial letter of credit

TO: CITIBANK, N.A.

P.O. Box 78, 336 Strand, London WC2R 1HB.

DOCUMENTARY CREDIT IRREVOCABLE	CREDIT NUMBER OF ISSUING BANK	OF ADVISING BANK
ADVISING BANK	APPLICANT	
BENEFICIARY	AMOUNT	
	EXPIRY DATE AT THE COUNTER OF:	

Available by the beneficiary's draft(s) drawn at:
☐ Sight ☐ _____ days Sight ☐ _____ days Date (Drafts to be dated same date as Bill of Lading)
☐ _____ Other
drawn on ☐ Citibank, N.A. London for _____ % invoice cost.
☐ _____ for _____ % invoice cost.
accompanied by the following documents which are indicated by "X", duly in order:
☐ Commercial Invoice in _____ copies.
☐ Marine and War Risk Insurance Policy or Certificate, in negotiable form, in the currency of the credit including _____
☐ Full set clean on Board original Ocean Bills of Lading or Container Bills of Lading or Bills of Lading bearing container endorsement, issued to order of: _____
marked notify _____
Marked: Freight ☐ Collect ☐ Paid
☐ Airway Bill consigned to _____
☐ Other documents _____
☐ Insurance covered by applicant:
COVERING:

Terms: ☐ FOB _____ ☐ C&F _____ ☐ CIF _____ ☐ C&I _____
(Location) (Location) (Location) (Location)
Imported under: ☐ Open General Licence ☐ Import Licence No _____
Each draft or presentation of documents must indicate the credit number of the issuing bank and the credit number of the advising bank (if indicated)

Despatch/Shipment/Taking in Charge Latest _____ From _____ To _____	Partial Shipments ☐ Permitted ☐ Prohibited	Transhipments ☐ Permitted ☐ Prohibited

Drafts and documents must be presented to negotiating or paying bank within _____ days after the date of issuance of the Bills of Lading or other Shipping documents but within expiry.

1248 5/77

256 International Borrowing

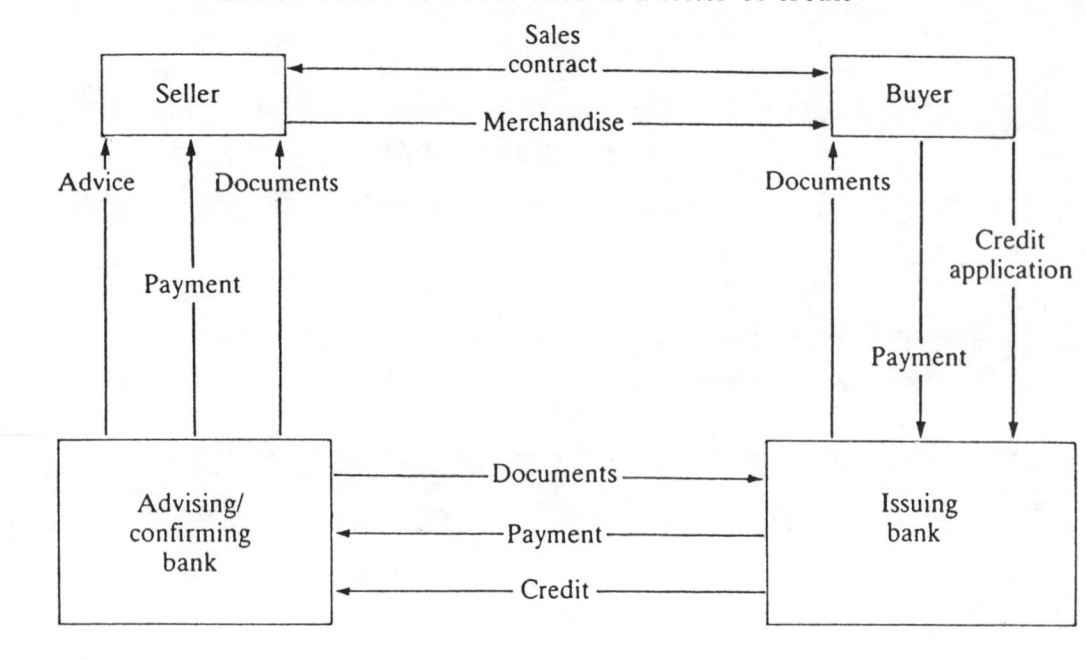

Exhibit 306: Procedure used in a letter of credit

For the simple case of a straight credit, the whole of this procedure is summarized in Exhibit 306, and the typical form of such a credit is shown in Exhibit 307.

3.6. Documents required in a letter of credit

The bank letter of credit imposes no greater requirement than the buyer would impose on the seller under any other trade terms save that negotiable transport documents must be included if the issuing bank is to obtain security over the documents (which is normally required). This is a key point in the banking system's availment of credits. Banks may well be willing to issue payment guarantees without security for some of their customers, but certainly not for as many as they will issue letters of credit. The reason is that *in extremis* the issuing bank can sell the merchandise to repay itself because the negotiable transport documents give it title. There may be a loss but not as much as without the merchandise.

Usual transport documents are the following:

3.6.1. Bill of lading

Details on the bill of lading should include:

i. description of the merchandise consistent with the credit;

ii. identifying marks or numbers on the merchandise;

iii. vessel's name;

iv. evidence of loading usually by the imposition of the words "on board";

v. loading and discharge ports;

vi. names of shipper (the seller) and consignee (the buyer, his agent or sometimes "to order");

vii. whether freight is pre-paid or not;

viii. the number and date of bills. The date is perhaps the most important requirement. Firstly it shows whether the goods are shipped within a required time for shipment under the credit; secondly it enables determination of presentation within the validity of the credit or, if no date is specified, 21 days of the date of the bills; thirdly, it permits determination of the acceptability of the accompanying insurance document.

The law affecting bills of lading is fairly complicated but, in essence, these are common sense documents. Any marks or comments on bills should be treated with care. For example, if the credit calls for merchandise to be stowed, and the bills are marked that goods are loaded on deck, they are not acceptable and indeed the insurance cover may not be effective either.

A bill of lading is shown in Exhibit 308. The name of the

Exhibit 307: Typical form of a letter of credit

DEUTSCHE BANK

Munich, Germany

JULY 26, (CURRENT YEAR)

A. SELLER CORP
1000 BROAD STREET
NEW YORK, NEW YORK 10015

IRREVOCABLE STRAIGHT CREDIT NO. 315

GENTLEMEN;

AT THE REQUEST B. BUYER CORP., 2 LINDENSTRASSE, MUNICH, GERMANY, AND FOR THE ACCOUNT OF SAME, WE HEREBY OPEN IN YOUR FAVOR OUR IRREVOCABLE CREDIT NO. AS INDICATED ABOVE, FOR A SUM OR SUMS NOT EXCEEDING A TOTAL OF U.S. $200,000. - (TWO HUNDRED THOUSAND UNITED STATES DOLLARS) AVAILABLE BY YOUR DRAFT(S) AT SIGHT ON US, TO BE ACCOMPANIED BY:

1.
2.   REQUIRED DOCUMENTATION
3.

EACH DRAFT DRAWN RELATIVE HERETO MUST BE MARKED, "DRAWN UNDER CREDIT NO. 315".

DOCUMENTS MUST BE PRESENTED AT OUR OFFICE WITHIN 10 DAYS OF BILL OF LADING DATE.

THIS CREDIT IS SUBJECT TO THE UNIFORM CUSTOMS AND PRACTICE FOR DOCUMENT CREDITS (1974 REVISION) INTERNATIONAL CHAMBER OF COMMERCE PUBLICATION NO. 290.

WE HEREBY AGREE TO HONOR EACH DRAFT DRAWN UNDER AND IN COMPLIANCE WITH THE TERMS OF THIS CREDIT, IF DULY PRESENTED (TOGETHER WITH THE DOCUMENTS AS SPECIFIED) AT THIS OFFICE ON OR BEFORE OCTOBER 15, (CURRENT YEAR).

VERY TRULY YOURS,

AUTHORIZED SIGNATURE

Exhibit 308: Bill of lading

SHIPPER: H. K. EXPORTER CORPORATION 1000 BROAD STREET NEW YORK, NEW YORK 10005			CONSIGNEE: ORDER OF THE SHIPPER	
NOTIFY PARTY: L. B. IMPORTER COMPANY RIO DE JANEIRO, BRAZIL				
VESSEL: S/S QUOVIS		PORT OF LOADING: NEW YORK		PORT OF DISCHARGE RIO DE JANEIRO
MARKS AND NUMBER	NO. OF PKGS.	PARTICULARS FURNISHED BY SHIPPER DESCRIPTION OF MERCHANDISE		GROSS WEIGHT
LBIC 1/500 LOADED ON BOARD JULY 14, (CURRENT YEAR) CARRIER LINE INC. AGENT _____	500 CTNS.	WIDGETS FREIGHT PREPAID		25 000 LBS.
FREIGHT CHARGES PAYABLE AT NEW YORK BY SHIPPER				
DETAILS OF FREIGHT CHARGES			SHORT FORM BILL OF LADING IN WITNESS WHEREOF, THE CARRIER MASTER OR AGENT OF SAID VESSEL HAS SIGNED AND THE SHIPPER HAS RECEIVED THIS <u>ONE</u> ORIGINAL BILL OF LADING DATED AT <u>NEW YORK</u> CARRIER LINE INC. BY_____ <u>JULY 13, (CURRENT YEAR)</u> B/L. NO. 1	
PREPAID	COLLECT			
TOTAL				

consignee is sometimes not specified but shown as "to order" to allow the issuing bank to obtain title, as otherwise the buyer (presuming he is the consignee) alone would be entitled to obtain possession. This does not affect the implied lien of the issuing bank over the goods, but enables it to obtain immediate possession of the merchandise.

3.6.2. *Combined transport document*

Where several modes of transport are to be employed, say, ocean-going vessel, inland waterways barge and trucks for container loads, either a *through* bill of lading or combined transport document is used. The word *transhipment* is more generally used to describe use of more than one mode of transport of the same kind, but can refer to multiple modes.

Whilst there is probably no greater significant risk of loss or damage of container loads in multiple modes of transport, it is desirable to have one document only, as railway bills, airway bills, truckers' bills and such like are not in themselves strictly negotiable.

3.6.3. *Insurance certificate*

Such a certificate is shown in Exhibit 309. Essentially, it only needs to be consistent with the other documents called for in the credit and cover the required risk. However, in the absence of specific requirement the certificate must:

i. be issued by an insurer;

ii. provide cover from date of shipment;

iii. be for at least the c.i.f. value of the merchandise.

The policy should also be endorsed so that the issuing bank becomes the beneficiary.

Exhibit 309: Insurance certificate

NAME OF INSURANCE COMPANY

SPECIAL MARINE POLICY   ORIGINAL

PLACE AND DATE, NEW YORK, JULY 13 (CURRENT YEAR)

INSURED: H. K. EXPORTER CORPORATION NEW YORK, N.Y.

SUM INSURED: $1,000,000.00 (ONE MILLION AND 00/100 DOLLARS)

SHIPPED BY VESSEL: S/S QUOVIS B/L NO.1 DATED JULY 13, (CURRENT YEAR) OF CARRIER LINE INC.

FROM: NEW YORK   TO: RIO DE JANEIRO

LOSS, IF ANY, PAYABLE TO THE ORDER OF: H. K. EXPORTER CORPORATION

MARKS AND NUMBERS	NO. OF PKGS.	NO. OF UNITS	DESCRIPTION OF GOODS
LBIC 1/500	500 CTNS.	1000	WIDGETS

TERMS AND CONDITIONS

VARIOUS TERMS AND CONDITIONS INCLUDING MARINE AND WAR RISKS.

NOT TRANSFERABLE UNLESS COUNTERSIGNED BY AN AUTHORIZED REPRESENTATIVE
COUNTERSIGNED:

IN WITNESS WHEREOF THIS COMPANY HAS EXECUTED AND ATTESTED THESE PRESENTS.

Various other documents are needed for specific cargoes, and it is the responsibility of the buyer and seller to ensure that these are adequate for the export of the merchandise. A widely used document is a certificate of origin (Exhibit 310), stating where the goods originate; unless the issuer is specifically stated, or qualifying words are used in the credit, the beneficiary can prepare this himself.

Most transactions also call for a series of invoices prepared by the beneficiary and a quality or inspection certificate prepared by professional inspectors.

3.7. Problem areas

As with most documentary transactions, discrepancies occur from time to time which are generally simple to correct, and which arise more from oversight than fundamental problems in the credit system. Most commonly, discrepancies arise with bills of lading either through clauses written on the bill stating defective condition of the merchandise, by which the bills are said to be *unclean,* or through presenation of the wrong kind of bill, usually a charter party bill.

If bills of lading are marked "freight prepaid" and the shipper is the owner of the vessel, the applicant and the issuing bank are safe in assuming that the applicant has title to the goods and the issuing bank has an indefeasible lien. However, if the shipper is a charterer, the owner of the vessel has a prevailing claim against the deadweight for unpaid charter fees, and indeed the carriage of certain merchandise may amount to a fundamental breach of the charter.

If the credit request by the buyer permits charter party bills of lading, the issuing bank will usually ask to see a summary of the charter party which will be required to be in acceptable form, i.e., that loading and discharge parts are permissible under the charter, that the merchandise is not prohibited, and that the charter, if it is a time charter, will not expire during the voyage.

For some cargoes, especially crude petroleum, control of the vessel may be a crucial point in the issuing bank's willingness to open the credit. Cargoes of oil frequently exceed US$50 million in value, and the risk of diversion of the vessel after a credit is opened to more profitable buyers is not insignificant where unscrupulous owners who are also sellers of oil are

Exhibit 310: Certificate of origin

Consignor: Noxell Corporation (UK) Ltd., Flanshaw Way, Wakefield WF2 9NA West Yorkshire England	**CERTIFICATE OF ORIGIN** A/ 115112
Consignee: Modern Pharmaceutical Co., P.O. Box 1566 Dubai United Arab Emirates	**CERTIFICATE OF ORIGIN** The undersigned authority certifies that the goods shown below originated in: **UNITED KINGDOM**
Consigned by: Vessel: Margorie Y From: South Shields	ARAB-BRITISH CHAMBER OF COMMERCE

Marks and Numbers:	Quantity and Kind of Packages:	Description of Goods:	Weight (gross & nett):
ModernPharm/ 125/78/UK/Dubai	NOXELL – COVER GIRL Cosmetics 120 Shippers — Nail Polish Remover 6 Shippers — Eye Make Up Remover Manufactured by: Vanda Beauty Counsellors, Gladden Place Skelmersdale. Lancs.		319.38Kgs 266.80K

KIRKLEES AND WAKEFIELD
CHAMBER OF COMMERCE AND INDUSTRY

CERTIFIED BY
19 MAY 1978
Arab-British Chamber of Commerce
AUTHORISED SIGNATURE

ARAB-BRITISH CHAMBER OF COMMERCE

Place and Date of Issue — Issuing Authority

tempted by rising oil prices. Banks are also concerned with the difficult question of liability for pollution damage which may occur with large oil cargoes. The charter party should make clear whose is the primary responsibility in such risk, and whose secondary risk such as inspection of cargo holds, the condition of which may affect the quality of the merchandise. Generally speaking, deterioration of volatile materials (which would include even animal fats) is a risk which should be clearly stated between owner and charterer.

All bills of lading tendered under credits must be *order* bills and not straight bills, unless specifically stated otherwise. An order bill directs the carrier to deliver the goods to the order of a designated party, and is a proper negotiable document of title granted to the addressee (sometimes a notify party is also shown on the bill but such a party has no title in the bill). A straight bill, which is always so described in its heading, states a specific consignee without use of the words "to the order", or "order of". It is not a title document and is, therefore, not good security for the issuing bank. Normally, straight bills are used only where the buyer has made payment in advance, and they seldom arise under documentary credits.

There is a more far-reaching problem with credits extending beyond the technical issues which arise from discrepancies, which is best described as the ambiguous role of the banks. Just as the ICC have produced a uniform Code for Collections, so they have for credits, and it is called the Uniform Customs and Practice for Documentary Credits, 1974 Revision (see Appendix II). Although this does not have the force of law, it does have the practically universal support of major banks in prescribing their obligations. The key article is article 8, which states that: "In documentary credit operations all parties concerned deal in documents and not in goods".

On the face of it, therefore, the issuing and the paying bank have no responsibility for innocent or fraudulently misrepresentative documentation—the risk is the applicant's. This responsibility is controversial, and of considerable importance to an issuing bank faced with misrepresentative documents which it must pay, and also an applicant unwilling or perhaps unable to pay the issuing bank. Innocent misrepresentation (that is not fraudulent) on documents usually arises through incompetence or negligence. For example, an inspection certificate called for under the credit may have been negligently made out, with resulting loss to the buyer.

If a leading or properly qualified inspection firm is used, such problems are less likely to arise. However, the uniform code excludes the use of phrases such as "first class" or "qualified" on documents, so that banks are not concerned with even the minimal restraint on incompetence which such wording would allow. Only the identity, and not the capacity, of issuers of documents is of concern to banks, and even this is only partially true of origin certificates, unless specifically described in detail in the credit application.

Whether or not this is reasonable depends on the applicant's understanding of the role of issuing banks—they do not offer counsel on the commercial risks of the transaction for the buyer, nor do they monitor the implementation of the underlying contract between buyer and seller through the credit. Banks merely facilitate payment.

The ambiguity in this definition of role arises in one of the cases where the bank is entitled not to pay. There are only three grounds on which the bank may refuse to pay: failure of the beneficiary to meet the conditions precedent which there may be under the credit; a common mistake between buyer and seller leading to issue of the credit; and lastly, fraud by the seller.

It is fraud by the seller as grounds for refusal to pay that creates the ambiguity, since detection of fraud, or even reaction to suggestion of fraud, requires the bank to go beyond the documents. In the straightforward case of the paying bank being aware of fraud before documents are presented by the seller, the refusal to pay is clearly not only morally laudable but entirely sensible: the seller keeps his fraud and the buyer keeps his money.

Complications only really arise where there are other parties involved who have given consideration for the proceeds of the credits, or where there are other banks which, after negotiation or payment, are requesting re-imbursement from the opening bank on documents or on a transaction now found to be fraudulent. In such cases, should issuing banks do any more than just look at the documents on their face value and ignore the underlying transaction? Or should the risk of fraud, surely remote in most credits, make them enquire deeper?

Since 1976, the celebrated case of Singer and Friedlander ("Singer") on behalf of itself and 10 other banks, against Creditanstalt-Bankverein ("Creditanstalt") has been pursued in Vienna on *(inter alia)* the issue of fraud as a defence to payment by the issuing bank. The facts of the case are somewhat complicated but, in outline, what happened was that Creditanstalt opened letters of credit for the purchase of pharmaceuticals by two Austrian companies from a Dutch company, which subsequently transferred the credits to a consortium of banks led by Singer. The pharmaceuticals were, in fact, to be on-sold to a Yugoslavian trading company, which Creditanstalt subsequently claimed was acting as agent for the Dutch seller, so that the sale was merely a pretence designed to obtain value for the pharmaceuticals which in reality, so Creditanstalt also claimed, were rubbish. Singer, having given consideration for the transfer of the

Creditanstalt credits by the Dutch company, presented the documents to Creditanstalt for payment, which it refused on certain technical grounds, and because of the alleged fraud in the transaction and in the goods.

The case is as yet undecided and the leading European legal authorities are divided, as are many banks, as to which side they support. The case really arises because there is a loss, and the disputants are attempting to ensure it does not fall on them. Most banks agree that it is right not to pay against fraudulent documents to prevent any loss arising, but enquiry into fraudulent transactions or goods is an onus which the banking system seems unable to bear, particularly at the low rates now charged for credits and within the time frame allowed by commercial pressures for transactions to proceed. However, the ambiguity remains and probably will, even after the Singer-Creditanstalt decision. The lesson for applicants, who in the great majority of cases will bear the loss on frauds is, as with all buyers, to beware their sellers.

Some protection for buyers may be had from a cross-credit or performance bond opened by the seller in their favour. Usually, these are limited to 10% only of the amount of the credit, and are difficult to obtain in sellers' markets which are normally those in which credits are opened by buyers anyway.

3.8. Costs

Although more expensive than collections because the issuing bank does take a risk on the applicant and charges for it, credits are a relatively cheap way for buyers to facilitate international transactions. Rates vary, depending on the credit standing of the applicant, the tenor of the credit, the amount of the credit and the merchandise, but a normal scale would be ¼% *ad valorem* commission for opening, plus ⅛% per month for a credit permitting time drafts. Very large credits with sight drafts are frequently charged at considerably less than this, however.

In addition to opening charges, banks other than the issuing bank involved in the credit have charges, and tariffs vary widely depending on the country in which the bank is located. Negotiating banks also charge for interest for the time between negotiation and their re-imbursement. On a currency negotiation credit, an overall cost of ½% or more might be typical.

Part of the cost, normally charges other than opening commission, may be met by the beneficiary, but against this he can set certainty of payment and also the time value of money paid earlier than later. Generally, credits are paid within 14 days from start to finish, even on long sea voyages, as bills of lading may be sent ahead of the vessel by air.

3.9. Recent developments in letters of credit

Letters of credit without the requirement for presentation of transport or commercial documents are called *clean* credits, and are analogous to, although not legally identical with, guarantees. These credits are extremely flexible and may be used in an almost unlimited variety of situations, from construction bonding to the finance of margin requirements on futures markets, where some kind of financial surety is required of the applicant.

Two kinds of clean credit which are relatives of the documentary letter of credit and which are making an increasingly common appearance are of particular interest. The first is the standby letter of credit, in which the issuing bank undertakes to pay if the applicant does not. Documents normally called for are evidence of the underlying transaction (such as non-negotiable copies of bills of lading), and the beneficiary's certificate of non-payment by the applicant. Such credits are useful in the purchase of crude oil, where it is particularly difficult to present negotiable documents speedily.

Sometimes the standby credit is coupled with a credit in favour of the applicant, used in lieu of negotiable documents as security for the issuing bank, which represents a particularly tricky instance of the back-to-back credit discussed earlier. The issuing bank will probably have to rely more on its knowledge of the parties and the transaction, than on the goods in such transactions.

The second is the indemnity for missing documents given to shipping companies, so that they will release merchandise to the applicant. This is a document of long standing in itself, but increasingly shipping companies are requesting such indemnities to have long expiry periods or no expiry date, and to be for a considerable multiple of the c.i.f. value of the cargo. Their reason for doing this is to protect themselves against unanticipated incidental damages, if at any time in the future the real owner of the cargo should appear.

Clearly, the banks must know their applicants well before issuing such indemnities, but such large contingent risks, unlimited in time, are undesirable from both the banks' and the applicants' point of view, and it may be that the ease with which such indemnities have been issued will diminish.

The great boom in letters of credit was after World War II when there was much financial uncertainty. Since then, the decline of the letter of credit on the grounds of cost and, in some arguments, on the grounds that credits foster excessive trust in documents, has been continuously forecast. In fact, this has not happened, save possibly in the area where credits would be of most use because of the amounts of money involved, i.e., in the financing the crude oil trade. For a number of reasons, but chiefly that major oil routes (for example, across the Mediterranean) are short and vessels arrive before documents, whilst demurrage is highly expensive or that vessels sail to save time before documents are ready, it is difficult to compose classical documentary letters of credit in the finance of oil. Instead, a guarantee for payment similar to a standby credit is frequently used.

3.10. Advantages and disadvantages of letters of credit

Advantages for seller

i. Letters of credit generally provide immediate finance, either by payment or bank acceptance.

ii. There is an effective guarantee of payment against the proper documents, regardless of the buyer's capacity to make payment. The bank cannot refuse payment for proper documents.

iii. Simple and minimal communication is necessary between seller and buyer, once the credit is established.

Disadvantages for seller

i. Really none, except that even a letter of credit is not as good as payment in advance.

Advantages for buyer

i. Deferred credit terms are simpler and easier to get, as the seller can be offered a bank rather than trade acceptance.

ii. Erroneous protest for non-payment is not possible.

iii. Buying is always easier with a letter of credit as incentive to the seller to sell.

Disadvantages for buyer

i. The buyer is sure of getting the documents he wants, but not necessarily the goods. Where there is a difference between the two, he must rely on the contract of sale for recovery of any loss, having already paid the issuing bank. Letters of credit are less favourable to buyers than collections.

ii. Letters of credit are more expensive and more work than collections.

Section III:
Selected Financing Techniques
Chapter 12: Countertrade

How to Negotiate Countertrade Deals
Stanley J. Marcuss and Jay D. Grushkin

Countertrade is perhaps the world's oldest form of commerce. It evolved as a means of exchange in the absence of money. In its simplest form, it is known as barter—the direct exchange of goods between one party and another without any transfer of currency. Despite their relative simplicity, however, barter transactions rarely occur among industrialised nations since it is difficult to find parties who have a matching interest in each other's goods.

Today countertrade exists in an endless variety of complex forms that are tailored to meet the unique modern commercial needs of the parties to the transaction. Some of these transactions defy description to anyone not versed in countertrade's art. Yet despite its modern complexities, countertrade can be viewed simply as an export-import transaction in which an export sale is expressly conditioned on the exporter's willingness to take back—or cause another to take back—all or a portion of his sales price in the form of goods of the importing country.

Ranging from simple two-party swaps to complex multiple-party transactions, countertrade florishes today and is expected to continue to grow in the future as a result of the same exigency that gave rise to its creation in the earliest days of commerce—lack of shortages of liquid capital. A sizeable portion of the global community simply lacks the convertible currency to engage in commerce with the industrialized world. This is especially true of the debt-ridden less developed countries of the South and currency-starved non-market economies of the East.

The purpose of this article is to provide a general primer on countertrade to the international practitioner who must advise or deal with parties wishing to engage in trade with a country or party imposing a countertrade obligation. To the modern banker and businessman, countertrade is not a goal to be attained but rather a 'necessary evil' that must be mastered.[1]

MOTIVATIONS UNDERLYING COUNTERTRADE

As a consequence of unforeseen global inflation during the past decade (largely a result of drastic increases in the price of oil), hard, or convertible, currency has become a precious commodity in many countries. Overwhelming levels of external debt have been accumulated by many countries in their attempts to meet domestic plans for internal development, and stringent foreign exchange controls have followed. As a result, a company seeking to export to these countries (the exporter) must choose between either foregoing an export opportunity, or selling only those goods for which hard currency is readily available, or selling goods on credit with the risk that repayment may never be made or engaging in countertrade transactions. As might be expected, many exporters have opted for the last alternative.

Countries that impose countertrade requirements often have other reasons in addition to those relating to hard currency shortages for doing so:

— countertrade may provide additional foreign currency to the country if the countertrade obligation exceeds the value of the import;

— countertrade is compatible with the import and export schedules of centrally planned systems (many of which have been thrown into a state of disarray as a result of unanticipated foreign currency shortages and credit restrictions);[2]

— countertrade can promote an upgrading of the countertrade provides lesser industrialised countries with access to the marketing and distribution channels of the industrialised nations; and

— countertrade can promote an upgrading of the countertrade nation's production facilities as it gears up to meet demanding specifications of foreign markets, especially in the case of compensation arrangements in which the countertrade partner may provide not only technological goods, but also training, quality control and a host of other improvements.

One of the more elusive motivations for engaging in countertrade is to adjust artificially the sales prices of goods in international transactions.[3] The party imposing the countertrade obligation (the importer) may demand a higher price for its goods than the international market can realistically bear. Although the exporter will simply increase the sales price of his own goods to compensate for the inflated value of the countertrade items, the importer has nonetheless superficially manipulated the international sales price of its goods, thus enabling it to meet hard currency export quotas imposed by its government. On the other hand, both parties to a countertrade transaction may wish to deflate their sales prices without others knowing about it. In the case of OPEC oil, for example 'a country (can) attract customers by means of a lower price than is officially available from OPEC countries without violating price guidelines, since the value of the imported good would never be stated in monetary terms.'[4] In addition, by deflating the price of the transaction, the parties may avoid certain international and domestic tariffs, a practice that is, for the most part, illegal.

FORMS OF COUNTERTRADE

Perhaps the most confusing aspects of countertrade is its lexicon, with differing versions advanced by nearly every commentator in the field. Unlike pure barter, which is easily recognised and labelled, contemporary countertrade transactions exist under such rubrics as buyback, clearing agreements, compensation, cooperation, counterpurchase, domestic use of blocked currency, evidence accounts, offset, parallel trading, swap and switch. While it is extremely difficult to place a single label on any particular countertrade transaction, virtually all countertrade transactions fall generally under one of two headings— counterpurchase or compensation.

COUNTERPURCHASE

A counterpurchase transaction is one in which the exporter is required to purchase from the buyer (or a third party designated by the buyer) a specified quantity of goods sometimes equal to, but typically less than, the value of the export. Although the counterpurchase obligation may be contained in the sales contract itself, it is generally evidenced by a separate contract between the two parties, the sales and counterpurchase contracts being connected by a protocol.

The protocol is simply a bilateral statement of intent to engage in the two-way transaction. A counterpurchase obligation typically must be fulfilled within a relatively short period—most often within one or two years.

A counterpurchase is the preferable form of countertrade in the eyes of the exporter, because, in a pure counterpurchase transaction, the exporter receives the full sales price for his goods upon delivery and is merely subject to a default under the separate contract in the event the counterpurchase is not consummated within the prescribed period. However, the contractual penalty imposed on the exporter for default on the counterpurchase obligation may constitute as much as 15 per cent of the value of the export.[5]

While the counterpurchase transaction, comprised of separate sales and counterpurchase obligations with separate settlements, is favourable to the exporter, it requires a significant degree of trust and cooperation among the parties—often rare commodities in East-West and North-South trade relations. A party imposing a counterpurchase obligation will be hesitant to pay hard currency for an export in the absence of an absolute guarantee of payment, if not some form of prepayment, for the counterpurchase. Similarly, an exporter will be reluctant to provide, in advance of the counterpurchase, money or goods, or for that matter to enter into a binding obligation to pay for a counterpurchase of goods—typically of indefinite nature and quality—within a prescribed period. As a consequence, several mechanisms have been developed to ensure that the importer's precious supply of hard currency will not be diminished and to provide the exporter with greater assurance that it will receive countertrade goods that can be easily converted into hard currency. These mechanisms include evidence accounts, clearing agreements and escrow arrangements.

EVIDENCE ACCOUNTS

The evidence account is a means of providing the exporter with flexibility in the conduct of counterpurchase transactions.[6] Once the parties to the countertrade transaction have agreed to offset a specific portion of the export with a counterpurchase, an evidence account may be established, typically in a foreign trade bank in the East or a central bank in the South. The evidence account is credited for the amount of any purchase by the exporter and debited for the proportionate amount of any export subject to a countertrade commitment. In this manner, the countertrade party need only expend hard currency to cover that portion of its import that will not be offset by a counterpurchase. Agreements establishing evidence accounts typically require that the exporter's counterpurchase constitute as much as 80 per cent of the value of the export.[7] If the exporter is unable to meet its counterpurchase obligation, the unsatisfied portion may be added to its obligation for the succeeding year.[8] The use of an evidence account is particularly appealing to the exporter, because 'instead of facing an immediate and uncertain counterpurchase demand at the signing of a ... sales contract, the evidence account allows the (exporter) time to leisurely "shop around" ... for products that can be marketed back home.'[9] An evidence account also enables the exporter to perform countertrade obligations resulting from numerous contracts with the same or different parties in the importing countertrade country over a relatively long period. Under such an arrangement, however, the exporter must anticipate a relatively long-term trade relationship with the countertrader or countertrade country.

ESCROW ARRANGEMENTS

Escrow or 'blocked account' arrangements are generally used when one of the countertrade parties, typically the exporter, feels insecure about the ability of the other party to meet its obligations.[10] Under this arrangement, the proceeds of a counterpurchase are typically placed in escrow prior to consummation of the export and subsequently used to pay for some or all of such export. Thus, to the extent of the counterpurchase obligation, the exporter's funds never actually fall into the hands of his countertrade partner, and any risk of loss to the exporter upon default by the importer is largely minimised. The drawback of this arrangement is that the counterpurchase (or some portion of it) must be consummated prior to the commencement of the export, and that may delay the export sale for a considerable period.

CLEARING AGREEMENTS AND SWITCH TRADING

A clearing agreement is 'a bilateral trade and payment arrangement under which the value of goods exported from country A to country B is not actually paid but is credited to country A in the clearing account and *vice versa* as goods are shipped in the other direction.'[11] Virtually all clearing agreements exist only between centralised governments. Unlike an evidence account, which is directed toward the individual exporter, a clearing agreement is, in effect, 'a long-term barter arrangement between two countries.'[12] Clearing agreements typically provide for an accounting at the end of each year and the imposition of an interest charge on any outstanding balance, which is often allowed to run into successive years.[13] Should too great an imbalance occur in the clearing account, trade between the nations may be halted until the imbalance is corrected or compensated.

Although a credit balance in a clearing account is not directly convertible into currency, bilateral clearing currencies may sometimes be used to finance multilateral trade arrangements that ultimately give rise to cash payments.[14] A clearing agreement may provide that the parties may transfer any credit surplus to a third party, which will acquire the right to purchase items from the party maintaining a deficit in the account. The third party typically designated is a specialist in switch trading that purchases (often at a considerable discount) the clearing rights of the party having a surplus. Once the switch trader purchases goods from the party maintaining the deficit, it will then conduct as many transactions as necessary until the sale of those goods ultimately results in a hard currency payment. The customer maintaining a surplus is, therefore, able to exchange nonconvertible clearing credits into hard currency.

The term 'switch' is also used loosely to describe the situation in which a party unable to meet a counterpurchase obligation either transfers this obligation to a third party or discounts to that party commodities that it has purchased in a countertrade and thus conducts a 'switch' to a party better able to sell the countertrade products for hard currency.[15]

COMPENSATION

Compensation arrangements, encompassing most forms of countertrade falling outside the broad parameters of a counterpurchase, are the most expensive and time-consuming of the countertrade mechanisms. Also known as buybacks or turnkey operations, compensations are agreements whereby an exporter of equipment, technology or often a complete manufacturing plant, takes as partial or complete payment some portion or percentage of the resultant products of the importer. As in the case of a counterpurchase, a compensation arrangement typically entails two separate contracts, connected by a protocol.

Unlike a pure counterpurchase, however, the exporter is not compensated in whole upon delivery, and the repayment in the form of resultant products may take many years (a 20 year compensation arrangement is not unusual). Since the amount of the buyback involved is usually substantial, third-party credit arrangements must typically be negotiated to protect the exporter. In addition, the exporter must often provide technical training and assistance, as well as quality control over the operations of the importer.

HARSH REALITIES

While most exporters accept countertrade as a necessary evil in transacting business in the international arena, many non-market and lesser developed countries at least outwardly view countertrade as a temporary solution to the two principal problems currently confronting them: lack of funds and lack of knowledge in the manufacture and export of domestic goods.[16] As an executive of a large Yugoslav bank recently stated, 'countertrade ... is a temporarily needed vehicle to help the countrry that has a shortage of foreign currency and it should be used in the way which should bring these countries in position to become normal partners in the international market.[17] Yet many exporters reject such notions and view countertrade as a permanent imposition upon them for the benefit of the lesser industrialised nations.

A recent commentary provides a somewhat jaundiced view of countertrade:

> When a company exports to a nation requiring countertrade, it must take back goods that the country can't (or won't try to) sell in international markets. To unload these goods, the company usually has to cut prices. Since it can't afford to absorb all that loss, it may pad the price of the goods it sells to its countertrade customer. When a French computer manufacturer sells to Hungary, for instance, it might raise prices by 10 per cent. Then when it has to unload the Hungarian shoes it gets in return, the premium covers the reduction in price. Usually, an exporting company wants to avoid the trouble of marketing those shoes, so it hands over the 10 per cent premium to a countertrade specialist. This middleman splits the premium with a shoe buyer, keeping maybe two per cent and passing the remaining eight per cent along in price cuts. The result: Hungary pays above the market for imports, making international trade less attractive than it should be, and dumps its own goods through back-door price shaving. Some might argue that, lacking hard currency or borrowing power, Hungary has no other course. In the long run, however, the practice is self-defeating. Having failed to set up continuing relationships with customers, Hungary never learns what the market really wants—what style shoes, for instance—or how it might improve its competitiveness.[18]

A number of these observations have real merit:

Unmarketable countertrade items. The nature of the countertrade product is such that it is generally inferior in quality, in surplus worldwide and thus often difficult to sell. Obviously, if a Third World nation has a product or commodity that can readily be sold on the international market for desperately needed hard currency, that product will typically not be offered in a countertrade transaction.

Pricing problems. The pricing mechanisms of importers imposing countertrade obligations, particularly those operating in non-market economies, are often irrational by free market standards, and, hence, it is difficult to measure accurately the price of the countertrade product (leading to a problematic situation in the assessment of tariffs). Furthermore, trading organisations in countertrade countries are cognisant of the inflated prices (secret padding) that exporters utilise in countertrade deals and, consequently, they often inflate the price of their own goods.[19]

Timing problems. Another concern to the exporter is the risk of market fluctuation pending delivery of the countertrade products. While the exporter is typically obligated to deliver its goods almost immediately after the sale is agreed, the countertrade obligation may not accrue for years, particularly in the case of a compensation arrangement, and even when it does accrue, the items agreed upon may not be available. This situation has led one commentator to state:

> Indeed, banking on the market value of goods at the time they are received is much like trying to speculate in commodities futures on a long-term basis. If, for example, a company builds a soda-ash plant for an East Bloc nation and accepts a specific number of tons of soda ash as payment, by the time the Eastern European country delivers the soda ash, the market for that product may have gone flat...[21]

As a result of the problems described above, a US industry executive has noted that '(a)nyone who uses countertrade as a means of building a business, instead of as a means of overcoming trading or currency problems, is asking for trouble ... Too much can go wrong.'[22] Indeed, the idealistic benefits of countertrade are questioned even in those countries that mandate such activities. Vice President Adam Malik of Indonesia believes that his country 'would be better off developing new markets by pricing aggressively and responding rapidly to customer needs.'[23]

Political risk. An additional and unpredictable pitfall of countertrade, which businessmen can easily overlook, involves the associated political risks. Many of the industrialised nations, including the United States, are currently developing formal positions on countertrade. It goes without saying that, if the government of any party to a long-term countertrade arrangement were to limit the ability of its nationals to continue such arrangements, the consequences could be costly.

For example, although the United States has not yet published its official policy statement on countertrade, various government officials have indicated that the United States will neither encourage nor discourage voluntary countertrade arrangements. Nonetheless, the United States believes that countertrade generally restricts international trade, adversely affects the ability of currency-short countries to repay international debts and is generally costly and cumbersome.

Moreover, the United States has indicated, that it will take an active diplomatic role in curbing coercive countertrade practices. Recently, the United States entered into consultations with the Government of Mexico regarding Mexico's dollar-for-dollar countertrade obligation imposed upon manufacturers selling auto parts within Mexico.

National governments also have within their arsenals trade legislation and export controls that can be used to curb countertrade. In the case of the United States, the antidumping, countervailing duty, escape clause and market disruption laws could be more strenuously enforced against countertrade should the United States perceive countertrade to be a serious threat to its domestic economy.[24]

NEGOTIATIONS

It is imperative that international businessmen appreciate the many pitfalls of countertrade.[25]

Before sitting down at the bargaining table with a prospective foreign trading partner, the exporter should know his opponent's bargaining position, which is a function of how many competitors the exporter has and the importer's need for the exporter's product(s). The exporter must inquire into his opponent's countertrade rules, which are more often than not informal,[26] and then assess the possibility that the foreign party will impose a countertrade obligation. This can be accomplished, in part, by examining whether such obligations have been imposed on similar exports to the targeted country. If there is even a possibility that the foreign party will suggest countertrade, the exporter must know the extent, if any, to which he would be willing to engage in such a transaction. It is imperative that the exporter carefully plan for the countertrade contingency. Negotiations regarding exports to a countertrade country are typically conducted in the countertrade country itself. It is therefore impractical for the exporter to leave the bargaining table upon the mention of countertrade in order to return home and reformulate the deal.

Thus, in the face of a potential countertrade obligation, the exporter's preparation should be twofold. First, he should prepare to negotiate a straight, outright sale to the countertrade country in the event that a countertrade obligation is not proposed. Second, the exporter should prepare an alternative and flexible export plan that considers the costs, delays and hazards of assuming a countertrade commitment.

Once the exporter has done his homework, he is ready to sit down with the potential countertrader. A word of caution, however, which cannot be overstated—the exporter must determine whether countertrade is an issue at the outset of the negotiations. If countertrade will in fact be necessary, it is advisable to conduct the negotiations for the sale and the purchase simultaneously in an effort to avoid the bargaining tactic, common when dealing with foreign trade organisations of the Eastern Bloc, of being confronted with a counterpurchase obligation only after all the conditions of the export itself have been negotiated.[27] Should the latter occur, 'it is then no longer possible to adjust the selling price to take account of the unforeseen costs which the marketing of these counterpurchases will inevitably entail,' and the exporter must be then prepared to walk out of the negotiations.[28]

SEPARATE AGREEMENTS

Virtually every commentator in the countertrade field suggests that, prior to a discussion of the terms of any countertrade commitment, the exporter insist that the sales and counterpurchase(s) be evidenced by two separately enforceable agreements linked by a third agreement, known as a protocol, rather than by a single contract encompassing the entire series of transactions. 'The reason is that if the purchase commitment is included in the contract of sale and if it cannot be fulfilled—even for reasons beyond the control of (the exporter)—the (importer) can stop payment on products already received on grounds of a unilateral breach of the contract as a whole.'[29] Moreover, for the same reason, it is widely stated that the use of a single agreement linking the two transactions will make the acquisition of bank financing or export guarantees a difficult task.

Regardless of the number of contracts constituting a countertrade transaction, the entire deal can best be viewed as being comprised of two transactions—an export sale and a counterpurchase.

EXPORT SALES AGREEMENT

The export sales agreement, also known as the primary agreement, is a straightforward international sales contract describing the products to be sold. It typically contains provisions governing the following:

— price;

— time and place of delivery;

— quantity of goods to be sold;

— quality of goods;

— currency in which goods are to be paid;

— terms of payment;

— security for any deferral in payments;

— dispute resolution mechanisms;

— choice of law; and

— details of arbitration.[31]

COUNTERPURCHASE AGREEMENT

The basic elements of the counterpurchase agreement are the same as those of the export sales agreement, but they must be tailored to provide the exporter with the greatest amount of protection against the common pitfalls of countertrade. In particular, there are six general elements that must be carefully considered:

— the counterpurchase ratio;

— the available countertrade products and permissible countertrade entities;

— the financial and credit terms;

— the restrictions, if any, on resale of the counterpurchase products;

— the time-limits for fulfilling a counterpurchase obligation; and

— events of default, appropriate penalties and dispute resolution mechanisms.[32]

COUNTERPURCHASE RATIO

The counterpurchase ratio (CR), also known as the compensation ratio, is simply the percentage of the value of the export that will be subject to a counterpurchase. Of course, it is in the interest of the exporter to keep the CR as low as possible. CR guidelines vary from one country to another but, in the Eastern bloc countries, tend to range between 15 and 50 per cent, the Soviet Union being on the low end of the range and Bulgaria and Romania at the top.[33]

The CR will depend upon three factors. First, the amount of hard currency available in the country at issue for importation of the products involved. Second, the importance of the imports to the countertrade country—ie, 'if (the) goods are essential to the industry of the ... country concerned, their purchase may be accompanied by a lower demand for countertrade than would be the case for non-essential supplies.'[34] Third, the details of the central economic plan. If funds have been allocated for the import in question, it is less likely that a significant countertrade obligation will be required.

COUNTERTRADE PRODUCTS AND ENTITIES

The selection of available countertrade products is perhaps the most arduous task of the exporter. Entities imposing countertrade obligations will generally not make available their entire range of domestic products for such purposes. Instead, they will typically provide the exporter with a list of available countertrade products, a list that may occasionally be open to negotiation. However, these lists provide only 'a theoretical selection of what is, in some cases, a very mixed bag of products,' subject to a multitude of problems:

— the products mentioned are not always *available*, because the lists are rarely up-to-date (this is particularly frequent in the case of Bulgaria);

— the lists are changed without warning as products are *unexpectedly withdrawn* (ie a domestic or foreign market has meanwhile been found for these products, or the manufacturer has not achieved his production target, etc); in some cases the lists get shorter as year-end nears (which can be annoying if the Western firm has spent time and money finding an outlet for products which are no longer available);

— product descriptions are *not specific* (quality, quantity, etc); [and]

— foreign trade organisations are reluctant to agree that the contract should include a *cancellation clause* concerning the counterpurchase commitment in the event that they are unable to make satisfactory product available.[35]

In view of these problems, it is advisable to negotiate the broadest possible range of countertrade products. The exporter should also obtain the right to satisfy its countertrade obligation through purchases from other foreign trade organisations or entities in the importing country in an effort to secure the widest range of products available.

In addition, the exporter involved in a countertrade deal will likely discover (1) that he will not be provided with an opportunity to inspect the goods that his counterpart has listed as available and (2) that it is extremely difficult, if not impossible, to obtain any form of after-sales service for the counter-purchased products. In order to ensure at least a minimal degree of quality control, the exporter should insist upon a right to inspect the countertrade items prior to delivery or, in the alternative, a similar inspection by a neutral third party. The exporter should also attempt—yet not be surprised if unsuccessful—to obtain a warranty of merchantability from the countertrader.

FINANCIAL AND CREDIT TERMS

After the counterpurchase ratio has been negotiated, the parties must agree upon the value of the countertrade products that will fulfill that ratio. Specified in hard currency or clearing currency, the price of the countertrade items should be expressed in a manner so as to avoid any overreaching on the part of the importer—a most favoured customer clause might prove useful in this regard.[36] The price should also account for hidden costs that are often overlooked. First, the price should account for the financing costs incurred by the exporter during the period between the original export and delivery of the counterpurchase. Second, the price should reflect the costs of obtaining guarantees for non-execution of the counterpurchase by the exporter. Third, the price should account for the costs of commissioning middlemen (eg, export trading organisations and switch traders) and any discounts that may have to be made in disposing of the countertrade items.

RESALE RESTRCTIONS

The importer will usually attempt to impose geographic and commercial marketing restrictions on the resale of the countertrade goods in order to avoid the discounting of such items in existing cash markets. Restrictions of this sort can be extremely harmful to the exporter if it is unable to resell countertrade items in accordance with those stringent guidelines. The exporter should attempt to limit such restrictions in the counterpurchase agreement. In particular, the exporter should, at minimum, insist upon a limited ability to sell countertrade items to third parties. If the exporter is restricted in the geographic markets in which he may resell the countertrade items, he should attempt to secure from the importer the exclusive right to distribute such items in those limited markets in order to avoid being undercut by competing sellers.[37]

TIME LIMITS

The time limit imposed by a countertrade agreement typically ranges from one to two years, except in the case of long-term compensation arrangements. While many trade experts suggest negotiating for the longest possible time (to allow for selection of the best available items, manufacturing delays and administrative delays involved in international shipping), the exporter should also consider the financing costs resulting from such time lags. On the other side of the coin, the exporter should attempt to get some form of credit for counterpurchases made ahead of schedule.[38] The counterpurchase agreement should also provide that any bank or other guarantee of performance should be reduced *pro rata* as counterpurchase obligations are fulfilled.

EVENTS OF DEFAULT AND DISPUTE RESOLUTION

If the exporter fails to fulfill its countertrade obligation within the period of time prescribed by the agreement, it will be required to pay the hard currency penalty. As noted above, such penalties can constitute a significant portion of the value of the export, and the foreign party will typically require, prior to executing the countertrade agreement, a bank guarantee for this penalty. The importance of negotiating as small a penalty as possible cannot be overstated. The default penalty is more than just a form of liquidated damages—it is an alternative to the counterpurchase obligation, which may become commercially impossible for the exporter to satisfy. If small enough, the default penalty may become a preferred course of action for the exporter at the outset (eg, the price of the export can be inflated to cover the penalty).

While an exporter should attempt to negotiate default remedies should the countertrade party be unable to meet its counter-obligations, the inclusion of such provisions are discouraged by countertrade importers, who would be hard pressed to meet hard currency penalties. Nonetheless, the exporter should attempt to obtain reciprocal penalties in the event that the importer defaults in the delivery of countertrade items when and as promised (eg, defective products, untimely delivery or failure thereof, etc).

The counterpurchase agreement should also contain detailed force majeure provisions that anticipate international and domestic export controls dumping actions, countervailing duty imposition and perhaps even antitrust liabilities.

Finally, the counterpurchase agreement should contain an explicit arbitration provision if insurmountable problems arise in the countertrade deal. This is especially important because traditional litigation might not be effective in policing a countertrade transaction due to language problems, cost and the difficulty in conducting discovery. Such a provision should spell out the details of arbitration, such as the place of arbitration, governing rules, languge of arbitral proceedings and costs. The exporter should ensure that the place chosen for any such arbitration subscribes to the 1958 UN Convention on Recognition and Enforcement of Aribtral Awards. The importer should also be asked to waive the defence of sovereign immunity.

NOTES

1. Organisation for Economic Cooperation and Development, *East-West Trade—Recent Developments in Countertrade* 133 (1981) (hereinafter cited as OECD).

2. US International Trade Commission, *Analysis of Recent Trends in US Countertrade* 10 (1982) hereinafter cited as ITC).

3. L. Welt, *Countertrade—Business Practices for Today's World Market* 9 (1982) (hereinafter cited as Welt).

4. *Id.*

5. OECD, *supra* note 1, at 54.

6. See generally ITC, note 2, at 4.

7. *Id.*

8. *Id.*

9. *Id.*

10. 'Why Banks Have to Barter.' *Euromoney Trade Finance Report* 18 (May 1983).

11. *Id.*

12. *Id.*

13. *Id.*

14. US Department of Commerce (International Trade Administration), *Countertrade Practices in East Europe, the Soviet Union and China: An Introductory Guide to Business* 11-13 (1980).

15. ITC, *supra* note 2, at 7.

16. Address by Budimir Kostic (Executive Vice President, Udruzena Beogradska Banka), in Ehrenhaft, *Countertrade: International Trade Without Cash* 237 (1983) (hereinafter cited as Ehrenhaft).

17. *Id.* at 239.

18. Dizard, 'The Explosion of International Barter,' *Fortune,* Feb, 7, 1983, at 89-90 (hereinafter cited as Dizard).

19. *Id.* at 90.

20. 'Growing Worries Over Buy-Back Deals,' *Chemical Week,* June 2, 1982 at 38 (quoting Frank R. Popoff, President of Dow Chemical Europe).

21. *Id.*

22. Maidenberg, 'Bartering Aids Poor Nations,' *New York Times,* Jan 17, 1983, at D8, col 4.

23. Dizard, *supra* note 18, at 95.

24. For a detailed discussion of domestic and international export controls in the context of countertrade, *see* Cunningham, 'US Import Laws Affecting Countertrade,' Fleischmann, 'Existing Legal Framework in US Applicable to Countertrade,' Gadbaw, 'The Implications of Countertrade Under the General Agreement on Tariffs and Trade,' and Marcuss, 'Export Controls and Countertrade,' in Ehrenhaft, *supra* note 16, at 39-106.

25. For an excellent discussion of countertrade agreements, *see* Park, 'Countertrade Requirements in East-West Transactions.' 10 *International Business Lawyer* 122-124 (April 1982).

26. Only two countries have specifically enacted legislation imposing CT requirements—Romania and Indonesia. Many other countries have implemented CT arrangements by means of regulation, administrative guidance or informal encouragement.

27. OECD, *supra* note 1, at 24.

28. *Id.*

29. *Id.*at 25.

30. Marks, 'Counselling US Clients in Countertrade Transactions', in Ehrenhaft, *supra* note 16, at 150. Despite the admonitions against the use of a single agreement, however, if the terms of either of the two contracts are reviewed by a competent tribunal, they will likely be viewed as a single, albeit two-part, transaction. In any event, a single contract can be drafted to defeat the expectations of the exporter if the export and the counterpurchase are not made contingent upon one another and if the default on either side of the transaction is expressly contemplated and provided for in the contract. In fact, a carefully drafted contract encompassing the entire transaction may be more advantageous to the exporter than dual contracts linked by a protocol, for such a contract would clearly evidence the parties' intent in the event of a default and not leave any issues open to speculation.

31. *Id.* at 150-151.

32. *See* OECD, *supra* note 1, at 37-56. *See also* Marks, 'Counselling US Clients in Countertrade Transactions', Ehrenhaft and Nelson, 'Counselling US Clients in Countertrade Transactions,' in Ehrenhaft, *supra* note 16, at 149-89.

33. OECD, *supra* note 1, at 38-43.

34. Park, 'Countertrade Requirements in East-West Transactions,' 10 *International Business Lawyer* 123 (April 1982).

35. OECD, *supra* note 1, at 43-44.

36. Nelson, 'Counseling US Clients in Countertrade Transactions,' in Ehrenhaft, *supra* note 16, at 168.

37. *Id* at 172.

38. *Id.* at 164.

Section IV: Negotiating and Structuring Loan Agreements

Chapter 13: Financial Issues

13A. Country Risk and International Bank Lending

Ingo Walter

I. INTRODUCTION

Economics and law are closely interwoven in international bank lending. An event of default may portent economic losses to international banks, and the legal sanctions that accompany such an event may significantly influence borrower behavior. At the same time, legal protection offers only limited comfort to banks lending to private or sovereign foreign borrowers. To minimize the risk of severe economic losses, a bank must carefully analyze the borrower's ability and willingness to service its external debt, whether that borrower is an individual, a corporation, or a country.

This article gives an economist's perspective on country risk, beginning with a discussion of the nature of country exposure, and how that exposure relates to a bank's global loan portfolio. The article outlines an approach to country risk assessment and suggests the manner in which that assessment can be built into international lending decisions.

II. EXPOSURE TO COUNTRY RISK

International bank lending involves several sources of risk that differ from purely domestic lending. One source of risk is that the foreign borrower resides in a politically sovereign national state different from that of the lender. Even though the creditworthiness of a particular foreign borrower may have been established to the bank's satisfaction, events may occur that could prevent the borrower from meeting its obligations under the terms of the loan. For example, the economy of the country in which the borrower is located may take a sudden turn for the worse, seriously threatening the borrower's ability to service its debt. The borrower's country may experience a balance of payments emergency and impose exchange controls that, in turn, would prevent a financially healthy borrower from meeting foreign debt obligations. The lender also risks violent political upheavals that could close or destroy a borrower's factories. By making such a loan, therefore, the lender takes on two kinds of risk: *credit risk* associated with the borrower itself and *country risk*[1] associated with conditions in the nation where the borrower resides.

If, on the other hand, a bank lends directly to a foreign government, or to a non-governmental borrower under unconditional government guarantee, the bank incures no credit risk because the government has unlimited power to create money to servie the debt. The bank still carries country risk, however, because the government may be unable or unwilling to service the external debt, which usually is denominated and payable in currencies other than its own.[2]

Diversification—lending to a wide variety of borrowers to reduce the chances that repayment problems on the part of any single borrower will seriously affect bank earnings and capital—is a fundamental principle of banking. By diversifying, a bank can reduce the total level of risk in its overall loan portfolio. Diversification, however, assumes that the financial fortunes of borrowers are substantially independent. Unfortunately, the assumption that several borrowers will not simultaneously encounter difficulties is not always valid, and a severe recession could bring about a flood of failures among a bank's clients and, conceivably, failure of the bank itself. Risk associated with individual borrower performance may be termed *unsystematic risk*. Risk associated with the broader environment within which the borrower exists is called *systematic risk*. Unsystematic risk can be reduced, conceivably even to zero, by means of careful diversification of a bank's loan portfolio. Systematic risk, however, cannot be reduced by diversification without changing the rules of the game. Using this terminology, credit risks associated with cross-border loans to borrowers in Country X are unsystematic and can be reduced by means of portfolio diversification. Yet, if all borrowers are located in Country X, the bank remains subject to country risk, which is systematic. Country exposure, therefore, defines an important source of risk in international lending and demands careful monitoring and evaluation.

This analysis does not mean that country risk is ultimately systematic and therefore completely irreducible. Country risk can be made unsystematic simply by diversifying a bank's loan portfolio across borrowers located in a variety of different countries. Based on an analyst's evaluation of future political and economic conditions in different countries, and on the profitability of lending in those countries, a bank will set exposure limits for each country so that the global loan portfolio achieves the desired degree of internatinal diversification.

The extent of risk-reduction that can be achieved even by global portfolio diversification, however, is limited. To be reducible, risk must be unsystematic; the economic and political futures of countries in which the bank is exposed must be substantially independent. Certain events, however, have worldwide impact. If, for example, OPEC doubles oil prices[3] or global interest rates rise, numerous countries simultaneously may suffer economic troubles. Similarly, if Vietnam invades Thailand, or Russia invades Poland, many countries would be affected, destroying the assumption of country-risk independence. This phenomenon constitutes another form of systematic risk called *ambient risk*.

Banks thus face a constellation of unsystematic and systematic risks. Management's job is to maximize the bank's returns subject to an "acceptable" overall level of risk or, stated differently, to minimize the overall level of risk subject to a target rate of return. The bank can do this, to a degree, by carefully balancing the rate of return it seeks and its exposure to risk entities, setting maximum limits for such exposure in order to achieve the desired degree of portfolio diversification. Careful monitoring of exposure risk is essential for management to succeed in maximizing the value of the bank to its shareholders. Earnings failures will be reflected quickly in the share prices of a bank's stock, but an increase in the perceived riskiness of a bank's position will create immediate effects in the stock market.[4]

Exposure to country risk probably is the most difficult source of risk for a bank to measure. Consequently, it must first develop a system for tracking its exposure in individual countries. Every cross-border loan or investment should be captured by a centralized information system set up for that purpose. All cross-border loan arrangements, no matter where they originate in the bank's global operations, must be reported into this system and classified by the term of the loan (for example, less than one year, one to three years, or more than three years).[5] Moreover, a cross-border loan to Country X which is guaranteed by an entity in Country Y is booked as Y-risk and not X-risk, so that the country of lending and the country of risk may be different—a particularly troublesome problem with complex financings such as shipping loans.

Once a tracking system has been set in place, the bank always will know its country exposure, both credits extended and drawdowns, by terms. The system allows the bank to determine quickly whether its exposure is within the country limits established by management. In some banks, the same system also can provide information on exposure to individual borrowers, industry, sectors, and other risk-relevant categories.

In addition, an exposure tracking system generally will record claims on the bank by countries.[6]

Thus, a bank can use country risk analysis to evaluate the political and economic future of nations in order to establish the risks and returns associated with country exposures, set appropriate exposure limits, and construct diversified global asset portfolios which maximize the bank's economic value to its shareholders. For an established rate of return, the level of a bank's exposure in a particular country will be lowered as the perceived risk associated with that country rises. Table 1 presents the output of one bank's risk evaluation system, as of mid-1981. Such rankings are difficult to derive and defend because country risk assessment is still an art rather than a science. Nevertheless, careful economic, political, and social analysis will continue to be extremely important for international lenders.[7]

III. ELEMENTS OF RISK ANALYSIS

A. Structural Aspects

The first question in risk analysis is whether developments in the internal workings of a national economy, both on the supply and demand sides, will seriously threaten the country's ability to service its external debt obligations. Analysts are particularly interested in the linkages between the supply side's capability to produce export, import-competing, and non-traded goods, and in the qualitative and quantitative dimensions of the labor force, capital stock, natural resource base, technology, and entrepreneurship that combine to determine this capability. At the same time, they evaluate the contributions of real capital inflows to these supply capabilities made possible by foreign borrowing, foreign direct investment, and other types of financial transfers.

Historical measures of supply-side economic performance abound, including labor force growth and paricipation rates, unemployment rates, migration and labor force distributional trends, savings and investment trends, productivity trends, and natural resource availability. The quality, timeliness, and comparability of the relevant data, however vary widely. Further analyzing the past may not be a good guide to forecasting for the future. For example, a great deal of judgment is required to identify and project various types of quantitative or qualitative labor-supply ceilings and possible market disruptions, social and economic infrastructure bottlenecks, capital adequacy problems, and natural resource constraints. The evaluation of governmental policies and the underlying complex of incentives and disincentives built into the nation's fiscal and regulatory system are especially important in establishing a sound investment scheme. In many cases such policies are anchored in government planning documents. An assessment of the degree of realism embodied in these plans may be quite important; government attempts to force the supply side of an economy into a mold that does not fit, but to which a political commitment has been made, can lead to severe domestic and international distortions in the real sector, ballooning of external borrowing, and, ultimately, to debt service problems.

On the demand side, lenders consider factors affecting taxes, government expenditures, transfer payments, and the overall fiscal soundness of the public sector. Also important are prospective patterns of demand for goods and services from the private and export sectors. As with supply-side analysis, historical data series covering consumption spending, government taxation and expenditures, gross national product or gross domestic product, and other conventional economic indicators usually are available on a reasonably timely basis to permit an evaluation of the demand picture over a number of years. Forecasts depend in large part, however, on the ability to predict government demand management and income distribution policies, as well as external demand-side shocks that may emanate from the foreign sector, changing expectations, or other sources.

In attempting to develop a defensible prognosis of the structural aspects of country futures, therefore, the analyst must start with complete information about the historical track-record of the domestic economy and its current situation and then try to project both the demand-side and supply-side dimensions. Short-term forecasts usually do not pose serious difficulties: the sources of error multiply as the forecasting period is extended because few of the important determinants of economic performance can be considered constant. Analysts simply cannot achieve certainty when projecting what will happen to taxes, government regulation, consumption and saving patterns, and other economic factors five or ten years in the future. Forecasting over the longer term must rely in large measure, therefore, on the basic competence of the policymakers, their receptivity to outside advice, and the pattern of social and political constraints under which they operate. Assuming the cast of political characters remains the same, experience in macroeconomic management and reactions to outside shocks may be a fair guide to the future.

B. Monetary Aspects

Understanding the monetary sector is a crucial element in projecting future country scenarios. While most country analyses contain extensive descriptions of the national financial system, prices and exchange rates are the most important factors. The domestic monetary base, the money supply, net domestic credit, and net foreign official assets and debt also may be useful indicators. Monetary disturbances can originate domestically or from the foreign sector. In addition to inflationary and exchange-rate effects, such disturbances can have real-sector influences on consumption and savings, capital formation, and income distribution.

The mechanisms relating monetary developments to debt service problems are well understood, and the requisite data usually is readily available to analysts. As with structural analysis, however, near-term assessments are far easier to formulate than defensible long-range outlooks.[8] The more difficult task of forecasting government responses to monetary problems such as devaluation, liberalization of controls, and domestic monetary stringency, and the timing of such measures, boils down to competence of the monetary policymakers and the political pressures bearing upon them. Accuracy is crucial to banks which often have exposures extending over a decade or more.

C. External Economic Aspects

Because of the importance of foreign exchange availability in projecting debt service, country assessments usually must reflect outside factors affecting a country's balance of payments and external finance. This includes, for example, the long-term trends and short-term instabilities of exports. Increasing product and market diversification might be a sign of greater export stability and reduced vulnerability to shifting economic and political conditions, or protectionist trends in a country's major markets. In addition, shifts in the ratio of exports to gross national product may signal changing future debt service capabilities, and an analysis of demand and supply elasticities for major export products may indicate possible sources of future instability in export receipts. Domestic export-supply constraints and export-competing demand elements relate to the analysis of structural problems, outlined above. Export policies and exchange-rate policies set by the national government, and by governments of competing exporters, also may be important. In general, lenders review the alignment of a country's exports with its international competitive advantage, the diversification of export risk, and the home and third-country policies that might pose a threat to future export earnings.

Analysts must also examine the long-term trends and short-term instabilities of a country's imports. The ratio of imports to gross national products reveals little about country risk, but abrupt and sizeable shifts in this ratio may be important. A country's ability to compress imports in times of balance of payments trouble may be considered in measures such as the ratio of food and fuel to total imports, or the ratio of food, fuel, intermediate goods, and capital equipment to total imports. Import price volatility, supplier concentration among trading partners, and trends in import-replacement production are other measures that may help identify risk elements originating on the import side. Here also, as with exports, the policy context is telling; the structure of effective tariff and non-tariff protection and its impact on domestic resource allocation and efficiency in production will sway long-term lending policies.

Foreign direct investment, on the supply side of a national economy, contributes to aggregate and sectoral capital formation, technology transfer, development of human resources, management and entrepreneurial activity, access to markets, and access to supplies. In addition, while the balance of payments gains are associated with capital inflows, induced export and import-replacement production, outflows may occur via induced imports of goods, services, and profit remittances. Each foreign investment project, therefore, constitutes a unique balance of payment profile, in magnitude as well as in timing.

Many countries have policies that directly affect foreign investment, such as taxation, restrictions on earnings remittances, indigenization pressures, nationalization, and expropriation. All of these factors may influence the international lenders' evaluation of a country's prospects. Multinational companies often are extraordinarily sensitive to changes in national policy environments; because they can protend change in the overall creditworthiness of countries, shifts in foreign direct investment patterns deserve careful attention. Capital outflows on the part of domestic residents also can reflect the domestic outlook, especially in times of possible discontinuous policy changes.

A final important factor in analyzing the external factors in a country's economy is the magnitude and types of grants and concessional loans that a country receives or is likely to receive from abroad. The domestic policies of the country will play a major role in determining the likelihood of aid from foreign sources. Moreover, countries of strategic or economic importance obviously are prime candidates for future intergovernmental "rescues" which may backstop private bank lending exposure in severe problem situations and increase likelihood of successfully concluding "workout" situations.[10]

D. Liquidity Aspects

The issues already discussed usually involve medium and long-range forecasts of such aggregates as the balance of trade, net capital movements, and various other "flow" measures. These measures are reflected in a country's future international reserve position and in its access to international financial markets for future financing needs. Near-term "liquidity" assessments, in contrast, generally focus on changes in a country's owned reserves and International Monetary Fund position and on ratios such as reserves to monthly imports, which are intended to indicate the degree of security provided by reserve holdings. The ability to borrow additional sums abroad, or to refinance existing debt, naturally depends on the projected state of financial markets and assessment of country creditworthiness by international banks and official institutions at the time of need. Favorable financial-market and country conditions sometimes lead to preemptive borrowing by countries to restructure outstanding debt at market terms and to build up reserves for future use or to improve future creditworthiness.

The size and structure of country indebtedness and debt service payments also indicate a country's short-term financial condition. Ratios such as total debt to exports or to gross national product and long-term public debt to exports or to gross national product are used in virtually all country analyses as are the amount and trends in overall external indebtedness, current versus term debt, and total and short-term bank claims. The "debt service ratio"—debt service payments to exports or "normal" exports—is perhaps the most common, but it can be inaccurate. For example, because the debt service ratio uses only exports in the denominator, it ignores the potentially equivalent contributions of import-substitution to debt-service capabilities. Moreover, a particular debt-service ratio may not mean equivalent creditworthiness for two different countries.

In addition, lenders commonly use the ratios of foreign capital inflows to debt service payments; exports plus capital inflows and aid receipts to current debt; vital imports plus debt service payments to exports plus capital inflows and aid receipts ("compressibility ratio"); and the reciprocal of the average maturity of external debt ("rollover ratio") to measure liquidity.

Banks' fondness for ratios in country analysis is derived in part from the techniques of financial analysis they apply to commercial borrowers. The similarities, however, clearly can be exaggerated. All such ratios must be interpreted cautiously; each has a different meaning for different countries as well as for the same country at different times and stages of development. There are no valid generalizations. The analytical skill lies in the interpretation of any ratios used, and changes therein, and in the specific context of particular country situations. Yet, even if a good bank analyst recognizes the limitations of some of the more pedestrian indicators, the indicators nevertheless may figure heavily and perhaps mechanically into how other banks view the situation in a debt rollover context, and therefore must be monitored carefully.

E. Political Aspects

In addition to charting domestic structural and monetary factors and external stock and flow variables, country analyis related to bank exposure always requires astute political forecasting. A crucial variable is the "competence" or "wisdom" of the economic managers which, insofar as it relates to the cast of characters on the stage, is basically a political matter. Small changes in the actors can cause enormous changes in the quality of the play. The issues are whether the technocrats have a full political mandate to "do what is necessary" to service the country's debt and, ultimately, whether the government itself is stable and has the political power to fulfill its policies. Recent turmoils in Argentina, Turkey, Zaire, Jamaica, Peru, and Poland illustrate the critical importance of evaluating and forecasting the political "overlay" of national economic policymaking—the degree of resolve, the power base, and the tools available for implementing sound policy decisions. The leading banks that engage in country analysis generally stress this particular dimension, which requires an entirely different information base than some of the more mechanical aspects of risk analysis. Political analysis is very difficult, however, due to the immense number of developments that analysts must monitor and forecast.

Internal political change may range from gradual to abrupt, systemic to nonsystemic, and cataclysmic to trivial in terms of its importance to international lenders. Political drift to either the right or left may sharply change the internal and external workings of a national economy and the quality of economic management, as demonstrated by the recent history of countries like Brazil, Mexico, Chile, and Sri Lanka. The symptoms of such change are felt in domestic fiscal and monetary policies, relations with foreign countries, pressures for nationalization or indigenization of foreign direct investments, and imposition of exchange controls. Adverse political shifts may result in soaring imports, reduced capacity to export, drying-up of foreign direct investment, capital flight, aid cutoffs, and problems in accessing international capital markets. The direction, magnitude, and timing of political drift, therefore, must be fixed before future macroeconomic scenarios can be understood.

More dramatic consequences arise from violent internal political conflict. These conflicts may produce rapid political change or the type of drift discussed above; in the meantime, the conflict itself can have major direct economic consequences. Strikes, terrorism, sabotage, and popular insurrection seriously disrupt a national economy, with potentially dramatic consequences for the balance of payments. Export industries such as tourism are particularly sensitive to such conflicts. In addition, the direct and indirect import requirements of government anti-insurgency efforts can be significant. The strength of the insurgency movement balanced against the government's strength will help forecast the duration and outcome of the conflict, which, if it results in systemic change, may even lead to repudiation of external debt. As the Iranian revolution demonstrated, such forecasts are as treacherous as they are critical to the whole process of country analysis. The assassination of South Korean President Park Chung Hee also illustrates the broad range of possible outcomes of violent political events: from total insignificance to a fundamental political and economic overthrow of the existing order.

External political conflict likewise takes a variety of forms, ranging from invasion and foreign-inspired or supported insurgency to border tension and perceived external threats. Threats from abroad often require far-reaching domestic resource reallocation in the form of inflated defense spending, causing probable adverse trade shifts, and large direct foreign exchange costs. Military hardware, human resources, and the economic infrastructure generally are not productive in terms of the domestic economy or the balance of payments, and thus contribute nothing to the basis of effective future debt service. These distortions alone may have a serious bearing on the risk profile of a country.

Economic threat to lenders lies in both potential and actual external conflict. The latter simply exacerbates the various distortions if the costs are not absorbed by foreign political allies. Actual conflict also results in supply-side damages of physical and human-resource destruction and dislocation, obsolescence, and reconstruction costs to the extent these are not offset by reparations or aid-receipts. Even if the external conflict is won, derivative internal political upheavals and possibly sizeable costs of occupation sway country risks. If the conflict is lost, however, continued internal resistance and reparations obligations may have a debilitating effect on the home economy. Further, a successor regime may repudiate the country's debt. Consequently, lending to countries such as South Korea, Taiwan, Thailand, Yugoslavia and Pakistan, where tensions always are evident, requires careful consideration of external political influences.

Shifting political alliances, regional political developments and bilateral relations over such peripheral issues as human rights and nuclear proliferation can provide additional sources of political conflict. All are influenced heavily by global, regional, and national political events. Major lending exposure in Eastern Europe and China carries risks related both to future political developments as well as the ability of the borrowers to sever links to Western trade and financial markets at acceptable economic cost to themselves.

Political forecasting is an art which, despite its central role in plotting the creditworthiness future of countries, remains in its infancy. Indices of political stability developed by political scientists are not reliable indicators of future political events which will have implications for debt service.[11] More sophisticated projections, and even on-line information systems detailing possible sources of internal and external political conflict, while useful and necessary, usually leave the critical judgments to the user of the information. Furthermore, political information often is incomplete or out-of-date, and is laced with the biases embedded in external and in-house information which consensual approaches such as the "delphi" technique have only begun to attack.[12] It is not surprising, therefore, that political forecasts by banks and others misjudged the dramatic changes in Iran and South Korea, the external conflicts affecting Argentina and Zaire, and the less dramatic shifts elsewhere. Significant forecasting advances, however, are still possible.[13]

Country analysis as applied to international banking exposure amounts to nothing more than astute political-economic forecasting, cutting across a variety of disciplines, sources of information, and analytical techniques. Ideally, a country risk assessor is a true "renaissance person": exceedingly intelligent, with doctorates from respectable institutions in economics, political science, law, sociology, psychology, and a few other fields as well; totally objective, with a great deal of common sense. In addition to being well-traveled, the person would be up-to-date on development in all countries of interest to the bank, and personally acquainted with key policymakers. Obviously, few people meet these qualifications. The question, therefore, is whether international banks as institutions, can put together all of these qualities in a sensible way, using "ordinary" people and traditional organizational structures to develop expertise in accurately forecasting the economic and political futures of countries. Such forecasts would bear on the economic value of the bank's exposed assets and shape its global portfolio management.

IV. MANAGING INTERNATIONAL LENDING

A. System Design

The flow of information within the organizational structure of an international bank, and its assembly in a form that is useful for decision makers are important aspects of risk analysis. A completely defensible portrayal of a country's future and its creditworthiness implications would fill a book for each nation in which the bank has actual or potential exposure; the book would be updated every six months, or whenever there is a significant change in bank interest or country circumstances.[14] However, such analyses would be rather useless for decisionmaking by the bank. Although the analyses probably would give the only conceptually correct and comprehensive overview of all the critical variables, each highly country-specific, and the various interrelationships among them, banks usually operate under severe time pressures and under fiscal and human resource constraints. Consequently, extensive, unwieldy analyses would be unfit for day to day decisionmaking.

More useful than the custom-tailored, encyclopedic country analyses are purely "descriptive" country studies, with responsibility for judgments vested in country economists or in line personnel. Employing a format particularly well suited to the country in question, such studies typically try to cover all of the political and economic bases, using often-voluminous data but relatively little analysis.[15] These studies tend to be heavily retrospective and subjective, using no standardized formating in order to avoid straightjacketing the discussion. This approach is particularly conducive to political assessments, which are unavoidably "soft." Although comparability suffers, the focus on specific country-attributes and prospects is maintained. The descriptive structure of the analysis, however, inhibits updating the information, and, therefore, distilling the essence of unstructured descriptive studies for use in landing decisions is difficult.

The evident shortcomings of this approach are alleviated in part by "structured qualitative" country analysis. By using a standard, relatively short format for all countries under review, this technique severely reduces narrative and greatly expands use of data, standard ratios, and trend-assessments.[16] The analysis retains qualitative elements to the extent possible in the abbreviated format. Country-specific sources of risk are kept in the analysis if possible, but usability is enhanced by requiring overseas or headquarters line personnel to prepare carefully worded summaries in standardized formats. The major American international banks have used their staff economists to prepare such summaries, with each economist typically following several countries in a particular part of the world. In addition to conventional sources of country data, periodic country visits and information flows from bank representatives in the field are supposed to update country files and improve the quality of analysis. The standard format in the structured qualitative approach is intended to facilitate cross-country comparisons without loss of too much qualitative country-specific information. In fact, the analysis sometimes deemphasizes political risk and adopts a heavily restrospective focus.

Efforts to overcome such weaknesses in qualitative assessments, and at the same time enchance usability in decisionmaking, have produced "check-list" systems.[17] By using the same kind of information base as the structured qualitative analysis, backed up by a formal narrative country study, analysts attempt to assign grades both to quantitative and qualitative variable. Each grade is then assigned a weight, and one or several weighted summary scores are computed. Summary scores capture not only the historical evidence, but also the future outlook as reflected in the score-assignment and weighting process. The weighted checklist approach supposedly facilitates country risk monitoring and cross-country comparisons by using a portfolio approach to international exposure management, as well as permitting an audit of the performance of the system.

In addition to weighted country scores, several banks have developed more spohisticated systems to generate composite measures of debt service capacity, political stability, and adaptability to external shocks. Weighted input measures are used to generate the composite indicators which are then sometimes displayed in grid or matrix format. Table 1 above represents a country-classification typical of such a system.

Despite their advantages in country comparisons and usability in lending decisions, weighted checklist systems suffer from a variety of ills. The selection of indicators tends to be subjective and often is not based on a coherent underlying behavioral model. Grading of indicators likewise tends to be subjective, as is the assignment of weights. The same indicators and weights are used for all countries examined, despite obvious differences between the countries' situations. Nonquantifiable information often is ignored, which may deemphasize some country-specific elements that can have a strong bearing on risk. Perhaps the greatest potential problem, however, lies in overreliance upon, and abuse of, such systems in lending decisions. In an area where the use of forecasting in decisionmaking, especially in the long term, is akin to grasping at straws, this technique may be particularly dangerous in the wrong hands.

Finally, lenders chart "market-related" indicators of country risk based on the maturity-weighted mean spreads over the London Interbank Offered Rate that countries have had to pay in syndicated Eurocurrency borrowings. As the weighted means spread grows, the relative degree of risk that banks must perceive with regard to a particular country's borrowings increases. However, such market rankings often neglect fee-type income and relationship considerations, which may substitute for narrow spreads. Moreover, low spreads in a particular country simply may reflect erroneous country assessments by the banks involved, especially where the number of loans is small. Special-purpose loans and portfolio-diversification considerations—the diversification value of incremental exposure in a particular country—also may be higher than some others simply because a country is relatively independent of factors affecting others; this encourages banks to accept lower spreads.

The twin temptations of "quick and dirty" and "overloaded" country assessments constantly seem to confront international banks. The first approach promises mechanical short-cuts and the use of low-priced talent to grind out results at reasonable cost, but often appears to succeed only in producing nonsense; there is no substitute for high-quality analysis, flexibility, judgment, and familiarity. The second approach may rely on well-qualified internal personnel at high cost, yet encounter a dangerous narrowing of country expertise, possibly cause dissension, and create bottlenecks in the decisionmaking process.

The conflicting demands of country assessment, the need for levels of usability and comparability, the need to capture exceedingly complex and country-specific qualitative judgments over extended periods of time, and the need to avoid abuse of the results in decisionmaking, probably preclude development of an "ideal" system. "Appropriate" systems certainly will differ for different banks. The key may be to efficiently use human resources as well as technology. Training line bankers to use reasonably unsophisticated yet sensible country assessments properly and to be sensitive to changing country risk profiles may contribute more to sound portfolio decisions than devoting comparable resources to the design and implementation of elegant analysis systems. For example, multinational banks seems to have a competitive advantage through the use of "information factories," to which their global operations and headquarters-affiliate links are ideally suited. Whether in systems-design or in the training function, resources devoted to the assessment of country risk clearly are subject to constraints, and some implicit optimum exists when the incremental costs in country assessment begin to outweigh the economic losses implicit in sub-optimal international loan portfolios.

The country analysis function is the beginning, not the end, of the portfolio management task in international lending. Approaches that try to be overly precise can trigger arguments among users over irrelevant points. Too general approaches may fail to concentrate on true sources of risk in country exposure and on specific concerns facing a particular bank.

B. Institutional Considerations

Once the nature of the country evaluation problem is discovered within the context of portfolio decisions in international lending, and the available analytical techniques are reviewed, lenders must establish the institutional setting within which this process will occur. As noted above, information on cross-border exposure of a bank generally is maintained by a monitoring system at its head office. The office receives and consolidates information on the size and tenor of credit facilities granted, draw downs, redeposits, and other pertinent data both from the originating offices and from the country offices where the exposure is incurred. Exposure data, along with the established country limits and term sublimits, usually are updated frequently and made available to responsible officers within the bank in periodic printed reports or through on-line systems.

The officers responsible for running the bank's country analysis system normally are in close communication with the line bankers; sometimes bank officers perform both functions. When a major credit is contemplated, or a shift in exposure limits seems justified by loan demand, profitability trends, or alterations in perceived risks, the bank may form an *ad hoc* country review group consisting of responsible lending officers, senior officials with regional responsibility, country economists, and other specialists. The group would recommend a course of action based upon the overall strategic goals of the bank and its positioning in the market concerned. The purpose is to bring together as many different viewpoints as possible, often with conflicting opinions.[18]

Each bank's institutional information flow and decision-making set-up with respect to country risk has its own profile, depending on such factors as the bank's size and structure. Some banks incorporate country assessments into portfolio decisions quite flexibly and informally, while others rely on rigid and formalized review procedures.[19] In some cases the review process is closely tied to the annual budget cycle and to the allocation of lending authority to countries and regions. Again, the system may be quite rigid in some banks, while in others decisions are relatively easily altered as perceived market and risk conditions change. In some banks, the determination of "loan loss provisions" is an integral part of the process. The standard affects the anticipated net profitability of loans by adjusting for risk and presumably permits improved performance evaluation within the bank's organizational framework.

While almost all international banks maintain adequate cross-border exposure measurement, allocation, and monitoring, the state of country assessment systems in those banks varies widely.[20] Some systems are devised carefully, while others are largely cosmetic or pseudo-scientific. Some are integrated into the life of the organization, while others seem separate and even isolated. Until fairly recently, smaller U.S. banks tended to rely on the risk evaluations of the larger money center banks, particularly when participating in loan syndications. Besides being unsatisfactory from a regulatory point of view, the appropriate risk-return calculus of the lead banks is not necessarily the same as that of the smaller banks. With some exceptions, on the other hand, banks in Europe and Japan traditionally have placed less emphasis on the design of formal approaches to country assessment and incorporating them into international lending decisions, preferring instead to rely more informally on the collective experience and wisdom of senior bank offiers.

V. CONCLUSION

Country risk analysis represents a complex, difficult, yet critical function in international banking. Without it, individual country-related economic losses related to default, reschedulings, forced refinancings, and other problems cannot be avoided. More importantly, only astute country risk assessment can ensure the ability of bank management to design and implement rational asset portfolios worldwide.

Whatever approach international banks use, rational portfolio decisions demand that forecasts of country futures be maintained on a comparable basis and modified in the light of country-interdependencies arising out of factors such as common export markets or sources of supply, conditions in and access to international financial markets, and regional and global political developments. Moreover, in assessing the impact of a particular change in country exposure on the value of a bank's asset portfolio as a whole, both the specific country-related profile of returns and the intercountry linkage of those returns are important. The latter factor is easily masked by an exclusive focus on country-specific sources of risk. Big lenders envision the application of country risk in a portfolio context with risk-aversion dictated by top management, correctly attributed returns estimated by formal or informal approaches to country evaluation, and country-interdependencies brought into the picture by setting limits and term sublimits.

†*Ingo Walter is Professor of Economics and Finance, Graduate School of Business Administration, New York University. A.B. 1962, M.S. 1963, Lehigh University; Ph.D. 1966, New York University.*

NOTES

1. Country risk encompasses what is often refered to as "sovereign risk."

2. *See* Long & Veneroso, *External Finance and the Balance of Payments of the Non-Oil Less Developed Countries: An Overview,* in The New International Economic Order (D. Denoon ed. 1979).

3. *See, e.g.,* P. Volcker, The Recycling Problem Revisited (Mar. 1980) (Federal Reserve Board mimeograph).

4. G. Feiger & B. Jacquillat, *International Bank Lending,* in International Finance Test and Acses (1982).

5. Association of Reserve City Bankers, *Country Exposure Measurement and Reporting Practices of Member Banks* (Mar. 1977).

6. Prudence does not permit netting out such redeposits against the bank's country exposure, but information regarding the bank's claims can be useful with regard to the right of set-off.

7. This discussion is based in part ofn Walter, *International Capital Allocation,* in Internationalization of Financial Markets and National Economic Policy (R. Hawkins, R. Levich & C. Wihlborg eds. 1982).

8. Analysts can evaluate the relationship of the existing exchange rate to some hypothetical market determined rate based on a calculated purchasing power parity index and project this deviation for the near term based on relative inflation trends. The larger the degree of currency overvaluation, for example, the greater the need for increased external borrowing will tend to be, and the greater the likelihood of reserve losses and/or the prospects for a tightening of controls on international trade and payments.

9. *See* T. Gladwin & I. Walter, Multinationals Under Fire: Lessons in the Management of Conflict (1980).

10. For a fascinating account of the Zaire rescue efforts, see *Erwin Blumenthal is Zaire's Last Hope,* Euromoney, Feb. 1979, at 9.

11. *See* Korbin, *Politicaal Risk: A Review and Reconsideration,* 10 J. Int's Bus. Stud. 67 (1979).

12. *See* Harner, *Rating Investment Risks Abroad,* 56 Bus. Horizons 49 (1979).

13. *See* T. Gladwin & I. Walter, *supra* note 9.

14. *See* Y. Maroni, Approaches for Assessing the Risks Involved in Lending

to Developing Countries (1977) (Federal Reserve Board mimeograph).

15. *See* Goodman, *How the Big U.S. Banks Really Evaluate Sovereign Risks,* Euromoney, Feb. 1977, at 105. *See also* Fry, *International Lending Risks,* Banker, Sept. 1977, at 126.

16. *See* van Agtmael, *Evaluating the Risks of Lending to Developing Countries,* Euromoney, Apr. 1976, at 16.

17. *See, e.g.,* Nagy, *Quantifying Country Risk: A System Developed by Economists at the Bank of Montreal,* 13 Colum. J. World Bus. 135 (1978).

18. For example, the country economist may emphasize the risks while the bankers emphasize business opportunities, competitive positioning, and the associated returns. Ultimate responsibility generally lies with a senior international credit officer, who reports directly to top management of the bank and is charged with monitoring and planning the bank's international loan portfolio within broad policy guidelines.

19. R. Senkew, Utilizing Risk Assessment in Decision-Making (Jan. 1980) (Bank of Montreal mimeograph).

20. D. Eiteman & J. Branin, Sovereign Risk Analysis by Commercial Banks (June 1979) (UCLA mimeograph). *See also* Assessing Country Risk (R. Ensor ed. 1981).

13B. The Mechanics of Eurodollar Transactions
Thomas Moffett

Editor's note: This extract discusses the key financial issues that borrowers should consider when negotiating a loan transaction. Each of the issues discussed will affect the overall cost and utility of the loan to the borrower.

ROLLOVER CONCEPT

A lending bank acts as an intermediary transforming short-term deposits into medium-term loans. While banks have been willing to accept the risk of continuing availability to them of funding deposits throughout the term of the loan and the credit risk that the borrower will be able to repay, banks have not been willing to take on the risk that rising costs of funds might erode or eliminate their profit margin. The spectacular swings of interest rates during the past year boldly underscores the magnitude of an unmatched funding risk, and so the concept of lending at a fixed margin over banks' incremental funding has grown up.

FUNDING AND BUSINESS DAYS

The most familiar funding base to which the margin or spread is added is cost of deposits in the eurocurrency inter-bank market. While interest rates have been determined at a spread over Certificates of Deposit (CD) rates or other domestic money market rates, and a growing number of loans are priced on U.S. banks' prime rates, the majority of syndicated loans are still priced over LIBOR, the London Interbank Offered Rate for deposits.

A bank participating in a syndicated loan must determine whether it will match fund or take a view on future interest rate movements. Assuming the bank adopts the prudent course of match-funding, a deposit must be taken for the exact period until the next interest setting date. This may be nominally 6 months but is adjusted if the next rollover date does not fall on a business day. In this case the interest period is extended to the next business day. If such translation would extend the interest period over month end into the next month, the date moves to the preceeding business day. Such a practice has led to considerable concentration of rate settings at the end of each month and a heavy work load for the agent bank during one or two days. Concern has also been voiced by the British Bankers Association which currently is consulting its members on their views with respect to permitting rollover dates to pass onto the following month.

Business days are usually defined as days on which banks and foreign exchange markets are open for business in New York, because that is where dollar payments are made, and in London because that is where rate settings take place. For purposes of determining interest periods, there is no reason to include the city of the borrower in the business day definition and can in practice lead to problems if it is not uncommon for holidays to be declared on short notice in the borrower's country.

Eurodollar deposits are usually paid through New York Clearing House Interbank Payment System on the same day funds, or as it is commonly known, through CHIPS. The settlement made of Clearing House Funds used to be a source of confusion because good funds were not available until the next day following payment. On October 1, 1981, procedures were adopted in New York for transactions cleared through CHIPS, which now gives same day value to transactions cleared prior to the new cut-off time, which is 4:00 pm. Fortunately the new clearing procedures came on-stream very smoothly.

Clearing House Funds now have the same day value as fed funds and as settlements in the major European currencies and Yen have. However in Europe the cut-off times for clearing tend to be early in the day.

Taking into account the difference between the time zones, instructions from London can seldom reach the Continent, and certainly not Japan, in time for clearing the same day, thus London eurocurrency rates in syndicated loans tend to be quoted on the basis that good funds will be made available two days following dealing.

In the case of a loan denominated in a currency other than dollars, the chief financial city of the country of that currency must replace New York in the definition of "Business Days". Reference rates can still be quoted in London if a eurocurrency is used as opposed to the domestic currency. The practicality of seeking quotations in London depends on how widely deposits in a currency are traded in London. Quotations for Sterling, Deutsch Marks, French Francs, Swiss Francs, and Yen are easy to obtain. The Scandinavian currencies are Dutch Guilders and have a pretty thin market here and there can be considerable discrepancies between quotations. You could find few banks to quote Saudi Rials and some of the deposits less commonly traded in London but rates may present wide discrepancies.

INTEREST PERIODS

Borrowers have been offered a wide number of interest rate periods in syndicated loans and their selection would normally depend on the view the borrower holds of future interest rate movements. One month periods result in a lot of administrative work for the agent because of the large number of rollovers. It can also be expensive for the borrower to make monthly interest payments if the time value of money is taken into account. Three and six month interest periods are the most commonly used. Nine month periods are occasionally seen in agreements but have always seemed to me an awkward period. At twelve months the deposit market begins to thin and a large rollover can move the rate considerably. Many lenders insist that if a 12 month period appears as an alternative, it should be subject to availability. For 2 or 3 year rates the constraints of availability and thinness of the market become more severe.

Nonetheless, there are phases in the interest rate cycles when the cost of a syndicated bank loan at a spread over 5 year LIBOR is lower than that of a 5 year bond issue. The situation last occurred for dollars in June and July of 1980 and the current pattern (May 1982) of interest rates indicate that a medium-term fixed rate LIBOR based loan could be of interest to some borrowers again. The total amount available was very limited and drawings had to be staggered to avoid over-extending the market and moving rates unduly.

Does lengthening or shortening an interest period by a few days for administrative reasons have any meaningful impact on the rate? The answer is normally no; that one would have to shift half a month before the yield curve displays a significant movement.

In order to simplify administration of the loan, a clause in the agreement usually permits the agent to draw together rollover dates of each tranche (disbursement) so that they coincide with each other and with principal repayment dates. The first drawing sets the semi-annual rollover pattern and the agent has the right to set the initial periods on subsequent drawings at less than six months, for example, so that rollover dates coincide. Similarly the interest period immediately prior to the first principal repayment date may have to be shortened.

In the event that the borrower fails to notify the agent of his selection of interest period, the agreement states what period applies, usually 3 or 6 months. A common alternative is for the same period to apply as was last selected. However, I find the latter alternative unsatisfactory if the borrower had previously chosen a one month period, which calls for unnecessary administration costs.

My last observation with respect to interest periods is with regard to the risk of high interest costs that has become a problem of new dimensions during the past twelve months. We have seen unprecedented swings in dollar interest rates. An interest setting date in February instead of January, raised the interest expense of a $200 million loan to $3 million because interest rates climbed 3%. A borrower may be prepared to live with high interest rates but now runs the risk if his rate setting date falls during an unfavorable month, that the interest costs on his loan may be significantly higher than the average interest rates during the year. Some borrowers spread out interest setting dates on their various loans throughout the year so that their borrowing cost will approximate the average 6 month LIBOR rates.

Are periodic rate settings adequate today and during times of widely swinging interest rates? Perhaps we should develop an interest basis which adjusts with rate movements and ensures borrowers they will not pay more than the average of interest rates throughout a year. Although a borrower would forego windfall gains of a favorable interest setting, he would be protected against getting locked into temporarily high rates. The main obstacle to realizing this goal is finding a continuously adjusting interest rate basis that accurately reflects the lenders' funding costs. I believe solutions exist and if they are used in syndicated loans, the interest sections of the agreements will change. For example we have seen several syndications in the past year structured to limit either the potential gains or losses to lenders and borrowers against the highly volatile swings in interest rates.

An $80 million loan for the Kingdom of Sweden in 1981 successfully tested a formula which established upper and lower limits on interest rates and this example has been successfully copied on a number of credits subsequently.

I shall briefly discuss U.S. based prime based mechanics in a few minutes.

INTEREST CALCULATIONS AND REFERENCE BANKS

Eurocurrency interest payments by custom are usually

higher than the figure of LIBOR plus spread would indicate. The interest is calculated by multiplying the principal and interest rate by the actual number of days in the interest period and dividing by 360. This is frequently referred to as a 365/360 days basis. LIBOR deposit rates are quoted on this basis, in regard to most eurocurrencies, and therefore must be reflected in the calculation of interest the borrower pays. Also, interest rate calculations in domestic currencies may differ, for example, domestic Sterling, Belgian Francs and Japanese Yen are on a 360/365 days basis and domestic Deutsch Marks are on a 360/360 days basis. It is most important to understand the specific days basis for specific currencies, be they domestic or eurocurrencies. Keep in mind therefore that while domestic UK Sterling in calculated on a 365/365 days basis, Eurosterling is calculated on a 365/360 days basis.

Interest on eurocurrency deposits is paid at the end of the interest period for tenor up to 12 months. On longer term deposits, interest is usually paid annually. Such practices are reflected in the interest payment dates stipulated in the loan agreement. It may be of interest to compare the syndicated loan practice with the AIBD convention of eurobonds whereby interest is paid annually on the basis of a 360 day year comprising 12 months of 30 days each.

The agent determines LIBOR by requesting quotations from several reference banks two days prior to the commencement of the interest period. They are typically asked for rates in an amount equal to their participation in the credit to avoid unrepresentative quotations. It is not unusual for rates to move up during the morning by 1/4% or 3/8% if several large loans are rolling over the same day. Rates are set at 11:00 am London time as that is a convenient time when the market could be expected to be free of any erratic influences. However, the concentration of rate settings at 11:00 am has become a problem for the agent bank. Because the reference bank must have a branch in London, the UK clearing banks are frequently among the reference banks. The resulting high demand for their quotes at 11:00 am means that the agents may have to wait 15 to 20 minutes to get through by telephone.

From time to time there are discussions among borrowers, banks and their lawyers about whether the quotations should be the rates offered by prime banks to the reference banks or rates offered by the reference banks to prime banks. A borrower might hold out some hope that the latter could be lower with a smaller reference bank but I doubt it. In practice I find both alternatives give identical rates. I have seen more agreements with the former alternative, that is, rates offered *to* the reference bank. This question is an old chestnut we won't crack today.

The agent adds the margin to LIBOR quotations from the reference banks and calculates the arithmetic mean, rounding the result up to the nearest integral fraction specified in the loan agreement, usually 1/16% or 1/8%. This is appropriate, since deposit rates in eurocurrencies are quoted in fractions of eighths, sixteenths, and unusually in 32nds. One would therefore expect the calculation to be simplified by having two or four reference banks but three is the most common number of reference banks I have observed. It is interesting to note Special Drawing Rights (SDR) deposits are an exception due to their characteristics, and can be quoted in decimal fractions because they must be calculated as a weighted average of five interest rates. I would have expected to see the interest rates of SDR denominated syndicated loans rounded up to the nearest one-sixteenth of one percent. However, early SDR loans went so far as calculating four decimal points in each currency then going through the complicated 6 month swap for each currency into the SDR unit. This has been abandoned to my knowledge as most reference banks now quote an SDRs LIBOR.

If the agent is unable to obtain a rate from a reference bank, the rate is determined by quotations from the remaining reference banks. Although it was not the original intention of this clause, it has become important in light of difficulties sometimes encountered in reaching the Clearers due to telephone congestion as previously mentioned.

The selection of reference banks tends to be determined by the lead manager in consultation with the borrower. He normally endeavors to select reference banks which are representative of the makeup of the lending syndicate, in the case of a eurodollar loan typically a large U.S. bank, a medium sized bank and a non-dollar based international bank.

Should reference banks charge for their rate setting services? Several banks have begun to charge modest fees to act as reference banks and this may be a trend of the future. For instance one major American bank charges $350 as a "one time only" charge for normal syndications and $350 per year for SDR syndications, where the syndication is not business related. If a reference bank is paid a fee, it should commit to making itself available to the agent at the rate setting hours.

It seems to me that the capacity is already in place to broadcast a suitable rate setting through the Reuters terminals at 11 o'clock. To be acceptable to the lenders, the rate would have to be representative of large and small banks and not the 11:00 am rate published in the Financial Times which is based only on several of the largest banks in the world.

What should be done if the borrower complains that the quotations he independently solicited from the reference banks in his loan are lower than those quoted to the agent at the same time? This is not a hypothetical question and I have seen it come up. Perhaps a confusion may exist between bid and offered rates; perhaps the period is not exactly 6 months; perhaps the reference bank is bidding for deposits at that time from the borrower and wants to keep its offered rate put forward directly in relationship to such bid; there are a number of possible explanations. In the end the rate certified by the agent is conclusive except for manifest error.

MECHANICS OF PRIME-BASED CREDITS

A relatively new departure in the euromarket is for an increasing number of credits to be priced over the U.S. prime rate rather than traditional LIBOR pricing. The U.S. prime rate basis moreover dispenses with the need for any reference banks since the prime rate of a single bank, usually the agent bank, is typically used. Furthermore, there is no one "prime rate" and no given bank's prime rate is an interbank rate or "cost". Prime rate will bear some relationship to a bank's nominal "cost" but it already has a spread built in. A U.S. bank's prime rate is the rate at which it will lend to its best commercial credits and so represents a competitive lending rate but not an interbank rate. Because of possible U.S. government influence on prime rates in the interests of domestic monetary policy, successful structures have been developed in a few instances employing so-called "cap" and "floor" rates.

In setting out minimum and maximum rates within which prime rate is to prevail, the funding cost is taken to be the adjusted 90 day secondary CD rate in the U.S.A. The base rate for this notional cost of funds is a three-week moving average of 90 day secondary CD rates which is then adjusted for the reserve requirement "cost" under Regulation D for a given bank's non-personal time deposits of over U.S. $100,000, and the assessment rate of the Federal Deposit Insurance Corporation (FDIC) premium. This adjusted CD rate can be calculated by polling reference banks for the base CD rate and then adjusting it for reserve requirements and the FDIC assessment rate or the rate published by the Federal Reserve in its weekly release H.9 (511) can be used.

The applicable rate for a prime based credit is basically a computed rate consisting of a given bank's prime rate plus the spread. However, this computed rate must not exceed certain parameters established by the notional cost of funds represented by the adjusted 90 day secondary CD rate. For this example, let us assume that the return to the lenders must not exceed 100 basis points over the the adjusted CD rate (the "cap"). Nor may it be less than 25 basis points over the same rate (the "floor"). The adjusted CD rate will be determined by the Federal Reserve release already mentioned. The agent determines the borrowing rate for the credit according to the applicable rate. This will basically be the computed rate (prime plus the spread) unless that rate exceeds the "cap" and "floor" parameters. If the computed rate exceeds the "cap" rate then the applicable rate for the credit will be 100 basis points over the adjusted CD rate. Likewise, should the computed rate fall below the "floor" rate then the applicable rate will be a spread of 25 basis points over the adjusted CD rate.

In this structure both borrowers and lenders are protected against undue "windfall" profits to lenders as well as unwarrantedly low returns. Essentially the prime basis of the credit ensures a good reception in the burgeoning U.S. regional market. The "cap" and "floor" provisions retain the "cost plus" basis of the pricing—smoothing out unduly high or low returns.

The mechanics are more complex than in the traditional LIBOR based credit. In the LIBOR priced credit, quotes are solicited every six months, the arithmetic mean calculated and the spread added to determine the rate for the forthcoming interest period. However, in a prime based credit the prime rate is monitored on a weekly basis and could change during the course of an interest period. In addition, the adjusted CD rate has to be monitored constantly and when there is no Federal Reserve release published or this is not provided for, it actually has to be calculated. The contrast between averaging three quoted rates and adding a fixed spread, and calculating a three week moving average of quoted 90 secondary CD rates adjusted for reserve requirements and FDIC insurance premiums is stark. To ease the administrative burden and to prevent constant changes in the basis of the calculation of the applicable rate, the "cap" or "floor" parameters sometimes have to be exceeded for two consecutive rate adjustment dates, before they apply as the applicable rate.

A new pricing structure is emerging which is analogous to that used in LIBOR based credits and which has been a logical development from the growth of the prime based market over the past year. This is pricing on a margin over the adjusted rate of issuing 90 days Certificates of Deposit in the primary market.

INCREASED COSTS

Returning to standard LIBOR credits, the interest rate on the loan has now been set but the quoted rates may not be the same as the funding costs to each participating lender. For those banks that have reasonable amounts of deposit placement lines, short term LIBOR quotes are not a problem. The difference between quotes to larger and smaller banks varies approximately 1/8% to 3/16% today. In 1975 tiering was much more pronounced and some banks paid as much as 2 1/2% premium. How can a participant protect himself in an adverse market against its funding costs exceeding the interest received?

Most agreements contain a section making provision for changes in circumstances. One of the provisions stipulates that if circumstances arise affecting the ability of a bank to obtain funds in the London Interbank Market, the borrower will prepay the bank on the next rollover date if an alternate funding structure cannot be negotiated. A weaker form of protection to the lender restricts the circumstance to one "affecting the London Interbank Market generally" but still allowing each bank to claim protection individually.

It is fundamental to the concept of lending over the incremental cost of funds that the fixed spread must be protected against erosion from changes in circumstances in its markets in which the lender obtains funding. Generally indemnification provisions shift the burden of increased costs to the borrower. Clearly borrowers are unwilling to accept unqualified cost-increase provisions and one of the major difficulties of a loan agreement is striking a balance between these contrary objectives.

The unregulated aspect of the eurocurrency market is a key to the growth of floating rate lending. The threat of unilateral or joint government regulation, is the cause of a second set of provisions under the "Change of Circumstances" section. It protects the lender from any reserve requirements or changes in taxation basis arising from a change of law or regulation. The wording of the clause is quite broad so as to include any form the taxation problem might take, other than income tax, to include special deposits and related forms of reserves, and to acknowledge their impact whether or not they have the force of law. The agreement stipulates the bank shall first notify the agent and borrower, then the borrower shall reimburse the amounts of additional costs certified by the bank to make it whole. The borrower then has the option to prepay that bank at the next rollover date without penalty.

An example occurred in October 1979 when U.S. banks became subject to reserve requirements if their 'so-called "managed" liabilities' exceeded the level outstanding. Although it only applied to loans to U.S. clients, increased cost claims were made. The whole exercise demonstrated how difficult it is to allocate increased costs to specific loans.

When the Ministry of Finance of Japan introduced guidelines a few years ago which led Japanese banks to fund a major portion of their foreign currency rollover loans with medium term deposit commitments, the banks began issuing floating rate certificates of deposit. FRCD's normally carry at a spread of 1/4% over LIBOR as well as a small management fee. This represents an increased cost to Japanese banks in funding their participation in syndicated loans and the circumstances would seem to benefit from the type of protection I have been discussing. Nonetheless, I am not aware of any of the Japanese banks requesting reimbursement. I would be interested to learn if any did. Similar matching requirements exist in other countries too.

We may not have to go so far from home to find an example of a change of law resulting in increased costs. The enlargement of eligible banks on August 20th last year led to a 6% reserve requirement on eligible sterling liabilities. The impact of this increased cost is limited to sterling loans or disbursements under multicurrency loans. The revision of monetary control requirements in the previous year had a somewhat similar effect on sterling loans of Licensed Deposit Takers. Also some banks contend that classification as a "Deposit Taking Institution" instead if a "Bank" has increased the cost they pay for deposits.

This same section of the loan agreement contemplates a change of law making it illegal for the lender to continue making the loan. In most countries, it is uncharacteristic for a new regulation to have retroactive effect on loans already in the books of a bank. If it did arise, the bank and the borrower are typically required to negotiate for 30 days to find another jurisdiction or manner to extend the loan which is not unlawful. Perhaps a good example of a situation of this nature might be the recent U.K. budget. The Inland Revenue is concerned with revenue losses they feel the UK has been deprived of due to various "tax-spared loans"—loans by UK banks which take advantage of certain loopholes in tax-reciprocity agreements between various governments which are often priced at extremely low margins or negative margins and which generally benefit the foreign borrower. Many of these loans have been on the books for 10 or more years. However, more recently signed loans form part of packages offering export credits with subsidized interest rates and leasing along with beneficial tax features. I believe this question was just resolved this week.

A last part of the "Change of Circumstances" section of the loan agreement is of an apocryphal nature—the so-called "disaster" clause. If the agent decides that due to circumstances affecting the London Interbank Market, reasonable means do not exist to ascertain the interest rate for the next period, a procedure for negotiating interest rates is set in motion. The majority banks may also determine that this situation exists. Upon notification to the borrower, the first step is for the agent, banks and borrower to negotiate in order to agree on a mutually satisfactory interest rate and period. There will be a deadline on negotiations, for example 30 days, at which time if no agreement has been reached the agent sets the rate in consultation with the lenders. This may well be a set of separate rates at the contractual margin over each bank's certified funding costs and perhaps in different currencies. The process would be repeated until normal rate setting could resume. The borrower has the option of prepaying any or all of the banks as long as an irregular circumstance continues. If an event occurred which resulted in the disaster clause coming into operation, we might ask whether it is likely a borrower would have sufficient liquidity to prepay any portion of its debt.

MULTICURRENCY LOANS

It has become common to offer the borrower on each rollover date the option to select any freely convertible currency, subject to its availability. Enormous savings have been made over the past two years when the differentials between 6 months dollar and Swiss Franc rates were 14% in 1980, 11% in 1981 and 7% today. During the same period the Swiss Franc weakened against the dollar. Typically upon receipt of notice from the borrower of its currency selection, the agent determines whether quotations in desired period and currency are available. However each bank has the right to certify that deposits in the selected currency are not available to it at reasonable rates. The bank would then fund in the nominal currency of the loan, which would probably be dollars.

At the end of each interest period, the agent calculates whether the value of the loan has appreciated or depreciated against the originally contracted amount of the loan. He uses the spot FX rate prevailing at the end of the interest period. If the cumulative changes in value since drawdown exceeds a certain percentage, typically 5%, either the borrower repays that excess, or the banks top up the shortfall for the subsequent period. The purpose of the topping up clause is to avoid the lenders' commitment exceeding, inadvertently, board approvals, country limits or legal lending limits if the selected currency revalues strongly against the nominal currency of the loan.

Borrowers have expressed their concern to me that during periods of widely fluctuating foreign exchange rates, they may be forced to make unanticipated payments under the topping up clause. They are worried about getting whipsawed between rapid revaluing currencies and high interest rates. There are several solutions to this problem such as denominating the loan in a strong currency or alternately increasing the percentage differential before the topping up clause comes into play.

In drafting a multicurrency agreement it may be necessary to allow extra time for drawdown notices and determination of availability. The agent may need time to open an account if a less common currency is selected on one of the rollover dates. Particular care must be taken to keep the structure simple and in order to simplify administration of the loan. I recommend only allowing 2 or 3 currencies drawn at one time. Interest periods should be limited to 3 or 6 months and the same period should apply to all currencies outstanding at one time. The agent should have discretion to shorten periods to avoid maturities on holidays in the country of each currency drawn and to ensure all periods are coterminous. If too many permutations are permitted, a multicurrency loan can become a nightmare for the agent.

Selection of a different currency on a given rollover date can present an important credit risk that I am not sure is always taken into account by the lenders. To illustrate it with an extreme example, let us suppose the loan was drawn in U.S. dollars and the borrower elected Yen for the next period. At 10 am Tokyo time the participating banks would disburse their commitment in Yen, but the borrower would not repay the dollar outstanding until 10 am New York the same day. For a period if 15 hours the lenders would have doubled their exposure to the borrower.

DRAWDOWN/DISBURSEMENT

Notice of drawdown must be given to the agent at least three business days prior to the intended date of drawing in order to allow time for the participants to be advised and order funds two days before drawdown. If there is a large number of participants, five business days is a more manageable notice period. A text is specified as an appedix to the agreement in order to avoid incomplete instructions and such notice is irrevocable. The availability of the first drawing is subject to receipt of the borrower's statutes, proof of the powers of the signatories to execute the loan agreement, with binding effect, any necessary approvals of regulatory authorities and the opinions of legal counsel. The drawdown notice reaffirms the representations of the agreement and that no events of default exist. The subject of condition precedent and representations is in the presentation of one of my colleagues.

The timing of the events which are monitored at drawdown must be carefully taken into account in drafting the agreement, otherwise a drawing may inadvertently be blocked. It is desirable to have as few days as possible between drawdown and the date of the legal opinions to avoid an adverse intervening event. On the other hand, sufficient time must be allowed for the local counsel to receive the borrower's counsel's opinion and the English counsel in turn to receive his, and for the agent to complete the technicalities between the date of notice and the date of drawing. Therefore the time slot between the earliest controlled date, usually an opinion of legal counsel to the borrower, and the date the borrower needs his funds should be judiciously calculated. Similarly the sequence and interrelationship of timing each step in the series should be checked to make sure they are practical in light of the location of each party and likely transmittal times. I would include in these considerations the travel plans of the borrower if he intends to bring the documents to the signing in order to make an early drawing.

Frequently the drawings are not allowed within five to ten days of each other due to similar reasons.

It may be convenient to specify in the agreement a minimum amount of each drawing. This will avoid the smallest participant in the loan having to purchase an inconveniently small deposit. Drawings in round million figures are also easier to accommodate. Sometimes this is not possible. For example the loan may be financing sale of capital equipment and drawings may be tied to specific value of shipments. If some of the shipments are in small amounts, for example spare parts, administration of the credit can be simplified by establishing a special disbursement account through which the agent makes short-term advances directly. The loan agreement would then provide for the agent to be reimbursed through a drawing on the syndicated loan once advances under the special disbursement account reach a predetermined level.

If such an arrangement is employed, three aspects require special attention. While short-term advances are outstanding, the syndicate members will want to receive their commitment fee and the agent will want a spread plus LIBOR on his advances. However the borrower will not want to pay both if the total exceeds the margin he has contracted to pay on borrowings in the mandate letter. Secondly the special disbursement account will have to be funded in a manner which takes into account the uncertainty of when advances will reach the level permitting drawings on the syndicated loan. Finally if shipments are made under an irrevocable letter of credit which the loan refinances, the participating banks may have to accept drawings even if an event of default has occurred after the letter of credit was opened.

The participating banks are typically required to pay their participation by 10 am in order to give time for the agent to transfer funds to the borrower on the same day. Many agents will monitor the receipt of each participant's payment and only pay the total amount received. This is difficult to do. Other agents will proceed to pay the borrower the requested drawing and rely upon collecting the delinquent subscription later, together with interest. In either case the agent is protected by a so-called clawback clause which requires the borrower to refund any amounts advanced by the agent but not made available to the agent by a participant. The same clause allows the agent to assume each participant will pay its commitment unless a participant has notified the agent to the contrary prior to drawdown date.

I once encountered a borrower who felt the agent should advance funds that any participating bank failed to provide and that the agent, who was also the lead manager, should limit the syndicate to banks which it felt confident would honor their commitments under the loan agreement. This is a variation of the concept of joint and several commitments of the managers which is sometimes advanced by certain Eastern European borrowers. In fact it has a precedent in some Swiss Franc domestic loan syndication practices, although arising there due to tax implications.

Finally, I should mention that drawdown is usually limited to a specified availability period after which the undrawn commitments of the banks expire. In the case of a revolving credit, the borrower may make drawings, repayments and further drawings throughout the term of the loan. A commitment fee is paid in both cases on the undisbursed amount of the loan, frequently quarterly in arrears, and is calculated on actual days/360 day basis.

REPAYMENTS

Payments of principal installments and interest by the borrower are to be made by 10 am in New York on a business day in same day funds. Receipt of this payment is much easier for the agent to monitor than the numerous payments from the banks on drawdown. The agent is only required to forward payments to the lenders promptly to the extent funds are made available to it. A "clawback" clause requires the lenders to return with interest any funds advanced by the agent but not received by the agent from the borrower. Occasionally a borrower has objected to the clawback clause as a matter of pride, finding the clause suggests the borrower would not honor its obligations to repay. It would be unwise for lenders to accept such arguments.

Semi-annual repayments of principal are the most common spacing and their dates should tie in with interest payments. Coordination becomes more complicated if several different lengths of interest periods may be elected, particularly with longer periods such as 12 months. The situation may be further complicated if repayments must be tied into repayment structures of other loans, such as export credits, and due attention to detail is called for in drafting the agreement to ensure the agency has sufficient scope to have all dates coincide.

The amount of each repayment installment tends to be equal with provision in the agreement for the agent to adjust the final installment to the remaining amount outstanding. Payments are also tailored to cash flow generation in many project financings.

From time to time we encounter loans with balloon repayments, that is, a final repayment considerably larger than the preceding ones. In one variation of this theme, upon request of the borrower, the lenders have the option to reschedule the balloon payment and accept instead a further series of semi-annual installments. Such a structure usually appears in a tight market when saleable terms are too short to meet the needs or aspirations of the borrower. For an extension structure to be marketable, the option should be exercised by each bank individually rather than by decision of the majority banks. Even then there may be concern by the lenders that they may come under pressure from the borrower to go along with the extension because of a long standing relationship. To mitigate to some extent the concern of an anonymous polling arrangement is sometimes used whereby the request for extension must first receive approval of the majority banks before each bank individually makes its own decision to extend.

If additional security of repayment is deemed necessary, the funds may come from an escrow account which is replenished, for example, from the proceeds of sales of a project's output.

This might be an appropriate place to mention that the payment sector of the loan agreement frequently contains a clause requiring each bank to maintain accounts evidencing principal lent, interest and repayments. The agent is required to maintain memorandum accounts with full details of all payments.

PREPAYMENT

In order to allow the borrower flexibility to adjust his financing strategy to new circumstances, an agreement provides for prepayment of all or a part of the loan prior to the contracted amortizations. The borrower must give notice, typically 30 days, which is irrevocable.

Prepayments may be made on interest payment dates only in order to protect the banks' yield on deposits already taken. Principal amounts may not be prepaid unless accrued interest is also paid. Amounts received are applied to reduce installments in the inverse order of their maturity. A minimum amount of prepayment is specified to simplify administration of the loan and repaid amounts may not be reborrowed.

All amounts prepaid are distributed prorata among the lenders except involuntary prepayments arising from changes in circumstances affecting a single bank or group of banks. If any bank receives a payment other than as mentioned, the agreement provides that it is to be shared prorata among the other lenders. Frequently the language stipulates that in so doing the sharing bank will purchase an identical amount of the obligation of the receiving bank. This gives the sharing bank a right in the loan equal to the amount of debt owed to it. Claims under this clause were instigated as Iranian loans but the issue was not resolved prior to prepayment.

Somewhat similar claims for prorata sharing of repayments have been made recently by British banks on their non-British co-participants in Argentinian credits. It is a matter of negotiation between borrower and lenders whether a penalty is to be paid on amounts prepaid.

A loan with several tranches presents additional complications. It must be decided how to share prepayments. Will they be prorata between tranches or prorata between banks? All lenders may not be represented in each tranche. Will application in inverse of order of maturities prevail if the tranches have different tenors? If one tranche carries special security or attractive return, the lenders may want it prepaid last.

PENALTY INTEREST

In the event of the borrower failing to make any payments when due, he will have to pay interest at a higher rate on overdue amounts. Several questions arise and they are not always treated identically in all agreements. How will the penalty interest be calculated? On principal only, or also on past due interest payments? What funding periods should the agent select? When a loan payment falls past due it is usually expected to be brought current within a few days. However, this would lead agents to fund overnight. When no payment comes, the interest must be included in the following overnight funding. As some banks discovered during the events of the past year over Iran, daily compounding at overnight rate prevailing over the last fifteen months caused a $1 million debt to rise to $12 million in that period.

This leads to the question of whether such a claim would be enforceable. In some countries compound interest may not be. My colleagues here can give a much better explanation than I on probable treatment by an English judge. In simple terms I understand English courts will only enforce an increased margin which is a reasonable prior estimate of damages the lender expects to suffer if payments are late.

WITHHOLDING TAXES

Another yield protection provision arises because some countries require a borrower, when remitting currency outside the country to pay a foreign bank interest, to withhold a portion of the interest payment as withholding tax. Governments do this to ensure that the tax is paid. The loan agreement shifts this economic burden to the borrower who has to pay the tax for the lenders or in some way assure that the net yield to the lenders is the full interest yield agreed upon.

The concept is reflected in two places in the loan agreement. First there should be a representation by the borrower as to whether or not there are withholding taxes. Secondly there should be a provision that all sums payable will be free of any deduction. If any deduction is made, the borrower is obliged to pay additional amounts so that the lender receives the full amount he would otherwise have received if no deduction had been made. This frequently takes the form of "grossing up" or increasing the interest rate. For example if the margin and LIBOR total 12% and the withholding tax is 20%, the interest would be increased to 15%. After payment to the authorities of the withholding tax which is 3% in this example, the lender receives the full interest of 12% for which he contracted. Finally the borrower undertakes to provide lenders with copies of the tax receipts which evidence taxes have been paid. The tax impact on the borrower must be considered. This is a highly technical matter which we cannot cover in my brief presentation.

Protection in the agreement addresses present and future taxes; it is a matter of negotiation whether it covers taxes everywhere (other than income taxes) or is limited to those imposed in the borrower's country.

The borrower may seek to avoid the burden of withholding taxes by borrowing only from banks which have branches in his country and are not therefore subject to withholding since they pay local income tax. Alternatively, in certain competitive circumstances, the lenders may be willing to absorb withholding taxes with the intention of offsetting them against their general income taxes. Such was the situation last year with the best private sector borrowers in Mexico. The opposite extreme was seen in Brazil a few years ago. The borrowers paid the withholding tax and gave the lending banks tax receipts which some banks were able to apply against their home country income tax thereby boosting their yields enormously (to as much as 4-5% pa with top quality names).

The borrower did not do badly either because his government refunded to him most of the tax he paid on behalf of the lenders. The tax laws have changed and this arrangement is no longer possible.

There are many special arrangements under bilateral tax treaties. Many reduce or eliminate withholding tax between their countries in certain circumstances. Others give specially advantageous credits. The case of Belgian banks and the United Kingdom tax sparing loans to several Far Eastern countries are some of the most sensational examples I am aware of.

An imaginative scheme was rendered ineffective by a change of Mexican tax law last year. Borrowers had previously benefitted from treatment of forward premiums. To lower the interest rate on which withholding tax is levied, the lenders lent Swiss Francs. Simultaneously they sold forward for dollars to the borrower the same Swiss Francs due for repayment. The Mexican authorities have closed this loophole. The burden of withholding taxes has led many Mexican borrowers to document their syndicated loans from banks in the form of Floating Rate Note issues of Euro-Note programmes which are exempt from withholding taxes if listed publicly on a Stock Exchange.

EURO-NOTE FACILITIES

One of the major roles for a Manager who underwrites a syndicated credit can be to bring in participants who will provide a new source of funding. Typically, participants in a syndicated credit live with the transaction for its full term. However, a new structure has evolved in the euromarkets which makes it possible for participants to lend to the borrower for short periods of time. This structure is the note issuance facility more popularly known as a euro-note or euro-commercial paper facility. In this form of transaction, the underwriting banks make a medium-term commitment to underwrite the sale of consecutive issues of short-term notes. Typically, the borrower will issue six bearer-denominated month notes which will have a stated interest rate. This will be determined by obtaining the normal form of LIBOR quotes from reference banks and adding the applicable margin. These notes are bearer denominated and are issued to the underwriting banks who may then sell them to investors who wish to lend to the borrower for the limited maturity of six months. The major advantage of the euro-note facility is that investors do not have to feel comfortable with the credit for the full term of the facility. Typically the underwriting banks will be those line banks of the borrower who are comfortable with the credit for the full term. However, the structure of bearer denominated notes issued with limited maturities of less than one year enables the banks in effect to sell off or participate the credit extended to the borrower in a convenient form. The advantage for investors is that the process of credit analysis is greatly eased since they are able to in effect get out of the credit at the maturity of any particular note series which they hold.

13C. Checklist of Items for Negotiation with Commercial Banks
Merrill Lynch & Co., Inc.

PART A

1. Form of Loan
   a. Revolving credit
   b. Term loan
   c. Line of credit
   d. Roll overs
   e. Standby commitment
   f. Various combinations of the above

2. Maturity of the Loan

3. Interest rate considerations:
   a. Formulas for computing
      (1) Prime based: prime-plus vs. Time prime
      (2) LIBOR based:
         (a) spread
         (b) choice of reference banks
      (3) Cap-rate floating rate loans (i.e., average not more than an agreed rate over the life of the loan)
      (4) US Money Market Based: commercial paper rate or secondary CD rate.
   b. Capitalization of interest during construction
   c. Various method of calculating interest

4. Loan commitment and disbursement
   a. Analysis of loan draw-down, commitment fees and trade-offs between the two may save money for the client.

5. Replayment schedule
   a. Grade periods
   b. Various alternative methods of repayment

6. Prepayment privileges and premia

7. Need for compensating balances
   a. Trade-offs in compensating balance and the nominal interest rate.

8. Security considerations
   a. Nature of collateral
   b. Ability to substitute collateral

9. Various fees
   a. Management, participation and other placing fees
   b. Agency fees
   c. Commitment (or facility) fees
      (1) Fee on unused portions of new commitments
      (2) Fee on renewals of existing commitments
   d. Legal fees
   e. Printing costs
   f. Financial advisor's fees

10. Financial and other Restrictive Governors

PART B

There is great variety in the terms and conditions associated with the various types and sources of finance that will be available to help fund projects in [state]. Differences in such factors as interest rate levels, currency of repayment, maturity, repayment methods, procurement requirements, and various non-financial terms need to be carefully considered in selecting the source of finance best suited to long-term needs.

In order to evaluate sources of finance and devise the most favorable finance plan for our clients, Merrill Lynch uses an evaluation checklist and matrix. Included in this section are examples of the type of checklist and matrix which are often helpful in selecting the most favorable source of finance.

Checklist of Questions Should Ask in Evaluating Sources of Finance

1. Will the total cost of the goods or services be affected by the type or source of financing?
   a. If finance is provided directly by the supplier, will the price be increased to cover the supplier's own financing cost? If so, would it be cheaper for [state] to borrow the funds in the international markets and purchase the goods without supplier financing?
   b. Does the lender require that the goods or services being financed be obtained from suppliers in the lender's country? Does this mean that the price of the goods would be higher than if the supplier were faced with competition from other countries?

c. Are the potential benefits of international competitive bidding so great that [state] should reject tied loans and seek sources of finance (e.g. syndicated bank loans or World Bank funding) that permit bids from several countries?

2. What percentage of the total cost of the goods and services will be financed by the loan in question?
   a. Does [state] have to provide a portion of the funds out of its own resources or by other borrowing?
   b. Does the loan fund foreign exchange costs only or can the loan be used to help fund all or some of the local costs involved in the transaction?

3. Are the proceeds of the loan available to fund construction or development or are they available only after the project begins operation?

4. What factors affect the overall cost of the loan to the borrower?
   a. Interest Rate Considerations
      (1) What is the absolute level of the interest rate compared to other available sources?
      (2) Is the interest rate fixed or floating?
      (3) If floating, what is the reference rate (e.g., LIBOR, SIBOR, US Prime or CD's) and how is the reference rate determined?
      (4) If a project is being funded out of [state] State Budget or other internal sources, what is the return [state] could earn by using the same funds for other projects?
   b. Currency Considerations
      (1) What is the currency in which principal and interest payments must be made?
      (2) Will [state] have any foreign exchange exposure or currency risk in connection with the loan?
      (3) Does the lower interest rate available on some hard currencies (e.g., Swiss franc, Japanese yen or German DM) fully offset the added costs associated with future appreciation of the currency against the [state] or other currencies readily available to [state]?
      (4) Can the currency of repayment be matched against expected receipts of the currency?
      (5) Can [state] use the forward exchange markets, currency swaps or parallel loan transactions to protect against foreign exchange risks involved in foreign borrowing?
   c. Hidden Cost Considerations
      (1) Are there other fees and cost that [state] must pay in connection with the loan that will add to the overall cost of the loan? If so, how much do these add to the overall cost of borrowing?
      (2) Does the lender charge management fees, commissions or other "front-end" fees in connection with the loan?
      (3) Are there commitment fees charged on the loan?
      (4) What are the legal, accounting, printing and other expenses associated with the loan?
      (5) Does the lender require insurance as a pre-condition to his loan? If so, are the insurance premium costs passed on to the borrower by adding to the price of the goods?

5. What factors affect the amount and timing of the yearly loan repayments?
   a. Is interest during construction capitalized and added to the principal amount of the loan? Or does interest have to be paid while the project is being constructed or the oil field developed?
   b. What is the maturity of the loan?
   c. Are there sinking fund, purchase fund or other prepayment obligations that reduce the average life of the loan?
   d. Is there a grace period on principal repayments?
   e. What is the method of loan repayment? (e.g., equal level payments including principal and interest? Equal payments of principal? Lump sum payment of the entire principal at maturity? Lower repayments of principal in the early years and higher repayments in the latter years?)

6. What type of security does the lender require in connection with the loan?
   a. Is a Bank of guarantee required?
   b. Will the lender want to obtain a mortgage or other security interest in the goods being financed?

7. Are there legal and other non-financial conditions that make the source of finance more or less desirable than other sources of finance?
   a. Does the lender attempt to impose requirements on the way the project is managed or operated?
   b. Does the lender require negative pledge clauses, pari passu treatment and other terms and conditions common in Euro-currency agreements?
   c. What sort of choice of law and dispute settlement mechanisms does the lender expect?
   d. Does the lender expect a waiver of sovereign immunity in connection with the loan?

Section IV: Negotiating and Structuring Loan Agreements
Chapter 14: Legal Issues

14A. Legal Aspects of International Lending: Basic Concepts of a Loan Agreement

Michael Gruson

CONDITIONS OF LENDING

Need for Closing Conditions

A loan agreement between a bank and a borrower (the following assumes a loan agreement drafted in accordance with U.S. practice and governed by New York law) is usually signed by the parties well in advance of the actual making of the loan (the disbursement of funds). The loan agreement represents a legally binding obligation of the bank to make the loan, and if the bank refuses to advance funds after having signed the loan agreement, it may be liable to the borrower for damages. The bank can protect itself by specifying in the loan agreement conditions, so-called closing conditions, that must be satisfied before it is obligated to disburse funds. If one of the conditions is not met, the bank may have the legal right to refuse to make the loan. If all conditions are satisfied, the bank is normally legally obligated to make the requested advance even though there have been significant changes in the borrower's circumstances. Thus these conditions assure the bank that the factors that constitute the basis for the bank's credit decisions are true and that the legal aspects of the loan are in order not only at the time of signing the loan agreement, but also remain unchanged at the time of disbursement of funds.

Customarily, most of these documentary closing conditions must be met only when the bank makes the first advance under the loan agreement and not also at the time of subsequent advances. At a minimum, banks generally require evidence that the loan was and still is duly authorized by the appropriate governing body of the borrower (usually banks require resolutions of the borrower's board of directors authorizing the loan transaction and authorizing certain officers to execute and deliver the loan documents) and that the loan agreement was duly executed and delivered by an authorized officer.

Governmental Approvals; Exchange Control

It is customary to require the borrower to deliver copies of any necessary governmental approvals. Although the bank will require the borrower's representation and an opinion of borrower's counsel that all necessary governmental approvals have been obtained, it is advisable to receive copies of such approvals so that the bank and all its counsel are able to verify for themselves that the transactions contemplated by the loan agreement have been approved. If it is known at the time of drafting the loan agreement which governmental approvals will be required, they should be specifically referred to in the loan agreement. This procedure helps counsel to focus early on the legal requirements.

A bank lending U.S. dollars or Eurodollars expects to be repaid in U.S. dollars; however, exchange-control laws of the country of the borrower may restrict availability, convertibility, or transferability of U.S. dollars. Accordingly, the bank should obtain the agreement or other assurance from the appropriate authorities that (1) U.S. dollars will be available to the borrower when needed to pay interest and principal and other amounts under the loan agreement, and (2) the convertibility of the borrower's currency into U.S. dollars and the transferability of U.S. dollars for purposes of the loan will not be restricted.

The International Monetary Fund (IMF) Articles of Agreement prohibit enforcement in any member country of an exchange contract involving the currency of any other member country that is in violation of the exchange-control laws of such other member country (assuming such laws are consistent with the IMF agreement). Though a loan agreement itself may not be an exchange contract for purposes of the IMF agreement, an exchange-control license or other approval would be such an exchange contract. Furthermore, the refusal by a foreign government to honor agreements by its currency-exchange agency to provide U.S. dollars for local currency is an act of state the validity of which is not reviewable by a U.S. court (French v. Banco Nacional de Cuba, 23 N.Y. 2d 46, 295 N.Y.S. 2d 433 1968).

Legal Opinions

Most major loan agreements contain a closing condition that the bank obtain a favorable opinion of counsel. The purpose of this requirement is to obtain counsel's judgment that the legal assumptions upon which the credit decision has been made are correct. In addition, negotiating the scope of the opinion may bring into the open legal problems and uncertainties before the loan agreement is signed or the loan proceeds are disbursed. In some cases these problems can be solved, whereas in other cases the bank must decide whether it will accept these problems and uncertainties as a credit matter. The opinion of counsel has the additional function of helping to establish the bank's prudence and good faith in making the loan.

Traditionally, banks require an opinion from borrower's counsel. This opinion usually covers the same subject matters as the representations made by the borrower in the loan agreement relating to legal matters, but does not cover representations by the borrower relating to financial matters. The borrower's counsel is usually more familiar than the bank's counsel with the subject matter covered by the opinion, and his opinion reinforces his client's representations. In many loan transactions the bank is satisfied with a legal opinion by the borrower's inside counsel. In more difficult transactions where the opinion requires more specialized expertise, or in unusually important transactions where the bank desires the safeguard of perhaps more independent judgment, the bank may insist on a legal opinion from borrower's outside counsel. In addition, some banks do regularly require an opinion of their own outside counsel about the validity and enforceability of the loan agreement or other matters.

In the case of loans to foreign borrowers, the bank, because of its unfamiliarity with the foreign law, usually insists on an opinion by a foreign counsel of its own selection, which may cover substantially the same subject matters as the opinion of borrower's counsel. But even where the bank retains local counsel in a foreign country, the bank usually expects its U.S. counsel to make a diligent effort to uncover problems that might arise under the relevant foreign law and to ascertain that these problems have been addressed and solved. In addition, U.S. counsel should ascertain that foreign counsel is familiar with the purpose and meaning of the proposed opinion. This requires close interaction between the bank's U.S. counsel and foreign counsel.

In the case of syndicated loans, the loan agreements usually provide for an opinion of special counsel selected by the lead manager who represents all members of the syndicate or the agent bank or both. This opinion is much more limited than the opinion of borrower's counsel and frequently is simply to the effect that the loan agreement and notes are legal, valid, binding, and enforceable against the borrower. Sometimes this opinion is to the effect that the legal documentation is "in substantially acceptable legal form" and that the closing documents are "substantially responsive to the requirements of the loan agreement."

Foreign borrowers, in particular foreign sovereign borrowers, have sometimes expressed annoyance at the requirement of an opinion of counsel. They do not understand why the opinion of a private attorney should determine whether or not the borrower obtains the loan. The answer is simply that a prudent bank will make a loan only if the loan agreement is legal, valid, and enforceable, and the legal opinion is a method of ascertaining whether the loan agreement meets these requirements.

Conditions for Each Disbursement

If the loan is not disbursed in a lump sum but in a series of disbursements or advances, the loan agreement usually contains conditions designed to permit the bank to refuse to make advances if changes have occurred in the legal or financial assumption underlying the credit decision. Normally the loan agreement will require as a condition of each advance that the representations and warranties remain true and accurate as of the date of the advance and that no event of default, or event that may become an event of default upon giving of notice or lapse of time, has occurred and is continuing at the time of the advance. If the loan agreement contains a representation that no material adverse change has occurred in the borrower's financial condition or operations since the date of the financial statements upon which the credit decision was based, this representation is repeated as of the date of each advance, and the bank could refuse to make an advance if there were a material adverse change. The requirements that no default has occurred picks up, through the provision making a breach of a covenant an event of default, all the covenants of the borrower, and again would permit the bank to refuse to make advances if the borrower were not in compliance with a covenant.

REPRESENTATIONS AND WARRANTIES

Purposes of Representations

The representations and warranties set forth in the loan agreement state the legal and, to some extent, the financial assumptions upon which the bank's credit decision is based. They serve several functions. If the loan agreement provides that it is a condition of the bank's obligation to make advances that the representations be correct on the date of each advance, the bank could refuse to make an advance if a representation were not correct on that date. If a material misrepresentation were to occur—either on the date of the loan agreement or on the date of an advance—it would constitute an event of default and would permit the bank to accelerate the loan. These rights are not conditioned upon a misrepresentation being the fault of the borrower. Rather, the representations operate to allocate the risk to the borrower for the matters covered by them. Borrowers unwilling to give a representation sometimes argue that they themselves are not certain whether the representation is correct; this argument is misdirected. The proper question is who should bear the risk if certain factual assumptions upon which the credit decision is based are not correct.

In addition, the representations serve as a disclosure device during the negotiations by requiring the borrower to disclose information inconsistent with the requested representations. finally, the representations may assist the bank in establishing that it acted in good faith in the transaction.

Typical Representations

Representations relating to legal assumptions typically cover (1) the proper incorporation and good standing of the borrower in the jurisdiction of its incorporation; (2) the corporate power of the borrower to enter into the loan transaction; (3) the proper authorization of the loan transaction; (4) the absence of the need for obtaining authorizations or approvals from governmental entities for the loan or, if such authorizations or approvals are required, their validity and effectiveness; (5) the absence of violations of law or any contract binding on or affecting the borrower resulting from the loan (e.g., the loan may violate other financing agreements of the borrower that limit the amount of indebtedness that the borrower is permitted to incur, and such violation could permit the other creditors either to declare defaults under their agreements or to bring suit against the bank for causing or inducing a breach of contract); and (6) the fact that the loan agreement is a legal, valid, and binding obligation of the borrower, enforceable against the borrower.

In each loan, the bank must consider whether its credit decision is based on any particular assumptions that should be covered by representations. If, for example, the business of the borrower depends upon a particular contract or permit, it may be useful to have a representation of the borrower concerning it. If the credit decision is made on the basis of certain nonpublic information supplied by the borrower (for example, projections or cash-flow statements), the loan agreement may contain representations as to the accuracy of such information.

A loan agreement normally contains a representation as to the accuracy of the financial statements upon which the bank based its original decision to extend the credit. This representation usually refers to the latest audited financial statements as well as any more recent interim financial statements.

The representations relating to financial assumptions reflect only the minimum assumptions as to financial matters; usually the borrower provides much more financial information to the bank than is set forth in the representations.

Absence of Material Adverse Change

A common representation is that there has been no material adverse change in the financial condition or operations of the borrower since the date of the latest financial statements. Such change may or may not be reflected in the balance sheet or income statement of the borrower. This provision enables the bank to refuse to lend to a borrower whose financial situation has materially deteriorated. It does not permit the bank to declare outstanding loans due and payable unless the representations was materially false when made (at the time of signing or of any advance).

The material adverse change standard is designed to cover circumstances in which the borrower's ability to perform its obligations under the loan agreement has become doubtful. The standard lacks precision and the bank's refusal to make further advances to the borrower because of a material adverse change is likely to cause disagreement. The bank's position obviously would be more certain if it were able to point to a violation of a financial covenant or some other provision of the loan agreement, However, because of the difficulty in defining clearly all possible material adverse changes, having the ability to invoke this standard, however imprecise, remains very important. Even in cases where the bank and the borrower disagree on whether a material adverse change has occurred, the existence of the clause alone may improve the bank's negotiating position.

COVENANTS OF THE BORROWER

Functions of Covenants

The affirmative and negative covenants bind the borrower in the conduct of its business during the period of the commitment and for the duration of the loan. Covenants permit the bank to influence the future conduct of the borrower in a manner that will reduce the risk that the loan will not be repaid. Violations of covenants serve as warning signals of difficulties. Covenants accomplish this in several ways: by requiring the borrower to comply with applicable legal requirements, by restricting excessive leveraging (restrictions on debt and leases), by preventing the borrower from preferring other creditors (the negative pledge), by maintaining assets in the borrower (restrictions on dividends and the net-worth covenant). Also typically included in the covenants is an agreement by the borrower to supply financial and other information so that the bank can monitor the condition of the borrower and take corrective action if the situation warrants such action. If the borrower has subsidiaries, the bank must decide whether to apply the covenants to the borrower alone, the borrower and its subsidiaries generally, or the borrower and a group of specified subsidiaries (frequently referred to as restricted subsidiaries).

A violation of these agreed-upon minimum standards for the borrower's future conduct should give the bank the right to refuse to make additional advances because such violation (in some cases upon notice and passage of an applicable grace period) creates an event of default, which should prevent the conditions of lending from being met and which should permit the bank to accelerate the loan and cancel its commitment.

Negative Covenants

The negative covenants may be more significant than the affirmative covenants, because they provide clear restrictions upon managerial decisions. These restrictions normally cover such areas as creation of liens, incurrence of indebtedness and lease obligations, payment of dividends, mergers, sale of assets, and investments.

The negative-pledge covenant usually prohibits the borrower from granting any security interest, lien, or mortgage on its property or its income to secure the payment of obligations to other lenders. The problem created by any such security interests, liens, or mortgages in favor of other creditors is that they subordinate the bank's loan to the borrower's obligations to other creditors in case of financial difficulty of the borrower. The purpose of a negative pledge is to provide a pool of assets that will be available for payment of the claims of unsecured creditors equally without any preference of one over the other; it does not create a security interest in favor of the bank. The negative-pledge covenant should apply to the borrower's right to receive income as well as its properties to prevent the use of devices that dedicate income streams to the payment of certain debts.

There are a variety of possible covenants. Which covenants the bank wishes to include in a loan agreement depends on the nature of the borrower's business, its financial condition, and the term of the loan. The covenants may be tied directly to detailed financial projections provided by the borrower if the credit risk is high, or may be limited to a few general financial benchmarks if the credit risk is low. In devising financial covenants for foreign borrowers, the bank should take into account the foreign accounting principles applicable to the borrower.

EVENTS OF DEFAULT

Events of default are circumstance in which the bank has the right to declare the loan immediately payable and to terminate the bank's commitment to extend credit under the loan agreement.

Typical Events of Default

Most loan agreements contain at least the following events of default: nonpayment of principal or interest, inaccuracy in the representations and warranties, violations of covenants, cross-default to other debt of the borrower, bankruptcy events, expropriation, and failure to pay a final judgment in excess of a certain amount.

A cross-default provision is important in circumstances in which the borrower has defaulted under another credit agreement, thus enabling other creditors to demand payment or negotiate improvements in their positions. The cross-default provision gives the bank the right to accelerate its loan in such event. The cross-default can be broadened to include events that have not yet become events of default under other credit agreements because notice requirements or cure (grace) periods are still applicable. This latter type of cross-default gives the bank the same opportunity to negotiate with the borrower as the other creditors prior to the occurrence of a formal event of default under their credit agreements.

In addition to the events of default mentioned above, the bank must consider whether, in the context of the particular loan transactions, there are other circumstances in which the banks should have the right to call the loan. However, many of these circumstances could more appropriately be located in other parts of the loan agreement. For example, if the purpose of the credit is to finance the construction of a hotel, the loan agreement could provide for mandatory prepayment rather than an event of default if the hotel is destroyed. If it is important for the bank that the borrower continues to be owned by its parent corporation, then instead of simply making the transfer of the borrower's stock an event of default, it might be preferable to have the parent corporation covenant to continue to hold the stock of the borrower, and then make the violation of this covenant an event of default. The advantage of covering these circumstances in parts of the loan agreement other than the events of default is that because of the requirement for notice and grace periods or because of the wording of the cross-default clauses in other credit agreements, such circumstances may not immediately trigger a cross-default in other credit agreements, and under proper circumstances, may enable the bank to obtain a court order enjoining the borrower or its parent corporation from violating a covenant.

Grace Periods and Notice Requirements

Certain events of default may contain grace periods or notice provisions, whereas other are considered so significant that the mere occurrence of the event gives the bank the immediate right to accelerate. Grace periods are granted very infrequently in the case of a default for failure to make principal payments. Since the representations and warranties reflect the fundamental assumptions upon which the credit is extended, any material inaccuracy is considered serious and usually treated as an automatic event of default. A cure period is usually not provided because misrepresentations often are not susceptible to being remedied. Violations of covenants become events of default frequently after notice is given by the bank to the borrower and a grace period lapses without the borrower correcting the default. However, a loan agreement may create an automatic event of default upon violation of certain covenants, especially financial covenants, because they are fundamental to the basic credit decision or because the opportunity for correction is limited.

Automatic events of default may be disadvantageous to the bank because they may trigger cross-default provisions in credit agreements between the borrower and other creditors and may thereby introduce an element of instability in the borrower's financial affairs. This consideration would not be relevant, however, if another credit agreement contained a cross-default provision that was violated irrespective of notices and cure periods in the loan agreement or waivers by the bank.

Remedies

Upon the occurrence and during the continuance of an event of default, the bank has the right to accelerate the loan and terminate its commitment. An event of default sometimes accelerates the loan automatically, especially upon the occurrence of bankruptcy or similar events, but automatic accelerations are unusual. This right to accelerate is not intended to be the only remedy available to the bank. In addition, the bank has the right to set off deposits of the borrower against the borrower's obligation to repay the loan either by virtue of a specific provision contained in the loan agreement, or by statute or by common law. If the borrower is not in bankruptcy, the bank is normally able to obtain a judgment against the borrower for the amount of the debt due and then has available the remedies under the legal system for the enforcement of judgments. Furthermore, the bank may be able to resort to legal proceedings to enforce certain provisions of the loan agreement. For example, the bank may be able to obtain a court order requiring the borrower to comply with a covenant or enjoining the borrower and third parties from violating a covenant.

In practice, banks rarely exercise the right to accelerate the loan, because an acceleration is likely to trigger acceleration by other creditors of the borrower and thus cause a bankruptcy. The most frequent result of an event of default is a renegotiation by the bank and the borrower of the loan agreement together with a renegotiation of the borrower's other credit relationships. Even though rarely used, the right to accelerate is an essential remedy, because having this right substantially strengthens the bank's negotiating position with the borrower and other creditors. It also serves as a powerful incentive for the borrower to remain in compliance. However, the bankruptcy appears inevitable, or other creditors accelerate, or if there exists fraud or some other situation with which the bank cannot live, the bank may be forced to acclerate and set off deposits.

14B. Annotated Sample Loan Agreement

PREFACE

The following annotated sample loan agreement is an illustration of the kind of document that might be used for an unsecured, syndicated Eurodollar term loan made to a public-sector corporation with a governmental guaranty. The sample should not, of course, be used for an actual transaction; each transaction will have its own special features, and the agreement drafted to document it will have to be carefully tailored to address the legal and business problems that it presents.

For the most part, the annotations relate to provisions of two kinds. The first are provisions that are generally found in agreements relating to Eurodollar financings but that have functions that might not be readily apparent to a reader unfamiliar with lending funded in the London interbank market. The second are provisions that have special importance in cross-border transactions and that might not be fully self-explanatory to readers accustomed to dealing with purely domestic transactions.

Most of the annotations are intended to explain the rationale for an important section of the sample agreement. Others point to the ways in which one provision is related to another or others. A third kind of annotation lists additional reading on the subject dealt with in a given clause. Most of the bibliographical entries are articles and books that address the practitioner's concerns, as opposed to theoretical sources.

Over the years lawyers at Cleary, Gottlieb, Steen & Hamilton have given valuable suggestions on how we might improve earlier versions of annotated sample loan agreements. We are very grateful for their help. Our special thanks to Marc Hansen for his assistance in preparing this version of the agreement and its annotations.

Anthony C. Gooch
Linda B. Klein
May 19, 1986

U.S. $100,000,000

LOAN AGREEMENT

Dated as of May 15, 1986

among

STATE-OWNED COMPANY, S.A.

as Borrower

THE REPUBLIC OF SOMEWHERE

as Guarantor

INFALLIBLE AGENT BANK

as Agent

BIG BANK, S.A.
BIGGER BANK, PLC
BIGGEST BANK, N.A.

as Managers

and

THE BANKS NAMED HEREIN

as Lenders

STATE-OWNED COMPANY, S.A.

$100,000,000

Dated as of May 15, 1986

Table of Contents

1. DEFINITIONS; INTERPRETATION
    1.1. Definitions....................................
    1.2. Interpretation................................

2. COMMITMENTS; DISBURSEMENT
    2.1. Commitment to Lend............................
    2.2. Notice of Intention and Commitment
         to Borrow....................................
    2.3. Disbursement..................................

3. REPAYMENT
    3.1. Repayment.....................................
    3.2. Optional Prepayment...........................
    3.3. Illegality....................................

4. INTEREST
    4.1. Basic Rate....................................
    4.2. Interest on Late Payments.....................
    4.3. Substitute Rate...............................
    4.4. Interest Notes................................

5. FEES
    5.1. Commitment Fee................................
    5.2. Management Fee................................
    5.3. Agency Fee....................................

6. TAXES
    6.1. No Setoff, Counterclaim or
         Withholding; Gross-Up........................
    6.2. Stamp Taxes...................................

7. PAYMENTS; COMPUTATIONS
    7.1. Making of Payments............................
    7.2. Computations..................................

8. CONDITIONS PRECEDENT
    8.1. Conditions to be Satisfied in Advance
         of the Disbursement Date.....................
    8.2. Further Conditions to be Satisfied at or
         Before Disbursement..........................

9. REPRESENTATIONS AND WARRANTIES
    9.1. Representations and Warranties of
         the Borrower.................................
    9.2. Representations and Warranties of
         the Guarantor................................
    9.3. Repetition of Representations
         and Warranties...............................

10. COVENANTS
    - 10.1. Use of Proceeds.........................
    - 10.2. Governmental Authorizations..............
    - 10.3. Financial Statements.....................
    - 10.4. Inspection Rights........................
    - 10.5. Notices of Default.......................
    - 10.6. Liens and Encumbrances...................
    - 10.7. Insurance................................
    - 10.8. Maintenance of Current Ratio.............
    - 10.9. Maintenance of Ratio of Debt to Equity..................................
    - 10.10. Notice of Tax Exemption.................

11. THE GUARANTY
    - 11.1. The Guaranty.............................
    - 11.2. Endorsement on Notes.....................

12. EVENTS OF DEFAULT
    - 12.1. Events of Default........................
    - 12.2. Default Remedies.........................
    - 12.3. Right of Setoff..........................
    - 12.4. Rights Not Exclusive.....................

13. APPLICATION, DISTRIBUTION AND SHARING OF PAYMENTS
    - 13.1. Application and Distribution of Payments............................
    - 13.2. Sharing of Payments......................

14. THE AGENT AND THE MANAGERS
    - 14.1. The Agent and the Managers...............
    - 14.2. Covenant to Reimburse....................
    - 14.3. Non-receipt of Funds by the Agent........

15. INDEMNIFICATION
    - 15.1. Initial Expenses.........................
    - 15.2. Amendment and Enforcement Expenses.......
    - 15.3. Other Expenses...........................
    - 15.4. Increased Costs..........................

16. GENERAL
    - 16.1. Choice of Law............................
    - 16.2. Jurisdiction.............................
    - 16.3. Loan Currency............................
    - 16.4. Replacement of Notes.....................
    - 16.5. Notices..................................
    - 16.6. Remedies and Waivers.....................
    - 16.7. Amendment................................
    - 16.8. Assignment...............................
    - 16.9. Determinations by the Agent or any Bank..
    - 16.10. Survival................................
    - 16.11. Severability of Provisions..............
    - 16.12. Counterparts............................
    - 16.13. Language................................
    - 16.14. Integration of Terms....................

EXHIBIT A - Schedule of Addresses......................
EXHIBIT B - Form of Promissory Note....................
EXHIBIT C - Form of Notice of Borrowing................
EXHIBIT D - Form of Certificate of the Borrower........
EXHIBIT E - Form of Certificate of the Guarantor.......
EXHIBIT F - Form of Opinion of Counsel to
            the Borrower...............................
EXHIBIT G - Form of Opinion of Counsel
            to the Guarantor...........................
EXHIBIT H - Form of Opinion of Special
            Local Counsel to the Agent.................
EXHIBIT I - Form of Opinion of Special
            New York Counsel to the Agent..............
EXHIBIT J - Form of Acceptance by the Agent
            for Service of Process.....................
EXHIBIT K - Schedule of Governmental
            Formalities................................
EXHIBIT L - Schedule of Liens and Other
            Encumbrances on Property of the Borrower...
EXHIBIT M - Schedule of Liens and Other
            Encumbrances on Property of the Guarantor..

LOAN AGREEMENT, dated as of May 15, 1986, among STATE-OWNED COMPANY, S.A., as borrower (the "Borrower"), THE REPUBLIC OF SOMEWHERE, as guarantor (the "Guarantor"), INFALLIBLE AGENT BANK, as agent (in such capacity, the "Agent"), BIG BANK, S.A., BIGGER BANK, PLC and BIGGEST BANK, N.A., as managers (collectively the "Managers" and each individually a "Manager"), and the several banks and financial institutions named as Banks on the signature pages hereof, as lenders (collectively the "Banks" and each individually a "Bank").

WHEREAS the Borrower proposes to borrow from the Banks, and the Banks, severally but not jointly, propose to lend to the Borrower, an aggregate amount of $100,000,000, the parties agree as follows.

> See the annotations to Section 2.1 and Section 12.4 on the several nature of the banks' obligations.

1. DEFINITIONS; INTERPRETATION

   1.1. *Definitions*. For purposes of this Agreement, the following terms shall have the meanings indicated.

   "Banking Day" means a day on which banks are not required or authorized by law to close in New York City that is also a London Banking Day.

   > The documentation for Eurocurrency loans is prepared on the assumption that each lender will fund its loan, for each interest period, by obtaining a matching deposit in the London interbank market. Interest and principal payments on the loan should be due precisely on the dates the matching deposits would mature (which are sometimes called "rollover dates"), so that the amounts received in connection with the loan can be applied to make payments on the deposits. Since only London and New York holidays are relevant for dollar deposits in the London interbank market, it is not advisable to take holidays in other jurisdictions into account in this definition. For that reason, there may be Banking Days which are holidays in the borrower's home jurisdiction.

   "Commitment Termination Date" means July 15, 1986.

   > 1. Before the loan agreement is drafted, the basic terms of the financing are generally set out in a commitment letter sent to the borrower by the lead lender or lenders (who are often referred to as the "managers"). That letter usually contains the managers' commitment to use their best efforts to put together a syndicate and, assuming certain conditions are met (including the completion of satisfactory documentation), to join with the other members of the syndicate to make loans in a specified aggregate amount.

> The period for which the commitment is good usually
> begins on the date the borrower accepts the commitment
> letter and ends on a stated date (the Commitment Termi-
> nation Date).
>
> 2. Very lengthy commitment periods are not com-
> mon, because the banks are committed to lend to the
> borrower at a certain "spread" or "margin" over their
> cost of funds (which is assumed to be LIBOR) and, the
> longer the period, the greater the likelihood that
> market conditions or circumstances affecting the bor-
> rower might indicate a change in the margin the lenders
> would expect. See Section 5.1 on commitment fees.

"<u>Disbursement Date</u>" has the meaning assigned to that term in Section 2.2.

"<u>Dollars</u>" or "<u>$</u>" means lawful money of the United States.

"<u>Event of Default</u>" has the meaning assigned to that term in Section 12.1.

"<u>External Indebtedness</u>" with respect to any Person, means any Indebtedness of that Person that (a) is or, at the option of that Person or the creditor, may be payable in a currency other than the lawful currency of the Republic of Somewhere or (b) is payable to a Person situated outside the Republic of Somewhere.

"<u>Guaranty</u>" means the guaranty set forth in Article 11.

"<u>Indebtedness</u>", with respect to any Person, means any amount payable by that Person pursuant to an agreement or instrument involving or evidencing money borrowed or received, the advance of credit, a conditional sale or a transfer with recourse or with an obligation to repurchase, or pursuant to a lease with substantially the same economic effect as any such agreement or instrument, to which that Person is a party as debtor, borrower or guarantor.

> The reference to "money . . . received" is par-
> ticularly appropriate when the borrower or guarantor is
> a bank, if it is intended that the definition include
> deposits placed with the bank.

"<u>Interest Note</u>" means each promissory note, substantially in the form set forth in Exhibit B, evidencing interest on the Loan of any Bank.

> Under this sample agreement, interest notes must
> be completed for interest payable in respect of any
> interest period for which the lenders request interest
> notes pursuant to Section 4.4. This mechanism is use-
> ful for situations in which the law of the borrower's
> or guarantor's jurisdiction does not recognize as a
> promissory note, entitled to treatment as such (see the
> first annotation to Section 8.2), an instrument that

> relates to both principal and interest. Where that is the law, and where (as is the case in a Eurocurrency loan) the amount of interest payable in respect of any interest period cannot be determined until the floating rate for the period is set, this mechanism gives the lenders the discretion to request interest notes. Alternatives would be to require the borrower to issue new notes automatically for each interest period or to execute blank notes and authorize the agent to complete them with the appropriate amounts for each lender for each interest period -- an approach the borrower or the guarantor may not be willing to accept.

"<u>Interest Payment Date</u>" means the last day of each Interest Period.

"<u>Interest Period</u>" means (a) the period beginning on the Disbursement Date and ending in the sixth month thereafter on the same day of the month as the Disbursement Date and (b) each subsequent period beginning on the last day of the preceding Interest Period and ending in the sixth month thereafter on the same day of the month as that last day, but, in each case, subject to Section 7.1(b).

> 1. The successive interest periods overlap by one day because the market convention assumes that each lender will be repaying a matching deposit for one interest period when the deposit matures on the last day of that period and that, on the same day, it will be obtaining a new deposit to fund its loan for the next interest period.

> 2. This definition should be read in the light of Section 7.1(b), which deals with month-end and holiday problems.

> 3. Eurodollar loan agreements frequently give the borrower an option to select a duration of one, three or six months for each successive interest period. Provision is sometimes made for the borrower to select longer periods, <u>e.g.</u>, of one, two or even five years. In these cases more elaborate provisions are introduced to deal with the possibility that one or more lenders will be unable to fund for the longer period chosen.

> 4. Reading: Wall & Geary, "Interest rate options, funding practices and yield protection", <u>International Financial Law Review</u> (October 1982).

"<u>International Monetary Assets</u>" means all gold and other bullion, Special Drawing Rights, Reserve Positions in the Fund and Foreign Exchange owned or held by the Central Bank of Somewhere or any monetary authority of the Republic of Somewhere. For purposes of this definition, the terms "Special Drawing Rights", "Reserve Positions in the Fund" and "Foreign Exchange" have the respective meanings specified in the International Monetary Fund publication entitled "International Financial Statistics", dated January 1986, or such other meanings as the International Monetary Fund may adopt from time to time.

"Lending Branch", with respect to any Bank, means the office of that Bank named in Exhibit A or such other office of that Bank as that Bank may have last designated as its lending branch for purposes of this Agreement by notice to the Agent, the Borrower and the Guarantor.

"LIBOR", with respect to any Interest Period, means the rate of interest (expressed as an annual rate) determined by the Agent to be the arithmetic mean (rounded up to the nearest 1/16%) of the respective rates of interest communicated by the several Reference Banks to the Agent as the rates at which each of the Reference Banks would, at approximately 11:00 a.m. London time on the second London Banking Day before the first day of that Interest Period, offer major banks in the London interbank market a deposit in Dollars for a term coextensive with that Interest Period in an amount substantially equal to the reference amount (as defined below) for that Reference Bank and Interest Period; provided, however, that, if any of the Reference Banks fails so to communicate a rate, LIBOR shall be determined on the basis of the rate or rates communicated to the Agent by the remaining Reference Bank or Reference Banks. For purposes of this definition, "reference amount", with respect to any Reference Bank and Interest Period, means (a) if that Reference Bank is a Bank, the amount of that Bank's Loan scheduled to be outstanding during that Interest Period, or (b) if that Reference Bank is not a Bank, the amount scheduled to be outstanding during that Interest Period of the Loan of the office or affiliate of that Reference Bank that is a Bank, in each case, (i) without taking into account any reduction in the amount of any Bank's Loan through any assignment or transfer and (ii) rounded up to the nearest integral multiple of $1,000,000.

> 1. The interest rate applicable for each interest period is LIBOR for that period (assumed to be the lenders' cost of funds) plus a "spread" intended to compensate the lenders for making their loans and assuming the credit risk of lending to the borrower. This spread, or gross profit element of the interest rate, is also called the "margin" -- the term used in this sample agreement.
>
> 2. LIBOR for each interest period is determined on the second London banking day before the beginning of that interest period because the convention in the London interbank market for deposits in dollars is to quote for value two days later or, if that day is not a "Banking Day", the next Banking Day. The conventional delay between a bank's commitment to take a deposit and the so called "value date" for the deposit (on which

the deposit will be available) facilitates the processing of payments, which are settled in New York, the principal financial center in the country of the currency. Where these geographical and time zone concerns do not exist, the same delay is not necessary. For example, quotations for deposits in pounds sterling in the London interbank market are for value on the same day and, so, are obtained on the first day of an interest period.

3. LIBOR in a syndicated transaction is usually an average of the rates quoted by several (often three) reference banks. It is important to note whether the rate used is the one at which the reference banks would offer to place deposits with other banks in the London interbank market, or the rate quoted by other banks in that market as the one they would be willing to receive if they placed deposits with the reference banks, since the identity of the offeree may affect the rate. "Large banks . . . can usually obtain funds at rates below LIBOR . . . . Tiering of interest rates is a normal feature of the inter-bank market. There are several tiers to reflect different bank quality ratings but the usual range of rates is only around 1/4% overall . . . . Immediately after the Herstatt crisis in 1974, the number of tiers increased and the range of rates expanded to exceed 1%." "Eurobanks and the interbank market", <u>Bank of England Quarterly Bulletin</u> (September 1981).

4. It is not the practice in Eurocurrency loan agreements to use LIBOR as obtained from a published source. The reluctance of lenders to look to a published rate quite possibly had its origins in single-bank lending, where the lender was actually obtaining matched funding for each loan and wanted to pass through the precise cost of that funding. In other types of financial instruments, such as interest rate exchange, or "swap", agreements, it is becoming increasingly common for the parties to use a published rate, often one taken from a display screen of a rate-quotation service such as the Reuter Monitor Money Rates Service.

5. The details of the rounding provision can involve a lot of money. In the case of a $100,000,000 syndicated loan, the difference between rounding up to the nearest 1/8% and the nearest 1/16% can amount to as much as $62,500 per annum.

6. In theory, the amount of the deposit can affect the rate though, in practice, we understand that quite large deposits can currently be obtained in the three-month and six-month deposit markets without affecting rates. In the case of "jumbo" loans, it may be desirable to provide for a series of partial drawdowns and to include provisions designed to ensure that

> rollover dates for different tranches do not coincide.
>
> 7. Under some circumstances, a bank will be subject to reserve requirements under Regulation D of the Board of Governors of the Federal Reserve System with respect to the bank's loan or the funding acquired by it to make the loan. This will generally be the case, in particular, for loans by U.S. banks (whether through a domestic or a foreign office) to U.S. borrowers. In such cases, the lender may seek to have the borrower agree that the interest rate on the loan will be adjusted to reflect the lender's cost of maintaining the reserve. Regardless of the outcome of negotiations on this point, market practice would require the borrower to run the risk of any increased cost resulting from new or increased reserve requirements (see Section 15.4).

"<u>Loan</u>", with respect to any Bank, at any time, means (a) the loan to be made hereunder by that Bank after that time or (b) the loan made by that Bank hereunder in the principal amount outstanding at that time, and "Loans", at any time, means the aggregate of the Loans of all the Banks at that time.

"<u>Loan Commitment</u>", with respect to any Bank, means the amount designated as such and set forth opposite the name of that Bank on the signature pages hereof.

"<u>London Banking Day</u>" means a day on which dealings in deposits in Dollars are carried on in the London interbank market.

> A distinction is drawn between "London Banking Days" (when banks are open in London) and "Banking Days" (when banks are open in both London and New York) because rates can be fixed on London Banking Days even though banks in New York are closed, but payments in dollars can be made only when banks in New York are open.

"<u>Majority Banks</u>" means (a) at any time before the disbursement of the Loans, Banks with Loan Commitments totalling more than 50% of the Total Loan Commitment, and (b) at any time thereafter, Banks maintaining loans hereunder that represent more than 50% of the aggregate principal amount of the Loans at the time.

> Depending on the make-up of the syndicate, some number other than 50% may be appropriate. Other frequently used figures are 60% and 66-2/3%. This point is particularly important if the power to accelerate the maturity of the loans upon the happening of an event of default is reserved to "Majority Banks" (see Section 12.2).

"Margin" means 2%.

"Note" means each Interest Note and each Principal Note.

| Promissory notes are often used in Eurocurrency
| transactions because they afford procedural advantages
| in legal proceedings in the borrower's jurisdiction.
| See the first annotation to Section 8.2.

"Person" means any corporation, natural person, firm, joint venture, partnership, trust, unincorporated organization or government, or any political subdivision, department or agency of any government.

"Principal Note" means each promissory note, substantially in the form set forth in Exhibit B, evidencing a repayment installment of the Loan of any Bank.

| In loan agreements for U.S. domestic lending
| transactions, when principal is repayable in install-
| ments, each lender generally receives only one promis-
| sory note, which specifies the installments and their
| due dates. This sample agreement requires the borrower
| to deliver one promissory note for each repayment in-
| stallment of the loan made by each bank (see Section
| 8.2) to illustrate the mechanism used when the law of
| the borrower's or guarantor's jurisdiction does not
| recognize installment instruments as promissory notes.

"Reference Banks" means the respective principal London offices of Biggest Bank, N.A., Average Quoter Bank, Limited and Small & Obscure Banking Company.

| It is customary to name as the reference banks the
| principal London offices of the institutions that will
| be supplying the quotations on which LIBOR will be
| based. If the quotations reflect the rates the refer-
| ence banks would be willing to pay for a deposit placed
| with them by major banks in the London interbank mar-
| ket, as opposed to the amounts the reference banks
| would be willing to receive for a deposit placed by
| them with major banks in that market (see the annota-
| tions to the definition of "LIBOR"), the borrower would
| be well advised to select reference banks that would
| not be expected to pay a premium for deposits. It
| would also be advisable to choose reference banks from
| different geographical regions, since a problem with a
| major bank in a particular region might affect the cost
| of deposits to other banks from the same region.

"Subsidiary", at any time, means any entity in which a controlling interest is owned at the time by (a) the Borrower, (b) the Borrower and any other such entity or (c) one or more such entities. For purposes of this definition, the direct or indirect beneficial ownership of more than 50% of the outstanding voting stock of an entity (or of any other equity interest entitled ordinarily to vote in the election of the directors or other governing officials of the entity) shall constitute ownership of a controlling interest.

> Even if the borrower has no significant subsidiaries at the time the loans are made, provisions dealing with subsidiaries are often included in case the borrower establishes one or more subsidiaries after the loan agreement is signed.

"Total Loan Commitment" means $100,000,000.

"United States" means the United States of America.

1.2. Interpretation. The table of contents and the headings of the articles and sections of this Agreement are for convenience of reference only and shall not affect the meaning or construction of any provision hereof.

2. COMMITMENTS; DISBURSEMENT

2.1. Commitment to Lend. On the terms and subject to the conditions set forth herein, each Bank shall make a loan through its Lending Branch to the Borrower in a principal amount equal to that Bank's Loan Commitment. Failure by any Bank to make a loan to the Borrower as provided in this Section shall not relieve any other Bank of its obligations hereunder. No Bank shall have any responsibility for any failure by any other Bank to fulfill its obligations hereunder.

> 1. It should be noted that the lenders' commitments are several, not joint. If a given bank fails to lend, the other banks have no responsibility to take up that bank's loan. By the same token, they are not released from their own obligations to lend.

> 2. The conditions precedent to the banks' obligations to lend under this sample agreement are listed in Article 8. If those conditions are not met, the banks are under no obligation to make their loans. It should be noted that a borrower that believes it has been damaged by a lender's refusal to make a loan might bring a judicial action for damages. In such a proceeding, a court might examine the lender's refusal to see whether it was made in good faith and in the reasonable exercise of the lender's discretion, and, at least in some circumstances, the court might determine that a refusal would be consistent with those standards only if there were some advance notice from the lender to the borrower. See K.M.C. Co., Inc. v. Irving Trust Co., 757 F.2d 752 (6th Cir. 1985).

2.2. _Notice of Intention and Commitment to Borrow_. If the Borrower wishes to borrow hereunder, it shall, on or before the fifth Banking Day before the date on which it wishes to borrow, give the Agent notice, substantially in the form set forth in Exhibit C, of (a) that date (the "Disbursement Date"), which shall be a Banking Day and shall not be later than the Commitment Termination Date, and (b) the account in New York City to which it wishes the proceeds of the Loans to be credited. That notice shall constitute the Borrower's irrevocable commitment to borrow an amount equal to the Total Loan Commitment on the Disbursement Date.

> 1. This sample loan agreement assumes that the full amount of the loan commitments will be borrowed on one day. A borrower that needs funds disbursed to it in varying amounts at times linked, for example, to the stages in the development of a project, would require a multiple disbursement, or "drawdown" facility. The mechanics for each separate disbursement under such a facility could be expected to be substantially the same as those set forth for the single disbursement contemplated in this sample agreement, and there would be separate conditions precedent (see Article 8) to be met in connection with each disbursement. For a summary of some features of multiple disbursement Eurocurrency loans, see Crozer & Wall, "The Eurodollar market: Loans and Bonds", in 1 _International financial law_ (R. Rendell, ed., 1983 ed.), 63, 64.

> 2. Unlike agreements and commitment letters relating to fixed-rate loans, which may impose on the borrower an obligation to borrow, or require it to pay damages if it fails to do so (see, _e.g._, _Teachers Insurance & Annuity Association of America v. Butler_, 626 F. Supp. 1097 (S.D.N.Y. 1986)), loan agreements providing for LIBOR-priced loans usually do not at the outset place any obligation on borrowers to borrow; they create a right to borrow if the conditions precedent are met. Once the notice of intention to borrow is given, however, the borrower becomes irrevocably committed to borrow on the designated disbursement date because, in reliance on that notice, the lenders may commit to take matching funding deposits. Section 15.3 deals with the consequences of a failure by the borrower to fulfill that commitment to borrow.

> 3. The borrower is generally required to give the agent at the very least three Banking Days' prior notice of its intention to borrow, so that there will be time for the agent to give notice of the intended disbursement date to the lenders, and for the lenders to fund their loans on the second London Banking Day before that date. It is advisable to provide for five Banking Days' notice or more, in the case of large syndications, to leave time for the agent to review the documents delivered in satisfaction of the conditions

> precedent to the making of the loans, most of which must be delivered by the last day on which the borrowing notice may be given (see Section 8.1), and to allow time for the borrower to deal with any problems that become apparent as a result of the agent's review of those documents.

    2.3. <u>Disbursement</u>. The Agent shall give prompt notice to each Bank by telex or cable of the Disbursement Date. By 10:00 a.m. New York City time on the Disbursement Date, each Bank shall, subject to the conditions set forth herein, make available to the Agent an amount equal to that Bank's Loan Commitment, in funds settled through the New York Clearing House Interbank Payments System or such other same-day funds as the Agent may at the time determine to be customary for the settlement in New York City of international banking transactions denominated in Dollars, by deposit to the Agent's account specified in or pursuant to Section 7.1(a). Subject to the conditions set forth herein, the Agent shall, on the Disbursement Date, credit the funds so received to the account specified by the Borrower pursuant to Section 2.2.

> Since October 1981, Eurodollar transactions have been settled in "same-day funds" through the New York Clearing House Interbank Payments System. Until that time, Eurodollar transactions were settled in "next-day funds".

3. REPAYMENT

    3.1. <u>Repayment</u>. Except as otherwise expressly provided herein, the Borrower shall repay the Loans in nine semiannual installments, each of which shall be in an amount equal to one ninth of the Loans outstanding on the Disbursement Date; <u>provided</u>, <u>however</u>, that the first eight of those installments shall each be rounded down to the nearest integral multiple of $1 and the last of them shall be in the amount necessary to repay in full the outstanding balance of the Loans. Each installment shall be allocated <u>pro rata</u> among the Loans, subject to such rounding of the installments of the Loan of each Bank as may be determined by the Agent. The installments of the Loans shall be repaid on successive Interest Payment Dates commencing with the eighth Interest Payment Date.

> Repayments take place on the last day of each interest period because the repayments are scheduled to coincide with the maturity dates for any matching deposits that the banks may have obtained to fund their loans. If repayment is early, there is a risk of loss to the banks, because they may be unable to invest the amounts so repaid at rates equal to those they are paying on the matching deposits plus the Margin. Section 15.3 deals with the consequences of repayment on a day other than an interest payment date.

3.2. _Optional Prepayment_. The Borrower may prepay the Loans in whole or in part in an integral multiple of $5,000,000 on any Interest Payment Date, and as provided in Section 3.3, but not otherwise. If the Borrower wishes to make a prepayment, it shall, on or before the fifteenth Banking Day before the date it wishes to designate for the prepayment, give the Agent notice of that date and of the amount to be prepaid on that date. That notice shall constitute the Borrower's irrevocable commitment to prepay the specified amount on that date, together with interest accrued on that amount to that date and a premium for the account of each Bank of 1/2% of the amount being prepaid to that Bank. Each notice pursuant to this Section shall be accompanied by evidence satisfactory to the Agent that all governmental approvals necessary for the prepayment have been obtained. Any partial prepayment hereunder shall be allocated _pro rata_ among the Loans and applied sequentially to the installments provided for in Section 3.1 in inverse order of their maturities. Any amount so prepaid may not be reborrowed under this Agreement.

> Prepayment is permitted, if at all, only on interest payment dates. (See annotation to Section 3.1.) Unlike revolving credit agreements, this sample term-loan agreement does not permit reborrowings of amounts prepaid. The prepayment premium reflects the fact that the lenders have invested time and administrative resources in preparing to participate in the financing, with the expectation that their efforts will produce a profitable asset for a specific term.

3.3. _Illegality_. If any Bank determines at any time that the adoption of, or any change in, or any change in the interpretation of, any law, regulation or treaty makes or will make it unlawful for that Bank to fulfill its commitment pursuant to Section 2.1, to maintain its Loan or to claim or receive any amount payable to it hereunder, that Bank shall give notice of its determination to the Borrower, whereupon the obligations of that Bank hereunder shall terminate. If any Bank gives any such notice after the disbursement of the Loans, the Borrower shall prepay the Loan of that Bank in full on the Interest Payment Date following the date that notice is given (or on such earlier date as that Bank certifies to be necessary in order to enable it to comply with that law, regulation or treaty), without premium but together with interest accrued to the date of prepayment on that Bank's Loan and all other amounts then payable to that Bank by the Borrower hereunder.

> 1. The illegality clause excuses a bank from its obligation to make or maintain its loan if it becomes illegal for it to do so. The possible types of illegality that most concern lenders are (a) situations (like the Falklands/Malvinas crisis) where diplomatic relations deteriorate between the government of the country of the lender and that of the borrower and

| (b) situations where newly-imposed foreign currency exchange controls make it impossible for the lender to make or maintain its loan.

| 2. It has become fairly common practice to provide that the bank involved will use its best efforts to transfer its commitment or its loan to one of its other branches or affiliates or to another bank if the illegality can be cured by such a transfer.

| 3. Reading: Buffo, "The Illegality Clause Raises More Problems Than It Solves", <u>Euromoney</u> (February 1978); Group Legal Department, Royal Bank of Canada, London, "Illegality clauses in syndicated loan agreements", <u>International Financial Law Review</u> (March 1983)

4. <u>INTEREST</u>

4.1. <u>Basic Rate</u>. (a) Except as otherwise expressly provided in Section 4.2 or Section 4.3, interest shall accrue on each Loan during each Interest Period, from and including the first day of that Interest Period, to but excluding the last day thereof, at a rate per annum equal to the sum of the Margin and LIBOR for that Interest Period.

(b) Except as otherwise expressly provided herein, accrued interest on each Loan shall be payable on each Interest Payment Date.

(c) The Agent shall give notice to the Borrower and the Banks of LIBOR promptly after each determination thereof.

4.2. <u>Interest on Late Payments</u>. If any amount payable by the Borrower hereunder is not paid when due (whether at stated maturity, by acceleration or otherwise), interest shall accrue on that amount, to the extent permitted by applicable law, during the period from and including the due date thereof, to but excluding the date that amount is paid, (a) during the week beginning on that due date, at a rate per annum equal for each day to the sum of (i) the Margin, (ii) 1% and (iii) the Agent's overnight offered rate (expressed as an annual rate) for a deposit in Dollars in the London interbank market in that amount for value on that day, and (b) thereafter, during each period of one day, one week or one or three months selected by the Agent in its sole discretion after consultation with the Borrower (to the extent practicable) concerning the date on which the overdue amount is likely to be paid, at a rate per annum equal to the sum of (i) the Margin, (ii) 1% and (iii) the rate at which the Agent would offer major banks in the London interbank market a deposit in Dollars for a term coextensive with that period in an amount equal to the overdue amount, determined by the Agent at approximately 11:00 a.m. London time (A) in the case of a period of one day, for value on that day, and (B) in the case of a period longer than one day, on the second London Banking Day before the first day of that period. However, if the Agent is not offering deposits in Dollars to major banks in the London interbank market at the time for any rate setting for any period under this Section, interest on the relevant overdue amount for that period shall accrue at a rate (expressed as an annual rate) equal to the sum of (i) the Margin, (ii) 1% and (iii) the Agent's effective cost (expressed as an annual rate) of funding a loan in an amount equal to that overdue amount for that period (as determined by the Agent). Interest accruing pursuant to this Section shall be payable from time to time on demand of the Agent.

> 1. The rule of the clause is stated to govern "to the extent permitted by applicable law" because a court might hold that the clause is unenforceable to the extent that it requires the payment of interest on interest. Lawyers may have difficulty in giving favorable opinions on the enforceability of the clause if this qualification is not included.

> 2. A common alternative to the approach taken in the sample clause is to apply as the overdue interest rate for any day a rate equal to the sum of the Margin, 1% and LIBOR (or the rate substituted for LIBOR under the substitute rate provision (see Section 4.3)) for the interest period during which the overdue amount falls due or, if it falls due on the first day of an interest period, for that interest period.

4.3. *Substitute Rate*. (a) If the Agent, after consultation with the Banks to the extent practicable, determines at any time that (i) it will not be possible to determine LIBOR for the following Interest Period or (ii) LIBOR for that Interest Period will not adequately reflect the costs to Majority Banks of funding the Loans for that Interest Period in the London interbank market, the Agent shall forthwith give notice of its determination to the Borrower and the Banks, whereupon the Banks shall cease to be under any further obligation to make Loans to the Borrower.

(b) If a notice of the kind referred to in Section 4.3(a) is given after the disbursement of the Loans, the Borrower and the Agent (for and on behalf of the Banks) shall enter into negotiations in good faith with a view to establishing a satisfactory alternative basis for computing interest on the Loans for the Interest Period to which the notice relates. If the Agent (after consultation with the Banks to the extent practicable) and the Borrower agree in writing upon such an alternative basis on or before the last day of the 30-day period beginning on the date that notice is given to the Borrower, the Agent shall forthwith give notice of that agreement to the Banks by telex or cable. If Majority Banks approve the alternative basis on or before the fifth day after that notice is given to the Banks, interest shall accrue on the Loans during that Interest Period in accordance with that alternative basis.

(c) If the Agent and the Borrower fail to agree on such an alternative basis during the 30-day period specified in Section 4.3(b) or if Majority Banks fail to approve that alternative basis on or before the day specified therein, the Agent shall forthwith give notice of the failure to the Borrower and the Banks. As soon as practicable after receipt of that notice, each Bank shall give notice to the Borrower of the rate of interest which that Bank determines is equal to the sum of the Margin and the effective cost (expressed as an annual rate) to that Bank of funding that Bank's Loan for that Interest Period, and interest shall accrue on that Bank's Loan during that Interest Period at the rate set forth in that notice.

> 1. This provision is an example of the "Eurodollar disaster clause". In this version, the determination that a problem has arisen is made by the agent, after consultation with the lenders "to the extent practicable". In other versions, the determination might require a decision of a majority of the lenders or (at the other extreme) might be left up to individual lenders.
>
> 2. With respect to timing, the sample clause calls for the agent to advise the borrower if it judges that there is a reasonable likelihood of a problem with respect to the next interest period at any time when it forms that judgment. The purpose of this feature of the sample clause is to give the parties as much time as possible before the commencement of an interest period to work out a solution. A more common version of the Eurodollar disaster clause provides that such a notice will only be given immediately in advance of the next interest period.
>
> 3. Another feature of the sample clause is that it operates anew for each interest period. Under this approach, for example, if it were impossible to determine LIBOR for deposits in dollars with respect to a given interest period and "Majority Banks" and the borrower agreed to redenominate the loans in another currency, that agreement would hold only for that interest period, and everything would return to normal, if possible, for the next interest period; if not, another deal would have to be struck for the next interest period.
>
> 4. The sample clause attempts to deal with two different kinds of problems (often referred to as "triggers"): first, that which would arise if it were not possible to determine LIBOR and, second, that which would arise if LIBOR did not adequately reflect the

cost of funding by Majority Banks. Sometimes a third trigger, that deposits in the relevant currency are not available in the amounts necessary to fund the loans, is added. It would appear that this third trigger is not really necessary, since, in any case where deposits are not available, there will be no way of ascertaining LIBOR, so the first trigger will apply.

5. In the sample clause, the second trigger relates to Majority Banks; sometimes it is phrased in terms of any lender -- an approach that is less favorable to the borrower.

6. The sample clause provides for negotiations involving the borrower and the agent, on behalf of the banks, for the purpose of establishing an alternative interest rate in the event of a problem. If the rate so negotiated is approved by Majority Banks within the specified period, it is applicable for the relevant interest period. If the negotiations are not successful, or the rate they produce is not approved by Majority Banks within the specified period, the substitute rate is determined on a lender-by-lender basis. There are other approaches: one approach authorizes the agent to agree to a substitute basis on behalf of the lenders; a second requires unanimity of the lenders or, at least, permits any lender not satisfied with the substitute basis to negotiate a separate substitute basis or have its loan prepaid; and a third operates on a lender-by-lender basis without a negotiation period. A somewhat more sophisticated variation of the second approach provides that certain kinds of substitute bases can be agreed to by the agent or by a majority of the lenders but that other kinds (most notably, a decision to redenominate the loans in a currency other than the original currency) would have to be agreed to on a lender-by-lender basis.

7. It is not uncommon to provide that the borrower may prepay the loan of any lender that has given the borrower notice of a substitute rate that the borrower finds too high. The borrower's election not to prepay the loan of any lender that has given the borrower notice of a substitute rate should be stated to constitute acceptance by the borrower of that rate if the lender's right to interest at a rate determined by the lender alone might be unenforceable in the borrower's jurisdiction.

8. Reading: Gooch, "The Eurodollar disaster clause", _International Financial Law Review_ (June 1983).

4.4. _Interest Notes_. On or before the fifth day after each demand therefor from the Agent, the Borrower shall deliver to the Agent for each Bank an Interest Note, duly executed by the Borrower, endorsed with the guaranty of the Guarantor, dated the date of that demand and payable to the order of that Bank, evidencing interest payable pursuant to Section 4.1 or Section 4.3 (as the case may be) on the Loan of that Bank scheduled to be outstanding during the Interest Period with respect to which that demand is made.

5. FEES

5.1. *Commitment Fee*. The Borrower shall pay for the account of each Bank a commitment fee at the rate of 1/2% per annum on the Loan Commitment of that Bank. This fee shall accrue from and including the date hereof, to but excluding the earlier of the Disbursement Date and the Commitment Termination Date, and shall be payable on the earlier of the Disbursement Date and the Commitment Termination Date.

> 1. Often the commitment fee runs from a date earlier than the date of the loan agreement, for example, the date a commitment letter is accepted by the prospective borrower. On the other hand, lenders sometimes agree that the commitment fee will only start to accrue at a date (*e.g.*, thirty days) after the loan agreement is signed.

> 2. Bankers refer to one hundredth of a percentage point as a "basis point", and amounts of less than 1% are often expressed in terms of basis points. Thus, in bankers' jargon, the commitment fee reflected in the sample provision is fifty basis points per annum.

5.2. *Management Fee*. The Borrower shall pay for the account of the Managers a management fee equal to 1% of the Total Loan Commitment. This fee shall be payable on the date hereof.

> This fee is payable as compensation for the managers' role in organizing the syndicate of lenders. It is usually due regardless of whether the borrowing actually takes place. Since the managers, as such, have no function under the loan agreement, few of the provisions of the agreement refer to them, and the managers generally do not assume any responsibility in connection with the agreement. See Section 14.1.

5.3. *Agency Fee*. The Borrower shall pay for the account of the Agent an annual agency fee in the amount of $2,500. This fee shall be payable (a) on or before the sixtieth day after the earlier of the Disbursement Date and the Commitment Termination Date and (b) on each anniversary of the Disbursement Date on which any amount payable or repayable by the Borrower under this Agreement remains outstanding (after taking into account all payments made by the Borrower on that anniversary).

6. TAXES

     6.1. *No Setoff, Counterclaim or Withholding; Gross-Up.* (a) Except as otherwise required by law, each payment by the Borrower or the Guarantor under this Agreement or the Notes shall be made without setoff or counterclaim and without withholding for or on account of any present or future taxes imposed by or within the Republic of Somewhere or any political subdivision or taxing authority thereof or therein. If any such withholding is so required, the Borrower or the Guarantor (as the case may be) shall make the withholding, pay the amount withheld to the appropriate governmental authority before penalties attach thereto or interest accrues thereon and forthwith pay such additional amount as may be necessary to ensure that the net amount actually received by each Bank, each Manager and the Agent free and clear of such taxes (including such taxes on such additional amount) is equal to the amount which that Bank, that Manager or the Agent (as the case may be) would have received had such withholding not been made. If the Agent or any Bank or Manager pays any amount in respect of any such taxes, penalties or interest, the Borrower or the Guarantor (as the case may be) shall reimburse the Agent or that Bank or Manager in Dollars for that payment on demand. If the Borrower or the Guarantor (as the case may be) pays any such taxes, penalties or interest, it shall deliver official tax receipts evidencing that payment or certified copies thereof to the Agent on or before the thirtieth day after payment.

> 1. The sample clause provides for a full "gross-up" by the borrower and the guarantor for local withholding taxes. If a withholding tax is applicable, an additional remittance by the borrower or the guarantor will be required so that the banks will receive the amount they would have received had no tax been withheld. This additional payment may itself be subject to withholding. For example, if the withholding tax rate is 25% and the "gross-up" payment is itself subject to tax, $400 must be remitted in order for the lenders to receive $300 net. The sample provision also applies to the payments to be made to the managers and the agent.

> 2. Borrowers often question the fairness of such provisions, on the theory that lenders will be able to recover the withholding taxes through the operation of foreign tax credits in the lenders' home jurisdictions. Such borrowers seek to have inserted in loan agreements a provision to the effect that each lender will pay to the borrower an amount equal to any tax credit received by that lender in respect of taxes borne by the borrower. Lenders rarely accept this provision, for various reasons. First, it is very difficult to allocate foreign tax credits to particular loans. Second, it may be many years after the interest is paid before a lender's tax credit for the year of payment is finally

determined. Third, lenders fear that such a provision may lead the borrower to assert rights of access to confidential records of a lender, in order to permit the borrower to check the lender's computation of the portion of the tax credit allocable to the borrower's loan.

3. Borrowers should not assume that U.S. lenders can automatically recover through tax credits whatever is paid to the tax authorities of the borrower's country. There is a limitation on the foreign tax credit, which, simply stated, limits the total credits for foreign taxes on foreign source taxable income of a U.S. lender to an amount equal to the total U.S. taxes allocable to that income. Suppose a lender receives $100 in interest from country X and the borrower pays $15 to its government in withholding taxes on that interest. For U.S. tax purposes, the lender is considered to have received income of $115. If this were the lender's only foreign source income, the taxable income would be the difference between $115 and the lender's own interest and other costs allocable to the loan. If, for example, the lender's profit is $5, taxable income will be $5 plus the $15 paid in taxes to country X, or $20, on which the U.S. tax is roughly $10, which would be the limit on the foreign tax credit. Tax reform proposals now under consideration by the U.S. Congress would make it more difficult to derive a full U.S. tax benefit for foreign taxes on interest income.

4. The borrower's obligation to deliver tax receipts is important to the lender because the local tax in many countries is, technically, imposed on the lender, so the lender may well be liable if the borrower fails to pay.

5. Reading: Wood, _Law and Practice of International Finance_ (1983 ed.), Chapter 12.

(b) If any Bank, any Manager or the Agent is or becomes entitled under any applicable law or treaty to a reduced withholding rate, or a complete exemption from withholding, with respect to taxes imposed by or within the Republic of Somewhere or any political subdivision or taxing authority thereof or therein on payments to it by the Borrower or the Guarantor under this Agreement or the Notes, that Bank, that Manager or the Agent (as the case may be) shall complete and deliver from time to time to the Borrower or the Guarantor (as the case may be) any form that the Borrower or the Guarantor (as the case may be) is required to obtain from that Bank, that Manager or the Agent (as the case may be) in order to give effect to the reduced rate or exemption.

6.2. **Stamp Taxes**. The Borrower shall pay any registration or transfer taxes, stamp duties or similar levies, and any penalties or interest that may be due with respect thereto, that may be imposed by any jurisdiction in connection with this Agreement or the Notes. If the Agent or any Bank or Manager pays any amount in respect of any such taxes, duties, levies, penalties or interest, the Borrower shall reimburse the Agent or such Bank or Manager for that payment in Dollars on demand.

7. PAYMENTS; COMPUTATIONS

7.1. **Making of Payments**. (a) Each payment by the Borrower or the Guarantor under this Agreement or the Notes shall be made in Dollars, in funds settled through the New York Clearing House Interbank Payments System or such other same-day funds as the Agent may at the time determine to be customary for the settlement in New York City of international banking transactions denominated in Dollars, by 11:00 a.m. New York City time on the date that payment is due, to the Agent by deposit to the Agent's account no. 00-0000, maintained at Infallible Agent Bank, 1000 Wall Street, New York, New York 00000, or to such other account as the Agent may have last designated by notice to the Borrower and the Guarantor.

(b) Any payment stated to be due hereunder or under the Notes, and any Interest Period stated to end, on a given day in a specified month shall instead be made or end (as the case may be) (i) if there is no such day in that month, on the last Banking Day of that month or (ii) if that day is not a Banking Day, on the following Banking Day, unless that following Banking Day falls in a different calendar month, in which case that payment shall be made or that Interest Period shall end (as the case may be) on the preceding Banking Day.

> 1. This clause is important because it reflects, and makes applicable to the loans, the conventions of the London interbank market that will apply to any matching deposits obtained to fund the loans, so that interest and principal payments on the loans will be made in time to provide the banks with funds to make payments in respect of their matching deposits.
>
> 2. If an interest period is lengthened or shortened because of the operation of this provision, interest on the loans will accrue at the rate applicable for that interest period for the actual number of days in the period. Another, and we think less desirable approach, freezes interest payment dates (and interest periods) and separately states that, if a period must be extended, or a payment date must be changed, because of a holiday, interest will accrue on the loans for the period of the extension at the rate applicable for the period ending just before the extension.

7.2. <u>Computations</u>. Interest and commitment fees payable hereunder shall be computed on the basis of a 360-day year and actual days elapsed.

> The computation basis, or day-count fraction, reflected in this clause is usual in Eurodollar lending. It is commonly referred to as "actual/360" or "actual over 360". Other day-count fractions are used in computing other interest rates on loans and investments. For example, LIBOR for loans in pounds sterling and the "prime rate", which is also called the "base rate", are usually computed on the basis of actual days over 365. The computation basis is an important financial term of a loan transaction. For example, a year's interest at 10% per annum on a $100,000,000 loan computed on an actual/360 basis is $138,889 more than interest at the same rate on the actual/365 basis in a year that is not a leap year and $166,667 more in a leap year.

8. <u>CONDITIONS PRECEDENT</u>

> Reading: Clark & Taylor, "Conditions precedent and covenants in Eurocurrency loan agreements", <u>International Financial Law Review</u> (August 1982).

8.1. <u>Conditions to be Satisfied in Advance of the Disbursement Date</u>. The obligation of each Bank to make the Loan to be made by it hereunder is subject to the condition that the Agent receive on or before the fifth Banking Day before the Disbursement Date seven executed copies of each of the documents listed below, each dated the date of its delivery, in form and substance satisfactory to the Agent.

(a) A certificate of the Borrower, substantially in the form set forth in Exhibit D, together with the attachments specified therein.

(b) A certificate of the Guarantor, substantially in the form set forth in Exhibit E, together with the attachments specified therein.

(c) An opinion of counsel to the Borrower, substantially in the form set forth in Exhibit F.

(d) An opinion of counsel to the Guarantor, substantially in the form set forth in Exhibit G.

(e) An opinion of Local Law Office, special local counsel to the Agent, substantially in the form set forth in Exhibit H.

(f) An opinion of Messrs. X, Y & Z, special New York counsel to the Agent, substantially in the form set forth in Exhibit I.

1. The legal opinions required of counsel for the borrower and the guarantor usually deal with each of the subjects addressed by the representations and warranties made by the borrower and the guarantor (see Article 9) to the extent that the subjects involve matters of law, as opposed to pure questions of fact. Local counsel for the lenders or the agent is generally asked to cover most of the same matters in his or her opinion, although his or her lesser familiarity with the day-to-day operations of the borrower and the guarantor may lead local counsel to the lenders or the agent to limit his opinion to matters known to him or her, on some points.

2. Reading:

"Legal Opinions to Third Parties: An Easier Path" (A Report By The Special Committee on Legal Opinions in Commercial Transactions, New York County Lawyers' Association, In Cooperation with The Corporation Law Committee, Association of the Bar of the City of New York, and The Corporation Law Committee of the Banking, Corporation and Business Law Section, New York State Bar Association, 34 The Business Lawyer 1891 (1979).

Babb et al., "Legal Opinions to Third Parties in Corporate Transactions", 32 The Business Lawyer 553 (1977).

Committee on Developments in Business Financing, "Legal Opinions Given in Corporate Transactions", 33 The Business Lawyer 2389 (1978).

Fuld, "Legal Opinions in Business Transactions -- An Attempt to Bring Some Order Out of Some Chaos", 28 The Business Lawyer 915 (1973).

Fuld, "Lawyers' Standards and Responsibilities in Rendering Opinions", 33 The Business Lawyer 1295 (1978).

Jacobs, Opinion Letters in Securities Matters (Clark Boardman Company, Ltd., New York, 1980).

Landau, "Legal Opinions Rendered in Securities Transactions", Eighth Annual Institute on Securities Regulation (1976).

Segall & Arouh, "How to Prepare Legal Opinions", 25 The Practical Lawyer 29 (1979).

Wood, Law and Practice of International Finance (1983 ed.), Chapter 18.

Youard, "And If You Want My Opinion ...", Euromoney, September 1982.

(g) An irrevocable written acceptance by Eternal Mail Box of its appointment as the agent of the Borrower and the Guarantor to receive service of process, substantially in the form set forth in Exhibit J.

> When the borrower or the guarantor is a foreign sovereign that agrees to submit to the jurisdiction of the courts of another country for purposes of judicial actions relating to the loan agreement, the agent appointed by it to receive service of process is often the consul general or charge d'affaires of the sovereign state in the city in which the court proceedings may take place. In those cases, the form of letter of acceptance of appointment obtained from the process agent is often more elaborate than the form set forth in Exhibit J. Counsel for the sovereign borrower or guarantor is often asked to address the binding nature of the appointment in these cases. The form of acceptance letter should be drafted to ensure that the appointment is binding on anyone occupying the same post in the future, and not merely the individual who occupies the post at the time the loan agreement is entered into.

8.2. <u>Further Conditions to be Satisfied at or Before Disbursement</u>. The obligation of each Bank to make the Loan to be made by it hereunder is subject to the further conditions that (a) no event shall have occurred and be continuing at the time of disbursement of the Loans that constitutes, or that, with the giving of notice or the lapse of time or both, would constitute, an Event of Default and (b) the Agent shall have received at or before the time of disbursement of the Loans (i) for that Bank, nine Principal Notes evidencing the Loan of that Bank, in an aggregate amount equal to that Bank's Loan Commitment, each such Note in an amount equal to one repayment installment of that Loan, as determined pursuant to Section 3.1, duly executed and delivered by the Borrower, duly endorsed with the guaranty of the Guarantor and delivered by the Guarantor and dated the Disbursement Date, and (ii) such other documents as the Agent or any Bank may reasonably request, in form and substance satisfactory to the Agent.

> 1. The availability of expedited judicial proceedings and other procedural advantages to lenders suing on promissory notes over those suing on loan agreements is one of the many important areas of interplay between the law chosen to govern the interpretation of the loan agreement (usually English or New York law) and the law of the jurisdiction of the borrower.

> 2. Provisions relating to the delivery of closing documents for syndicated financings often give the agent discretion to waive compliance with conditions precedent, or to permit compliance with them after the time specified, if the non-compliance is not material.

> 3. Reading: Helpful articles on the use of promissory notes in lending transactions from the point of view of U.S. law (by Bruce W. Nichols) and English law (by Richard G.A. Youard), among others, appeared in <u>International Business Lawyer</u>, Volume 4(ii) (April 1976).

9. REPRESENTATIONS AND WARRANTIES

    9.1. <u>Representations and Warranties of the Borrower</u>. The Borrower makes the following representations and warranties to the Agent and each Bank and Manager.

    (a) The Borrower is a company duly organized and validly existing under the law of the Republic of Somewhere and has the power and authority to own its property, to conduct its business as currently conducted and to consummate the transactions contemplated in this Agreement.

    (b) The Borrower has taken all necessary action to authorize the execution and delivery of this Agreement and all other documents to be executed and delivered by it in connection with this Agreement, the performance of its obligations under this Agreement and the Notes and the consummation of the transactions contemplated in this Agreement.

    (c) This Agreement has been duly executed and delivered by the Borrower and constitutes, and each of the Notes, when duly executed and delivered by the Borrower, will constitute, a legal, valid and binding obligation of the Borrower, enforceable against the Borrower in accordance with its terms.

    (d) Except for the formalities referred to in Exhibit K, all governmental authorizations and actions of any kind necessary to authorize the Loans or required for the validity or enforceability against the Borrower of this Agreement or the Notes have been obtained or performed and are valid and subsisting in full force and effect.

> Reading: Wood, <u>Law and Practice of International Finance</u> (1983 ed.), Chapter 5 -- "Exchange Controls"

    (e) No event has occurred and is continuing that constitutes, or that, with the giving of notice or the lapse of time or both, would constitute, an Event of Default or a default under any agreement or instrument evidencing any Indebtedness of the Borrower, and no such event will occur upon the making of the Loans.

    (f) No consent or approval of, or notice to, any creditor of the Borrower is required by the terms of any agreement or instrument evidencing any Indebtedness of the Borrower for the execution or delivery of, or the performance of the obligations of the Borrower under, this Agreement or the Notes or the consummation of the transactions contemplated in this Agreement, and that execution, delivery, performance and consummation will not result in any breach or violation of, or constitute a default under, the charter or by-laws of the Borrower or any agreement, instrument, judgment, order, statute, rule or regulation applicable to the Borrower or to any of its property.

(g) There are no actions, proceedings or claims pending or, to the knowledge of the Borrower, threatened the adverse determination of which might have a materially adverse effect on the financial condition of the Borrower or impair its ability to perform its obligations under, or affect the validity or enforceability of, this Agreement or the Notes.

(h) Except as set forth in Exhibit L and except for liens of the types referred to in the proviso in Section 10.6(a), the Borrower has good title to its property free and clear of all liens and other encumbrances, and its obligations under this Agreement rank, and its obligations under the Notes will rank, at least _pari passu_ with all its other Indebtedness.

| This provision is an example of the "_pari passu_
| clause". The clause in effect states that there are no
| legal provisions which would cause the loans to be
| subordinated to other indebtedness of the borrower, and
| that the borrower has no secured indebtedness other
| than that referred to in Section 10.6(a) or the sched-
| ule of liens and encumbrances appended to the loan
| agreement. Borrowers often seek to limit the applica-
| tion of this provision to external indebtedness. See
| Section 9.2(g), which includes such a limitation for
| the guarantor.

(i) The Borrower's financial statements as at December 31, 1985 and for the fiscal year ended on such date are complete and correct, have been prepared in accordance with generally accepted principles of good accounting practice in the Republic of Somewhere, consistently applied, and have been certified by a firm of independent accountants as fairly presenting the financial condition of the Borrower as at such date and the results of its operations for such fiscal year.

| If the borrower has provided the lenders with
| quarterly financial statements (which would not nor-
| mally have been audited), the borrower should also be
| asked to represent that those financials have been
| prepared in accordance with generally accepted princi-
| ples of good accounting practice, often referred to as
| "GAAP". The borrower is entitled to ask that the rep-
| resentation as to the accuracy of the quarterly finan-

cial statements be "subject to normal year-end adjustments".

(j) There has been no material adverse change since December 31, 1985 in the financial condition of the Borrower or in the Borrower's ability to perform its obligations under this Agreement or the Notes.

> If the borrower has delivered quarterly financial statements, some drafters provide that the representation as to the absence of any material adverse change (sometimes called a "MAC" clause) runs from the date of the quarterly statements. Our practice, however, is to have it run from the date of the most recent audited statements, which are not subject to year-end adjustments. If there has in fact been a material adverse change in the financial condition of the borrower between the two dates, the relevant circumstances should of course be reviewed in detail between the lenders and the borrower, and the representation should be adapted to reflect those circumstances, assuming the change is not so drastic that the lenders will call off the transaction.

(k) The execution and delivery of this Agreement and the Notes are not subject to any tax, duty, fee or other charge, including, without limitation, any registration or transfer tax, stamp duty or similar levy, imposed by or within the Republic of Somewhere or any political subdivision or taxing authority thereof or therein.

(l) Neither the Borrower nor its property has any right of immunity on the grounds of sovereignty or otherwise from jurisdiction, attachment (before or after judgment) or execution in respect of any action or proceeding relating in any way to this Agreement or the Notes that may be brought in the courts of the Republic of Somewhere.

> Reading:
>
> Bistline & Stephenson, "Development of the United States Foreign Sovereign Immunities Act", _International Financial Law Review_ (August 1982).
>
> Stevenson, Browne & Damrosch, "United States law of sovereign immunity relating to international financial transactions", in 1 _International financial law_ (R. Rendell, ed., 1983 ed.), 97-116.
>
> Wall, "Waiver of sovereign immunity under United States law", _International Financial Law Review_ (November 1982).
>
> Wood, _Law and Practice of International Finance_ (1983 ed.), Chapter 4.

Youard, "Sovereign Loans -- Your Problems Solved", *Euromoney* (July 1982).

(m) The execution and delivery of this Agreement and the Notes by the Borrower and performance of its obligations hereunder and thereunder constitute commercial transactions.

(n) All information relating to the Borrower heretofore delivered to the Agent or any Bank in connection with this Agreement is complete and correct in all material respects.

9.2. <u>Representations and Warranties of the Guarantor</u>. The Guarantor makes the following representations and warranties to the Agent and each Bank and Manager.

(a) The Guarantor has taken all necessary action to authorize the Guaranty, its execution and delivery of this Agreement, endorsement of its guaranty on and delivery of the Notes, the execution and delivery of all other documents to be executed and delivered by it in connection with this Agreement and the performance of its obligations under this Agreement and the Notes.

(b) This Agreement has been duly executed and delivered by the Guarantor and constitutes, and each of the Notes, when duly executed and delivered by the Borrower and duly endorsed with the guaranty of and delivered by the Guarantor, will constitute, a legal, valid and binding obligation of the Guarantor, enforceable against the Guarantor in accordance with its terms.

(c) Except for the formalities listed in Exhibit K, all governmental authorizations and actions of any kind necessary to authorize the Loans, the Guaranty or the endorsement of the Notes by the Guarantor with its guaranty or required for the validity or enforceability against the Guarantor of this Agreement or the Notes have been obtained or performed and are valid and subsisting in full force and effect.

(d) No event has occurred and is continuing that constitutes, or that, with the giving of notice or the lapse of time or both, would constitute, an Event of Default or a default under any agreement or instrument evidencing any External Indebtedness of the Guarantor, and no such event will occur upon the making of the Loans.

(e) No consent or approval of, or notice to, any creditor of the Guarantor is required by the terms of any agreement or instrument evidencing any Indebtedness of the Guarantor for the execution or endorsement (as the case may be) or the delivery by the Guarantor of, or the performance of its obligations under, this Agreement or the Notes, and that execution, endorsement, delivery and performance will not result in any breach or violation of, or constitute a default under, any agreement, instrument, judgment, order, statute, rule or regulation applicable to the Guarantor or to any of its property or under the Constitution of the Republic of Somewhere.

(f) There are no actions, proceedings or claims pending or, to the knowledge of the Guarantor, threatened the adverse determination of which might have a materially adverse effect on the financial condition of the Guarantor or impair the ability of the Guarantor to perform its obligations under, or affect the validity or enforceability of, this Agreement or the Notes.

(g) Except as set forth in Exhibit M and except for liens of the types referred to in Section 10.6(b), the Guarantor has good title to its property free and clear of all liens and other encumbrances, and the obligations of the Guarantor under this Agreement rank, and its obligations under the Notes will rank, at least *pari passu* with all its other External Indebtedness.

(h) The execution and delivery of this Agreement and the delivery of the Notes endorsed with the guaranty of the Guarantor are not subject to any tax, duty, fee or other charge, including, without limitation, any registration or transfer tax, stamp duty or similar levy, imposed by or within the Republic of Somewhere or any political subdivision or taxing authority thereof or therein.

(i) Neither the Guarantor nor its property has any right of immunity on the grounds of sovereignty or otherwise from jurisdiction, attachment (before or after judgment) or execution in respect of any action or proceeding relating in any way to this Agreement or the Notes that may be brought in the courts of the Republic of Somewhere.

(j) The execution and delivery of this Agreement by the Guarantor and performance of its obligations hereunder and endorsement of its guaranty on and delivery by it of the Notes and performance by it of its obligations thereunder constitute commercial transactions.

(k) The full faith and credit of the Guarantor is pledged for the due and punctual performance of its obligations under this Agreement and the Notes.

(l) The Guarantor is a member of, and is entitled to use the general resources of, the International Monetary Fund.

(m) All information relating to the Guarantor heretofore delivered to the Agent or any Bank in connection with this Agreement is complete and correct in all material respects.

9.3. <u>Repetition of Representations and Warranties</u>. Each of the representations and warranties set forth in Section 9.1 and Section 9.2 shall be deemed to be repeated at the time of disbursement of the Loans as if made at and as of that time and on each Interest Payment Date as if made on and as of that date.

> Borrowers routinely represent to lenders that there has been no material adverse change in the financial condition of the borrower during the period between the date of the borrower's most recent financial statements and the date of the loan agreement. See Section 9.1(i). Moreover, loan agreements usually provide that the lenders will not be required to disburse the loans if there is a material adverse change between the date of those financial statements and the disbursement date for the loans. See Section 8.2(a). Borrowers frequently seek to have that representation excluded from the provision for repetition of representations and warranties. If that representation is not excluded, the lenders will be able to require repayment of the loans whenever there is a material adverse change in the financial condition of the borrower between the date of the financial statements and the date when the representation and warranty is repeated.

10. <u>COVENANTS</u>

> Reading: Clark & Taylor, "Conditions precedent and covenants in Eurocurrency loan agreements", <u>International Financial Law Review</u> (August 1982); Logan & Rowntree, "Term loan agreements", in 1 <u>International financial law</u> (R. Rendell, ed., 1983 ed.) 5-6; Wood, <u>Law and Practice of International Finance</u> (1983 ed.), Chapter 6.

10.1. <u>Use of Proceeds</u>. The Borrower shall use the proceeds of the Loans as working capital.

> See Logan & Rowntree, "Term loan agreements", in 1 <u>International financial law</u> (R. Rendell, ed., 1983 ed.), 4, for a discussion of special concerns on the use made of loan proceeds by foreign public-sector borrowers for federally-chartered U.S. banks attempting to determine which loans must be aggregated for purposes of the single-borrower limit applicable to those banks.

10.2. <u>Governmental Authorizations</u>. Each of the Borrower and the Guarantor shall obtain, make and keep in full force and effect all authorizations from and registrations with governmental authorities that may be required for the validity or enforceability against the Borrower and the Guarantor of this Agreement or the Notes.

| This area is primarily the responsibility of local
| counsel and will be covered by his opinion to the agent
| or the lenders. A principal concern is compliance with
| exchange controls, since the sanctions for failure to
| comply with them can be quite severe and may even ren-
| der the loan agreement unenforceable.

10.3. <u>Financial Statements</u>. (a) The Borrower shall furnish to the Agent, with a copy for each Bank, not later than the forty-fifth day after the close of each quarter of each of its fiscal years, its balance sheet as at the close of that quarter and its income statement and statement of changes in financial position for that quarter, prepared in accordance with generally accepted principles of good accounting practice in the Republic of Somewhere, consistently applied (except insofar as any change in the application thereof is disclosed in those financial statements and is concurred in by a firm of independent accountants of international standing selected by the Borrower and acceptable to the Agent), certified by the Borrower's chief financial officer as fairly presenting the financial condition of the Borrower as at the close of that quarter and the results of its operations for that quarter.

(b) The Borrower shall furnish to the Agent, with a copy for each Bank, not later than the ninetieth day after the close of each of its fiscal years, its balance sheet as at the close of that fiscal year and its income statement and statement of changes in financial position for that fiscal year, prepared in accordance with generally accepted principles of good accounting practice in the Republic of Somewhere, consistently applied (except insofar as any change in the application thereof is disclosed in those financial statements and is concurred in by a firm of independent accountants of international standing selected by the Borrower and acceptable to the Agent), certified by those accountants as fairly presenting the financial condition of the Borrower as at the close of that fiscal year and the results of its operations for that fiscal year, which certification shall include or be accompanied by a statement that, during the examination by that firm of those financial statements, that firm observed or discovered no event that constituted, or that, with the giving of notice or the lapse of time or both, would have constituted, an Event of Default (or a detailed description of any such event so observed or discovered).

(c) The Borrower shall furnish to the Agent from time to time such other statements and information as the Agent or any Bank may reasonably request.

(d) The Guarantor shall deliver to the Agent from time to time such financial, statistical and general information relating to the Guarantor as the Agent or any Bank may reasonably request.

10.4. _Inspection Rights_. The Borrower shall enable representatives of the Agent or any Bank to examine its property and records at any reasonable time.

> This clause, though seemingly innocuous, may be troublesome to borrowers. Borrowers in certain businesses, and particularly banks, may be subject to confidentiality requirements that would render compliance with this clause unlawful. Other borrowers may be concerned about the confidentiality of their business plans. Public-sector borrowers that have policy as well as operational objectives are particularly sensitive to clauses of this kind.

10.5. _Notices of Default_. Each of the Borrower and the Guarantor shall promptly give notice to the Agent of each event that constitutes, or that, with the giving of notice or the lapse of time or both, would constitute, an Event of Default and each other event that has or might have a materially adverse effect on its ability to perform its obligations under this Agreement or the Notes.

> The principal purpose of this clause is to place an obligation on the borrower to give notice to the lenders of the occurrence of events of default that are likely to be known to the borrower before they would otherwise be known to the lenders, such as defaults on other debt instruments. It should be noted that a borrower that fails to give the required notice in a timely manner may forfeit the grace period (also known as a "cure period") that the borrower would otherwise have to remedy the default. Agreements are sometimes written to require periodic delivery by the borrower and the guarantor of a certificate to the effect that no event of default (or event that could ripen into one) exists.

10.6. _Liens and Encumbrances_. (a) The Borrower shall not create or permit to be created any lien or other encumbrance on any of its property; _provided_, _however_, that this Section shall not apply to (i) any lien created on property at the time of purchase thereof by the Borrower solely as security for the payment of the purchase price thereof, (ii) any lien arising in the ordinary course of banking transactions and securing Indebtedness of the Borrower, maturing not more than one year after the date on which it is originally incurred or (iii) any lien on inventory securing Indebtedness of the Borrower, maturing not more than one year after the date on which it is originally incurred and to be repaid out of the proceeds of the sale of that inventory.

(b) The Guarantor shall not create or permit to be created any lien or other encumbrance on any of its property (including, without limitation, International Monetary

Assets) or revenues, except liens arising in connection with contracts entered into substantially simultaneously for sales and purchases at market prices of precious metals.

> 1. This provision is an example of the "negative pledge clause." It works together with Section 9.1(h) and Section 9.2(g), the _pari passu_ clauses. More elaborate exceptions will often be necessary in light of the particular business of the borrower and other circumstances affecting it or the guarantor. When the borrower or guarantor is a foreign sovereign, the lenders may seek to have the negative pledge clause applicable to the sovereign include a prohibition against liens on property of public-sector entities in general. Where this is the case, the exceptions tend to be numerous, so that the prohibitions do not hamper the conduct of the country's foreign trade or have unintended, adverse effects on its economy.

> 2. Negative pledge clauses are sometimes written to prohibit the creation of any lien or other encumbrance (other than any expressly excepted) to secure any indebtedness unless the lenders under the agreement are equally and ratably secured. A variant of this approach is to provide that the creation of any prohibited lien or encumbrance will automatically constitute the grant of an equal and ratable security interest to the lenders being protected by the negative pledge clause. This approach may not suffice to create or perfect the security interest that is sought, but it may prove helpful in certain circumstances as the basis for an action to prevent other lenders with knowledge of the prohibition from completing their arrangements for financing that would violate the clause. See the complaint in _Citibank, N.A. v. Export-Import Bank of the United States_, 76 Civ. 3513 (S.D.N.Y. 1976) (in an action that seems not to have proceeded beyond the complaint stage).

10.7. _Insurance_. The Borrower shall maintain insurance on its property, with financially sound and reputable insurers, to the extent and against the risks customary for companies in similar businesses.

10.8. _Maintenance of Current Ratio_. The Borrower shall at all times maintain a ratio of current assets to current liabilities of not less than 1.5:1. For purposes of this Section, "current assets" means, at any time, cash, accounts receivable due within 12 months after that time (less an appropriate reserve for bad debts), prepaid expenses, inventories and all other assets that could in the ordinary course of business be converted into cash within 12 months after that time, and "current liabilities" means, at any time, accounts payable due within 12 months after that time, customer advances, amounts due for income taxes, dividends, bonuses and all other liabilities payable, or that could be called for payment, within 12 months after such time.

> This clause and Section 10.9 are examples of "financial covenants". These covenants are much more elaborate in cases where the borrower has found it necessary, in order to obtain financing, to make more detailed commitments to the lenders as to how the borrower will conduct its business during the life of the loan. Financial covenants are more frequently included in domestic U.S. loan agreements than in Eurodollar financings. Elaborate financial covenants are negotiated, in particular, in project finance situations and when loans are made to finance leveraged buy outs of businesses. They can be difficult to monitor in agreements with borrowers from jurisdictions where accounting practices and principles change frequently and should be examined in light of local accounting principles to ensure that they make sense. Similar caution should be taken with other kinds of business-related covenants, such as those which restrict distributions of dividends, since such matters may be regulated by applicable local law.

10.9. <u>Maintenance of Ratio of Debt to Equity</u>. The Borrower shall at all times maintain a ratio of debt to equity not greater than 1.2:1. For purposes of this Section, "debt" means any Indebtedness incurred by the Borrower and maturing more than one year after the date on which it is originally incurred, and "equity" means the sum of the Borrower's unimpaired paid-in capital, surplus and free reserves.

10.10. <u>Notice of Tax Exemption</u>. If an exemption is obtained at any time from any present or future taxes imposed by or within the Republic of Somewhere or any political subdivision or taxing authority thereof or therein that would otherwise be due in respect of any payment to be made by the Borrower or the Guarantor under this Agreement or the Notes, the Borrower or the Guarantor (as the case may be) shall promptly deliver to the Agent a certified copy of the documents evidencing that exemption.

11. <u>THE GUARANTY</u>

11.1. <u>The Guaranty</u>. (a) The Guarantor irrevocably guarantees (as primary obligor and not merely as surety) payment in full as provided herein, of all amounts payable by the Borrower under this Agreement and the Notes, as and when those amounts become payable (whether at stated maturity, by acceleration or otherwise).

(b) The Guarantor's obligations under this Guaranty shall be unconditional, irrespective of the validity or enforceability of any other provision of this Agreement or of the Notes.

(c) This Guaranty is a guaranty of payment and shall remain in full force and effect until all amounts payable by the Borrower under this Agreement and the Notes have been validly, finally and irrevocably paid in full, and shall not be affected in any way by the absence of any action to obtain those amounts from the Borrower or by any variation, extension, waiver, compromise or release of any or all of the obligations of the Borrower hereunder or under the Notes or of any security from time to time therefor. The Guarantor waives all requirements as to promptness, diligence, presentment, demand for payment, protest and notice of any kind with respect to this Agreement and the Notes.

> Section 11.1(a) and Section 11.1(c) are examples of guaranty provisions used in guaranties of payment, as opposed to guaranties of collection. Under a guaranty of payment, the beneficiaries of the guaranty need not seek to enforce their claims for payment against the borrower in order to be entitled to payment from the guarantor. Under a guaranty of collection, such prior action would be required before the beneficiaries could turn to the guarantor for payment.

(d) This Guaranty shall not be affected by the occurrence of any Event of Default, by any change in the laws, rules or regulations of the Republic of Somewhere or by any present or future action of any governmental authority or court amending, varying, reducing or otherwise affecting, or purporting to amend, vary, reduce or otherwise affect, any of the obligations of the Borrower under this Agreement or the Notes or by any other circumstance (other than by complete, irrevocable payment) that might otherwise constitute a legal or equitable discharge or defense of a surety or a guarantor. If the Borrower merges or consolidates with or into another entity, loses its separate legal identity or ceases to exist, the Guarantor shall nonetheless continue to be liable for the payment of all amounts payable by the Borrower under this Agreement and the Notes.

(e) This Guaranty shall remain in full force and effect or shall be reinstated (as the case may be) if at any time any payment of the Borrower, in whole or in part, is rescinded or must otherwise be returned by the Agent or by any Bank or Manager upon the insolvency, bankruptcy or reorganization of the Borrower or otherwise, all as though such payment had not been made.

> This provision is an example of a "claw-back clause". Bankruptcy and similar laws in some jurisdictions provide for return to a troubled company, or to a trustee or similar official appointed with respect to the company or its property, of certain kinds of payments made to the company, often within specified periods before the filing or commencement of bankruptcy

or similar proceedings. The "claw-back clause" provides for the guaranty to continue in effect, or to be reinstated, if all or part of any payment by the borrower to the agent or any of the banks or managers must be returned or is rescinded under such circumstances.

(f) The Guarantor recognizes that this Guaranty is governed by the law of the State of New York and expressly agrees that any rights or privileges that it might otherwise have under Articles 1, 2 and 10 of the Civil Code and Article 50 of the Commercial Code of the Republic of Somewhere shall not be applicable to this Guaranty.

Lenders seek to have this provision included when local counsel indicates that special statutory protections for guarantors should be expressly waived to protect the lenders in the event legal proceedings are brought in the guarantor's jurisdiction.

(g) If at any time when any amount payable by the Borrower under this Agreement or any Note is overdue and unpaid the Guarantor receives any amount as a result of any action against the Borrower or any of its property or assets or otherwise for or on account of any payment made by the Guarantor under this Guaranty, the Guarantor shall forthwith pay that amount received by it to the Agent, without demand, to be credited and applied upon any such amount payable by the Borrower.

Guaranties customarily include limitations on the guarantor's rights of subrogation against the borrower in respect of payments made by the guarantor under the guaranty. The sample provision requires that the guarantor pay the agent any amount received by the guarantor in respect of any such payment made by it, if any amount payable by the borrower is overdue and unpaid at the time. Other versions of this provision seek to limit the guarantor's rights further, by requiring it to pay the agent amounts received by the guarantor through the exercise of its subrogation rights whether or not any payment by the borrower is overdue at the time.

11.2. <u>Endorsement on Notes</u>. As further evidence of this Guaranty, the Guarantor shall endorse its guaranty of payment on the Notes, but no failure by the Agent or the Banks to insist upon such endorsement shall affect the existence, validity or terms of this Guaranty, and the form of guaranty endorsed on the Notes by the Guarantor shall not be construed as in diminution of or substitution for any of the obligations or agreements of the Guarantor under this Guaranty.

12. <u>EVENTS OF DEFAULT</u>

12.1. <u>Events of Default</u>. If one or more of the

following events of default (each an "Event of Default") shall occur and be continuing, the Agent and the Banks shall be entitled to the remedies set forth in Section 12.2.

> Reading: Clark & Taylor, "Events of default in Eurocurrency loan agreements", <u>International Financial Law Review</u> (September 1982); Wood, <u>Law and Practice of International Finance</u> (1983 ed.), Chapter 7.

(a) The Borrower fails to pay any amount payable hereunder as and when such amount becomes payable or fails to deliver any Interest Note to the Agent as provided in Section 4.4 or Section 8.2.

> Borrowers often request a grace period for defaults, particularly those involving interest payments. Although it is not unusual to find a short grace period for interest defaults in domestic U.S. loan agreements, Eurocurrency lenders are reluctant to agree to such a grace period because the matching deposit mechanism assumes that each lender will be able to obtain a deposit in the London interbank market for precisely the term of each interest period, at LIBOR, and be confident that it will receive interest at the end of the period, at LIBOR (which it will apply to pay interest on the deposit it obtained) plus the agreed-upon "margin", or "spread".

(b) The Borrower or the Guarantor fails to perform or observe any covenant or agreement contained herein to be performed or observed by it other than those referred to in Section 12.1(a), if that failure is not remedied (i) on or before the fifteenth day after it occurs, in the case of the covenant set forth in Section 10.5, or (ii) on or before the thirtieth day after it occurs, in the case of any other such covenant.

(c) Any representation or warranty of the Borrower or the Guarantor in this Agreement or any other document delivered in connection with this Agreement proves to have been incorrect, incomplete or misleading in any material respect at the time it was made or repeated or deemed to have been made or repeated.

(d) The Borrower or any Subsidiary (i) fails to pay any of its Indebtedness as and when that Indebtedness becomes payable or (ii) fails to perform or observe any covenant or agreement to be performed or observed by it contained in any other agreement or in any instrument evidencing any of its Indebtedness if, as a result of that failure, any other party to that agreement or instrument is entitled to exercise, and has not irrevocably waived, the right to accelerate the maturity of any amount owing thereunder.

> 1. The sample cross-default clause applies only

to defaults in connection with the payment of money and to defaults that permit lenders to accelerate payment of the indebtedness with respect to which the default occurs. Lenders sometimes seek broader cross-default clauses that include all defaults under other credit agreements.

2. Borrowers often seek to include a de minimis provision in the cross-default clause, specifying that a default in a borrowing of a small amount will not trigger defaults on other debt. Borrowers (and particularly sovereign borrowers) often seek to exclude internal debt from the coverage of cross-default provisions. See Section 12.1(e), which includes such limitations in the cross-default clause applicable to the guarantor.

3. Reading: Carroll, "The Worst Clause in the Euromarkets", Euromoney, June 1981; Youard, "Why the Cross-Default Clause Won't Go Away", Euromoney, July 1981.

(e) The Guarantor (i) fails to pay any of its External Indebtedness as and when that External Indebtedness becomes payable or (ii) fails to perform or observe any covenant or agreement to be performed or observed by it contained in any agreement or instrument evidencing any of its External Indebtedness if, as a result of that failure, any other party to that agreement or instrument is entitled to exercise, and has not irrevocably waived, the right to accelerate the maturity of any amount owing thereunder; provided, however, that such failure shall not constitute an Event of Default under this subsection if (A) the overdue amounts in the aggregate do not exceed $10,000,000, or the equivalent thereof in any other currency or currencies, (B) the obligation to pay the overdue amounts has not resulted from acceleration and (C) that failure is remedied on or before the thirtieth day after it occurs.

(f) The Borrower or any Subsidiary (i) is dissolved, (ii) fails or is unable or admits in writing its inability to pay its debts generally as they become due, (iii) commences a voluntary case in bankruptcy or any other action or proceeding for any other relief under any law affecting creditors' rights that is similar to a bankruptcy law, (iv) consents by answer or otherwise to the commencement against it of an involuntary case in bankruptcy or any other such action or proceeding, (v) is the subject of an order for relief or a decree in an involuntary case in bankruptcy or any other such action or proceeding in respect of it or any of its property or (vi) has a receiver, custodian or similar official appointed for it of any of its property, if that order or decree or appointment is not dismissed or stayed or terminated on or before the sixtieth day after the entry of the order or decree or the appointment or if any such dismissal or stay ceases to be in effect.

(g) Any governmental authorization necessary for the performance of any obligation of the Borrower or the Guarantor under this Agreement or the Notes fails to become or enter into or remain valid and subsisting in full force and effect.

(h) Any governmental authority or court takes any action that, in the reasonable opinion of Majority Banks, adversely affects the condition of the Borrower or the Guarantor or the ability of the Borrower or the Guarantor to perform its obligations under this Agreement or the Notes, if that action is not rescinded on or before the thirtieth day after it occurs or if that rescission ceases to be in effect.

(i) The aggregate amount of unsatisfied judgments, decrees or orders for the payment of money against the Borrower or any Subsidiary or the Guarantor exceeds $500,000, in the case of the Borrower or any Subsidiary, or $10,000,000, in the case of the Guarantor, or the equivalent thereof in any other currency or currencies.

(j) The Borrower or any Subsidiary sells or otherwise disposes of all or a substantial part of its assets or ceases to conduct all or a substantial part of its business as now conducted, or merges or consolidates with any other company without the prior written consent of the Banks, unless the entity surviving the merger or consolidation is the Borrower (in any case involving the Borrower) or a Subsidiary (in any other case).

(k) The Guaranty is disaffirmed or questioned as to its validity or enforceability by the Guarantor or ceases for any reason to be valid and in full force and effect.

(l) The Guarantor fails or is unable to pay its debt generally as they become due or admits in writing its inability to pay its debt generally or declares a moratorium on payment of its debts.

(m) The Guarantor ceases to be a member of, or entitled to use the general resources of, the International Monetary Fund.

12.2. *Default Remedies*. (a) If any Event of Default shall occur and be continuing, the Agent shall, upon the request of Majority Banks, by notice to the Borrower and the Guarantor, (i) declare the obligations of each Bank hereunder to be terminated, whereupon those obligations shall terminate, and (ii) declare all amounts payable hereunder by the Borrower or the Guarantor that would otherwise be due after the date of that termination to be immediately due and payable, whereupon all those amounts shall become immediately due and payable, all without diligence, presentment, demand of payment, protest or notice of any kind, which are expressly waived by the Borrower and the Guarantor; provided, however, that, if an event of a kind referred to in Section 12.1(f) occurs, the obligations of the Banks hereunder shall immediately terminate, and all amounts payable hereunder by the Borrower or the Guarantor that would otherwise be due after the occurrence of that event shall become immediately due and payable, without any such notice or other formality waived by the Borrower and the Guarantor in this Section.

(b) Each Bank is acting hereunder individually. Nothing herein, and no action taken by the Banks, the Managers or the Agent hereunder shall be construed to constitute them or any of them a partnership, an association, any other entity or a joint venture. Without limiting the generality of the foregoing, each Bank, each Manager and the Agent shall be entitled to act independently, whether by court action or otherwise, to enforce or protect its rights under this Agreement and the Notes, subject, in the case of each Bank, to the provisions of Section 12.2(a) regarding any declaration that any unmatured obligations of the Borrower hereunder or under the Notes shall be immediately due and payable upon the occurrence of an Event of Default.

> 1. As indicated in the opening recital of the agreement and in Section 2.1, the banks' obligations under the agreement are several, and not joint. Therefore, each of the banks should also be entitled to exercise its rights and remedies individually, except to the extent that it has agreed otherwise. The sample provision is intended to make that clear and to avoid a determination that the syndicate of lenders is analagous to a joint venture and, therefore, that its members should be entitled to take court action to enforce their rights only jointly or through the agent bank. See Credit Francais International, S.A. v. Sociedad Financiera de Comercio, C.A., 490 N.Y.S.2d 670 (Sup. Ct. 1985).

> 2. The final sentence of the sample provision represents a concession made by the lenders in exchange for the benefits of participating in a syndicated financing (e.g., the opportunity to lend to a borrower that may not have an established relationship with a given bank, the ability to lend on terms available in a major financing but perhaps not to an individual lender willing to offer only a fraction of the total amount, and the shifting of administrative burdens to the agent). Each bank has agreed to limit its right to accelerate to circumstances that Majority Banks agree warrant that kind of action. Borrowers generally expect this kind of protection, which can be particularly important when there is an established relationship between the borrower and the major participants in the syndicate, but not the smaller participants. In such instances, if there is a default, the major lenders may

> well have greater confidence in the borrower's ability
> to cure the situation, or be more willing to partici-
> pate in a restructuring, than the smaller participants.
>
> 3. Reading: Buchheit, "Is syndicated lending a
> joint venture?" _International Financial Law Review_
> (August 1985).

12.3. <u>Right of Setoff</u>. If any amount payable hereunder is not paid as and when due, each of the Borrower and the Guarantor hereby authorizes each Bank and each affiliate of each Bank to proceed, to the fullest extent permitted by applicable law, without prior notice, by right of setoff, banker's lien or counterclaim, against any assets of the Borrower or the Guarantor in any currency that may at any time be in the possession of that Bank or affiliate, at any branch or office, to the full extent of all amounts payable to the Banks hereunder. Any Bank that so proceeds or that has an affiliate that so proceeds shall forthwith give notice to the Agent of any action taken by that Bank or affiliate pursuant to this Section.

> The sample clause seeks to confer broader setoff
> rights than would exist under New York law, either as a
> matter of common law or by statute. Note, in particu-
> lar, that the clause extends setoff rights to affili-
> ates and permits each bank to exercise rights of setoff
> to the extent of all the banks' loans under the agree-
> ment (to the extent permitted by applicable law). This
> clause operates in conjunction with Section 13.2 on
> sharing of payments.

12.4. <u>Rights Not Exclusive</u>. The rights provided for herein are cumulative and are not exclusive of any other rights, powers, privileges or remedies provided by law.

13. <u>APPLICATION, DISTRIBUTION AND SHARING OF PAYMENTS</u>

13.1. <u>Application and Distribution of Payments</u>. All payments received by the Agent from the Borrower or the Guarantor pursuant to this Agreement or the Notes shall, regardless of the application designated by the Borrower or the Guarantor (as the case may be), be applied, first, to any sum due and owing pursuant to Article 15, second, to any fees due and owing pursuant to Article 5, third, to any premium due and owing pursuant to Section 3.2, fourth, to any interest due and owing on the Loans and, fifth, to the repayment of the principal of the Loans. Such payments shall be distributed promptly upon receipt among the Agent, the Banks and the Managers in like funds as received, in proportion to the respective amounts of the sums payable pursuant to Article 15, fees payable pursuant to Article 5, premium, interest or principal, as the case may be, at the time due and owing to each of them.

13.2. <u>Sharing of Payments</u>. If any Bank at any time obtains total or partial payment of any amount payable hereunder other than pursuant to Section 3.3 or by distribution by the Agent pursuant to Section 13.1, that Bank shall forthwith give notice to that effect to the Agent, which shall forward the notice to the other Banks. Unless Majority Banks determine that the amount so obtained need not be shared as provided herein, that Bank shall forthwith pay that amount to the Agent, and the Agent shall apply and distribute that amount pursuant to the provisions of Section 13.1 as if that amount were a payment made by the Borrower or the Guarantor; <u>provided</u>, <u>however</u>, that, if any Bank at any time obtains total or partial payment of any amount payable hereunder by exercising a right of setoff, banker's lien or counterclaim, unless such a determination is made by Majority Banks, that Bank shall forthwith purchase from the other Banks such participations in the principal of or interest on the Loans made by those other Banks as shall be necessary to cause the purchasing Bank to share that amount ratably with those other Banks; and <u>provided</u> <u>further</u>, <u>however</u>, that, if all or any portion of that amount is thereafter recovered from that purchasing Bank, the purchase shall be rescinded and the purchase price restored to the extent of that recovery, but with such adjustments of interest as Majority Banks shall determine to be equitable. Any Bank so purchasing a participation from another Bank pursuant to this Section may, to the fullest extent permitted by law, exercise all its rights of payment with respect to that participation as fully as if that Bank were the direct creditor of each of the Borrower or the Guarantor in the amount of that participation. Nothing herein contained shall in any way affect the right of any Bank to retain any amount obtained with respect to indebtedness other than indebtedness under this Agreement or the Notes.

> 1. This provision, known as a "sharing clause", operates together with Section 12.3, which permits the lenders to set off against deposits of the borrower and the guarantor. The sharing clause has undergone substantial changes in light of experience with its use following the freeze of Iranian assets imposed by the United States and following the Falklands/Malvinas crisis, when Argentine borrowers made debt repayments only to non-British lenders. The sharing clause requires a Bank that has exercised setoff rights to acquire the other banks' rights to receive payments from the borrower in amounts sufficient effectively to redistribute the amount obtained by setoff among all the banks. The clause is sometimes written to require the banks to share amounts recovered by them net of the costs of any legal proceedings brought to obtain the recovery. Some lenders seek to restrict their obligations to share amounts obtained through legal proceedings so that other lenders that could have participated in the proceedings, but chose not to, do not benefit from the recovery obtained.

2. Sharing provisions sometimes include more detailed procedures on how the sharing will be effected (including guidelines on how frequently the agent should calculate the amounts to be shared by participation purchases), and some agreements now include a form of the participation agreement to be used to implement purchases under the clause. The sharing clause may also provide that, for purposes of provisions requiring the vote of the lenders, each lender's voting rights will be determined on the basis of its loan interests determined without taking into account any purchase of participations effected pursuant to the sharing clause.

3. Reading: Cates & Isern-Feliu, "The Real Purpose of the Sharing Clause", *Euromoney* (November 1982); Ludwig, "International Crisis May Lead to Improved Loan Documentation", *American Banker*, September 7, 1983; Youard, "Enough is Enough", *Euromoney* (November 1983).

14. THE AGENT AND THE MANAGERS

14.1. *The Agent and the Managers*. (a) Each Bank authorizes the Agent to exercise on its behalf the powers specifically delegated to the Agent herein and all other powers reasonably incidental thereto. The relationship between the Agent and each Bank is that of agent and principal only, and nothing herein shall be deemed to constitute the Agent a trustee for any Bank or to impose on the Agent any obligations other than those for which express provision is made herein.

Reading: Cates, "The role of managers and agents in syndicated loans", *International Financial Law Review* (June 1982); Ryan, "International bank loan syndications and participations", in 1 *International financial law* (R. Rendell, ed., 1983 ed.), 15-30; Youard, "The Agent's Role Revisited", *Euromoney*, May 1982.

(b) Neither the Agent nor any Manager nor any director, officer, employee or agent of any of them shall have any responsibility for (i) any failure of the Borrower or the Guarantor to fulfill any obligation under this Agreement or the Notes, (ii) the truth of any representation or warranty made by the Borrower or the Guarantor in this Agreement or any other document delivered in connection with this Agreement or (iii) the validity or enforceability of this Agreement or the Notes against the Borrower or the Guarantor.

(c) Neither the Agent nor any of its directors, officers, employees or agents shall have any responsibility for any action taken or omitted to be taken in connection with this Agreement or the Notes, except for gross negligence or willful misconduct, and neither any Manager nor any of its directors, officers, employees or agents shall have any duty, obligation or responsibility of any nature whatsoever with respect to this Agreement or the Notes.

(d) The Agent shall be entitled to rely in good faith on any document believed by it to be genuine and to have been sent or signed by the proper person and on the opinions and statements of any independent legal counsel or other professional advisors selected by it and shall not be liable to any other party for any consequence of any such reliance.

(e) Each Bank has made such investigation and evaluation of the creditworthiness of the Borrower and the Guarantor as it has judged appropriate and prudent in connection with the making of its Loan. Except as expressly provided herein, the Agent shall have no duty to provide any Bank with any credit or other information with respect to the Borrower or the Guarantor, whether such information comes into its possession before or after the disbursement of the Loans.

(f) The Agent shall promptly (i) transmit to each Bank each notice or other document received by the Agent from the Borrower or the Guarantor addressed to, or calling for action by, that Bank, (ii) advise each Bank upon receipt of all the documents referred to in Section 8.1, (iii) advise each Bank upon its receipt of all documents referred to in Section 8.2, (iv) forward to each Bank all Notes received by it for that Bank and (v) forward to each Bank copies of any documents delivered to the Agent pursuant to Section 6.1. The Agent shall, as soon as practicable, forward to each Bank copies of the documents received pursuant to Section 8.1 and Section 8.2.

(g) The Agent shall not be under any obligation to inquire as to the performance by the Borrower or the Guarantor of its obligations under this Agreement or the Notes; provided, however, that the Agent shall give prompt notice to each Bank of any event of which it receives actual notice in its capacity as Agent hereunder that constitutes, or that, with the giving of notice or the lapse of time or both, would constitute, an Event of Default.

(h) Except as otherwise expressly provided herein, neither the Agent nor any Manager shall be obligated to account to any Bank for any amount received in respect of any loan maintained by the Agent or any Manager or any affiliate of any of them or for the profit related thereto. The Agent and the Managers and the affiliates of each of them may, without liability to account to any Bank therefor, make loans to, accept deposits from, and generally engage in any kind of business with, the Borrower and the Guarantor as though the Agent were not the Agent and the Managers were not Managers.

(i) The Agent may treat each Bank as the holder of each Note delivered for that Bank pursuant to this Agreement for all purposes whatsoever unless and until the Agent receives notice of a transfer or assignment thereof and the written agreement of the person or persons to whom that Note has been transferred or assigned to be bound by the terms of this Agreement.

(j) The Agent may resign at any time by giving written notice to the Banks, the Borrower and the Guarantor or be removed with or without cause by Majority Banks by notice to the Agent. Upon the giving of a notice of either kind, Majority Banks shall have the right to appoint a successor Agent. If a successor Agent has not accepted an appointment hereunder on or before the thirtieth day after the notice of resignation or removal of the retiring Agent is given, the retiring Agent may appoint a successor Agent, which shall be a bank having a combined capital and surplus of at least $50,000,000, or the equivalent thereof in another currency or currencies, or an affiliate of such a bank. When a successor Agent has accepted its appointment as Agent hereunder and notice of its acceptance has been given to the Borrower, the Guarantor and the Banks, the successor Agent shall succeed to and become vested with all the rights, powers, privileges and duties of the retiring Agent, and the retiring Agent shall be discharged from its duties and obligations under this Agreement. Notwithstanding the resignation or removal of any retiring Agent hereunder, the provisions of this Article shall continue to inure to the benefit of that retiring Agent in respect of any action taken or omitted to be taken by it in its capacity as Agent.

14.2. *Covenant to Reimburse*. Each Bank shall reimburse the Agent (to the extent not reimbursed by the Borrower or the Guarantor) ratably for all expenses incurred by the Agent in the exercise of its responsibilities as Agent, including, without limitation, the reasonable fees and expenses of legal and other professional advisors. The proportionate share of each Bank for purposes of ratable reimbursement of expenses hereunder shall be determined (a) if the Agent seeks the reimbursement before the disbursement of the Loans, on the basis of the respective Loan Commitments of the Banks, or (b) if the Agent seeks the reimbursement thereafter, on the basis of the respective principal amounts of the Loans maintained at the time.

14.3. *Non-receipt of Funds by the Agent*. (a) The Agent may assume that the Borrower has made each payment to be made by it hereunder as and when that payment is due unless the Agent has received written notice to the contrary from the Borrower before the due date. The Agent, acting in reliance upon that assumption, may (but shall not be required to) make available to each Bank on the date that payment is due an amount equal to the portion of that payment which that Bank is entitled to receive hereunder. If the Borrower has not in fact made that payment to the Agent, each of the Banks shall, on demand, repay to the Agent the amount so made available to it, together with interest on that amount for each day from and including the due date for that payment to but excluding the date of repayment of that amount by that Bank, at a rate per annum determined by the Agent to be the Agent's overnight offered rate for a deposit in Dollars in that amount in the London interbank market for value on that day.

(b) On the Disbursement Date, the Agent shall be entitled to assume that each Bank (other than any Bank that has given the Agent notice to the contrary) has made funds available to the Agent as required by Section 2.3, and the Agent, acting in reliance upon that assumption, may (but shall not be required to) credit funds to the Borrower in an amount equal to the aggregate of the respective Loan Commitments of all Banks from which the Agent has not received such a notice. If any Bank that has not given such a notice fails to make funds available as required by Section 2.3 and the Agent has credited to the Borrower an amount equal to that aggregate, the Agent shall be entitled at its option to recover an amount equal to the Loan Commitment of that Bank on demand from either that Bank or the Borrower (without prejudice to the rights of the Borrower against that Bank), together with interest on that amount for each day from and including the Disbursement Date to but excluding the date of the recovery, at a rate per annum determined by the Agent to be the sum of 1% and the Agent's overnight offered rate for a deposit in Dollars in that amount in the London interbank market for value on that day.

> The sample provision is necessary because the lenders are required to put the agent in funds by 10:00 a.m. New York City time on the disbursement date for the loans, but in same-day "CHIPS" funds, for which settlement is not made until 4:00 p.m. New York City time. See Section 2.3 and Section 7.1(a). Thus, if the agent disburses the aggregate amount of all the lenders' commitments to the borrower before 4:00 p.m. in New York, the agent may not know whether it has received from each lender the amount it committed to provide.

15. **INDEMNIFICATION**

15.1. *Initial Expenses*. The Borrower shall reimburse the Agent in Dollars on demand for all reasonable expenses incurred by the Agent on its own behalf or on behalf of the Managers in connection with the negotiation, preparation and execution of this Agreement and the Notes and the syndication of the Loans. Those expenses shall include, but shall not be limited to, printing and other reproduction costs, travel and communication costs, the costs of any advertisement incident to the transactions contemplated herein and the fees and expenses of special local and special New York counsel to the Agent.

> 1. This clause provides for reimbursement of expenses incurred by the agent, whether on its own behalf or on behalf of the managers, but not those directly incurred by the managers or the banks. Borrowers often seek to have a maximum, or "cap", placed on the amount of expenses they will be required to reimburse.
>
> 2. Reading: Youard, "How Can that Straightforward Deal Justify Your Fee?" Euromoney, January 1982.

15.2. **Amendment and Enforcement Expenses**. The Borrower shall reimburse the Agent and each Bank and Manager in Dollars on demand for all reasonable expenses incurred as a consequence of, or in connection with, (a) the negotiation, preparation or execution of any amendment to this Agreement, (b) any Event of Default or (c) the preservation or enforcement of any right of the Agent or any Bank or Manager under this Agreement or the Notes.

> Borrowers often seek to limit the expenses they will be required to reimburse with respect to amendments to those relating to amendments requested or agreed to by the borrower.

15.3. **Other Expenses**. If the Borrower (a) fails, after giving the notice referred to in Section 2.2, to fulfill the conditions set forth in Article 8 at or before the respective times specified for their fulfillment or otherwise defaults in its irrevocable commitment pursuant to Section 2.2, (b) fails to pay any amount payable hereunder as and when due or (c) makes any prepayment of principal of any Loan other than on an Interest Payment Date, the Borrower shall reimburse each Bank in Dollars on demand for all reasonable expenses incurred as a consequence thereof, including, without limitation, any loss of margin or expense incurred by that Bank in liquidating or employing deposits acquired to make its Loan, to fund the overdue amount or to fund that Bank's Loan during the Interest Period in which that prepayment occurs (as the case may be).

> This clause is designed to protect the banks against the "broken funding" costs that may arise if the borrower fails to carry through with the borrowing after having given notice of its intention to borrow or if the borrower makes a principal payment early or late. In these cases, the banks may be required to find an alternative use for funds acquired for the purpose of making or maintaining the loans.

15.4. **Increased Costs**. The Borrower shall reimburse each Bank in Dollars on demand for all costs incurred and reductions in amounts received or receivable (as determined by that Bank) that are attributable to that Bank's Loan or the performance of its obligations under this Agreement, if that cost or reduction occurs by reason of the promulgation of any law, regulation or treaty or any change therein or in the application or interpretation thereof or by reason of compliance by that Bank with any direction, requirement or request (whether or not having the force of law) of any governmental authority. The amount reimbursable to each Bank hereunder shall include, without limitation, any such cost or reduction that results from (a) the imposition or amendment of any reserve, special deposit or similar requirement against assets of, liabilities of, deposits with or for the account of, or loans by, that Bank or (b) the imposition or amendment of any tax which is neither (i) a tax referred to in Section 6.1 nor (ii) a tax measured by the net income of that Bank or its Lending Branch and imposed by the jurisdiction in which that Bank's principal office or Lending Branch is situated.

> 1. Underlying this clause is the "net-lending" concept, according to which the margin, or spread, component of the LIBOR-based floating rate is meant to compensate the lenders for making their loans and running the risk of the continued creditworthiness of the particular borrower, but not any other risks. Other risks are for the account of the borrower. Borrowers often seek the right to repay the loan of any lender that claims reimbursement of the costs referred to in the sample clause.

> 2. Reading: Wall & Geary, "Interest rate options, funding practices and yield protection", _International Financial Law Review_ (October 1982).

16. GENERAL

16.1. <u>Choice of Law</u>. This Agreement shall be governed by and construed and interpreted in accordance with the law of the State of New York.

> 1. An important purpose of this clause is to afford predictability as to which country's law will apply. If there is no express choice of law, a court might apply the law of the borrower's country, the law of the country of the lenders (or some of them) or the lead manager, the law of the jurisdiction where suit is brought, the law of the jurisdiction with the most contacts with the transaction, the law of the place where the loan agreement is signed, the law of the place where the loan agreement is to be performed, the law of the place with the greatest "interest" in the transaction or, under the "principle of validation", a law which the court deems will give effect to the intent of the parties.

> 2. The desire of the lenders for predictability as to the future development of the law that is chosen usually leads to a choice of U.S. or U.K. law. The

lenders perceive certain dangers in applying the law of the borrower's country, such as possible future moratoriums, interest limitations, exchange controls or rules voiding loans deemed "odious".

3. The governing law provision is only as good as the court interpreting the agreement says it is, and that might be a court of the borrower's country or a court of some other jurisdiction. Under New York law in effect since July 19, 1984, a choice of law provision in a Eurocurrency loan agreement relating to an obligation arising out of a transaction covering at least $250,000 in the aggregate will be upheld, irrespective of whether the agreement bears a reasonable relation to the State of New York. With respect to proceedings in the borrower's country, the lenders will need to rely on local counsel to advise on enforceability of the choice of law.

4. Particularly in the case of sovereign loans or guaranties, there may be legal or policy considerations that make it difficult or even impossible to choose New York or English law. Other exceptions to the general choice of New York or English law to govern loan documentation for international transactions relate to secured transactions and project finance. For example, even though the loan agreement itself may be governed by New York law, agreements creating security interests in property situated in the borrower's country will normally have to be governed by the law of that country. Still other exceptions may be made for loans to private-sector borrowers that have no assets located outside their own countries. A lender to such a borrower might elect to have the loan agreement governed by local law, with the intention of bringing suit directly in the borrower's country if suit becomes necessary. This choice usually occurs only if the lender has extensive operations in the borrower's country and has reached such a high level of familiarity with that country and integration into its business and banking circles that the lender feels that documentation governed by local law -- and perhaps even written in the local language -- will be as satisfactory as documentation governed by New York or U.K. law, or even better.

5. An unusual dual choice of law provision gained favor with certain banks a few years ago. One version reads as follows:

> "This Agreement shall be governed by and construed in accordance with New York law, provided that in any suit, action or proceeding with respect to this Agreement brought by any Bank in the courts of the Republic of _____, this Agreement shall be governed by and construed in accordance with the law of the Republic of _____."

> The proponents argue that, if it becomes necessary to
> bring a law suit in the local courts, proving New York
> or English law will impose an additional burden on the
> lenders which can be avoided by the use of the clause.
> In our view, this type of clause introduces an unneces-
> sary element of uncertainty into the governing law
> provision. In particular, there is a theoretical pos-
> sibility that suits could be brought both in the local
> jurisdiction and abroad and that, since different laws
> could be applied to the same question in the two suits,
> conflicting results could be produced.
>
> 6. Reading: Carroll, "The Biggest Fallacy in the
> Euromarkets", _Euromoney_, October 1981; Carroll, "Last
> Words on Governing Law", _Euromoney_, December 1981;
> Wood, _Law and Practice of International Finance_ (1983
> ed.), Chapters 1 & 2; Wood, "External governing law --
> Either a fortress or a paper-house", _International
> Financial Law Review_ (July 1982); Youard, "Jeeves and
> the Governing Law", _Euromoney_, November 1981.

16.2. _Jurisdiction_. (a) Any action or proceeding against the Borrower or the Guarantor relating in any way to this Agreement or any Note may be brought and enforced in the courts of the State of New York or of the United States for the Southern District of New York, and each of the Borrower and the Guarantor irrevocably submits to the jurisdiction of each such court in respect of any such action or proceeding. Each of the Borrower and the Guarantor irrevocably appoints Eternal Mail Box, which currently maintains a New York City office situated at Broad and Narrow Streets, New York, New York 00000, as its agent to receive service of process or other legal summons for purposes of any such action or proceeding. So long as the Borrower or the Guarantor has any obligation under this Agreement, it will maintain a duly appointed agent in New York City for the service of such process or summons, and if it fails to maintain such an agent, any such process or summons may be served by mailing a copy thereof by registered mail, or a form of mail substantially equivalent thereto, addressed to it at its address as provided for notices hereunder.

(b) Any such action or proceeding may be brought and enforced in the courts of the Republic of Somewhere or any other jurisdiction where the Borrower or the Guarantor or any of its property may be found, and each of the Borrower and the Guarantor hereby irrevocably submits to the jurisdiction of each such court in respect of any such action or proceeding.

> 1. As subsections (a) and (b) of the sample il-
> lustrate, the lenders wish to be able to bring suit in
> a jurisdiction where they can obtain a fair and speedy
> judgment, which they then can seek to enforce where the
> borrower has assets, but they also wish to be able, at

their option, to sue directly where the borrower has assets. Particularly in the case of sovereign borrowers, the benefits of a speedy judgment extend beyond the possibility of enforcing against assets, because it is unlikely that a sovereign will let a judgment go unsatisfied.

2. Both the lenders, on the one hand, and the borrower and the guarantor, on the other, wish to be certain that any suit will be heard by an unbiased tribunal. An effort to insist on exclusive jurisdiction of the borrower's or the guarantor's own courts is unlikely to be successful.

3. The courts of New York or the U.K. are most frequently chosen, because those jurisdictions have an institutional interest in continuing to be perceived as providing a fair forum to borrowers and lenders. They are the home jurisdictions of major borrowers as well as lenders, which works to ensure an even-handed legislative and judicial approach to problems. The relevant substantive law in these jurisdictions is well developed, and the courts have a good record for fair treatment of litigants.

4. Until 1984, there were statutory limitations on the jurisdiction of New York state courts to entertain actions brought by foreign corporations against other foreign corporations and non-residents (unless the defendant was a "foreign state" under the U.S. Foreign Sovereign Immunities Act of 1976). However, under New York law in effect since July 19, 1984, any person may bring an action in a New York state court against a foreign corporation or other non-resident if (i) the action arises out of an agreement with an appropriate New York choice-of-law provision (see the annotation to Section 16.1) and a provision whereby the foreign corporation or non-resident agrees to submit to the jurisdiction of the New York courts and (ii) the action relates to an agreement arising out of a transaction covering at least $1,000,000 in the aggregate.

5. The borrower and the guarantor will normally be expected to appoint an agent for service of process in the jurisdiction whose courts are selected to decide disputes arising under the loan agreement. In determining whether there should be an agent for service of process and who that agent should be, it is important to take into account not only the laws of the jurisdiction whose courts are selected but also the laws of the borrower's home country.

6. Some sovereign governments cannot or will not submit to the jurisdiction of foreign courts. In such cases, loan agreements sometimes provide for arbitration as a means of settling disputes. See Rowntree

> "Arbitration -- Is it the right solution?" Unpublished paper dated January 30, 1980; Crawford & Johnson, "Arbitrating with foreign states and their instrumentalities", International Financial Law Review (April 1986).

> 7. Additional reading: Wood, Law and Practice of International Finance (1983 ed.), Chapter 3.

(c) Each of the Borrower and the Guarantor irrevocably waives, to the fullest extent permitted by applicable law, all immunity (whether on the basis of sovereignty or otherwise) from jurisdiction, attachment (both before and after judgment) and execution to which it might otherwise be entitled in any action or proceeding relating in any way to this Agreement or any Note in the courts of the Republic of Somewhere, of the State of New York, of the United States or of any other country or jurisdiction, and neither the Borrower nor the Guarantor will raise or claim or cause to be pleaded any such immunity at or in respect of any such action or proceeding.

> This waiver is stated to be "to the fullest extent permitted by applicable law" because the law of the borrower's or guarantor's jurisdiction may prohibit waiver of certain types of immunity and because the United States Foreign Sovereign Immunities Act of 1976 may make it impossible for the borrower or guarantor to waive certain kinds of immunity. For instance, immunity from pre-judgment attachment for purposes of obtaining jurisdiction may not be waived, and the central bank of a country may not be able to waive immunity from pre-judgment attachment in respect of reserves. See Banque Compafina v. Banco de Guatemala, 583 F. Supp. 320 (S.D.N.Y. 1984).

(d) Each of the Borrower and the Guarantor irrevocably waives, to the fullest extent permitted by applicable law, any objection that it may now or hereafter have to the laying of venue of any such action or proceeding in the Supreme Court of the State of New York, County of New York, or the United States District Court for the Southern District of New York and any claim that any such action or proceeding brought in any such court has been brought in an inconvenient forum.

> Under New York law in effect since July 19, 1984, if an action arises out of an agreement containing an appropriate contractual choice of New York law and a submission to the jurisdiction of the courts of the State of New York, a New York State court may not dismiss the action on the grounds of forum non conveniens.

(e) Each of the Borrower and the Guarantor irrevocably waives, to the fullest extent permitted by applicable law, any claim that any action or proceeding commenced by the Agent or any Manager or Bank relating in any way to this Agreement or any Note should be dismissed or stayed by reason, or pending the resolution, of any action or proceeding commenced by the Borrower or the Guarantor relating in any way to this Agreement or any Note, whether or not commenced earlier. To the fullest extent permitted by applicable law, each of the Borrower and the Guarantor shall take all measures necessary for any such action or proceeding commenced by the Agent or any Manager or Bank to proceed to judgment or award prior to the entry of judgment in any such action or proceeding commenced by the Borrower or the Guarantor.

> The sample provision is a waiver of the defense of lis pendens, pursuant to which the borrower or guarantor might seek to have a suit brought, say, in New York dismissed, or stayed, pending resolution of a suit commenced by the borrower or the guarantor in its own jurisdiction. Lenders sometimes also seek to include an agreement by the borrower that it will not assert the "act of state" doctrine, under which a borrower might rely on the law of its own country as an excuse for nonperformance of its obligations, if that law prohibits that performance. On some questions raised by such a provision and on the act-of-state doctrine in general, see Ebenroth & Teitz, "Winning (Or Losing) By Default: The Act of State Doctrine, Sovereign Immunity and Comity In International Business Transactions", 19 The International Lawyer 225 (Winter 1985).

16.3. *Loan Currency*. (a) If any expense required to be reimbursed pursuant to Article 15 is originally incurred in a currency other than Dollars, the Borrower shall nonetheless make reimbursement of that expense in Dollars, in an amount equal to the amount in Dollars that would have been required for the person that incurred that expense to have purchased, in accordance with normal banking procedures, the sum paid in that other currency (after any premium and costs of exchange) on the day that expense was originally incurred. Any interest accruing thereon pursuant to Section 4.2 shall be computed on the basis of that amount in Dollars.

(b) Each reference in this Agreement to Dollars is of the essence. To the fullest extent permitted by applicable law, the obligation of the Borrower in respect of any amount due under this Agreement or the Notes shall, notwithstanding any payment in any other currency (whether pursuant to a judgment or otherwise), be discharged only to the extent of the amount in Dollars that the person entitled to receive that payment may, in accordance with normal banking procedures, purchase with the sum paid in that other currency (after any premium and costs of exchange) on the Banking Day immediately following the day on which that person receives that payment. If the amount in Dollars that may be so purchased for any reason falls short of the amount originally due, the Borrower shall pay such additional amounts, in Dollars, as may be necessary to compensate for the shortfall. Any obligation of the Borrower not discharged by that payment shall, to the fullest extent permitted by applicable law, be due as a separate and independent obligation and, until discharged as provided herein, shall continue in full force and effect.

> 1. This provision is an example of the "judgment currency clause", which is designed to protect the banks against a foreign exchange loss they might suffer if they are paid in a currency other than dollars and the amount received, when converted into dollars, is insufficient to pay the full amount owed. This might occur, in particular, if a judgment in favor of the lenders is expressed in a foreign currency and the exchange rate used to compute the amount of the judgment is different from that in effect when the judgment is paid. Borrowers sometimes ask that any corresponding exchange profit be turned over to the borrower.

> 2. The clause is stated to be the rule "to the extent permitted by applicable law" because of the possibility that a court will not entertain an independent lawsuit for the "shortfall" referred to in the clause, on the theory that the lender's cause of action merged into the earlier judgment. Lawyers may have difficulty in giving favorable opinions on the enforceability of the judgment currency clause if this qualification is not included.

> 3. Reading: Freedman, "Judgments in foreign currency -- when to convert?" _International Financial Law Review_ (September 1984).

16.4. _Replacement of Notes_. Upon the loss, theft, destruction or mutilation of any Note and (a) in the case of loss, theft or destruction, upon receipt by the Borrower of indemnity or security reasonably satisfactory to it (except that if the holder of that Note is the payee thereof or any other financial institution of recognized responsibility, the holder's own agreement of indemnity shall be deemed to be satisfactory) or (b) in the case of mutilation, upon surrender to the Borrower of the mutilated Note, the Borrower shall execute and deliver in lieu thereof a new Note, endorsed with the guaranty of the Guarantor and dated the Disbursement Date, in the same principal amount.

16.5. _Notices_. Except as otherwise expressly provided herein, all notices in connection with this Agreement shall be given by telex or cable or by notice in writing hand-delivered or sent by facsimile transmission or by airmail, postage prepaid. All such notices shall be sent to the telex or telecopier number or address (as the case may be) specified for the intended recipient in Exhibit A, or to such other number or address as that recipient may have last specified by notice to the other parties. All such notices shall be effective upon receipt.

16.6. *Remedies and Waivers*. No failure or delay on the part of the Agent or any Manager or Bank in exercising any right hereunder shall operate as a waiver of, or impair, any such right. No single or partial exercise of any such right shall preclude any other or further exercise thereof or the exercise of any other right. No waiver of any such right shall be effective unless given in writing. No waiver of any such right shall be deemed a waiver of any other right hereunder.

16.7. *Amendment*. This Agreement may be amended only by an instrument in writing executed by the Borrower, the Guarantor and Majority Banks; *provided*, *however*, that execution of such instrument by the Borrower, the Guarantor, the Agent and all the Banks shall be required for any amendment that (a) increases the Loan Commitment of any Bank or otherwise subjects the Banks to any additional obligation hereunder, (b) reduces the Loans or any fee payable hereunder, (c) alters any provision of Article 4, (d) postpones any date fixed for, or changes the currency of, payment of the Loans or any other amount payable by the Borrower or the Guarantor under this Agreement or any of the Notes, (e) changes the number of Banks, or the manner of determining the number of Banks, required for the Banks or any of them to take any action hereunder or (f) alters this Section; and *provided* *further*, *however*, that amendment of any provision of this Agreement affecting the rights or duties of the Agent or the rights of the Managers hereunder shall, in addition, require execution of such instrument by the Agent or the Managers (as the case may be).

> Clause (d) of this provision makes any restructuring of the loans impossible without the participation of all the lenders. During the negotiation of restructuring agreements, the basic rule is that the lenders should all be treated equally. As a result, familiar provisions of Eurodollar lending agreements that permit prepayment of an individual lender's loan under circumstances affecting only that lender (see Section 3.3, Section 4.3 and Section 15.4) are generally rejected as unacceptable in restructuring agreements. For other features of restructuring agreements, and descriptions of the sovereign debt restructuring process in general, see Buchheit & Walker, "Legal issues in the restructuring of commercial bank loans to sovereign borrowers", in *Sovereign Lending: Managing Legal Risk* (Gruson & Reisner eds., Euromoney Publications 1984); Karat, "The Eurodollar disaster clause and corporate restructuring", *International Financial Law Review* (September 1983); Kurz, "Problem loans and sovereign restructuring," in 1 *International financial law* (R. Rendell, ed., 1983 ed.), 117-53; "Symposium: Default by Foreign Government Debtors", *University of Illinois Law Review* (1982).

16.8. _Assignment_. (a) This Agreement shall be binding upon and inure to the benefit of the Borrower, the Guarantor, the Agent, each Manager and each Bank and their respective successors and assigns; _provided_, _however_, that neither the Borrower nor the Guarantor may assign any of its rights or obligations under this Agreement without the prior written consent of the Agent and all the Banks.

(b) Each Bank may at any time assign or otherwise transfer any of its Notes or any of its rights or obligations hereunder. Each of the Borrower and the Guarantor shall, from time to time at the request of any Bank, execute and deliver such documents as may be necessary to give full force and effect to such an assignment or transfer, including, without limitation, a new Note, endorsed by the Guarantor, in exchange for any Note held by that Bank. If any Bank assigns or otherwise transfers any of its rights or obligations hereunder, subject to Section 14.1(i), each reference in this Agreement to that Bank shall be deemed to be a reference to that Bank and the person or persons to whom those rights or obligations were assigned or transferred to the extent of their respective interests. Any request, authority or consent of any holder of any Note shall be conclusive and binding on any subsequent holder thereof.

| Borrowers sometimes seek to impose limitations on the right of the lenders to transfer their loans, such as a requirement that consent of the borrower be obtained for transfers other than to affiliates. Borrowers also seek provisions to the effect that no transfer will be made under circumstances that would create an increased cost or additional tax that the loan agreement would allocate to the borrower. Where local law affords special tax treatment to certain kinds of lending institutions or permits lending to borrowers or certain classes of borrowers only by institutions registered with a governmental agency or office, such as a registry of public debt, the borrower may insist that assignees be limited to qualifying institutions.

16.9. _Determinations by the Agent or any Bank_. Each determination by the Agent or any Bank hereunder shall, in the absence of manifest error, be conclusive and binding on the parties.

16.10. _Survival_. The obligations of each of the Borrower and the Guarantor under Section 6.1, Section 6.2 and Article 15 shall survive the repayment of the Loans and the cancellation of the Notes and the termination of the other obligations of the Borrower and the Guarantor hereunder.

16.11. _Severability of Provisions_. Any provision of this Agreement that is prohibited or unenforceable in any jurisdiction shall, as to that jurisdiction, be ineffective to the extent of that prohibition or unenforceability without invalidating the remaining provisions hereof or affecting the validity or enforceability of that provision in any other jurisdiction.

16.12. <u>Counterparts</u>. This Agreement may be executed in any number of counterparts, and all the counterparts taken together shall be deemed to constitute one and the same agreement.

16.13. <u>Language</u>. Each document to be delivered by the Borrower or the Guarantor with respect to this Agreement shall be in the English language or shall be accompanied by an English translation thereof certified by the Borrower or the Guarantor (as the case may be) to be complete and correct.

16.14. <u>Integration of Terms</u>. This Agreement contains the entire agreement of the parties relating to the subject matter hereof and supersedes all oral statements and prior writings with respect thereto.

IN WITNESS WHEREOF, the parties have caused this Agreement to be duly executed and delivered in New York City as of the day and year first written above.

STATE-OWNED COMPANY, S.A.,
   as Borrower

By:_____

Title:_____

THE REPUBLIC OF SOMEWHERE,
   as Guarantor

By:_____

Title:_____

INFALLIBLE AGENT BANK,
   as Agent

By:_____

Title:_____

MANAGERS:

BIG BANK, S.A.

By:_____

Title:_____

BIGGER BANK, PLC

By:_____

Title:_____

BIGGEST BANK, N.A.

By:_____

Title:_____

BANKS: Loan Commitment

BIGGEST BANK, N.A. $30,000,000

By:_____

Title:_____

BIGGER BANK, PLC $20,000,000

By:_____

Title:_____

BIG BANK, S.A. $20,000,000

By:_____

Title:_____

EUROPEAN BANK $10,000,000

By:_____

Title:_____

ASIAN BANK $10,000,000

By:_____

Title:_____

MIDDLE EASTERN BANK $ 10,000,000

By:_____

Title:_____

    TOTAL LOAN COMMITMENT: $100,000,000

EXHIBIT A - Schedule of Addresses

STATE-OWNED COMPANY, S.A.,
   as Borrower
100 Lethe Street
Federal Capital
The Republic of Somewhere
Telex: 99999 ABC
Telecopier: 00 000

THE REPUBLIC OF SOMEWHERE,
   as Guarantor
Rescue Road
Federal Capital
The Republic of Somewhere
Telex: 00000 CDE
Telecopier: 00000

INFALLIBLE AGENT BANK, as Agent
One Money Center
New York, New York 00000
Telex: 00000 QUICK
Telecopier: 00000

MANAGERS:

BIGGEST BANK, N.A.
100 Vault Street
International Financial Center
Telex: 00000
Telecopier: 00000

BIGGER BANK, PLC
101 Bullion Street
International Financial Centre
Telex: 00000
Telecopier: 00000

BIG BANK, S.A.
102 Bourse Street
Centre Financier International
Telex: 00000
Telecopier: 00000

BANKS:

BIGGEST BANK, N.A.
100 Vault Street
International Financial Center
Telex: 00000
Telecopier: 00000

BIGGER BANK, PLC
101 Bullion Street
International Financial Centre
Telex: 00000
Telecopier: 00000

BIG BANK, S.A.
102 Bourse Street
Centre Financier International
Telex: 00000
Telecopier: 00000

EUROPEAN BANK
Avenue des Interets
Centre Financier Europeen
Telex: 00000
Telecopier: 00000

ASIAN BANK
Yen Place
Asian Financial Center
Telex: 00000
Telecopier: 00000

MIDDLE EASTERN BANK
Petro Money Oasis
Middle Eastern Financial Center
Telex: 00000
Telecopier: 00000

EXHIBIT B - Form of Promissory Note

$ _____ Federal Capital, Somewhere
  _____, 19__

    For value received, STATE-OWNED COMPANY, S.A. hereby unconditionally promises to pay to the order of _____ on _____, 19__, the sum of _____ Dollars ($_____) in lawful money of the United States of America at Infallible Agent Bank, 1000 Wall Street, New York, New York 00000.

    Each of the undersigned hereby waives all requirements as to diligence, presentment, demand of payment, protest and notice of any kind with respect to this promissory note.

                      STATE-OWNED COMPANY, S.A.

                      By:_____

                      Title:_____

PAYMENT GUARANTEED:

THE REPUBLIC OF SOMEWHERE

By:_____

Title:_____

> The proper form for endorsement of a guaranty of payment on the promissory notes is a subject that should be reviewed with local counsel.

EXHIBIT C - Form of Notice of Borrowing

N O T I C E

_____, 19__

Infallible Agent Bank
One Money Center
New York, New York 00000
As Agent

    We refer to a loan agreement dated as of May 15, 1986 (the "Agreement") providing for loans to State-Owned Company, S.A. (the "Borrower") in an aggregate principal amount of $100,000,000. All terms defined in the Agreement and used but not defined herein have the meanings given to them in the Agreement.

    Pursuant to Section 2.2 of the Agreement, the Borrower hereby gives the Agent notice that (1) the Borrower irrevocably commits itself to borrow under the Agreement the aggregate principal amount of $100,000,000 on _____, 19__ (the "Disbursement Date") and (2) the proceeds of that borrowing are to be credited to the Borrower's account No. _____, maintained at the offices of _____ _____
at _____, New York, New York _____.

    The Borrower hereby certifies that the representations and warranties made by the Borrower in the Agreement are true and correct as if made on and as of the date hereof. If any such representation or warranty ceases to be true and correct at and as of any time before the disbursement of that amount on the Disbursement Date, the Borrower will immediately give the Agent notice to that effect.

                          STATE-OWNED COMPANY, S.A.,
                           as Borrower

                           By:_____

                           Title:_____

EXHIBIT D - Form of Certificate of the Borrower

CERTIFICATE

Pursuant to Section 8.1(a) of a loan agreement dated as of May 15, 1986 (the "Agreement") providing for loans to State-Owned Company, S.A. (the "Borrower") in an aggregate principal amount of $100,000,000, the Borrower certifies that:

(a) Attachments I through _____ hereto are true and correct copies of the charter and by-laws of the Borrower and of all resolutions and other actions adopted or taken by the Borrower to authorize the execution and delivery of the Agreement and all other documents required to be executed or delivered by the Borrower in connection with the Agreement and the performance by the Borrower of its obligations under the Agreement and the Notes, and all such documents and actions remain in full force and effect.

(b) Attachments _____ through _____ hereto are true and correct copies of documents evidencing the truth and accuracy of Section 9.1(d) of the Agreement.

(c) The name, title and specimen signature of each person who has executed the Agreement on behalf of the Borrower or who will execute any other document (other than this certificate) in connection with the Agreement on behalf of the Borrower are as set forth below, and each such person is in office on the date hereof and thereunto duly authorized:

Name and Title	Specimen Signature
_____	_____
_____	_____
_____	_____
_____	_____
_____	_____

If any certification contained herein ceases to be true and correct at and as of any time before the disbursement of the Loans on the Disbursement Date, the Borrower will immediately give the Agent notice to that effect.

All terms defined in the Agreement and used but not defined herein have the meanings given to them in the Agreement.

IN WITNESS WHEREOF, this certificate has been executed on and as of _____, 19__.

                        STATE-OWNED COMPANY, S.A.,
                        as Borrower

                        By:_____

                        Title:_____

EXHIBIT E - Form of Certificate of the Guarantor

CERTIFICATE

Pursuant to Section 8.1(b) of a loan agreement dated as of May 15, 1986 (the "Agreement") providing for loans in an aggregate principal amount of $100,000,000 to State-Owned Company, S.A., with the guaranty of The Republic of Somewhere (the "Guarantor"), the Guarantor certifies that:

(a) Attachments I through _____ hereto are true and correct copies of all resolutions and other actions adopted or taken by the Guarantor to authorize the execution and delivery of the Agreement and all other documents required to be executed or delivered by the Guarantor in connection with the Agreement and the performance by the Guarantor of its obligations under the Agreement and the Notes, and all such documents and actions remain in full force and effect.

(b) Attachments _____ through _____ hereto are true and correct copies of documents evidencing the truth and accuracy of Section 9.2(c) of the Agreement.

(c) The name, title and specimen signature of each person who has executed the Agreement on behalf of the Guarantor or who will execute any other document (other than this certificate) in connection with the Agreement on behalf of the Guarantor are as set forth below, and each such person is in office on the date hereof and thereunto duly authorized:

Name and Title	Specimen Signature
_____	_____
_____	_____
_____	
_____	_____
_____	
_____	_____

If any certification contained herein ceases to be true and correct at and as of any time before the time of disbursement of the Loans on the Disbursement Date, the Guarantor will immediately give the Agent notice to that effect.

All terms defined in the Agreement and used but not defined herein have the meanings given to them in the Agreement.

IN WITNESS WHEREOF, this certificate has been executed on and as of _____, 19__.

                        THE REPUBLIC OF SOMEWHERE,
                          as Guarantor

                        By:_____

                        Title:_____

EXHIBIT F - Form of Opinion of Counsel to the Borrower

_____, 19__

Biggest Bank N.A.
  and the several other
  banks and financial
  institutions named as
  Banks in the Agreement
  herein described

c/o Infallible Agent Bank
One Money Center
New York, New York 00000
As Agent

Dear Sirs:

In my capacity as counsel to State-Owned Company, S.A. (the "Borrower"), I have examined originals or copies certified or otherwise identified to my satisfaction of the following documents relating to a loan agreement dated as of May 15, 1986 (the "Agreement") providing for loans in an aggregate principal amount of $100,000,000 (the "Loans") to the Borrower:

1. The Agreement;

2. The form, attached to the Agreement as Exhibit B, of the promissory notes to be delivered in accordance with Section 8.2(b) of the Agreement (the "Notes"); and

3. Such other documents as I have deemed necessary or appropriate as a basis for the opinions expressed herein.

The opinions expressed herein are limited to questions arising under the law of the Republic of Somewhere ("Somewhere") and its political subdivisions, and I do not purport to express an opinion on any question arising under the law of any other jurisdiction.

All terms defined in the Agreement and used but not defined herein have the meanings given to them in the Agreement.

Subject to the foregoing, it is my opinion that:

1. The Borrower is a company duly organized and validly existing under the law of Somewhere and has the power and authority to own its property, to conduct its business as currently conducted and to consummate the transactions contemplated in the Agreement.

2. The Borrower has taken all necessary action to

authorize the execution and delivery of the Agreement and all other documents to be executed and delivered by it in connection with the Agreement, the performance of its obligations under the Agreement and the Notes and the consummation of the transactions contemplated in the Agreement.

 3. The Agreement has been duly executed and delivered by the Borrower and constitutes, and each of the Notes, when duly executed and delivered by the Borrower, will constitute, a legal, valid and binding obligation of the Borrower, enforceable against the Borrower in accordance with its terms, subject to applicable insolvency, moratorium and similar laws affecting creditors' rights generally.

 4. Except for the formalities referred to in Exhibit K to the Agreement, all governmental authorizations and actions of any kind necessary to authorize the Loans or required for the validity or enforceability against the Borrower of the Agreement or the Notes have been obtained or performed and are valid and subsisting in full force and effect.

 5. To the best of my knowledge, no event has occurred and is continuing that constitutes, or that, with the giving of notice or the lapse of time or both, would constitute, an Event of Default or a default under any agreement or instrument evidencing any Indebtedness of the Borrower, and no such event will occur upon the making of the Loans.

 6. No consent or approval of, or notice to, any creditor of the Borrower is required by the terms of any agreement or instrument evidencing any Indebtedness of the Borrower for the execution or delivery of, or the performance of the obligations of the Borrower under, the Agreement or the Notes or the consummation of the transactions contemplated in the Agreement, and that execution, delivery, performance and consummation will not result in any breach or violation of, or constitute a default under, the charter or by-laws of the Borrower or any agreement, instrument, judgment or order known to me, or any statute, rule or regulation, applicable to the Borrower or to any of its property.

 7. There are no actions or proceedings pending or, to my knowledge, threatened the adverse determination of which might have a materially adverse effect on the financial condition of the Borrower or impair the ability of the Borrower to perform its obligations under, or affect the validity or enforceability of, the Agreement or the Notes.

 8. Except as set forth in Exhibit L to the Agreement and except for liens of the types referred to in the proviso in Section 10.6(a) of the Agreement, the Borrower has good title to its property free and clear of all liens and other encumbrances, and its obligations under the

Agreement rank, and its obligations under the Notes will rank, at least *pari passu* with all its other Indebtedness.

9. The execution and delivery of the Agreement and the Notes are not subject to any tax, duty, fee or other charge, including, without limitation, any registration or transfer tax, stamp duty or similar levy, imposed by or within Somewhere or any political subdivision or taxing authority thereof or therein.

10. Neither the Borrower nor its property has any right of immunity on grounds of sovereignty or otherwise from jurisdiction, attachment (before or after judgment) or execution in respect of any action or proceeding relating in any way to the Agreement or the Notes that may be brought in the courts of Somewhere.

11. The execution and delivery of the Agreement and the Notes by the Borrower and performance of its obligations thereunder constitute commercial transactions.

12. The Borrower has the power to submit, and pursuant to the Agreement has legally, validly, effectively and irrevocably submitted, to the jurisdiction of the courts of the State of New York and of the United States for the Southern District of New York in respect of any action or proceeding relating in any way to the Agreement or the Notes.

13. The choice by the parties to the Agreement of the law of the State of New York as governing law is legal, valid and binding.

Unless and until I give the Agent notice of any change in this opinion before the disbursement of the Loans, you and your counsel may rely on this opinion at all times from the date hereof to and including the disbursement of the Loans as if this opinion were dated on and as of the day of, and delivered at, each such time.

Very truly yours,

| The final paragraph imposes an affirmative obligation on counsel to advise the agent of changes in the opinion, and most lawyers would be reluctant to agree to it unless the period that it covered was very short. An alternative to this approach is to provide for a supplemental, or "bring-down", opinion of counsel to be issued before the loans are disbursed. Although the alternative is more cumbersome, it should be used when there is a long availability period, as in the case of multiple-disbursement loans.

EXHIBIT G - **Form of Opinion of Counsel to the Guarantor**

_____, 19__

Biggest Bank N.A.
  and the several other
  banks and financial
  institutions named as Banks
  in the Agreement herein
  described

c/o Infallible Agent Bank
One Money Center
New York, New York 00000
As Agent

Dear Sirs:

      In my official capacity, I have examined originals or copies certified or otherwise identified to my satisfaction of the following documents relating to a loan agreement dated as of May 15, 1986 (the "Agreement") providing for loans in an aggregate principal amount of $100,000,000 (the "Loans") to State-Owned Company, S.A. (the "Borrower"), with the guaranty of The Republic of Somewhere (the "Guarantor"):

    1. The Agreement;

    2. The form, attached to the Agreement as Exhibit B, of the promissory notes to be delivered in accordance with Section 8.2(b) of the Agreement (the "Notes"); and

    3. Such other documents as I have deemed necessary or appropriate as a basis for the opinions expressed herein.

      The opinions expressed herein are limited to questions arising under the law of the Republic of Somewhere ("Somewhere") and its political subdivisions, and I do not purport to express an opinion on any question arising under the law of any other jurisdiction.

      All terms defined in the Agreement and used but not defined herein have the meanings assigned to them in the Agreement.

      Subject to the foregoing, it is my opinion that:

    1. The Guarantor has taken all necessary action to authorize the Guaranty, its execution and delivery of the Agreement, endorsement of its guaranty on and delivery of the Notes, the execution and delivery of all other documents to be executed and delivered by it in connection with the Agreement and the performance of its obligations under the Agreement and the Notes.

2. The Agreement has been duly executed and delivered by the Guarantor and constitutes, and each of the Notes, when duly executed and delivered by the Borrower and endorsed with the guaranty of and delivered by the Guarantor, will constitute, a legal, valid and binding obligation of the Guarantor, enforceable against the Guarantor in accordance with its terms, subject to applicable moratorium and similar laws affecting creditors' rights generally.

3. Except for the formalities listed in Exhibit K of the Agreement, all governmental authorizations and actions of any kind necessary to authorize the Guaranty or the endorsement of the Notes by the Guarantor with its guaranty or required for the validity or enforceability against the Guarantor of the Agreement or the Notes, have been obtained or performed and are valid and subsisting in full force and effect.

4. To the best of my knowledge, no event has occurred and is continuing that constitutes, or that, with the giving of notice or the lapse of time or both, would constitute, an Event of Default or a default under any agreement or instrument evidencing any Indebtedness of the Guarantor, and no such event will occur upon the making of the Loans.

5. No consent or approval of, or notice to, any creditor of the Guarantor is required by the terms of any agreement or instrument evidencing any Indebtedness of the Guarantor for the execution or endorsement (as the case may be) or the delivery by the Guarantor of, or the performance of its obligations under, the Agreement or the Notes, and that execution, endorsement, delivery and performance will not result in any breach or violation of, or constitute a default under, any agreement, instrument, judgment or order known to me, or the Constitution of Somewhere or any statute, rule or regulation, applicable to the Guarantor or to any of its property.

6. There are no actions or proceedings pending or, to my knowledge, threatened the adverse determination of which might have a materially adverse effect on the financial condition of the Guarantor or impair the ability of the Guarantor to perform its obligations under, or affect the validity or enforceability of, the Agreement or the Notes.

7. Except as set forth in Exhibit M to the Agreement and except for liens of the types referred to in Section 10.6(b), the Guarantor has good title to its property free and clear of all liens and other encumbrances, and the obligations of the Guarantor under the Agreement rank, and its obligations under the Notes will rank, at least _pari passu_ with all its other External Indebtedness.

8. The execution and delivery of the Agreement and the delivery of Notes endorsed with the guaranty of the

Guarantor are not subject to any tax, duty, fee or other charge, including, without limitation, any registration or transfer tax, stamp duty or similar levy, imposed by or within Somewhere or any political subdivision or taxing authority thereof or therein.

9. Neither the Guarantor nor its property has any right of immunity on grounds of sovereignty or otherwise from jurisdiction, attachment (before or after judgment) or execution in respect of any action or proceeding relating in any way to the Agreement or the Notes that may be brought in the courts of Somewhere.

10. The execution and delivery of the Agreement by the Guarantor and performance of its obligations thereunder, and endorsement of the Notes by the Guarantor with its guaranty and delivery by it of the Notes so endorsed constitute commercial transactions.

11. The Guarantor has the power to submit, and pursuant to the Agreement has legally, validly, effectively and irrevocably submitted, to the jurisdiction of the courts of the State of New York and of the United States for the Southern District of New York in respect of any action or proceeding relating in any way to the Agreement or the Notes.

12. The choice by the parties to the Agreement of the law of the State of New York as governing law is legal, valid and binding.

13. The full faith and credit of the Guarantor is pledged for the due and punctual performance of its obligations under the Agreement and the Notes.

Unless and until I give the Agent notice of any change in this opinion before the disbursement of the Loans, you and your counsel may rely on this opinion at all times from the date hereof to and including the disbursement of the Loans as if this opinion were dated on and as of the day of, and delivered at, each such time.

Very truly yours,

EXHIBIT H - Form of Opinion of Special Local Counsel to
the Agent

_____, 19__

Infallible Agent Bank, as Agent
  under the Agreement
  herein described
One Money Center
New York, New York 00000

Dear Sirs:

We have acted as your special local counsel in connection with a loan agreement dated as of May 15, 1986 (the "Agreement") providing for loans in an aggregate principal amount of $100,000,000 (the "Loans") to State-Owned Company, S.A. (the "Borrower"), guaranteed by The Republic of Somewhere (the "Guarantor"). All terms defined in the Agreement and used but not defined herein have the meanings given to them in the Agreement.

In our capacity as such counsel, we have examined originals or copies certified or otherwise identified to our satisfaction of the following documents:

1. The Agreement;

2. The form, attached to the Agreement as Exhibit B, of the promissory notes to be delivered in accordance with Section 8.2(b) the Agreement (the "Notes");

3. The opinion of counsel to the Borrower delivered in accordance with Section 8.1 of the Agreement (the "Opinion of Counsel to the Borrower");

4. The opinion of counsel to the Guarantor delivered in accordance with Section 8.1 of the Agreement (the "Opinion of Counsel to the Guarantor");

5. The opinion of Messrs. X, Y & Z delivered in accordance with Section 8.1 of the Agreement (the "Opinion of New York Counsel"); and

6. Such other documents as we have deemed necessary or appropriate as a basis for the opinions expressed herein.

The opinions expressed herein are limited to questions arising under the law of the Republic of Somewhere ("Somewhere"), and its political subdivisions, and we do not purport to express an opinion on any question arising under the law of any other jurisdiction. We have relied on the

Opinion of New York Counsel as to matters of New York law that are relevant to the opinions expressed herein. We have assumed, with your permission, that the signatures on all the documents that we have examined are genuine.

We have made no special investigation of the matters as to which our opinion is stated herein to be to the best of our knowledge, and we are relying on the Opinion of Counsel to the Borrower and the Opinion of Counsel to the Guarantor in regard to such matters.

Subject to the foregoing, it is our opinion that:

1. The Borrower is a company validly existing under the law of Somewhere, has the power and authority to consummate the transactions contemplated in the Agreement and, to the best of our knowledge, has the power and authority to own its property and to conduct its business as currently conducted.

2. The Borrower has taken all necessary action to authorize the execution and delivery of the Agreement and all other documents to be executed and delivered by it in connection with the Agreement, the performance of its obligations under the Agreement and the Notes and the consummation of the transactions contemplated in the Agreement.

3. The Guarantor has taken all necessary action to authorize the Guaranty, its execution and delivery of the Agreement, endorsement of its guaranty on and delivery by it of the Notes, the execution and delivery of all other documents to be executed and delivered by it in connection with the Agreement and the performance of its obligations under the Agreement and the Notes.

4. The Agreement has been duly executed and delivered by the Borrower and constitutes, and each of the Notes, when duly executed and delivered by the Borrower, will constitute, a legal, valid and binding obligation of the Borrower, enforceable against the Borrower in accordance with its terms, subject to applicable insolvency, moratorium and similar laws affecting creditors' rights generally.

5. The Agreement has been duly executed and delivered by the Guarantor and constitutes, and each of the Notes, when duly executed and delivered by the Borrower and endorsed with the guaranty of and delivered by the Guarantor, will constitute, a legal, valid and binding obligation of the Guarantor, enforceable against the Guarantor in accordance with its terms, subject to applicable moratorium and similar laws affecting creditors' rights generally.

6. Except for the formalities listed in Exhibit K to the Agreement, all governmental authorizations and actions of any kind necessary to authorize the Loans, the Guaranty or the endorsement of the Notes by the Guarantor

with its guaranty or required for the validity or enforceability against the Borrower and the Guarantor of the Agreement or the Notes have been obtained or performed and are valid and subsisting in full force and effect.

7. The execution and delivery of the Agreement and the Notes by the Borrower, the execution of the Agreement and the endorsement of the Notes with the guaranty of the Guarantor, the performance by each of the Borrower and the Guarantor of its obligations under the Agreement and the Notes and the consummation of the transactions contemplated in the Agreement will not result in any breach or violation of, or constitute a default under, the charter or by-laws of the Borrower or the Constitution of Somewhere or, to the best of our knowledge, any agreement instrument judgment or order, or any statute, rule or regulation, applicable to the Borrower or the Guarantor or to any property of either of them.

8. The execution and delivery of the Agreement and the Notes by the Borrower, and the execution and delivery of the Agreement and the delivery of the Notes endorsed with the guaranty of the Guarantor, are not subject to any tax, duty, fee or other charge, including, without limitation, any registration or transfer tax, stamp duty or similar levy, imposed by or within Somewhere or any political subdivision or taxing authority thereof or therein.

9. Each of the Borrower and the Guarantor has the power to submit, and pursuant to the Agreement has legally, validly, effectively and irrevocably submitted, to the jurisdiction of the courts of the State of New York and of the United States for the Southern District of New York in respect of any action or proceeding relating in any way to the Agreement or the Notes.

10. Neither the Borrower nor the Guarantor nor any property of either of them has any right of immunity on the grounds of sovereignty or otherwise from jurisdiction, attachment (before or after judgment) or execution in respect of any action or proceeding relating in any way to the Agreement or the Notes that may be brought in the courts of Somewhere.

11. The execution and delivery of the Agreement and the Notes by the Borrower and performance of its obligations thereunder, the execution and delivery of the Agreement by the Guarantor and performance of its obligations thereunder and endorsement of the Notes by the Guarantor with its guaranty and delivery by it of the Notes all constitute commercial transactions.

12. The choice by the parties to the Agreement of the law of the State of New York as governing law is legal, valid and binding.

Unless and until we give you notice before the disbursement of the Loans of any change in this opinion, you and your counsel may rely on this opinion at all times from the date hereof to and including the disbursement of the Loans as if this opinion were dated on and as of the day of, and delivered at, each such time.

We are furnishing this opinion letter to you solely for your benefit. You may furnish a copy of it to the Banks, and they may rely on it as if it were addressed to them. It may also be relied on by your counsel and counsel for the Banks in connection with the Agreement and the Notes. It is not, however, to be used, circulated, quoted or otherwise referred to for any other purpose.

                                          Very truly yours,

                                          LOCAL LAW OFFICE

                                          By:_____

EXHIBIT I - <u>Form of Opinion of Special New York Counsel to the Agent</u>

_____, 19__

Infallible Agent Bank, as Agent
  under the Agreement
  herein described
One Money Center
New York, New York 00000

Dear Sirs:

We have acted as your special New York counsel in connection with a loan agreement dated as of May 15, 1986 (the "Agreement") providing for loans in an aggregate principal amount of $100,000,000 (the "Loans") to State-Owned Company, S.A. (the "Borrower"), guaranteed by The Republic of Somewhere (the "Guarantor").

In arriving at the opinions expressed herein, we have examined originals or copies certified or otherwise identified to our satisfaction of the following documents:

1. The Agreement;

2. The form, attached to the Agreement as Exhibit B, of the promissory notes to be delivered in accordance with Section 8.2(b) of the Agreement (the "Notes");

3. The opinion of counsel to the Borrower delivered in accordance with Section 8.1 of the Agreement (the "Opinion of Counsel to the Borrower");

4. The opinion of counsel to the Guarantor delivered in accordance with Section 8.1 of the Agreement (the "Opinion of Counsel to the Guarantor");

5. The opinion of Local Law Office delivered in accordance with Section 8.1 of the Agreement (the "Opinion of Local Counsel"); and

6. Such other documents as we have deemed necessary or appropriate as a basis for the opinions expressed herein.

The opinions expressed herein are limited to questions arising under the law of the State of New York and of the United States of America. We are relying upon the Opinion of Local Counsel, the Opinion of Counsel to the Borrower and the Opinion of Counsel to the Guarantor as to matters relating to the law of the Republic of Somewhere that are relevant to the opinions expressed herein, and we have made no independent investigation thereof. We have assumed and have not verified that the signatures on all the documents that we have examined are genuine.

> 1. "By relying on an opinion, a lawyer ordinarily indicates that in his or her judgment it is reasonable to do so. Generally, to establish the reasonableness of reliance the opinion lawyer must ascertain the reputation for competence of local counsel and whether the opinion on its face responds to the questions posed to local counsel." "Legal Opinions to Third Parties: An Easier Path" (A Report By The Special Committee on Legal Opinions in Commercial Transactions, New York County Lawyers' Association, In Cooperation with The Corporation Law Committee, Association of the Bar of the City of New York, and The Corporation Law Commitee of the Banking, Corporation and Business Law Section, New York State Bar Association), 34 <u>The Business Lawyer</u> 1891, 1902 (1979).
>
> 2. Reading: Janis, "The Lawyer's Responsibility for Foreign Law and Foreign Lawyers", 16 <u>The International Lawyer</u> 693 (Fall 1982) (on a lawyer's responsibility to identify questions of foreign law and then either to deal competently with them or to advise his client that foreign counsel should be retained).

We express no opinion as to the effect, if any, under the laws of the State of New York, the United States of America or any other jurisdiction on the enforceability of the Agreement or the Notes of any future action of the Republic of Somewhere or any of its political subdivisions, agencies or instrumentalities that may constitute an act of state or be given effect, for reasons of comity or otherwise, by the courts of the State of New York or the United States of America.

Based on and subject to the foregoing, and upon such investigations of law as we have deemed appropriate, we advise you that in our opinion the Agreement is, and each of the Notes, when duly executed and delivered by the Borrower, will be, a legal, valid and binding obligation of the Borrower, enforceable against the Borrower in accordance with its terms, and the Agreement is, and each of the Notes, when so duly executed and delivered and duly endorsed with the Guarantor's guaranty and delivered by the Guarantor, will be, a legal, valid and binding obligation of the Guarantor, enforceable against the Guarantor in accordance with its terms, subject, in both cases, to applicable bankruptcy, insolvency, moratorium and similar laws affecting creditors' rights generally, and subject, as to enforceability, to general principles of equity (regardless of whether enforcement is sought in a proceeding in equity or at law).

Unless and until we give you notice before the disbursement of the Loans of any change in this opinion, you may rely on this opinion at all times from the date hereof to and including the disbursement of the Loans as if this opinion were dated on and as of the day of, and delivered at, each such time.

We are furnishing this opinion letter to you solely for your benefit. You may furnish a copy of it to the Banks, and they may rely on it as if it were addressed to them. It may also be relied on by your counsel and counsel for the Banks in connection with the Agreement and the Notes. It is not, however, to be used, circulated, quoted or otherwise referred to for any other purpose.

Very truly yours,

| This form of opinion is appropriate for a transac-
|tion in which special New York counsel will represent
|the agent alone, not the agent and the lenders, in
|connection with the transaction. Lenders should be
|conscious of this distinction, since they may wish
|their own separate counsel to take a more active role
|in such cases.

EXHIBIT J - <u>Form of Acceptance by the Agent for Service of Process</u>

_____, 19__

Biggest Bank N.A.
 and the several other
 banks and financial
 institutions named as
 Banks in the Agreement
 herein described
Infallible Agent Bank, as Agent

c/o Infallible Agent Bank
One Money Center
New York, New York 00000
As Agent

Dear Sirs:

We understand that, pursuant to a loan agreement dated as of May 15, 1986 among State-Owned Company, S.A. (the "Borrower"), The Republic of Somewhere (the "Guarantor"), Infallible Agent Bank, as agent, and others (a copy of which has been supplied to us), we have been irrevocably appointed agent of the Borrower and the Guarantor to receive service of process or other legal summons. We hereby irrevocably accept such appointment.

Very truly yours,

ETERNAL MAIL BOX

By:_____

EXHIBIT K - Schedule of Governmental Formalities

[To be completed with
information to be supplied
by local counsel.]

EXHIBIT L - Schedule of Liens and Other Encumbrances
on Property of the Borrower

[To be completed with
information to be supplied
by the Borrower.]

EXHIBIT M - Schedule of Liens and Other Encumbrances
on Property of the Guarantor

[To be completed with
information to be supplied
by the Guarantor.]

Section IV: Negotiating and Structuring Loan Agreements
Chapter 15: Negotiations

Negotiations with Transnational Banks: A Sovereign Borrower's Perspective*
Jose Angel Gurria-Trevino

GENERAL PREPARATION AND FINANCIAL TERMS

Borrowing in general and sovereign borrowing in particular require considerable preparation before the first contacts with a prospective foreign lender take place. The degree to which such preparation is thorough and effective will determine the outcome of any specific negotiation to a greater extent than the negotiating skills of the individuals involved. Moreover, the foreign banks' estimations of the scale, quality, seriousness and depth of said preparatory work will crucially affect their attitudes and disposition towards the borrower in general and the loan at hand in particular.

1. Control and co-ordination, the crucial preliminary requirements

The most basic framework for any sovereign borrowing operation is the variety of laws, institutions, regulations and traditions which control and coordinate all acts relating to foreign borrowing by a sovereign borrower or its agencies. Outside the overall institutional and legal infrastructure for the whole of the economic and social system of a country, the existence of specific laws and regulations dealing with foreign borrowing is indispensable if a country intends to incur foreign debt in substantial amounts to support its development plans.

A sovereign borrower may approach capital markets either through the central Government, through its agencies, or through both. Larger developing countries generally use the names of the Government and of its agencies to borrow abroad, and in this case the question of institutional control becomes all the more important. Such control should be granted by law to a particular government agency—the foreign borrowing controlling agency (FBCA). Written authorization from FBCA should be a legal pre-condition of any loan. Furthermore, such an authorization should be based upon the analysis of FBCA of the loan's size, cost, maturity, instrument, market, currency, contractual provisions and so on.

Regulations issued by the controlling agency should clearly state the pre-conditions which a potential borrower must fulfill in order to have access to foreign loans. The pre-conditions should ideally include considerations of the nature of the projects to be financed, the use of proceeds as applied to specific portions of a project (the external component of a steel mill, for example), and considerations on the profitability of the loan, both social and economic. These control elements will tend to rationalize the use of foreign credit and thereby maximize its impact. Explicit provisions to avoid borrowing for current expenditure in local currency would reinforce the desired effect.

Control should also be exercised at the overall, macro-market level through a careful process of co-ordination. In the case of small countries with relatively small requirements or sovereign borrowers who only tap the market through their central Governments, the co-ordination of borrowing is relatively easy. However, the typical situation in many medium to large-size developing countries is that a host of agencies, both those guaranteed and not guaranteed by the central Government, as well as the central Government itself, are competing for foreign funds.

The role of FBCA must be to translate the resulting natural rivalry into a competition of performance and professionalism, rather than allowing the competition to result in simultaneous attempts to tap the market through borrowings which are comparable. Such action only brings about confusion in the market, an increase in costs and an overall deterioration in the image of the borrower. A careful, knowledgeable "queuing" system closely monitored by FBCA must therefore become an integral part of the control system.

The control function should also involve constant supervision of the performance of the different borrowers regarding the fulfillment of obligations under existing loan agreements (punctual payments, financial ratios, information requirements etc.), their capacities as negotiators, and the perfor-

*Reprinted from *Issues in Negotiating International Loan Agreements*, U.N. Centre on Transnational Corporations (New York 1983).

The author is Director General of Public Credit, Ministry of Finance and Public Credit Government of Mexico.

mance of their debt issues in secondary markets, when applicable (as in the case of fixed-rate public bonds).

The above-delineated responsibilities of FBCA are not meant to usurp the critical role of the agencies or the Government when negotiating foreign loans. In fact, a broad base of knowledgeable, experienced and skilled operators spread throughout the individual borrowing institutions is the best support that a successful FBCA can have. It is equally critical, however, that FBCA be able to intervene wherever and whenever it sees fit in order to ensure the achievement of general goals which might be jeopardized by independent actions of individual borrowers, however beneficial such actions might be for the agencies concerned.

The foreign borrowing controlling agency should also be vested with an absolute screening function. Naturally, not all potential governmental end-users of foreign exchange should be allowed to borrow abroad. FBCA should carefully control the number and quality of the "names" which are given clearance and, if necessary, create financial institutions which specialize in intermediation of foreign loans to serve the needs of a multiplicity of smaller users.

Negotiating financial terms with transnational banks: a multiple-step process

(a) Selecting the financing method

A foreign borrowing programme, especially a relatively large one, must be established within a policy framework which will give it continuity and which will warrant the necessary flexibility to achieve its stated goals both in terms of the quantity and quality of debt contracted. The starting point, at the country level, should be an absolute figure which must be raised, generally related to the expected current account gap of the economy for the target year. Such a figure, however, is only a starting point. A comprehensive effort must be made in order to break down the total foreign exchange requirement into its partial components in order to approach foreign exchange markets with the best possible results.

For each specific need, there is a source of foreign credit that is better suited than others. Identifying the needs and finding the most appropriate source is as important as finding the right bank with which to deal. The major focus of the present paper is the negotiation of medium-term, syndicated bank loans. Such loans will certainly predominate among the external commercial borrowings of virtually any developing country Government. However, it should be clearly noted that such loans are not in every instance the best way to finance a foreign currency need.

If there are imports or exports of commodities, for example, acceptances will be less costly, more flexible and more expeditious than bank loans. Currently, acceptances both in dollars and in sterling can be syndicated for large amounts, and renewal commitments may be obtained from banks so that the maturity of the instrument can in fact be stretched from three and six months to at least two years and sometimes more.

Further, there is a wide world of capital markets. Floating rate certificates of deposit (mostly for financial institutions), and ultimately fixed-rate bond issues (both private and public) in the different markets and currencies also represent a possibility to avoid over-reliance on the bank market. Access to these instruments is substantially restricted, but it may be possible to start with debt issues in small amounts and undertake extensive "road-shows" to educate potential investors about the borrower involved. Once a foothold in the market is established, it is a question of time and of "nursing" the capital markets before a borrower can use it more extensively.

Finally, we come to the primary market for developing country sovereign borrowers, the syndicated bank loan markets. The effort to avoid this market to the greatest possible extent stems from one simple consideration: the less one borrows from banks, the less costly will borrowings be; the more a sovereign borrower diversifies its sources and markets, the more "appetite" there will be in those markets for the next loan, increasing in the same measure the chances for a good reception.

(b) Selecting the lenders

From the outset of the actual negotiation process, confidence and fluid communication between borrower and lender are crucial. No intermediaries should be utilized. A fully empowered representative of the borrower (or a team with advisers but with an easily identified head) should contact the bank or banks and conduct negotiations from beginning to end. Acting through a local financial institution should be avoided, although someone from said institution could join the negotiating team as adviser, if specialized expertise is lacking on the borrower's team.

The question of the choice of bank depends very much on the type of instrument chosen; some banks are noted for their skills in specific fields. For example, a Eurodollar bond issue will be best left to a European bank, although United States investment banks are increasingly active in the field. When dealing in dollar acceptances and commercial paper, United States investment banks have a virtual monopoly, while sterling acceptances can be dealt with by both commercial and merchant banks, as long as they are United Kingdom banks. Obviously, any securities issued in domestic markets should be led by banks or investment houses of the country where the issue is launched. The same rule applies to credits.

The choices are less clear when it comes to our primary concern regarding medium-term Eurodollar syndications. Two options exist: the bidding system or the "confidence" system. The bidding system is relatively simple and straightforward: one announces to the market the intention to borrow and a dead-line is set for the offers to be delivered. The borrower can then appraise the offers and choose the one which is most convenient. This approach is most useful for first-time borrowers or borrowers with little experience in the markets.

The "confidence" approach requires greater expertise and skill on the part of the borrower, but gives him a greater degree of control over the whole process of negotiation and the actual marketing of the operation. The approach requires selecting a single institution which the borrower trusts either on the basis of previous experience or as a logical conclusion after having discussed and sounded out the possible loan with a number of banks. The bank selected is granted a mandate to co-ordinate the formation of a lending syndicate.

Large money-centre banks usually constitute safe choices to play this role of "lead bank". However, the lead banks must also show a strong commitment to the borrower's potential in the market. At the same time, it should be cautioned that granting a mandate to a bank from a sovereign lender means both prestige and the largest share of the fees involved in the lending arrangement made. Overly aggressive offers should be discarded, no matter how tempting; accepting them could lead to failure in the market.

These guidelines impose on the borrower the need to be well informed, well connected and in possession of a clear idea of the "slot" in which it belongs among the world's borrowers. Using comparable countries as benchmarks is extremely useful, and even the country ranking efforts of specialized publications can prove handy in providing an approximate idea of the right pricing for the borrower involved. Most big banks tend to be cautious and this reinforces the argument of using them as leaders, but FBCA and/or the borrower must have made the rounds and spoken to several potential candidates before the "confidence" choice is made.

Once the bank is selected, it must then be asked to openly discuss its ideas with the negotiating team and FBCA in order to arrive at a generally acceptable set of indicative terms and conditions. Most operations for major borrowers involve amounts in the hundreds of millions of dollars. In this situation, no single bank will alone wish to provide a major loan. The next step thus involves asking the chosen bank to go to a limited number of other banks in order to put together and present to the borrower a fully underwritten offer. This means that the banks involved are willing to commit firmly to lend the amount offered in the proposed terms and conditions, in the event that this group of bankers, the "lead managers", are unable to attract participation from other banks. In this case, the financial terms of the loan are secure, regardless of the results of the marketing effort.

Best effort offers, in which the lead managers selected make no such commitment, should be avoided. They leave all the market risk on the borrower's side, and banks are bound to launch a more effective marketing effort if they are fully committed.

The list of banks which are invited to act as lead managers or underwriters must be carefully screened by both the lead bank and the borrower. The criteria for inviting these other lead managers is the same: those banks who might have expressed interest during the sounding out process should be uppermost on the list and banks with previous experience in the country should rank ahead of newcomers.

The formation of the lead management group is fundamental to a successful borrowing. Geographic balance, selling or "placing" power and market expertise are basic requirements for the group. The inclusion of local banks must not be made a condition unless they genuinely add to the group's "muscle". The borrower can co-operate with the lead bank at this stage not only by suggesting names of other banks, but by actually inviting them directly. Banks favour a direct link with the borrower, and will respond better than if only invited by the lead bank.

When the borrower receives the fully underwritten offer, it must carefully analyse the terms and conditions, and use its educated judgment to decide whether they are acceptable or not. There is almost always some room for negotiation and improvement in the borrower's favour, although the fact that any change has to be accepted by all lead managers makes this room for manoeuvre rather limited. This stresses the importance of establishing the main terms and conditions with the lead bank before and not after the lead group is formed.

Before granting a firm mandate, the borrower must discuss and agree with the lead bank (and maybe with some of the other members of the lead group, to save time and effort) on the appropriate marketing strategy and perhaps even going into the details of how fees are going to be distributed. Although some lenders will regard the distribution of fees as strictly the banks' affair, borrowers should not share this view. Fees are becoming an increasingly important element of loan arrangements. If the lead bank or the lead group of banks attempt to capture too large a share of the fees, they can jeopardize the success of the marketing effort. There is an almost direct relationship between the distribution of the fees and the success in the marketing of any operation.

Where the borrower is finally prepared to give the mandate in writing, it must make sure the mandate contains, besides all the basic terms and conditions of the loan, some of the key contractual provisions which it should have negotiated previously. Because loan agreements are usually negotiated during or after the placing of the loan, there should be no surprises when the draft is presented to the borrower. Once a loan is sold on a certain basis, it is highly inconvenient to attempt to change any key clauses or provisions.

Finally, the mandate is given and the operation goes to the market. It is legitimate for the borrower once again to contact banks during the marketing period in order to sway those whose decision might depend on the borrower's request. This exercise, however, should be done in careful coordination with the lead bank.

(c) Strategic aspects

In addition to the various institutional, legal and market considerations that must be brought to bear on the bargaining process in order to give the borrower greater leverage, negotiating strategy can play a critical role. The borrower's team should never give the impression that it has the final say. This should be left to FBCA, with which the borrower should be in constant contact. It is convenient both strategically and in actual practice to establish from the beginning that all decisions must be double-checked with FBCA. It gives the borrower greater flexibility and it reinforces the negotiating capacity of the country as a whole, because there will be many issues which might ultimately have to be decided by FBCA anyway.

A final word of warning is warranted. Countries and agencies of a country must take full advantage of the competitive nature of the bank market, but they must also be concerned with creating loyalty (or at least a minimum of sympathy) from banks towards it. If a borrower is seen to take every single advantage it can take, the borrower-lender relationship will become a very short-sighted one: in the end it may not work in the borrower's favour, particularly if one considers the possibility that a country might at some point find itself in financial difficulties requiring expanded transnational bank support.

Banks and borrowers are natural adversaries, but the market is a greater equalizer, and after all, what both the borrower and the banks need are successful operations that leave a good aftertaste and an unsatisfied appetite which will assure the success of the next loans that are brought to the market.

B. THE NEGOTIATION OF CONTRACTUAL PROVISIONS

Practically all clauses in a loan agreement are negotiable; at least all clauses which are important to the borrower's position *vis-a-vis* its lenders. The stronger the borrower's economic, political and market situation the better negotiating capacity and its chances of obtaining a fair, equitable and balanced loan agreement.

Although each country has laws and regulations which will be brought to bear on the process of negotiating legal clauses, a set of general rules must be applied: all clauses have to be negotiated fully; all implications studied at length; each scenario explored in depth; every option must be discussed; and all texts must be self-explanatory in order to avoid misunderstandings.

While it is true that the limits to which a borrower can go in conceding legal points to lenders are the boundaries defined by the borrower's laws. it is also true that no borrower should have to go all the way to those limits; all negotiations should stay well within such boundaries if the banks are serving the borrower's interests in addition to serving their own.

The guidlines established by FBCA should be known to all agencies within a country and, just as important, to all banks wanting to lend to such country or agencies. This will save time and effort and will result in more homogeneous and, hopefully, more equitable contractual provisions. It will also take care of the cases where a relatively weak borrower would otherwise concede too much, in detriment of the other public sector borrowers.

This chapter will consider some of the more relevant legal issues which normally arise during contractual negotiations, and the particular experience which Mexico has had in this field.

In the chapter on definitions, a constant concern should be to obtain the inclusion of a narrow definition of "indebtedness" that makes a clear distinction between foreign debt and domestic debt. This definition should refer only to currencies other than the local currency and owed to a non-resident. When applied to the cross-default, the negative pledge and the *pari passu* clauses, a narrow definition of indebtedness will limit the possibility of a loan being accelerated because of a default with a domestic institution or with a foreign institution lending in domestic currency, as the case may be. The rationale in support of such a narrow definition is that sovereign borrowers can clearly deal with domestic credit difficulties in a much more flexible way than with debts denominated in foreign currencies.

In the representations and warranties chapter, experience advises that the borrower should negotiate the drafting of clauses in the present tense. Banks normally ask for these determinations of the borrower's situation to be projected into the future. Borrowers should avoid such constructions because conditions might change, officers may be removed and administrative regulations can be altered without these changes necessarily being to the detriment of the lenders.

The *pari passu* clause normally appears in the representations and warranties section. Because borrowers might have previous loans or liabilities which were incurred on a different basis, it is best to equate the ranking of any new foreign debt to that of "other unsecured external indebtedness for borrowed money". Typically, sovereign borrowers and their agencies and public bodies (at least those fully owned) will not pledge any of their assets as securities for foreign loans, so that all foreign banks are left in the same relative position when the above-cited text is adopted. This is precisely the result lenders seek.

Moving on to the chapter on terms and conditions, the most relevant topics would be:

(a) Interest rate. The borrower must make sure that the rate applied to the relevant borrowing period is that of at least three to five reference banks which provide a representative sample of the totality of the banks involved in a loan, both geographically and by size. This will ensure that said rate is truly a market rate, without circumstantial distortions which might inflate it;

(b) Penalty for late payment. Although any borrower should make it a matter of highest priority to ensure that all payments are made when due in order to enhance its creditworthiness, it must nevertheless negotiate that the additional cost incurred by any delay in paying its obligations is not excessive. Some banks seek to capitalize unpaid interest, for example. One way of circumventing the problem is simply to negotiate a flat increase in the applicable rate (in Mexico, thus far, the penalty has been limited to 1 per cent).

Another critical aspect of the negotiation involves the documentation used as evidence of indebtedness. Here the option is between a loan agreement, promissory notes, or both. The borrower's position should be to attempt to simplify documentation as much as possible and, ideally, to eliminate the issuance of promissory notes. Notes tend to reappear in the secondary market over and over, while sales of bank participation are made in a more discrete fashion, ordinarily with the approval of the borrower, who shall not unreasonably withhold said approval. Sometimes, notes are requested by banks because they protect their right to apply for execution action before the courts. To the extent that such right can be exercised on the basis of a loan agreement only (as in the case of Mexico), lenders should be satisfied that their interests are fully protected.

Prepayment at the option of the borrower is a crucial provision which should always be pursued. Such an option should be without premium or penalty, as long as it coincides with an interest payment date in a typical medium-term roll-over syndication. The existence of a no-penalty prepayment clause places the borrower in a much stronger position to renegotiate when the market improves in its favour, and hence allows for a more flexible debt-management policy.

Regarding the definition of interest rates, some sovereign borrowers have been borrowing United States dollars on the basis of the London interbank offered rate (LIBOR) or prime rate, at the option of the lender, in order to increase their market penetration. It should be clearly established that lenders must from the beginning commit to lend over one or the other rate for the whole duration of the loan, and should not have the option of choosing the base rate at every rollover date.

When defining the prime rate, United States offer a language which identifies such rate as the higher of either the prime rate or the cost of the three-month adjusted rate for certificates of deposit in the secondary market, plus reserve and insurance costs. This is sought by banks in order to avoid funding losses if ever the prime rate is held at artificially low levels for any reason, while their cost of funds goes up. The borrower must seek a more equitable solution which should require the majority banks (holding at least 66 per cent of the loan) to declare that prime rate no longer covers their costs and then the borrower and the banks will negotiate in good faith to find an alternative base rate for the period during which the phenomenon occurs. Upon failure to reach agreement, the respective tranche of the loan (not the entire loan) could then be prepaid by the borrower.

Closely related to the above-mentioned item is the chapter referring to changes is circumstances. Typically, banks try to introduce every possible contingency that might affect them, and make these reasons for early repayment of the loan. Borrowers should, on the one hand, recognize the possibility of some of these events actually happening, but should also search for remedies short of repaying the loan. The "legitimate" cases of change in circumstances which a borrower might accept are: illegality, increased costs, and non-quotation of the base rates.

(a) Illegality. If changes in laws or regulations in lending jurisdiction should make the loan illegal, the banks must commit (on a best effort basis) to try to transfer their participation to other branches of their own bank or to other banks not affected by the illegality. Failing this, the borrower should be able to repay the loan, but such prepayment should be made without any premium or penalty. Asking for a penalty would be tantamount to assuming that the loan was illegal when closed, and it would involve a retroactive application of the laws that made it illegal. Besides being clearly inequitable, retroactivity is generally prohibited by legislation based both on Roman right and on common law.

(b) Increased costs. These might arise when changes in laws or regulations require from the banks higher reserve requirements, for example, or higher taxes on the banks' lending activity. Borrowers in negotiations should strive to require that banks attempt to reassign their assets to other branches not thus affected. Failing this provision, in situations where a borrower feels that the higher costs are not reasonable, it should be allowed to prepay the loan, without premium or penalty, after a relatively short period of previous notice (five days, for example) in order to avoid paying such higher costs for an extended period.

(c) Non-quotation of base rates. If the market were in such a state of disarray that it would be impossible to obtain quotations of the base rate as specified in the loan agreement, provisions should be made for a friendly good faith search for an alternative rate which, if not found, would lead to prepayment without premium or penalty. The borrower, however, has to be cautious to ascertain that the problem is affecting the majority banks (66 per cent) and not only one or a few who might have a special problem.

Contrary to the case of representations and warranties, covenants and undertakings must be projected into the future. Because of this, special attention must be paid to this chapter. Borrowers must make sure that no future actions, either administrative or legal, which it might take in the pursuit of its objectives, become cause for early repayment.

The *pari passu* clause appears again in this section, but this time in the future tense. Borrowers must clearly define and set in writing their degrees of freedom to pledge their assets under either existing or future commitments and, as mentioned before, insist on equating the ranking of the new foreign credit to that of "other unsecured foreign indebtedness for borrowed money".

Although not applied to a sovereign borrower engaged in general purpose borrowing, the inclusion of financial ratios is sought by banks when dealing with public agencies or corporations engaged in some form of market activity (that is, utilities, banks etc.) in order to ensure their financial soundness. While it is legitimate to ask for these ratios when dealing with private sector borrowers, where the only guarantee of repayment lies in the continued soundness of the firm involved, this is not the case with public agencies, and even less so with a central Government. Governments frequently adopt pricing and taxing policies for public goods and services which have a direct impact on the agencies which provide them.

These policies might cause an agency to show low profits, for example, or a higher debt/equity ratio than would otherwise be advisable. The situation, however, would not reflect the Government's chosen way of allocating resources among the members of this society, and the presence of compulsory financial ratios might jeopardize this aim.

The chapter on causes of default or early repayment is perhaps the most difficult to negotiate. As more and more elements have been added to it over the years, this section appears to have evolved against the interest of borrowers. Some basic precautions are warranted when approaching these provisions.

First, the clause should contemplate only matters which are imputable to the borrower, not to the lenders or third parties. Borrowers should also attempt to make sure that the default is declared by the "majority banks", either directly or through the agent, and not only by one or a few, in order to be valid.

The possible sources of default should be explicitly distinguished in the provisions. Default may result from the violation of or non-compliance with the covenants (technical default), or it may arise from the non-payment of amounts due under the loan agreement (administrative or "blatant" default). In the first case, the borrower should negotiate the inclusion of a reasonable grace period (30 days) in order to remedy the situation, before default can be declared. In the second case, a grace period of at least five working days should be given to the borrower before default is declared, in order to avoid acceleration because of lost payments and other mechanical problems which might not be fully imputable to the borrower.

With respect to the cross-default clause, borrowers should fight as hard as they can to avoid the "open" cross-default which links all their liabilities in a cascade effect which would accelerate all loans when default is declared on any of them. First and foremost, the cross-default clause should only relate to other cases of "external indebtedness" as earlier defined, rather than to any and all liabilities of the borrower.

In syndicated bank loans, borrowers should strive for clauses in which cross-default can only be declared when the borrower fails to pay other loans to any of the banks participating in the operation at hand; a default to a non-participant in the loan should not be enough to invoke this clause. This is often termed a "limited" cross-default clause.

Finally, in this section, a clause is sometimes found which states that a loan can be accelerated if there has occurred a situation which constitutes a "material adverse change" in the condition of the borrower. Borrowers should attempt to avoid all clauses which leave it to the subjective judgment of the banks whether they accelerate a loan or not. Phrases like "may be declared", "capable of being declared" or "in the judgment of the banks" leave all the risk on the side of the borrower and expose it to situations where political or ideological considerations might prevail over strictly economic and financial realities. If a borrower cannot avoid this clause, it should eliminate the potential for arbitrariness by qualifying it as much as possible. For example, "if an extraordinary situation shall occur which gives reasonable grounds to conclude, in the judgment of the majority banks, after consultation with the borrower, that a material adverse change has occured...".

In the chapter referring to the agent, the manager and the banks, the borrower should take the precaution of ensuring that an agent is only removed from its role by the banks with the prior consent of the borrower (who chose the agent in the first place). Otherwise, this section deals with relationships among the banks only.

Concerning the chapter on applicable law and jurisdiction: sovereign immunity, one must define clearly which law will be applicable for the loan agreement and, just as clearly, set out which courts will have jurisdication over any dispute that might arise between the parties. The question is both theoretical and practical. Borrowers should not allow any law to be applied, as banks could choose a body of law which does not render fair treatment. The same applies to jurisdiction. One must avoid the typical clause stating that "the borrower submits to the nonexclusive jurisdiction of the courts of..." Sovereign borrowers in particular must be extremely careful to negotiate law and jurisdiction with which they are familiar. Another approach would be to grant jurisdiction to the courts where the parties have their main place of business or, if unavoidable, the courts where the borrower has assets, but not yield to the non-exclusive solution.

In the case of sovereign immunity, although a waiver of such immunity is always included in standard loan agreements, some countries (like Mexico, for example) will not allow attachment prior to judgment or in aid of execution, although their laws allow for a foreign law to govern their agreements, and accept the jurisdiction of a foreign court.

Related also to this item is the question of set-off, that is, the capacity of the banks to automatically seize as payments the assets of the borrower held by them or by other banks or entities (that is, deposits of a borrower). The only acceptable possibility is that banks might file a claim and that a judge will grant permission to do so, but not without first going to court.

In the case of sovereign Governments or their agencies, their assets are immune from attachment unless they have explicity waived this immunity. But countries cannot go beyond what their own laws state, and if no attachment prior to judgment will be ordered by a court in Mexico, for example, even if it waives its immunity the attachment will not be executed.

Because the right of set-off is not clearly applicable in all courts when immunity is waived, it is convenient to exclude it from loan agreements, even if one waives sovereign immunity in general as an inevitable result of the forces at play. The mention of set-off should be deleted completely.

The question of law and jurisdiction is also crucial for purposes of this clause, as some court clearly are more adequate than others when protecting a borrower's interest. New York State laws, for example, require more evidence and conditions to consent to attachment prior to judgment than California or Illinois, but will grant the right to set-off even if it is not explicitly accepted in the loan agreement, whereas in California and Illinois set-off is not automatically allowed.

Section V: International Monetary Fund
Chapter 16: International Monetary Fund

16A. The International Monetary Fund: An Overview of its Structure and Functions

Daniel D. Bradlow

I. INTRODUCTION

The International Monetary Fund (hereinafter IMF or Fund) was established to foster international monetary cooperation by serving as a forum for consultation and collaboration between member states and to promote a stable monetary order by functioning as an international regulatory and financing institution.[1]

All IMF member states are required to maintain exchange rate, and other economic policies designed to promote international financial stability and orderly economic growth.[2] The Fund is empowered to exercise surveillance over these policies through consultations with member states.[3]

The IMF uses its financial resources to assist members to resolve their balance of payments problems in a manner that is consistent with a stable international monetary order and that is not destructive of either international or national prosperity.[4] Conditionality refers to the adjustment policies that the Fund expects a member state to pursue in exchange for its use of IMF financial resources.

Through its regulatory and financing functions the IMF influences the level of global liquidity. This influence was enhanced by the creation, in 1969, of the Special Drawing Right (hereinafter SDRs). The IMF has been mandated to use SDR allocations to avoid both international economic stagnation and excess demand and inflation.[5]

It is the purpose of this paper to describe each of the above IMF functions in greater detail so as to allow for an understanding of the IMF's role in international finance. Before discussing the role of the IMF, it is necessary to first describe the organizational structure of the IMF. Having then discussed the functioning of the IMF, the paper will conclude with a discussion of the IMF's relationship with the World Bank and with private commercial lenders.

II. ORGANIZATION

Membership in the IMF is open to every sovereign state that is willing and able to fulfill the obligations of IMF membership. As of June 1986, 150 nations belong to the IMF. All Western industrialized countries except Switzerland, most developing countries, and a few Eastern bloc countries are members of the Fund.

Each member state, upon joining the IMF, is assigned a quota by the Board of Governors. The quota is calculated on the basis of a complex formula that utilizes two sets of data that reflect the relative position of the member state in the international economy.[6] The quotas are weighted so as to give small and poor developing countries a somewhat greater quota than their relative position in the world economy warrants. This is done so as to ensure that they have some say in IMF affairs.[7]

The Articles of Agreement provide for adjustments to quotas. These adjustments can be selective, that is, limited to one or more member states or of general applicability. The Board of Governors, at intervals of no more than five years, is required to conduct general quota reviews and to make appropriate adjustments.[8] The eighth general review was concluded in 1983. This review resulted in an increase in aggregate quotas from SDR 61.1 billion to SDR 90 billion, equal to a 47.5% increase. Pursuant to the Articles of Agreement, the next quota review is due to be held in early 1988.

A member state's quota is of fundamental importance because it determines the member state's rights and duties in the IMF. Voting power, subscriptions to the IMF, SDR allocations, and access to the IMF's resources are all determined by quotas.[9]

A member state's subscription to the IMF is the contribution that the member state must make to the IMF's funds. The member state's subscription, expressed in SDR's, is equal in value to its quota. 75% of the subscription is payable in the member state's own currency and 25% is payable in SDR's or in one of the designated reserve currencies.[10] The member state is responsible for maintaining the above proportions in the IMF's holding of its quota.[11]

A) Voting

The IMF uses a system of weighted voting. This system incorporates both the principle of the equality of sovereign states and the fact that member states make substantially different financial contributions to the Fund. In recognition of the former, each member is assigned a basic allotment of 250 votes and because of the latter, each member state is then given one additional vote for each 100,000 SDR's of its quota.[12]

Thus,

Member State's Vote $= 250 + \dfrac{\text{Quota (expressed in SDR's)}}{100{,}000}$

As of May 1986 the total votes in the IMF were 930,018. Member states' votes ranged from 179,433 (=19% of total vote) for the United States of America to 270 (=0.03% of total vote) for the Maldives.

The member state's governor casts its vote at meetings of the Board of Governors and the Executive Director representing the member state casts its votes on the Executive Board of Directors (hereinafter Executive Board).

Most Fund decisions require a simple majority of the votes cast. Certain important operational issues require a 70% majority of the total IMF vote for approval. An example of such an issue is a change in the interest rates charged on the use of Fund reserves. Issues of fundamental importance require an 85% majority of the total IMF vote for approval. This requirement applies to changes in the Articles of the Fund, changes in quotas, and changes in SDR allocations.[13] It will be noted that in the case of an issue requiring an 85% vote, the USA has an effective veto. In decisions requiring 85% or 75% majorities, large voting blocs such as the EEC or the developing countries acting as a group, can also exercise a veto.

While the Articles establish voting majority requirements, the practice in the Fund is to operate by consensus. The consensus, however, does pay due regard to the relative strengths of member states' voting power.

B) Board of Governors[14]

The Board of Governors is the highest decision making body in the IMF. It is composed of one governor and one alternate governor from each member country. Governors are high government officials, usually Ministers of Finance or officials of comparable rank.

According to the Articles of Agreement, the Board of Governors has a number of enumerated powers and all powers not expressly given to other organs of the IMF. The Board of Governors can delegate all of its powers except its authority to admit new members, to determine quotas, and to make SDR allocations. The Board of Governors, in fact, has delegated all of its delegable powers to the Executive Board.

The Board of Governors meets annually, usually in conjunction with the meeting of the World Bank's Board of Governors. A quorum of the Board of Governors is two-thirds of the total voting power of the IMF. A special meeting can be called by a minimum of 15 member states or by member states holding 25% of the total IMF vote. As shown above, different decisions of the Board of Governors require different voting majorities.

C) Executive Board of Directors[15]

The Executive Board consists of twenty-two executive directors and the Managing Director of the IMF, who acts as chairman of the Executive Board. Each executive director appoints an alternate director who may attend all Executive Board meetings but does not vote unless the executive director is absent.

There are six appointed and sixteen elected executive directors. The member states holding the five largest quotas in the IMF each appoint one executive director. Currently, the United States of America, the United Kingdom, France, the Federal Republic of Germany and Japan each appoint one director. The Articles provide that, if at the time of the regular election of the Executive Director, the member states with the five largest quotas do not include one or both of the two member states whose currencies have been most often used in outstanding IMF transactions during the preceding two years, then one or both of these member states may appoint an executive director. Since 1978 Saudi Arabia has appointed an executive director pursuant to this provision.

The remaining members of the IMF are divided into sixteen groups that each elect one director to represent the group. Since 1980 the People's Republic of China has constituted its own group and has elected its own executive director. The executive director for each of the remaining fifteen groups casts one ballot equal to the combined voting power of the group's member states. All elected directors serve for a term of two years and may be re-elected.

The Executive Board is responsible for conducting the day-to-day business of the IMF. To perform this task the Executive Board is in continuous session. Among the Executive Board's most important functions is the approval of all requests for IMF financing.

D) Interim Committee[16]

The Interim Committee is one of the two committees that succeeded the Committee of Twenty. The latter was formed by member states in the early 1970's to conduct the negotiations that led to the Second Amendment of the IMF's Articles of Agreement. The Interim Committee, like the Committee of Twenty, consists of one representative from each member state that appoints an executive director and one representative from each group that elects an executive director. Interim Committee members, who each may appoint seven associate members, tend to be the Governors of the Fund or someone of comparable rank. All executive directors and the Managing Director are entitled to attend Interim Committee meetings.

The Interim Committee, which meets twice a year, gives advice to the Board of Governors on the IMF's role in managing the international monetary system, including the operation of the balance of payments adjustment process and on any proposed amendments to the Article of Agreement. It is important to note that the Interim Committee only has advisory powers. The Articles of Agreement do provide for the creation of a body with decision making power, known as the Council, to supercede the Interim Committee.[17] To date the Board of Governors has refrained from creating the Council.

E) Development Committee[18]

The second committee to succeed the Committee of Twenty is the Joint Ministerial Committee of the Board of Governors of the Bank and the Fund on the Transfer of Real Resources to Developing Countries, known as the Development Committee. Its function is to study and to recommend measures designed to promote the transfer of resources to developing countries, especially the least developed countries.

The Development Committee has the same structure as the Interim Committee except that the Executive Board constituencies of the IMF and the World Bank alternate in electing representatives to the Development Committee. The Development Committee usually meets at the same time and place as the Interim Committee.

F) Managing Director[19]

The Managing Director is selected by the Executive Board for a five year term. He is chairman of the Executive Board and is accountable for his actions to it. To date, the Managing Director has always been a national of a European member state and his deputy has been a citizen of the United States of America.

The Managing Director is the chief of the IMF staff and conducts the ordinary business of the IMF. In addition to chairing the Executive Board, he participates in the meetings of the Board of Governors and the Interim and Development Committees.

G) IMF Staff[20]

The IMF staff, which is drawn from about one hundred member states, is organized into a number of departments. There are five area departments — the African, Asian, Middle Eastern, European and Western Hemisphere departments. Staff members in these departments are responsible for providing economic advice to member states, and for assisting in the formulation of IMF policy towards each member state.

Other IMF departments include the Exchange and Trade Relations, Legal Research, Treasurer's and Fiscal Affairs departments. These departments are involved in the development of Fund policies and in working in their special areas of expertise.

Staff members give technical assistance to member countries through the Fiscal Affairs and Central Banking Departments and through the IMF Institute.

III. SPECIAL DRAWING RIGHTS[21]

Special Drawing Rights (SDR's) were created by the first Amendment to the Articles of Agreement to serve as an international reserve asset for those IMF member states who chose to participate in the Fund's Special Drawing Rights Department. To date, all member states participate in the Special Drawing Rights Department. The SDR is the IMF's unit of account and it is becoming a unit of account for some non-IMF related purposes.

Originally the value of the SDR was expressed in terms of gold. Since 1974, the SDR's value has been based on a basket of currencies whose composition is reviewed every five years. At present this basket consists of a weighted average, expressed in U.S. dollars, of the currencies of the countries having the five largest shares of total world exports of goods and services. The value of the SDR is calculated on the basis of the U.S. dollar equivalents at the market exchange rates prevailing in the London foreign exchange market of the following currencies in the following proportions — U.S. dollar 42%, German mark 19%, Japanese yen, French franc, UK pound sterling 13% each.

Article XV Section 1 of the Articles gives the IMF the authority to create unconditional liquidity by allocating SDR's to participants in the Special Drawing Rights Department. The IMF cannot allocate SDR's to itself or to other authorized holders of SDR's. SDR allocations are made for a stated period of time after which another decision on allocation is made. The Articles of Agreement allow the IMF to cancel SDR allocations. To date this has not occurred.

The procedure for deciding to make an SDR allocation is complex.[22] The allocation or cancellation is proposed by the Managing Director with the concurrence of the Executive Board. It is then voted on by the Board of Governors, who must approve the allocation with an 85% majority of total IMF votes. Each member state's share of the allocation is calculated on the basis of its quota.

Since SDR's affect the level of global liquidity, the IMF, in deciding to make allocations, must take care not to create excess liquidity and fuel inflation or to create too little liquidity and thereby induce stagnation. Some commentators have argued that the link between global liquidity and SDR allocations should be exploited to assist development in developing countries.[23] The idea of using SDR allocations as a means of transferring capital to developing countries is very controversial, in part, because it may have inflationary effects. It has not yet been adopted by the IMF.

The SDR is treated as a reserve asset of the member states by the IMF.[24] Member states are not required to maintain any minimum SDR balance with the IMF. There is no conditionality attached to the use of the member state's SDR account. The Fund, however, does pay member states an interest payment on that portion of their SDR holdings with the IMF that exceeds their SDR allocation.

The only condition attached to SDR's is that they may only be used in transactions with other authorized holders of SDR's. This means that members may use SDR's in their transactions with the IMF and with those IMF member states who participate in the Special Drawing Rights Department. Inter-member state use of SDR's may be by agreement or by designation.[25] Designation means that the IMF has mandated certain member states to receive SDR's and to exchange them for freely usable currencies. The amount of SDR's that the designated member state is obliged to receive is specified by the IMF and cannot exceed the member state's balance of payments deficit.

The IMF has certified fourteen official financial institutions as being allowed to hold SDR's.[26] IMF member states can use SDR's in their transactions with these institutions.

Growing international acceptance of SDR's has led to the appearance of occasional SDR denominated transactions in private capital markets. These private SDR's are not subject to IMF control and need not follow IMF alterations in the valuation of SDR's and in the legal requirements pertaining to SDR's. At present, however, the private SDR's are valued in an identical fashion to official SDR's.[27]

IV. REGULATORY FUNCTIONS[28]

When the international monetary system relied on fixed exchange rates, the IMF was responsible for monitoring member states' observance of their exchange rate obligations. The present international monetary system grants member states much more autonomy and flexibility in devising an exchange rate policy and thus allocates a less well defined regulatory role to the IMF. The IMF's surveillance policy is intended to clarify its regulatory function.

The IMF's surveillance policy is based on Article IV of the Articles of Agreement and on a 1977 Executive Board decision. Together they establish the principles underlying surveillance and the procedure for surveillance. The 1977 decision is reviewed each year and, when necessary, is updated to ensure its continuing relevance and comprehensiveness.[29]

The surveillance policy is based on three principles, which provide guidance to member states in their formulation of an exchange rate policy and to the IMF in its surveillance of these policies. The first principle states that member states should avoid manipulating exchange rates in order to prevent effective balance of payments adjustments or to gain an unfair trade advantage over their trading partners. Secondly, members should intervene in exchange markets to counter disorderly short-term conditions affecting their currency's value on international money markets. Finally, members should consider the impact of their actions on other member countries when they decide on a course of action.

IMF surveillance is conducted through regular consultation with member states. The consultations cover the overall economic situation of the member state in order to assess the sustainability of its exchange rate policy and the impact of these policies on other countries. Discussions will also cover means of reducing structural rigidities in the economy, the impact of the exchange rate policy on the member state's international competitiveness and its debt servicing capacity. The consultations are designed to encourage exchange rate policies that are consistent with medium term global adjustment requirements. In its consultations with the member state the IMF should take into consideration the member state's economic policies and its social and political situation.

The IMF is required, pursuant to a decision of the Executive Board, to hold annual consultations with member countries. This requirement has proved to be too onerous. Consequently, annual consultations are conducted only with those countries receiving IMF financial assistance, those member states whose economies have a substantial impact on the world economy and those whose medium term balance of payments prospects are uncertain. For all other countries consultations are held at least every two years.

If it appears to be necessary or beneficial, the IMF may hold more frequent consultations with member states. The types of events that are likely to trigger such special consultations are exchange rate movements unrelated to underlying economic conditions, heavy and unsustainable government intervention in the money markets, external debt problems, economic policies that disproportionately affect capital flows. It should be noted that in a number of recent sovereign debt restructurings the IMF has agreed to institute "enhanced surveillance" over debtor countries in return for pledges from commercial banks to provide additional funding to the debtor nation. The purpose of the enhanced surveillance is to ensure that the debtor country follows IMF approved economic policies, even though the debtor state has not entered into a standby arrangement with the IMF.

If the Managing Director suspects that a member state's exchange rate policy is not in accordance with IMF principle, he may enter into informal consultations with the member state about its policies. If he deems these informal consultations inadequate, the Managing Director may initiate formal consultations with the member state.

Consultations between the IMF and a member state are designed to give the IMF a better understanding of the economy of the country concerned and also of the international monetary system. This enhanced understanding should enable the IMF to develop more effective adjustment programs. The consultations also provide member states with an opportunity to request advice on its policies from the IMF. This advice has no binding effect and, in theory, can be disregarded by the member.

The IMF draws on the information obtained in all its consultations, both regular and special, with member states when composing its periodic publication, World Economic Outlook.[30] This publication contains the IMF's assessment of the functioning of the international economy and the international monetary system from a medium term perspective. It should be noted that during the drafting of the World Economic Outlook, the IMF may consult member states about specific aspects of their policies.

V. FINANCING FUNCTION

A) IMF Financial Resources[31]

The IMF's financial resources consist of paid-in member states' subscriptions and borrowed funds. Subscriptions, equal to total quota allocations, are the primary source of funds. While not legally so restricted, the IMF only borrows from official sources. Pursuant to a 1982 guideline, IMF borrowing is limited to 50% of the total quota allocation.

The most important source of borrowed funds for the IMF is the General Agreement to Borrow (hereinafter GAB). This is an agreement between the IMF and ten leading industrial states or their central banks, which assures the IMF of additional funding to help finance drawings in the reserve or credit tranches by any one of these ten states.[32] GAB was created so as to ensure that a drawing by one of the rich IMF member states would not unexpectedly or unduly deplete IMF resources to the detriment of other member states.

The GAB was first established in 1962 for a specified period of time and has been periodically renewed and updated since then. The last revision was in 1983 when the GAB participants agreed to expand GAB resources from SDR 6.4 billion to SDR 17 billion. An adjunct agreement to the GAB, between the IMF and Switzerland, allows the IMF to borrow from the Swiss National Bank to finance transactions with both GAB and non-GAB member states.[33]

The Saudi Arabian Monetary Authority has been another important source of borrowed funds. It loaned the IMF SDR 8 billion over two years to establish the enlarged access policy. An SDR 1.5 billion credit arrangement with the Saudi Arabian Monetary Authority grants the IMF access to funds for similar purposes and under similar terms to the GAB. Similar arrangements have also been concluded with the Bank for International Settlements, Japan, and the National Bank of Belgium.[34]

When the IMF relies on borrowed funds to finance a facility it has to charge member states, who use the facility, an interest rate that reflects the cost to the IMF of the borrowed funds. Since this interest charge may be quite onerous for some member states, the IMF has created a Supplementary Financing Facility Subsidy Account to assist poorer nations in paying the interest charges. This Subsidy Account is financed by donations from member states.[35]

The IMF's resources are managed by one of two departments — the General Department or the Special Drawing Rights Department.[36] The General Department consists of four separate accounts. The General Resources Account holds member states' subscriptions and administers all IMF financing facilities except the IMF administered facilities. The Borrowed Resources Suspense Account contains borrowed funds not immediately required for IMF transactions. The Special Disbursement Account receives repayments from Trust Fund loans and transfers these funds to the Supplementary Financing Facility Subsidy Account. The Investment Account, which is not yet operative, will administer IMF investments.[37]

The General Department is also responsible for the Fund administered facilities. Though the IMF administers these facilities, their funds are legally distinct from IMF resources. The IMF administered facilities are all financed from donations, borrowed funds, or investment proceeds such as from IMF gold sales.

The Special Drawing Rights Department conducts all the IMF's SDR operations. This means that it is responsible for SDR allocations, cancellations and IMF's SDR transactions.

B) Form of Financing

The IMF's financing facilities are designed to assist member states finance balance of payments adjustments. While each facility is a response to an economically distinct cause of balance of payments disequilibrium, they all share some common characteristics.

Due to the IMF's policy of uniformity,[38] all financing facilities are open to any member state who can demonstrate that it suffers from the balance of payments problem for which the particular financing facility is designed. The IMF recognizes, however, that some balance of payments problems are characteristic of developing countries and that, therefore, they are the primary beneficiaries of certain IMF financing facilities.

IMF assistance is made available to member states through exchange transactions or standby arrangements. Exchange transactions, in reality, are limited to drawings in a member state's reserve tranche. Exchange transactions outside the reserve tranche are known as extensions of credit, but are not common.[39]

An exchange transaction consists of a member state purchasing, from the IMF, another member state's currency in exchange for the purchasing member state's own currency. The purchasing member state is obligated to repurchase its own currency from the IMF for an equivalent amount of SDR's or a reserve currency. The repurchase must occur within three to five years after the initial purchase but may occur earlier if the member state's balance of payments position improves more rapidly than expected.

Legally, an exchange transaction is different from a loan because it involves a purchase rather than an extension of credit. The repurchase obligation, however, distinguishes an exchange transaction from an outright purchase. This legal distinction is important because it means that an exchange transaction does not create a debtor-creditor relationship between the IMF and the member state and that the Fund has none of the rights of a creditor against the member state.[40] However, the repurchase obligation does establish a legal relationship between the IMF and the member state that differs from that normally arising between a seller and a buyer. Exchange transactions should, thus, be viewed as *sui generis*, legal relationships.

The currencies involved in an exchange transaction depend upon the purchasing member and the IMF. No member can veto the use of its currency in an exchange transaction, but the IMF is not obliged to give the purchasing member state its first choice of currency. In deciding what currency to make available to the member state, the IMF considers the member state's needs and the balance of payments and reserve position of the member state whose currency has been requested. If the member state's first choice of currency is denied, the IMF will give the member a currency which is easily converted into its first choice in the private money markets.

C) Standby Arrangements[41]

A standby arrangement is a decision by the IMF according to which a member state is assured that it will be able to make purchases from the General Resources Account in accordance with the terms of the decision.[42] The decision will specify the time period and the amount of the standby arrangement and will also specify the conditions attached to the member state's access to the funds.

The standby arrangement is used by member states for three different purposes. It can be used to satisfy an immediate need for foreign exchange. The arrangement may also be used by members for the precautionary purpose of ensuring a source of foreign exchange in case of future need. Finally, members may use standby arrangements to demonstrate to actual and potential creditors, that the member state's financial policy has the "seal of approval" of the IMF. This symbolic function may be important for member states seeking to negotiate or renegotiate their debt with public- or private-sector creditors.

The terms of the standby arrangement are arrived at after extensive consultation between the member state and the IMF. After a member state requests financial assistance, the IMF sends a mission, acting under the Managing Director's authority, to the member state. The mission consults with the member state about its payments problem and its currency needs. The member, based on these negotiations, drafts a Letter of Intent for the IMF. The Letter of Intent states the policies the member intends to pursue during the period of the standby arrangement. The letter is signed by the Minister of Finance and/or the Governor of the Central Bank.

Once the IMF has received the Letter of Intent, it begins drafting the standby arrangement. The contents of the Letter of Intent, the amount and type of financing requested by the member state and the IMF's own policies all influence the terms of the standby arrangement. The most contentious terms of the standby arrangement are the performance criteria and the phasing of the payments, because they constitute the legal formulation of the conditionality attached to the financing.

The performance criteria are derived from elements of the member state's adjustment program which are easily measured and which adequately indicate the degree to which the member is observing the adjustment program described in its Letter of Intent. The performance criteria used in each standby arrangement depend on the circumstances of the member state but they tend to be macro-economic variables reflecting the member state's success in controlling demand and credit creation. Typical performance criteria are ceilings on the expansion of credit by the banking system, on public sector debt, and, on the government's budget deficit; minimum levels of foreign reserves; and the removal of import restrictions.[43]

The IMF uses performance criteria not only to measure the member states' observance of its adjustment program but also to enforce such observance. Enforcement is achieved through the IMF's policy of phasing. Phasing means that the member state is only able to obtain specified fractions of the total financing at agreed-upon intervals over the life of the standby arrangement. Consequently, when a member state fails to meet a performance criteria the IMF can delay making future payments as they fall due under the standby arrangement. It should be noted that while the IMF does have the power to suspend future payments, it tends to use the member state's failure to satisfy a performance criteria more to reassess the member state's adjustment program and, if necessary, to amend the program and the terms of the standby arrangement, than to permanently deprive the member state of the promised future payments.[44]

Standby arrangements usually extend over a one-year period but may have a life of up to three years. These longer standby arrangements are not very different, in form, from extended fund facility arrangements which are usually of three years' duration and which also contain performance criteria and phasing of purchases.[45] In the longer standby arrangements, performance criteria are established for twelve-month periods at a time. This means that at the end of the first year of the arrangement the member state and the IMF meet to establish the performance criteria for the next twelve month period. A similar meeting is held at the end of the second year to establish performance criteria for the third year.

Once the IMF has drafted the standby arrangement, the Managing Director submits it, together with an explanatory staff memorandum and a recommendation for approval, to the Executive Board. The Executive Board, which is not bound to accept the Managing Director's recommendations, has the final decision.

A standby arrangement is a unique legal arrangement and should be treated as such.[46] It is not a contract because the member state's Letter of Intent and the IMF's standby arrangement are parallel, rather than reciprocal, documents. Furthermore, the Letter of Intent, with its description of future governmental policy is too vague to be a legally sufficient promise.

The legal distinction between a contract and a standby arrangement is important. The standby arrangement, because it is not legally binding on the member state, does not have the status of an international agreement. Consequently, it does not bind the member state's future freedom of action and departures from the terms of the agreement do not expose the member state to legal liability. Furthermore, since it is not an international agreement, the standby arrangement does not have to be registered with the United Nations.

Purchases under the standby arrangement do impose on the member state a repurchase obligation. This obligation, however, arises from the Articles of the IMF rather than from the standby arrangement itself. Standby arrangements usually require members to make their repurchases in eight equal quarterly installments beginning three years three months after the final drawing and ending five years after that drawing. Members are expected to make quicker repurchases if they are in a position to do so.

D) Conditionality[47]

Conditionality refers to the adjustment policies that the IMF expects member states to follow in return for being granted IMF financing. The purpose of conditionality is to ensure that the member state uses the IMF's resources in a manner that is consistent with the IMF's purposes and policies. This means that the member state must use the resources to correct its balance of payments problem "without resorting to measures destructive of national or international prosperity."[48] Conditionality is also designed to protect the revolving character of the IMF's resources, by ensuring that the member state is able to perform its repurchase obligations.

All IMF financing facilities except the reserve tranche are subject to some form of conditionality. The degree of IMF conditionality is dependent on the severity of the balance of payments problem, the amount of financing involved relative to the member state's quota, and the susceptibility of the balance of payments disequilibrium to adjustment through governmental action. In determining the conditionality it attaches to a member state's use to IMF financing, the IMF is required to pay "due regard to the domestic, social and political objectives, the economic priorities and the circumstances of members, including the cause of balance of payments disequilibria.[49]

Balance of payments disequilibria may be described as follows:[50]

a) *Temporary balance of payments deficits.* These deficits are caused by cyclical or climatic conditions. Such problems are self-correcting and require short-term financing rather than adjustment programs;

b *Excess demand.* Such balance of payments deficits are caused by an excess of demand over supply. This type of problem requires an adjustment program to reduce demand to the level of supply or to increase supply to the level of demand. Some financing is needed to facilitate the adjustment process;

c *Fundamental disequilibria.* These are balance of payments problems caused, primarily, by an overvalued currency. The solution to the problem is likely to be a currency devaluation to improve international competitiveness, coupled with a program to restrain demand for imports;

d *Structural deficits*. These deficits are caused by distortions in production and trade, that result in an economy that is characterized by slow growth and an inherently weak balance of payments position that prevents pursuit of an active development policy.

These categories are not mutually exclusive, and a member state's balance of payments problem may exhibit features of all four categories.

The IMF was originally created to deal with the first three categories, all of which are susceptible to relatively short-term solutions. Structural deficits, on the other hand, require longer term adjustment programs and longer periods of financial assistance. To meet these needs the IMF has lengthened the potential period of its standby arrangements, has created the extended fund facility and has begun to place more emphasis on supply side measures in its adjustment programs. In addition, in October 1985 the Interim Committee decided to create a Structural Adjustment Facility.

The goal of a balance of payments adjustment program is to achieve a sustainable balance of payments position. This is defined as a position in which the member state is able to finance any current account deficit with capital flows which it is able to borrow and for which it has a sustainable debt servicing capacity.

Balance of payments adjustment programs utilize one or both of two techniques.[51] They will either adopt measures designed to reduce the level of aggregate demand to the level of the society's ability to pay or they will adopt measures to increase the country's supply capacity, particularly of exportable goods and service. While demand management techniques are relatively fast acting, supply side measures require longer time periods that do not fit comfortably into the IMF's relatively short-term financing periods. Consequently, IMF adjustment programs are a mix of demand and supply side measures with the balance between the two dependent on the urgency of the need for adjustment, the precise cause of the balance of payments problem, and the ease of fitting supply side adjustment into the schedule of the IMF program.

IMF demand management policies are concerned with limiting the level of demand to a level that allows the country to service its external debts. To do this the government must manipulate the rate of growth of the money supply and bank credit; and must reduce government spending by making appropriate adjustments to the level of government debt, subsidies, taxes and interest rates. In order to limit demand for imports, the IMF will often order a currency devaluation which will increase the price of imports and decrease the price of exports.

IMF supply side measures are concerned with improving the allocation of resources and the quantity and quality of investments so as to accelerate growth and the availability of tradeable products. To achieve these results the IMF will recommend measures, such as devaluations, removal of government subsidies and exchange regulations, which are designed to increase the incentives to produce tradeable goods. Such policies should not only expand the volume of exports but should reduce imports through encouraging the production of import substitutes.

It can be seen that the conditions attached to IMF funding may result in austere adjustment programs being imposed on member states. The impact of such policies can be dramatic and, on occasion have resulted in food riots and the overthrow of governments. The controversy surrounding IMF conditionality therefore, is not surprising.

The major issue in the debate on IMF conditionality is not whether the IMF should have conditionality policies but is what the content of such policies should be.[52] Most commentators agree that some form of conditionality is necessary if the IMF is to retain the revolving character of its financing facilities and is to make its financing available to all member states.

Critics have argued that the IMF's adjustment policies are too much like a text book solution to a balance of payments problem and that they do not make sufficient allowance for the adjustment capacity of member states. Developing countries, which are dependent on imports for many necessities, such as food, cannot afford the inflationary consequences of devaluations nor can their populations accommodate to sharp contractions in the level of demand. These critics argue that the IMF should accept the limited adjustment capacity of its member states and should develop policies that are less austere and allow for adjustment with growth. In addition, it is argued that the IMF, in developing its adjustment policies pays too little attention to the specific development policy of the member state concerned, and imposes uniform policies on all member states.

IMF policies are also criticized for paying insufficient attention to the nature of member states' exports. Most developing countries rely on a small number of primary commodities for their export earnings. Such commodities tend to be demand and supply inelastic. Consequently, currency devaluations and increased levels of production are unlikely to raise export volumes or earnings and may even result in reduced revenues. This is especially true when commodity prices are falling and many developing countries are concurrently following similar IMF-inspired, export-led adjustment policies.

Critics argue that it may be misguided to emphasize demand management policies in developing countries. The payments problems of these countries are often due more to international economic factors beyond their control than to excess demand. In addition, these countries tend to have underutilized productive resources. Consequently, by improving utilization of these resources it is possible to achieve equilibrium at a higher level, albeit more slowly, than is possible with demand management techniques.

In addition, it is alleged, the IMF's policies fail to take into account the political realities of their client states. In most states, it is the politically powerful parastatal corporations and urban elites that are in greatest need of demand adjustment measures. These sectors, however, are able to use their political power to avoid the burdens of demand adjustment and to force this burden onto less powerful groups, such as the rural peasantry. The result is that the IMF adjustment program exacerbates the social imbalances already existing in the member state.

The IMF defends its policies by arguing that the need to restrain demand is independant of the IMF. They argue that a balance of payments deficit, regardless of its cause, means that the country is living beyond its means and must reduce its demand to the level of its ability to pay. They argue that their policies are stringent because member states delay approaching the IMF until their balance of payments problem is so serious as to require emergency treatment. The IMF maintains that if members would approach it earlier, the adjustment process could be less severe and could make more use of slower working but less painful supply side measures.

The IMF also argues that many developing countries are dependent on private lenders for a large portion of their project and balance of payments financing. These lenders look on IMF adjustment policies as a "stamp of approval", indicating IMF confidence that the member state will resolve its balance of payments problem and, thus, can be considered creditworthy. Conditionality, therefore encourages lenders to continue lending to member states who might otherwise be cut off from their usual sources of funds. The IMF contends that if it lowered its conditionality standards its credibility would be harmed and its ability to generate funds from other sources for its member states would be reduced.

E) IMF Financing Facilities

The IMF makes its resources available to its member states through a number of financing facilities. In each of these facilities the amount of funding available to the member state is dependant on the member state's quota and is expressed as a percentage of that quota.

(i) Reserve Tranche[53]

A member state's reserve tranche is the excess of its quota over the IMF's holding of the member state's currency in the General Resources Account, excluding holdings arising out of member state purchases under IMF policies and facilities other than the credit tranche and extended fund facilities.

Member states treat their reserve tranche as a reserve asset. They can purchase foreign currency from the IMF up to the amount of their reserve tranche without prior challenge by the IMF and, thus, without any form of conditionality attached to the purchase. It should be noted that the IMF can challenge the member state's purchase after the event on the grounds that the member state had no need for the funds or that it used the purchase for purposes inconsistent with IMF policy.

A consequence of the reserve tranche being viewed as a reserve asset is that member states are reluctant to use it. Member states are allowed to make drawings from the Compensatory Financing, Buffer Stock and Supplementary Financing facilities before they draw on their reserve tranches.

(ii) Credit Tranches[54]

The credit tranche facility is the basic lending policy of the IMF. This facility gives member states access to IMF reserves for amounts up to 200% of their quota. The credit tranche facility consists of four tranches each equal to 25% of the member state's quota. Drawings within these tranches are effected through standby arrangements and, on occasion, by extensions of credit.

All credit tranche drawings are subject to prior IMF approval. Before being allowed to make a drawing in the first credit tranche member states are required to show that they have a need for the funds and that they are making "reasonable efforts" to solve their balance of payments problem. Drawings within the three upper credit tranches are subject to prior IMF approval of the member state's adjustment program and involve performance criteria and phased purchases.

It is often stated that the more credit tranches a member state uses the stricter the IMF's conditions for approval of a purchase become. Even though this statement often appears to be *de facto* true, it is more accurate to treat all upper credit tranche purchases as subject to the same conditionality requirement. The severity of the conditionality will, however, vary with the seriousness of the member state's balance of payments problem. Since member states making purchases in the third or fourth credit tranches are more likely than not to have serious balance of payments problems, the conditions to which their purchases are subject are likely to be more stringent than those pertaining to purchases in the second credit tranche.

(iii) Compensatory Financing Facility[55]

The Compensatory Financing Facility provides financing to member states who are experiencing balance of payments problems because of temporary shortfalls in export earnings, cause by factors largely beyond the member state's control.[56] The facility is designed to provide assistance to exporters of primary commodities. Earnings from such products are unstable because of their sensitivity to both climatic and international economic conditions and because of their inelasticity of demand and supply. In 1981 the facility was also made available to member states' experiencing balance of payments problems due to unexpected increases in the cost of their cereal imports.

The Compensatory Financing Facility allows member states to make drawings in amounts that do not exceed the member state's quota or the extent of its export shortfall or cereal import increase, whichever is less. Separate drawings can be made in the case of an export earnings shortfall and a cereal import increase but the member states' total drawing under this facility may not exceed 83% of its quota.

It should be noted that the compensatory financing facility "floats" next to the credit tranche policy. This means that drawings under the Compensatory Financing Facility do not affect the member states access to the Credit Tranche Facility and vice versa.

Compensatory Financing drawings are subject to mild conditionality. The reason for this is that the causes of the problems motivating the member state to utilize this facility are largely beyond its control. Consequently, the IMF does not demand a rigorous adjustment program from the member state. Nevertheless, in order to make drawings of up to 50% of the member state's quota, the member state must be willing to cooperate with the IMF to find appropriate solutions to its payments problems. For any drawings above this level the member state must satisfy the IMF that it is cooperating with the IMF to formulate and apply a solution to its balance of payments problem.

Drawings from the Contemporary Financing Facility do involve repurchase obligations. Repurchases must be made in eight equal quarterly installments during the period three to five years after the final drawing from the facility. The IMF, in its discretion may approve a different repurchasing schedule.[57]

(iv) Buffer Stock Financing Facility[58]

The Buffer Stock Financing Facility provides financial assistance to member states participating in approved commodity price stabilization arrangements. In the past, the IMF has made the Buffer Stock Financing Facility available for tin, sugar and rubber arrangements.

The IMF cannot legally contribute to the commodity arrangement because it is not a party thereto but it will assist the member state to meet its obligation to the arrangement. The IMF will help the member state pay its share of the financing of commodity stockbuilding, the operating expenses of the buffer stock and the refinancing of short-term debt incurred as a result of buffer stock operations.

The amount of assistance available to a member state under this facility is determined by the extent of the member state's obligations to the buffer stock organization but there is a ceiling equal to 45% of a member state's quota.

(v) Extended Fund Facility[59]

The Extended Fund Facility provides financing to member states whose balance of payments problems are structural. This means that the member state's problems are caused by cost and price distortions, and distortions in trade and production patterns. As was discussed above, these problems require corrective measures that are of longer duration than the traditional one year life of standby arrangements. Consequently, the Extended Fund Facility provides financing for up to three years and has a longer repurchase period than standby arrangements. The repurchase obligation matures four years after the final drawing under the facility and repurchases are made in twelve equal semi-annual installments. Members are expected to accelerate their repurchases if they are in a position to do so.

The form in which Extended Fund Facility financing is provided, known as extended arrangements, is similar to standby arrangements in that it involves Letters of Intent and performance criteria and phased payments. However, the IMF conditionality involved in an extended arrangement tends to place more ephasis on supply side measures than on demand management.

Before being eligible for Extended Fund financing a member state must have used its reserve tranche and is encouraged to have used its first credit tranche facility. A member state may draw up to 140% of its quota from the Extended Fund Facility provided the IMF's total holding of the member state's currency, from the credit tranche and Extended Fund facility, does not exceed 165% of the member states' quota.

(vi) Supplementary Financing Facility and Enlarged Access Policy[60]

The Supplementary Financing Facility was only operational between 1979 and 1981. It was available to member states with large balance of payments needs relative to their quotas. In order to obtain access to the Supplementary Financing Facility, member states had to demonstrate that their problems were such, that satisfactory balance of payments adjustment would require more than a one year adjustment period, that the amount of financing required for this adjustment would exceed the amount available to them under the credit tranches or the Extended Fund facility, and that they were requesting supplementary financing in conjunction with an upper credit tranche standby arrangement or an extended arrangement.

The IMF financed the Supplementary Financing facility out of borrowed funds. In order to cover the cost of the borrowed funds, the IMF charged member states interest on their use of Supplementary Financing funds.

By 1981 all the resources of the Supplementary Financing Facility were committed and the IMF decided to replace the facility with its Enlarged Access policy.[61] This policy, like the Supplementary Financing Facility, is financed by borrowings and thus involves an interest charge.

The enlarged access policy provides financing to member states under the same conditions as the supplementary financing facility. Originally the enlarged access policy gave member states access to financing equal to 150% of their quota per year for a total of three years, for a total of 450% of their quota, excluding compensatory financing and buffer stock financing purchases. However, the resources of the original enlarged access policy were fully committed by 1983 and the renewed policy provides lower levels of financing. It allows member states access to financing equal to 95 or 115% of their quota per year with a total of 280 or 345% of quota and overall limits, over the life of a three year program, and cumulative limits of 408% or 450% of quota (net of scheduled repurchases). The precise amount provided to a member state will depend on its economic condition and its need for such financing.

(vii) Fund Administered Facilities [62]

Fund Administered Facilities are IMF facilities which are not financed out of the IMF's General Resources Account and which are legally distinct from, but administered by, the IMF. These facilities are designed to serve a specific function and usually have a limited life. They are financed by donations and loans from member states.

The first of these facilities were the 1974 and 1975 Oil Facilities. These facilities made loans to oil importing countries who were experiencing payments problems because of the sudden increase in the cost of oil. The accounts were fully disbursed and closed in 1983.

The Trust Fund was established in 1976. It was financed through IMF gold sales, with the excess of the IMF receipts over the official gold price being placed in the Trust Fund. By 1980, the Trust Fund's resources, enhanced by some member states' donations, were fully disbursed or committed to qualifying developing countries on highly concessional terms. Repayments to the Trust mature six years after disbursement and are completed over a four year period. In 1985, the Interim Committee decided to use these repayments to fund a new Structural Adjustment Facility for the least developed countries. This facility will provide financing for qualifying member states who adopt IMF-approved structural adjustment policies.

The Supplementary Financing Facility Subsidy Account was established in 1980 to allow the IMF to reduce the interest cost to developing country member states using the Supplementary Financing Facility. The Account receives funding from donation, loans, investment income and the repayment of Trust Fund transactions.

VI. Technical Assistance [63]

The IMF provides a variety of technical services to its member states. These services are designed to help member states to better manage their exchange rate and balance of payments policy. IMF assistance can be divided into three categories—publication, technical assistance and training.

A) Publications

Each year the IMF's Executive Board publishes an annual report. This report reviews the state of the world economy and the IMF's activities during the previous year. Pursuant to its Articles of Agreement, the IMF also publishes an annual report documenting exchange arrangements and exchange restrictions on both a global and a country-by-country basis. The IMF also publishes, on an annual basis, *International Financial Statistics,* which provides detailed financial statistics about each member state, and *World Economic Outlook,* which is a report on the world economy and financial system, based on IMF research and consultations with member states.

Together with the World Bank, the IMF publishes a quarterly magazine called *Finance and Development,* which contains reports on the activities of the IMF and the World Bank and short analytical articles by staff members. Finally the IMF publishes a variety of staff papers containing technical analyses of topical issues and issues of relevance to the Fund's activities.

B) Technical Assistance

The IMF will provide advisory assistance to member states who request such assistance and who are unable to obtain it elsewhere. In providing such assistance the IMF will either use staff members or will recruit outside experts for assignment in the member state.

The IMF assists member states in developing appropriate tax structures and fiscal organizations through its Fiscal Affairs Department. The Central Banking Services of the IMF will advise member states on managing their Central Bank operations. Less formal technical assistance may be provided to member states during their regular consultations with the IMF. This assistance is of an advisory nature.

C) Training

The IMF Institute, conducts courses in Washington, D.C. for nominated officials from member states. These courses are technical and are on such subjects as financial analysis and policy making, public finance, balance of payments methodology and management, central banking, and economic analysis techniques.

The IMF Institute will, upon request, give assistance to training institutions in member countries.

THE IMF AND THE WORLD BANK[64]

The IMF and the World Bank (hereinafter Bank) were both created at the Bretton Woods Conference in 1944 to perform separate but related functions. The IMF was established to oversee the international monetary system and to assist member states to correct balance of payments disequilibria. The Bank's function was to provide financing for economic reconstruction and development. Given the nature of their respective functions, the IMF concentrated on short term balance of payments financing while the Bank was concerned with long term project financing.

There have always been formal and informal links between the IMF and the World Bank. Only IMF member states may join the Bank. Their Boards of Governors hold concurrent annual meetings. Informal contacts between the two institutions has been facilitated by the fact that they are located across the street from each other.

The increased size and changed character of their memberships, developments in the world economy and their concentration on the problems of developing countries, have caused both the IMF and the Bank to alter their *modus operandi*. The IMF has increased the number of its financing facilities and has lengthened its financing periods in order to help developing countries undertake the supply side adjustment measures needed to correct their balance of payments positions. The Bank, on the other hand, has been forced to consider the impact of a country's macroeconomic position on the success of specific projects. Consequently, the Bank has begun to make programme and structural adjustment loans which are designed to improve the country's overall economic condition.

As the IMF has begun to make financing available for purposes that are more project related than heretofore and the Bank has begun to make loans for purposes related to balance of payments adjustment, the need for closer collaboration between the two organizations has grown. In order to meet this need the Development Committee monitors the activity of both organizations in regard to the transfer of resources to developing countries; and Bank and IMF staff members collaborate through joint missions, sharing of information and joint studies. This collaboration should increase the efficiency of the operations of both institutions and should reduce the risk of duplication of effort.

Despite this growing collaboration between the two institutions, they still maintain their independence. This means that each institution makes its own policy and financing decisions. In addition, each remains dominant in its own area of primary expertise and responsibility.

VII. THE IMF AND PRIVATE LENDERS[65]

The IMF has no formal relationship with or obligations to private lenders. The IMF will not give commercial lenders access to the confidential information it obtains from member states nor will it give banks advice on the creditworthiness of member states.

Given the IMF's superior access to information, commercial lenders have viewed the IMF as being in the best position to determine a particular country's creditworthiness and, in their sovereign lending operations, have attempted to devise means of establishing the IMF's view of the member state's economy and economic policies. As a result, some bank loan documents require the sovereign borrower to warrant that it is a member "in good standing" with the IMF. Under the IMF's Articles of Agreement "good standing" is a technical term relating to the member state's fulfillment of its obligations to the IMF rather than to its commercial creditworthiness. Consequently, such a warranty is of marginal value to private lenders.

Another method used by banks to test the IMF's view of a member state's creditworthiness is to try and establish the extent of the member state's access to IMF funding. In order to accommodate member states, the IMF will issue the member state a letter stating that the member state is eligible to obtain financing from the IMF. This letter is of limited value because all it certifies is that the member state has not violated any of its obligations to the IMF and, thus, legally, is entitled to access to the IMF's resources. The letter does not state that the member state would, in fact, be granted IMF funding if it so requested.

The final method used by banks to test the IMF's perception of a member state is to rely on the existence of an IMF stand-by arrangement with the member state. The arrangement and its associated conditionality is taken by the banks to signify an IMF "stamp of approval" on the member state's economic policies.

The banks' reliance on this "stamp of approval" has no legal standing but it does have practical significance. The stand-by arrangement is an arrangement between the IMF and the member state.[66] It involves no legally binding promises to commercial lenders who, therefore, cannot enforce its terms against the member state or the IMF. Despite this, many private lenders will delay lending to IMF member states until the member state has entered into a standby arrangement with the IMF. This catalytic effect is often cited by the IMF in defense of its conditionality policies.

In the wake of the debt crises of the 1980's, the relationship between the IMF and private lenders began to change.[67] The IMF, in order to ensure a sufficient flow of funds from the commercial lenders to the sovereign debtors, began to delay approving its funding arrangements with member states until the private banks committed a certain amount of funds to the member state. This form of IMF-commercial bank cooperation helped to alleviate the position of the debtor countries but it also increased the commercial banks' bargaining power with the IMF.

This growing IMF-commercial bank relationship has resulted in some benefits for all parties but it does raise some troubling issues. The relations may result in the commercial banks being able to demand and obtain access to IMF information hitherto denied them, with adverse consequences for the debtor countries. This problem is probably avoidable through IMF awareness of the problem and through the banks need for such information being met through other sources, such as the Washington D.C.-based Institute for International Finance.

NOTES

1. Article I of the IMF's Articles of Agreement states:

The purposes of the International Monetary Fund are:

(i) To promote international monetary cooperation through a permanent institution which provides the machinery for consultation and collaboration on international monetary problems.

(ii) To facilitate the expansion and balanced growth of international trade, and to contibute thereby to the promotion and maintenance of high levels of employment and real income and to the development of the productive resources of all members as primary objectives of economic policy.

(iii) To promote exchange stability, to maintain orderly exchange arrangements among members, and to avoid competitive exchange depreciation.

(iv) To assist in the establishment of a multilateral system of payments in respect of current transactions between members and in the elimination of foreign exchange restrictions which hamper the growth of world trade.

(v) To give confidence to members by making the general resources of the Fund temporarily available to them under adequate safeguards, thus providing them with opportunity to correct maladjustments in their balance of payments without resorting to measures destructive of national or international prosperity.

(vi) In accordance with the above, to shorten the duration and lessen the degree of disequilibrium in the international balance of payments of members.

The Fund shall be guided in all its policies and decisions by the purposes set forth in this Article.

2. Article IV Section 1 of Articles of Agreement. The full text of this provision is as follows:

Recognizing that the essential purpose of the international monetary system is to provide a framework that facilitates the exchange of goods, services, and capital among countries, and that sustains sound economic growth, and that a principal objective is the continuing development of the orderly underlying conditions that are necessary for financial and economic stability, each member undertakes to collaborate with the Fund and other members to assure orderly exchange arrangements and to promote a stable system of exchange rates. In particular, each member shall:

(i) endeavor to direct its economic and financial policies toward the objective of fostering orderly economic growth with reasonable price stability, with due regard to its circumstances;

(ii) seek to promote stability by fostering orderly underlying economic and financial conditions and a monetary system that does not tend to produce erratic disruptions;

(iii) avoid manipulating exchange rates or the international monetary system in order to prevevnt effective balance of payments adjustment or to gain an unfair competitive advantage over other members; and

(iv) follow exchange policies compatible with the undertakings under this Section.

3. Article IV Section 3 which reads as follows:

(a) The Fund shall oversee the international monetary system in order to ensure its effective operation, and shall oversee the compliance of each member with its obligations under Section 1 of this Article.

(b) In order to fulfill its functions under (a) above, the Fund shall exercise firm surveillance over the exchange rate policies of members, and shall adopt specific principles for the guidance of all members with respect to those policies. Each member shall provide the Fund with the information necessary for such surveillance, and, when requested by the Fund, shall consult with it on the member's exchange rate policies. The principles adopted by the Fund shall be consistent with cooperative arrangements by which members maintain the value of their currencies in relation to the value of the currency or currencies of other members, as well as with other exchange arrangements of a member's choice consistent with the purposes of the Fund and Section 1 of this Article. These principles shall respect the domestic social and political policies of members, and in applying these principles the Fund shall pay due regard to the circumstances of members.

4. Article I(v).

5. Article XVIII Section 1 which reads as follows:

(a) In all its decisions with respect to the allocation and cancellation of special drawing rights the Fund shall seek to meet the long-term global need, as and when it arises, to supplement existing reserve assets in such manner as will promote the attainment of its purposes and will avoid economic stagnation and deflation as well as excess demand and inflation in the world.

(b) The first decision to allocate special drawing rights shall take into account, as special considerations, a collective judgement that there is a global need to supplement reserves, and the attainment of a better balance of payments equilibrium, as well as the likelihood of a better working of the adjustment process in the future.

6. *The Role and Function of the International Monetary Fund,* International Monetary Fund (Washington, D.C., 1985) at 15-17 (hereinafter cited as *IMF*); *The International Monetary Fund: Its Evolution, Organization and Activities,* A.W. Hooke, IMF Pamphlet Series No. 37 (3rd Ed., IMF, Washington, D.C. 1983) at 10. (hereinafter cited as *Hooke*); *The International Monetary Fund: Its Financial Organization and Activities,* Anand G. Chandavarkar, IMF Pamphlet Series No. 42 (IMF, Washington, D.C.

1984) (hereinafter cited as *Chandavarkar*) at 10-16.

The two sets of data are:

Set I data — gross domestic product, reserves, exports, imports and the variability of exports.

Set II date — gross domestic product, reserves, current receipts, current payments, variability of current receipts.

7. *Id.* The weighing in favor of small countries is achieved by increasing the weight attached to trade and the variability of trade and decreasing that attached to gross domestic product and reserves in the calculation of quotas.

8. Article III, Section 2.

9. *supra,* note 6.

10. The designated reserve currencies are the U.S. dollar, the pound sterling, the German mark, the Japanese yen and the French franc.

11. *supra,* note 6.

12. Article XII Section 5. Also see *IMF, supra* note 6 at 27; *Hooke, supra* note 6 at 17.

13. J. Gold, *Voting Majorities in the Fund: Effects of Second Amendment of the Articles,* IMF Pamphlet No. 20 (IMF, Washington, D.C. 1977)

14. *IMF, supra* note 6 at 17; *Hooke, supra* note 6, at 11.

15. *IMF, supra* note 6 at 18; *Hooke, supra* note 6 at 11.

16. *IMF, supra* note 6 at 20; *Hooke, supra* note 6 at 13.

17. See Article XII, Section 1 and Schedule D of Articles of Agreement.

18. *IMF, supra* note 6 at 21; *Hooke, supra* note 6 at 13-14.

19. *IMF, supra* note 6 at 23; *Hooke, supra* note 6 at 14.

20. *Id.*

21. See generally *IMF, supra* note 6 at 73; *Chandavarkar, supra* note 6 at 62; *Hooke, supra* note e6 at 58. Also see *User's Guide to the SDR,* IMF Treasurer's Department (1982)

22. Article XVIII.

23. See e.g. Brandt Commission, *Common Crisis,* (MIT Press 1983) at 56-68.

24. Articles XIX, XX, XXI, XXII, XXIIII.

25. Article XIX, Sections 4, 5.

26. The following institutions are authorized to hold SDR's—the Andean Reserve Fund; the Arab Monetary Fund; the Asian Development Bank; the Bank of Central African States; the Bank of International Settlements; the Central Bank of West African States; the East African Development Bank; the East Caribbean Central Bank; the International Bank for Reconstruction and Development; the International Development Association; the International Fund for Agricultural Development; the Islamic Development Bank; the Nordic Investment Bank and the Swiss National Bank.

27. J. Gold, *Development of the SDR as a Reserve Asset, Unit of Account and Denominator: A Survey,* 16 George Washington J. of Int'l. L. and Ec. 1 (1981).

28. IMF, *1985 Annual Report; IMF, supra* note 6 at 28-35; *Hooke, supra* note 6, at 18-25.

29. Executive Board Decision No. 5392-(77/63) (April 29, 1977) in *Selected Decisions of the International Monetary Fund,* 10th Issue (IMF, April 30, 1983) at 20 *et seq.*

30. The most recent publication is: *World Economic Outlook,* International Monetary Fund Occasional Paper No. 43, IMF (Washington, D.C. 1986).

31. J. Gold, *Financial Assistance by the International Monetary Fund,* IMF Pamphlet No. 27 (IMF, Washington, D.C. 1980) at 6-10 (hereinafter cited as *Financial Assistance*), *Chandarvarkar, supra* note 6; *IMF, supra* note 6 at 39. *Hooke, supra* note 6, at 29-30.

32. Michael Ainley, *The General Agreement to Borrow,* IMF Pamphlet Series No. 41 (Washington 1984). The participants in the GAB are: United States, United Kingdom, Italy, Canada, Netherlands, Belgium, Sveriges Riksbank.

33. *Id.* Also see *Chandavarkar, supra* note 6 at 19; *IMF, supra* note 6 at 39-43. The amount of this adjunct agreement is SDR 1020 million. This amount is part of total GAB resources.

34. *Id.*

35. *Chandavarkar, supra* note 6 at 73; *Hooke, supra* note 6, at 55. Also see discussion, *infra* on IMF financing facilities.

36. Chandavarkar, *supra* note 6.

37. *Financial Assistance, supra* note 30; *Chandarvarkar, supra* note 6. Each of the facilities is discussed in Section V of this article.

38. Uniformity ensures that all member states in a similar position receive equal treatment. Uniformity is designed to prevent both discrimination in favor of and against member states. For more on the principle of uniformity see, J. Gold, *Uniformity As A Legal Principal of the International Monetary Fund,* 7 Law and Policy in International Business 765 (1975).

39. *Financial Assistance, supra* note 30, at 10-11.

40. *Id.*

41. *Financial Assistance, supra* note 30 at 11-19.

42. Article XXX(b) of the Articles of Agreement. It states:

Standby arrangement means a decision of the Fund by which a member is assured that it will be able to make purchases from the General Resources Account in accordance with the terms of the decision during a specified period and up to a specified amount.

43. *Financial Assistance, supra* note 30, at 14.

44. See generally J. Gold, *Conditionality,* IMF Pamphlet No. 31 (IMF, Washington, D.C. 1979) (hereinafter cited as *Conditionality*).

45. *Id.*

46. J. Gold, *The Legal Character of the Fund's Stand-by Arrangements and Why It Matters,* IMF Pamphlet No. 35 (IMF, Washington, D.C. 1980).

47. See generally, M. Guitian, *Fund Conditionality: Evolution of Principles and Practices,* IMF Pamphlet No. 38 (IMF, Washington, D.C. 1981), *Conditionality, supra* note 44.

48. Article I(v) of Articles of Agreement.

49. *Guidelines on Conditionality,* Executive Board Decision No. 6056—(79/28) of March 2, 1979 quoted in *Selected Decisions of the International Monetary Fund,* 10th Issue (IMF, April 30, 1983) at 21 (hereinafter cited as *Decisions*).

50. See e.g. *The IMF and Stabilization,* Tony Killick (ed) (St. Martins Press (1984) and its companion volume *The Quest for Economic Stabilization: The IMF and the Third World,* Tony Killick (ed) (St. Martins Press 1984);

R.F. Mikesell, "Appraising IMF Conditionality", in *IMF Conditionality*, J. Williamson (ed) (Institute for International Economics, Washington, D.C. 1983) at 49.

51. E.g., Killick, *supra* note 50. A. Crockett, "Issues in The Use of Fund Resources", Finance and Development, June 1982 at 10 *et seq.*

52. *IMF Conditionality, supra* note 49. Killick, *supra* note 50. Also see N. Kaldor, "Devaluing the Myth", South Magazine, October 1983 at 32 *et seq;* Kaldor, "Devaluation and Adjustment in Developing Countries" Finance and Development, June 1983 at 35 *et seq.* (republished as Chapter 5.3D in this volume). Also see sources cited *supra* note 49; Cheryl Payer, *The Debt Trap*, (Monthly Review Press 1974).

53. *IMF, supra* note 6 at 58; *Chandavarkar, supra* note 6 at 38. *Hooke, supra* note 6, at 41-42. *Financial Assistance, supra* note 30, at 27.

54. *Financial Assistance, supra* note 30, at 27-9; *IMF supra* note 6 at 59. *Chandavarkar, supra* note 6 at 40. *Hooke, supra* note 6, at 42-3.

55. *Financial Assistance, supra* note 30, at 29-30, *IMF, supra* note 6. Also see *Compensatory Financing of Export Fluctuations*, Executive Board Decision No. 6224-(79/135), Aug. 2, 1979. *Compensatory Financing of Fluctuations in The Case of Cereal Imports*, Executive Board Decision No. 6860-(81.81) May 13, 1981, both in *Decisions, supra* note 49, at 61 *et seq.*

56. *Id.* The member states' export shortfall is calculated by means of a formula that measures the deviation in export earnings from a five year geometric average centered on the twelve months in which the shortfall occurred. At the discretion of the member, the export shortfall calculation may exclude receipts from travel and migrant worker remittances. A similar formula is used in calculating the increase in cost of cereal imports.

57. Executive Board Decision No. 6224-(79/135), Aug. 2, 1979, *supra* note 49, at 64.

58. *Financial Assistance, supra* note 30, at 30-1, *IMF, supra* note 6 at 66; *Hooke, supra* note 6, at 48-9. Also see Executive Board Decision No. 2772-(69/47), June 25, 1969 as amended by Decision No. 4913-(75/207), December 24, 1975 in *Decisions, supra* note 49, at 70 *et seq.*

59. *Financial Assistance,* supra note 30, at 32-4. *IMF, supra* note 6 at 60; *Chandavarkar, supra* note 6 at 46; *Hooke, supra* note 6, at 44-6. Also see Executive Board Decision No. 4377-(74/114), September 13, 1974, as amended, in *Decisions, supra* note 49, at 27 *et seq.*

60. *Financial Assistance, supra* note 6, at 49-50. Also see, Executive Board Decision No. 5508-(77/127), August 29, 1977 in *Decisions, supra* note 49, at 32 *et seq.; Chandavarkar, supra* note 6 at 47.

61. *IMF, supra* note 6, at 67.

62. *Financial Assistance, supra* note 30, at 31-36. *Chandavarkar, supra* note 6.

63. *Technical Assistance Services of the International Monetary Fund,* IMF Pamphlet Series No. 30 (IMF, Washington, D.C. 1979).

64. J. Gold, *The Relationship Between the International Monetary Fund and The World Bank,* 15 Creighton L.R. 499 (1981-82).

65. J. Gold, *Order in International Finance, the Promotion of IMF Standby Agreements and the Drafting of Private Loan Agreements,* IMF Pamphlet Series No. 39 (IMF, Washington, D.C. 1982).

66. For discussion of the legal significance of standby arrangements see *Gold, supra* note 46.

67. Bahram Nowzad, "The Role of the IMF in Rescheduling International Debt", in *Default and Rescheduling: Corporate and Sovereign Borrowers in Difficulty,* D. Suratgar (ed) (Euromoney Publications, 1984).

16B. Enhancing the Effectiveness of Surveillance
G.G. Johnson

"Surveillance" entered the international monetary lexicon in 1978 when the Second Amendment of the Fund's Articles of Agreement came into effect. The international monetary system, as it is now constituted, allows Fund member countries great latitude in their choice of exchange rate regime—in fact, they may choose virtually any regime other than pegging their currencies to gold. Members nonetheless have obligations regarding their exchange rate policies—and the Fund is required to exercise "firm surveillance" over those policies.

The introduction of surveillance gave the Fund broader responsibilities with respect to oversight of its members' policies than existed under the par value system. Under that system, a member was required to consult with the Fund regarding its exchange rate policy only when it proposed a change in the par value of its currency, and the Fund's role was limited to concurrence in, or objection to, the change. By contrast, to exercise surveillance, the Fund engages in a continuous review of members' exchange rate policies, and its appraisal must consider the extent to which members' economic policies in general—not only their exchange rate policies—are compatible with the objectives set out in Article IV of the Fund Agreement (see box on Article IV). The Fund's purview has thus been broadened under the new system but, by the same token, its members are no longer obliged to seek its concurrence in changes in exchange rates.

Since Fund surveillance began, its effectiveness has repeatedly been questioned. The continuing volatility of exchange rates, and their prolonged divergence from levels that appear to be sustainable over time, have been matters of growing concern. Some have concluded that a new exchange system is needed—one that circumscribes the range of exchange arrangements that the Fund's members may adopt, or that specifies more precisely the types of policies that members may pursue (see Morris Goldstein, "Whither the exchange rate system?" *Finance & Development,* June 1984).

Others would argue that it is neither feasible nor desirable to move to a more defined system, at least under present circumstances. They acknowledge the shortcomings of the present system, but consider that any corrections should be made within the context of that system—that is, by enhancing the effectiveness of surveillance. After outlining the main elements and recent improvements in the Fund's surveillance procedures, this article reviews current proposals for enhancing effectiveness.

RECENT DEVELOPMENTS

The general obligations of Fund member countries regarding exchange arrangements are spelled out in Article IV of the Fund Agreement. The principles and practices of surveillance were reviewed by William C. Hood in "Surveillance over exchange rates," *Finance & Development,* March 1982. While the principles underlying surveillance have remained unchanged since their adoption in 1977 by the Fund's Executive Board (see box on principles of surveillance), the implementation of surveillance has evolved considerably, as explained below.

World Economic Outlook and Other General Studies

An essential backdrop to surveillance over the policies of individual members is the Fund's review of developments in, and prospects for, the world economy. The World Economic Outlook exercise continues year-round, culminating in a major review early each year and a supplementary review prior to the Fund's Annual Meeting (which normally takes place in late September). Besides analyzing developments and considering prospects at the global level, the WEO assesses the policies of member countries, particularly the major industrial countries, that impinge on the world economy. In recent years this assessment has increasingly been carried out in a medium-term context, and the WEO now includes medium-term scenarios for the world economy that permit the implications of alternative national policies to be analyzed.

Preparation of the Fund's *Annual Report* provides another occasion for review of issues of international economic policy. The Fund also produces studies of developments in particular policy areas, such as external debt, international capital markets, and international trade, and is a major compiler and publisher of international economic statistics. All of these activities have greatly expanded since the inception of surveillance.

Besides providing a basis for review and discussion of policy issues within the Fund and the official international community, these aspects of the Fund's work provide an opportunity for the Fund to focus public attention on the issues involved. In recent years, the Fund has published the *World Economic Outlook* and many of its studies in these areas, as part of an expanding program of public information. (Those published in 1984-85 included *Exchange Rate Volatility and World Trade; Formulating Exchange Rate Policies in Adjustment Programs; International Capital Markets: Developments and Prospects, 1984; Issues in the Assessment of Exchange Rates of Industrial Countries;* and *The Exchange Rate System—Lessons of the Past and Options for the Future,* all in the Occasional Paper Series.)

Article IV Consultations

These consultations between the Fund and member countries are the basic vehicle for the Fund's exercise of surveillance. The process of consultation was described in an article by Eduard Brau, "The consultation process of the Fund," in the December 1981 issue of *Finance & Development.* As noted in that article, the consultation process includes preparatory work by country authorities and Fund staff, discussions in the country between the authorities and the Fund staff team, the preparation of staff reports for the Fund's Executive Board, the discussion of reports in the Board, and the conclusion of the consultation through the Chairman's summing up.

The policy focus of Article IV consultations evolves as new issues come to the fore. In recent years, for example, external debt and protectionism have received increasing attention; currently there is a major emphasis on fiscal imbalances and the need for structural adjustment. The techniques of analysis used for Article IV consultations have also evolved over time; as in the WEO, for example, considerable attention is now given to the medium-term implications of policy choices.

The surveillance principles specify that Article IV consultations with each member are to take place annually. This proved difficult to achieve in practice, and up to 1983 the intervals between consultations tended to lengthen. This gave rise to the present system of specifying, at the end of each consultation, the date by which the next one is to be concluded. Under this system the one-year cycle applies to a large majority of members. Longer cycles of up to two years may be specified for countries that are small enough for their policies not to have a substantial impact on other countries, that do not have Fund-supported programs in effect, and whose balance of payments viability over the medium term is not substantially in doubt.

Besides regular Article IV consultations, the surveillance principles provide for supplemental consultations when requested by the Fund. There has been some reluctance to single out member countries in this way, and the resulting rarity of supplemental consultations has itself reinforced this reluctance.

Monitoring

Under the amended Articles, members are required to notify the Fund promptly of changes in their exchange arrangements. This requirements includes, for members that peg their currencies, any changes in the level of the peg. For members that maintain more flexible exchange rate arrangements, such as individual or joint floating, small day-to-day changes in exchange rates are not subject to a notification requirement. In practice many such currencies, which include those of the major industrial countries, have experienced large cumulative changes in exchange rates over a few weeks or months, and as a result it was decided in 1983 that the Fund's Executive Board should be kept informed of changes in exchange rates for all member countries.

In a world where the major currencies change continuously against each other, it was considered more useful to monitor indices of effective exchange rates (which measure changes in the value of a currency against a weighted average of the currencies of trading partners) than bilateral exchange rates. In view of the large differences in rates of inflation among countries, it was also considered that each country's effective exchange rate index should be adjusted for inflation differentials (thus giving real effective exchange rates). Information is provided to the Board through comprehensive quarterly reports and through special reports when the rate of an individual country shows a large cumulative change since the country's exchange rate policies were last reviewed by the Board.

Reflecting the growing concerns about protectionism, the practice of providing information to the Board on important trade policy developments in member countries as they occur is also being developed.

Multilateral Aspects

The Fund collaborates with various other international organizations on matters relating to surveillance. The European Community, the Organization for Economic Cooperation and Development, and the Bank for International Settlements all address many of the issues with respect to industrial countries that are of concern in Fund surveillance. Joint statistical working parties are one example of the collaboration among these bodies. The Fund collaborates particularly closely with the General Agreement on Tariffs and Trade on trade policy issues, with the GATT supplying information on trade policy developments and the Fund, besides helping to concentrate members' attention on key trade policy issues, providing the GATT with needed information on balance of payments developments. The World Bank and the Fund, which have similar broad objectives and complementary responsibilities, maintain continuous close consultation. In each of these cases the areas of collaboration have been greatly extended in recent years.

Fund management or staff participate in various forums of the Fund's membership where surveillance issues are discussed. The Managing Director participates in meetings of the Ministers of the G-5—the five largest members of the Fund. The Fund also plays a role in forums such as aid consortia and the Paris Club, which deal with the flow of resources to individual developing countries and the resolution of external debt problems, respectively.

Fund's Public Role

One aspect of surveillance not specifically addressed by the surveillance principles is the Fund's role in informing interested public opinion on key policy issues, a role that has grown considerably in recent years. Public statements by the Managing Director have focused attention on such issues, including the identification of policy problems in individual member countries that are particularly important for the international community. The Fund's publication program has already been mentioned.

ISSUES IN EFFECTIVENESS

The current process of analysis and discussion means that the Fund and the member usually have a good understanding of each other's views, so that the obligation to consult, which is inherent in surveillance, is fully met. Often, moreover, the process of consultation leads to a convergence of views.

Concerns about the effectiveness of surveillance, however, focus on the fact that at any time the policies of a member may diverge to some extent from those advocated by the Fund, and that often these divergences persist for long periods. As already indicated, under the Fund's Articles, a member has the procedural obligation to provide information and undertake consultation at the request of the Fund. There is no requirement that the Fund and the member reach agreement on the appropriateness of actions taken or not taken. In that sense, the effectiveness of surveillance rests on the ability of the Fund to persuade members of the desirability of changing their policies, and the willingness of members to take the international interest into account. Many countries have, in fact, demonstrated a willingness to take actions consistent with the views expressed by the international community.

Surveillance also can have a less direct impact through keeping international economic issues before the eyes of domestic policy makers, so that international implications are always considered, at least to some degree, in policy decisions. In this sense, surveillance has helped to prevent a retreat from the considerable progress made toward greater international economic integration since the Fund was founded, despite the severely strained economic environment of recent years. In some areas, particularly financial integration, further progress has been achieved. Moreover, following the spurt of inflation in the early 1980s, inflation rates in most countries have come down to levels not seen since before the advent of floating. The external debt crisis, if not resolved, has at least been contained.

Other developments must be considered as failures of surveillance. The debt crisis could be seen as resulting from the failure of surveillance to discourage many developing countries from taking on too much external debt in the 1970s and early 1980s. The consequences of that failure were exacerbated by a second major failure of surveillance—the severe imbalance of macroeconomic policies in a number of industrial countries, notably the United States, compounded in some instances by structural rigidities; particularly in Europe. It is such failures that have led to the widespread calls for more effective surveillance.

ENHANCING EFFECTIVENESS

To provide effective surveillance, the Fund must focus on its members' attention on the key policy issues and maintain an adequate flow of information on developments and policies in member countries. This is important both for the dialogue the Fund has with its members and for the exercise of "peer pressure" by member countries on each other.

Effective surveillance requires, in the first instance, cogent analysis by the Fund. Significant advances have taken place since surveillance was introduced, particularly in evaluating country policies in terms of their medium-term implications and their international consequences, and further work is under way in these areas. While there will always be room for improvement in analytical techniques, current concerns about effectiveness focus on other aspects of surveillance—in particular, the means by which countries can be persuaded to act on the conclusions reached through consultation.

Some proposals call for the more frequent use of supplemental consultations, provision for which already exists in the surveillance principles. Such consultations could be triggered either by particular developments, such as large changes in exchange rates, or by a decision by the Executive Board, at the time of an Article IV consultation, that shortcomings in a member's policies indicated a need for further review before the next regular consultation. The aim would be to have a more continuous dialogue with the member in situations of concern.

Greater continuity of dialogue is also an aim of proposals that the Fund follow up Article IV consultations more systematically, extending a recent innovation whereby developments and policies are discussed against the background of the conclusion of the previous consultation. A related proposal is that members be asked to reply formally to the views of the Fund.

Proposals for extended follow-up often are linked to proposals for calling the attention of authorities at the highest level to the Fund's views. One such proposal calls for the Fund's Managing Director, in selected cases, to be in contact with the finance minister of the member concerned regarding the outcome of the consultation.

Some of the most controversial proposals relate to publicizing the views of the Fund. As already mentioned, the Fund has actively expanded its role in multilateral forums and has taken on a more public role. But Article IV consultations have thus far been treated as confidential. The new proposals envisage the public release of staff reports, or parts of them, or, in selected cases, a public statement by the Fund's Managing Director at the conclusion of the consultation. Such approaches have strong potential for focusing attention on key policy issues, but they raise the question of the extent to which international organizations should become involved, however indirectly, in domestic political processes. The traditional confidentiality of the Fund's relations with member countries has been an integral part of the consultation process and the consequences of departing from that confidentiality would need to be considered carefully.

These ideas and others are currently being discussed both inside the Fund and in a variety of forums outside (see box G-10 and G-24 views). Some of them may eventually be adopted, and will no doubt contribute to a strengthening of surveillance. In the last analysis, however, procedural innovations cannot ensure that surveillance is effective. The sovereign nations that make up the Fund's membership are responsible for formulating their own policies, and only insofar as such policies are formulated within the broad framework of the international interest can surveillance be said to be truly effective.

16C. Procedures in Establishing Adjustment Programs
Andrew Crockett

INITIATION

There is no fixed procedure for initiating discussions on a program to be supported by the Fund's resources. The Fund has regular contact with member authorities through annual Article IV consultations (on exchange rate arrangements), through the Executive Directors, and through other visits either by Fund staff to member countries or by member government officials to Washington, D.C. Whenever BOP[*] trends suggest that a financing gap is or may be emerging, the nature and scope of possible adjustment measures is a central feature of discussions during these contacts. At such times, the member country may request Fund assistance in designing a suitable program, or the Fund staff may itself suggest the advantages of comprehensive adjustment measures supported by use of the fund's resources. If, as occurs in quite a significant number of cases, a country is already using resources in the first credit tranche, a dialogue would already have begun, albeit on a less comprehensive basis than would be needed for a program supported by resource use in the upper credit tranches.

REQUEST FOR ASSISTANCE

The actual request to initiate discussions on the use of Fund resources, whether in the upper credit tranches or under the Fund's other facilities, need not be formal. Typically, the authorities of a member country will indicate to the Fund staff or to their Executive Director their wish to discuss a possible arrangement, and this will be immediately communicated to the Managing Director. The request and the subsequent discussions are confidential and, as far as possible, unpublicized. This is because the policies that will be under discussion are sensitive and the success of the discussions cannot be assured; in the event that agreement cannot be reached, it is often desirable to avoid unnecessary speculation on the reasons for the disagreement.

The Author is a staff member at the International Monetary Fund.

[*] Editor's Note: BOP stands for balance of payments.

PREPARATIONS BY FUND STAFF

The Fund is prepared to try to respond to a request for discussions on the use of its resources as rapidly as the situation requires. Prior to its departure the staff team, or "mission" as it is called in the Fund's terminology, prepares a comprehensive briefing paper that sets out the member's current economic situation, reviews recent discussions between the staff and the authorities on adjustment policies, and considers in as much detail as possible the nature and scope of the options the staff believes are open to the authorities to bring about the needed adjustment. This briefing paper is reviewed within the Fund staff to ensure both a consensus on the adjustment measures proposed and consistency with the Fund's uniform (which does not, of course, mean identical) treatment of all members. The briefing is then forwarded for review to the Managing Director, who will frequently call a meeting to discuss its contents with the mission head and other senior staff. When he is satisfied that the briefing is consistent with the guidelines established by the Executive Board, he gives it his approval, at which time it becomes the instructions under which the staff will operate.

NEGOTIATING PROCEDURES

While the staff always negotiates ad referendum to the Fund's management and Board, the degree of latitude given to a mission in its brief can vary If, as often happens, the economic information on a member country available at headquarters is incomplete or not fully up-to-date, some flexibility is needed to enable the staff to respond to the actual situation when discussions take place. Further, the policy instruments that the authorities are prepared to consider may not be precisely those that the staff is able to foresee when it prepares its briefing. Since staff missions do not normally refer to headquarters for additional instructions during the course of their work, it is important for them to have adequate discretion to respond authoritatively to proposals by member authorities, even when these have not been foreseen.

MISSION COMPOSITION

A typical mission consists of four to six economists. The mission chief is usually a senior staff member of the area department concerned, and he is accompanied by one or two staff members from that department who specialize in the country involved. In addition, there will be a staff member from the Exchange and Trade Relations Department, whose specific assignment includes work on the external trade and payments aspects of the program, and often also a staff member from another department (such as the Fiscal Affairs Department), if a particular area of economic management warrants special attention. An increasing number of recent missions have been accompanied by a staff member from the World Bank. This has been found particularly useful, and even necessary, in adjustment programs stretching over more than one year to ensure that the BOP adjustment process is consistent with such longer-term goals as improving the efficiency of domestic resource use, promoting economic diversification, and rationalizing the development program.

A mission usually remains in the field for about two to three weeks, through this timetable can vary depending on the difficulty of obtaining necessary information, the complexity of the program, and the constraints faced by member authorities in marshaling a consensus for needed adjustment measures. This latter factor not infrequently prevents full agreement being reached during a single mission. In such circumstances, discussions are adjourned, which offers the authorities of the member country the chance to reflect on the scope of an adjustment program and permits the Fund staff the opportunity to present the Managing Director with a more comprehensive picture of the latest economic developments and the authorities' thinking.

FORMS OF AGREEMENT

Once understandings have been reached between the staff and the authorities on needed adjustment measures, the staff assists the member country in drawing up a formal request for its use of Fund resources. The manner in which this request is presented varies slightly from case to case but, in a typical one, the Minister of Finance, on behalf of his government, will address a "letter of intent" to the Managing Director. This document, besides requesting use of resources, describes in some detail the measures that are being undertaken to improve economic and financial performance, the policies that will be followed during the life of the program, and the circumstances under which the member will request (or refrain from requesting) drawings under the arrangement.

When the staff returns to headquarters, the mission chief prepares a brief note summarizing the discussions for the Managing Director and attaches the draft letter of intent. This is also circulated to interested departments within the Fund. At this stage, it is not uncommon for minor changes in the letter of intent to be proposed to the authorities for legal or technical reasons. Once the Managing Director is satisfied that the policies described in the member's request are appropriate to the situation, the staff prepares a report for the Executive Board that describes the background to the request, the economic developments and prospects, and the manner in which the proposed program will restore a viable economic position. Preparation of this document usually takes several weeks, though this timetable is shortened when the need for financial support is urgent.

BOARD DISCUSSION

The staff report, together with the member country's request, is circulated to the Executive Directors and put on the Board's agenda for discussion and decision four weeks later. Since the program will have been framed against the background of the Executive Board's guidance (both from specific decisions and from comments made in the course of Board discussions on other subjects), a management recommendation to make resources available to a member country is likely to be approved. Nevertheless, Board discussion, which frequently extends over several hours, has an important influence on the way in which programs are put into effect. First, since usually a detailed record of the Board's discussion, together with the Managing Director's summing up, is transmitted to the authorities, it can affect the manner and pace at which measures contemplated for the program period are actually implemented. Second, it can guide the staff in conducting periodic reviews of performance under the program. This is particularly important when certain measures have been left for subsequent decision under "review clauses." Lastly, the tenor of the Board's views on a given program gives guidance to the staff in the negotiation of other programs. For example, if the weight of opinion is that, say, fiscal performance could have been more ambitious or that inadequate attention was being paid to the energy sector, additional emphasis would be given to these points, where appropriate, in subsequent programs.

16D. Do Fund-Supported Adjustment Programs Retard Growth?

*Mohsin S. Kahn and
Malcolm D. Knight*

The International Monetary Fund's Articles of Agreement make it clear (Article I) that promoting the growth of output and trade is a primary objective of economic policy and that eliminating payments disequilibria should be sought in accordance with this objective. Fund-supported adjustment programs consequently have to be designed to achieve a viable balance of payments within the context of improved long-term growth performance and price stability. Nevertheless, Fund policies and programs have come under mounting criticism in recent years in the press, as well as in certain academic circles, for failing to encourage economic growth. Indeed, it has been frequently argued that rather than fostering the growth of output, Fund programs tend to cause a slowdown in economic activity, increased unemployment, and a general worsening of living standards...

OBJECTIVES

In analyzing the effects of Fund-supported adjustment programs on the level or rate of growth of output, it is crucial first to consider the circumstances in which such programs are introduced. Typically the need for a stablization program, whether supported by the Fund or otherwise, arises when a country experiences an imbalance between aggregate domestic demand (absorption) and aggregate supply, which is reflected in a worsening of its external payments position. While it is true that such external factors as an exogenous deterioration of the terms of trade or an increase in foreign interest rates can be responsible for the basic demand-supply imbalances, often these imbalances can be traced to inappropriate domestic policies that expand aggregate domestic demand too rapidly relative to the productive potential of the economy and seriously distort relative prices. If foreign financing is available, the relative expansion of domestic demand can persist for extended periods—albeit at the cost of a widening current account deficit, a loss of international competitiveness owing to rapid domestic inflation, an inefficient allocation of resources because of the distortions in relative prices, and aheavier foreign debt burden.

Clearly, this disequilibrium cannot continue indefinitely, as the country steadily loses international competitiveness and eventually creditworthiness. In the absence of appropriate policy action, a cessation of foreign financing would impose adjustment on the country, and this forced adjustment is likely to be very disruptive. The basic objective of the Fund in these circumstances is to provide for a more orderly adjustment of the imbalance between absorption and aggregate supply so as to achieve a viable balance of payments position within a reasonable period of time. A viable balance of payments has two aspects. First, it implies that the balance of payments problems will not merely be suppressed but eradicated, and second, that the improvement in the country's external position will be durable.

The Fund's task is, in the first instance, to ensure that foreign financing attains a level consistent with the country's present and future debt-servicing capacity. This may involve setting limits on foreign borrowing or, as has been more evident in recent years, ensuring that the requisite inflow of foreign capital is in fact forthcoming to fill the financing gap. (For example, during 1983 lending by the Fund exceeded $12 billion and the Fund helped to secure over $21 billion in additional bank lending to countries with programs.) The permissible rate of foreign borrowing defines the necessary degree of adjustment of the imbalances in the economy. To achieve the required adjustment, the Fund designs a stabilization program that includes measures to restore a sustainable balance between aggregate demand and supply and simultaneously to expand the production of tradables, thereby easing the balance of payments constraint.

POLICY CONTENT

Description of Fund programs.

Although stand-by arrangements with the Fund are often viewed as synonymous with devaluation and domestic credit restraint, Fund programs are in fact complex packages of policy measures geared to the particular circumstances of the country. More important, the choice of policies and the nature of the policy mix in programs result from extensive negotiations between the country authorities and the Fund. Aside from monetary and exchange rate policies, a typical Fund program calls for fiscal measures, such as reductions in government expenditures and increases in taxation, increases in domestic interest rates and producer prices to realistic levels, policies to raise investment and improve its efficiency, trade liberalization, and wage restraint. Considerable overlap among these various policies does not preclude the convenience of grouping them into the following three categories: demand-side policies supply-side policies, and policies to improve international competitiveness.

Demand-side policies are measures that influence the aggregate level or rate of growth of domestic demand and absorption. Such policies include the whole range of fiscal, monetary, and domestic credit measures associated with traditional macroeconomic policy. Although these policies also affect production and supply, it is useful at this level of abstraction to label policies that primarily affect aggregate absorption as "demand-oriented" policies.

Supply-side policies are intended to increase the volume of goods and services supplied by the domestic economy at any given level of domestic demand. Such supply-oriented policies can be divided broadly into two groups. First, there are policies designed to increase current output by improving the efficiency with which factors of production, such as capital and labor, are utilized and allocated among competing uses. This category includes measures to reduce distortions caused by price rigidities, monopolies, taxes, subsidies, and trade restrictions. The second group encompasses policies designed to raise the long-run rate of growth of capacity output. Under this heading are incentives for domestic saving and investment. Also important are policies designed to increase the inflow of foreign savings, whether in the form of private lending, foreign direct investment, or increase development assistance. These two groups of supply-side policies are obviously interrelated, since policies that increase current output may, by themselves, led to a larger flow of saving and investment and a higher rate of growth of capacity output.

Policies to improve international competitiveness contain elements of both demand-side and supply-side policies, since they are based on combinations of measures (such as devaluation cum wage restraint) intended to affect the program country's real exchange rate. Improving competitiveness is why considerable importance often attaches to the role of exchange rate policies in stabilization programs. In general, to the extent that a combination of policies alters the real exchange rate, it will affect both real domestic absorption and the incentive to produce tradable goods.

In summary, it would be misleading to suggest that Fund programs rely exclusively on one or two policy instruments directed solely at restraining domestic demand. As the above discussion has indicated, much more is involved in the design of Fund programs than a mechanical application of the simply monetary approach to the balance of payments, supplemented perhaps by an exchange rate change. From this standpoint, it may be noted that many alternative policies proposed by critics, particularly those relating to the supply side, already form an integral part of Fund programs...The basic difference, if any, arises from some critics' proposal to use controls as a policy to correct balance of payments problems. Fund policy leans heavily in the direction of eliminating controls and restrictions on trade and payments; nevertheless, the Fund has on occasion accepted the temporary use of import controls and export subsidies and, as an interum arrangement, the continuation of dual exchange markets. What the Fund has consistently opposed is the introduction of new restrictions, as well as the intensification on a permanent basis of existing restrictions, as well as the intensification on a permanent basis of existing restrictions and other distortions in the trade and payments system. (The use of controls on trade and payments also is inconsistent with the objectives of the Fund as set forth in the Articles of Agreement.) Although a theoretical case can be made for controls and restrictions in the short run, in practice it has proved difficult to manage such systems efficiently and effectively over time. Furthermore, such policies, by introducing rigidities in the economy and creating incentives for the inefficient use of resources and forms of production, can turn out to be counterproductive in the long run and damaging to the growth potential of the economy.

Choice of policy instruments.

A crucial concern that arises in the design of adjustment programs is how much emphasis should be placed on supply-side policies relative to demand-side policies. As the need for a stabilization program typically reflects excess demand, all programs must involve some degree of restraint of aggregate domestic demand. This does not mean, however, that adjustment should be based exclusively on reducing absorption—the imbalance could in principle also be eliminated through expanding domestic supply. In fact, demand-side and supply-side policies are closely interrelated. Policies designed to achieve a higher growth rate in the medium term generally require an increase in the rate of productive investment, while demand-management policies require a reduction in the savings-investment gap. The policy package, therefore, must be designed to reduce the level of aggregate domestic demand and simultaneously to cause a shift in its composition away from current consumption and toward fixed capital formation.

Notwithstanding the difficulties of implementing supply-side policies as part of an adjustment progra, the Fund has stressed their importance in improving efficiency and the long-term rate of growth. The first difficulty is that many types of supply-side measures improve output only after a significant delay...

A second constraint on the use of certain supply-side

measures is the possibility that they may affect the political and social objectives of governments. Many government policies that create distortions (that is, deviations of prices from marginal costs are designed to achieve objectives other than economic efficiency and may have been implemented with full knowledge of their likley adverse effect on resource allocation. Such policies may include food subsidies, employment programs, restrictions on imports of certain categories of goods and services, and capital controls. Changes in such policies often have a strong impact on equity as well as economic efficiency, and the Fund is enjoined to respect the views of sovereign governments in these matters, although it can, and frequently does, render advice on the budgetary costs of such policies.

Even if these difficulties with supply-side policies are somehow overcome, this does not imply that demand-side policies can be dispensed with. Supply-side policies by themselves do not guarantee an improvement in the balance of payments because, other things being equal, aggregate demand can rise beyond sustainable levels even with increasing aggregate supply, unless it is restrained from doing so. Consequently, stablization programs have to use both sets of policies, and the decision on the relative emphasis that is to be placed on demand and supply measures in Fund programs is based on a number of criteria. These include:

(i) The nature, magnitude, and likely duration of the external payments imbalance. For example, if a deterioration in the country's external terms of trade causes the balance of payments deficit, the appropriate response would include supply-side measures designed to change the basic structure of production in the economy. In other words, an adverse external development may alter the mix between demand and supply measures. By contrast, if the initial disequilibrium is the result of excess aggregate domestic demand, owing perhaps to exessively expansionary fiscal and domestic credit policies, then the response would normally rely more heavily on demand restraint than on supply-side measures.

(ii) The initial level of the country's external indebtedness and the amount of additional financing that can be expected. These conditions determine the length of time over which the adjustment process can take place.

(iii) The nature and importance of the constraints facing the government in pursuing policies that have important social and political implications.

ISSUES RELATING TO GROWTH

...a distinction needs to be drawn between the short-term issues and the longer-term issues relating to the effects of Fund programs on growth.

Short-term issues.

If the initial problem is excess aggregate domestic demand, then, in order to achieve the objectives of the adjustment program, absorption must be reduced in the short run. Although this reduction in absorption can be perceived as representing a decline in living standards, it should not be regarded as a "cost" of the program, since absorption is merely being brought back into line with availablity of resources. The real issue is how the reduction in absorption—whether brought about by appropriate demand-side policies or by exchange rate action—will influence the level and rate of growth of output or real income...In practice... the reduction in absorption necessary to achieve the objectives will generally be accompanied by some fall in the growth of output, particularly if inflation has become ingrained in the system. This decline in the growth rate is a necessary part of the adjustment to eliminate underlying imbalances in the economy. In other words, the adjustment aims at leading the economy onto a more stable and sustainable path that generally accompanies the supply-demand imbalances. The critical question, of course, concerns the size and duration of the short-run effects of policies designed to reduce absorption.

...Fund programs are not intended to reduce a country's absorption of goods and services below the level that can be financed (out of current savings and capital inflows) on a sustainable basis. Any reductions in absorption and growth that go beyond the levels necessary to achieve the objectives of the program can be fairly viewed as the true "costs" of a program. Since the "necessary" reduction in absorption and the consequent decline in growth, however, are not measurable precisely, such a notion of costs is difficult to quantify...

Long-term issues

...Even if it was determined that stabilization programs reduce output in the short run, this deficiency could be outweighed by the long-term benefits resulting from the adoption of suitable adjustment policies. Indeed, it is a basic premise of Fund program that balance of payments recovery does not conflict with economic growth when the time-horizon of both objectives is properly specified to be the medium term.

This view is based on a number of condierations, First, even if a reduction in absorption impairs growth over the short run, to the extent that a Fund program succeeds in avoiding the drastic cut in absorption that accompanies a complete loss of creditor support, the program can be said to protect the growth of the economy currently and in the future. Second, the supply-side, or structural, policies in adjustment programs are intended to enhance the productive potential of the economy by improving the allocation of resources and stimulating domestic savings and investment. If such policies are successful, they diminish any inescapable impact upon growth of measures that focus on reducing absorption. Furthermore, by raising the capacity of the country to service debt in the future, these structural policies allow for a higher level of sustainable growth in the long run. Lastly, financial stability resulting from a successful stabilization program can have a beneficial effect on the state of confidence in the economy. This confidence can encourage both domestically financed and foreign-financed investment, leading to gains in employment, productivity, and output.

CONCLUSIONS

...The main patterns to emerge from the present survey can be briefly summarized. First, the studies reviewed generally indicated that, while the size of the effect varied, tighter monetary and credit policies would result in a fall in the growth rate in the first year after they were implemented. Furthermore, if monetary and credit restraint took the form of a reduction in the flow of credit to the private sector, the empircal evidence showed that private capital formation and possibly the long-run rate of growth would be adversely affected. Second, no studies showed any clear empirical relation between growth and fiscal policy. There are close institutional links between monetary and fiscal policies in developing countries and thus, once monetary policy variables are taken into account, the various studies have found it difficult to measure the independent role of fiscal policy. Third, there is some evidence that supply-side policies, particularly policies to increase producer prices and the domestic interest rates, have favorable effects on production and savings. For example, price elasticities of supply of agricultural commodities tend to be higher than normally assumed, so that increases in prices encourage the production of primary goods. The effect of variations in real interest rates on savings is, however, quite small, implying that it would take fairly sizable increases in nominal interest rates to change the savings rate. Fourth, a number of studies find a close relationship between the growth rate and capital formation. Therefore, policies directed at increasing investment and improving its efficiency will tend to have a beneficial effect on long-run development. Finally, such empirical evidence as is currently available is consistent with the view that devaluation would, on balance, exert an expansionary rather than contractionary effect on domestic output, even in the short run. This result clearly has an important bearing on the use of exchange rate policy in developing countries.

One explanation of the view that Fund programs systematically reduce growth is perhaps the misconception that programs are designed solely to reduce aggregate demand through the use of contractionary monetary and fiscal policies. Since some empirical evidence indicates that such policies slow growth temporarily, it is concluded that Fund programs must therefore be deflationary. As discussed in this survey, this interpretation of the policy content of Fund programs is far too narrow, and account has to be taken of the other growth-inducing measures contained in Fund programs. This aspect is brought out clearly in the results of cross-country studies measuring the effects of Fund packages that combined the whole range of demand-management and supply-side policies. These studies found that the rate of growth declined in a number of countries during the course of a program, but this result was matched by a number of cases where the growth rate in fact rose. Once the influence of all relevant policies on the growth rate is recognized, there is no clear presumption that Fund-supported adjustment programs adversely affect growth.

In conclusion, this paper has shown the serious limitations of existing empirical analysis of Fund-supported adjustment programs and economic growth. To evaluate the criticism that Fund programs are unnecessarily deflationary would require more systematic empirical studies. Such studies would have to be in the nature of a case-by-case approach, taking the whole range of Fund policies into consideration rather than focusing on individual elements of programs. They would also have to be supplemented by some type of modeling and simulation analysis so as to handle the issues that arise in comparing the set of policies included in a Fund program with a hypothetical alternative package of measures or in comparing the effects of a Fund program with the outcome that would occur in the absence of a program...

16E. Towards a Real Economy Approach

Tony Killick, Graham Bird, Jennifer Sharpley and Mary Sutton

I. INTRODUCTION

(a) A large proportion of oil-importing ldcs is faced with persistent, unviable BoP deficits. A great deal of the deterioration in their payments situation in recent years has been the result of largely irreversible adverse movements in their commondity terms of trade-a deteriorating current account is no longer prime facie evidence of the pursuit of excessively expansionary domestic demand policies; and restoration of a healthy BoP requires longer-term changes in the structure of production and demand.

(b) Even though often emanating from a more hostile world environment, economic adjustments to strengthen the BoP are inevitable, for there are no grounds for assuming that enough funds will become available on concessional terms for long-term financing to be a sustainable alternative to corrective measures. Adjustment is thus inevitable in most deficit ldcs and it is the *costs of adjustment* which turn the BoP into a 'problem'. There are, however, both domestic and global factors which severly limit ldc governments' abilities to achieve adjustment without heavy social costs.

(c) The key task is to minimise the adjustment costs associated with the required strengthening of the BoP. Conceptually, the approach presented in this chapter is set in a cost-minimising framework (although we admit that we are using the language of quantification loosely and that the costs cannot be reduced to some simple measure of welfare foregone). The most important single determinant of adjustment costs is the extent to which adjustment is achieved by suppressing demand rather than stimulating supply. Closely related to this is the availability of financing and, therefore, the required speed of adjustment. In the face of a BoP crisis a government must look for quick-acting measures, which almost certainly means opting for cuts in demand.

(d) Unfortunately, the IMF has not set its programmes within a cost-minimising framework. It has tended to treat the BoP objective as an overriding one and has been reluctant to give weight to other government objectives as constraints upon the design of stabilisation programmes. Reasons were given in chapter 6 for believing that, *potentially*, the Fund approach is a rather high-cost one: the limited volume of its resources; the stress on demand management; the short-term nature of its programmes; the preoccupation with a small number of quantified performance criteria. However, were emphasise the word 'potentially' in the above sentence, because we suggested in chapter 7 that the actual impact of Fund programmes has been limited. While it seems clear that the more extreme complaints about the deflationary effects of Fund programmes cannot be generally substantiated, it also seems that with existing resources and policies the Fund is unable to achieve its own objectives in the area of global BoP management.

It must be admitted, however, that most of the Fund's past critics have not gone far in setting out constructive alternatives. It is clear to us that a policy of neglect by ldc governments offers the worst outcome of all—an involuntary 'adjustment' brought about by an inability to borrow abroad and by interruptions in import supplies, resulting in greatly reduced capacity utilisation, large reductions in investment, shortages of key consumer goods and much hardship. We are also clear that a policy of 'de-linking', advocated by members of the dependency school, does not offer a cost-efficient alternative because, even in the unfavourable climate of the early l980s, ldcs were still deriving major benefits from international trade.

The onus is thus upon those who are interested in reformist solutions to suggest alternatives to the present arrangements which promise to be more cost-efficient. It is the purpose of this chapter to make suggestions along these lines, advocating what we call a 'real-economy' approach. Part II

---

*Editor's Note: This chapter is the conclusion of a two volume study of the IMF and its policies by the authors of this article. All references to previous chapters refer to these volumes, namely, *The Quest for Economic Stabilization* and *The IMF and Stabilization* (St. Martins Press, New York 1984).

provides a general description of this approach; Part III makes a range of specific suggestions concerning IMF policies; Part IV examines implications for developing countries; Part V takes up some objections that have been raised to our ideas; and Part VI briefly considers the tactics of international monetary reform. Finally, the appendix provides an illustrative application of a real economy approach to the situation in Kenya.

II. TOWARDS A REAL ECONOMY APPROACH

First principles

The best approach to economic management will often be the adoption of a programme primarily aimed at re-orienting the productive system. This may be called a 'real economy' approach and it places greater weight on supply-side measures in contrast with approaches emphasising the control of aggregate demand. There are strong *a priori* reasons for expecting such an approach to be most cost-efficient if it can be successfully implemented. Such a strategy of 'adjustment with growth' would permit equilibrium to be restored at a higher overall level of economic activity; it would minimise the conflicts between policy objectives of stabilisation, growth and social welfare. A wide variety of problems is more amenable to solution in the context of economic growth than in a recession: it is easier to secure sectoral shifts and industrial restructuring because what is chiefly in question is differential rates of expansion rather than the absolute decline of the disfavoured lines of activity; it is easier to sustain the level of saving and thus investment; it is easier to solve the absorption problem by raising income than by cutting spending; financing the government's budget becomes easier; the politics of adjustment becomes less sensitive.

What we are urging then is an approach which emphasises the importance in designing BoP programmes of measures which stimulate output and productivity, focusing on key bottlenecks and constraints within the productive system, and going beyond conventional macro aggregates to a wide variety of specific microeconomic measures.

The objective of a strategy of adjustment with growth is to create a viable BoP in a manner which also promotes, or at least minimises conflicts with, that group of government objectives called 'economic development'. The key target variable will generally be the *current account* of the BoP; it is only by reducing the current deficit that the country can safeguard against the danger of generating a financing gap that cannot be filled or against building up an unsustainably large volume of external debt-servicing obligations. The emphasis will thus be upon increasing the volume and value of exports, reducing *net* dependence on imports through efficient import-substitution, and maximising net inflows (minimising net outflows) on invisibles and transfers account (e.g. through the tourist industry), measures to encourage the repatriation of earnings from nationals working abroad, the more efficient domestic provision of insurance and shipping services.

The growth of output envisaged in this strategy can be thought of as stemming from two sources: from the improved utilisation of existing productive capacity and from increases in that capacity. Greater capacity utilisation may be of particular importance (a) because it is common for countries experiencing a payments crisis to be operating well below the trend level of output and (b) because, in principle, greater output from existing capacity should not be subject to long gestation lags in a situation where time is of the essence.

When it comes to the enlargement of productive capacity, what is necessitated by an adjustment with growth strategy is a relative increase in the output of tradeables *vis-a-vis* non-tradeables, described under the heading of 'expenditure switching' in chapter 4. By 'tradeables' we means all goods and services which enter significantly into world trade. From the view point of a specific country these will be made up of items which are, or could potentially be exported, imports and home produced substitutes for imports. Almost all goods are traded or are potentially tradeable but some goods, and a larger proportion of services, do not normally lend themselves to international commerce—domestic water supplies, health services, buildings. As will be shown shortly, a wide range of policy instruments can be deployed to assist the relative expansion in the output of tradeables but measures to change the structure of commodity and factor price incentives will be of crucial importance. However, to the extent that the payments crisis has been largely caused by rapidly rising import prices, this trend will itself create new profitable import-substituting investment opportunities as well, perhaps, as improved ability to compete in non-traditonal export markets.

The strategy so far described may produce quick results but only when there is much excess capacity in the traded goods sector which it is possible to bring rapidly into use. In many circumstances it would be unwise to plan on the basis of major improvements in utilisation, for although most countries operate well within their production frontier, the obstacles to remedying this situation are often deep-seated— otherwise the problem would be less widespread. The alternative of expanding the production frontier, although in a sense a more fundamental solution, is bound to be slower-acting because of gestation lags. In the meantime, BoP deficits must be expected to persist, even if on a diminishing scale, and these will have to be financed somehow. While there are no grounds for being dogmatic, there must also be a general presumption in favour of gradual *vis-a-vis* shock programmes. In large part this follows from what we have already said about the need for actions that will stimulate output which, however, will involve gestation lags. However, it is also plausible to think that the loss to 'psychic welfare' is less when people have time to adjust their lives to altered circumstances and policies than if traumatic changes are suddenly thrust upon them. Gradual programmes are also likely to be easier to monitor and control; the risks of major policy mistakes are thus probably lessened. The discussion in Chapter C_2 of the Chilean experience suggests the large costs of the shock approach in that case. What we particularly fear is the danger of overkill through a combination of devaluation, interest rate reform, budgetary stringency and credit restrictions.

A general preference for gradual programmes further emphasises the need for longer term financing, however. The strategy advocated here envisages a more adequate flow of financing than is often available, including concessionary flows to those countries which cannot (or should not) meet their needs from commercial sources. The role of supporting finance is particularly important because a country's abililty to meet its import needs will have a great influence on the utilisation of productive capacity and the volume of new capital formation. One criticism of programmes emphasising the limitation of imports is that they may starve of essential intermediate and capital goods precisely those sectors that need to expand if the structural problem is to be overcome. But while increases in the production of tradeables are at the heart of our strategy, this does not mean that demand management can be abandoned. To go back to essentials, payments adjustment entails a reduction in absorption (consumption plus investment) relative to income (reduced A/Y). One of the attractions of the approach advocated here is that the primary emphasis is on the expansion of Y, thus obviating or reducing the need for an absolute reduction in A. But in the absence of demand management and incomes policies there is every likelihood that A would expand quite as fast as Y, thus subverting the entire programme. With our approach it would be essential to protect the investment component of A; it is chiefly consumption that would have to be restrained. The same destination is reached by another route when we recall that the objective is to reduce the *current account* deficit. In terms of the basic model of income determination in an open economy, if X must rise relative to M, then S must rise relative to I. Since we have already determined that I should not be cut, it follows that S must be raised, again entailing that the chief burden must fall upon consumption. This is an unwelcome fact, since we are writing about countries with generally low average incomes and many people living in absolute poverty. But in the absence of much enlarged, near-permanent internatonal flows of concessionary finance we see no alternative to austerity. This is the sharp end of the truth that the adverse movement in the terms of trade suffered by most oil-importing ldcs represents a transfer of real income from them to their suppliers. All that can be said in mitigation is that the real economy approach offers less draconian consumption curbs than an approach based more centrally upon demand restraint.

But is not the restraint of consumption likely to require conventional fiscal and monetary policies of the type associated with IMF programmes and, if so, are we really offering an alternative? There are, in fact, major differences, the most important being the level of activity (and consumption) at which a viable BoP may be restored. Furthermore, if successful, supply-oriented measures will increase the demand for real money balances, which is primarily a function of real income (see chapter 3). Other things being equal, this will mean that a given payments outcome will be consistent with a larger real volume of domestic credit which, in turn, may assist a further round of increased capacity utilisation and capital formation. In addition, suggestions will be made shortly for safeguarding against the danger that fiscal and monetary restraint may undermine the pattern of structural change advocated above. We do not wish to exaggerate the extent to which our suggestions would offer an alternative to IMF policies. In the present context, we see the change as being an important one of emphasis; of viewing demand management as an essential supporting measure to a supply-oriented strategy, rather than treating demand management as the centre-piece, with or without supplementary supply measures.

One other 'first principle' to mention is that, in common with the Fund, we also see BoP adjustment as requiring a package of measures, which is why it is called a strategy. There are, however, inherent dangers in any such strategy since the effective implementation of a large number of mutually reinforcing and carefully phased policy measures is likely to test the most powerful government and the most efficient public administration, and their abilities vary greatly across countries. This is partially what is meant by 'the capacity to adjust' and it would be essential to tailor the programme to the practical limitations of the country in question. In this regard, the technical assistance and training offered by the IMF can make a vaulable contribution.

Some elaboration

First principles are all very well...but they are also all very general. Adjustment with growth cannot be critically evaluated at this level; it needs elaboration. The difficulty in this is the great diversity of country situations and potentialities. In some countries, improving agricultural performance may deserve the first priority; in others, it may be the composition of public investment, or the system of industrial protection, or the development of mineral resources. The extent to which the country has access to international finance will be a key determinant of the length of time over which adjustment must be completed and, therefore, of the programme design itself. The composition of domestic production, exports and imports will also be among the key variables influencing programme design, as will the size of the country, with its correlate of the openess of the economy. Country size, in combination with geographical location and political orientation, will have an additional effect on the availability of Western financial assistance, which is strongly influenced by military-strategic considerations.

But while there is little scope for generalised solutions, it is possible to say something about the sectoral implications of a strategy of adjustment with growth and what these mean for the role of the public sector. The priority, remember, is to encourage the production of tradeables *vis-a-vis* non-tradeables. In the broadest terms, tradeables can be equated with industry and agriculture; non-tradeables are mainly various kinds of services, although there are important exceptions to this. Among the most important are services provided by government. The strategy being presented thus seems to imply a relative decline in the share of the public sector or, anyway, of government services, as well as some private service industries. Moreover, since they are labour-intensive activities, the strategy appears to have serious implications for employment.

However, we should beware the danger of ignoring the network of sectoral interdependencies. Agriculture, for example, depends heavily upon the transportation and marketing systems, just as industry relies upon the urban infrastructure. On this view, roads, the postal services, banks, rural storage facilities and the like really belong in the 'tradeables' category. We need an input-output analysis to obtain a more refined view of the matter but what remains unambiguously in the non-tradeables category is private and public services *for final consumption*. In what is normally the private sector, these include some transport; much of commerce; entertainment; personal and household services; real estate; housing construction. In what is normally the public sector, they include general administration and defence; health and welfare services; and much of the educational system. Of course, it is possible to argue that even these make essential contributions to the production of tradeables, for example by providing people with the incentives to expand their incomes, by providing a necessary framework of security, by supporting a trained and healthly labour force, etc. But to argue along these lines is simply to draw attention to the complex interdependencies within an economy, the existence of which does not, however, remove the basis or need for setting priorities among sectors.

The complexity and diversity of real-economy approaches to BoP adjustment can be illustrated further by reference to the range of policy instruments available to governments for achieving the objectives set out earlier. A *partial* inventory of such is set out in Table 8.1. It is partial (a) because it is largely confined to measures affecting the agricultural and industrial sectors, and (b) because even within this restricted area it would be quite easy to add to the list. Each country has its

Table 8.1

TAX MEASURES
    Import tariffs (and the associated pattern of industrial protection)
    Export taxation
    Taxation of land values
    Taxation of gasoline and other fuels
    Investment incentives (tax holidays, etc)
    Reform (strengthening of tax administration)

GOVERNMENT EXPENDITURE MEASURES
    Agricultural research and development; extension; training
    Rural infrastructure (roads, storage facilities, boreholes, cattle dips, etc)
    Land conservation/reclamation
    Food and other buffer stocks
    Subsidies on food and other essentials
    Agricultural input subsidies (fertilisers, etc)
    Geological surveying and exploration
    Export subsidies and insurance
    Industrial infrastructures (power, water, communications, etc)
    Industrial estates
    Research and development of more appropriate industrial technologies
    Investments in local resource-based energy projects (hydro-electricity, etc)
    Port facilities

LEGAL AND REGULATORY
    Export quality and health controls
    Land reform; land registration
    Import and export controls
    Price controls

OTHER INSTITUTIONAL MEASURES
    Strengthening relevant parastatal bodies
    Improved distribution of agricultural inputs
    Co-operative development
    Export advice and technical assistance
    Promotion of tourism
    Strengthening public sector project selection and execution procedures
    Improved negotiating stance *vis-a-vis* multinational corporations (e.g. on oil exploration, mineral exploitation, etc)

FINANCIAL, PRICING AND RELATED MEASURES
    Interest rate and other financial reforms
    Sectoral credit allocations (including rural credit, and allocations as between public and private sectors)
    Pricing policies, e.g. for agriculture, some parastatals
    Exchange rate adjustments
    Incomes policies

own peculiarities by way of institutional framework, policy traditions, sectoral needs and so on, and comparisons of specific country policies reveal an exceedingly rich variety of instruments in use.

No attempt is made in the table to go beyond mere listing in order to indicate the relative importance of various instruments. For one thing, this will depend upon specific circumstances, although some are clearly of far greater potential importance than others. What is clear from the inventory is the wide range of policy instruments available and relevant. The familiar distinction between macroeconomic and microeconomic policies (which has been used to limit the coverage of IMF programme conditionality) tends to break down in the context of adjustment with growth. Apparently macroeconomic instruments (say, the exchange rate) affect the productive sectors in differential ways, just as microeconomic measures aimed at a particular activity (say, tourist promotion) can make an important contribution to the macroeconomic objective of payments adjustment.

We delve further into the specifics of the real-economy approach shortly when making suggestions for IMF policies, which are illustrated by particular reference to Kenya, Before turning to this, however, mention should be made of the World Bank's structural adjustment programmes, which also illustrate a real-economy orientation and have much influenced our own thinking.

World Bank structural adjustment programmes

The Bank opened its window of structural adjustment loans (SALs) early in 1980.[1] They are designed to provide quick-disbursing finance in support of a package of measures aimed at strengthening the borrowing country's BoP. They are particularly addressed to payments deficits resulting from permanent adverse changes in the external environment, although it is recognised that no hard and fast distinction can be drawn between these and more domestic sources of payments deficits. Adjustment is anticipated over a period of 5 years or more. The loans themselves are for disbursement within 12-18 months but the Bank normally expects to undertake a succession of such loans over a 4-5 year period.

By contrast with the IMF, the Bank's conditionality relates to specific policy actions, to be undertaken over 12-18 months. In order to give its conditionality teeth, the policy actions in question must be 'monitorable'. Disbursement of a loan is generally in two instalments, with the release of the second dependent upon satisfactory progress with the implementation of a few key measures. The chief sanction which the Bank possesses, however, is with respect to agreement on future SALs (and perhaps project loans too). Reasonable progress with the policies supported by one SAL in effect becomes a pre-condition for the next loan. The nature of the policy conditions written into the Bank's first nine SALs is summarised in Table 8.2.

On the face of it, the SALs are a very different approach to payments adjustment from that adopted by the IMF. The contrast is reduced, however, by the practice, if not the formal policy, of requiring the government to have agreed a Stand-by or EFF programme with the IMF before an initial SAL will be recommended for approval, as was the case with all eight countries listed in Table 8.2. It seems likely, however, that SALs beyond the initial one will not necessarily require an IMF programme to be in place, so long as the Bank is satisfied with progress to date and that its supply side measures will not be undermined by irresponsible demand creation. While the Bank's staff generally agree with the Fund about the importance of demand management, disagreements do arise between them about the desirable levels of public sector investment and of other 'development' categories of government spending, and also about the possibly adverse effects on structural adaption and capacity utilisation of restrictive credit ceilings.

Although it is as yet too early to form any rounded judgement about the effectiveness of this innovation, and the record to date has been mixed, there is overall satisfaction amoung the Bank's staff with progress so far. The programme originally encountered opposition within the Exeuctive Board, which until recently insisted that SALs should account for no more than 10% of the Bank's new lending. Moreover, the SALs compete with other uses of the Bank's resources-they do not represent any net addition to total lending and their value remains small in relation to total payments financing needs (loan commitments in 1982 amounted to slightly over $1bn and disbursements were no doubt a good deal smaller).

Another problem that has already become apparent is a particular bias in the nature of the governments with which SALs have been negotiated. Although the countries listed in Table 8.2 appear to have neither more nor less authoritarian governments than a random sample of ldcs, there is an evident bias towards governments with market-oriented policies. While admitting that their programmes have a market orientation, Bank staff deny that this results from any ideological predilection and insist that as a pragmatic matter the Bank's experiences have taught that market forces are more effective allocative devices than controls and planning. Be that as it may, it remains the case that the policy content of the Sal innovation in uncongenial to some left-wing governments, which may help to explain why the Bank itself has stated that the expansion of SALs is primarily constrained by 'political and technical difficulties'. A further apparent bias is one against the least developed ldcs. Of the countries listed in Table 8.2 only Malawi falls into the Bank's category of low-income countries and the unweighted average per capita income of the eight in 1979 was $650.

These limitations notwithstanding, the SAL programme is an imaginative attempt to adapt the policies of a major international agency to the changing nature of ldc problems and to the increased severity of the foreign exchange constraint. It is an innovation which will be watched with particular interest as a test of the practicability of a supply side approach to economic stabilisation.

III. SUGGESTIONS FOR FUND POLICIES

The case for a change

Lest it be thought that we are wanting to convert the IMF from its traditional role into another purveyor of long-term development aid it is as well to begin this exploration of the policy implications for the Fund of our study by setting out our initial premise. Specifically, we start from the statement of objectives set out in the Articles of Agreement, reproduced on page 129. Among those who created the Fund at Bretton Woods and those who have joined it since there was presumably a belief that all members stood to benefit from having an effective organisation that would facilitate international monetary co-operation, the growth of international trade and exchange stability, and which would provide material assistance to members seeking to correct payments imbalances. We share that belief but our results have suggested ways in which existing Fund policies are an obstacle to the effective execution of its responsibilities, at least *vis-a-vis* some developing country members.

Consider the case for a change. The influence of deteriorating terms of trade and other exogenous factors has increased and worsened the BoP situation of most oil-importing ldcs. At the same time, the control of domestic demand remains the thrust of Fund programmes and we have suggested that attempts at structural adaptation chiefly by means of demand restraint are likely to be high-cost solutions. It is, moreover, universally accepted, not least by the Fund, that structural adaptation is necessarily a lengthy process. Conventional one year Stand-by programmes are not well designed to assist with this long-term task, even if they are set within some kind of medium-term framework (although the Fund would maintain that, whatever its limitations, credit restraint remains the most practical available instrument).

The changing geography of the Fund's clients must also be considered. As is shown in chapter 5, the great majority of Stand-by and EFF credits have in recent years been lent to the least developed countries in Africa and elsewhere (although Argentina, Brazil and Mexico were major exceptions in early 1983), but it is precisely for the circumstances of this type of country that the Fund's traditional policies are least well suited (particularly for reasons set out in chapters 3 and 6). It is worth recalling here one of the conclusions of the Kenya study in chapter C5 of the companion volume: in terms of attitudes towards economic policies, an appreciation of the gains to be had from maintaining an open-economy stance, and the avoidance of the grosser forms of economic mismanagement, Kenya appears to be precisely the type of ldc which could most easily do business with the Fund. And yet, the relationship has been a troubled one. All programmes have broken down and the question is posed, if the IMF and Kenya cannot work out an effective relationship where else in Africa is this likely to be possible? This, we suggest, is a specific illustration of the general difficulty of applying the Fund's approach to stabilisation to the circumstances of the poorer developing countries.

We have already provided reasons why the Fund's conventional programmes may often not be very effective and why they could potentially impose heavy costs on the economy in output and employment foregone. The Articles of Agreement (I.ii) refer to the maintenance of high levels of employment, income and economic development as 'the primary objectives of economic policy' which the Fund can assist through the balanced growth of international trade. But in practice the Fund has sometimes appeared to treat these objectives as secondary to the restoration of payments equilibrium and has tended to neglect the potentially negative impact of its programmes on these 'primary objectives'. We have also suggested, however, that in practice Fund programmes often have only a modest impact, for good or ill (chapter 7). For reasons that are far from exclusively attributable to the Fund, a high percentage of programmes become inoperative during their intended lifespans, even though they are generally for only one year periods. Even when a credit is fully drawn, it seems that only limited improvement can be claimed in the BoP and other macroeconomic variables. Finally, we have already mentioned that while the Fund sought hard to adapt its resources, facilities and conditionality to the changing circumstances following the first oil shock, some of that adaptation was undone by a return during 1981-82 to a policy stance nearer to the late-1960s position than to the late-1970s. As others have pointed out (Williamson, 1982) one of the effects of the tightening-up in conditionality in 1981-82 was to give a further contractionary twist to a world economy already in recession.

For all these reasons, there is an overwhelming case for a major change in the content of conditionality—at a minimum, a reversion to the late-1970s attempts to adapt and to accommodate ldc Fund members. The case flows simply from the Articles of Agreement: given the changing nature of its clientele and their problems, the Fund's traditional conditionality reduces its ability to carry out certain of the purposes written into its Articles.

It should in all honesty be added that in urging the need for changes we are not merely concerned with Fund ability to perform the responsibilities set out in its Articles. We are also concerned with the desirability of redressing the present tendency for international monetary arrangements to widen income disparities between nations. In the past few years the powerful OPEC surplus and OECD countries have been able to shift much of the burden of adjustment onto ldc oil-importers, which is precisely why this group of countries is plagued with such intractable deficits. It is also difficult to dismiss the accusation (by President Nyerere among others) that the IMF has been employed as an instrument of control by the rich and powerful nations over the poorer, as an active agent in an asymmetrical adjustment process which places the greatest burdens upon those least able to bear them.[2] At a minimum, it is surely desirable that the Fund's policies be designed to minimise this burden andd its adverse welfare effects on those already living in poverty. In our view, the equity case is an immensely strong one but, alas, it is not one that will find a ready acceptance by those benefiting from present arrangements. But whether or not that case is accepted, we reiterate that there is a no less strong efficiency case for change.

Perhaps at the heart of some of the Fund's difficulties is the view that there should be a fairly standard stabilisation programme, a well-defined 'conventional' approach. We are not urging the Fund to switch from a standard demand-management approach to a standard real-economy approach. In fact, we place importance on the role of demand management and would be the last to deny that governments often worsen their external problems by domestic mismanagement or inertia. Rather, what is urged is that the Fund utilise a richer *mix* of policies, recognising the mutual interdependence of demand- and supply-oriented policies and adapting stabilisation programmes to country circumstances within a less confining intellectual frontier. Fundamental to the approach taken in this chapter is the premise that the design of stabilisation programmes must be related to the causes of the problems to which they are addressed.

For expositional purposes, it is convenient to identify two polar cases. First, there is what might be called 'a classical IMF problem' of a persistent payments deficit attributable largely to excessively expansionary fiscal policies. Among our case studies, Indonesia under Sukarno provides the clearest example of this. With the terms of trade assumed to be roughly steady, the chief task is to bring aggregate demand (and therefore the budget) under control, to increase the incentive to export, reduce the incentive to import and create domestic conditions conducive to an inflow of supporting finance.

At the other extreme, we may take the case of a country confronted with an enormous increase in the unit cost of imports, a depressed foreign demand for its traditional exports and presistent, serious deteriorations in the terms of trade, prusuing responsible fiscal and monetary policies at home. These factors may be aggravated by weaknesses of a more domestic origin, or such weaknesses may themselves be the principal source of difficulty—lagging agriculture; high-cost industry; an inefficient marketing system. Such problems can be described as 'structural'. Of our case studies, Keny comes nearest to this model, although it is not a pure case. Obviously, most countries experiencing payments difficulties will fall somewhere between these polar cases and will therefore require a blend of policies designed to tackle both the demand and supply weaknesses. What is equally obvious, however, is that in the last decade or so, particularly since the second oil shock and the general recession of the early 1980s, the structural sources of deficit have become more important relative to excess-demand sources.

Having made this expositional distinction, we now divide our suggestions on IMF policies into two categories: those of fairly general applicability to all programmes, no matter what the source of difficulty; and those relating specifically to programmes designed to deal with structural problems. The 'general' recommendations could largely be carried out within the Fund's existing resources, whereas those relating to real economy problems would necessitate substantially enlarged resources.

General recommendations

First, we see scope for narrowing the differences between the objectives of the Fund and of its member governments for these differences underlie many of the disagreements and programme break-downs. This could be promoted if the Fund were to design its programmes much more explicitly within a cost-minimisation framework that it has in the past. We are not here suggesting that it will normally be possible to quantify all the costs but rather that greater explicit weight should be given to designing measures that will do most to promote, or least to hamper, other major economic objectives of governments. The Fund would claim that it already does this in some measure, at least with respect to economic growth and inflation. On the other hand, it was suggested in chapter 6 that the Fund has tended to place limited weight on such factors. It was also reported that there remains a body of opinion among Fund staff that economic growth per se is no concern of the Fund, except in the indirect sense that restoration of a healthy BoP is conducive to growth.

Nevertheless, one of the Fund's most thoughtful economists has recognised that, whatever be the case with short-term programmes, such an attitude cannot be defended in the context of longer-term approaches:[*]

> Apart from the implications for the requisite financing, the lengthening of the period of adjustment reduces the number of economic variables that can be considered exogenous for the purposes of policy formulation. This is particularly the case with the ef-

fect of policy on economic activity and the rate of real economic growth, which for short periods of time can be disregarded as being either nonexistent or of small order of magnitude. Such assumptions lose plausibility when the time frame is extended. The experience of countries undertaking an adjustment effort with respect to their rates of growth is generally mixed. In a large number of cases, this was perceived as a problem area and it led to the question of whether, in the process of adjustment, too much emphasis was placed on demand management measures and whether the appropriate strategy would be to supplement them with measures directly aimed at improving the allocation of resources and stimulating the growth of productivity and aggregate supply.

It was further shown in chapter 6 that the Fund has always declined to take explicit account of distributional consequences when designing its programmes. While we accept that this is both a sensitive area and one on which it is often difficult to obtain firm evidence, sensitivity of subject-matter has not deterred the Fund from other policy areas, for example on the respective roles of the public and private sectors. Moreover, its programmes frequently include measures which directly affect the distribution of income: changes in the pricing policies of parastatals, in the structure of taxation and subsidisation, in incomes policies. No doubt it is often necessary for programmes to be addressed to such measures but surely no rounded view of theie desirability can be formed without explicitly assessing their likely distributional consequences? This is particularly true of the poorest members of society who must be protected from the potentially adverse effects on their precarious hold on life of the general need to restrain consumption. Quite apart from this the distributional factor has a crucial bearing upon the likelihood that an agreed programme will be executed and sustained, as repeated difficulties over the reduction of food subsidies and devaluation have demonstrated.[3]

The greater attention to costs advocated here should be further extended to a more systematic and explicit consideration of the political consequences of stabilisation programmes; indeed, one of the chief reasons for programme breakdowns is, as suggested in chapter 2, that governments often perceive the political costs of carrying through a programme to be greater than the payments crisis to which it is addressed. While the Fund does form political judgements, it is weak in this area. A sound political 'feel' is perhaps the most important attribute of a successful mission chief. But the Fund's staff is not professionally qualified to undertake systematic political analysis and the weight given to political factors in the judgements of the management is unclear. There have been well-known cases where considerable insensitivity was shown, for example the 1979 credit to Nicaragua in the dying days of the hated Somoza regime.

There are both moral and efficiency grounds for urging the Fund to strengthen its capacity in this area. At the moral level, and to quote Foxley, if one prefers an open, democratic society then policies 'that require a good deal of political repression to have a reasonable chance of success are certainly not a satisfactory solution'. At the efficiency level, programmes designed with sensitivity to the probable political consequences simply stand a better chance of being implemented. It is perhaps symbolic of insensitivity that Fund missions generally arrive with a Letter of Intent (ostensibly a letter from the government to the Managing Director) already drafted, albeit one that is open to negotiation. We urge an end to that practice. To be a political document to which there is a real commitment, a Letter of Intent must essentially emanate from the government. The legal language of the Fund, which is at present written into the letter, could be handled in another way.

This brings us to a further recommendation, concerning the Fund's principle of uniformity of treatment among members. This, recall from chapter 6, is defined as requiring 'that for any given degree of need the effort of economic adjustment sought in programmes be broadly equivalent among members'. Some have suggested, however, that the Fund should replace this principle by one of 'positive discrimination' in favour of its least developed member countries. In our view the problem is not with the priciple of uniformity of treatment, which is a sound one as defined, but with its application. It may be helpful here to use Kindleberger's notion of the 'capacity to transform', which he described as the 'capacity to react to change, originating at home or abroad, by adapting the structure of foreign trade to the new situation in an economic fashion'. Uniformity of treatment requires that the nature of stabilisation programmes be designed in the light of countries' differing capacities to transform—a rule that would result in less draconian, more gradual adjustment programmes in the poorer developing countries.

In the context of a mixed economy, the capacity to transform will be determined by the efficiency of the market mechanism, by the structure and technical characteristics of production, and by the efficiency of the policy-making and implementation processes. It is widely accepted that the efficiency of the market system (and of the information flows upon which it depends) is likely to be at its lowest in the least developed countries. Poor communications and transport, low educational levels, social and other obstacles to labour mobility, dualistic capital markets, heavy concentrations of monopoly and monopsony power, quite apart from the often malign influence of state interventions, all conspire to make it so. The price responsiveness of the productive structure will also be much affected by the stage of development. In support of this proposition we may quote an internal Fund document on supply oriented adjustment policies:

The short-term responsiveness of aggregate real supply differs markedly across countries with different structures of production, particularly between developed and developing countries... In primary-producing developing countries...the responsiveness of aggregate supply depends on cost conditions in the industries producing these basic commodities. Most agricultural commodities, by their very nature, are in relatively inelastic supply over periods of less than one year, owing to the harvest cycle; other products, such as rubber and coffee, have a long gestation period. Even the price elasticity of the supply of mineral extraction industries in developing countries may be low in the short run, owing to the limited availability of skilled labour and specialised capital equipment. Thus, in contrast to the industrial countries, aggregate supply in primary-producing developing countries may often be relatively unresponsive to changes in the prices of their primary commodities relative to industrial-country output in the short run, and may be more elastic in the long run.

Quite so. And, if so, the less developed countries require longer term adjustment periods than the more developed. It is similarly a plausible generalisation that the efficiency of policy-making and of the execution of policies is also an approximately increasing function of the level of development. The same is likely to be true, in a rough-and-ready way, of the stability and efficacy of socio-political institutions.

The notion of the capacity to transform can be extended to include 'the capacity to restrain aggregate demand'. Here, too, the same general point is valid: that this is likely to be a rising function of the level of development. For reasons presented generally in chapter 3 and illustrated in a number of the studies in the companion volume, governments' ability to use the conventional instruments of fiscal and monetary management will be severely constrained in an economy still largely based on primary production, subject to unpredictable distrubances emanating from the international economy and the weather, with a narrow tax base, only rudimentary government services, an underdeveloped banking system and a public administration of suspect efficiency.

One other factor which may be mentioned is the size and openness of the economy. This will largely determine, for any given magnitude of a BoP deficit, the size of the required adjustment relative to total economic activity. The adjustment problem in a country like India is likely to loom much less large than in a Jamaica or Tanzania, simply because foreign trade impinges much less upon economic life.

What is being suggested here, then, is that the Fund's principle, that the effort of adjustment be broadly equivalent among members, points in the direction of more gradual adjustment programmes among the poorer and small ldc members who have made up the majority of borrowers in recent years. As a modification of this principle, however, there is a good case for discriminating between member governments according to their access to commercial sources of international capital.

The above should not be taken as a plea for 'softness'—rigorous conditionality is still needed to encourage adjustment. Another change we suggest, however, is that the Fund should move away from its emphasis on quantified performance criteria and concentrate instead on achieving a consensus with member governments about the *policy measures* necessary to achieve the desired stabilisation. A shift towards achieving a consensus on policy changes would carry a number of implications. First, it would require substantial give and take among *both* parties, including more flexibility on the part of the Fund than it has sometimes shown in the past. It would also require more time, or a more continuous interaction between the Fund and the government, than has typified past Stand-bys. For this and other reasons set out shortly, we favour more extensive use of resident Fund representatives.

The case for dispensing with quantified performance criteria in a wide range of circumstances has already been set out in chapter 6: the attention biases they create; the large margins of error to which they are subject; the sometimes rather tenuous connection between them and the economic variables they are intended to influence; the barrier they may set up against a rounded judgement of the overall extend of the programme execution. An example of what we suggest is set out in the appendix to this chapter. An essential feature is that in many cases continuing access to Fund credit should depend upon an overall judgement about the extent of programme execution—what are known in Fund parlance as 'review clauses'—rather than upon observance of conventional performance criteria. We recognise that this suggestion may be unwelcome to both the Fund and member governments because of the extra burden placed upon staff members and the loss of objectivity in determining continuing success. But the widespread use of waivers and modifications (see chapter 6) has reduced this objectivity and already throws much judgmental responsibility upon the staff. Given the grave difficulties which performance criteria create, the recommended change would be an improvement in many cases. Of course, if governments preferred conventional performance criteria (or some more flexible variant of these), where the variables in question are not subject to large uncertainties and are tolerably susceptible to government manipulation they could still be used.

Whether or not they are used as performance criteria, governing access to Fund credit, there remains a role for quantified indicators of programme execution so long as the uncertainties are small enough for them to be meaningful as indicators. Subject to this qualification, there is, however, a case for utilising a wider range of economic indicators than has been in the past. It is not typically the case any more that monetary indicators are the only tolerably reliable statistics which are quickly available. Depending on the specific country, reasonably up-to-date and disaggregated data are likely to be available on imports and exports, government revenues and expenditures, domestic prices, inventory levels, industrial and perhaps agricultural production, urban employment and wages, weather conditions, and so on. Monitoring these, probably in relation to a targeted range of values, could provide valuable evidence on progress with the programme and an early warning system when things are going wrong. When a red light is flashed, this could serve as a triggering device for a review mission from Washington to determine whether overall execution of the programme is sufficiently poor for the government to be declared ineligible for continued access to the credit until policy performance is improved.

A final general recommendation concerns the balance between the high and low conditionality resources of the Fund. As shown in chapter 5, this balance shifted markedly away from low conditionality finance during the late-1970s and early-1980s. It this shift desirable? The explanation offered by the Fund runs as follows. Given the nontransitory nature of most deficits experienced in developing countries there is a clear need for adjustment; the Fund is best able to encourage this through the conditions it attaches to its financial support. Left to their own devices developing countries have insufficient political commitment to adjustment so that low conditionality finance would tend to encourage the postponement of necessary changes, leading to a further deterioration in the BoP. This argument sees the causes of payments deficits as largely irrelevant.

Against this it is frequently argued that the causes of deficits have an important bearing on the balance between high and low conditionality. Since a principal cause of the deteriorating payments situation in many developing countries has been externally generated by adverse movements in the terms of trade, the inference is drawn that countries should not be penalised through strict conditionality for problems for which they are not responsible.

Our view is that the way in which this debate has been framed is unhelpful and serves to confuse the crucial issues. While the causes of deficits are relevant, external causation is not a sufficient reason for attaching low conditionality to Fund finance, for a number of reasons. First, while temporary deficits should be financed rather than corrected, in order to do minimum damage to economic and social welfare, non-transitory deficits do require correction. Second, conditionality does have a role to play in encouraging BoP correction but, third, such conditionality should be appropriate to the economic characteristics of the countries concerned, with the causes of deficits being an important determinant of appropriateness.

Key problems here are to distinguish ex ante between temporary and permanent deficits, and to identify the significance of external factors in explaining the deficit. In this connection, the Fund already possesses the low-conditionality CFF, described in chapter 5. However, the relative size of this facility has declined over recent years and there is a good case for making more resources available under it by raising the quota limits on drawings and the percentage of shortfall that may be covered. Furthermore, the logic of the CFF argues in favour of extending its coverage to include all aspects of externally generated short-term adverse movements in the income terms of trade. This implies compesation for import excesses arising from increases in import prices as well as against export shortfalls. While such modifications would assist countries in dealing with temporary payments problems, they would also ensure that where a deficit is persistent, ineligibility for CFF finance would drive the country towards the stricter conditionality facilities, even if the deficit results from external factors. Expansion of low conditionality lending through a modified CFF rather than through the first credit tranche has the advantage that it avoids the 'moral hazard' associated with the sub-market interest charges on some Fund finance. Without the external causation element contained in the CFF, countries might be encouraged to pursue over-expansionary domestic policies which result in access to relatively cheap, and in effect subsidised, resources from the Fund.

Of course, if the nature of the Fund conditionality is inappropriate then judging the 'right' balance between low and high conditionality is very complex. Is it better to have few and weak conditions in circumstances where policy changes are indeed needed, or strictly imposed yet inappropriate conditions? The only clear answer would appear to be that it is better still to have conditions that are appropriate and it is with this proposition that much of this chapter is concerned.

Real economy programs

We turn now from suggestions that relate to all types of BoP deficits to recommendations more specific to programmes designed to deal primarily with problems at the 'structural' end of the spectrum. Hopefully, enough has already been said to establish the rationale for such programmes. This is not a very radical approach for it is essentially the rationale presented by the Fund itself for introducing the EFF and subsequently for the policy adaptations of 1979-80 described in chapter 6. The analysis presented in an internal Fund document in mid-1980 was scarcely less relevant, 2½ years later.[4]

The problems of adjustment in present circumstances are particularly complex. It is clear that the correction of the large payments imbalances cannot be achieved within a short period... Moreover, important structural changes in the oil importing countries will be necessary, if these countries are to achieve a gradual correction without seriously endangering growth prosects. The task of bringing about the necessary adjustment is made more difficult in the present circumstances by the fact that inflationary expectations have become deeply entrenched in most countries. Sustained anti-inflationary corrective actions, taken simultaneously, tend to dampen the growth of world trade and this makes it more difficult for each country to shift more resources into the export sector. In order to maintain a reasonable and durable rate of economic growth, adjustment has to be set within a relatively long time frame and it has to be concerned with structural improvements in the pattern of output and demand.

Publications by IMF staff members have similarly urged the importance of measures to change the structures of demand and supply.

To a large extend then, what we are proposing for the Fund is not new. We are essentially asking it to have the courage of its own analyses and to continue the process of adaptation begun in the later 1970s but seemingly aborted in 1981-82.

The general nature of real economy programmes has already been set out in Part II: a primary emphasis on shifting the distribution of productive resources in favour of tradeable goods and services plus supporting demand management measures. The change from demand management as the primary means of payments adjustment to a supporting role would only be a shift of emphasis but a significant one for the Fund. In the context of a strategy of adjustment with growth, it would be most important to design demand control measures so that they protect saving and investment to the fullest possible extent, leaving the chief burden of reducing absorption relative to income to be borne by consumption. Similarly, to the extent that the programmes continue to incorporate relative or absolute reductions in government spending, it would be essential to include safeguards to prevent the cuts from falling on those public expenditures which could promote the needed changes in the economic structure. This is a more subtle task than simply trying to protect the capital budget *vis-a-vis* the recurrent budget. The captial budget includes military equipment, office building and a wide variety of other items unlikely to make much contribution to payments adjustment, just as the recurrent budget contains items, such as agricultural research and extension, which can be essential to programme success. Some reclassification of the budget would be required for the protection of 'adjustment items' to be feasible but an effort along these lines is likely to be well worthwhile.

Adaptations would similarly be needed in the Fund's traditional approach to credit control. The role of domestic credit in a real economy approach is far more ambiguous than under a monetary approach. Monetarists stress the negative effects of increased credit on the overall BoP. This is likely to occur partly because of the use of credit to finance imports. However, domestic credit is also likely to have a positive effect on investment and thus on the potential pace of structural adjustment. Thus, Keller draws attention to the positive effects of credit on the productive system and suggests that 'at least in the longer run, increased levels of profitable credit will strengthen the current account performance rather than place a burden on the balance of payments' (p. 464). One way in which excessively tight credit restrictions could be an obstacle to supply-side adjustment would be to reduce industrial capacity utilisation, by making it more difficult or costly to finance adequate inventories of inputs and work in progress.

The upshot of these considerations is that more credit is likely to be justified in a structural programme than in a demand-oriented programme and also that more attention will have to be given to credit allocation across the economy, perhaps through the use of selective controls. This is not, however, an invitation to print money; increased credit to finance consumption (broadly defined to include housing and other durables) is particularly to be discouraged.

For reasons given earlier, there is limited scope for going beyond the rather general prescriptions offered above except in the context of a specific country situation. *That programme should be tailor made to fit the specifics of the particular case is a the heart of the changes we are urging.* On the other hand, it is desirable to give a concrete idea of what a real economy programme, incorporating the various suggestions made above, would be like, so that the reader may assess it. We have therefore prepared a specific illustration based upon Kenya as at mid-1982. Since it runs to several pages and is fairly detailed, it is placed as an appendix to this chapter in order not to disrupt the continuity of the present discussion. However, this illustration is an important aspect of our conclusions and readers anxious to obtain a clearer view of the nature and practicability of our recommendations are urged at this point to turn to the appendix. Among its chief features are:

(a) It is set in a cost-minimising, growth-oriented framework and is also designed to be consonant with the government objective of poverty alleviation.

(b) It is a medium-term programme, designed to be executed over five years.

(c) The emphasis is upon a programme arrived at as a consensus, reflecting a genuine government commitment.[5] We place some importance on the role of an IMF resident representative in this context, as also in monitoring the programme.

(d) A substantial number of measures to stimulate the production of exportable and import-substituting goods and services relative to non-tradeables are included, with at least the same status as other provisions of the programme.

(e) Quantified performance criteria are replaced by a broader set of 'review indicators'. Performance under these indicators would not govern eligibility for continued access to the credit, as in the case of existing performance criteria, but—like these criteria—they would trigger a review mission whose job it would be to form a rounded judgement of overall progress with the programme and to make recommendations about continued access on that basis. A review mission could be despatched at the initiative of either the government or the IMF.

(f) There would be an agreed timetable of execution of all, or a large proportion, of the programme elements and explicit provision for the ways in which progress would be monitored.

(g) In addition to lending its own resources, the Fund would initiate actions to attract additional supporting finance from other multilateral, bilateral and, perhaps, commercial sources.

There is no doubt a good deal to argue about in the specifics of our proposals and gaps to be filled in. But one point is unquestionable: they do not offer deficit countries a soft option, a way of obtaining a lot more money without taking tough policy measures. No-one who reads the appendix, especially anyone who knows the Kenyan scene, should think that the programme would be either popular or easy.

It might at this point be objected that the IMF has already conducted an experiment in the EFF which went some way towards what we are suggesting, but that this experiment did not work well, and consequently the EFF is now much less used than was the case a few years ago. The effectiveness of the EFF is considered in chapter 7 (pp. 247-50) so we need do no more here than summarise the conclusions of that examination. These were (a) that in 1978-81 EFFs were more likely to break down than Stand-bys; (b) that by comparison with prior outcomes, EFF programmes produced weaker results for the BoP but the outcome was ambiguous if compared with programme targets; (c) by both types of comparison EFF programmes were notably more successful in protecting real economic growth; (d) neither type of programme made much impression on the inflation rate but, by comparison with programme targets, the EFF result was clearly the better; and (e) that the unpopularity of the EFF within the Fund had a great deal to do with special presentational and cash-flow difficulties resulting from EFF programme breakdowns.

If comparison is made with Stand-by programmes and the most relevant test is against the targets set, then evidence on the relative merits of the two approaches is ambiguous: no clear EFF inferiority (or superiority) emerges. However, as shown in chapter 6, a far greater reluctance by the Executive Board to agree to new EFF credits was part of the conditionality freeze of the second half of 1981. The Reagan Administration and certain European governments were not happy with the Fund's move towards medium-term programmes and towards a more active role in global recycling. There were, as mentioned, internal Fund reasons for not resisting very strongly the political pressures against continued extensive use of the EFF and, in all fairness, it must be said that its supporters were not able to point to a strong performance record.

We would, in any case, dispute whether the EFF represented a definitive test of a real economy approach. As is brought out in chapters 5 and 6 and in the Kenya case study (chapter C$_5$), the 'structural' elements in this facility had a somewhat uncertain status, being essentially superimposed upon conventional demand-management measures, with the key performance criteria remaining the conventional ones of quarterly credit ceilings and the like. Any effective supply-side conditionality contained in EFF agreements was *additional to* the Fund's conventional conditions. It was, in other words, an uneasy compromise and it is argued in chapter 6 that it did not satisfactorily bridge the gap between the Fund's intellectual recognition of the need for a changed approach to adjustment and its traditional practices—a point reinforced by the data in chapter 7 (Table 7.2) suggesting credit ceilings were *more* stringent in EFFs than in Stand-bys. As can be perceived from the appendix to this chapter, what is proposed is a more thorough-going integration of supply-side conditionality, with demand management among a number of essential components of adjustment in the face of structural problems.

Financial and organisational implications of a real economy approach

If much Fund lending were to take the form advocated above it would require more funds. From what sources might such money come? We identify the following five possibilities.

(i) *Increased quotas.* In many ways this is the most straightforward alternative. The ratio of quotas to world imports has fallen dramatically since the 1960s, over a time when the size of payments disequilibria has been increasing. Furthermore, using increased quotas to raise resources would permit the Fund to expand that part of its lending which is at sub-market interest rates. On the other hand, part of the value of increased quotas would be expected to be used for the low-conditionality facilities, and, given that an increase in quotas may be used to replace policies on enlarged access, the proportion of low conditionality finance will rise. It should also be expected that increased quotas would not only increase the Fund's resources but also increase demand for them.

(ii) *Ad hoc borrowing*. Although offering a useful and often expedient way of meeting potential crises of liquidity, this form of borrowing does not seem to offer a satisfactory long-term solution to the shortage of resources because it does not provide a reliable source of finance. For example, the scope for future borrowing from Saudi Arabia hinges crucially on the price of oil and size of the Saudi BoP surplus which, however, is highly sensitive to conditions on the world oil market and OPEC politics. Moreover, this is a rather expensive source of finance.

(iii) *Borrowing from the private sector*. Direct borrowing by the Fund from private captial markets raises a number of questions. Would the Fund on-lend at commercial terms similar to those under which it borrowed or would it attempt to transform the maturity of terms of loans? If it were to on-lend at softer terms than those on which it was borrowing, where would the finance for such subsidisation come from? Would all ldcs benefit form such arrangements or would there be distributional variations, particularly between the more and less creditworthy developing countries?[6]

Any incentive for private banks to lend to the Fund would have to arise from the rate of return offered and their own assessment of the risks involved, which could be influenced by the uses to which the extra resources were put. Since the banks would presumably assess the risks as less than those involved with lending directly to developing countries, they would probably be prepared to accept a lower rate of return. As a means of widening their asset portfolio, lending to the Fund could be attractive to commercial banks since it would enable them to combine high-return, high-risk lending directly to developing countries with lower return, low-risk lending to the IMF. However, it might also induce them to pull out of direct BoP financing, an area in which the Fund has the greater expertise. Furthermore, IMF lending financed by commercial borrowing might be concentrated particularly on the higher-income idcs unless an interest rate subsidy could be devised.[7] It could thus be unpopular with low-income countries. At the same time, it might also be unpopular with middle-income countries who might regard IMF borrowing as crowding out their own direct borrowing, compelling them to turn to the Fund and it conditionality.

(iv) *Gold sales*. This, of course, is not a new idea since the Fund has already used sales of its gold to finance operations of the Trust Fund (chapter 5). The Fund has thus accepted that this constitutes an appropriate use of its gold. The pros and cons of using gold in this way have been thoroughly investigated elsewhere (Brodsky and Sampson, 1980, 1981). What emerges is that there is a strong case on equity grounds for such sales and no legitimate argument against them on efficiency grounds.[8]

The principal problems with gold sales arise, first, from variations in the market price of gold, causing fluctuations in receipts from any given volume of sales; second, from the fact that the major beneficiaries may turn out to be the purchasers of gold, mostly industrial countries, rather than developing countries; third, because it leaves unanswered the question of what happens when all the gold has been sold; and finally from the question of the way in which the finance is to be used once acquired.

The first problem simply makes the exercise of maximising receipts that much more complex, with further complications resulting from the fact that ldcs will have their own time preference rate for resources. It has not, however, prevented the auctioning of gold in the past. The second problem could, in principle, be dealt with by introducing some form of international gold capital gains tax, although it seems highly unlikely that such a tax would prove acceptable. The only practical solution would then be to use IMF gold as collateral for raising private loans, rather than selling it, but in this case the finance made available would not be concessionary. The third problem may be resolved by using only the interest from the investment of receipts from gold sales rather than the full capital value; although this would imply a continuing flow of finance it would, of course, also mean that less finance would be available initially. Finally, the revenue raised through gold sales could be used to help finance the IMF programmes suggested above or it could subsidise Fund credits.

(v) *An SDR link*. Most proposals for an SDR link keep the creation of SDRs separate from the activities of the General Account. In principle, however, the link could be so organised as to provide extra resources for the General Account, and schemes of this nature have been discussed within the Fund.[9] In effect, SDRs would be used to augment other Fund resources. Although the mechanics of this type of link are various, one important implication is that the SDRs thus created would be allocated to borrowing countries on a conditional and quite possibly repayable basis, and would thus lose many of their previously distinctive features. Under this form of link the appropriateness of IMF conditionality would again be a crucial issue.

The various methods of increasing the Fund's resources discussed above are, of course, not mutually exclusive. While all deserve consideration and accepting that there may be technical as well as political difficulties associated with each of them, we would prefer a package that included methods (i), (iv) and (v). Not the least of our reasons for preferring this combination is that it would leave the IMF in a position to provide special financial relief (for example, through interest subsidies and the SDR link) to the poorer ldcs whose poverty and BoP situations make it inappropriate for the standard borrowing terms to be applied.[10]

Our proposals would require an augmentation of the Fund's human, as well as its financial, resources. Indeed, a standard, and entirely justified, response within the Fund to proposals of the type set out earlier is that it simply does not have the expertise. In terms both of numbers and specialisation, the Fund is not staffed in a way that would permit it to get heavily into the type of real-economy programme advocated here; it already leans heavily upon the expertise of the World Bank on occasions when it needs to go beyond its own traditional fiscal and monetary remit.[11] Indeed, and despite its image as a well-heeled organisation, the Fund is run on a personnel shoe-string and there has been no increase in staff commensurate with the enlarged number of country programmes in recent years.

As a reason for not adapting in desired directions, this is important but not insuperable. Much of the required expertise could probably be hired, the Fund is still sufficiently small that there are no overriding arguments of organisational efficiency to prevent expansion and it will hopefully continue to augment its own manpower by borrowing from the World Bank. What is lacking is not so much the human resources but the political will, on the Board of Governors and elsewhere. If the will were there the personnel problems could be overcome, albeit not quickly or easily. In this event, we would strongly favour a far more common use of resident Fund representatives—certainly in all the major borrowing countries and perhaps in all member countries (there were 20 such representatives in member countries as at late-1982). Although it is no panacea and the quality of the representatives would be a crucial factor, we see this as a potentially very valuable way of improving communications and relations between the Fund and governments; of increasing the Fund's knowledge of individual country circumstances and its capacity to take a view of a wider range of economic policies; of monitoring programmes once they are in place; and of providing a far more continuous flow of advice than is possible on the basis of occasional missions of uneven quality and changing composition.

In concluding this section, it should be apparent that the view taken above of the role of the Fund is both positive and cast within its historical terms of reference as being primarily concerned with assisting member governments to overcome BoP imbalances. To the extend that we are critical of IMF practices, it is because we do not think they are currently framed in a manner which is likely to achieve the Fund's stated objectives—and because we believe that in the past the Fund has placed insufficient weight on other economic (not to mention political) objectives of policy as setting constraints upon the design of stabilisation programmes. As we argue later (p. 304), ours is not an attempt to convert the IMF into yet another development aid agency but rather an assertion that in contemporary circumstances it is impossible to draw any sharp distinction between BoP management and the design of development strategies.

Indeed, the changes we have suggested are rather modest. It is worth repeating that essentially our aim is to urge the Fund to bring its practices into line with its own case set out when introducing the EFF in the mid-1970s—a case which has certainly been strengthened by subsequent events in the world economy. Our real economy approach is, in effect, a redesign of the kind of proramme that should—in appropriate cases—be supported by EFF-type credits. Even some of our more radical sounding suggestions, such as the replacement of performance criteria by review indicators, would actually require only modest changes in Fund practices, although no less worthwhile for that. Overall, our approach has been to opt for useful and achievable changes rather than a radical return to square one.

Naturally, ours is only one way of viewing these matters. Some see no case for substantial change; others see the problems as systemic, incapable of solution except through a radical restructuring of post-war institutions. Even those who share our own reformist bent will not necessarily agree with the specifics of our suggestions. There are, as we have discovered during the course of this project, many alternative perceptions of 'the same' issue and we make no claims to a uniquely clear vision. What we have sought to offer is a constructive input into the debate, not a panacea nor a blueprint that has been developed in the finest detail.

IV. IMPLICATIONS FOR DEVELOPING COUNTRIES

If the stress so far has been on changes in IMF policies, this is not because we see these as exclusively responsible for the difficulties to which we address ourselve. The real world never does offer a black and white picture and the country studies in the companion volume not only bring out some of the complexities but point to numerous weaknesses in ldc government policies as well. In short, the case for change within many ldcs is no less strong than the case for change at the IMF.

At the core of the deficiencies we found in ldc policies was a reluctance to come to terms with the harsh realitics of the two oil shocks and the recession in the industrial world; and a reluctance to place sufficient weight upon economic stabilisation as a policy objective. That many of their problems have been wished upon them by convolutions in the world economy over which they has no control is obviously true and we have already argued that this should influence the design of adjustment programmes. On the other hand, external causation does not remove the need for adjustment. And while the worsened external environment has been increasingly a cause of ldcs' payments deficits during the past decade, domestic policy weaknesses have often compounded the difficulties. Undoubtedly the best policy advice is for ldcs to avoid situations in which it becomes necessary to seek IMF assistance and chapters 3 and 4 are devoted to an exploration of the stabilisation potential of domestic policy instruments. Prevention is better than a cure—but easier said than done!

The pressure of events in the early-1980s has left ldc governments in little doubt that shortages of foreign exchange today constitutes a massive obstacle to the fulfilment of the material aspirations of their peoples. Once shortages of foreign exchange are recognised as the binding constraint upon development, it follows as a matter of logic that policies designed to deal with this constraint *are part of the development effort*. Quite apart from loosening the hold of the foreign exchange constraint, successful stabilisation will also reduce uncertainties and risks, which is a key task of planning and is itself likely to have a beneficial effect on economic performance. The task then becomes one of building adjustment into the country's development strategy and planning. It is rather obvious that the description in Part II of the real-economy approach has much to say about the desirable content of ldcs' development strategies, although such strategies will necessarily deal with other problems as well.

One source of difficulty in this context is that planning in developing countries has conventionally been regarded as a once-every-five-years effort to write a medium-term development plan. Quite apart from the numerous other difficulties and disappointments which this has led to, it has the great defect of inflexibility, of being incapable of accommodating the kind of exogenous shocks to which the developing world has been subjected in recent years.[12] If stabilisation policy is to be effectively co-ordinated with other aspects of the development effort—and plans are commonly very weak in this area—planning will have to be much more flexible than it has typically been in the past to permit more successful adaptation to changing economic conditions and to facilitate the co-ordination of short-term fiscal and monetary measures with long-term policies. This is not the place in which to spell out detailed proposals for the machinery of planning, although the appendix on Kenya does include components along these lines. In general, we see a strong case in favour of rolling plans which can be re-written every year in the light of changing circumstances and the provisions of each year's budget. We should also like to draw attention to the suggestion in chapter 3 (p. 62) for what is called there 'structural budget planning'.

Turning to more concrete matters, we would urge ldc governments to accept a number of propositions about their domestic policies to which some have demonstrated resistance in the past.

First—and at the risk of undue repetition—demand management *is* crucially important if adjustment and therefore development are to be achieved. This case has been sufficiently argued already. Suffice it to say here that we are not advocating fine tuning—which, for reasons explored in chapter 3, is impracticable—but rather the achievement of some general control over the level of absorption (particularly consumption) relative to income, including the avoidance of large-scale deficit financing.

Second, we urge the view that relative prices do matter crucially in the allocation of resources and, therefore, in achieving structural adjustment. There has accumulated over the years a large volume of empirical research which gives the lie to any generalised elasticity pessimism, except in the very short term, some of which is reviewed in chapter 4.[13] While 'getting prices right' can only be part of the answer to the adjustment problem, programmes that swim against the tide of perverse price signals are unlikely to be successful.

This view is, of course, particularly directed at 'left-wing' governments, for it is they who are most likely to be sceptical of the market mechanism. Our Jamaican case study provides an illustration, as also do the chapters dealing with Latin America and Indonesia. That there is no intrinsic incompatibility between socialism and the use of market signals as an allocative mechanism is suggested both by the existence of a large literature of venerable pedigree giving a positive role to prices in a socialist economy and by the practices of various socialist governments.

> In Hungary and Yugoslavia, state-owned firms operate in a market system and respond to price signals, with domestic prices being linked to world market prices through the exchange rate, import tariffs, and export subsidies. Of greater relevance to economies of lower levels of development, China also attempts to decentralise the process of decision-making, with increased use made of the market mechanism.

Since the distinctive feature of socialism is its concern to reduce inequalities, left-wing governments tend to cling to systems of price controls and subsidies as means of achieving this objective. But price controls often have perverse effects, for reasons beiefly surveyed in chapter 3, and the major beneficiaries of subsidies are by no means invariably the poorest of the poor. This is particularly true of subsidies to a wide range of parastatal organisations. In a high proportion of cases it is the relative affluent urban population which gains the most; the persistence of subsidies is more a tribute to the political clout of the town-dwellers than to the idealism of th government. Of course, when a subsidy truly does alleviate poverty in an important way it should not be abandoned unless and until other ways have been found of providing equal protection.

It also appears that left-wing governments are the more likely to reject calls for demand and wage restraint, and to neglect the BoP. But we would urge that a disregard of the basic tenets of demand management is bound to undermine attempts to build a socialist society, just as it did in a number of the countries studied in the companion volume. Socialists should ponder seriously the advice of a sympathetic writer on this matter:

> The great importance of correct financial policies during attempts at transition to socialism and the fact that it is precisely socialist governments . . . which need most to follow deliberate and often strict financial policies is very rarely recognised by economists and politicians on the Left . . . [Such policies are needed] so as to avoid too large an expansion of total demand, as this will inevitably lead to scarcities, high inflation and foreign exchange crisis. Very high levels of inflation will not only disrupt market links with the remaining private sector, but even more importantly will make an effective system of planning and control of the rapidly growing State sector very difficult, if not meaningless.

She goes on to stress the importance of proper BoP management and incomes policy. The danger otherwise is that economic disruptions will undermine the political foundations of social reforms. Active policies of economic management should thus be seen as a necessary feature of any transition to socialism and what should be clear is that our approach to adjustment envisages a large and active role for the state, as is amply illustrated in the appendix. In no sense are we advocating a *laissez-faire* solution.

As a particularly important application of our general plea for governments to make positive use of the price mechanism, we would urge an active exchange rate policy, as presented in chapter 4. On this matter we are in general agreement with the IMF but the 'structural' case for this is overwhelming because it is the exchange rate which determines the relative prices of tradeable and non-tradeable goods. Moreover, the evidence surveyed in chapter 4 gives little support to the 'elasticity pessimism' school which argues that production is not responsive to such alterations in price incentives, although there are, of course, particular circumstances in which elasticities are indeed small. There is, no doubt, much force in the argument that what ultimately determines the export prospects of ldcs is the income elasticity of demand for their goods (mainly in industrial countries) but this is not an argument against the use of exchange rates. It is precisely non-traditional exports—which, in general, are likely to have the larger income elasticities of demand—which respond most to exchange rate depreciations. Moreover, for reasons given in chapter 4, we see use of the exchange rate as generally preferable to wholesale exchange controls—which are actually liable to weaken the underlying BoP situation by discriminating against exports—although we acknowledge that ther are crises in which controls are inevitable.

The active use of the exchange rate weapon can also be urged as a more positive (and perhaps more distributionally progressive) alternative to severe demand repression. Far more weight is thrust upon the control of aggregate demand in a country facing a payments crisis if it insists on an unchanged exchange rate. Currency depreciations reduce the need for additional measures of demand restraint (a) because of their own deflationary effects but (b) because they do more to stimulate appropriate supply (production of exports and import substitutes), thus limiting any requirement for absolute reductions in absorption.

But what actually do we mean by 'an active exchange rate policy'? Three points on this. First, conceptually, governments (or at least their economists!) should focus on the 'real' exchange rate (ie. adjusted for differential inflation rates) as the variable to be addressed. The IMF complies estimates of trends in the real exchange rates of member states and these could usefully be made generally available as aids to analysis and prescription. Second, we see no grounds upon which to advocate a single type of policy for all country circumstances. Adjustable peg; crawling peg; 'compensated devaluation',[14] a two or multiple tier system; fiscal simulations of devaluations; even, hypothetically, anti-inflation policies—all these are means by which governments can seek to manipulate real exchange rates. But third and for reasons already mentioned in chapter 4, we believe there is a strong general case for overt (as against simulated) manipulation of a single, uniform rate and that frequent small adjustments—the crawling peg—have considerable advantages over occasional large devaluations, not the least because they help to de-politicise exchange rate decisions.

It should not be thought that we see the maintenance of a 'realistic' real exchange rate as some sort of panacea. Such a policy would not be able to achieve the required changes by itself. For one thing, it is important to recognise the price-raising effects of a currency devaluation and the danger that this will set up sufficiently strong reactions by groups seeking to protect the real value of their incomes as to undermine the incentive/comparative-advantage effects of the depreciation. Thus, there will be a need for supporting demand management and income policies but there will also be a need to operate on a wider range of price incentives, and of supporting institutional and investment policies in the public sector. Thus, the Krueger (1978. p. 274) study found that the longer term growth stimulating effects of a devaluation were not likely to be large and that what was needed was 'a reversal of signals in the entire gamut of policy instruments . . .'. Nashashibi's (1980) valuable study of the Sudanese case similarly stresses the key importance of supply-side measures in support of a devaluation. It must also be recognised that depreciation of a uniform exchange rate may well create additional profits in traditional export industries that are unwanted as incentives for additional production and/or because of their distributional consequences. In such circumstances taxation can be used as a way of eliminating excess profits. The Kenya programme in the appendix provides an illustration of this: any large increase in coffee production would be undesirable because of restrictive export quotas under the international coffee agreement, so a coffee export tax is proposed in conjunction with a general devaluation.

The maintenance of an appropriate real exchange rate is thus advocated not as a panacea but rather in the belief that a seriously overvalued currency is likely to prove an insuperable obstacle to the type of adjustment required.

We are also concerned about the possible adverse consequences of 'financial repression', as discussed in chapter 3. In the context of payments adjustment, there is a general presumption against policies which hold nominal interest rates well below the inflation rate. Interest rate reforms which create positive (or less negative) real interest rates are likely in principle to have a number of advantages. They will tend to encourage domestic saving and inflows (or reduced outflows) of capital from the rest of the world; they will tend to channel investible resources into higher productivity employments; by increasing the demand for money and near-money, they may reduce the necessary degree of credit restraint and its potentially adverse effects on production and employment; they are likely to enhance the effectiveness of the conventional instruments of demand management, particularly by increasing central bank control over the money base.

Caution is necessary, however, for experiences with financial reforms have been far from uniform. Positive effects are noted for Indonesia in chapter C3; South Korea and Taiwan are also commonly cited as success stories. But there have been some negative results too, as exemplified by the experiences of Chile described in chapter C2. More generally, evidence is accumulating that financial reform is less potent than its more enthusiastic advocates sometimes suggest, and this includes an internal IMF finding, based upon its experiences with Stand-by programmes, that higher interest rates do not have a significant effect on saving or the demand for money.

The degree of efficiency of the financial system as a means of mobilising savings and channelling them into productive investment is a key factor, especially in many of the poorer ldcs. It should not, however, be taken for granted that a sufficient array of investment opportunities promising high rates of return will always exist, or be perceived to exist; if it does not, interest rate reform can result in a seriously reduced investment rate. Finally, if interest rate policy is not carefully coordinated with exchange rate policy it can lead to unwanted results via the foreign asset component of the money base, as stressed by Mathieson and in the discussion of Chile in chapter C2: the greater the degree of exchange rate flexibility, the greater the danger of 'overkill' through higher interest rates, with an unwanted inflow of capital tending to appreciate the exchange rate and/or swell the money base. The case against financial repression remains nonetheless, so long as due caution is exercised in the design of policies to eliminate it.

V. OBJECTIONS AND REBUTTALS

The subject matter of this study is highly contentious. Widely opposing views are held about the proper role of the IMF and the design of economic policy in developing countries. In setting out our arguments we tried to deal with potential criticisms, but it may be useful in this seciton to deal more explicitly, if briefly, with some of the objections raised against preliminary statements of our views. In particular, we would like to guard against ill-founded criticisms based upon any misunderstanding of our position.

Objection I

The proposals would fundamentally change the nature of the Fund, turning it into a soft aid agency. This would be inconsistent with the Articles of Agreement, and would involve wasteful duplication with the World Bank.

Rebuttal

A certain proportion of Fund finance is already 'soft' in the sense that it involves a significant grant element, and the Fund has already used the Trust Fund and subsidies to assist low income countries without seeing these activities as contravening its Articles. Using 'soft' as applied to conditionality, it should be repeated that our proposals involve strict conditionality; in some ways stricter than is currently the case. What we are chiefly concerned with is to ensure that the conditionality should become more appropriate. By making the conditions more cost effective the Fund will be in a better position to achieve the objectives set out in the Articles and encourage payments correction. To repeat, the thrust of our suggestions is to urge the IMF to act more upon the rationale it originally presented for introducing the EFF, which is hardly a radical recommendation. It is an important part of our argument, however, that in the context of the need for structural adjustment the distinction between development strategy and BoP policy is largely spurious. As a result, there is bound to be some overlap of the Bank and Fund activities. However, provided their activities are co-ordinated this should be a source of strength not weakness. While accepting this margin of overlap, the micro-cum-project-orientation of the Bank may be demarcated from the more macro-economic orientation of the Fund. With close co-operation, a consistent set of economic policies which assist the realisation of both development and BoP objectives should be attainable. Under our proposals the Fund retains the role of providing BoP assistance linked to a programme of adjustment in circumstances where the deficit is other than temporary. Moreover, it does so within the context of a liberalised, multilateral trading system. This does not constitute any break from its traditional role.

Objection 2

The switch to real economy conditionality is ill-conceived because supply-side programmes are difficult to specify and monitor. Credit ceilings are the only practicable performance criterion and to ignore credit creation will simply mean that the programmes will fail dismally.

Rebuttal

As the World Bank's experience with structural adjustment lending shows, it is not impossible either to specify or monitor supply-oriented programmes. Specification can take the form of detailed policy actions, compliance with which may be conveniently monitored. We have provided in the appendix an example of the sort of programme we have in mind. The remainder of this objection involves a misconception. Our argument is for more flexibility in programme design, not for a uniform switch to supply-side conditionality in all cases. Indeed, we recognise that in some circumstances the traditional form of conditionality is appropriate and there is a continuing role for credit ceilings. Similarly, even in cases where more emphasis should be placed on inducing changes in the real economy we are not arguing that demand management should be abandoned, but rather that it should occupy a supporting role.

Objection 3

Programmes fail not because they are economically inappropriate but because there is a lack of political commitment in developing countries to payments adjustment and in some cases a lack of technical competence to carry through the programme.

Rebuttal

We have tried to deal with this in chapter 7, where we recognise the poor implementation record but show that programme impact is only weakly correlated with implementation. We have stressed the desirability of planned adjustment in circumstances where a deficit is not self-correcting. However, we also argue that developing countries are more likely to agree to execute programmes which are perceived as working on the root causes of the problem and as causing minimum damage to other policy objectives. We see a con-

tinuation of the Fund's technical assistance as a valuable contribution in raising technical competence in this area.

Objection 4

Our proposals would greatly widen the scope of Fund conditionality, breaking down the distinction between macro- and micro-measures and contravening the insistence of the Group of 24 that only a small number of 'objective' performance criteria be included in the conditionality guidelines. As such, our proposals would be unacceptable to ldcs.

Rebuttal

First, it was shown in the discussion of Table 8.1 that, if it ever did, the macro/micro distinction no longer makes much analytical sense,[15] and it is only asking for failure and frustration to lumber an agency with flawed operational ground rules. Second, we have suggested the elimination of performance criteria as such, replacing them with review indicators and overall judgements about programme execution. In other words, we are seeking to replace the tyranny of quantification, constituted by credit ceilings and the like, with something more flexible, which should be welcomed by developing country governments. Third, supply-side and microeconomic conditionality has always been presented as additional to conventional demand management conditions (as in the case of the EFF), whereas we are presenting it within a different framework. Finally, we have stressed the inevitability of adjustment in the face of a non-reversible worsening in the external environment; and that a far larger effort be made in future to design programmes on the basis of consensus. We therefore do not see adjustment programmes as IMF 'interference' imposed upon a reluctant government. Indeed, we believe imposed conditionality has little chance of success.

Objection 5

Our proposals will also be unacceptable to some industrial countries because we are suggesting an enhanced role for a public multi-national agency and, in effect, enlarged flows of concessional finance for ldcs. International monetary policy is based upon national self-interest and it is not in the interests of industrial countries to agree to the proposed changes.

Rebuttal

We would not deny that those overly-enamoured of the virtues of private capital markets might well resist an expanded role for the Fund. Furthermore, they might argue that any further transfer of financial resources to developing countries, or additional international credit creation, will only serve to raise world inflation. However, we argue that much of this concern is ill-founded. First, we have been at pains to show that we are not proposing a 'soft option' for ldc governments and that our case is firmly grounded in the objectives of the Fund as set out in its Articles. The industrial countries presumably saw it in their interests to create the IMF and, by virtue of their continued membership, appear to continue to regard it in that way. If so, our suggestions are constructive since they would assist the Fund to realise its original objectives. Second, in the international financial sector, as in other areas of economic activity, there are significant aspects of market failure for which the Fund may compensate. The turmoil in international capital markets in the latter half of 1982 and subsequent moves by the Reagan Administration and others to strengthen the IMF in the face of those problems have scarcely strengthened the position of those who stress the virtues of unregulated private markets. Third, the inflation argument would appear to us to be quantitatively insignificant, particularly in the context of a world recession.

Undeniably our proposals would require extra financial resources. However, expanding the Fund along the lines we suggest would seem to offer an efficient and equitable means of channeling resources to deficit countries. Given an approach to conditionality which more effectively encourages adjustment, such expansion might be attractive to the industrial and OPEC countries that provide most of the resources. Moreover, the specific suggestions made for raising the additional funds would minimise the budgetary and resource-costs. Indeed, any remaining 'costs' may be more beneficial than burdensome for industrial countries concerned with stagnating output and high unemployment. Finally, even those major powers of the West concerned with a rather narrow conception of national self-interest might hesitate at the possible political consequences of enforcing an involuntary adjustment via a traumatic loss of income upon poor countries with already fragile social systems.

Objection 6

The proposals will so reduce the rigour and viability of Fund programmes as to destroy the catalytic effect they have on commercial lending.

Rebuttal

A number of points may be made. First, as noted in chapter 5, the importance of the catalytic effect is often exaggerated, since the Fund and the banks employ different lending criteria and are often invloved in different countries. Second, the apparently poor record of past Fund programmes has already undermined the confidence of the banks and encouraged them to formulate their own views on the credit-worthiness of potential borrowers. It is more likely that bank confidence would be restored by more effective programmes, which is what our proposals are designed to achieve. The banks have come to realise that the existence of a Stand-by agreement far from ensures a sustained improvement in commercial credit-worthiness. Finally, where the Fund and the banks are simultaneously involved, mainly in certain middle-income ldcs, it is quite possible that an appropriate Fund programme would not be very dissimilar from past programmes, for we agree that where payments problems have been caused chiefly by over-expansionary fiscal and monetary policies, then conventional demand restraint is an essential component of any adequate policy response. Overall, we see the need to strengthen the catalytic effect as one of the strongest arguments for changes that would increase the effectiveness of IMF programmes.

Objection 7

The proposals attempt to shore up the old international economic order; they are conservative, pro-capitalist, anti-socialist and anti-egalitarian; they would perpetuate the dependence of the periphery on the core.

Rebuttal

Following on from objection 5, if our rather modest modifications were to seem unacceptable to industrial countries how much more unacceptable would more radical changes be? The fact that our proposals involve only incremental changes would seem to have the advantage that they may have some chance of being accepted. But we also believe that these changes could yield major benefits for developing countries.

The necessity for payments adjustment unfortunately observes no ideological boundaries. We have already suggested that left-wing governments which neglect economic management are undermining their own political objectives and that our proposals are in no way inconsistent with socialism. We would also argue that, depending on the specifics of a country's situation, the real-economy approach to adjustment is congruent with efforts to alleviate poverty; for example through the expansion of smallholder agriculture and small-scale industry, and the imaginative use of progressive taxation. The appendix illustration on Kenya is explicitly set within a poverty-alleviating framework.

Similarly, our suggestions should not be regarded as inconsistent with proposals for strengthened south-south co-operation. Strengthened southern arrangements and institutions could be useful complements to existing multi-lateral arrangements but they do not seem to us to constitute adequate replacements.[16] Exclusive reliance on southern institutions would in our view leave the majority of developing countries worse off. Furthermore, the advocacy of such arrangements, fuelled by frustration at the slow progress of north-south negotiations, is based on the doubtful proposition that it would be easier to get agreement amongst developing countries.

Finally, we would emphasise the negativism of the hard-line 'dependency' school. To the extent that it offers any policy advice at all, it is for disengagement from capitalist trading relationships. We cannot believe that such advice is helpful. It seems to amount to a suggestion that, having lost some of the gains from trade through adverse increases in import prices, developing countries may as well give up all the other gains, through a policy of near-autarky and through reliance on trade with socialist countries — who have not proved particularly generous trading partners in the past.

V. THE PATH TO REFORM

But if there is to be reform, how might it be achieved? Some of the suggestions made earlier could be implemented administratively by the IMF, just as changes in ldc policies could be undertaken unilaterally. But the scope for effective unilateral action is limited. The Fund management is kept on a tight rein by the Executive Board and, more remotely, by the Board of Governors and the Interim Committee. Any adequate modification in Fund conditionality would have to be sanctioned politically at those levels — on bodies, therefore, in which the preponderant voice is still that of the industrial countries' Group of 10.[17] Similarly, the ability of ldc governments to design adequate policy responses to the payments crises which many of them face cannot be considered independently of international arrangements made to support their efforts.

Where the IMF is concerned especially, any major changes will *perforce* be an outcome of international diplomacy and this places the issue of IMF policies towards ldcs firmly within the context of the north-south 'debate'. As such, it raises major questions of differences in the objectives and perceived interests of different country groups. It has been argued elsewhere (Killick and Sutton, 1982, pp. 48-54) that such differences are perhaps the most fundamental obstacle to reform in this area. The task of international diplomacy is thus to change these perceptions and reconcile remaining differences on the basis that it is in no one's interest to continue with policies that are manifestly not working well in an area where there is an acknowledged international need. It is particularly important to reduce the uncertainties surrounding the future role of the IMF. There have been two contradictory trends in the post-war period. First, there has been a trend towards greatly increased interdependence between nations, with international trade growing much faster than total output and with vastly increased movements of capital. But this has not been matched by a parallel development of institutions for translating this greater interdependence into a closer co-ordination of national economic policies. It is the IMF, above all other agencies, which is equipped to perform that task but it has not been given the authority nor resources with which to carry it out successfully. Indeed, we noted on page 132 how the real value of its resources has been allowed to shrink drastically during the past three decades; and in the early 1980s the American government was not alone in viewing supranational agencies in an unfavorable light.

In such an environment, how might ldcs best go about the task of securing needed reforms? We have already indicated that there is not much mileage in the fashionable stress on strengthening south-south co-operation; it can help, of course, but probably not very much. We similarly see limited scope for achieving reforms through increased voting strength of ldcs within the councils of the IMF, as is sometimes urged. This poses a number of difficulties but the overriding one is that the industrial (plus the surplus OPEC) countries are the primary net providers of the Fund's financial resources and there is no way in which they will allow their money to be used in pursuit of policies with which they seriously disagree. If by some means the ldcs were able to force through a reform despite their opposition, the end result would almost certainly be a withdrawal of resources from the Fund, perhaps its actual demise, leaving a situation in the end even worse than that at the beginning. Moreover, it is important not to be misled by the use of convenient shorthand expressions such as 'ldcs' and 'the Third World', into thinking that this large and exceedingly diverse number of developing countries have similar or consistent interests.[18] In this area of international monetary reform, as on many other subjects, there are major differences within the 'ldc' group which both complicate the process of reform and strengthen the case for doing so on the basis of an international consensus.

Whatever the difficulties and frustrations, and however unpromising the present state of north-south relations, there is in the end no alternative to patient negotiation. To this rather obvious truth we would add a corollary: that the tactics of confrontation apparently favoured by some are more likely to be a hindrance than a help. The stirring rhetoric of IMF-bashing may go down well at home and sound impressive at international gatherings, but it is an obstacle to understanding and to the persuasion of those who must be convinced. We hope this study will at least help to improve understanding and the prospects for reform.

APPENDIX: AN ILLUSTRATIVE APPLICATION OF THE REAL-ECONOMY APPROACH TO KENYA

By 1982 Kenya was facing a critically difficult BoP situation despite extensive import controls, considerable external borrowing and past assistance from IMF. The general nature of the payments problem, as well as the recent history of the government's relations with the Fund, is presented in some detail in chapter C5. However, this appendix is intended mainly as a hypothetical illustration of how the 'real economy' approach advocated in this chapter might be applied in a specific country situation and does not presuppose any detailed background knowledge of the Kenyan case. It is based on the situation as of mid-1982. The following falls into two parts. The first summarises the modalities by which an adjustment programme might be agreed between the government and the Fund, and subsequently executed. The second part sets out the programme itself — the diagnosis on which it is based; the objectives which it is to further; and the policies to be pursued.

A. Modalities

1. For the purposes of this illustration, it is assumed that by mid-1982 the Government of Kenya (hereafter GoK) decided that it required IMF assistance (a conventional Stand-by having just lapsed because of failures to comply with credit ceilings). It is important in our approach that the initiative should come from the Government, but it is consistent with this that it might be prompted by discussions with a regular consultation mission from Washington. The initial approach would probably be informal. It would provide an initial sketch of the problem, objectives and policy measures, and of the scale of assistance sought.

2. If the initial sketch is thought to provide a basis for discussion and elaboration, the Fund would assign a resident representative (or would preferably already have one in situ) based in Nairobi in order to assist in the preparation of a detailed programme and to arrive at a consensus with GoK. The GoK and IMF representative would be able to draw upon such technical assistance, from the Fund and World Bank staffs and other sources, as is necessary for completion of the programme.

3. The GoK, in consultation with the Fund representative, would prepare a draft detailed programme (equivalent to a draft Letter of Intent under existing practices, except that it would be drafted by the Government, not by Fund staff). This would form the basis for detailed discussions with a full-scale Fund mission (probably supplemented by personnel from the Bank and/or outside consultants).

4. Through iteration, the draft would be brought to a mutually acceptable state and at the same time detailed estimates prepared of the country's financing needs. The emphasis throughout would be on achieving a consensus, on the grounds that an imposed programme is unlikely to be executed satisfactorily. The agreed programme, with implementation envisaged over a medium-term period, say five years, would include a detailed schedule for implementation. It would also identify a limited number of 'review indicators' (marked with a star in the detailed programme below).

5. On the basis of the agreed programme, the IMF would commit itself to a five-year credit payable in five annual instalments (or perhaps ten six-monthly instalments) and repayable over ten years. There would be a form of agreement between the two parties containing the Fund's necessary legal formulations. It is preferable that these should be separate from the programme, rather than incorporated in it as is the case with the present Letters of Intent, because our stress is upon the programme being a *Government* document and one to which it is fully committed. It is envisaged that the Fund's representative would remain in Nairobi to monitor progress and advise the GoK. The Fund would also take an active part in mobilising additional multilateral, bilateral and commercial resources in support of the programme, eg. through the Consultative Group on aid to Kenya.

6. The role of the performance criteria in conventional agreements would be taken over by the 'review indicators'. When, in the opinion of *either* party, these are being implemented in a seriously unsatisfactory manner a review mission would be despatched from Washington. The task of this mission would be to reach an overall judgment of the extent to which the programme is being executed based particularly on the record of review indicators and in the light of such unforeseen factors as may have come into play. On the basis of this overall assessment it would recommend whether or not the government should remain eligible to draw upon future instalments of the credit. In either event, it would seek to work out with the GoK ways of improving programme execution and of modifying it in the light of changing circumstances. The Government would remain ineligible for this credit or any other higher-conditionality credit until such time as it is judged that programme execution has sufficiently improved or agreement can be reached on a new programme. Note, however, that it is the programme review which provides the test of eligibility, rather than the failure of some specific performance criterion.

B. The Programme

The following sets out in a highly condensed form the hypothetical outlines of an adjustment programme, in support of which Fund assistance is sought. It is in the form of a summary submission by the GoK to the IMF.

Diagnosis of the Problem[19]

1. The BoP problem has reached unviable proportions and has become the binding constraint on the realisation of the Government's objectives of alleviating poverty and main-

taining the expansion of the economy. It is for this reason that the growth of the economy has been relatively static since the emergence of a payments problem in the mid-1970s.

2. Most of the payments deterioration during 1972-81 can be attributed to the rising import bill. In turn, all this was due to rising import prices because there was a sharp fall in the volume of imports relative to total economic activity. With the exception of 1976-77, the trend in the terms of trade during the past decade has been sharply adverse. A 24-fold increase in the price of oil, all of which must be imported, was a principal cause of this but non-oil import price trends were also strongly adverse over most of the period.

3. The BoP has, however, been undermined by a relatively poor export performance, particularly outside the traditional staples of coffee and tea. The break-up of the former East African Community and the movement of relative prices, in combination with the pre-1981 policy of maintaining a constant nominal exchange rate, acted as a disincentive for exports. Export performance and import demand have also been adversely influenced by the relative stagnation of agriculture and the inefficiencies of the manufacturing sector.

4. Poor demand management policies have also contributed to the difficulties, particularly the mis-handling of the 1976-77 coffee and tea boom. Deficit financing by the GoK, reflecting an increasingly stringent fiscal situation, has also been an occasional contributory factor, particularly in 1981-82.

5. Inflows of capital have been crucial in protecting the country's international reserves and its import capacity from the full impact of the payments deterioration. However, an increasing proportion of the inflows has been from commercial sources at high interest rates, and debt servicing costs absorb a growing share of total foreign exchange availabilities.

6. The period of difficulties with the BoP has coincided with an inflation rate well above the historically normal level. This is only partly attributable to the influence of rising import prices and structural factors; here too demand pressures have played a part.

7. On the basis of the above, it is clear (a) that a large part of the country's payments problems are of external origin; (b) that much of the deterioration in the terms of trade is unlikely to be reversed and that the present unviable payments difficulties are likely to persist; (c) that it is therefore essential to strengthen the BoP; (d) that this will necessitate structural changes in the economy to stimulate exports and diminish dependence on imports, but (e) that those structural changes will need to be supported by policies to restrain aggregate demand and reduce absorption relative to income.

Statement of Objectives

In the economic sphere, the GoK's overriding objective remains the development of the economy. However, since shortages of foreign exchange are the binding constraint on that development, the improvement of the BoP is the single most important immediate step towards accelerated development. It is essential, however, that BoP policies be designed in such a way as to minimise any possible adverse effects on the growth of the economy, the alleviation of poverty and other components of the development objective. The objective of the programme may thus be summarised as *least-cost adjustment*.

Since Independence in 1963 the GoK has favoured a mixed economy, open on a generally liberal basis to trade with the rest of the world. The GoK intends to maintain this mixed and open economy stance druing the period of the programme.

As regards BoP indicators, the programme is particularly geared to strengthening the current account. This needs to be qualified in a number of ways, however. First, it is regarded as essential to the success of the programme to maintain a reasonable volume of essential imports of intermediate and capital goods. It is especially for this reason that it is important to mobilise as much financial support as possible. Second, due regard must be paid to the desirability of effecting some early reduction in the amount of external commercial debt, so as to reduce debt servicing claims on scarce foreign exchange. It is also important to rebuild international reserves, which by the end of 1981 had fallen to less than two months-worth of imports on a gross basis and were actually negative when calculated net of liabilities to the IMF. It will thus be important to monitor a variety of payments indicators and it is not possible to reduce the payments objective to any single target.

An approximate idea of the size of the adjustment problem can be given, however. The current account deficit in 1981 was equivalent to 13% of GDP. In the past two years sustainable inflows of concessional finance have been equal to about 4% of GDP. Taking into account the desirability of rebuilding the country's international reserves and, perhaps, of retiring some commercial debt, it appears that the size of the needed adjustment might be put as equivalent to about 10% of GDP. This was equal to 25% of imports and 34% of exports in 1981, and was about four times the size of Kenya's quota in the IMF. The required changes are therefore large in relation to total economic activity and can only reasonably be expected to be achieved over a period of years.

The policies to be pursued in this programme are summarised below, under various headings.[20] Since this is only a summary statement, no attempt is made to offer a detailed justification of each measure but brief explanations are provided for items which are not self-explanatory. It is envisaged that the policies would be spelled out in more detail in an actual creidt request and that each item would be accompanied by a date or time-table for its proposed execution. While we have not identified any pre-conditions, there is no reason in principle why they should not be included.

Fiscal Measures

*— Increased recurrent government expenditures will only be sanctioned to the extent that they are at least covered by expected increases in current revenues, ie. no reduction in the size of the current surplus.

— Government expenditure items will be reclassified according to whether they are to be given high, average or low 'adjustment priority'. This classification will cut across the conventional recurrent/capital classification. The objective will be to protect high priority items and capital formation generally, and that the burden of any cuts should fall on low priority items.

— Educational expenditure, which has been growing very rapidly and absorbs a high proportion of total revenues, will not be allowed to exceed 30% of the total recurrent budget; the provision of other social services will be held constant on a per capita basis (nb. population is growing at nearly 4% p.a.) In the absence of any unforeseen security threat, the real value of military spending will be reduced by 10% during the programme period.

— There will be closer Treasury scrutiny of draft budget estimates. Any ministry overspending will have the amount of its over-expenditure subtracted from its budgetary allocation in the following year.

— The following new taxes will be introduced:
  On land values (to encourage better utilisation as well as raise revenues in a progressive matter).
  On real estate transaction.
  A tariff surcharge on imported intermediate inputs to reduce existing tax biases against domestic production of such goods.
  Extension of the 15% sales tax to all personal service activities.
  On coffee exports (to discourage production in excess of the country's export quota under the international coffee agreement and to encourage diversification into other agricultural crops).

— The corporation tax will be reformed so as to reduce the acute seasonality of the present tax and facilitate fiscal planning.

— All budget estimates to be adjusted for the systematic biases that have marked most estimates in previous years and have resulted in over-optimistic budgeting.

— The GoK to introduce new, or utilise existing, powers for discretionary tax changes between budgets (eg. by varying the sales tax and import duty surcharge).

*— Expansion of public sector borrowing from the banking system not to exceed xxx m Kenya pounds. However, this amount is based upon certain assumptions about the behaviour of other fiscal items, including receipts of grants and loans from abroad, and will be varied (according to a procedure to be agreed with the Fund) in the light of unexpected departures from assumed values. If, on an annualised basis, actual government borrowing exceeds the adjusted ceiling, the discretionary tax powers mentioned in the previous item will be used to restore borrowing to within the agreed limit.

Monetary Measures

*— The GoK will continue its policy of gradually rising interest rates towards positive real levels, but will carefully monitor the effects of this on saving, investment and the financial system.

— The GoK will extend the full range of central bank control to non-bank financial institutions and will define domestic credit to include lending by these bodies.

*— The increase in the value of domestic credit to the private sector will be held to yyy m Kenya pounds, subject to an adjustment provision similar to that set out for credit to the public sector.

— The statutory reserve ratios of the banks and other financial institutions will be varied so as to keep credit within the adjusted value mentioned in the previous paragraph.

— Credit to the private sector will also be based on sectoral allocations, with top priority going to credit to sectors producing tradeables and a lower priority for credit to finance consumption, other imports and sectors producing non-tradeables.

Other Macroeconomic and General Measures

*— The GoK will strengthen its capacity for short-term economic management by setting up a system of economic indicators and a machinery by which the policy implications of the trends revealed can be considered at the official and political levels on a continuous basis.

— The GoK will institute a system of 'rolling' development plans in order to increase flexibility and assist the co-ordination of medium-term planning with short-term economic management.

*— The GoK will undertake an initial currency devaluation and will then pursue a policy of frequent small adjustments in order to sustain the real effective exchange rate established by the devaluation. (nb. since there were two devaluations in 1981, with a cumulative size of 24%, it is not expected that the devaluation mentioned here will need to be large — say 10-15%).

— The GoK will continue with its policy of liberalising and reducing the coverage of price controls and also intends to liberalise export licensing.

*Items marked with an asterisk are identified as review indicators, as already explained.

— Recognising the detrimental long-term effects of rapid population growth on saving, productive investment and agricultural performance, the government will raise the priority of its population policies and will formulate proposals for making family planning services widely available in the rural areas.
— The GoK will pursue a policy of wage restraint with respect to public sector employment and wage employment in the organised private sector. However, in recognition of the decline in real wages over the past decade, the policy will be one of limiting the size of wage increases to the rate of increase in the Nairobi consumer price index. However, this falls short of full indexation and contains an anti-inflation provision to the extent that labour productivity increases.
— The GoK will seek to improve the rate of modern-sector capacity utilisation. This is partly expected to result from measures listed above to safeguard against excessive demand deflation and to improve the efficiency of resource allocation, including the proposed land tax. In addition, the stress placed upon mobilising outside assistance in support of this programme is intended to ensure adequate supplies of imported inputs for the productive sectors.
— The GoK will continue with its subsidy scheme for non-traditional exports and with its efforts to improve the administration of this. It will also set in place the proposed export insurance and financing scheme as a matter of urgency.

Sectoral Measures

— The government's agricultural pricing policies will be based upon the import-parity principle, except for milk, for which a seasonal pricing formula will be announced. In conjunction with the exchange rate policy announced above and the proposed changes in tariffs and industrial protection, application of the import-parity principle should give improved agricultural incentives and help reverse the apparent long-term trend towards a deterioration in the domestic terms of trade of the agricultural sector.
— A Land Commission will be created to review the existing land-use situation and to advise the GoK on the formulation of a comprehensive land policy.
*— The GoK will prepare a detailed schedule for the execution of the other agricultural policies set out in its 1981 Sessional Paper on food policy. A special unit will be created in the Office of the President to monitor and chase implementation of these policies.
*— The GoK will continue with its present policy of standardising the system of industrial protection and of reducing the more extreme levels of protection which currently exist for some industries. Here too a detailed schedule of implementation will be agreed.

— The GoK will use its own investment programme to encourage industrialisation chiefly through the provision of supporting infrastructure. Its general policy will be to limit its own further direct participation in industrial production. All proposals for new investment by public enterprises and parastatals, and for joint ventures with private concerns, will be subject to the most careful scrutiny by the Treasury.
— The GoK will foster the development of informal industrial activities through the provision of building sites, pre-investment advice, concessionary loan facilities, extension services, marketing facilities, preferential treatment in GoK purchase programmes, and the liberalisation of licensing and other regulations which have the effects of discriminating against the informal sector and of inviting harassment.
— The GoK will formulate a comprehensive policy for the development pf non-oil energy sources based on domestic resources. This is in process of preparation and will form part of this programme when it has been approved.
— The GoK will pursue petroleum tax policies intended to ensure that the full proportionate cost of rising world prices is passed on to final users. This has been the general policy in the past but the gap betwen imported and final prices has narrowed a little and will be restored.

NOTES

1. Discussions of the SAL programme are offered by members of the World Bank staff in Landell Mills, 1981; Stern, 1982; and Wright, 1980.

2. See Killick and Sutton, 1982, pp. 53-4, for a fuller statement of the 'asymmetry' argument; also Tew, 1982.

3. Johnson and Reichmann, 1978, p.13, draw a clear connection between the distributional effects of Fund programmes and the extent of implementation.

4. From an unpublished Fund document on its policies for adjustment in 1980 conditions.

5. Interestingly, there are similarities to our approach to this matter in a 1982 paper by the European Commission (1982) setting out its view of the desirable relationship between the EEC and Third World countries, which proposes 'inverted conditionality' where EEC assistance is aimed at supporting policies freely chosen by governments but, no doubt, partly as an outcome of a dialogue with representatives of the Commission.

6. For a more thorough attempt to answer these questions, see Bird, 1981b.

7. Private banks' assessment of the creditworthiness of the Fund would also depend on their estimation of the Fund's usable resources, its holdings of gold, SDRs and currencies, and the degree of international support for its activities. Certain technical problems would be associated with direct borrowing by the Fund. For instance, its holdings of particular currencies, which could be affected by borrowing, in turn affects countries' access to Fund finance (Morgan Guaranty Trust, 1980)

8. That gold sales are not neutral with respect to resources flows is insufficient argument when it is recalled that the existing system is not distributionally neutral.

9. For more details of these schemes see Bird, 1982a.

10. For a fuller discussion of the use of the subsidies in this context and some attempt at estimation see Bird, 1982b. For a discussion of why the SDR link may still be relevant to low income countries in particular and an estimation of the benefits that may in certain cases be derived, see Bird, 1981d.

11. Stern, 1982, particularly emphasises the differing orientations of the staffs of the Bank and the Fund.

12. See Killick, 1976 and 1981b, chapter 3 for a fuller statement of this argument and, in the latter reference, for a discussion of ways of overcoming this defect.

13. See Tolley et al, 1982, and sources cited there on the price responsiveness of farmers.

14. See Schydlowsky, 1982, for a discussion of this and related notions which is all the more interesting for being addressed to the need for structural adjustment.

15. See Guitian, 1982, pp. 96-7, for a statement of the practical difficulties created by this distinction.

16. For a discussion of south-south co-operation in the monetary sphere see Stewart et al, 1982.

17. See Tew, 1982, for a statement of this view.

18. See Bird, 1982a, for an exploration of differing ldc interests in international monetary reform.

19. The following paragraphs are largely based on a special survey of balance of payments trends in Kenya since 1972 in the Central Bureau of Statistics, *Economic Survey, 1982,* chapter 3. See also chapter C5 of the companion volume.

20. A high proportion of the policies listed below are taken from official policy statements in the following sources. Use has also been made of a paper submitted to the GoK by Killick on the strategy of the fifth development plan.
Development Plan, 1979-1983, Part I (1979)
Sessional Paper No. 4 of 1980 on Economic Prospects and Policies.
Sessional Paper No. 4 of 1981 on National Food Policy.

Section VI: Loan Renegotiation
Chapter 17: Loan Renegotiation

17A. Coordination of Paris and London Club Reschedulings
Karen Hudes

I. INTRODUCTION

This Article discusses the coordination of debt reschedulings between governments of developing countries and their creditors in the private and public sectors. Private sector creditors, such as banks and other commercial lending institutions, generally reschedule their credits to developing country governments in an informal forum commonly referred to as the "London Club." Public sector creditors, such as official government agencies,[1] generally reschedule with developing country governments on an ad hoc basis in the "Paris Club."

Debt reschedulings require the contribution of various governments and financial institutions. The governments of developed and developing countries are involved as well as central banks, commercial banks, and other lending institutions. However, the citizens who incur the costs of the necessary economic adjustments upon which the sovereign debt reschedulings are predicated make the biggest contribution to debt reschedulings.[2]

All of the parties involved in debt reschedulings must work in a cooperative effort, because if any participant fails to contribute to the effort, others will be forced to compensate. If a debt rescheduling is unsuccessful, that is, if a country must reschedule previously rescheduled debt, then it will be increasingly difficult for that country to become bankable again.

This Article will examine the procedures used in the Paris Club and the London Club to ensure that timely, orderly, and equitable debt relief is provided on a comparable basis by both public and private creditors to countries experiencing difficulty in paying their debt. The Paris Club and London Club have operated in tandem to meet the challenge of adjusting the immediate debt servicing burdens of developing countries. However, if the debt situation deteriorates over the longer term,[3] additional financial backing may be needed to support the adjustment efforts of developing countries.

II. THE PARIS CLUB

In countries experiencing payment difficulties, government and private debt to official creditors is rescheduled in the Paris Club.[4] The Paris Club was organized in 1956 when a small group of European governments invited Argentina to meet with their senior representatives in Paris to consolidate approximately $350 million of bilateral trade debts and renegotiate certain insured supplier credits. Occasionally, official creditors will reschedule debt outside the framework of the Paris Club in such multilateral form as aid consortia, the Organization for Economic Cooperation and Development (hereinafter OECD), and special creditor groups.[5]

The Paris Club has no fixed membership; participation is limited to the major creditors of countries whose request for rescheduling is examined. Normally, there are from five to twenty creditor countries present at a Paris Club rescheduling. Representatives of the OECD, the European Economic Community, and the United Nations Committee on Trade and Development (hereinafter UNCTAD) are also invited to attend the Paris Club. In 1978, creditor countries agreed to greater participation by the Secretary-General of UNCTAD or his representative, in response to developing countries' request for reform of the Paris Club.[6]

The Paris Club is not an official institution; it has no offices and no secretariat. The creditor countries have deliberately retained the ad hoc nature of the Paris Club in order to reinforce the policy that debt reschedulings are exceptions to the normal sanctity of contracts. French Finance Ministry officials staff the negotiations. A senior member of the French Finance Minsitry serves as the Paris Club chairman.[7]

To qualify for debt relief in the Paris Club, debtor countries must satisfy two conditions. First, they must be in a situation of "imminent default." Second, they must have negotiated a program with the International Monetary Fund (hereinafter IMF) for drawings in the upper credit tranches. Official creditors have always insisted that an IMF program be in place before Commencing Paris Club negotiations. Nicaragua has been the only exception.[8]

Negotiations in the Paris Club are generally completed within thirty-six hours. The terms are embodied in an "Agreed Minute" which is signed ad referendum by the heads of delegations.[9] These terms are then incorporated into separate bilateral agreements between the debtor country and the creditor countries to give the rescheduling the force of law. In addition, several countries including the United States require an implementing agreement between the debtor country and individual credit agencies. The interest rates charged in Paris Club reschedulings are determined bilaterally between the official creditors and the debtor country. In many cases, official creditors reschedule at below-market interest rates.

The debt to be rescheduled may be limited to sovereign debt to creditor governments. On the other hand, some reschedulings may include private debt as well.[10] Paris Club reschedulings have increased sharply in recent years. Between 1956 and 1978, eight countries were granted debt relief totaling $5 billion.[11] Between 1978 and 1983, twenty-three countries rescheduled $22 billion in debt.[12]

The amount of debt relief granted can be measured in relation to a number of indicators; export earnings, current account deficits, external debt service payments, and stock of outstanding debt.[13] A survey of 37 Paris Club reschedulings between 1975 and 1983 involving 19 debtor countries demonstrated the extensive amount of relief granted.[14] The official creditors' cost of granting debt relief is generally less than 10% of the amount of debt rescheduled.[15]

A. The Role of the Export-Import Bank

The Export-Import Bank of the United States (hereinafter Eximbank) is the export credit agency of the U.S. Government.[16] Eximbank finances U.S. exports by making loans, supplying export credit insurance, and providing guarantees to buyers of U.S. goods and services. Although a majority of Eximbank's business is with sovereign borrowers, Eximbank also extends financing to private borrowers, typically through supplier credit programs. Consequently, private borrowers in developing countries may become involved in sovereign debt rescheduling when their government does not provide them with foreign currency to service their debt.[17]

Eximbank's total loan portfolio exceeds $38 billion and involves 133 countries. As a result, Eximbank is involved in almost all of the debt reschedulings. Debt owed to Eximbank is rescheduled in the Paris Club, together with the debt owed to other U.S. Government agencies such as the Agency for International Development, the Commodity Credit Corporation and the Defense Security Assistance Agency. As a creditor, Eximbank participates in the U.S. Government's Paris Club reschedulings in various capacities: it negotiates the terms of the sovereign debt rescheduling; it prepares and executes the implementing agreement with the developing country government;[18] it serves as a member of the National Advisory Council; and it extends new coverage to countries rescheduling in the Paris Club.

B. U.S. Policy Parameters

The National Advisory Council on International Monetary and Financial Policies sets out the policy parameters within which the U.S. Government will negotiate sovereign debt reschedulings.[19] The National Advisory Council is an interagency group composed of the following members: the Secretary of the Treasury, who chairs the Council, the Assistant to the President for Economic Affairs, the Secretary of Commerce, the Chairman of the Board of Governors of the Federal Reserve System, the Director of the International Development Cooperative Agency, and the President of the Eximbank.[20]

The U.S. Government has worked out a division of labor regarding the Paris Club negotiations. The Treasury Department has the lead in formulating and preparing the government position. It also prepares an economic analysis demonstrating that the preconditions for debt relief exist—imminent default and an economic program approved by the IMF.[21] The Treasury Department then circulates this analysis as the negotiating position and obtains interagency clearances through the National Advisory Council. The State Department heads the actual negotiations in Paris. The State Department also drafts the bilateral agreement enacting the Paris Club Agreed Minute. The Minute is then sent to Congress for a thirty day notification period.[22] The State Department and the Treasury Department share the stand in congressional hearings and informal consultations on debt relief.

The debt relief is granted in the Paris Club without going through the normal appropriations process of the U.S. Congress. Obviously, it would be extremely difficult to negotiate viable multilateral reschedulings if U.S. contributions were predetermined. Therefore, neither House of Congress requires that the level of debt relief be authorized in advance in order to provide the government agencies flexibility in debt rescheduling. This arrangement is conditioned upon the requirement that the Secretary of State keep the Foreign Relations and Appropriations Committees in both Houses informed of the status of all debt relief negotiations.

III. THE LONDON CLUB

Debt owed to commercial creditors by governments and private entities in countries experiencing payment difficulties is restructured[23] in the London Club. Before agreeing to reschedule in the London Club, commercial banks frequently require that these sovereign debtors have an IMF arrangement with drawings in the upper tranches and that the sovereign debtors have a Paris Club rescheduling in place or have agreed to a Paris Club rescheduling.

Restructuring debt in the London Club is difficult and time-consuming because many creditor banks must reach agreement.[24] Although no formal framework exists for commercial debt negotiations, a common procedure has evolved. A coordinating or steering committee of bankers is established to act as an advisory and liaison group to all bank creditors.[25]

The early practice in London Club reschedulings required all parties to sign a single complex agreement. In several Latin American reschedulings, however, commercial banks have adopted a procedure similar to that of the Paris Club.[26] Banks agree in principle to the terms of the reschedulings and develop a model restructuring agreement. Subsequently, each individual bank creditor enters into a separate agreement with the government based upon the model.

Since 1980, the number of countries that have approached commercial banks for formal debt restructuring has increased sharply, particularly in late 1982 and early 1983. The amount of commercial debt restructured rose from an annual average of approximately $1.5 billion from 1978 to 1981 to approximately $5 billion in 1982, and to nearly $60 billion by early October 1983.[27]

Commercial banks generally do not reschedule interest because such rescheduling has negative tax, income, and regulatory implications. In some rescheduling agreements, banks have required a commitment from the debtor countries to become current by a specified date on interest in arrears and to remain current on all future interest payments. In refinancings, banks may lend to creditors the funds to pay interest on existing loans. Interest paid in such a new receivable may be shown as income in banks' financial statements as long as the receivable remains collectible.[28]

From a banker's perspective, the amounts restructured between 1978 and 1983 are significant, ranging from 15% to 60% of the debt outstanding.[29] From the perspective of the debtor countries, these amounts are also significant. The amount of debt relief granted by commercial banks during this period has ranged from 4% to 8% of the respective country's gross national product.[30] Moreover, during 1983, the debt relief granted in the eight largest bank debt restructuring cases enabled the debtor countries' debt service ratio to decline from over 80% to less than 50%.[31] Typically, the interest rates on these restructurings ranged from 1.75% to 2.25% above the London InterBank Offered Rate (hereinafter LIBOR) or U.S. prime rate, while fees amounted to 1% to 1.5% of the amounts restructured.[32]

IV. COMPARABLE TREATMENT

Government creditors maintain that commercial creditors must give debt relief to developing countries in the London Club comparable to the debt relief that official creditors have given these developing countries in the Paris Club. This policy of comparable treatment was formulated in response to the 1976 debt reschedulings of Zaire and Indonesia.[33] The Paris Club Agreed Minute incorporates this requirement in the "comparable treatment" clause.[34] Basically, comparable rescheduling treatment means that the measure of debt relief given by the commercial creditors is as generous (in the context of normal commercial lending) as the relief offered by creditor governments in the Paris Club.

Comparable treatment is very hard to quantify. In 1976, official creditors refused to provide additional relief to Zaire until after Zaire had obtained some relief from commercial banks.[35] Three years later, the government creditors invoked the comparable treatment clause against Peru. The terms of Peru's previous reschedulings in the Paris Club and the London Club were identical and provided for two years of debt relief. Government creditors revoked the second year of debt relief when Peru cancelled the banks' second year of rescheduling. In most other cases, the terms have been sufficiently similar that official creditors did not feel they were "bailing out" the banks.

V. THE INTERNATIONAL MONETARY FUND

The coordination of debt reschedulings in the Paris Club and the London proceeded informally until 1982. In that year, the number of heavily indebted developing countries seeking such reschedulings increased dramatically. In response to this crisis, the IMF adopted the role of the "honest broker" to determine the appropriate balance needed between the adjustment effort required of the developing countries experiencing payment difficulties and the commitment of new external finance from the commercial banks.[36]

The IMF fulfills three functions as an honest broker: it helps formulate an adjustment program incorporating the performance criteria for debtor countries' drawings under the upper credit tranches; it provides IMF resources under standby or extended arrangements; and it acts as a catalyst in raising external finance from commercial banks.[37] The IMF first began its role as honest broker in November 1982, when it advised bankers with heavy exposures in Argentina and Mexico that the IMF would not commit its resources under an adjustment program until the banks had increased their exposures in these two countries.[38]

The IMF's practice of obtaining commitments from commercial banks for new loans as a prerequisite to making its resources available has been referred to in various contexts as "nonspontaneous lending"[39] or "involuntary lending."[40] The IMF's decision to require involuntary lending from commercial banks was considered by some to be a radical step. However, the IMF's informal efforts to persuade the banks to continue lending to a few countries in Eastern Europe provided some precendent for this policy. Also, if the IMF had not required involuntary lending from the banks, it might have been in breach of the U.S. requirement to uphold the comparable treatment policy of private and public creditors.[41]

To meet the increased demand on its funds due to the numerous debt restructurings, the IMF has expanded its resources. In 1983, the IMF's ability to extend intermediate term credit was improved through an increase in IMF quotas of nearly 50%, from approximately $60 billion to $90 billion.[42] In authorizing the 1983 quota increase, the U.S. Congress also enacted measures to ensure that the expansion of the IMF's resources would not be used to bail out the banks. This legislation also incorporated procedures for U.S. banking regulatory agencies to supervise international lending to debtor countries.[43]

In addition, IMF resources have been increased by changes in the General Arrangements to Borrow (hereinafter GAB), a line of credit from the major industrial countries to the IMF. IMF resources have increased under this credit line from approximately $7 billion to $18 billion. In circumstances involving an international liquidity crisis, the IMF has now been authorized to lend funds derived from the GAB to countries that are not contributors to that arrangements.[44]

VI. LENDERS OF LAST RESORT

Sometimes bridge financing is needed while IMF arrangements, London Club restructurings, and Paris Club restructurings are being negotiated. Developing countries may procrastinate in adopting adjustment programs since austerity measures are unpopular and may prove politically difficult to implement. However, developing countries will not qualify for debt relief in the Paris Club or the London Club until they have negotiated or have immediate prospects of negotiating an IMF arrangement.[45]

Debtor countries may experience an immediate liquidity crisis when official creditors, commercial banks, and the IMF are unable to agree to a restructuring. In this situation, official agencies have provided foreign reserves on a temporary basis during the time period necessary for debtor countries to negotiate a standby agreement with the IMF and reschedule commercial as well as official debt. In the following instances, the Bank for International Settlement (hereinafter BIS) has had to advance short-term credit facilities to serve as bridge financing.[46]

1. In 1982, the BIS advanced $1.85 billion to Mexico as bridge financing for a $4 billion IMF program pending a $1.5 billion and $5 billion commercial bank loan in 1982 and 1983 respectively.

2. In 1982, the BIS advanced $510 million to Hungary as bridge financing for a $580 million IMF program pending a $260 million commercial bank loan.

3. In 1982, the BIS advanced $1.45 billion to Brazil as bridge financing for a $5.4 billion IMF program pending a commercial bank restructuring involving $1.2 billion of new short-term credits. In addition, in 1983 commercial banks refinanced maturities due, extended short-term credit, reconstituted interbank positions, and provided an additional $6 billion in credits.

4. In 1983, the BIS advanced $500 million to Yugoslavia as bridge financing for a $600 million IMF program pending a commercial bank loan of $600 million, refinancing of medium-term maturities, rollover of short-term debt, and new commitments by foreign governments of $1.3 billion.

5. In 1983, the BIS advanced $500 million to Argentina as bridge financing for a $2.2 billion IMF program.

The BIS bridge operation was supported by central banks and other monetary authorities in industrialized countries. In the United States, the Treasury Department utilizes the Exchange Stablization Fund (hereinafter ESF) to underwrite its commitment to the BIS.

ESF financing may assist the BIS in providing a bridge during the period it takes to obtain an IMF standby arrangement. Thus, during Mexico's liquidity crisis in August 1982, the ESF entered into a $600 million swap arrangement (in the form of Mexican peso/U.S. dollar swaps) with the Bank of Mexico, at the same time that the Federal Reserve System entered into a $325 million swap. These arrangements were parallel to the $925 million credit arrangement between the Bank of Mexico and the BIS.[47]

Funds in the ESF are available when foreign international financial difficulties threaten the stability or orderliness of the international monetary system.[48] There are restrictions on the size of the ESF and the period during which funds may be used. The ESF facilities may be used for no longer than six months at a time.[49] Since the ESF must be repaid within six months, credits extended under these facilities are well secured and typically undertaken through swap agreements.[50] Such security arrangements may violate "negative pledges" given by the borrowing country in its agreements with other creditors.[51]

The willingness of the BIS to extend bridge financing acts as a stabilizing factor. However, the BIS relies upon the cooperation of BIS central banks to ensure that adequate resources will be available to face potential liquidity shortages. The swap network between the BIS and member central banks amounts to $32 billion.[52] The size of the swap network has not been broadened or expanded in recent years.

Its present size needs to be considered in relation to potential risks:

Central bankers have not committed themselves in advance to any precise action as lenders of last resort in an international liquidity crisis which would call for liquidity in excess of the $32 billion swap network. However, in 1974, when facing the first postwar crisis of confidence in the international banking system, the central bank governors of the Group of Ten and Switzerland stated that adequate means were available in liquidity crisis. The central bank governors stated that: "they recognized that it would not be practical to lay down in advance detailed rules and procedures for the provision of temporary liquidity. But they were satisfied that means are available for that purpose and will be used if and when necessary."[53]

VII. IMPROVED HANDLING OF DEBT CRISES

Although the procedures for sovereign debt reschedulings developed during the debt crises of 1982 to 1983 have demonstrated the international community's ability to face major challenges, further efforts must be made to restore the developing countries' access to the market place. However, there is disagreement among commentators whether to require fundamental changes in debt rescheduling procedures or simply improve current practices.

A. Global Approaches

Finding the current procedures for rescheduling sovereign debt inadequate, several critics believe that fundamental changes must be made in debt reschedulings to avoid global default. Examples of these proposals include: capitalizing interest;[54] indexing principal;[55] converting existing claims;[56] sharing foreign exchange earnings;[57] stretching out maturities;[58] and increasing marketability of claims.[59]

These proposals for a global solution to sovereign debt rescheduling vary considerably in the amounts of debt relief they would provide and who would bear the costs. Those proposals advocating across-the-board relief would treat all debtors identically, thereby decreasing incentives for economic adjustment measures. Moreover, those proposals allocating losses to the commercial banks would reduce the banks' willingness to extend new credits to debtors in the future. Similarly, commercial banks would be reluctant to advance new money to protect their existing portfolios if those proposals converting commercial bank debt into claims on international organizations were adopted.

Regardless of the merits of these new proposals, agreement on any of the global solutions presented would be difficult to obtain since commercial banks and official creditors with divergent interests would have to approve the solution. Even if such approval could be obtained, implementation would be problematic because several of the proposals require new legislation.

B. Improvements to Current Practices

Although the prospects for a global solution to sovereign debt rescheduling are remote, there is room for improvement in current debt rescheduling practices. Developing countries need to have better debt management in order to keep their debt servicing burden within manageable proportions. As a preventive measure, developing countries should limit future borrowings by presenting only high-priority projects for financing. In addition, developing countries should maintain accurate records of their external debt to improve the exchange of information between developing countries, commercial banks, the IMF, and offical creditors concerning prospective balance of payments requirements and capital flows.

Critical imports of raw materials and spare parts frequently need to be resumed during a developing country's debt rescheduling. New credit is required from both commercial and official creditors to finance these emergency imports. The IMF sets the levels of involuntary lending from commercial banks to assure that commercial banks continue to provide the necessary financing for this purpose. However, there is no formal mechanism to coordinate the extension of new credit to developing countries by official creditors.

In 1982 to 1983, several official creditors committed additional trade credits in an informal procedure involving major financing packages in the Paris Club reschedulings for Brazil, Mexico, and Yugoslavia. In the case of Brazil, Eximbank provided special trade facilities of $15. billion, and $488 million in regular lending programs. Moreover, Eximbank provided Mexico with a special trade facility of $500 million and $516 million in normal credits. In addition, Eximbank provided Yugoslavia with $128 million in credits.

Although Japan and Germany participated in the special export credit package to Mexico and Brazil, and Germany participated in the new credit facility to Yugoslavia, the United States has pledged a larger proportion of new credits in the Paris Club than can be justified on burden-sharing grounds. Better cooperation among official creditors is needed to assure that adequate levels of new financing are provided to developing countries by all official creditors.

Unfortunately, some official export credit agencies have suspended coverage for shipments to developing countries when a Paris Club rescheduling seems evident.[60] Indeed, pulling out export credit places an increased burden upon such countries as the United Kingdom to finance the necessary imports. However, the United Kingdom has stated that it will resume cover to developing countries rescheduling their debt at an earlier stage to facilitate the developing countries' ability to export.[61]

One commentator has suggested that a central export credit agency be created which would monitor IMF adjustment programs and coordinate insurance by the export credit agencies.[62] However, this proposal is likely to meet resistance from creditor countries which generally consider the case-by-case approach more expedient. In addition, the export credit agencies in several countries are autonomous from their governments and would not be controlled by a central pledging forum.

Export credit agencies have not equally shared in the burden of additional exposure to the developing countries which reschedule in the Paris Club. The burden-sharing problem is likely to become more acute in the future. Demand for export credit financing insurance has increased in light of the levels of accumulated external debt.[63] In addition, the proposal that export credits supply longer-term capital requirements of developing countries experiencing external debt problems has received growing attention.[64]

VIII. CONCLUSION

Debt restructuring involves a careful balancing of the policies and constraints of various parties. One of the challenges in a restructuring is to obtain agreement on the appropriate combination of debt relief, structural adjustment, and new lending commitments. Although the institutional procedures for restructuring debt are ad hoc, fairly standard patterns for burden-sharing have gradually been developed by official creditors, commercial banks, the IMF, the BIS, and developing countries. To restore the developing countries' access to the international marketplace, continued cooperative efforts will be needed to improve the procedures for restructuring the developing countries' debts.

The author is Attorney Adviser, Export-Import Bank of the United States. B.A. New York University, Doctoral University of Amsterdam, J.D. Yale Law School. The views expressed herein do not necessarily represent the views of any agency of the U.S. Government.

NOTES

1. These agencies include export credit agencies, development assistance agencies, and defense agencies.

2. A member of the International Monetary Fund (hereinafter cited as IMF) may draw funds from the IMF above the amount of its quota in units of 25%, or "tranches." Access to drawings in the upper tranches is subject to performance criteria which typically include limitations on expansion of internal credit, currency devaluation, restrictions on subsidy programs as well as other government spending, and modifications of wage and price controls. See J. GOLD, CONDITIONALITY 2 (IMF Pamphlet No. 31, 1979); Kincaid, *Conditionality and the Use of Fund Resources,* FINANCE & DEVELOPMENT, June 1981, at 18-21; see also Robinson, *One by One, They Come to Terms,* EUROMONEY, Mar. 1984, at 38.

3. Some observers believe that the worst of the debt crisis is now over. Economic projections indicate that there would be a deterioration in the debt situation if the following events occur:

(1) the growth of the member countries of the Organization for Economic Cooperation and Development (hereinafter cited as OECD) in 1984 to 1986 is less than 2.5% per annum;

(2) oil prices decline at a rate which has a greater negative impact on oil exporting countries than the benefit to oil importing countries;

(3) the dollar appreciates (for every 10% appreciation, an improvement of developing countries' ratios of debt to exports is halved); and

(4) interest rates increase (one percentage point in OECD growth has seven times as much impact as one percentage point change in the interest rate).

W. CLINE, INTERNATIONAL DEBT AND THE STABILITY OF THE WORLD ECONOMY 52-71 (Institute for International Economics, Pol'y Analyses in Int'l Econ. No. 4, 1983).

4. The history of the Paris Club is outlined in Bee, *Lessons from Debt Reschedulings in the Past,* EUROMONEY, Apr. 1977, at 33; Cizauskas, *International Debt Renegotiations; Lessons from the Past,* WORLD DEVELOPMENT 199, World Bank Reprint Series No. 101 (1979), at 201-203; Camdessus, *Governmental Creditors and the Role of the Paris Club,* in DEFAULT AND RESCHEDULING CORPORATE AND SOVEREIGN BORROWERS IN DIFFICULTY 125 (D. Suratgar ed. 1984). For a study of post-1956 reschedulings see C. HARDY, RESCHEDULING DEVELOPING COUNTRY DEBTS 1956-1981: LESSONS AND RECOMMENDATIONS, (Overseas Development Council Monograph No. 15, June 1982).

5. In 1979 and 1980, Turkey rescheduled its debt through a Working Party of the OECD's Consortium for Turkey. In 1981, Poland restructured its debt in a special creditor's meeting. In 1983, Mexico rescheduled its debt at the OECD.

6. Resolution No. 165, S-IX of the United Nations Conference on Trade & Development, UNCTAD Report of the Trade and Development Board, 35 U.N. GAOR Supp. (No. 15) 68, U.N. Doc. A/35/15 Vol.II (1981) (a compromise between developing countries seeking an independent and multilateral framework and creditor countries).

7. Since 1978, the Chairman of the Paris Club has been Michael Camdessus, Director of the French Treasury.

8. In the case of Nicaragua, all OECD creditors except the United States extended relief on a bilateral basis without an IMF program in place. This exceptional approach has not been repeated for Nicaragua or any other country. For a general discussion of Nicaragua's debt rescheduling, see Weinert, *The Restructuring of Nicaragua's Debt,* in DEFAULT AND RESCHEDULING CORPORATE AND SOVEREIGN BORROWERS IN DIFFICULTY 137 (D. Suratgar ed. 1984).

9. For a description of the negotiation procedures in the Paris Club, see Rieffel, *The Paris Club, 1978-1983,* 23 COLUM. J. TRANSNAT'L L. 83, 97-98 (1984).

10. A creditor government may have made a loan directly to a private entity in a developing country, or may have guaranteed or insured loans made by a commercial lender. When private borrowers have made debt service payments in local currency to the central bank, the debtor government assumes responsibility for repayment of the private credits. In effect, the government then becomes the debtor vis a vis the creditor. Loans to private borrowers, which at the time of the rescheduling were judged to be unable to meet debt service payments in local currencies, are excluded from the reschedulings.

11. Camdessus, *supra* note 4, at 126.

12. Rieffel, *supra* note 9, at 108 n. 45.

13. In over 40% of the agreements surveyed, debt relief was more than 20% of exports in the year of rescheduling; in over 33% of agreements surveyed, debt relief was more than 50% of the current account deficit; when rescheduling included arrears, the ratio of amount rescheduled to

total debt service payments was over 100% in almost 50% of the cases surveyed. P. MENTRE, THE FUND, COMMERCIAL BANKS, AND MEMBER COUNTRIES 21 (IMF Occasional Paper 26, 1984).

14. *See* E. BRAU & R. WILLIAMS, RECENT MULTILATERAL DEBT RESTRUCTURINGS WITH OFFICIAL AND BANK CREDITORS 15 (IMF Occasional Paper 25, 1983).

15. *See* C. HARDY, *supra* note 4, at 25. There was a difference of 10% between the discounted value of streams of debt service payments before and after rescheduling. During the period of 1956 to 1974, the cost of rescheduling was $2 billion for a total outstanding debt rescheduled of $400 billion. The cost of debt rescheduling was 41% for Turkey between 1978 and 1980; 45% for Ghana between 1966 and 1974; and 56% for Indonesia between 1966 and 1970.

16. 12 U.S.C. § 635 (1945). Eximbank was first organized in 1934 under Exec. Order No. 6581, 12 C.F.R. 401, *reprinted in* 12 U.S.C. § 635 (1982).

17. *See supra* text accompanying note 10.

18. Each U.S. creditor agency reschedules its debts with developing countries bilaterally in an implementing agreement.

19. The National Advisory Council issued a policy statement on debt rescheduling on January 6, 1978. This policy statement includes the following elements;

(1) rescheduling is to be on a case by case basis when necessary to ensure repayment and should not be given as a form of development assistance;

(2) rescheduling is to take place in the context of a multilateral creditor club agreement;

(3) reschedulings must incorporate the principles of nondiscrimination among creditor countries, comparable treatment of private credits, and an IMF standby arrangement;

(4) amounts of principal and interest must be rescheduled on the basis of the debtor country's balance of payments needs; and

(5) debt falling due after more than one year of the rescheduling shall be excluded.

Address by Peter J. Wallison, General Counsel of the U.S. Dept. of Treasury, The Role of Treasury in International Debt Matters 7-8 (June 13, 1983) (presented at Workshop on Sovereign Debt: Recent Regulatory and Lending Issues and Practices, sponsored by Legal Times and Law & Business, Inc./Harcourt Brace Jovanovich) (hereinafter cited as Wallison Address).

20. 22 U.S.C. § 286b (1945).

21. The January 1981 debt rescheduling for Pakistan was an exception to the requirement that the debtor country be in a state of imminent default. The U.S. Government had suspended aid to Pakistan after legislation to cut off development assistance to countries building nuclear weapons was enacted. 22 U.S.C. §2429a (1977). However, U.S. security interests in Pakistan intensified after the Soviet Union invaded Afghanistan. Consequently, President Carter waived the two rules for debt reschedulings: existence of an imminent default and an IMF-supported economic stabilization program, to allow the U.S. to participate in a multilateral debt rescheduling for Pakistan. The President granted this waiver after inquiries with members of Congress showed support for this approach.

22. 22 U.S.C. § 2395(a) (1979).

23. Bank debt restructuring is defined here to cover both the rescheduling and refinancing of debt service payments in arrears (generally principal repayments). It also covers future service payments on short-term and medium-term debt. Rescheduling is a formal deferral of debt service payments over a period exceeding one year, with new maturities applying to the deferred amounts. Refinancing is either a straight rollover of maturing debt obligations or involves the conversion of existing and/or future debt service payments into new medium-term loans.

24. For instance, in Mexico, 530 commercial banks were involved in the rescheduling. DeVries, *Historian Details Improved Debt Outlook and Policies Needed to Sustain Progress,* 1985 IMF SURVEY 2, 4.

25. To speed up the negotiation process, many creditors would like the steering committee to be formed quickly. Perhaps the Institute of International Finance, Inc. might contribute to a more rapid selection of the steering committee participants. For a description of the Institute of International Finance, Inc., see Surrey & Nash, *Bankers Look Beyond the Debt Crisis: The Institute of International Finance, Inc.,* 23 COLUM. J. INTERNAT'L L. 111 (1984).

26. Mudge, *Sovereign Debt Restructuring: A Current Perspective* in DEFAULT AND RESCHEDULING CORPORATE AND SOVEREIGN BORROWERS IN DIFFICULTY 85, 90 (D. Suratgar ed. 1984).

27. BRAU & WILLIAMS, *supra* note 14, at 22.

28. Link, *The Value of Bank Assets Subject to Transfer Risk,* 23 COLUM. J. TRANSNAT'L L 75, 80 (1984).

29. BRAU & WILLIAMS, *supra* note 14, at 27.

30. *Id.*

31. *Id.*

32. *Id.* at 26.

33. H.R. REP. No. 853, 95th Cong., 2d Sess. 25-27, *reprinted in* 1978 U.S. CODE CONG. & AD. NEWS at 2530.

34. The following language is boilerplate in every Paris Club Agreed Minute, but it is not publicly available:

"In order to secure comparable treatment of public and private external creditors on their debts, the Delegation of _____ stated that their Government will seek to secure from external creditors, including banks and suppliers, rescheduling or refinancing arrangements on terms comparable to those set forth in this Agreed Minute for credits of comparable maturity, making sure to avoid inequity between different categories of creditors."

35. H.R. REP. No 853, *supra* note 33, at 26.

36. Robichek, *The International Monetary Fund: An Arbiter in the Debt Restructuring Process,* 23 COLUM. J. TRANSNAT'L L. 143, 146 (1984).

37. *Id.*

38. *Id.*

39. DeVries, *supra* note 24, at 5.

40 P. MENTRE, *supra* note 13, at 13.

41. The comparability requirement applies when official U.S. credits are involved. 22 U.S.C. § 286E—8 (1982).

42. DeVries, *supra* note 24, at 18.

43. Pub. L. No. 98-181, 97 Stat. 1278 (1983) (to be codified at 12 U.S.C. §§ 3901-13). Pursuant to the International Lending Supervision Act of 1983, U.S. supervisory authorities are directed to adopt the following reforms:

(1) establishment of prudential reserves against certain international assets (12 U.S.C. § 3904);

(2) an increase in the requirements for disclosure of exposure in relation to assets and capital (12 U.S.C. § 3906(b));

(3) an increase in the frequency of U.S. bank reporting on country exposures to supervisory authorities (12 U.S.C. § 3906(a));

(4) the adoption of regulations for the accounting for fees on restructured international credits (12 U.S.C. § 3905); and

(5) the adoption of tightened policy guidelines for the capital adequacy of large U.S. banks (12 U.S.C. § 3907).

44. M. AINLEY, THE GENERAL ARRANGEMENTS TO BORROW (IMF Pamphlet Series Pub. No. 41, 1984).

45. *But see supra* text accompanying note 8.

46. P. MENTRE, *supra* note 13, at 12-13.

47. Wallison Address, *supra* note 19, at 5.

48. *See* 31 U.S.C. § 5302(b) (1934).

49. However, a loan or credit to a foreign entity or government of a foreign country may be made for greater than six months in any 12-month period only if the President gives the Congress a written statement that unique or emergency circumstances require the loan or credit be for more than six months. *Id.*

50. "A swap is an arrangement between two parties to exchange a certain amount of one currency for another and to reverse that transaction at a specified date." Wallison Address, *supra* note 19, at 4.

51. *See geneally* Bradfield & Jacklin, *The Problems Posed by Negative Pledge Covenants in International Loan Agreements,* 23 COLUM. J. TRANSNAT'L L. 131-42 (1984).

52. P. MENTRE, *supra* note 13, at 34.

53. Bank for International Settlements, Press Communique (Basle, Sept. 9, 1974), *cited in* P. MENTRE, *supra* note 13, at 33 n.54.

54. *See* Rutledge & Bell, *Facing Reality on Sovereign Debt,* EUROMONEY, Nov. 1984, at 103.

55. Proposal by John Williamson that "an international institution issue bonds of 50-year maturities, denominated in SDRs (Special Drawing Rights), with a real interest payment and redemption value which are indexed to some internationally weighted price index," *cited in* P. MENTRE, *supra* note 13, at 19 app.

56. The exchange of existing short-term loans for long-term, low-interest notes to be issued by a national or multinational agency, Heineman, *Third-World Debt Problem,* N.Y. Times, Mar. 10, 1983, at D1, D5, col. 2.

57. Proposal for debtor countries to give creditors negotiable Exchange Participation Notes, which would entitle them to a certain percentage of the country's future foreign exchange earnings. *See* P. MENTRE, *supra* note 13, at 20 app.

58. Plan to stretch out maturities of short-term loans by issuance of certificates by subsidiary of the World Bank, *See* Pine, *World Bank Weighs New Entity to Raise More Funds for Use in Developing Nations,* Wall St. J., Oct. 13, 1983, at 6, col. 2.

59. A discounting device whereby banks could sell rescheduled developing country debts to central banks or other agencies. Feder, *The World Banking Crises: Phase Two,* N.Y. Times, Mar. 27, 1983, § 3 at 1, col. 1.

60. Japan has suspended export coverage for short-term commitments after a Paris Club rescheduling.

61. Export Credits Guarantee Department, Press Notice 84-44 (Dec. 19, 1984).

62. Lever, *The International Debt Threat,* ECONOMIST, July 9, 1983, at 14, 15-16.

63. Export trade credits extended or guaranteed by official creditors to developing countries grew by 7% to $190 billion at the end of 1983, from $178 billion at the end of 1982. This amounted to roughly one-fourth of these countries' outstanding external debt. E. BRAU & C. PUCKAHTIKOM, EXPORT CREDIT COVER POLICIES AND PAYMENTS DIFFICULTIES 33 (1984).

64. Bolin & Del Canto, *LDC Debt: Beyond Crisis Management,* 61 FOREIGN AFF. 1099, 1110-11 (1983); Roett, *Democracy and Debt in South America,* 62 FOREIGN AFF. 695, 718 (1984).

17B. Legal Issues in the Restructuring of Commercial Bank Loans to Sovereign Borrowers

Mark A. Walker and Lee C. Buchheit

INTRODUCTION

Since 1981 there has been a virtual epidemic in the number of countries experiencing "liquidity crises" of the kind which have become the familiar symptom of an incipient external debt restructuring.[1] The amount of debt subject, or likely to become subject, to these renegotiations is staggering and the practical and legal complexities entailed by sovereign debt restructurings on this scale are equally formidable.

The external debt subject to a typical restructuring may have been incurred by dozens of borrowers in the public and private sectors pursuant to hundreds if not thousands of separate credit instruments. In the case of large sovereign borrowers such as Mexico and Brazil, the universe of the country's external creditors will include virtually every major commercial bank in the world active in the international financial markets together with many smaller or regional banks and financial institutions.[2] Other external creditors may include holders of publicly-issued debt instruments, trade creditors (including suppliers), official government agencies (such as export/import agencies), multilateral development banks, and so forth. These creditors will vary widely in terms of nationality, perspective and sophistication. The credits to be restructured may have been advanced in a number of different currencies, for varying maturities and at differing interest rates and margins. The documentation relating to these credits — ranging from one-paragraph promissory notes or telex exchanges to hundred-page loan agreements — will contain a bewildering array of representations, covenants, and cross-default clauses. Moreover, these instruments may by their terms be subject to interpretation and construction under the laws of a number of different jurisdictions.

If one attempts an Olympian perspective on this complex subject, however, the outlines of a "market practice" in dealing with sovereign external debt problems appear to be coalescing out of the recent spate of these renegotiations. Developing countries attempting to resolve their external debt service problems often go through remarkably similar stages, and their international creditors are beginning to adopt increasingly predictable responses to the practical and legal issues raised by this process.[3] This chapter will highlight some of the more important legal issues which must be confronted when a country elects to restructure all or a portion of its external commercial bank debt. There will, of course, be other elements in a country's overall debt profile which will require concurrent attention (such as dealing with interbank credits exempt from restructuring, official creditors, international development banks, trade creditors, and so forth), but the special legal issues involved in these negotiations are beyond the scope of this chapter.

It should be noted at the outset that many of the strictly legal issues involved in a sovereign debt renegotiation are present in some form in most typical international loan transactions and will therefore be familiar to sophisticated borrowers, lenders and their legal counsel. This is not surprising. A restructured international loan is, after all, still an exercise in international lending and will continue to reflect customary market practices and concerns. And many lawyers given the task of documenting sovereign restructurings have tended— for better or worse—to address these concerns by cannibalizing standard Eurocurrency loan forms.

Although the legal questions may for the most part be familiar, it is often the sheer size and complexity of a sovereign debt restructuring—the large number of creditors and borrowers, and the amounts involved—which intensifies the interest of the parties in these shop-worn issues. For example, what might have been regarded as a matter of acceptable risk for either a borrower or a lender in the context of documenting a $5 million loan in good times may become a subject of acute concern when the negotiations relate to a $25 billion debt restructuring.

One final introductory comment is in order. It would be incorrect to suppose that any trend toward an increasing standardization of the documentation for sovereign debt restructurings results entirely from a considered and rational judgment by the parties concerned that a particular format is the most effective way of dealing with this task. There may be a more human explanation for this phenomenon. Many large international banks sit on the steering or advisory committees for a number of sovereign debt negotiations and they are often represented on those committees by the same bank officers. Similarly, the community of lawyers around the world actively engaged in sovereign debt workouts is surprisingly small. It is not uncommon to find a single law firm representing either the lenders or the borrowers in a number of different negotiations all taking place simultaneously.

Given the natural human instinct to follow precedents when confronted with new and complicated assignments (an instinct with which lawyers are generally thought to be hopelessly afflicted), an increasing standardization in documentation relating to sovereign debt restructuring is probably inevitable. Thus, legal documentation and even communications from borrowers to their creditors prepared in the context of one negotiation not only can be, but often are, marked up as the basis for another borrower's restructuring. Provisions which may play a useful role in one agreement are sometimes uncritically incorporated into its progeny. A solution to a particular problem worked out between a borrower and a steering committee for purposes of that borrower's restructuring may cross-fertilize concurrent negotiations between other borrowers and their respective steering committees in large part because the same bankers and lawyers are involved in each case. Whatever one's views on the merits of the resulting standardization of restructuring documentation, however, it is important to keep in mind that this consequence is probably attributable more to the human element in this process than to any consensus regarding the proper way to document a sovereign restructuring.

THRESHOLD ISSUES

Commercial banks are only one group of external creditors involved in a typical sovereign debt renegotiation. Commercial banks have the benefit (or liability, depending on one's perspective) of being easily identifiable and they can usually be dealt with as a group. They are also presumed to be "in the business of lending money," with all the attendant risks, and consequently they are a tempting candidate for restructuring. Commercial banks have staunchly insisted, however, that their loans cannot be dealt with in isolation when the causes of the country's inability to service its external debt, and the steps necessary to reform its finances, are much broader. Thus, likely sources of fresh funds and the proposed treatment of all other significant creditors (including the International Monetary Fund ["IMF" or the "Fund"] facilities, governments, trade creditors, and so forth) are likely to figure prominently in discussions regarding the restructuring of commercial bank debt.

Identifying the Debt Subject to Restructure

The first order of business for a country facing an external debt renegotiation will be to define (often in consultation with representatives of its creditors) the categories of debt which will be subject to the restructuring. These categories must be sufficiently broad to give the country an adequate respite from its current debt service burden, and yet cannot be so expansive as to risk alienating the creditors whose cooperation and willingness to continue to extend new credits is necessary to the restructuring process and to ultimate recovery.[4] There is, of course, an immediate economic disincentive for a country to expand the category of restructurable debt beyond what is reasonably necessary to overcome a temporary liquidity problem. Restructured debt will generally command margins and fees considerably higher than those which the borrower could insist upon in better days.

Four preliminary issues must be addressed in identifying the debt subject to restructure. First, what is meant by external debt for these purposes? Second, which borrowers in the country will be requested to enter into restructuring arrangements with their external creditors? Third, what types of debt will be covered by the restructuring? Finally, to what maturities of this debt will the restructuring apply?

The Definition of External Debt

Sovereign debt renegotiations are typically limited to the "external debt" of the country. It is rare that a sovereign will accept an attempt by foreign lenders to interfere in whatever arrangements the country undertakes in respect of debt payable in local currency. A country may also object to a definition of external debt which encompasses even foreign currency obligations payable to persons or entities resident in that country since payment of these obligations will not by itself result in any outflow of foreign currency but simply reallocate internal claims to such currency.[5] A typical definition of external debt for these purposes might therefore include only indebtedness (i) for borrowed money, or the deferred purchase price of property or services, (ii) payable in currency other than the local currency, and (iii) payable to a person having its head office or chief place of business outside of the country.

The concept of external debt may do more than serve as the definitional base for identifying the class of debt subject to restructure. For example, lenders generally accept that negative pledge clauses will only restrict the borrower's ability to secure *external* debt, and cross-default clauses will usually be drafted so as to limit the trigger to other agreements relating to the *external* debt of a specified category of borrowers.

Public vs. Private Sector Debt

At an early stage a country will need to decide whether it wishes to restructure its private sector debt (or a portion such as that contracted by the private financial sector) as well as its public sector debt. This decision will be influenced by the relative size of each category of debt and by the role of the central government in private sector affairs. If the country had in the past adopted the practice of giving government or public sector guarantees to private sector borrowers, the lenders under these agreements may be able to convert their debt into public sector obligations merely by calling on the guaranties. On the other hand, if such guaranties were not typically extended, the country might be cautious about requesting a formal restructuring of its private sector debt for fear that the private sector lenders would demand some form of government guaranty as a *quid pro quo* for their acceptance of the restructuring. The consequences of such a transformation could be both political and economic, and may strikingly affect the country's ability to comply with any applicable economic performance criteria established by the IMF as part of an IMF stabilization program.

A formal restructuring of private sector debt may be carried out in parallel with the restructuring of public sector debt or as part of the same exercise and on the same terms. The closer the two are linked, however, the more the country's credit standing and ability to reenter the financial markets will be dependent on the fortunes or recovery of the private sector.

Even if the restructuring is limited to public sector borrowers, it is unlikely that the issue of the treatment of private sector external debt can be avoided. For a large debtor country, the universe of its public sector bank creditors will probably be more or less congruent with its private sector bank creditors. For obvious reasons, these banks are unlikely to agree to restructuring terms for the public sector without some assurance that private sector arrearages will be paid and that the private sector will have access to foreign exchange on an equitable basis with which to service its debt in the future. The country may choose, however, to use its control over the foreign exchange required for private sector debt service to encourage (if not compel) private sector lenders and borrowers to negotiate on a case-by-case basis for the restructuring of that debt. This incentive can be provided in several ways, such as by offering forward sales of foreign currency at fixed exchange rates to private sector entities whose creditors have agreed to reschedule the maturities of their loans.[6]

"Excluded" Debt

For reasons of commercial necessity or market practice, a debtor country will probably resist any proposal that *all* of the external debt incurred by the specified category of borrowers be restructured. It is customary for sovereign borrowers and their creditors (each for their own reasons) to negotiate a category of "excluded debt"; *i.e.,* credits otherwise falling within the definition of the debt subject to restructure but which, for reasons relating to the nature of the debt or the identity of the payee, are exempted from the restructuring. A sovereign borrower may be understandably ambivalent about excluding certain types of debt in this way. On the one hand, the country will wish to restructure as much of its debt as is feasible in order to facilitate a quick return to manageable debt service levels. Cutting against this desire, however, is the genuine concern that certain types of obligations cannot be re-structured without serious adverse consequences for the country's economy and long-term credit status.

Among the types of debt which are sometimes excluded from a renegotiation are:

(i) publicly-issued bonds, floating rate certificates of deposit and notes;
(ii) privately-placed securities;
(iii) loans made, guaranteed or insured by foreign government agencies (including export credit agencies);
(iv) loans made by supranational or multilateral organizations (such as the International Bank for Reconstruction and Development and similar development banks);
(v) lease obligations with respect to, or financings secured by, tangible personal property;
(vi) loans which are the subject of interest make-up obligations or subsidies provided by official agencies;
(vii) short-term trade credits;
(viii) spot and forward exchange and precious metal contracts; and
(ix) debts payable to entities other than banks or financial institutions.

Decisions regarding the composition of a category of excluded debt have the inevitable result of favoring certain creditors. That is, creditors holding excluded debt can look to be repaid on time while other lenders will be asked to restructure. The favored treatment of any group is not likely to be popular with commercial bank lenders whose credits remain subject to the restructuring, and consequently the inclusion of any candidates on the list of excluded debt must be perceived by these banks as justifiable.[7] In the case of suppliers' credits, for example, it is generally recognized that a failure by the borrower to pay these obligations on a timely basis could result in severe constraints being placed on the country's continued ability to conduct foreign trade in a normal way. Similarly, most lenders are willing to accept the principle that multilateral development bank loans should either be exempted wholly from the restructuring or dealt with on an *ad hoc* basis. The terms under which these loans are extended are usually more favorable to the borrower than those obtainable from commercial banks, and the political circumstances of multilateral organizations are such that any pressure to join a commercial bank restructuring might jeopardize future concessional assistance from these organizations.

Nevertheless, the definition of excluded debt may spark heated internecine conflicts among classes of creditors. In some recent sovereign debt renegotiations, for example, commercial bank lenders have objected to proposals that bondholders be exempt from the restructuring,[8] notwithstanding a general market practice to exclude holders of publicly-issued debt instruments.[9] Banks may also question whether trade creditors who offer long-term suppliers' credits should be treated any differently from commercial bank lenders.

Maturities to Be Restructured

Finally, a country must determine which maturities of external debt it wishes to restructure. One approach is to request that all external credits (other than excluded debt) outstanding as of a particular date be restructured. If a temporary relaxation of debt service requirements is believed sufficient (or the most obtainable), however, a country may ask only for a restructuring of principal (and sometimes interest) maturities falling due between specified dates. Since the premium interest rates and fees charged for restructuring normally apply only to those maturities which are extended, the exclusion from the restructuring of later maturities will have immediate economic consequences.

An important legal consequence of this latter approach is that the principal maturities falling due within the restructuring "window" will become subject to the restructuring agreement while later maturities will continue to be subject to all the terms of the original credit instrument. This will give rise to legal issues relating to the continued effectiveness of the original credit instruments and the relationship of those instruments to the restructuring documentation.

Who Is the Obligor?

At the outset of the debt renegotiation a decision must be made as to the obligor under the eventual restructuring agreement or agreements. The obvious candidates are: (i) the original public sector obligors; (ii) the original public sector obligors with a sovereign or Central Bank guaranty; (iii) the Central Bank; (iv) the Central Bank with a sovereign guaranty; or (v) the sovereign itself. Different legal consequences may flow from each of these options.

The principal arguments for retaining the existing borrower as the obligor under the restructuring agreement are the preservation of the integrity of the financial affairs of the original borrower as well as the individual bank/customer relationship which was the basis for the extension of the original loan. At the opposite extreme, commercial bank lenders may urge using a single restructuring agreement with the sovereign or the Central Bank as primary obligor for all of the country's public-sector debt. If a single obligor is not feasible, the lenders may request that the sovereign or the Central Bank guarantee the obligations of each public sector borrower. The lenders will argue that this is the best way of assuring equal treatment among commercial bank creditors to the various individual borrowers. Moreover, the lenders will point to the fact that individual borrowers may (regardless of their particular condition) be unable to service their external debt because of a general scarcity of foreign currency in the country. In such a case, the lenders may ask for some form of sovereign or Central Bank guaranty as part of the restructuring package.

For the sovereign or Central Bank to act as obligor or guarantor, however, will have a highly centripetal effect on the country's debt picture. Instead of individual public sector borrowers being responsible under separate obligations, the government will have transformed all of the debt into a single sovereign risk. As will be discussed below, from a legal standpoint clauses in the restructuring documentation such as those providing for cross-defaults to other obligations of the borrower or guarantor, or contractual rights of set-off, may take on very different significance if the sovereign or Central Bank appears as a primary obligor or guarantor under each restructuring agreement.[10] Moreover, the effect of concentrating the debt into one obligor may have legal consequences for banks subject to lending limit restrictions.

The Form of Restructuring

Many recent restructurings have followed the practice of imposing a uniform agreement or form of agreement on all debt to be restructured. This uniform restructuring agreement then supercedes for legal purposes the individual credit instruments under which the debt was originally contracted (at least for those maturities being restructured). Some banks, however, particularly in Europe, have urged that the terms of existing agreements be preserved with appropriate adjustments to applicable maturities, interest rates and fees. The principal advantages of this approach from the banks' standpoint are simplicity of restructure documentation and the retention of previously bargained for covenants and other protective provisions.[11] The principal disadvantages are the possibility of unequal treatment of creditors, the perpetuation in the restructuring context of provisions with which the borrower may have already demonstrated an inability to comply, and the necessity of dealing with each instrument or agreement evidencing debt to be restructured on an individual basis. In some cases, this last consideration alone could introduce delays intolerable to all parties. The arguments for a single or uniform agreement are strongest when there is a common obligor or guarantor for all restructured debt.

THE LENDERS' CONCERNS AND THE BORROWER'S RESPONSES

From the standpoint of commercial bank lenders, a sovereign debt restructuring amounts to the renunciation of a present right to exercise legal remedies for non-payment and a deferral of the repayment of their loans. In return, the banks will expect that their loans will be repaid on an agreed schedule on a fair and reasonable basis, and they will generally seek higher margins and fees for the restructured credits. A commercial bank lender, but acquiescing in a request to restructure its loans, will *not* however expect to be disadvantaged in terms of the borrower's —

- repayment of other commercial bank debt which is similarly restructured;
- repayment of other debt satisfying the criteria of debt subject to restructure but which, for one reason or another, is not restructured on similar terms; and
- prepayment of the borrower's existing non-restructurable debt earlier than as required by the payment schedule for such debt in effect on the date of the restructuring.

To meet these concerns, certain contractual provisions and techniques are becoming a common feature in restructuring documentation.

Equal Treatment of All Restructurable Debt

Once a determination has been made of what debt is to be restructured, commercial bank lenders will look for assurances that the borrower will treat all lenders of that debt in an equal and even-handed manner. The banks may therefore insist that the restructuring agreement contain restrictions preventing the borrower from playing favorites among its bank creditors, whether these creditors choose to restructure or not. Two provisions intended to achieve this result are the so-called "sharing clause" and a clause inhibiting the repayment by the borrower on more favorable terms of other restructurable debt.

Sharing Clauses

The sharing clause, a mechanism designed to ensure that each bank in a syndicated credit facility receives rateable repayment of its loan, is a common feature in many international multibank credit agreements. The sharing clause is intended to place all bank lenders under a single loan agreement on an equal footing in the event that one bank receives a non-rateable payment from the borrower, or sets off its loan against deposits of the borrower held by it, or otherwise realizes on security for its loan.[12]

Two variations of the sharing clause are currently in vogue, although neither is completely free from legal worries.[13] Under one variation, generally favored by U.S. banks, each bank which has received or applied funds in excess of its rateable repayment entitlement purchases for cash a participation in the loan of each other bank with the goal of equalizing the position of all banks which are parties to the same loan agreement. The primary benefit of this approach is also its principal drawback. The benefit is that the banks will share non-rateable payments or applications of funds pursuant to formal participation agreements which might prove useful in the event of any subsequent litigation contesting the propriety of the sharing with other banks or any set-off against deposits of the borrower. In a restructuring which includes a large number of bank lenders, however, the preparation and execution of these participation agreements may be extremely burdensome, costly and time-consuming. Moreover, if rateable payment to all the banks is eventually made by or on behalf of the borrower, the participations may need to be reversed and this presumably would have to be evidenced by additional documentation, at additional cost.

A second variation of the sharing clause—often seen in English-law agreements—provides that any bank which receives or applies funds in excess of its rateable repayment entitlement will redistribute such excess amounts (through the agent) to each of the other lending banks in the syndicate so that, following such redistribution, each bank will have received a rateable repayment of its loan. This approach normally does not contemplate that any special legal documentation will be exchanged in connection with the sharing process.

Sharing clauses of either kind, when used in the context of a restructuring, must deal with the question of arrearages which may exist under numerous unrelated agreements at the time the restructuring agreement becomes effective. In addition, although not now prevalent, some lenders may urge that the principle of equality of treatment requires that all restructure agreements with the various borrowers be linked by a universal sharing provision. For example, a creditor of one borrower which sets off against deposits of that borrower would be required to share not only with all other creditors of that borrower, but with the creditors of other borrowers as well.

Assuming that the relevant agreements do not provide for sharing among creditors of different borrowers, the overriding concern with sharing clauses in a restructuring context is a practical one. In a large restructure agreement providing for payments to hundreds of banks in several different currencies on staggered repayment dates, the mechanical problems in administering a sharing clause can be enormous. Moreover, by operation of the expense indemnity provision found in most agreements, the cost of operating a sharing clause will ultimately be for the account of the borrower. The borrower will therefore want to be sure that the sharing mechanism cannot be set in motion unintentionally by, for example, bank errors in effecting or processing payments.

Remedies in the Event of More Favorable Repayment of Other Debt Subject to Restructure

Commercial bank lenders will want to ensure that no debt falling within the definition of debt subject to restructure is repaid on terms more favorable than their restructured loans. The intention here is obvious. If a lender has no basis to anticipate repayment of its loans earlier than those that are formally restructured, it will have every incentive to participate fully in the restructuring and thus benefit from the higher margins and fees. Moreover, if the restructuring takes place on a borrower-by-borrower basis, the lenders to each borrower will want to be sure that lenders to the other borrowers are not being paid out on a preferential basis. In other words, all holders of debt subject to restructure must march in lockstep.

These concerns are sometimes addressed through the use of a clause in the restructuring agreement requiring a rateable prepayment of each bank's restructured credits in the event that the borrower (or guarantor, if any) repays any amount of restructurable debt earlier than as contemplated by the repayment schedule set forth in the relevant restructuring principles. These clauses raise two troublesome legal issues. First, how is "rateable prepayment" to be defined in this context? Rateable prepayment may be determined on a maturity-by-maturity basis (for example, a $5,000 payment on a $10,000 maturity triggering a 50% prepayment of each restructured loan), or as a proportion of the borrower's aggregate debt owed to the specific lender being repaid, or owed to all lenders of restructurable debt, or on a dollar-for-dollar basis. Banks tend to favor the first interpretation and argue, for this purpose, that each existing "credit" of the borrower (a concept also requiring some definitional efforts) should be treated separately, with a payment under one triggering a proportionate payment under each of the credits of the other lenders. This can lead to absurd results. If a borrower repays in full a single $1,000 principal maturity which meets the criteria of debt subject to restructure, all of the borrower's restructured debt must, by operation of this clause, also be repaid in full. Moreover, similar clauses in the restructure agreements for each borrower would force the full repayment of all of the country's restructured debt.

A second issue raised by these mandatory prepayment clauses centers on the exceptions from the coverage of the clause. To avoid the Draconian results discussed above which can arise from the repayment in full of a small piece of debt, borrowers have occasionally sought an exception to these clauses for *de minimis* payments.[14] A well-advised borrower should also seek exceptions for any payments it might be required to make to avoid illegality or increased costs provisions under the original credit instruments or under the restructure agreement itself. Unless these exceptions are secured, the borrower may find itself in the unfortunate position of either having to pay increased costs, however burdensome these may become, or face the alternative of being required to prepay all of its restructured debt.[15] Similarly, such a total prepayment obligation might be triggered by another lender demanding payment of its loan as a result of a clause in its original credit agreement or its restructuring agreement requiring prepayment if a change in applicable law or regulation makes it illegal for that lender to maintain its loan.

Treatment of Non-Restructurable Debt

By definition, restructured debt consists of obligations whose maturities have been deferred, with the consent of the lenders, beyond the dates contemplated for their repayment by the original credit instruments. It is perfectly understandable, therefore, that the lenders of the debt being restructured will want to ensure that the borrower applies its available resources in the future first to discharge these extended obligations before any early repayment is made of other debt outstanding at the time the decision to restructure was made.[16] Moreover, lenders of restructured debt will not want to give the borrower the freedom to elevate subsequent creditors to a preferential legal position in the event of a future insolvency of the borrower, nor will they wish to leave unfettered the borrower's ability to pledge or encumber its assets or revenues in favor of future external creditors.

As in the case of the commercial bank lenders' desire to preserve equality *inter sese,* the borrower may be asked to undertake various contractual commitments in its restructure agreement whose purpose will be to inhibit any attempt to give such preferential treatment to lenders of non-restructurable debt.

Pari Passu and Negative Pledge Clauses

International credit agreements often contain both a representation by the borrower that the debt incurred pursuant to the agreement in question ranks at least *pari passu* with the borrower's other external debt, and a covenant requiring the borrower to refrain from subordinating that debt to any subsequently-incurred external debt obligations. Such clauses do not, of course, obligate the borrower to repay all of its debt at the same time. A *pari passu* covenant will, however, restrict the borrower from subordinating in a formal way the debt being incurred (or restructured) pursuant to the agreement containing this clause in favor of some other external obligation.

A negative pledge clause is designed to inhibit a borrower from granting security interests in its property or assets in favor of third parties without the express consent of the lender or lenders benefitting from the protection of the clause. A negative pledge clause thus is intended to complement the protection sought by the lender in the *pari passu* undertaking by ensuring that subsequent creditors of the borrower will share the lender's status as a general (*i.e.,* unsecured) creditor. When used in the context of typical corporate borrowers, negative pledge clauses are intended to ensure that the property and assets of the borrower will be unencumbered and available to satisfy the claims of all general creditors on a rateable basis in the event of the bankruptcy of the company.

It might be questioned whether *pari passu* and negative pledge undertakings play any useful role in a sovereign debt restructuring. It is well recognized that sovereigns do not go bankrupt in the same way as commercial corporations. One crucial difference is that a sovereign is most unlikely ever to permit a compulsory marshalling of its assets (at least those assets located within its territory) in order to satisfy the claims of its creditors. Nor is a court inside or outside its territory likely to presume, or have any real power, to dispose of all claims against it. A commercial bank accepting a restructuring of existing debt owed to it by a sovereign borrower or advancing new money to the borrower might, however, be legitimately concerned that the borrower not be permitted to encumber any of its assets or property (such as foreign currency receivables) located outside its own territory. The theory here is that in the event of a recurrence of the borrower's liquidity crisis, a creditor holding security in the borrower's overseas assets might choose to foreclose. At the very least, a creditor with the ability to do so would have little inclination to join in any future restructuring of the borrower's debt on an equal footing with all other creditors.

The context of a sovereign debt renegotiation, however, requires that the issue of negative pledge clauses be approached with great care. From the borrower's perspective, the negative pledge undertaking must not be so restrictive that a default may arise unwittingly, nor should the existence of such an undertaking prevent the borrower from engaging in its normal commercial activities. Thus, the first concern of a sovereign debtor should be to confirm that security interests existing at the time the restructure agreement is signed will not result in an immediate default under the negative pledge clause. In addition, certain kinds of security interests (such as mechanic's, materialmen's and banker's liens) may arise in the future by operation of law without the need for the borrower to make any special arrangements in favor of the creditor; others (such as purchase money mortgages) may be necessary for the borrower to receive favorable credit terms on future financing of capital equipment; and others (such as liens to secure short-term letters of credit opened in connection with the importation of goods or services) may be regarded as indispensable to the normal functioning of the country's transnational trade.

Parties Covered

The first issue to be addressed in connection with a negative pledge undertaking is the object of the clause. In a sovereign debt restructuring, the lenders are likely to request that the clause be drafted expansively to cover the government itself, the entities whose debt is being restructured, and all other present and future government-owned or controlled entities. The effectivenes of a negative pledge clause could easily be undermined, for example, if the government were to create a new agency or instrumentality, transfer its assets to that new entity, and allow those assets to be pledged to secure debt in a way which would be foreclosed to the government itself.[17]

Types of Security Interests Covered

Careful draftsmen of negative pledge clauses will take pains to enumerate the various forms of security interests which are intended to be covered by the undertaking. Technical differences may exist in certain legal systems between liens, pledges, mortgages, charges, encumbrances, deeds of trust and so forth, and omitting reference to a particular form of security interest may open a loophole through which the borrower could evade the restrictions of the clause. In addition, some sovereign borrowers have shown considerable imagination in devising arrangements which do not, strictly speaking, violate their negative pledge undertakings, but which may constitute an effective form of security or preference for subsequent borrowings. The placing of a blocked deposit with a bank under circumstances in which a default by the borrower on a loan made by that bank would, as a matter of law, give rise to an immediate right of set-off against the deposit is one example of such an arrangement which has enjoyed some popularity among borrowers. To preclude such efforts to evade the scope of negative pledge clauses, it is now common to see in these clauses, in addition to an enumeration of specific types of prohibited security interests, a broad catch-all provision along the lines of "any other preferential arrangement which has the practical effect of constituting a security interest with respect to the payment of any obligation with, or with the proceeds of, any asset or revenues of any kind."

Exceptions

Exceptions to the negative pledge clause must be drafted with equal care. A major sovereign borrower engaged in a restructuring may be forced to sweep dozens of public-sector agencies or companies within the scope of its negative pledge undertaking. Many of these entities may have assets subject to existing liens of various kinds and the normal functioning of their business activities may require them to grant future security interests which could result in technical violations of an expansively-worded negative pledge clause. It is therefore usually necessary to set out specific exceptions from the scope of the negative pledge clause.

The success of sovereign borrowers in securing exceptions from negative pledge undertakings in their debt renegotiations seems to vary considerably. The authors' informal survey of eight recent sovereign restructure or "new money" agreements showed a wide disparity between the exceptions to the negative pledge clause contained in those agreements. This disparity may be explained by the different economic situation of the sovereign borrowers or it may reflect a lack of appreciation by some borrowers of the importance of these exceptions.

The exceptions to negative pledge undertakings found in

these agreements include liens or security interests —

(i) incurred to secure the purchase price of property;
(ii) existing on property at the time of its acquisition;
(iii) in favor of multilateral monetary authorities or central banks;
(iv) securing obligations with respect to short-term letters of credit to finance the importation or exportation of goods;
(v) on property acquired under a financial lease;
(vi) arising pursuant to an order of attachment or similar legal process;
(vii) arising by operation of law;
(viii) incurred in connection with project financing;
(ix) existing on the date of the restructure or new money agreement;
(x) arising in connection with contracts for the sale or purchase of precious metals;
(xi) to finance exports;
(xii) incurred in connection with debt maturing in less than one year; and
(xiii) in favor of trade creditors under limited circumstances.

In addition, it is common to limit any negative pledge undertaking to liens and security interests securing external debt.

Prepayment of Non-Restructurable Debt

Contractual restrictions on a sovereign borrower's ability to prepay non-restructurable debt are often cast in the same form as those which guard against preferential repayment of debt which is to be restructured. These provisions obligate the borrower to repay each restructured credit (however that term may be defined) on a rateable basis with any prepayment of a credit not subject to restructure. As is the case with prepayments of restructured debt, the same problems of defining "rateable repayment" and determining what will constitute a specific "credit" for these purposes must here be addressed as well (see Part III.A.2 above). Moreover, if the non-restructurable debt consists of a revolving line of credit (such as those commonly used in trade-related financings), a prepayment which is followed within a reasonably short period by a redrawing under the same credit line should not trigger a mandatory repayment of all restructured credits.

Special care should also be taken in the drafting of these clauses to ensure that involuntary prepayments of non-restructurable debt do not result in a rateable payment obligation for restructured credits. The borrower will argue that an "involuntary" prepayment for these purposes should (at a minimum) include prepayments to avoid increased costs provisions, substitute interest rate provisions and illegality clauses.

To the extent that the injunction against prepayment of debt excluded from restructuring is limited to debt outstanding at the time of the restructuring, the borrower should not find this injunction completely unpalatable. It is frequently necessary for the borrower to offer interest rates for its restructured debt or "new money" borrowings higher than those applicable to prior loans as an inducement for the lenders to restructure or advance new money. A sovereign borrower finding itself at some point in the future in the happy position of having excess cash with which to repay external debt is therefore likely to have an economic motivation to retire first its most expensive debt, *i.e.,* its restructured or "new money" obligations.

Arrangements for Future Availability of Foreign Exchange

Sovereign debt crises are precipitated (whatever their root causes) by an insufficient supply of foreign exchange with which to carry on normal international trading operations and service the external debt of public and private sector borrowers. Many countries approaching a liquidity crisis of this kind will have previously imposed exchange controls of varying stringency. Some exchange control regimes require all foreign currency coming into the country or earned through exports to be sold to the Central Bank or other central monetary authority in return for local currency.[18] A common feature of these schemes is that external debt service payments by individual borrowers within the country require the approval of the governmental authorities before foreign exchange is released.

A sovereign's control over the foreign exchange entering or leaving the country will effectively allow that sovereign in times of shortage to allocate to selected borrowers sufficient foreign currency to pay their external debts on time, leaving others no choice but to slip into arrears. It is equally open for the sovereign to direct that certain borrowers will have access to foreign exchange at a preferential rate; other borrowers will thus be left to face the cruel choice of purchasing foreign currency at open-market or black-market rates or defaulting on their loans. There are many reasons why a sovereign might choose to favor one borrower over another in this way. The sovereign may wish to preserve the international credit standing of the public sector or of particular entities, or stay on the good side of certain lenders from whom additional credits may be expected in the future, or give special treatment to debts incurred in connection with specific types of transactions (such as arms purchases). It will come as no surprise that commercial bank lenders of restructured debt have a strong preference for restricting a sovereign's ability to discriminate among borrowers in this way.

The manner in which commercial banks may attempt to inhibit this discrimination will depend on the factual situation of each restructuring. Particularly if the debt of only one category of borrower within the country (such as the public sector) will be restructured, the lenders may ask for an express undertaking by the sovereign or Central Bank to the effect that other borrowers will have equal access (or at least access at comparable rates) to foreign exchange. Although recognizing that these concerns may be legitimate, most sovereigns will nevertheless resist expanding this undertaking into anything resembling a guaranty that foreign exchange will in fact be made available for future debt service purposes. Such an expansion would be regarded as an effort by the lenders to interfere with the sovereign's prerogative to decide how to apply its scarce foreign exchange in the overall best interests of the country (*e.g.*, to defense, importation of food stuffs, debt service and so forth). The most that the banks can reasonably hope to achieve in this regard is an undertaking that whatever foreign exchange may be made available for debt service will be allocated on equitable terms.

Access to Official Credit Sources

As noted above, the restructuring of commercial bank debt is rarely undertaken in isolation from other measures designed to normalize a country's economy and payments situation. In particular, commercial banks may be reluctant to advance new money, or restructure existing debt, unless they believe that the borrower has worked out, accepted politically, and intends to implement a sound and realistic adjustment plan. Moreover, they may wish to be certain that official sources of credit such as the IMF, multilateral development banks, and individual governments will contribute an equitable share to financing the adjustment program.

Relationship to IMF Credit Facilities

Most member countries of the IMF facing a liquidity crisis will at some stage approach the Fund for assistance in overcoming temporary balance of payments difficulties. If this assistance would significantly exceed the country's allowable quota for IMF drawings (a quota based on the size of the country's capital contribution to the Fund), it is made available pursuant to IMF stand-by or extended fund arrangements.[19] The Fund conditions these facilities on the country's willingness to implement changes in its economic policies, and meet certain economic goals, designed to ameliorate the circumstances giving rise to the liquidity crisis.[20] These measures are negotiated with the member country and will constitute an IMF stabilization and adjustment program for that country. The economic goals against which the Fund will monitor compliance with the program are set out in detail as performance criteria.

Commercial bankers typically encourage and applaud a country's acceptance of an IMF stabilization program. Assuming timely access to relevant and accurate information, commercial bankers are in a position to assess the creditworthiness of a particular borrower or group of borrowers, but they have neither the experience nor the standing to attempt to direct fundamental changes in a country's economy which will have the effect of enhancing a sovereign's credit standing. The assumption by a supranational body such as the IMF of such a didactic and supervisory role is, therefore, viewed by the commercial banks as contributing to a restoration of the country's economic health and ultimately its ability to repay its external loans.

It has not escaped the IMF's attention that commercial banks are thus often third-party beneficiaries of the Fund's stabilization programs. In recent years the IMF has chosen to use its leverage to encourage (some might say conscript) the banks to play a role in a sovereign debt workout which comports with the Fund's notion of the measures necessary to restore stability.[21] The IMF has, in a number of recent renegotiations, adopted an unabashedly paternalistic approach by calling together the borrower, major commercial bank creditors and representatives of central monetary authorities from other affected countries to discuss the Fund's views on each party's expected contribution to the workout. In the case of the 1982-83 Mexican debt renegotiation, for example, the banks were told that the Fund foresaw a need for Mexico to borrow an additional $5 billion of "new money" from commercial banks in 1982 in order to meet an anticipated foreign exchange shortfall that year.[22] This amount was ultimately raised by the international banking community and lent to Mexico.

The Fund does not purport to interfere in negotiations relating to the terms on which a sovereign borrows new money from its commercial bank creditors or restructures existing commercial bank debt.[23] The IMF may, however, exercise its influence on both the borrower and the banks to affect the level of such borrowings during any period in which a stabilization program is in effect. Thus, even though brought together at the encouragement of the IMF, the parties are left to negotiate the details of their arrangements, as long as some agreement is ultimately reached and that agreement is not inconsistent with the IMF program. For their part, the banks—who see themselves as advancing new money or restructuring existing credits on the assumption that an IMF stabilization program will be in operation and that anticipated official credits will in fact be forthcoming—will usually want to condition their own participation on the borrower's compliance with the other elements of the IMF's program. This desire can be reflected in several ways in new money or restructuring agreements.

Condition Precedent to Drawdowns

In the context of a new money agreement which contemplates multiple disbursements at stated intervals, the lenders may seek to condition drawings under the agreement on the borrower's making corresponding purchases under its IMF stand-by or extended fund facility as and when these become available. This correspondence serves two purposes. First, it assures the lenders that the borrower will first utilize all available IMF funds before drawing under its new money commitments (a policy which is, from a cost-of-funds viewpoint, highly desirable for the borrower). Second, the lenders will be disbursing new funds only after the IMF has reviewed the borrower's compliance with the performance criteria under the IMF program applicable to the corresponding IMF purchase. (Although the right to make purchases under an IMF facility may be suspended if the borrower fails to meet these criteria, the Fund maintains the ability to modify or amend specific performance criteria as it deems appropriate.) By linking new money drawings with disbursements under an IMF facility, therefore, the lenders indirectly ensure that the borrower will have available the resources contemplated to be required to make its adjustment program work and that it will be meeting (at least to the satisfaction of the IMF) the applicable economic goals set by the IMF before incremental borrowings may be made under a new money agreement.

Representations and Covenants

Lenders may also seek to include in new money or restructuring agreements a representation to the effect that the sovereign is currently a member of the IMF and is eligible to use the general resources of the IMF.[24] There may also be a corresponding covenant obligating the sovereign to maintain this membership and eligibility while the new money or restructured debt remains outstanding. These clauses are favored by lenders because they regard IMF membership and the ability to utilize the general resources of the Fund as providing a helpful source of long-term assistance to the country in dealing with its debt problems as well as some assurance that the country has not abandoned its commitment to a realistic adjustment program. In the period immediately following a restructuring, of course, the lenders will be more concerned that the sovereign continue to be in a position to make purchases under any IMF stand-by or extended fund arrangement which may then be in place. The principal significance of a covenant regarding IMF membership and eligibility is that it will typically extend beyond the term of such special IMF arrangements.

For several reasons, however, sovereign borrowers tend to resist covenants in their restructuring or new money loan documentation which would contractually commit them, vis-a-vis their commercial bank lenders, to meet applicable performance criteria under IMF stand-by or extended fund arrangements. Such a covenant goes well beyond a clause which merely conditions the availability of new money drawings on the borrower's having made corresponding purchases under its IMF facility. In effect, it incorporates directly all of the performance criteria of a Fund-sponsored stabilization program into the new money or restructuring agreement with the immediate consequence that failure to comply with performance criteria for any reason hurls the entire restructuring package into default. Moreover, unless it is made clear that any determination by the IMF is dispositive, such a covenant will entitle the banks themselves to monitor compliance with the IMF program. This might also entail the anomalous result that a failure to meet a particular performance criterion would constitute a default under the new money or restructure documentation even though the Fund might decide to waive the non-compliance and permit purchases under its stand-by or extended fund arrangement.

Events of Default

Draftsmen of loan documentation jealously protect the symmetry of their agreements; the same concept, in virtually identical terms, will often appear several times in an agreement under the guise of a representation, a covenant and, inevitably, an event of default. When applied to the issue of a sovereign's relationship to the IMF, this practice will result in the sovereign being asked to accept that its failure to remain a member of the IMF, or the loss of its eligibility to use the general resources of the Fund, will constitute an event of default under a new money or restructuring agreement. Most sovereign borrowers will not find this request objectionable.

As discussed above, however, sovereigns often do quarrel with an attempt to make any failure to meet a performance criterion under an IMF stand-by or extended fund arrangement an event of default under commercial bank loan documentation. The commercial banks will argue that such an event of default is necessary to preserve for the lenders the full benefit of linking their new money advances or restructuring efforts to the borrower's compliance with the Fund's prescriptions for economic recovery.

The sovereign may offer several responses to this position. First, if the commercial banks were willing at the outset to accept the terms of an IMF stabilization program without attempting to influence those terms or impose their own economic performance criteria, the banks should similarly be willing to accept a decision by the Fund to waive or modify a performance criterion in a particular case as the Fund deems appropriate. In practice, the Fund has not demonstrated that it will waive or amend performance criteria uncritically,[25] and the banks should not therefore be overly concerned that the IMF will lightly accept a dilution of its proposed stabilization measures. Second, in order to second guess the IMF on any decision to waive or modify particular performance criteria, the commercial banks would need to be in a position to replicate the Fund's analysis of the country's overall economic and political situation. It is not at all clear that commercial banks are prepared or even very anxious to assume this responsibility.[26] Finally, the sovereign would argue that if it fails to meet a performance criterion and the Fund is unwilling to waive or modify that criterion, the borrower will be penalized by an inability to make an incremental purchase under the IMF facility. If such purchases are linked to new money drawings under an agreement with commercial bank creditors, the penalty will be cumulative. No additional incentive is necessary or helpful to encourage the borrower to meet its IMF targets, and the threat of a default under new money or restructuring documentation (with all its probable cross-default consequences) amounts, the sovereign will claim, to a disproportionate penalty that in the end may do more harm than good to all concerned.

Sharing of Information

One of the most contentious issues raised by a sovereign debt restructuring centers on the extent to which the sovereign will be required to release to its commercial bank creditors economic information that it provides to the IMF, or disclose staff reports, assessments, economic projections and so forth that it receives from the IMF. The banks have argued that release of this information is necessary for them to make informed credit decisions. Indeed, in the wake of recent Congressional criticism of the international lending practices of major U.S. banks,[27] the banks' desire for complete credit files on "problem loans" has intensified. A sovereign borrower engaged in restructuring commercial bank debt may therefore expect to be confronted with a request that it promptly provide to its bank creditors copies of all information submitted to, or received from, the IMF during the term of the restructured debt.

For most sovereign borrowers this suggestion will have little appeal. A sovereign will argue that its relationship to an entity such as the IMF requires the protection of a certain degree of confidentiality if full and candid exchanges between the country and the Fund are to be encouraged. Moreover, much of the information sought by the banks through the use of this form of contractual covenant will be publicly available from other sources without requiring the sovereign to compromise its position that exchanges of information with the Fund are presumptively confidential.

The real motivation behind a country's objection to an information-sharing clause of this type, however, will be based on the recognition that some (but admittedly not all) of this information may be politically sensitive. Viewed realistically, distributing this information to a large restructuring syndicate is tantamount to public disclosure. It should be remembered that IMF remedial stabilization programs often call for severe domestic austerity measures.[28] A government may be understandably loath to have IMF staff projections of the effect of these measures on employment and standard of living, or IMF staff predictions regarding the need for future additional austerity measures, appear verbatim in local newspapers. All governments, even those in unquestionably democratic societies, like to have some control over the timing and circumstances of the release of important government economic projections. This concern is of course more acute in countries in which the belt-tightening measures urged by the IMF could result in political instability.

There is no easy solution to this issue. One approach that has been adopted in some restructurings is for the lenders and the borrower to negotiate the particular categories of information which will be supplied to the lenders. The borrower then compiles and provides this information to its commercial bank creditors separately from whatever submissions are made to, or received from, the IMF. The advocates of this approach hope that this will sufficiently distance the information or projections from the Fund, thus preserving the principle of the confidentiality of Fund/member exchanges and possibly reducing the danger that economic austerity measures summarized or proposed in the information will be perceived as emanating from forces outside the country itself.

Availability of Other Official Credits

It is principally the IMF's practice of conditioning its financial assistance on the borrower's willingness to adopt measures imposing a degree of economic discipline that stirs such a keen interest on the part of commercial banks in a sovereign borrower's relationship to the IMF. There may, however, be several other sources of official credits available to the borrower and, in the context of restructuring commercial bank loans, it may be proposed that the borrower undertake certain contractual obligations regarding its continued access to these sources. This is particularly likely to be the case where the Fund program itself contemplates and is premised on specified levels of borrowings from official sources.

Multilateral development banks such as the International Bank for Reconstruction and Development ("IBRD") and the Inter-American Development Bank are frequently potential sources of official funds for a sovereign borrower. Loans from these institutions usually take the form of project financing transactions and they are rarely, if ever, conditioned on the sovereign borrower's agreement to implement remedial changes in its economy. Nevertheless, it is not uncommon for commercial bank lenders to seek a covenant in their new money or restructuring documentation (often with a corresponding event of default) to the effect that the borrower will remain a member of the IBRD and any other multilateral development bank likely to be a significant source of future loans. In addition, because the IBRD communicates regularly with its member countries on the state of their economies and debt position, commercial bank lenders may seek access to information exchanges between the sovereign and the IBRD similar to that sought for IMF-related information. Sovereign borrowers sometimes object to this request for the same reasons they may oppose full disclosure to commercial bank lenders of all information exchanges with the IMF (see Part III.D.1.d. above).

Finally, the borrower may request that sister governments continue to make available official lines of credit and guaranty or insurance facilities to ease current payments difficulties. Lenders may also insist that the borrower seek a restructuring of arrearages and amounts becoming payable under such facilities under the auspices of the Paris Club.

Events of Default

There are at least two reasons why the event of default clause in a restructuring or new money agreement requires even closer scrutiny than in an ordinary loan agreement. First, since the restructuring process often has the effect of centralizing a country's debt profile (particularly when the sovereign or central bank acts in the role of borrower or guarantor), the consequences of a default under one agreement may have immediate cross-default ramifications for all of the country's external borrowings. Second, unlike an ordinary loan transaction, some of the lenders participating in a restructuring or new money loan may do so with a distinct lack of enthusiasm. The borrower can therefore safely assume that its conduct and compliance with the terms of the agreement will be closely watched by parties who may see it as in their interest to bring purported defaults to the attention of other lenders. The obvious lesson for the careful borrower (and, incidentally, the well-disposed lenders) is to ensure that the default clause is not drafted so rigorously as to force the borrower into technical default in circumstances that do not threaten the borrower's ability or willingness to repay its debt.

The Psychology of Default Clauses

Not all default clauses, however, are limited to circumstances signalling the borrower's inability or unwillingness to repay. The documentation in some recent restructurings reveals a tendency to use event of default clauses as a means of influencing other creditors, such as recalcitrant banks or official sources of credit, into accepting responsibilities that are compatible with the restructuring program. In its most benign form, this is typified by a clause making it an event of default under a new money or restructuring agreement if the country fails to obtain a contemplated level of official credits necessary to cover any anticipated residual foreign exchange shortfall. Viewed in one light, this merely reflects an understandable desire on the part of the commercial bank lenders to ensure that it is not they alone who will be performing their part in a sovereign workout. The clause also serves another purpose. If one believes that the threat of exercising normal legal remedies against a defaulting borrower has any efficacy in the context of a sovereign restructuring, then this clause gives the commercial banks considerable leverage over the official creditors who are asked to advance new funds.

Not only could the banks' new money or restructured obligations (not to speak of other pre-existing credit instruments linked by cross-default clauses) become immediately due and payable if this event of default were triggered by a failure of the official creditors to open and fund the necessary credit lines, but also the whole process of readjustment, of which the renegotiation of commercial credits is but one piece, could be brought to a standstill. At the very least, this may cripple the country's ability to participate normally in international trade.

There are other examples of the use of default clauses to influence the behavior of persons other than the borrower. Suppose the lenders decide that certain banks are taking advantage of an interbank placement or trade exclusion from the category of debt subject to restructure to demand immediate repayment of their interbank credit lines or trade credits to banks in the borrowing country. One obvious consequence of such repayment would be to drain off scarce foreign currency reserves which could otherwise be used to service payments on term loans. To discourage this behavior, the commercial banks agreeing to restructure their loans may suggest including in the new money or restructuring agreement a clause making it an event of default if interbank lines or trade credits to the country fall below some specified level.

In both of these examples, the stated event of default is not triggered by any misconduct on the part of the borrower. After all, the borrower cannot compel official creditors to advance funds nor can it prevent commercial banks from demanding repayment of their interbank lines or trade credits. The commercial bank lenders insisting on these clauses are in effect attempting to influence the behavior of third parties (in these examples, official creditors or sister commercial banks) by placing both the borrower and its universe of creditors in great jeopardy if the desired conduct is not forthcoming. In effect the lenders are using the default clause to create a third class of the borrower's indebtedness in addition to the classes of restructured debt and debt which is to be truly exempt from restructuring and expected to be repaid on a timely basis. This third category, be it interbank lines, trade credits or anything else, is expected to be rolled over indefinitely (or at least until things look better for the borrower) without any formal, binding commitment on the part of the holders of this debt to do so.

In the extreme case, the borrower can find that such default clauses place him in the very uncomfortable position of being, as it were, consigned to perdition if he does, and consigned to perdition if he doesn't. For example, the lenders will no doubt insist that the borrower's failure to make timely payment of principal or interest on external debt (including loans not subject to restructuring such as interbank lines or trade credits) will constitute an event of default. Thus, if a bank refuses to roll over substantial trade credits who maintenance is necessary to keep the borrower's aggregate trade credit balance above the stipulated level and instead sues the borrower for prompt repayment, the borrower will be in default (i) if he pays the bank suing him or (ii) if he doesn't pay the bank suing him. The same reasoning holds true in the case of debt subject to restructure where the lender declines to extend the original maturity and holds to his original payment schedule, thus triggering a choice between outright default and a mandatory repayment obligation with which the borrower cannot possibly comply (see Part III.A.2. above).

The justification advanced by commercial banks for placing the borrower in this disagreeable position is that it allows the banks to persuade a reluctant lender to accept the restructuring and to honor the existence of the third category of non-restructurable (but not to be repaid) debt. The banks will point out that if the lender doesn't play the game, an event of default can be declared and the borrower's available assets may quickly become subject to numerous attachment orders. Thus, a recalcitrant bank is warned that it may prove extremely difficult to satisfy any judgment it might receive. The moral which the perceptive lender is supposed to derive from this story is that all banks are better off if no one of them tries to get paid out early and this, the commercial bankers will tell the borrower, is in the borrower's best interest.

Cross-Default Clauses

It is generally thought that the primary purpose of a cross-default clause in a syndicated loan agreement is to place the lenders on an equal footing (in terms of bargaining position and available remedies) with the borrower's other creditors should the borrower default under one or more of its other agreements. If the borrower begins to show signs of financial instability, the argument goes, lenders will not want to be forced to wait until a payment default occurs under *their* agreement with the borrower before they become entitled to undertake remedial actions. If these lenders were forced to sit by while other creditors were set at liberty to initiate legal proceedings against the borrower, the assets of the borrower available to satisfy judgments could become smothered by pre-judgment attachments or similar conservatory measures long before such lenders could accelerate their loan and pursue their own legal remedies. This could be very prejudicial in a jurisdiction in which the application of the proceeds from the sale of a debtor's assets follows the order of pre-judgment attachments covering that asset.

This rationale will be equally applicable to cross-default clauses in restructuring or new money agreements. The justification for these clauses, however, may not be limited to this traditional explanation. Commercial banks involved in a restructuring may suggest that an enlightened borrower should actually welcome rigorous cross-default clauses at least in so far as concerns the payment of debt subject to restructure. Bearing in mind that restructuring is ultimately a consensual process, these banks will argue that the best way of persuading a recalcitrant lender that it would be ill-advised to attempt to stay out of the restructuring and to pursue independent legal remedies against the borrower is to make it clear that the initiation of such actions by any one lender will empower all of the borrower's other bank creditors to do likewise. It is sometimes claimed that this threat operates to keep all bank lenders within the restructuring fold.[29]

This prediction as to the likely response of maverick lenders in the face of broad cross-default clauses is not, however, entirely self-evident. An equally plausible case can be made for the proposition that faced with such a recalcitrant lender who has been given the ability to threaten the entire restructuring effort unless his debt subject to restructure is paid on its original maturity, the borrower (or, indeed, another bank creditor with more to lose than his renegade comrade) will in fact be forced to pay up precisely in order to avoid the default. Thus, a maverick lender threatening suit against an obligor rather than agreeing to restructure his debt may be able to hold the banks principally interested in the restructuring ransom to their own cross-default clause. Had the cross-default been drafted so as to exclude any defaults under other agreements which involve a lender's demand to receive early repayment of debt subject to restructure, however, such a lender would know in advance that neither the commencement of a suit nor the borrower's refusal to pay could jeopardize the entire restructure process.

Coverage

A salient feature of cross-default clauses in sovereign restructurings is that they generally embrace a large number of borrowing entities within the country. There is no rule that requires the draftsman of a cross-default clause to limit himself to defaults occurring under other agreements of that particular borrower. Consequently, if the goal is to cast the cross-default net as widely as possible, the draftsman will make reference to defaults by any borrowing entity within the public (and, in some circumstances, the private) sector under any agreement for borrowed money or the deferred purchase price of goods or services. Some limitation may be achieved by restricting the scope of the clause to agreements relating to external debt. Nevertheless, simply monitoring the compliance of each borrowing entity with all of its external debt obligations may pose a formidable task.

It should also be noted that the medium of a cross-default clause may provide lenders in a restructuring with an additional way of assuring equal treatment by the sovereign of all obligors whose debt is being restructured. If, for example, a failure to make payment by an obligor under one restructured credit risks by virtue of cross-default clauses placing *all* of the country's restructured debt in default, the sovereign will have a further disincentive to favor some obligors over others.

Triggering Events

Cross-default clauses are usually drafted so as to be triggered in one of two ways. The triggering event may be either (i) a default or event of default occurring under a credit instrument signed by a specified borrower which has the effect of permitting the lenders in that agreement to accelerate the debt, or (ii) actual acceleration of a debt owed by such a borrower. The first of these options gives the proponents of the cross-default clause the greatest latitude in being able to accelerate their own loan in the event that the borrower under their agreement (or any of the other specified borrowing entities whose financial condition the lenders regard as material to their loan) defaults in some fashion under another credit instrument. The significant feature of this approach is that actual acceleration of the other debt is not required to trigger the cross-default. Thus, it is of no significance that the lenders under the other credit instrument might agree to waive or ignore the default. It is the fact that the other lenders are capable of accelerating their loan—regardless of whether this right is actually exercised—which triggers the cross-default clause.

Borrowers disfavor these "capable of" cross-default triggers which do not require actual acceleration of some other debt.[30] Borrowers argue that their creditors are not seriously prejudiced unless other lenders begin positioning themselves to exercise legal remedies against the borrower by accelerating debt. They may also point out, for example, that lenders insisting on a "capable of" cross-default clause would theoretically need to grant a waiver under their agreement each time one of the specified borrowers covered by the clause defaults under some other credit instrument. Obtaining multiple waivers from a large syndicate can be onerous for the agent and expensive for the borrower.

The "capable of" formulation is sometimes defended by lenders who will openly admit that they want the widest freedom of action in the event that the borrower (or any other entity covered by the cross-default clause) begins to show signs of financial instability. These lenders may also claim that this formulation will allow them to participate in any negotiations or arrangements into which the borrower (or another party) may be forced by its other creditors in order to avoid an acceleration of its debt to those other creditors.

A sovereign may expect to be more successful in restricting the use of a "capable of" formulation of this clause where the triggering event is a default other than a failure to make a payment required under another agreement. For example, the devaluation of local currency and general economic downturn which often attend the need for a sovereign debt restructuring will make it almost inevitable that borrowers in the country who have financial covenants in the form of debt/equity ratios and the like will necessarily remain in default for much of the restructuring period and will require a continuous series of waivers by their lenders.

Cure Periods and De Minimis Tests

It is sometimes possible to inject flexibility into cross-default clauses by providing for grace or cure periods in which to remedy defaults arising under other agreements before a cross-default is triggered. If the sovereign or Central Bank will act as borrower or guarantor under the restructuring documentation, it may be in everyone's interest to provide for a short period (say 10 to 15 days) after notice is given to the sovereign or Central Bank of a default by one of the specified borrowers in order to allow the default to be cured. This greatly reduces the risks inherent in extending the cross-default clause to dozens of borrowing entities within the country because the failure or inability of the sovereign to police strictly the behavior of those borrowers in respect of their external debt obligations will not have automatic cross-default consequences.

It may also be prudent for the parties to agree on acceptable *de minimis* levels in order to ensure that the cross-default clause will not be triggered by payment defaults involving relatively minimal amounts. Even in the case of defaults not involving non-payment, the borrower may request that the cross-default clause not be triggered unless the default in question entitles other lenders to accelerate a principal amount of debt in excess of some agreed amount.

CONCLUSION

The legal issues raised by a sovereign debt restructuring must be addressed and resolved in a rather unique setting. Unlike conventional financial transactions, neither side in a sovereign debt restructuring would—if it had its choice—wish to be engaged in the process. The same economic necessity which forces the sovereign to embrace IMF-directed austerity measures and accept higher margins and fees on its restructured commercial bank debt will similarly dictate that the banks, in furtherance of their own enlightened self-interest, agree to a deferral of the repayment of their loans.

The sovereign cannot simply declare bankruptcy, distribute its assets among its various creditors and face the future absolved of its past debt problems. Nor will the banks, despite all the ingenuity and effort expended on legal documentation intended to improve their legal position in the event of non-payment, find that there are sensible legal remedies when none of the country's external creditors is being paid. It is by and large true that the best way of diluting the efficacy of any individual creditor's legal remedies is to empower all of one's creditors to pursue their legal remedies at the same time. Stated differently, there is a paradoxically inverse relationship between the enormity of a country's actual or threatened payment default and the practical danger that individual bank creditors will resort to legal remedies.

Even if one starts with the premise that sovereign debt restructuring will be a mutually distasteful exercise, however, it will almost certainly be true that some lenders will find the process more repugnant than others. For example, an obscure bank with a small exposure in the country may entertain hopes that, solely by virtue of its own relative insignificance, it will succeed in being paid (or bought out of its loan by another bank) when its more influential and visible sister banks have no choice but to restructure their credits. During the course of the negotiations, the sovereign borrower can expect to hear much about risks posed by such maverick lenders who may refuse to participate in the restructuring process. The sovereign may be told again and again that its approach to particular points in the negotiations, whether legal issues or strictly business terms, will increase the chance that maverick lenders may reject the restructuring and set off an uncontrollable *sauve qui peut* reaction on the part of other creditors. The sovereign will rarely be in a position to verify whether potential maverick lenders are in fact possessed of the sensitivities claimed for them by the bank advisory group during negotiations. Nevertheless, the sovereign will be asked to concede a great deal in order to forestall possible adverse reactions by some lenders when both the imminence and the relative importance of such reactions will remain largely speculative.

This negotiating tactic of appealing to spectral and often unquantifiable risks is not, however, entirely the prerogative of the banks. In less sophisticated times, Louis XIV embossed his cannon with the legend "Ultima Ratio Regis," or the King's Last Argument. A modern sovereign in a commercial bank debt renegotiation is likely to find its last argument in an appeal either to the potential for domestic political instability which could result from the sovereign's acceptance of excessively harsh terms, or the possibility that such terms would so undermine the country's financial stability as to place in jeopardy the prospects for eventual repayment of the loans. Fortunately, the broader political and economic implications of major sovereign debt restructurings are generally apparent to all the parties and "last arguments" of this sort are necessary very infrequently.

NOTES

1. Sovereign debt restructurings, for all their recent prominence, are not a new phenomenon. Between 1956 and 1976, there were thirty debt renegotiations for eleven countries, involving a total debt of $7 billion. During the period from 1975 through 1981, twenty-five such renegotiations took place involving fourteen countries and total debt of approximately $10 billion. See C. H. Hardy, *Rescheduling Developing Country Debts, 1956-1981: Lessons and Recommendations* 1-2 (Overseas Development Council, 1982).

2. The practice of granting so-called "silent subparticipations" in international credits may make it difficult to determine the precise number of banks with credit exposure in a particular country.

3. In 1982, Mexico and Brazil initially adopted very different approaches to their debt renegotiations but subsequent developments induced the Brazilians to modify their program in ways which more closely resembled the Mexican approach. Mexico, for example, appointed a single commercial bank advisory committee at the same time as it announced a moratorium on repayment of principal due on public sector debt in August 1982. Brazil delayed taking this step for five months after the first indications of a liquidity crisis. It became apparent by the end of 1982, however, that Brazil would also need to deal with a centralized committee of its bank creditors. See M. Mendelsohn, *Commercial Banks and the Restructuring of Crossborder Debt* 20-23 (Group of Thirty, 1983) (hereinafter "Mendelsohn").

4. "[T]here is an understandable fear on the part of the commercial banks that too easy an agreement involving longer-term maturities may remove one of the principal weapons in their hands: the borrower's consciousness of the need to put his house in order and keep the creditors sweet for the next rescheduling negotiations." Leslie, "Techniques of Rescheduling: The Latest Lessons," *The Banker* (April 1983) at 28.

5. When, however, a bank resident in the country is a participant in a syndicated loan denominated in a foreign currency, pragmatic considerations will likely dictate a restructuring of the entire loan.

6. *See, e.g.,* El Khoury, "Mexico's Foreign Exchange Programme for Private Sector Companies," *Int'l Financial L. Rev.* 18 (July 1983).

7. *See* P. Wood, *Law and Practice of International Finance* §4.13(2) (1982) for a discussion of the reasons advanced by some creditors in support of their claims for priority.

8. *See, e.g.,* Robinson, "Costa Rica's Plight Deepens as the Creditors Wrangle," *Euromoney,* December 1981 at 34.

9. *See,* Mendelsohn at 8-9.

10. Even if the sovereign does not appear as an obligor or guarantor in the restructuring, there is nothing to prevent lenders from linking (through cross-default clauses) a restructuring agreement to other loan or restructuring agreements signed by other public or private sector borrowers. The centralization of the country's external debt which would result from the sovereign or Central Bank acting as obligor or guarantor under each restructure agreement, however, makes such broad cross-default clauses almost inevitable.

11. To the extent that the original credit instruments may retain their legal vitality in respect of non-restructured maturities the lenders will, of course, continue to benefit from protective clauses (such as default clauses) contained in those instruments.

12. An additional benefit (from the bank's standpoint) is that a sharing clause justifies, or seeks to justify, set-offs against deposits in excess of the depositary bank's participation in the loan, up to the aggregate amount owed to all banks in the syndicate.

13. *See* Brown, "Sharing Strains on Euromarket Syndicates," *Int'l Financial L. Rev.* 4 (June 1982); Youard, "Enough Is Enough," *Euromoney* 107 (November 1983).

14. Consider, for example, the plight of a borrower which has no choice but to repay a recalcitrant lender with a small credit if that lender takes legal action to recover payment and refuses to be dissuaded from its course.

15. Despite the obvious (to the authors) equity of permitting prepayment without penalty of a lender who asserts a claim for reimbursement of substantial increased costs, a practice seems to be developing in the restructuring context of denying the borrower any right to prepay the claimants of those costs without rateably prepaying all of its restructured credits, notwithstanding the virtually universal prevalence of such a right in syndicated loans generally. A minor (though not insignificant) recompense should be that the claimant be put to a higher burden of proof in justifying its right to reimbursement.

16. Lenders will generally not try to interfere with the borrower's flexibility in respect of debt incurred after the restructuring because they do not wish to inhibit the borrower from obtaining the fresh loans which may be necessary to stabilize its financial position while the restructured loans remain outstanding.

17. Query, however, whether different treatment should be accorded for a private company nationalized after the restructuring is in place. It may, at the time of such nationalization, have existing security interests and a need to continue to borrow without a central government guaranty on a secured basis.

18. If the Central Bank does act as the repository of all foreign exchange, this may increase the lenders' desire to see the Central Bank take an active role (either as borrower or, if legally permissible, guarantor) in the restructuring in order to facilitate the banks' legal ability to attach or set off against foreign currency deposits of the Central Bank held abroad.

19. For a description of these arrangements, see J. Gold, *Financial Assistance by the International Monetary Fund, Law and Practice* 11-19 (1980).

20. *Id.* at 19-24.

21. *See* "The IMF and Latin America," *The Economist* (December 23,

1982) at 69.

22. *See* Bogdanowicz-Bindert, "IMF Is Emerging as Central Econmoic Coordinator," *American Banker* 33-34 (September 27, 1983).

23. *See* J. Gold, *Order in International Finance, The Promotion of IMF Stand-By Arrangements, and the Drafting of Private Loan Agreements* 15-16 (1982).

24. There are certain drafting subtleties involved in these clauses. *See* Gold, *id.* at 17-20.

25. *See* "Can the IMF Dare to Deny Loans to Brazil," *The Economist* 75-76 (July 9, 1983).

26. In the context of a new money loan to Peru during its 1976 debt renegotiation, for example, the banks attempted to impose economic performance criteria (modelled on an IMF stand-by arrangement) as a condition to advancing the loans. This effort was noticeably unsuccessful and the practice seems to have fallen out of favor with commercial banks in subsequent restructurings. *See* Marmorstein, "Responding to the Call for Order in International Finance: Cooperation Between the International Monetary Fund and Commercial Banks," 18 *Va. J. Int'l L.* 445, 454 (1978).

27. *See* Buchheit, "Restrictions on United States Banks' International Lending," *Int'l Financial L. Rev.* 24 (March 1983).

28. "While the *objectives* of the Fund may be entirely apolitical, the *consequences* of Fund recommendations can be highly political. Although the Fund has in recent years become increasingly aware of the political and social dimension of its policy recommendations, nevertheless, its principal concern is to bring a country's external accounts into balance; and it naturally stresses domestic economic policies which are geared to achieving that goal. But such "adjustment" policies may also bring about a low standard of living, higher unemployment, a cutback in social welfare programs, and greater emphasis in filling the demands of the export market than on producing to meet the needs of the domestic consumer. And these are consequences which few governments can afford to ignore; certainly not if they operate in a democratic system." Staff of Subcomm. on Foreign Economic Policy of the Senate Comm. on Foreign Relations, 95th Cong., 1st Sess., *International Debt, The Banks, and U.S. Foreign Policy* (Comm. Print 1977) at 66.

29. Of course, a cross-default clause does not *obligate* a lending syndicate to accelerate its loan if a default occurs under another agreement, but the threat to the recalcitrant bank will only be credible if it feels that its insistence on payment will in fact result in a default.

30. For a discussion of criticisms of the "capable of" cross-default formulation, *see* Carroll, "The Worst Clause in the Euromarkets," *Euromoney* (June 1981) at 90.

Mark A. Walker is a member of the New York Bar; Cleary, Gottlieb, Steen & Hamilton; New York.

Lee C. Buchheit is a member of the Pennsylvania and District of Columbia Bars; Cleary, Gottlieb, Steen & Hamilton; Washington, D.C.

(Copyright 1983: Mark A. Walker, Lee C. Buchheit)

17C. Terms and Conditions of Bank Debt Restructurings and Bank Financial Packages, 1978-June 1985

Table 17. Terms and Conditions of Bank Debt Restructurings and Bank Financial Packages, 1978–June 1985

Country, Date of Agreement, and Type of Debt Rescheduled	Basis	Amount Provided	Grace Period	Maturity	Interest Rate
		(US$ millions)	*(In years, unless otherwise noted)*		*(In percent spread over LIBOR/U.S. Prime)*
Argentina					
Bridging loan (1982) [1]		1,300 [2]	7 months	14 months	1⅝–1½
New medium-term loan (1983)	New financing	1,500	3	4½	2¼–2⅛
Agreement in principle [3] with Working Committee (December 3, 1984):					
Refinancing of medium- and long-term debt					
Public and publicly guaranteed debt					
Due in 1982 and 1983	100 percent of principal	16,552	3	10	1⅜–1⅜
Due in 1984 and 1985	100 percent of principal		3	12	1⅜–1⅜
Private sector nonguaranteed debt			3	10	1⅜–1⅜
New medium-term loan	New financing	3,700	3	10	1⅝–1¼
New trade credit deposit facility		500	—	4	1⅜–1
Trade credit maintenance facility	Banks would maintain trade credit at levels of September 30, 1984 (estimate)	1,200	—	—	1⅛–¾
Stand-by money market facility	Banks would make available to the Central Bank on request any amounts outstanding to foreign branches and agencies of Argentine banks on September 30, 1984	1,400	—	—	¼
Bolivia					
Deferment agreement of August 1980 and December 1980: short- and medium-term debt falling due August 1980–March 1981	100 percent of principal	200	—	to April 1981	1¾
Refinancing agreement of April 1981:					
Conversion and consolidation of:					
Deferred short-term debt	80 percent of principal	99	2	3½	2
Deferred medium-term debt	90 percent of principal	69	3	7	2¼
Refinancing of debt:					
Due April 1981–March 1982	90 percent of principal	120	3	6	2¼
Due April 1982–March 1983 [4]	90 percent of principal	124	2	5	2¼
Normalization plan of May 1983: [5]					
Principal payments falling due April 1–October 6, 1983	Moratorium on 100 percent of principal	87	—	—	Originally contracted rates
Arrears on interest payments	New schedule of payments [6]	118	—	Within September 1983	
Interim plan of October 1983:					
Deferment of:					
Obligations arising from 1981 rescheduling	100 percent of principal	48	2 more years	. . .	. . .
Maturities falling due April 1983–January 1984	100 percent of principal	261	4	. . .	. . .

Table 17. Terms and Conditions of Bank Debt Restructurings and Bank Financial Packages, 1978–June 1985 (continued)

Country, Date of Agreement, and Type of Debt Rescheduled	Basis	Amount Provided	Grace Period	Maturity	Interest Rate
		(US$ millions)	(In years, unless otherwise noted)		(In percent spread over LIBOR/U.S. Prime)
Chile					
Agreement of July 28, 1983:					
New loan agreed in principle	New financing	1,300	4	7	2¼–2⅛
Rescheduling of medium-term debt due:					
In 1983	100 percent of principal	1,200	4	8	2⅛–2
In 1984	100 percent of principal	1,000	4	8	2⅛–2
Rollover of trade related short-term debt:	100 percent rollover until December 1984	1,700	—	—	1½
Agreement of January 25, 1984:					
Short-term nontrade related debt converted to medium-term debt	100 percent of principal	1,200	4	8	2⅛
Agreement of June 14, 1984:					
New loan	New financing	780	5	9	1⅜–1½
Agreement of November 26, 1984:					
Continuation of rollover of short-term trade related line of credit until June 30, 1985	1,700	—	6 months	Originally contracted rates
Moratorium on public and private debt					
Due in January–March 1985	100 percent of principal	298	—	6 months	Originally contracted rates
Due in April–June 1985	100 percent of principal	. . .	—	6 months	Originally contracted rates
Costa Rica					
Agreement of September 10, 1983 (amendment agreed in principle in January 1985):					
Principal in arrears prior to 1983	97½ percent	363	3¼	7½	2¼–2⅛
Principal falling due in 1983	97½ percent	110	3¼	7½	2¼–2⅛
Principal falling due in 1984	100 percent	136	3¼	6½	2¼–2⅛
Certificates of deposit:[12]					
Falling due prior to 1983	100 percent of principal and interest accrued prior to 1983		4	8	—
Falling due in 1984	100 percent of principal	100	5	8	—
New revolving facility[13]	Revolving credit equivalent to 50 percent of interest payments actually paid in 1983	202	2	3	1⅞–1⅝
Agreement in principle with Steering Committee (January 1985):					
Increase in revolving facility originally agreed in September 1983	New financing	75	1½	6	1⅝–1⅜
Rescheduling of principal falling due in 1985 and 1986	100 percent	440	3	10	1⅝–1⅜ [14]

477

Dominican Republic					
Agreement of December 21, 1983:					
Letters of credit outstanding on November 30, 1982, and in arrears at that date					
Central Bank acceptances					
Public and private debt in arrears as of November 30, 1983	95 percent	500	1	5	2¼–2⅛
Public and private debt falling due between December 1, 1982–December 31, 1983					
Agreement in principle with Steering Committee (May 1985):					
Rescheduling of public and private debt					
In arrears as of December 31, 1984	100 percent	168	3	13	1⅜
Due in 1985–89	100 percent	707	3	13	1⅜
Ecuador					
Agreement of October 1983:					
Refinancing of private debt falling due in 1983	100 percent of principal	940	1	7	2¼–2⅛
Refinancing of public debt falling due in 1983 (effective December 31, 1983)[15]	90 percent of principal	895 (including 580 in short-term debt)	1	6	2¼–2⅛
New loan	New financing	431	1½	6	2⅜–2¼
Trade credit	100 percent rollover until December 1984	700	—	—	1½–1⅝
Agreement in principle with Steering Committee (December 1984):					
Refinancing of the 1985–89 public sector debt	100 percent of principal	4,360	3	12	1⅜
Rescheduling of deposit facility falling due in 1985–89					
Rescheduling of 1983 loan	100 percent of principal	431	2	10	1⅝–1¼
Extension of trade finance		700			

[12] Refers to those certificates which were issued by the Central Bank against existing arrears of the private sector (mainly with regard to imports) and which were held by the foreign commercial banks.

[13] The banks agreed to provide Costa Rica with a revolving trade related credit facility equivalent to 50 percent of interest payments actually paid in 1983, which were either in arrears or had accrued in 1983.

[14] These are 1⅝ percent over "domestic reference rate," equal to: U.S. dollar C/D rate adjusted to reserves and insurance; or a comparable yield for loans denominated in other currencies.

[15] Payments of 100 percent of the maturities falling due were deferred until December 31, 1984, when 90 percent of the amount was refinanced.

Table 17. Terms and Conditions of Bank Debt Restructurings and Bank Financial Packages, 1978–June 1985 (continued)

Country, Date of Agreement, and Type of Debt Rescheduled	Basis	Amount Provided	Grace Period	Maturity	Interest Rate
		(US$ millions)	*(In years, unless otherwise noted)*		*(In percent spread over LIBOR/U.S. Prime)*
Guyana					
Deferment agreement of June 1982:[16] Public and publicly guaranteed medium- and long-term debt due during March 11, 1982–March 31, 1983	100 percent of principal	15	—	—	2½
Deferment agreement of July 1983: Amount deferred in June 1982, plus amount due until January 1984	100 percent of principal	24	—	—	2½
Deferment agreement of January 1984:					
Amount deferred in July 1983, plus amount due until July 1984	100 percent of principal	29	—	—	2½
Deferment agreement of July 1984: Amount deferred in January 1984 plus amount due until July 1985	100 percent of principal	42	—	—	2½
Honduras					
Requested by the authorities in January 1982:[17] Refinancing of medium- and long-term debt (public entities):					
Due 1981 (arrears)	100 percent of principal	11	9 months	6	2¼
Due 1982 (arrears)	100 percent of principal	41	9 months	6	2¼
Due 1983 (arrears)	100 percent of principal	36	3–15 months [18]	6	2¼
Due 1984	100 percent of principal	32	3–15 months [18]	6	2¼
Agreement in principle with Steering Committee (December 1984):[19] Extension of principal due (including principal in arrears through 1984) until end of 1985	100 percent of principal	148	—	—	1⅞
Refinancing, in 1986, of:[20] Deferred principal due through end of 1985	100 percent of principal	148	2	10	1½
Principal falling due after 1986	100 percent of principal	72	1–2 [21]	7–9	1½
Ivory Coast					
Agreement of March 1, 1985: Public and publicly guaranteed medium- and long-term debt:					
Due December 1983 and 1984	100 percent of principal	280	2	7	1⅞–1⅝
Due 1985	90 percent of principal	221	3	8	1⅞–1⅝
New loan		104	3	7	1⅞–1⅝

Jamaica					
Agreement of September 1978:					
Due April 1978–March 1979	7/8 of principal	63	2 [22]	5 [22]	2
Agreement of April 1979:					
Due April 1979–March 1980	7/8 of principal [23]	77	2	5	2
Due April 1980–March 1981	7/8 of principal [23]	72	2	5	2
Agreement of June 1981:					
Due April 1981–March 1983	100 percent of principal	89	2	5	2
Of which: 1982–1983	100 percent of principal	41	2	5	2
Syndicated loan (July 1981)	New financing	71	3	7	2¼
Other new loans (March 1982)	New financing	18	2	7	2½
Agreement of June 1984:					
Due July 1983–March 1984	100 percent of principal	65	2	5	2½
Due April 1984–March 1985	100 percent of principal	100	2	5	2½
Liberia					
Agreement of December 1, 1982: [24]					
Due July 1, 1981–June 30, 1983	95 percent of principal	30	3	6	1¾
In process:					
Maturities falling due during July 1983–June 1985	95 percent of principal	35	3	6	. . .
Madagascar					
Agreement of July–November 1981:					
Rescheduling of arrears on overdrafts	100 percent of principal	147 [25]	—	3½	1½
Agreement of October 25, 1984: [26]					
Global restructuring of outstanding public debt [27]					
Of which: in arrears	100 percent of principal	70	2½	. . .	. . .
Medium-term		18	2½	8	2
Short-term		52	2½	6	1¾
Of which: future maturities	100 percent of principal	126	2½	. . .	. . .
Medium-term		60	2½	8	2
Short-term		65	2½	6	1¾

[16] In June 1982, banks indicated their intention to negotiate a refinancing agreement to convert the principal repayment into a longer-term loan prior to January 31, 1983, conditional upon successful completion of negotiations for an upper credit tranche program with the Fund. As negotiations with the Fund have not yet been completed, further deferments under the same conditions were agreed in July 1983 and January 1984.

[17] Agreement in principle was tentatively reached in early 1983.

[18] Original proposals were for repayments to start in March 1984, for the maturity due in 1983 and in March 1985, for the maturities due in 1984, but no agreement has yet been reached.

[19] The agreement covers all regularly scheduled maturities on debt incurred prior to November 30, 1982 by certain public entities; none of these refinanced maturities occurs after 1989.

[20] Conditional upon stabilization program acceptable to the banks.

[21] A down payment of $3 million has to be paid in 1987.

[22] Grace period and maturity were measured from the date of the first disbursement of the refinancing loan.

[23] The rescheduled amounts were rolled over on a short-term basis and were converted into medium-term loans on April 1, 1980 and on April 1, 1981 for the 1979/80 and 1980/81 reschedulings, respectively.

[24] Also, the bank that was owed most of the arrears informally agreed to allow Liberia to repay the arrears in 12 monthly installments.

[25] Includes about $50 million of arrears on overdrafts rescheduled on similar terms in late 1980.

[26] The agreement is subject to Madagascar being current on interest payments. The agreement also envisages the provision of a revolving trade facility, for an amount equivalent to the principal payments falling due in 1983 ($12 million) or a one-year grace period on that amount.

[27] Based on outstanding debt, including short-term debt, as of December 31, 1982, and including payments arrears on both short- and medium-term debt. Includes a special agreement for the rescheduling of Air Madagascar debt, secured by aircraft.

Table 17. Terms and Conditions of Bank Debt Restructurings and Bank Financial Packages, 1978–June 1985 *(continued)*

Country, Date of Agreement, and Type of Debt Rescheduled	Basis	Amount Provided	Grace Period	Maturity	Interest Rate
		(US$ millions)	*(In years, unless otherwise noted)*		*(In percent spread over LIBOR/U.S. Prime)*
Malawi					
Agreement of March 6, 1983:					
Medium- and long-term debt					
Due September 1982–August 1983	85 percent of principal	28	3	6½	1⅞
Due September 1983–August 1984	85 percent of principal	29	3	6½	1⅞
Mexico					
Agreement of August 27, 1983: [28]					
Rescheduling of public sector short-, medium-, and long-term debt [29] due August 23, 1982–December 31, 1984	100 percent of principal	18,800	4	8	1⅞–1¾
Syndicated loan [30]	New financing (net)	5,000	3	6	2¼–2⅛
Settlement of interest in arrears on private sector's debt [31]	—	1,367	—	—	1–⅞
Agreement of April 1984:					
New loan	New financing	3,800	5½	10	1½–1⅛
Agreement in principle of September 8, 1984: [32]					
Rescheduling of public medium- and long-term debt not previously rescheduled falling due from 1985 to 1990	100 percent of principal	20,100		14 [32]	⅞ in 1985–86; 1⅛ in 1987–91; 1¼ in 1992–98
Rescheduling of public medium- and long-term debt previously rescheduled					
Due in 1987	100 percent of principal	5,800	—	14 [32]	⅞ in 1985–86; 1⅛ in 1987–91; 1¼ in 1992–98
Due from 1988 to 1990	100 percent of principal	17,800	—	14 [32]	
Rescheduling of 1983 syndicated loan [33]		5,000	5	10	1½–1⅛
Morocco					
Agreement in principle of January 1984:					
Medium- and long-term debt due September 9, 1983–December 31, 1983	100 percent of principal	530	4	8	1¾
Medium- and long-term debt due in 1984	90 percent of principal		4	8	1¾
Rollover of short-term debt		750	—	—	—
People's Republic of Mozambique					
Preliminary discussions on bank debt	. . .	1,400	. . .	. . .	. . .

[28] Agreement took effect with disbursement of a new loan in March 1983.

[29] For the purpose of the rescheduling, Mexico's public sector debt (short-, medium-, and long-term) excludes: loans made, guaranteed, insured, or subsidized by official agencies in the creditor countries; publicly issued bonds, private placements (including Japanese yen-denominated registered private placements) and floating rate certificates of deposit and notes (including floating rate notes); debt to official multilateral entities; forward exchange and precious metal contracts; spot and lease obligations in respect of movable property, short-term import and export related trade credits; interbank obligations (including placements) of the foreign agencies and branches of Mexican banks, excluding guarantees on interbank placements; financing secured by legally recognized security interest in ships, aircraft, and drilling rigs; and the Central Bank's obligations arising from the arrangements to liquidate interest payments in arrears.

[30] The $5 billion loan was raised in the form of a medium-term international syndicated credit in which banks participated on the basis of their pro rata exposure to Mexico as of August 23, 1982. The loan document included a specific reference to a written explanation and confirmation from the Fund Managing Director with respect to $2–2.5 billion in financial assistance to be obtained from official creditors (other than the Fund), a requirement to provide information about the implementation of the financial program, a request on the part of the lending syndicate not to object to the final restructuring principles of the contemplated rescheduling operation, the customary cross-default clause, a specification of events of defaults (including the failure of Mexico to comply with the performance criteria agreed with the Fund in connection with the three-year extended arrangement, and nonmembership), and the implementation of the proposed mechanism to eliminate the interest arrears on the private sector debt. In addition, interbank exposure was restored and would be maintained through the end of 1986 at $5.2 billion.

[31] Specifically, Mexican private borrowers owing interest on foreign bank debts payable in foreign currency and outstanding prior to September 1, 1982 could use the procedures proposed by the Mexican authorities to settle interest payments due in the period from August 1, 1982 to January 31, 1983. Settlement had to be made by depositing the local currency equivalent of the amount of interest due in foreign currency, at the controlled exchange rate of the date at which the deposit was constituted. Special foreign currency deposits were being opened by the foreign lenders with the Bank of Mexico, and the amounts of interest owed were being credited to these accounts. Ten percent of the outstanding balance in these accounts was paid to creditors on January 31, 1983, while the remainder had to be settled subject to the availability of foreign exchange. As of March 7, 1984, all outstanding arrears were eliminated.

[32] There are no rescheduling fees and, under certain conditions, banks are allowed to switch their loans from dollars to home country currencies. Rescheduling of previously rescheduled debt falling due from 1987 to 1990 is conditional upon the achievement of Mexico's own economic targets to be monitored on the basis of enhanced Article IV consultations with the Fund beginning in 1986. Maturities shown relate to the date of the agreement in principle.

[33] $250 million of the 1983 syndicated loan was prepaid in 1985.

483

Table 17. Terms and Conditions of Bank Debt Restructurings and Bank Financial Packages, 1978–June 1985 (continued)

Country, Date of Agreement, and Type of Debt Rescheduled	Basis	Amount Provided	Grace Period	Maturity	Interest Rate
		(US$ millions)	(In years, unless otherwise noted)		(In percent spread over LIBOR/U.S. Prime)
Nicaragua					
Agreement of December 1980:					
Arrears on interest or due up to December 1980 [34]	75 percent of arrears and amount due	90	—	5	¾–1¼, but with deferred interest payment provision and interest recapture clause [35]
Arrears on principal as of December 1979 [35]	100 percent of arrears on principal	252	5	11	
Due after December 1979	100 percent of principal	240	5	12	
Agreement of December 1981 (debt of nationalized banks):					
Accumulated arrears	90 percent of interest and principal	192	5	10	¾–1¼, but with deferred interest payment provision and recapture clause [35]
Principal due after September 1981	100 percent of principal		5	10	
Agreement of March 1982 (debt of nationalized enterprises and of private enterprises):					
Accumulated arrears	90 percent of interest and principal	120	—	10	¾–1¼, but with deferred interest payment provision and recapture clause [35]
Due after March 1982	100 percent of principal	100	5	10	...
Agreement of February 1984: Rescheduling of principal and interest due July 1983–June 1984 (previously rescheduled in 1980–82)	95–100 percent of principal	145	—	8 [36]	1¼–1¾
In process of negotiation: Principal and interest due July 1984–June 1985 (previously rescheduled in 1980–82)	95–100 percent of principal	120	—		...
Niger					
Agreement of March 9, 1984: Rescheduling of medium-term debt:					
Due October 1983–September 1984	90 percent of principal	12	3½	7½	Originally contracted rate + 2 percent
Due October 1984–September 1985	90 percent of principal	15	3½	7½	Originally contracted rate + 2 percent
Nigeria					
Agreement of July 1983: Arrears as of end-March 1983	100 percent of arrears on letters of credit	1,350	5½ months	3	1½–1⅜
Agreement of September 1983: Arrears as of end-July 1983	100 percent of arrears on letters of credit	585	3½ months	2⅝	1½–1⅜

Panama					
In process of negotiation:					
Public sector debt					
Due in 1985	Principal	225	3½	12	1⅜
Due in 1986	Principal	377	3½	12	1⅜
New loan	New financing	60	3	9	1⅜–1¼
Short-term credit lines	Principal	190	—	—	. . .
Peru [37]					
Agreement of June 1978:					
Due during second semester of 1978	Rollover of 100 percent of principal	186 [38]	—	Due January 3, 1979	. . .
Agreement of December 1978:					
Due in 1979	90 percent of principal	} 200 [38]	2	6	1⅞
Due in 1980	90 percent of principal		2	5	. . .
Due in January 1979 as per June 1978 agreement	50 percent of amount rolled over		—	1	1¾
Agreement of January 1980: [39]					
Due in 1980	90 percent of principal	340 [38]	2	5	1¼
Agreement of July 1983:					
Medium- and long-term maturities falling due between March 7, 1983 and March 7, 1984	100 percent	380	3	8	2¼
Bridge loan	—	200	. . .	. . .	. . .
New loan	New financing	450	3	8	2¼
Short-term credit lines outstanding as of March 7, 1983	100 percent of principal	2,000 [40]	. . .	1	2¼
Agreement in principle of February 1984: [41]					
Medium- and long-term maturities falling due between March 7, 1984 and June 30, 1985	100 percent	460	5	9	1⅜–1¼
Short-term working capital outstanding on March 6, 1984	100 percent	965	5	9	1⅜–1¼
Loan covering the undisbursed portion of the 1983 new loan	New financing	200	3	8	2¼
Short-term trade related credit lines committed as of March 6, 1984	100 percent	800	—	Rollover	⅝ + 1½ percent acceptance commission

[34] On short- and medium-term debt. Banks agreed to recalculate the interest due but unpaid at a spread of ½ percentage point above the actual LIBOR during the relevant period, rather than at the higher spreads specified in the original contracts.

[35] All four categories of debt are subject to interest accrual at a spread of 1 percent above LIBOR between December 15, 1980 and December 14, 1983; of 1¼ percent between December 15, 1983 and December 14, 1986; of 1½ percent between December 15, 1986 and December 14, 1990; and of 1¾ percent between December 15, 1990 and December 14, 1992. However, actual payments of interest can be limited to 7 percent a year for the agreement of 1980, and to 6 percent for the agreements of 1981 and 1982. Any excess of accrued interest will be added to a deferred interest payment pool which will be repaid whenever the accrued interest rate payments are less than 7 percent per annum, or, if this does not exhaust the pool by December 15, 1985, the balance will be amortized between 1986 and 1990 with 10 percent due in each of 1986 and 1987, and the rest during the remaining three years. The agreement also contains an interest recapture clause. If Nicaragua fulfills all the terms of the contract, the interest rate spread would be reduced by ⅛ percentage point for every $20 million of principal repaid after 1985 for up to 1 percentage point.

[36] Backloaded in the last years.

[37] All rescheduling agreements cover only public sector obligations. Bank loans with creditor country guarantees were included in the Paris Club agreement, rather than the bank reschedulings.

[38] Under the 1978 and 1980 bank reschedulings, amounts were initially rolled over on a short-term basis to be consolidated into a medium-term loan at a specified date early in the following year.

[39] In January 1980, Peru prepaid the 1979 bank rescheduling and the terms of the 1980 rescheduling were renegotiated.

[40] $1.2 billion of working capital and $800 million of trade related lines.

[41] Signing of the agreement has been delayed inter alia by Peru's nonpayment of interest since July 1984.

Table 17. Terms and Conditions of Bank Debt Restructurings and Bank Financial Packages, 1978–June 1985 *(continued)*

Country, Date of Agreement, and Type of Debt Rescheduled	Basis	Amount Provided	Grace Period	Maturity	Interest Rate
		(US$ millions)	*(In years, unless otherwise noted)*		*(In percent spread over LIBOR/U.S. Prime)*
Philippines					
Agreement in principle with Advisory Committee (October 17, 1984):					
Rescheduling of public sector debt, medium- and long-term:					
Due between October 17, 1983 and December 31, 1985	100 percent of principal	918	5 [42]	10 [42]	1⅝
Due in 1986	100 percent of principal	574	5 [42]	10 [42]	1⅝
Rescheduling of private financial sector debt medium- and long-term:					
Due between October 17, 1983 and December 31, 1985	100 percent of principal	130	5 [42]	10 [42]	1⅝
Due in 1986	100 percent of principal	93	5 [42]	10 [42]	1⅝
Short-term debt		649	4	4	Less than 2
Rescheduling of corporate debt medium- and long-term:					
Due between October 17, 1983 and December 31, 1985	100 percent of principal	384	. . .	. . .	. . .
Due in 1986	100 percent of principal	270	. . .	. . .	. . .
Short-term debt		490	. . .	. . .	. . .
New medium-term loan	New money	925	5	9	1¼
Revolving short-term trade facility	Trade related outstanding and central bank overdrafts as of October 17, 1983	2,975	Revolving per annum	. . .	1¼
Romania					
Agreement of December 7, 1982:					
Arrears on the 1981 debt obligations	80 percent of such debt obligations }		3	6½	1¼
Due in 1982 on all debts (including short-term)	80 percent of principal }	1,598	3	6½	1¾
Agreement of June 20, 1983:					
Medium- and long-term due in 1983	{ 10 percent of principal	81	1½	1½	1¾
	{ 60 percent of principal	486	3½	6½	1¾
Senegal					
Agreement of February 1984:					
Due between May 1, 1981 and June 30, 1982 (including arrears)	100 percent of principal }	78	3	7	2
Due between July 1, 1982 and June 30, 1984	100 percent of principal }				
Agreement in principle with Steering Committee (May 7, 1985):					
Due between July 1, 1984 and June 30, 1986	80 percent of principal [43]	20	3	7	2

Sierra Leone				
Agreement of January 1984:				
Principal arrears	100 percent	25	2	7	1¾
Sudan				
Agreement of December 1981:				
Arrears on principal as of end-1979	100 percent	383	3	7	1¾
Arrears on interest due:				
Period January–June 1980	60 percent				
Period July 1980–April 1982	100 percent	115	1	3	1¾
Excess balances on Nostro accounts over end-1979 level	40 percent				
Modification of December 1981 agreement (March 1982)					
Arrears on interest as of end-1979	40 percent ⎫	55	5 months	9 months	1¾
Arrears on interest due January–June 1980	60 percent ⎭				
Excess balance on Nostro accounts over end-1979 level					
Modification of December 1981 agreement (April 1983)					
Principal and interest	100 percent	790	2	6	1¾
Modification of December 1981 agreement (April 1984)					
Principal and interest	100 percent	838	1	5	1¾
Togo				
Agreement of March 1980:				
Arrears as of end of 1979	100 percent of arrears	8	Settlement to be made in 1980 in 3 equal installments		Original rates maintained. However, spreads on Euroloan reduced to 1½.
Interest					
Principal					
Due in 1980 on a number of specific loans	100 percent of principal	17	6 months	1½	
		44	1	3½	
Agreement of October 1983:					Original rates maintained
Arrears as of end of 1982	100 percent of arrears	58	—	7¼	2
Due in 1983 and 1984 on medium- and long-term public and publicly guaranteed loans	100 percent of principal	26	—	7¼	2

---
[42] Ten years from the earlier of signing date or December 31, 1984; with 5 years of grace.
[43] The remaining 20 percent is to be paid in eight equal quarterly installments starting in 1985.

Table 17. Terms and Conditions of Bank Debt Restructurings and Bank Financial Packages, 1978–June 1985 *(continued)*

Country, Date of Agreement, and Type of Debt Rescheduled	Basis	Amount Provided	Grace Period	Maturity	Interest Rate
		(US$ millions)	*(In years, unless otherwise noted)*		*(In percent spread over LIBOR/U.S. Prime)*
Turkey					
Eurocurrency loan of June 1979 [44]	New financing (net)	407	3	7	1¾
Agreement of June 1979:					
Bankers' credits	100 percent of principal	429 [45]	3	7	1¾
Agreement of August 1979:					
Convertible Turkish lira deposits [46]	100 percent of principal	2,269 [46]	3	7	1¾
Agreement of August 1981:					
Third-party reimbursement claims	100 percent of principal	100	—	3	1½
Agreement of March 1982:					
Improve the maturity profile of the August 1979 rescheduling agreement	100 percent of principal	. . . [47]	2 [48]	3 [48]	1¾
Uruguay					
Agreement of July 29, 1983:					
New medium-term loan	—	240	2	6	2¼–2⅛
Short-term nontrade related credits	90 percent of principal	425	2	6	2¼–2⅛
Medium-term maturities falling due in 1983	90 percent of principal	39	2	6	2¼–2⅛
Medium-term maturities falling due in 1984	90 percent of principal	111	2	6	2¼–2⅛
Deferment agreement of December 14, 1984:					
Public sector debt due January–June 1985	Principal	120	—	6-month extension	Originally contracted rates
Venezuela					
Agreement with Steering Committee (September 1984): [49]					
Rescheduling of medium- and long-term debt falling due during 1983–88	Principal	21,203	—	12½ [50]	1⅛
Yugoslavia					
Agreement of September 1983:					
Refinancing of:					
Medium-term loans due in 1983	100 percent of principal	950	3	6	1⅞–1¾
Short-term debt	Rolled over (through either 1983 or 1984)				
Nontrade related credits		200	2	2	1⅜–1¼
Revolving trade facility		600	2	2	1⅜–1¼
New syndicated loan	New financing (net)	600	3	6	1⅞–1¾
Agreement of May 16, 1984: [51]					
Refinancing of:					
Medium- and long-term maturities falling due in 1984	100 percent of principal	1,200	4	7	1⅝–1½
In process:					
Refinancing of public sector debt falling due in 1985–89	100 percent of principal	3,500	5	11	

Zaïre [52]			
Agreement of April 1980:			
Arrears on principal as of end of 1979	76 percent of principal	287	5	10	1⅞ for first 5 years, 2 thereafter
Principal payments due after end of 1979	100 percent of principal	115	5	10	1⅞ for first 5 years, 2 thereafter
Deferment agreement of January 1983: [53]	Principal	58	...	...	Originally contracted rate
Deferment agreement of June 1984: [54]	Principal	64	...	...	Originally contracted rate
Zambia					
Agreement with Steering Committee (December 1984):					
Refinancing of medium- and long-term public and publicly guaranteed unsecured debt in arrears as of February 28, 1983	100 percent of principal	16	—	1 [55]	2¼
Due March 1, 1983–February 29, 1984	100 percent of principal	26	1	4	2¼
Due March 1, 1984–February 28, 1985	100 percent of principal	21	2	5	2¼
Due March 1, 1985–December 31, 1985 [56]	90 percent of principal	11	3	6	2¼

---

[44] The disbursement was to be based on letter-of-credit financing for imports. Other conditions for the first disbursement (50 percent) included making the first purchase under IMF stand-by arrangement and the signing of the agreement on convertible Turkish lira deposits. For the second and third disbursements (25 percent each), other conditions included making the purchases under the IMF stand-by arrangement scheduled for November 1979 and March 1980, and the implementation of programs for third-party reimbursement claims and arrears on nonguaranteed debts.

[45] All previously rolled over.

[46] Holders were allowed to switch currency of denomination, with liability being switched from commercial banks to the Central Bank. The amount includes $2 billion rolled over prior to June 30, 1979; and $0.2 billion due in second half of 1979.

[47] The amount rescheduled is equivalent to the sum of obligations rescheduled in June and August 1979, including a new syndicated credit extended at that time.

[48] The years shown represent the extension to the grace period and maturity granted under the original rescheduling arrangement.

[49] In March 1983, with the endorsement of the Steering Committee, Venezuela declared a deferral on principal payments of external public sector debt owed to foreign commercial banks. The amount of short-term debt involved was about $8.5 billion. The deferral was extended until October 1, 1983. It was twice further extended, first until January 31, 1984, and then until April 30, 1984. The rescheduling agreement is conditional on a solution to the arrears on the private sector debt.

[50] Maturity shown relates to the date of the agreement in principle. Payments are to be made in equal amounts; however, Venezuela will make an initial payment of $750 million during the second quarter and further debt service payment for 1985 will total $5.15 billion with regular payment not to exceed $5 billion per year thereafter.

[51] Conditional upon refinancing of $700 million in officially guaranteed loans.

[52] Bank debt refinancing agreement covers only syndicated loans (and other floating rate loans) without creditor country guarantee.

[53] Under this agreement Zaïre would make monthly payments of $5 million to the London Club banks. This amount is to be increased to $6 million if U.S. producer prices for copper rise above the threshold price of $.75 per pound.

[54] Under this agreement Zaïre would make monthly payments of $2 million in the first semester of 1984, of $5 million in the third quarter, of $7 million in the fourth quarter, and of $4 million in the first quarter of 1985.

[55] Arrears as of February 28, 1983, are to be paid in 12 equal monthly installments starting from January 15, 1985.

[56] The remaining 10 percent amounting to $1.2 million was agreed to be paid off in two equal installments in June and December 1985.

Table 17. Terms and Conditions of Bank Debt Restructurings and Bank Financial Packages, 1978–June 1985 (concluded)

Country, Date of Agreement, and Type of Debt Rescheduled	Basis	Amount Provided	Grace Period	Maturity	Interest Rate
		(US$ millions)	(In years, unless otherwise noted)		(In percent spread over LIBOR/U.S. Prime)

Memorandum items:
Non-Fund members
Cuba
  Agreement of December 30, 1983:
    Rescheduling principal payments on medium-term debt due between September 1, 1982 and December 31, 1984 | 100 percent of principal | 128 | 2 | 5½ | 2¼
    Rollover of short-term credit [57] | ... | 490 | ... | ... | 1¼

Poland
  Agreement of April 1982: [58]
    Medium-term debt due March 26, 1981–December 1981 | 95 percent of principal | 2,300 | 4 | 7 | 1¾
  Agreement of November 1982: [59]
    Medium-term debt due in 1982, including arrears on unrescheduled maturities due in 1981 | 95 percent of principal | 2,300 | 4 | 7½ | 1¾–1½
  Agreement of November 1983: [60]
    Medium-term debt due during 1983 | 95 percent of principal | 1,400 | 5 | 10 | 1⅞
  Agreement of April 28, 1984:
    Medium- and long-term debt due in 1984–1987 | 95 percent of principal | 1,615 | 5 | 10 | 1¾
    New trade credits [61] | New financing | 235 | — | 5 | 1⅝
    Rollover of short-term credit facility [61] | ... | 465 | ... | ... | ...

[57] All lines of credit with Banco Nacional de Cuba were scheduled to remain at the level of February 28, 1983.
[58] The agreement, which covers maturities due during March 26–December 31, 1981, was effective May 10, 1982. Short-term facilities and interbank deposits were specifically excluded.
[59] A six-month trade credit, revolving up to three years, was extended under separate agreement; the amount of the credit was equivalent to 50 percent of the $1.1 billion in interest due.
[60] A six-month trade credit, revolving up to three years, was extended under separate agreement.
[61] In 1985 the short-term credit facility was rolled over, and further trade credits, revolving every six months for up to 4–5 years, are to be extended.

Section VI: Loan Renegotiation
Chapter 18:
Proposed Solutions to Sovereign Debt Problems

The International Financial System and the Management of the International Debt Crisis

David Suratgar

INTRODUCTION

A veritable flood of articles, memoranda and reports on the subject of the external debt problems of the less developed countries has emanated from national and international institutions and distinguished commentators since the full force of the problems surfaced in 1982[1]. It is therefore perhaps excusable to omit a full history of the origins of the crisis and an assessment of the consequences for the international system in general or the Eurocurrency syndicated loan market in particular. Previous chapters have indeed provided a survey of the record of the handling of sovereign debt crises and overviews of the process of rescheduling of governmental debts through the Paris Club and of commercial bank debts. What remains to be assessed, however, is the efficacy of the process of rescheduling sovereign debt and also the difficulties inherent in the task facing borrowers and creditors in seeking equitable treatment and a lasting solution for each particular case.

THE SETTING

Seen from the perspective of the international financial institutions in Washington there is no simple explanation for the current predicament or solution for overcoming it. As the financial difficulties of the LDCs began to build up to the point of crisis at the end of the 1970s, it became increasingly clear that private non-concessional flows (the combination of export credits, tied aid and Eurocurrnecy syndicated loans) which had been resorted to by the LDCs, to supplement falling levels of concessional flows and by the OECD countries to help them export their way out of the difficulties created by the first oil crisis, could not continue to work.

The 1973-1974 oil crisis ocurred against the background of the abandonment of the Bretton Woods system of fixed exchange rates and was followed by inflation and a world recession. The OECD countries sought to stimulate demand through their fiscal and monetary measures. The international commercial banks also provided an unexpected and significant boost to the international economy through greatly expanded international lending, as they were used as the major vehicle for recycling OPEC surpluses.

Certain features of this growth in international commercial bank lending deserve to be highlighted. For example, it can be argued that the expansion in lending was frequently encouraged by many of the OECD governments and by OPEC countries which preferred to use intermediation by the major international banks for the recycling exercise rather than international institutions. The commercial banks of the OECD countries were quick to see the opportunity for profit. Their own central banks would provide security as lenders of last resort ready to protect the system from a failure.

The Basle Concordat of 1975 set out an understanding of the spheres of responsibility of the major central banks but at the same time much of the cross-border lending, particularly to the LDCs, took place outside the regulatory and supervisory network of these central banks.[2] Major commercial banks established offshore subsidiaries able to operate without the discipline of having to maintain minimum reserve requirements. Relatively low overhead costs and use of the floating rate mechanism made the business sufficiently attractive to attract a constant stream of new names to the lenders' circuit, many of them banks with little or no international lending experience. This in turn ensured constant competition for mandates and very low margins. Even more importantly banks moved increasingly from lending to finance trade and projects to balance of payments lending, hitherto the province of the IMF or the capital markets. Whereas the IMF demanded strict conditionality, borrowing for these purposes from commercial banks was relatively painless. The dollar was depreciating and the decline in real interest rates had the effect of lowering the cost of borrowing and seemingly buttressed the debt service capacity of LDC borrowers at a time of steady or rising commodity prices. For many of the banks, however, the great expansion carried with it potential problems since their capital and reserves could not keep pace with their rapidly growing balance sheets.

The second oil crisis, however, produced a very different setting for efforts to continue this pace of LDC borrowing. OPEC countries had less enthusiasm for building up even greater surpluses in a period of low or negative real interest rates. Nor were they as ready to embark on a second round of heavy investment in major projects at home while still trying to complete or digest those financed after the first oil price boom. The OECD countries led by the United Kingdom and the United States were anxious to avoid another inflationary spiral and this was seen as a more serious challenge than the threat of recession. The monetarist policies of these countries contributed to a major decline in the world economy and the world came face to face with a period of extraordinarily high real interest rates which were underscored by the continuing demand for funds on the part of major OECD countries to finance their own continuing government expenditures. The realities of a deep recession accompanied by continuing high real interest rates became clearly apparent. This time the non-oil producing countries were also faced with plunging commodity prices (UNCTAD's index of non-oil commodity prices in dollars fell by 33 percent between 1980 and the end of 1982), growing restrictions on their exports to the OECD, a strong dollar and continuing high oil prices. The oil exporters were in turn faced with cash flow problems as they sought to maintain their new found style of living. Thus some sovereign borrowers faced virtual insolvency while others, such as Mexico and Nigeria, were affected by acute liquidity problems.[3]

As one country after another came to the inevitable point of having to reschedule medium and long term external debt and to consolidate and lengthen the terms of trade debt, the commercial banks faced the added problem of the loss of confidence in major Latin American borrowers which followed the Falkland Islands adventure.[4] Yet large amounts of new money would be required as part of each rescheduling exercise. As a result little new LDC lending was possible other than that required for such rescheduling.

Once the major Latin American borrowers were forced to reschedule, the central banks and their own international institution, the Bank for International Settlements (BIS), had to recognize the dangers inherent in the situation for the stability and liquidity of the international banking system. With no world lender of last resort to look to they realized that they would have to help to bail out either the major borrowers or the banks. They had therefore little choice but to cooperate with the IMF and the Paris Club and to play a role in devising arrangements to meet each major rescheduling crisis as it arose.[5]

They and the Congress in the case of the United States have, however, sought to use the occasion to strengthen controls over future international lending by their commercial banks and to review the adequacy of the provisions for and treatment of existing bad and doubtful debts.[6] In the case of the United States, Congress has used the need for legislation to increase the resources of the IMF to stipulate a series of conditions which will require new strengthened regulatory controls by the U.S. monetary authorities over the conduct of international lending by U.S. commercial banks.

THE MANAGEMENT OF SOVEREIGN DEBT RESCHEDULINGS

What became clear, as the real scale of the LDC debt crisis broke in the second half of 1982, was that the OECD monetary authorities had no overall "solution" to offer. Each individual case has been handled on an *ad hoc* basis. Of course a broad pattern can be discerned with a typical rescue package involving the following elements: (i) an IMF programme based on domestic deflation, devaluation and pressure to push for increased exports; (ii) IMF funds for a three-year period; (iii) new commercial lending, where possible (often extracted under pressure from the IMF and central banks) with from two to four years of grace; (iv) deferrment of capital repayments on commercial bank and governmental loans for varying periods depending on the borrower and its situation, but often, it is argued, with little relation to a realistic assessment of ability to export or the capacity to repay.

It must, however, be recognized that the more complex and major reschedulings have constituted testimonials to *ad hoc* international cooperation between the IMF, creditor governments through the Paris Club, the BIS, central banks and commercial banks. Yet it must also be noted that they have constituted a series of somewhat overexciting and often last-minute cliff-hangers. Furthermore, there has been little progress in addressing many of the regulatory issues within the OECD countries and the demonstrable shortcomings of the framework of developmental and structural adjustment financing issues which face the non-oil LDCs.

The debtor governments for their part have also been faced with great difficulty in organizing themselves to deal with their creditors. They too have experienced the trauma of working their way through a series of separate *ad hoc* negotiations with each class of creditor and have found that neither the IMF nor the World Bank, creditors themselves, was well placed to act as an arbitrator or mediator. Indeed, the IMF, in effect a creditor of last resort as well as an international cooperative institution with both the creditor and debtor governments as shareholders, has found itself in the front line—sniped at by the debtors, member governments and the commercial banks.

The Paris Club is demonstrably not a disinterested forum but a political body representing OECD interests. Steering or advisory committees of lending banks are equally not impartial. They primarily represent the major lenders whose interests are not necessarily the same as those of the borrower or indeed of smaller commercial banks. The Fund and World Bank are also in a difficult position. They are lenders themselves with set lending policies and their own problems with their own constituents, be they the borrower members or the creditor members. Their loans are by convention not rescheduled and since money is fungible their continued support to a borrower in difficulty may be seen as, or alleged to be, an effort to bail out a country or a group of commercial banks. Where such institutions require continuing funding support they are calling ultimately on the taxpayers in the OECD countries. Legislation is thus often required to replenish or augment their resources and this brings political pressures directly into the negotiation process.

This ad hoc approach to external debt problems of the developing countries has thus enhanced the political dimension of the process of rescheduling. The dangers of the situation are equally apparent within the developing countries as they are in the domestic councils of member states of the OECD. In a difficult economic environment there is the ever present danger that over-reliance on draconian adjustment programmes imposed by the Fund, unaccompanied by new money (aid, export credits and private non-concessional flows for the poorer countries and commercial funds and export credits for the newly industrializing countries) and fair and free trading opportunities for nascent industries could propel extreme nationalist opinion in certain regions such as Latin America. This might in turn lead to unilateral debt moratoria.[7]

Thus a major lesson of the experience with international sovereign debt rescheduling during the period 1979-1983 is that the legal and institutional framework for international finance has not kept up with the pace of financial innovations since Bretton Woods. This was first brought home with vengeance to international lawyers faced in 1979 with the impact of the U.S. ordered freeze on Iranian assets. As the contributions in Part 1 of this book demonstrate, the shortcomings of the framework for international bankruptcy were also exposed as the impact of the recession, high real interest rates and falling demand for energy resulted in financial difficulties for major corporations such as Massey-Ferguson, Chrysler, AEG-Telefunken, Braniff, Laker, International Harvester, Korf, and institutions such as Penn Square, Banco Ambrosiano, Schroeder Muenchmayer Hengst to name a few recent cases.

The international rules governing the handling of default and of borrowers in difficulty be they sovereign or corporate are at best rudimentary. As noted in Chapter 1, this is an area of international law which has been neglected since the 1930s. The world's financial system has in effect raced ahead of the institutional infrastructure for crisis management. Significantly, however, one feature of the difference between the albeit rudimentary framework for dealing with international corporate borrowers in difficulty and the case of sovereign borrowers in difficulty stands out. In the case of international corporate bankruptcies a forum, or regrettable and more frequently a multiplicity of forums, exist with jurisdiction over the relations and issues between creditors and debtors. Statutory law, however inadequate, exists and the courts of most OECD countries have certain powers to assist in attempting to reorganize borrowers, reschedule their debts and implement a financial plan. No such framework or forum exists to cope with the issues that arise in sovereign debt reschedulings.

The contributions to this book that deal with corporate borrowers in difficulty and the legal framework for corporate 'workouts' served to focus attention on the shortcomings of existing national legislation in the principal OECD countries on corporate debt rescheduling even where the writ of a domestic court operates effectively. The possibilities of effective workouts under Chapter 11 of the U.S. Federal Bankruptcy Act and behind the protective umbrella of the Federal Courts are to be contrasted with the somewhat less helpful legal framework in the Federal Republic of Germany, the United Kingdom and France and with the *ad hoc* salvage operations for major companies that have taken place with varying degrees of government help in such countries as Canada and the United States. The inadequacies of the national legal framework, however, pale in comparison with the problems facing international creditors of multinational corporate borrowers in difficulty in the absence of a controlling forum and a workable treaty framework.

The short term reschedulings of government to government debt through the Paris Club, the *ad hoc* approach to rescheduling commercial bank debt and the inadequate methods of dealing with short term debts also compare unfavorably with the enlightened approach of U.S. courts under Chapter 11 to corporate borrowers in difficulty. No mechanism exists under international law for putting a sovereign borrower into effective quarantine from its creditors; thus allowing time for a reorganization of its financial affairs with a view to ensuring that creditors receive equitable treatment consistent with the objective of enabling the debtor to continue and develop its economy in an orderly way and in due course repay its creditors. No legal jurisdiction or statute exists to control a sovereign or its assets and set the framework for a court supervised settlement.

This facet of rescheduling sovereign debt underscores the problems that stem from the lack of an adequate forum in which a debtor country's total external debt and balance of payments difficulties can be debated by all interested creditors. The interests of the various classes of creditors are indeed different. Debt service competes with development as a priority. Even where debt service capacity and essential development and government operating needs can be reconciled, IMF conditionality and harsh austerity measures will be difficult for debtor governments to sell to their populations. Official lenders such as the international institutions and Paris Club creditors are naturally concerned to ensure that new loans or payment concessions on old loans are not used to permit a flow of non-essential imports or to "bailout" commercial lenders. Just as some debt inevitably has to be converted into equity or quasi-equity in corporate 'workouts', sovereign borrowers have an interest in transferring as much principal and interest of their external debt to low interest long-term creditors as possible. Much of their commercial borrowing in the period since the first oil price shock in 1973-74 has been to finance investment in infrastructure and industrial projects. Such commercial borrowing on a floating rate basis has been used in combination with export credit finance to fund projects which really should have been financed through long-term fixed rate finance, equity, and more importantly, aid or grant funds from the OECD.

One feature of the absence of a suitable legal framework or forum for dealing with sovereign borrowers in difficulty is that there has been little discernible effort to distinguish between borrowers in difficulty because of events outside their control and those whose difficulties are due to mismanagement or from events within their control. As we have noted each case has been handled on an ad hoc basis and often temporary contractual settlements have been reached with separate classes of creditors such as governments (through the Paris Club), commercial banks (through self-appointed steering committees), and trade creditors. We have therefore had no common standard or yardstick against which the fairness and workability of each settlement can be measured.[8]

NECESSARY ELEMENTS OF AN EQUITABLE AND EFFECTIVE APPROACH TO SOVEREIGN DEBT RESCHEDULING

The contributions to Part 2 of this book provide clear evidence of the importance in sovereign debt reschedulings, of an early clarification of the full extent of a country's external debt broken down by categories (short, medium and long term) and by the class of creditor (international institutions, governments, commercial banks, bondholders, suppliers etc.) Equally essential it would seem is an agreed procedure designed to provide a clear picture as to the categories of debt and classes of creditors to be excluded from the proceeding or covered in some other parallel exercise and the reasons for these differentiations. Several contributors stressed the importance of equal clarity on issues such as the need for new money and the purposes for which such money is to be used (i.e. the maintenance of necessary imports required for agreed overall needs of the economy) and on the assumptions with respect to the domestic economy, export performance and world prices on which the overall rescheduling and new money arrangements are based.

The previous contributors also appear to be in general agreement that the rescheduling of a particular class of debt in isolation is an unrealistic exercise. Meaningful rescheduling it seems, has to take place in the context of a comprehensive and accurate assessment of the country's demonstrable overall needs and prospects. It is equally apparent that the necessary coordinated access to reliable economic information has been lacking in many cases. The gaps and deficiencies in data resulting from the hitherto limited objectives of the World Bank external debt reporting system and its retrospective character and the lack of communication between the Fund and the commercial banks, have been major factors in this situation. The establishment of the new Institute of International Finance by the world's major banks is in effect a somewhat belated but nevertheless welcome response to this problem. What then are the necessary elements of a rational, comprehensive and equitable framework for rescheduling of sovereign debt?[9]

In an ideal world sovereign borrowers should only get into debt service problems as a result of factors outside their control rather than as a result of miscalculations or gross negligence in the management of their own financial affairs. Thus, contrary to what frequently occurs, they should be fully conscious of the scale of their external debt and its maturity profile and ideally will have borrowed on the longest possible maturities and at low fixed rates with little exchange exposure in terms of the currencies of their export sales. In the ideal situation they should be able to demonstrate a successful record in minimizing imports of essentials while maximizing export earnings. Equally they would be sble to show that they were balancing the government's books and limiting credit expansion to agreed planned levels.

In contrast, certain factors are only too clearly outside a government's control. Thus erratic currency and interest rate fluctuations and high real rates of interest and factors such as terms of trade and the price of essential commodities are not matters on which a typical LDC government has much influence. In an ideal world compensatory financing mechanisms would be set up and operating in such a way as to permit a sovereign borrower in difficulty to deal with the effects of such developments under a rational adjustment plan financed by soft funds in sufficient amounts to permit debt service to be maintained without the need for rescheduling. Only if such a compensatory mechanism were not in place or sufficient funding available, would a borrower have to resort to requesting existing lenders to accept stretched out maturities because of its recognized reduced debt service capacity. In this ideal world, creditors would have a clear picture of the total external debt and its break-down by categories and classes of creditor and by maturity structure. Creditors and borrowers would have an equally clear perspective of the possibilities of repayment and the extent of the funding gap. It would thus be possible to move quickly to agree on rescheduling agreements, possibly including a "bisque clause" with a built in revision mechanism to allow, in advance, for further smooth adjustments in debt service obligations, requiring either higher or lower payments depending on favorable or unfavorable developments in the world economy, interest rates and commodity prices.

Unfortunately, reschedulings do not occur in this ideal world. The analogy with the corporate world is also of only limited value. Under national law if a corporation cannot meet its bills and cannot agree on an arrangement with its creditors to give it breathing space to reorganize and develop its business more effectively, it can be wound up and and have its assets disposed. The applicable legislation determines the rules in this exercise and determines the order in which creditors' rights are satisfied. In contrast, nation states cannot be put into liquidation under international law except in the political sense consistent with the Charter of the United Nations. They do not normally surrender control of their own affairs because of sensitivities as to loss of sovereignty. As is shown by the chapter "Special Risks and Remedies in International Sovereign Loans", they may well have privileges such as sovereign immunity against suit and execution with respect to some of their debts. They may not permit execution against certain of their assets. Finally, public international law does not establish the ground rules or lay down any order in which creditors are to be treated.

In sovereign debt reschedulings the basic problem is the lack of a mechanism for putting the debtor into quarantine from its creditors while disinterested analysis establishes the true situation and prospects and satisfies all classes of creditors that they will receive equitable access to what is reasonably available for debt service. The chapter "Multilateral Debt Renegotiation: a Banker's Perspective," provides a clear explanation of the full scope of the term "external debt" for purposes of international debt rescheduling. The debts of the government and its central bank and state agencies are included.

The issue remains as to the status of commercial banks, corporations and individuals with the nationality of or domiciled in that state. It may be necessary to require a register of foreign exchange assets that the banks possess, if not a surrender to the national authorities of existing assets and subsequent foreign exchange coming into their hands. It may also be necessary to control their incurring of new foreign exchange liabilities and also their ability to net such liabilities against foreign assets or claims.

There is furthermore no clear picture from recent practice with respect to sovereign debt rescheduling as to whether a country's public sector can be effectively separated from its private sector for this purpose.

It is also clear that a rescheduling cannot work effectively and fairly unless all foreign exchange flows are taken into account and all future foreign borrowings and extensions of external credit are controlled. Equally, all creditors' claims would need to be registered and there would also need to be some agreed formula for determining the rate and method of calculation of interest accruals on them and on the rules of compounding. Similarly, controls would need to be established on a creditor government's behalf to limit extensions of credit by other governments on their agencies or private institutions and this in turn would have to take into account a debtor country's needs to meet agreed current import requirements or sound developmental objectives.

How should such a 'working out' of sovereign debt problems be handled given that no forum exists on the international scene with a writ running to all the participants in such situations? The Fund would appear to be the best qualified financial forum for governments but, as has been noted, the Fund has not been prepared to act in this capacity. Even an agreement reached under its auspices would need to be supported by an international system of exchange controls and domestic exchange controls in the debtor country. One possible alternative could of course be to return to some modern equivalent of the 19th Century answer—an externally selected exchange control policeman given full powers by the debtor government to assure fair play and equitable treatment. This seems highly unlikely and indeed undesirable in the context of the current system of international relations and there are likely to be few, if any, sovereign states which are likely to agree voluntarily to appoint such a czar over their financial affairs.

There could, however, be one partial answer to this lack of a forum, which could nevertheless go a long way towards assuring both debtor governments and their various classes of foreign creditors fair and equitable treatment. This would lie in the appointment by a debtor government in its own intrests of an ombudsman of undoubted international standing in the world of finance and economic affairs to act as a referee in such matters. It would of course be even more satisfactory if agreement could be reached on the use of such a third party by inclusion of a clause in all loan agreements or guarantee agreements with governments, providing in advance for the terms for reference to an ombudsman or mediator, or at the least for the method of his selection. The remit of such an ombudsman would be to develop and recommend a scheme of arrangements based on the realities of a debtor's situation and its legitimate developmental requirements. In return a debtor country would have to be assured of an adequate period of breathing space and insulation from its creditors to put such a scheme into operation and to secure the agreement of the Fund, World Bank, Paris Club and other international creditors.

The main elements of such a scheme would have to show that the payment burden would be adequate and not excessive, that the debtor country takes the necessary adjustment measures over a realistic period given its dependence on world economic developments, and that creditors will be treated equitably as between classes. The scale of the payment burden will need to take account of the level of aggregate existing credit which will have to be kept in place and will need to factor into the amount of new credit which will be required to assure the service of interest on outstanding debt and meet current account deficits until reasonable equilibrium is achieved. The adjustment process in turn presupposes a careful analysis of the characteristics of the running deficit. It could be that the deficit could be dealt with provided there was no net capital outflow or that in some way the interest rate burden was alleviated—for example by replacing debt at commercial rates by debt on concessionary rates. From the country's perspective there should be some effort, allowing for both inflation and some real growth, to provide for additional net capital inflows to permit its economy to maintain its relative position. Allowance should also be made for sufficient adjustment finance to compensate the debtor country for the effects of factors outside its control such as changes in the terms of trade. Given such an analysis the resulting scheme could carry sufficient evidence of its equitable basis to be acceptable as providing for reasonable adjustment measures over a demonstrably reasonable period of time. The international financial community would then have the responsibility for providing adequate and suitable adjustment finance over a set period providing the debtor country continues to adhere to the measures required on its part to make the scheme work.

CONCLUSIONS

The real problem, which has hitherto been largely ignored, is that there is no established framework or forum for impartial assessment of the reasonableness of a sovereign borrower's request for rescheduling or of the equity of the proposed terms of the rescheduling arrangements. Equity in this context means not only equity between creditor and debtor but also between creditors. What is needed is some international variation on the Chapter 11 approach to workouts under the United States Federal Bankruptcy Law. We need to have the ability to help countries in difficulty, due to events outside their control, to reorganize their external indebtedness on the basis (i) of an impartial assessment of their prospects for earning foreign exchange on a fair trading basis, (ii) of their need and access to new money for sound development and restructuring requirements and (iii) of their demonstrated commitment to necessary structural adjustments and reasonable austerity measures. As in all cases of *force majeure* or "unforeseen circumstances," the settlement procedures in such cases should be designed to spread the burden of adjustment and loss of profit or delays in repayment on an equitable basis between the various actors in the drama, creditors, borrowers and the taxpayers of both the capital exporting and importing countries.[10]

Close coordination is therefore certainly required in seeking to establish an acceptable framework between the Fund, the World Bank, OECD governments and the commercial banks acting through a common organisation such as the Institute of International Finance. No lasting solution, however, can be expected until a new framework allows for the real equities between creditors and debtors to be taken into account and also recognises the interdependence of the economies of the industrial and the developing countries. Leadership from the United States and other industrial countries is needed to establish the required institutional framework. This institutional framework, moreover, will need to be buttressed by greatly expanded financial resources to give the framework a chance to work.[11] It is a necessary cost. The lesson of the Great Depression is that short term ad hoc measures and a lack of leadership are a dangerous combination in an era of economic and political uncertainty.

It would be tragic if the World's financial system had to undergo once again the traumas of 1929-1939 due to an inability to learn the lessons of that period. It was only after "a sequence of improvisations which kept alive the semblance of solvency" that an overall debt rescheduling was put in place which recognised that only a German recovery based on stable money and the provision of finance to facilitate the conduct of Germany's foreign trade would make possible the repayment of its external debts on a non-discriminatory basis. The earlier *ad hoc* improvisations, however, had already done their damage, and, in political terms, had created the conditions for the destruction of German democracy.[12]

Total retreat by commercial banks from lending on most sovereign risks will, as has frequently been stressed, simply compound the problems currently facing the international financial system. Yet it is difficult to criticize the banks when there has been no concerted effort to establish a framework for debt rescheduling and no coherent overall effort to deal with the problems faced by major commercial lenders who originate from many varied jurisdictions, each with its own tax and bank supervision rules and regulations.[13] The *ad hoc* approach, however, breeds uncertainty, and uncertainty is the real enemy of those seeking to restore confidence in the international finance system. It also emphasizes the political aspects of the rescheduling process, and risks unfortunate overraction on the part of certain Third World borrowers.[14]

NOTES

1. See particularly William R. Cline, "International Debt and the Stability of the World Economy," in *No. 4 Policy Analyses in International Economies*—Intitute for International Economics, (Washington, D.C., September 1983); see also M.S. Mendelsohn, *Commercial Banks and the Restructuring of Cross-Border Debt* (Group of Thirty, New York 1983); Mario Henrique Simonsen "The Financial Crisis in Latin America" (Getulio Vargas Foundation, Rio de Janiero, 1983); William R. Cline "Mexico's Crisis, the World's Peril," *Foreign Policy* No. 49 (Winter 1982-83); Morgan Guaranty Trust Co. of N.Y., "Global Debt: Assessment and Long-Term strategy," *World Financial Markets* (June 1983); Paine Webber, Mitchell, Hutchins, Inc. "Earnings Models for Large U.S. Banks" *Status* Report (June 14, 1983); John Williamson, ed., *Prospects for Adjustment in Argentina, Brazil and Mexico: Responding to the Debt Crisis*, in Intitute for International Economics (Washington, D.C. June 1983); House of Commons, Fourth Report from the Treasury and Civil Service Committees Sess. 1982-83, *International Monetary Arrangements: International Lending by Banks* Vol. 1 (March 1983); U.S. Congress, House Committee on Banking, Finance and Urban Affairs; *International Recovery and Financial Stability*, H.R. 2957, 98 Cong., 1st Sess. 1983. A detailed case-by-case examination of the rescheduling saga is provided by Chandra Hardy, "Rescheduling Developing Country Debts 1956-80," Overseas Development Council Working Paper No. 1. (Washington, D.C. 1982) and also by Albert C. Cizarcskas, "International Debt Renegotiation: Lessons from the Past" *World Development* Vol. 7 pp. 199-210 (1979) reprinted in World Bank Reprint Series No. 101.

2. See Richard Dale, *Bank Supervision Around the World (Group of*

Thirty, New York, 1982); William R. Cline, *International Debt, op. cit. supra* 32-44 and 102-105; Compare Jack Gutentag and Richard Herring "The Lender of Last Resort Function in an International Context," Princeton Essays in International Finance No. 151 (Princeton University, May 1983) with Group of Thirty's more confident perspective on the lender of last resort arrangements in *Balance of Payments Problems of Developing Countries* (Group of Thirty, 1981); W.P. Cooke "Developments in Cooperation Among Banking Supervisory Authorities." *Bank of England Quarterly Review* Vol. 21, No. 2 (June 1981); Debora Ann Chan, "An International Code for Banking Supervision," *International Financial Law Review* 26-28, (July, 1983); Richard Dale, "Basle Concordat: Lessons from Ambrosiano" *The Banker* p. 55 (September, 1983); Wilfrid Guth, "International Debt Crisis: The Next Phase," *The Banker* pp. 25-32 (July, 1983); M.S. Mendelsohn "A Longer View of Debt," *The Banker* pp. 21-26 (November 1983).

3. See B. Nowzad, "The Rise of Protectionism," IMF Pamphlet Series No. 24 (Washington, D.C. 1978), and more recently the report of the international committee of experts, on *Protectionism: Threat to International Order—The Impact on Developing Countries,* Commonwealth Secretariat, (London 1982). See also Christopher Davis "Financing Third World Debt," *Chatham House Papers No. 4.* (R11A, London 1979).

4. See Guy P. Pfeffermann, "Latin America and the Caribbean: Economic Performance and Policies" Vol. 2, No. 1. *Southwestern Review of Management and Economics* (1982) also printed in World Bank Reprint Series No. 228; and particularly P.P. Kuczynski "Latin American Debt," *Foreign Affairs* pp. 344-364 (Winter 1982-83). See also The *Economist (30 April-6 May, 1983) Special issue on the international debt crisis ("A downpour of banks?"), section on Latin America pp. 17-30*, and S. Griffith Jones *"Transnational Finance and Latin American Development," Intitute of Development Studies, University of Sussex (July 1982).*

5. See William J. Gasser and David L. Roberts, "Bank Lending to Developing Countries—Problems and Prospects," *Federal Reserve Bank of N.Y., Quarterly Review* pp. 18-29 (Autumn 1982) "Sovereign Debt Rescheduling (the Implications for Private Banks)" No. 4, *The Amex Bank Review—Special Papers* (July 1982); M.S. Mendelsohn. "Firemen's Ball in Washington" *The Banker* pp. 25-29 (September 1983). See also speakers papers for the Financial Times' Conference on *World Banking in 1983* (Financial Times, London, December 1982) and for the Fourth International Monetary Conference sponsored by the Global Interdependence Center and the Group of Thirty (Philadelphia, Penn. November 1982).

6. See collected conference papers, "Sovereign Debt: Recent Regulatory and Lending Issues and Practices" from a London conference organized by Law and Business Inc. and published by Harcourt Brace Jovanovich (New York, 1983) and also the background analysis in *Risks in International Lending*, First Report of the International Banking Study Group of the Group of Thirty (Group of Thirty, New York, 1982) and the views expressed in the Group of Thirty's report *How Bankers See the World Financial Market (New York, 1982). Note also Franklin R. Edwards "Financial Institutions and Regulation in the 21st Century: After the Crash?"* Columbia Journal of World Business Vol. XVII No. 1 (special issue on External Debt of Developing Countries, Spring 1982) and W.P. Cooke, "The International Banking Scene: a Supervisory Perspective," *Bank of England Quarterly Bulletin* Vol. 23. No. 1 (March 1983), also G.G. Johnson and R.K. abrams "Aspects of the International Banking Safety Net," *IMF Occasional Paper* No. 17, (March 1983).

7. See William R. Cline, *International Debt,* op. cit. supra pp. 31-44, and also Martin Bronfenbrenner, "The Appeal of Confiscation in Economic Development" *Economic Development and Cultural Change* Vol. 3 pp. 201-218 (April 1955) and Doreen Hemlock "David and Goliath—Latin American Debtors Serve Notice of Future Strategies" *South* p. 71 (November 1983). See also C.R. Brown and C. deKay Wilson "Brazil the Restructuring that Almost Failed" *International Financial Law Review* p. 4 (August 1983).

8. See M.S. Mendelsohn, "International Debt Crisis: The Practical Lessons of Restructuring" *The Banker* pp. 33-38 (July 1983) and Morgan Grenfell & Co. Limited, *Economic Review* "World Banking: Prospects in the Eighties," (August 1983). A thorough review of the inadequacies of the current international mechanisms is provided by the report of the commonwealth study group of *Towards a New Bretton Woods—Challenges for the World Financial Trading System" (Commonwealth Secretariat 1983).*

9. I am particularly indebted to the help and assistance of my colleague William Higman in the preparation of the following section. The ideas set out *infra* were first presented in a paper on "The IMF and a World Financial System Under Strain" reprinted in the collection papers of the Financial Times' Conference on *World Banking in 1983* pp. 96-104 (Financial Times, London, December 1982). See also C. Bogdanowicz-Bindert, "Debt: Beyond the Quick Fix," *Third World Quarterly* Vol. 5 no. 4, pp. 828-838; Chandra Hardy, *op. cit. supra,* and Peter Leslie, "Techniques of Rescheduling: the Latest Lessons," *The Banker* p. 23 (April 1983).

10. One recent commentator has question whether it is practicable in the current climate of international relations to differentiate between debtors on the basis of the degree or responsibility they ha shown in the management of their affairs. See Barbara Stallings, "Latin America Debt: What Kind of Crisis," but compare with Susan Strange "The Credit Crisis: A European View" Vol. 3 No. 2 *SAIS Review* (School of Advanced International Studies, Johns Hopkins) pp. 27-29 and 171-181 (Summer/Fall). See also the support for this "equity" argument in Christine Bogdanowicz-Bindert "Debt: Beyond the Quick Fix" *op. cit. supra* at note 9. UNCTAD had adopted a resolution directed to a similar general objective but has received little support from the OECD countries for its approach to the debt problem. Res. 222 (XX1) 21 UNCTAD Trade and Development Board Official Records Supp. (No. 1) 3 UN DOC TD/B/830 (1981). The Group of 77 were behind these reform proposals. See *Proceedings of the UN Conference on Trade and Development,* Fifth Session Vol. 1, Reports and Annexes UN DOC.E.79 II.D.14 Annex VI (1981), (suggesting establishment of an International Debt Commission independant of the creditors and debtors).

11. See Overseas Development Institute, *Developing Country Bank Debt: Crisis Management and Beyond,* (Briefing Paper No. 2 London March 1983).

12. Paul Bareau, "The lessons of an Earlier International Debt Crisis" *The Banker* 35, (December 1983); for a further account Karl Eurich Born *International Banking in the 19th and 20th Centuries* pp. 256-286 (English translation Berg Publishers Ltd. 1983). See also Anatole Kaletsky "When Debtors Said No: Lessons of the 1930's" *Financial Times* p. 8 (Dec. 28, 1983).

13. An imaginative series of proposals for restructuring the current international indebtedness of Third World countries have recently been set out by prominent international financial figures such as William Bolin and Jorge Del Canto. "LDC Debt: Beyond Crisis Management," *Foreign Affairs* 1099-1112 (Summer 1983); Lord Lever, Felix Rohatyn, Minos Zombanakis, G.W. Mackworth-Young. See William R. Cline, *International Debt, op. cit. supra* pp. 117-127 for an excellent summary of such schemes. See also the ideas expressed in the 1983 Per Jacobsson lecture by H.J. Witteveen "Developing a New International Monetary System: A Long Term View" (International Monetary Fund September 1983). The World Bank has sought for its part to contribute to the effort to maintain credit flows to countries actively implementing programmes to restore their creditworthiness by expanding its lending for structural adjustment and by its newly announced system of cofinancing through "A" and "B" loans. It may prove necessary to explore the possibility of establishing a World Bank commercial banking subsidiary in New York or London if the co-financing programme does not succeed in its objectives.

14. See i particular Rimmer de Vries' speech "World Recession: Causes and Cures" pp. 8-10, reprinted in *World Finance Markets,* (Morgan Guaranty Trust Co. of New York—March 1983); "Global Debt: Assessment and Long-Term Strategy" *World Financial Markets* (June 1983).